22-
1760

Alvin E. Ford

La Vengeance de Nostre-Seigneur

The Old and Middle French Prose Versions

The Version of Japheth

Known in nearly fifty manuscripts, the Old and Middle French prose versions of the apocryphal *Vengeance de Nostre-Seigneur* represent at least nine different tellings of a tale based to varying degrees on three earlier Latin works: the *Cura sanitatis Tiberii*, the *Vindicta Salvatoris*, and the *Mors Pilati*. Together they relate the conversion of the Roman Empire to Christianity through the miraculous curing of the emperor by St. Veronica's Holy Veil, the vengeance the emperor takes on the city and people of Jerusalem because of Jesus' death, and the punishing of Pilate, enemy of both emperor and God.

This edition of the *Vengeance de Nostre-Seigneur* presents the Middle French redactions, the last and the longest before the fifteenth-century mystery plays treating the same subject. In addition to the edited text of the base-manuscript (Grenoble 468), the variants from the other twenty-one related manuscripts, explanatory notes, a detailed bibliography, a glossary, and a list of proper names, this volume includes an introduction outlining the origins and status of the legend of St. Veronica during the Middle Ages, in both its European and its specifically French developments.

STUDIES AND TEXTS 63

# LA VENGEANCE DE NOSTRE-SEIGNEUR

## The Old and Middle French Prose Versions: The Version of Japheth

EDITED BY

ALVIN E. FORD

PONTIFICAL INSTITUTE OF MEDIAEVAL STUDIES

The publishing program of the
Pontifical Institute is supported
through the generosity
of the De Rancé Foundation.

CANADIAN CATALOGUING IN PUBLICATION DATA

Main entry under title:
La Vengeance de Nostre-Seigneur : the Old and Middle French prose versions

(Studies and texts, ISSN 0082-5328 ; 63)
Text in Middle French, with introduction and notes in English.
Bibliography: p.
Includes index.
ISBN 0-88844-063-4

I. Ford, Alvin E. (Alvin Earle), 1937- II. Pontifical Institute of Mediaeval Studies. III. Series: Studies and texts (Pontifical Institute of Mediaeval Studies ; 63.

PQ1545.V3 1984 843'.1 C83-098197-7E

DONNÉES DE CATALOGAGE AVANT PUBLICATION (CANADA)

Vedette principale au titre:
La Vengeance de Nostre-Seigneur : the Old and Middle French prose versions

(Studies and texts, ISSN 0082-5328 ; 63)
Texte en français moyen, avec introduction et notes en anglais.
Bibliographie: p.
Comprend un index.
ISBN 0-88844-063-4

I. Ford, Alvin E. (Alvin Earle), 1937- II. Pontifical Institute of Mediaeval Studies. III. Collection: Studies and texts (Pontifical Institute of Mediaeval Studies) ; 63.

PQ1545.V3 1984 843'.1 C83-098197-7F



Pontifical Institute of Mediaeval Studies
59 Queen's Park Crescent East
Toronto, Ontario, Canada M5S 2C4

PRINTED BY UNIVERSA, WETTEREN, BELGIUM

*This book is dedicated*
*to the memory of*
*Elisabeth Frankfurter*

# Contents

Acknowledgments

I would like to take this opportunity to thank my friends for their unflagging support and forbearance, Dr. William Roach and Fr. Leonard E. Boyle for their interest, encouragement, and helpful suggestions, the Bibliothèque municipale de Grenoble for graciously allowing me to publish ff. 34-56 of their manuscript 468, and the American Philosophical Society. A grant-in-aid from the latter enabled me to visit sites in France identified with the legend of St. Veronica and to pursue research in various libraries and archives. The Introduction and critical notes are undoubtedly the richer because of their generosity.

# Introduction

The Old and Middle French documents being presented in this study are known collectively as the *Vengeance de Nostre-Seigneur* or the *Vindicta Salvatoris*. Representing at least nine differing versions of the base materials, they draw to varying degrees on three earlier works, each of which may be traced back to the first centuries of the Christian era. These apocrypha, the *Cura sanitatis Tiberii* (*The Curing of Tiberius*), the *Vindicta* proper, that is, the *Destruction of Jerusalem*, and the *Mors Pilati* (*The Death of Pilate*) were known throughout the Middle Ages, not only in France, but throughout Christian Europe and the Middle East.[1]

The works involved are, it must be noted, New Testament apocrypha, that is, works dealing with the characters and events of the New Testament, but which were never accepted into the canon of the Christian Bible, either because of doctrinal contradictions or because of unsure date of composition. Their unofficial standing, however, never stood in the way of their tacitly being approved, even encouraged, since the story they told – the conversion of the Roman Empire to Christianity and the concomitant punishment of those traditionally held responsible for the Crucifixion – fitted nicely into the Church's propaganda needs. It is therefore not difficult to imagine that the various tellings of the *Vengeance de Nostre-Seigneur* existed in many hundreds of manuscripts in most of the languages of the Christian world.

In this present study, we are limiting ourselves to the Old and Middle French prose versions[2] which are known today in at least forty-five manuscripts, excluding those of the fifteenth-century *mystères*. Of these forty-five, twenty-two contain the text referred to here as the "Version of

[1] The relationships of the nine versions (here designated families A through I) to the base-materials and to each other will be an important part of the Introduction to a future volume dealing with the other versions. Families A and B contain all three parts; families C to I are essentially versions of the *Cura sanitatis Tiberii*.

[2] Our apocryphon is also known in verse versions. See Gryting; Buzzard; and listings of verse versions in *Bulletin de la Société des Anciens Textes français*, 1 (1875): 53, n. 2; 25 (1899): 48-50; *Romania*, 16 (1887): 56. Full publication information for the books and articles cited throughout the Introduction and in the critical and explanatory notes is to be found in the Bibliography.

Japheth," a title adopted for the sake of convenience, for although Japheth is named as its author, it is a designation we need not take seriously. These twenty-two manuscripts make up families A and B, the subject-maker of this volume.

With the exception of Prof. Micha's redaction of MS Bib. Nat. fr. 187 (family H), there have been, to my knowledge, no modern editions of any of these manuscript families. However, in the last decade of the fifteenth century and the first half of the sixteenth century, there were at least twenty-three editions (excluding reprints) based on manuscripts related to those of families A and B.[3]

As is clear from the listing of these editions, Lyons seems to have been the city in which the *Vengeance de Nostre-Seigneur* was first and most frequently published (seventeen out of twenty-three editions). This is almost to be expected, given the important role of nearby Vienne in the final "Death of Pilate" section. Yet, two aspects of the publication history are perhaps surprising: first, the absence of editions printed in Bordeaux, in spite of the existence there of well-established presses, and what one would have expected to have been avid local interest in the legend of St. Veronica; and second: the failure of the text to be reprinted after the mid-sixteenth century.

This "failure" can be explained in at least three ways. First, we must not be misled by the seemingly large number of separate editions into concluding that the work was a best-seller, available in untold thousands of copies. Early printing runs were very small compared to today's, and several of the indicated editions are known in only one or two extant copies, while others have not survived at all, and are known only from booksellers' descriptions. These facts suggest only moderate, rather than intense, interest in this type of document. Second, and not unrelated, is the

[3] *Lyons*: c. 1485-1488 (Arnollet), 1494 (Maillet), 1495 (Arnollet), 1501 (Nourry), 1504 (Arnollet), 1510 (Cheney), 1512 (Nourry, reprinted in 1527 and in an undated edition by Nourry, in 1550 and 1555 by P. de Sainte-Lucie), 1515 (Nourry, reprinted in 1517), before 1525 (Arnollet), 1536 (Feu Barnabé Chaussard, reprinted in 1544), 1545 (Chaussard), plus four undated editions with no editor, one edited by Boutellier, one by La Veuve Barnabé Chaussard; *Poitiers*: 1524, c. 1530, 1535 (all De Marnef); *Rouen*: c. 1520 (G. de la Motte); *Paris*: 1491 (Trepperel), 1491 (Meslier). There were undoubtedly other Paris editions, but a complete listing of these could not be obtained as the hand-written Fiches Renouard, the most thorough cataloguing of books published in Paris in the sixteenth century, is being prepared for publication by the Bibliothèque Nationale, and hence is presently not available for general consultation. The Bibliothèque Nationale has no Paris editions in its collections (although it does have the 1501 and 1504 Lyons editions); the Bibliothèque de l'Arsenal has the 1491 Paris (Meslier) edition. On the basis of the *incipits* and *explicits*, none of the above twenty-three editions was based directly on a manuscript known today.

coincidence of the failure to print new editions of the *Vengeance* and the banning in 1548, at least in Paris, of the performances of the formerly very popular mystery plays, the literary genre of the fifteenth century made famous by Jean Michel, Eustache Marcadé, Arnould Greban, and others, a genre which incorporated into it much of the thematic material of our apocryphon. Although the banning was largely the result of an attempt to assure public safety and morality, it may in addition have been symptomatic of a turning away from apocryphal subject matter in the theater, coincident with the beginnings of renewed interest in "classical" themes. Third, the need to disseminate the new knowledge of the Renaissance, whether through translations of Greek and Latin authors or through new works in the vernacular, must have made heavy demands on the presses of the period. In such a situation, publishers would obviously have had to establish new priorities, priorities that would not have been favorable to the reissuing of a text such as our *Vengeance de Nostre-Seigneur*.

## A. The Legend of St. Veronica

### *1. The Biblical Tradition*

The development of the legend of St. Veronica seems to have followed the general principle at work in all apocryphal materials: the fewer the details in the "historical" sources, the more extensive may be the elaborations of those details. Less may be more. For examples of this, one has only to think of the fate of some of those people who play a role in Jesus' Crucifixion: Joseph of Arimathea, historically unknown after the burial of Jesus, becomes the custodian of the cup of the Last Supper and travels to Europe, where his legend is fused with Arthurian materials, particularly with reference to the Holy Grail; the Roman centurion, nameless and sighted, is made blind so he may be miraculously cured, and soon acquires the name Longinus and a complete *vita*; Nicodemus, known as a secret follower of Jesus and for his role in His burial, becomes the main character (after Jesus) in his own gospel; lastly, there is Pilate who disappears historically after being summoned to Rome, only to reappear in diverse forms in Middle-eastern and European literatures, either quietly in retirement or suffering a cruel death for his political and religious crimes, either converting or not to Christianity, even suffering martyrdom for the Faith.

In the case of Veronica, the Biblical specifics are few in number and, with one exception, exceedingly vague in nature. The potential for apocryphal expansion was therefore very great. In the following passages it should be noted that she is never named, and that there is no need to assume that the woman cured of hemorrhages is the same as one of those present along the *Via dolorosa* or at the Crucifixion. Of course, our author came at the problem from the opposite end. For him, as long as nothing stood in the way of these women all being the same woman, he could proceed, his only restraint being the need not to contradict accepted doctrines.[4]

The most specific reference to the woman who will become Veronica is to be found in Matthew 9:20-22:

> Then a woman who had suffered from hemorrhages for twelve years came up from behind, and touched the edge of his cloak; for she said to herself: "If I can only touch his cloak, I shall be cured." But Jesus turned and saw her, and said: "Take heart, my daughter; your faith has cured you." And from that moment she recovered.

The other passages that soon came to be identified with Veronica – and which were used to justify subsequent developments of the legend – are less precise, in that they deal with a group of women rather than a single woman. The only reference to women being present along the *Via dolorosa* is recorded in Luke 23:27-28:

> Great numbers of people followed, many women among them, who mourned and lamented over him. Jesus turned to them and said: "Daughters of Jerusalem, do not weep for me; no, weep for yourselves and your children."

And three gospelers tell of the presence of unnamed women at the Crucifixion:

> A number of women were also present, watching from a distance: they had followed Jesus from Galilee and waited on him. (Matthew 27:55)
>
> A number of women were also present, watching from a distance. Among them were Mary of Magdala, Mary the mother of James the younger and of Joseph, and Salome, who had all followed him and waited on him when he was in Galilee, and there were several others who came up to Jerusalem with him. (Mark 15:40-41)

[4] See as an excellent example of this the *Descensus ad inferos* section of the *Évangile de Nicodème* (ed. Ford, pp. 52-57, 92-98), in which the author has Jesus leading the saints out of the netherworld into Heaven. The "He descended into Hell" section of the *Apostles' Creed* was not officially sanctioned until the thirteenth century, although it had been in use since the fourth century. The author, writing perhaps even before the fourth century, was within doctrinal limits, basing himself on: Ephesians 4:8-10, 1 Peter 3:19-20, Mt 27:51-53, 2 Timothy 1:10, etc.

> His friends had all been standing at a distance; the women who had accompanied him from Galilee stood with them and watched it all. (Luke 23:49)

These three "facts" then (a woman cured of hemorrhages, women present on the road to Calvary and at Calvary itself) were the minimal but adequate materials that sparked the imaginations of the various elaborators. It should be noted in passing that, logically enough, the *Gospel of Nicodemus* limits the identification of Veronica to her role as the woman healed by Jesus. The *Nicodemus* is primarily an expanded narrative of Jesus' trial (at which Veronica testifies) and gives a very simplified account of the Crucifixion. The texts of the *Vengeance de Nostre-Seigneur*, if they mention this first identification at all, do so as a prelude to the curing of the emperor. They are generally much more interested in explaining how Veronica came into possession of an image of Christ, either along the *Via dolorosa* or during the Crucifixion itself.

## 2. *The Legend as It Appears in the Various Versions of the "Vengeance de Nostre-Seigneur"*

Before outlining the various problems connected with her legend (origins of her name, how she came to Rome, her fate thereafter, her presence in France, etc.), let us look quickly at some representative manuscripts of the *Vengeance de Nostre-Seigneur*, so as to have a more precise idea of the variables and invariables in the fully-developed forms of the legend as it was known in France, at least 1200 years after the events of the Biblical narratives. In all of these, we have a dying emperor (Tiberius or Vespasian) whose faithful servant (Volusian or Gaius) hears about Jesus' miracles, goes to Jerusalem only to learn that Jesus is dead, but that a woman possesses an object with miraculous powers that may cure the emperor. She and the image are sought out and brought to Rome, where the emperor is indeed healed.

a. MS Bib. Nat. fr. 19525 (13th cent., family E)

> Dunc vint un homme par nun Marcus qui sout le secrei d'une femme, si dist a Volusien: "Treiz ans a passé que Jesus sana une femme del corlun de sanc. Et quant ele fu garie, de la grant amor qu'ele out vers lui, si fist paindre un ymage del semblant Jesu, dementiers qu'il ert vivant." Dunc dist Volusien a celui: "Di mei comme la femm[e] a nun." Et il respundi: "Veronica." (f. $60^b$)

Note that here the image is painted. Although there is some confusion among the scribes of families E and C concerning the verbs *peindre* and *prendre*, the verb *peindre* is sufficiently frequent in occurrence to indicate that the tradition here did speak of a painted rather than an imprinted face. This may be the result of the influence of the Abgar-Edessa version of her legend. See pp. 9-10, notes 8 and 9.

b. MS Bib. Nat. fr. 413 (end 14th cent., family C)

Here the materials of family E are considerably expanded:

> Et lors vint un juif avant qui avoit nom Marchus, qui descouvri le secret d'une femme que ele lui avoit dit. Et dist a Volusien: "Or a trois ans passez que il gueri une femme qui decouroit de sanc pour ce qu'elle atoucha ses vestemens. Et quant elle se vit guerie, pour l'amour de lui, elle print s'ymage a sa semblance et la maiesté de Nostre Seigneur endementiers qu'il vivoit en une touaille, si qu'il le sot bien. Si mist en sauf moult honnourablement. Et encore l'a et la garde moult chierement." Lors respondi Volusien a celui: "Dis moy le nom de la femme." Et il lui dit: "Elle a nom Veronique." (f. 28[c])

Veronica denies having the Holy Veil, Volusian sends soldiers to her home, removes it and brings it and a somewhat uncooperative Veronica back to Rome. There:

> Volusiens s'aprisma de l'empereur et lui dist: "Ce sache, nostre sires li empereres, que une femme que Jhesus gueri d'une grant maladie / a son ymage painte pour l'amour de lui selon sa semblance et sa façon." (ff. 29[b-c])

And after the emperor is cured, he orders that:

> "... Celle ymage feust aovree d'or et d'argent et de pierres precieuses et mise en net lieu et en honnourable." (f. 29[c])

c. MS Bib. Nat. fr. 1850 (14th cent., family F, the "Bible en français" of Roger d'Argenteuil)

> Lors passa Nostre Seigneur pardevant une sainte fame qui avoit a non la Veronique. Et portoit un quevrechief pour vendre au marchié. Et quant elle vit Nostre Seignor ainsi villainement mener, si en ot moult grant dueil et commença a plorer. Et li bailla le ceurvrechief et li dit: "Sire qui me garicites dimenche qui passa d'une maladie que je avoie, moult sui dolente de cest martire que vous souffrez / sanz raison. Mez or tenez cest cuervechief et en essuiez vostre visage." Et Nostre Sire le prinst tantost et en essuia son visaige. Et lors fu le visages Jhesu Crist en cel cuervechief ausi comme c'il fust en char et en os. Lors li bailla le cuvrechief arriere et li dit que elle le gardast bien car il avroit encore moult grant mestier a maint malade garir. Et tantost la fame s'en retourna en sa meson et atoucha le ceuvrechief au visage et as cors de son seignor qui gisoit en lengueur. Et il fu gueriz et ce

leva sainz et haitiez, et rendi grassez a Dieu. Et furent maint malade gari par l'atouchement de cel saint cuvrechief. (ff. $18^v$-$19^r$)

d. MS Bib. Nat. fr. 181 (15th cent., family I)

In contrast to the manuscripts of family F, those of I make no reference to the *Via dolorosa*, nor to the earlier curing of Veronica herself. Several other differences are evident as well. Whereas elsewhere Veronica is reticent to reveal the existence of her treasure, she here is most helpful, from the very moment of her chance meeting with Volusian. Note that he is not directed to her by a Jacob or a Marcus or a Thomas, as in most of the other traditions. And here too, after the emperor is restored to health, she returns to Jerusalem:

> Maiz Verone oiant Volutien / tout desplaisant le reconforta moult doulcement et lui dist: "Mon bon amy, ne vous desconfortez de riens, car je vous dy pour certain que j'ay en mon hostel itelle chose de Jhesus, mon Dieu, que se vous me voulez croire, et l'empereur aussi, il demour[er]a tout net guery de sa maladie. Et je vous diray que c'est, car il est bonne verité que comme Jhesus, mon Dieu, aloit par le pays preschent sainte doctrine, gaires il n'arrestoit en ung lieu. Et pourtant il me desplaisoit quant si souvent je perdoie sa presence. Et pour moy de par lui donner aucun effois ung petit de reconfort et consolation, je proposay en mon cœur que par ung bon paintre je feroie pourtraire aprés le vif sa sainte face en ung linge drap pour la devotement regarder quant voulenté m'en prendroit." (ff. $184^d$-$185^a$)

On her way to the painter's home, she meets Jesus who understands her intention, takes the cloth and presses it to His face:

> Et lors tout soudainement il y empraigni et pourtraist sa sainte samblance, voire trop mieulx et plus proprement que paintre nul n'eust sceu pourtraire. (f. $185^b$)

The four manuscripts from which these extracts are taken represent the twenty-three manuscripts of families C through I, and as such present a literary transmission of the legend of St. Veronica based on a combination of her perceived role as the woman cured of hemorrhages and as a woman present on the road to Calvary (this is occasionally implied rather than specified), who at that moment comes into possession of a representation of the holy face of Jesus.

The second literary tradition is that of the twenty-two manuscripts which make up families A and B and are the subject of the present volume. In this tradition, Veronica is not identified with the woman healed relatively early in Jesus' ministry; nor is she connected to the *Via dolorosa*, but rather to the women present at the Crucifixion. Consider the following passage from our base-manuscript, Grenoble 468 (Jacob is speaking to Gaius):

> Il estoit une bonne dame qui s'apelloit Beronique laquelle vist ancoures et sy est de Galilee et estoit si plaine de lepre qu'elle ne s'ouzoit tenir entre les gens. Et elle avoit sa foy que le Saint Prophete Jhesu Crist la guerist. Et quant elle seut que les Juifs l'eurent mis en crois, elle eut grant duel et s'en vint au mont de Calvaire out il estoit mis en crois. Et vist la Vierge Marie emprés la crois avec ung sien disciple qui s'appelloit Jehan, si que Beronique ne s'auzoit aprocher d'eulx pour sa maladie, mes plouroit et crio[i]t fort et fesoit grant duel. Et quant la Vierge Marie la vist et vist qu'elle pleuroit, elle lui fist signe a la main qu'elle venist a elle. Et quant elle fust venue, la Vierge Marie print ung crevichié que Beronique avoit en sa teste et essuia le visage de Jhesu Crist. Et incontinent la figure du visaige de Jhesu Crist fust apparant au crevichief, et le bailla a Beronique. / Et encouirres l'a et si fust guarie. (ff. 36ᵛ-37ʳ, ll. 135-147)

### 3. *The Origins of the Name Veronica*

Although unnamed in the Biblical accounts, the central figure of our legend is universally known by some form of the name *Veronica*. What then is the origin of this name? If pressed to do so, anyone familiar with the popular versions of her story would probably not hesitate to explain that Veronica is derived from the Latin root *ver* meaning "true" plus the Greek root *eikon* meaning "image." However logical and appropriate this explanation may be, it likely represents nothing more than an example of post-factum folk-etymologizing, in which the object, the Holy Veil or "true image" has given its name to the person identified with it.[5]

If the "popular" explanation of the origins of her name is unacceptable, what are the other possibilities? The commentator Pearson (p. 9) is not alone in insisting on the fact that the legend in its earliest manifestations was eastern rather than western, Greek rather than Latin, and that the name *Berenike*, that is, "bringer of victory," could well have been applied to her. Baring-Gould (pp. 287-288) prefers *Prounike*, the form he finds

[5] That there was even some hesitation in the western (Roman) tradition is shown by Pope Benedict XIV (1740-1758): "Haemorhoissa, mulier videlicet sanguinis profluvio laborans (alii S. Martham, alli Veronicam, alii vero probabilius putant mulierem fuisse ex urbe Paneadis ad Jordanis fontem sitae...)" (pp. 57-58). This distinction between person and object is corroborated by the nineteenth-century visionary Catherina Emmerick, who frequently used the name *Seraphia* to designate the women (vol. IV, pp. 254-259). Cf. Mabillon: "Haec Christi imago a recentioribus VERONICAE dicitur: imaginem ipsam VERONICAM veteres appellabant" (p. 88).

used by the Gnostic Valentinians.[6] He offers as a second possibility the name *Berenice* given by the chronicler Julianus Petrus to Salome's daughter, and perhaps subsequently blended with the name of *Beronicus*, an early martyr of the city of Antioch.

It is important to note that any of these Greek forms of her name could have been latinized into *Veronica* without any reference to her possession of the Holy Veil, the *vera ikon*. It is therefore quite possible to believe with Maury (*Croyances*, pp. 296-297) that the typical pilgrim who came to Rome during the Middle Ages to venerate the Holy Veil, and who saw the words *Vera ikon* written above it: "... ne saisit ni le sens de ces mots, ni celui de l'image; il ne s'attacha qu'à la femme dont ce portrait n'était qu'accessoire, alors que le but principal était d'offrir à ses regards la sainte célèbre, nommée *Véronica*." (p. 296)

### 4. *The Story of Abgar: The Influence of Eusebius*

Before examining the cult of St. Veronica that grew up around the Holy Veil preserved in St. Peter's Basilica in Rome, let us mention two other legendary components of our story which undoubtedly served to intensify the interest of medieval Europe in this holy relic and in the woman to whom the task of safeguarding it had been entrusted.

First, we have the multi-faceted legend of Abgar, prince of the Mesopotamian city of Edessa.[7] In spite of the obvious anachronism, the prince in question is thought to be Abgar VIII, who reigned from 176 to 213 AD. According to his legend, the dying Abgar, having heard of Jesus' miracles in the Holy Land, writes to Him only to have Him reply that He cannot come as He is to die soon, but that He will send one of His disciples to Edessa. This disciple, Thaddeus or Addai, arrives and cures Abgar.[8] The letter from Jesus becomes the principal treasure of the city, but by the

[6] "The Valentinians, in their lying doctrine, speak of a certain Prounice, to whom they give the name of Wisdom, of whom they assert the woman of the Gospel, who had an issue of blood, was a symbol" (p. 287). See other comments in Reiske (pp. 66-67); Mabillon (p. 89).

[7] The present city of Urfa, in north-eastern Turkey.

[8] In the sixth-century Syriac version of the *Doctrine of Addai*, as translated and published by Phillips, Jesus' reply is brought back orally to Abgar by the servant Hannan, who had been dispatched to Judea to find Jesus: "When Hannan, the keeper of the archives, saw that Jesus spake thus to him, by virtue of being the king's painter, he took and painted a likeness of Jesus with choice paints, and brought it with him to Abgar the king, his master. And when Abgar the king saw the likeness, he received it with great joy, and placed it with great honour in one of his palatial houses" (p. 5). It is to be noted that in this version, the painting does not bring about Abgar's cure. Here too, this occurs only through the laying on of hands by the disciple Addai (p. 7). See von Dubschütz (*Christusbilder*, ch. v); Grimm (ch. IV).

fourth century, the letter has been supplemented by Hannan's portrait of Jesus' face. It is this painting that was sent from Edessa to Constantinople in the year 944 and is thought to have been forwarded to Rome soon thereafter.[9] King Louis IX is said to have possessed a copy of this Eastern *mandylion* (arabic *mindil*, handkerchief) which he placed in the treasury of the Sainte-Chapelle in 1252, where it remained until apparently destroyed during the Revolution of 1789. Other references to such an image date from 1063 (Moscow) and 1384 (Genoa).[10] The original may well be the image preserved in the Roman Church of San Sebastiani in Capite.[11] Other similar portraits are venerated in Turin and Jaen (Spain).[12]

The second tradition is based on the fourth-century Christian historian, Eusebius of Caesarea (Pamphilus), whose *Historia ecclesiastica* was written while he was bishop of that Palestinian city (314-339 AD). In chapter XVIII of Book VII, he describes as follows a work of art he has himself seen:

> § 2 ... The figure in bronze of a kneeling woman, her hands extended forward like a suppliant; before her is held another figure in the same material representing a man standing, magnificently draped with a cloak and holding out his hand to the woman; at his feet is to be found, on the *stele* itself, a sort of strange plant which climbs up to the fringe of the bronze cloak; it is an antidote for all sorts of illnesses.

[9] Fleury, in vol. 12 of his *Histoire ecclésiastique*, gives a somewhat fuller account. In his version (Livre 55, ch. 30, pp. 49-54), Jesus saw Hannan's sketch and completed it by pressing the cloth to His face. Jesus retained the cloth, entrusted it during the *Via dolorosa* to St. Thomas, who in turn gave it to St. Thaddeus (Addai), who of course took it to Edessa. Fleury relates as well the subsequent history of the painting: a) Abgar placed it on public display at the gates of the city, replacing the pagan idols; b) his successor having returned to idolatry, the Bishop of Edessa was obliged to wall up the image and it was lost from sight for several centuries; c) 500 years later, the image, miraculously found and now double, turned back a siege of the city; a third copy cured the besieging king's daughter; d) 400 years later (c. 944 AD), the Roman Emperor informed the Emir of Edessa that he wished to have all three images. The original was sent to Constantinople (and ultimately to Rome). Much of Fleury's account is based on Evagrius Scholasticus [Liber IV, c. XXVII, pp. 405-407 ["De Chosdrois expeditione adversus Edessam"]).

[10] See von Dobschütz; Cabrol; the very detailed bibliography and notes in Leclercq (vol. I, cols. 87-97); Molanus (Liber IV, c. II). For an excellent résumé of the arguments for and against the authenticity of the letter and portrait, see Le Nain de Tillemont (vol. I, partie III, pp. 1106-1117). For the texts of the letters, see Baronius (vol. I, anno Christi 31, n. LVIII [Latin text of the letter from Abgar to Jesus]; n. LIX [Latin text of the letter from Jesus to Abgar]; n. LX [the Gelasian decree declaring the texts apocryphal]; anno Christi 34, n. CXXXVIII ["Instrumenta passionis]); Fabricius (vol. I, pp. 317*-319 ["Epistola Christi ad Abgarum graece et latine cum notis"]).

[11] See Marangoni (p. 235); Marucchi (pp. 116, 123, 395, 400-402).

[12] Wilson (pp. 92-103) argues convincingly for the identification of the *mandylion* with the famed Shroud of Turin.

§ 3 People say that this statue reproduces the face of Jesus; it has survived even down to our time, with the result that we saw it ourselves when we came into the city.

§ 4 There is nothing astonishing in the fact that former pagans, recipients of the blessings of our Saviour, would have made such an object, as we have also seen that the faces of the apostles Peter and Paul and of Christ himself have been preserved in paintings: as was natural, the former [pagans], without distinction, were accustomed to honor them as saviours in this way, according to the pagan custom current among them.

Although there is nothing in his description that imposes the belief that the man is Jesus or that the woman is Veronica, Eusebius himself made the connection (§ 1), and as he was the earliest and most trusted of post-biblical Christian historians, his identification of the woman suffering from hemorrhages with an art-work representing the figure of Jesus must surely have encouraged the development of her legend.[13]

## 5. *The Holy Veil Preserved in St. Peter's Basilica in Rome*[14]

While it is impossible – and of dubious merit – to bring together all the medieval references to the presence in Rome of the Holy Veil (lat. *sudarium*), it will be useful here to list some of the most important moments in its history, if for no other reason than to show beyond any doubt that it was an object of veneration throughout the period, and as such, supplied a continuing source of inspiration for the writers who chose to speak both of it and of its guardian-transporter, Veronica.[15]

All authors of the period, whether they are theologians or mere tourists, repeat the common-place belief (which we find also in the *Vengeance de Nostre-Seigneur*) that Veronica herself brought the *sudarium* from Jerusalem to Rome.[16] The version in our apocryphon has her led there by a servant of the emperor, in order to heal either the emperor or a member of his family. The only significant variant to this has Veronica expelled

[13] For further commentary on Eusebius and the importance of the image, see Du Feis, particularly the résumé, beginning p. 191.

[14] For a brief physical description of the Holy Veil, see Eméric-David (p. 24, n5).

[15] The fullest account of the step-by-step development of the legend of St. Veronica is to be found in von Dobschütz' *Christusbilder*: "Die Entstehung der Veronica-Legende" (pp. 209-217); "Der Kultus der Veronica" (pp. 218-230); "Die Fortbildung der Legende" (pp. 230-262). In the *Belege* to ch. VI, he lists over 120 documents dealing with Veronica, including (as item # 2) the 65 known Latin manuscripts of the *Cura sanitatis Tiberii*.

[16] See "De S. Veronica" (p. 456); Marangoni (p. 70).

from Jerusalem with other disciples on a rudderless, sailless ship. They arrive in Marseilles, from which she returns to Rome with her treasure.[17]

However, the first incontrovertible mention of the *sudarium* in Rome does not occur until the beginning of the eighth century, when, in documents dealing with the death of Pope John VII in 707, it is said to be present among the treasures of St. Peter's Basilica. This is also the approximate date of the oldest Latin versions of the *Vindicta Salvatoris* as published by Tischendorf. The historian Marangoni reports that Pope Stephen III carried various relics in procession in 745 "... with great humility ... along with the most holy Image of our Lord God and Saviour Jesus Christ, which is called 'Acheropita' (='not made by human hands')." [18] In 1143, Peter Mallius describes the basilica as:

> The Oratory of the Holy Mother, the Virgin Mary, which is called Veronica, where without any doubt is to be found the *sudarium* of Christ, with which, as most of us believed, she wiped His face before His most holy passion, when His sweat became as drops of blood dripping to the ground.[19]

Then in 1208, Pope Innocent III instituted an annual procession in its honor on the first Sunday after Epiphany, a rite confirmed by Honorius III in 1223 and Alexander IV in 1255.[20] The year 1289 saw it declared the most important relic in St. Peter's, an honor surpassed only by Sixtus IV's affirmation in 1482 that St. Peter's was the most important church in Christendom because of the presence there of the *sudarium*.[21]

The year 1191 is the earliest recorded for a formal exposition of the relic other than on a feast-day, although this practice may have been usual

[17] "Hierosolymitani Judaei vehementer infensi B. Lazaro, Magdalenae, Marthae, Marcello, Maximino, Josepho ab Arimathia nobili decurioni, et aliis plurimis; navi sine remigio velisque ac sine gubernatore eos imponunt, et exulare mandant: qui per vastum mare divinitus delati, ad Massiliensem portum incolumes appellunt. Verenice sancta mulier, ex plurimis comitibus aliqua, tum a Gallia Romam venit, ibique Divino relicto vultu, miraculis clara, migrat ad Dominum anno LXX." Baronius, *Annales ecclesiastici* (anno 34), quoted in "De S. Veronica" (p. 455). See also Dexter ("Anno Christi 48").

[18] "Cum multa humilitate ... cum Sacratissima Imagine Domini Dei Salvatoris nostri Jesu Christi, quae Acheropita nuncupatur." (p. 70)

[19] "Oratorium Sanctae Genetricis Virginis Mariae quod vocatur Veronica, ubi sine dubio est Sudarium Christi, in quo ante passionem suam sanctissimam faciem, ut a maioribus nostris accepimus, extersit, quando sudor ejus factus est sicut guttae sanguinis decurrentis in terram." *Ordo romanus*, quoted by Frugoni (p. 565). Massmann (p. 576) records an alter in Rome dedicated to Veronica in the year 1011. See also Wilson (p. 89).

[20] Marangoni (ch. XXIII-XXVI) describes similar processions down to the year 1550.

[21] "... Basilicam S. Petri Romanam prae aliis Urbis orbisque ecclesiis excellere, ob Salvatoris nostri Sudarium...." Quoted in "De S. Veronica" (p. 454).

much earlier. In that year, it was shown to Philippe-Auguste (returning from the Third Crusade) and in the years 1217, 1342, 1409, and 1452, other dignitaries were similarly honored. During the period, the annual processions continued, with special expositions on Holy Thursday, on the feast-day of St. Veronica (4 February),[22] and in Holy Years of Jubilee.[23]

Two related events further increased interest in the legend of St. Veronica. First, Crusaders, such as Philippe-Auguste who had actually seen the relic or one of the numerous copies, must have helped spread enthusiasm for information about it. And second, those same Crusaders visited the Holy Land and particularly Jerusalem, where travellers as early as the twelfth century speak of a *Via sacra*, an itinerary of places important to the final hours of Jesus' life on earth. Sts. Bernard of Clairvaux (1090?-1153) and Francis of Assisi (1182-1226) may have played a significant role in this, as their writings did much to reorient western Christian thought to an interest in the sufferings of Jesus. It is, however, not until the fourteenth century that the holy places are in Franciscan hands and we can begin to identify the fourteen stopping places that will rather slowly impose themselves as the fourteen indulgenced Stations of the Cross.[24] Not until the end of the fifteenth century are travel accounts in any way numerous. Three examples will suffice. First, Bernardus Breydenbachius wrote that in 1483 he had gone:

> ... down that long street, down which Christ was led from the home of Pilate to the place of the Crucifixion, and they came to the home of St. Veronica which is five hundred and fifty feet distant from Pilate's home, where Christ imprinted in her cloth the form of His face, which may be visited in Rome today.[25]

[22] It should be noted that by the sixteenth century, the historical authenticity of St. Veronica had been questioned and found wanting. Pope Gregory XIII removed her from the list of martyrs (1582) and St. Charles Borromeo had her name deleted from the Roman Missal and the Calendar of the Saints. This did not affect the Ambrosian Missal, used in the Milan region.

[23] See Thurston (pp. 58, 67), and Dante, *La Divina Commedia* (Canto XXI, lines 103-108) and *Vita nuova* (XL). Both refer to the year 1300. Also Aurélien (pp. 258-261).

[24] The Stations did not come into general usage throughout Europe until the seventeenth century, and became popular in France only after the Revolution of 1789. During the fifteenth and sixteenth centuries, however, reproductions of the *Via dolorosa* or *Via crucis* in Jerusalem had been set up in various countries. See Alston, *Catholic Encyclopedia* (vol. XV, p. 569); Miserey (pp. 73-77); Cirot de la Ville (pp. 19-21).

[25] "Per viam illam longam, per quam Christus de domo Pilati usque ad crucifixionis locum ductus est; ac devenisse ad domum S. Veronicae, quae ad passus quingentos et quinquaginta distat a domo Pilati: ubi Christus eius peplo Imaginem faciei suae impressit, quae hodie Romae visitur." Quoted in "De S. Veronica" (p. 454).

Second, Felix Fabri (also 1483):

> Then we came to Veronica's place, who, they say, was that woman with the flow of blood for twelve years and who had been cured when she secretly touched the fringes of His garment ... and who, seeing His face covered in spit and blood, took out a cloth and wiped the Saviour's face; however the form of the face remained on the cloth as if it had been painted....[26]

And third, William Wey identifies the same spot as number six of the fourteen Stations in his *Loca sancta in Stacionibus Jerusalem* (1483), a position it still occupies today.

It should be pointed out also that belief in the authenticity of the *sudarium* and in the story of Veronica was encouraged by the awarding of indulgences for the veneration of the relics in St. Peter's, and later for participation in meditations on the Way of the Cross.[27]

### 6. *The Legend of St. Veronica in France*

In addition to what might be called the international or universal versions of her legend – those which were known throughout Europe, including France – there existed from the first centuries of the Christian era a second series of legendary developments limited exclusively to France.

The first of these purely French traditions involving St. Veronica is to be found in the apocryphal text *Nathanis Judaei legatio* or *La Vindicte du Sauveur*,[28] which represents a combination of elements concerning the origins of Veronica and the Holy Veil that are known in the versions already discussed, plus new materials clearly of French origin. According to the *Legatio*, the Palestinian Nathan arrives at the court of Tyrus, king of Aquitaine,[29] where, after recounting the life and miracles of Jesus (in-

[26] "Deinde ... venimus ad locum Veronicae, quae dicitur fuisse mulier illa sanguine fluens XII annis, et ad tactum fimbriae vestimenti occultum fuit curata ... videns vultum ejus sputo et sanguine repletum, sudarium extraxit, et faciem salvatoris tersit; mansit autem figura faciei in sudario ac ut fuisset ei impicta...." Baldi (p. 599).

[27] The earliest date recorded for this with specific reference to the Holy Veil is 1289 (Pope Nicholas IV). Cirot de la Ville (pp. 22-23) quotes Pius IV's *Bull* of 1561 ratifying the indulgences established by Sixtus V, Benedict XIII, Benedict XIV, and Gregory XVI. For those granted by John XXII, see Reiske (p. 73), and Rainoldus (Liber II, c. III, pp. 485-487).

[28] One manuscript of this document has been published by Darley, *Acta Salvatoris* (pp. 38-46). See also MS Egerton 613 (ff. 21r-25r, family I).

[29] Tyrus is also the name occasionally given to Pilate's father. See, for example, MS Bib. Nat. fr. 1553, f. 406c (408c) (13th century).

cluding the curing of Veronica), he heals the king who, upon accepting Christianity, changes his name to Titus. Titus and a companion at arms (Vespasian) set out for Jerusalem, both to destroy the city and to seek out Veronica, as she: "... avait un morceau d'un vêtement du Sauveur et elle le gardait précieusement et l'estimait à l'égal d'une image même du Christ." While they are in Jerusalem, Volusian arrives on behalf of the ill Tiberius, expropriates all known relics of Jesus' passion, including the Holy Veil, and these are returned along with Veronica to Rome, while Titus and Vespasian continue their sacking of the city.

A fascinating document, but one somewhat apart from the most frequently occurring French version of her legend, although both deal with events of the first century AD and with Aquitaine, understood here as most of southern France west of the Rhone. The more frequent versions have Veronica herself coming to France by one of two routes, in each case accompanied by holy companions and possessing relics (excluding the Holy Veil, now in Rome) which she distributes along the route.[30] The first itinerary is an overland one: Rome to Siena to Florence to Ravenna to Milan to Genoa to Marseilles to Mende to Le Puys to Clermont to Rodez to Toul (Creuse) to Ahun (Creuse) to Limoges to Bourges to Tours to Poitiers to Périgueux to Angoulême, etc., and finally to Soulac, on the Atlantic coast, north-west of Bordeaux.[31] This missionary expedition resulted from a vision of St. Peter, directing him to convert the Limoges area. Peter therefore organized a small group of disciples under the leadership of St. Martial, and consisting principally of Martial, St.

[30] As Veronica was reputed to have been an intimate of the Blessed Virgin and of St. John the Baptist, the relics distributed, although varying somewhat in nature depending on the particular version of the legend, are almost always items of their clothing, St. John's blood, and a phial of the Virgin Mary's milk. See, with reference to the latter, the section treating the origins of the name "Soulac" (p. 25). In all probability, Veronica's legend has here been combined with that of an unnamed "Dame bazadaise," the subject of an originally independent legend. In later developments, Veronica will be born in Bazas, and becomes, like Pilate, a Gallo-Roman. See Baillet (p. 10); Bourrières (ch. LXVII, pp. 388-395); Moniquet, *St. Fort* (p. 23); Maréchaux (p. 47); Darley, *Sainte Véronique* (pp. 1-3); Mezuret (p. 85-89). Cf. Gregorius Turonensis: "Tunc temporis a Gallis matrona quaedam Hiersololymis abierat, pro devotione tantum, ut Domini et Salvatoris nostri praesentiam mereretur. Audivit autem quod beatus Joannes decollaretur: cursu illuc rapido tendit, datisque muneribus supplicat percussori, ut eam sanguinem defluentem colligere permitteret non arceri. Illo autem percutiente, matrona concham argenteam praeparat, truncatoque martyris capite, cruorem devota suscepit: quem diligenter in ampulla positum patriam detulit, et apud Vasatensem urbem ( = Bazas), aedificata in ejus honore ecclesia, in sancto altari collocavit." (col. 717)

[31] See Aurélien (ch. 4); Bourrières (ch. XXXV, pp. 209-215); Cirot de la Ville (p. 56); Gaume (p. 64); Maréchaux (p. 55).

Veronica, and St. Amador, the latter frequently identified with the Zachaeus of Lk 19:2 and as the husband of Veronica.[32]

The second route is by water, from Palestine (from which she and her companions were expelled) to the Atlantic coast of Spain, where they visit St. James of Compostella before continuing their voyage to Soulac.[33]

Whatever the route taken and the stops made, her goal seems clearly to have been the village of Soulac, which over the centuries has been the undisputed French center of her cult. It was here she established a convent, here she died (reportedly in 70 or 71 AD, the date also of the destruction of Jerusalem), and here are to be found to this day, in the church of Notre-Dame-de-la-Fin-des-Terres, iconographical materials identified with her.[34] The origins of the name Soulac itself have been the subject of much speculation, with *etyma* from Iberian, Celtic, and Gallo-Roman sources having been suggested as possibilities. Popular belief derives Soulac from *solum* and *lac*, the *lac* referring, as mentioned earlier, to the legendary belief that a small phial of the Virgin Mary's milk had been brought to the area by Veronica.[35] Some years after her death, her body was removed from Soulac (either because the church building was in danger from the sea or because of Norman invasions) and installed in the crypt of St. Fort in the basilica of St. Seurin in Bordeaux, where what is believed to be her tomb may still be visited.[36]

[32] See Albe; Moniquet, *St. Fort* (ch. 2); Duchesne, "Saint Martial"; Ring (pp. 6-7); the "Acta Sancti Martialis" in *Acta Sanctorum* (IV Aug.); Rabinis (pp. 104-105); Robertus de Monte (anno 1170, p. 519, lines 43-56); Bonaventure de St-Amable (vol. II, livre VII, ch. XII; vol. I, livre X, ch. XI); Pinius (pp. 16, 24-25); Dexter (pp. 99-100).

[33] "De Jaffa, la barque vient aboutir en Espagne, et l'ermite va droit à l'église célèbre de l'apôtre S. Jacques. C'est le même tour que font Amadour et Véronique pour débarquer à l'embouchure de la Gironde, non sans avoir fait escale à Compostelle...." Albe (p. 58), based on MS Bib. Nat. n. acq. lat. 881.

[34] For listings of the local iconography and the history of this church, see Réau (vol. III, partie III, pp. 1314-1315); Darley, *Fragments* (p. 23); Aurélien (pp. 10-13); Maréchaux (chs. 2, 4, 5, 7, and Appendice n° 1 ["Sur le culte et les reliques de Sainte Véronique"]); Thomas (ch. 5).

[35] Aurélien's explanation is typical: "La chapelle de Soulac ... reçut son nom de ce que le *lait* de la Mère de Dieu était la *seule* relique que Véronique y déposa." (p. 93). See also Mezuret (pp. 120-125); Bonaventure de St-Amable (p. 287); Pinius (p. 17, § 4); Auracher (pp. 29-30).

[36] See Aurélien (pp. 131-134); Moniquet, *St. Fort* (chs. XXI, XXIV); Cirot de la Ville (ch. V); Darley, *St. Fort* (pp. 3, 11); *Apôtres* (pp. 28-29). The *Chronique saintongeaise*, as edited by Bourdillon, preserves in two thirteenth-century manuscripts listings of church treasures hidden because of these Norman invasions: "En liglise saint Seurin de bordeu . toz lo tresors e li cor saint furent seveli ... A solac iosta louter sainta Veroniqua mitrent lo tresor e la sainctuaire de liglises ... Apres ico vindrent li normant e destruissirent tota la terre..." (pp. 85-87).

It is of course impossible today to ascertain in any scientific way, whether Veronica the person existed, and if she did, whether she ever came to Gaul. All that is important is that her legend existed, that people believed she had been there after playing a significant role in the Crucifixion. And yet, in spite of what seem to have been firmly rooted local traditions concerning her, particularly in Aquitaine, those local traditions did not translate themselves into numerous literary and artistic monuments. With minor exceptions, she has not been the subject of paintings and statuary outside her portrayal in the sixth Station of the Cross. And with the exception of MS Egerton 613, all the manuscripts of the *Vengeance de Nostre-Seigneur* remain attached by content to the international rather than the intranational aspects of her story. Her literary world is limited to Jerusalem and Rome. It should be noted in addition that although the manuscripts of families A and B speak of Vienne, Bordeaux, and Narbonne, they do so in reference to the fate of the population of Jerusalem and to the punishing of Pilate. These cities are not seen as having anything to do with Veronica's presence in France. Even the *Nathanis Judaei legatio*, while dealing with the kingdom of Aquitaine, mentions Veronica only in her role as guardian of the Holy Veil in Jerusalem. And as her authenticity was sufficiently doubtful for her to be dropped from the Roman Missal, this precluded the naming of churches and chapels after her.

In northern France, the international aspects dominate as well, but the situation there is somewhat confused by the frequent use of an alternate name "Venisse," which, while being understood as identical with Veronica, may have originally referred to a different person, whose legend had been fused with that of Veronica.

The earliest reference to her in the north seems to be in the supplement to the *Chronicum Sigeberti*, composed by Robert, the abbot of Mont St.-Michel, in 1170 or 1171. It repeats the story of the arrival of Veronica and her companions in the Bordeaux region.[37] In 1249, the then archdeacon of the cathedral at Laon (the future Pope Urban IV) sent there a copy of one of the Holy Veils of Rome. A cult of St. Veronica is known to have developed soon thereafter at the nearby convent of Montreuil.[38] In 1382, Charles VI authorized the Paris cloth merchants to establish: "Une confrérie en l'honneur de sainte Venisse en l'église parrochiale de saint

[37] "De S. Veronica" (ch. 4).

[38] See Grabar.

Eustache." [39] It is this last identification that brought about her role in the fifteenth-century mystery plays as a blind clothmerchant, cured by the *sudarium*, who supplies the material for the Holy Shroud.[40] Her name is only very infrequently used for places of worship. Lebeuf, in his seven-volume study of the ecclesiastical province of Paris, lists only one chapel dedicated to St. Veronica, located in the Church of Notre-Dame de Pompone, a town on the Marne between Chelle and Lagny.[41] Maréchaux (p. 175) notes in addition an underground chapel in the cathedral at Chartres. The Veronica iconography of the north is all relatively late and must be seen as resulting from rather than antecedent to the development of the now traditional Stations of the Cross.

## B. Concerning the Manuscripts of the "Vengeance de Nostre-Seigneur"

### *1. The List of Manuscripts Containing Prose Versions*

a. Family A:

A. Grenoble. Bibliothèque Municipale 468

ff. 34, line 21 to 56, line 33; fourteenth century; 1 column per folio, 33 lines per column; no decoration.

Text preceded by the *Gospel of Gamaliel* (that is, the long version of the *Gospel of Nicodemus*).

*Titles*: "Si après s'ensuy la Vengence de Jhesu Crist et la Destruction de Jherusalem"
"Si finit la Destruction de Jherusalem et la Vengeance de Jhesu Crist et la Justice et la male fin de Pilate"

A1. Valenciennes. Bibliothèque Municipale 541

ff. 67$^{v}$, line 1 to 113$^{v}$, line 3; fifteenth century; 1 column per folio, 22-23 lines per column; no decoration.

Text preceded by the "Procés de la passion de Jhesu Crist et de la resurrection" (the *Gospel of Gamaliel*), and followed by "La Plainte de Nostre-Dame."

[39] Quoted in Réau (vol. III, partie III, p. 1315). See also Spadafora and Celletti, *Bibliotheca Sanctorum* (vol. XII, col. 1049). St. Venisse seems to have been known best in Normandy during the Middle Ages. See the listing of statuary in Blouet (although this article should be used with caution).

[40] Réau (vol. III, partie III, p. 1314).

[41] Vol. II, pp. 504-505. See also vol. I, pp. 61-63.

*Titles*: "Cy aprés s'ensieult la Vengance de Jhesu Crist et la Destruction de Jherusalem"
"Cy fine la Destruction de Jherusalem et la Vengance de Jhesu Crist et la Justice et mal fin de Pilate"

A2. Bern. Bürgerbibliothek A260

ff. 127r, line 1 to 148v, line 28; fifteenth century; 1 column per folio, 41-43 lines per column; no decoration.

Text preceded by the *Gospel of Nicodemus* (in French) and followed by a poem in French entitled "Pater noster qui as fait le monde."

*Title*: "Ci finist la Vengence de la mort Nostre Seigneur Jhesu Crist et la Destruction de Jherusalem."

A3. Paris. Bibliothèque Nationale, fonds français 981

ff. 40a, line 1 to 61c, line 34; fifteenth century; 2 columns per folio, 38 lines per column; no decoration.

Text preceded by "Aultrez huit Exortacions de saint Ancelmne, archidiacre de Cantorbie."

*Title*: "La Destruction de Jherusalem ... la Justice et la mort de Pilate."

A4. London. British Library Additional 32090

ff. 48v, line 1 to 88v, line 3; 1445 (f. 88v); 1 column per folio, 40 lines per column; 3 miniatures: f. 58v (Roman army leaving Rome); f. 59v (Roman army besieging Japheth's castle); f. 78r (Pilate kneeling before the emperor). Spaces left for additional miniatures on all folios except: 49r, 49v, 50r, 50v, 51r, 57v, 62v, 85v.

Text preceded by the *Gospel of Gamaliel*.

*Titles*: "Cy commenche la Destruction de Jerusalem au tamps de Vaspasian"
"Cy fine la Destruction de Jherusalem et la Vengance de la mort Nostre Seigneur Dieu Jhesu Crist et De la mort et de la justice du faulx traÿtre juge Pylate."

A5. Paris. Bibliothèque Nationale, nouvelles acquisitions françaises 1357

ff. 1r, line 5 to 25v, line 23 (text is incomplete); fifteenth century; 1 column per folio, 23 lines per column; no decoration.

Text followed by a poem in French entitled "Se ta famme de tes sers se complaint."

*Title*: "Cy commance la Vengeance de la mort de Nostre Sauveur Jhesu Crist et la Destruction de Jherusalem et la Male Fin de Pilate."

A6. Besançon. Bibliothèque Municipale 588

ff. 25$^{v}$, line 1 to 41$^{v}$, line 4; early sixteenth century; 1 column per folio, 31-39 lines per column; no decoration.

Text preceded by the *Gospel of Nicodemus* (in French) and followed by "En ce livre sont contenues et escriptes les choses qui appartiennent a faire pour le remede de l'ame."

*Title*: "Explicit la Destruction de Jherusalem."

A7. Paris. Bibliothèque Nationale, fonds français 12481

ff. 47$^{r}$, line 1 to 63$^{v}$, line 35; fifteenth century; 1 column per folio, 34-39 lines per folio; no decoration.

Text preceded and followed by religious tracts in Latin.

*Titles*: None.

A8. Brussels. Bibliothèque Royale IV.509 (formerly Phillipps 3657)

ff. 39$^{r}$, line 1 to 58$^{v}$, line 25; c. 1480; 1 column per folio, 34-35 lines per column; no decoration.

Text preceded by a "Passion de Jhesus Crist" in French, and followed by two religious treatises also in French: "Les Commandemens de la loy" and "Douze fruits de l'esprit."

*Title*: "Cy commence [ ] Destruction de J[ ]" (rest lost in trimming).

A9. Chantilly. Condé 38 (olim 898)

ff. 87$^{r}$, line 7 to 141$^{r}$, line 10; fifteenth century; 1 column per folio, 25-27 lines per column; no decoration.

Text preceded by the *Gospel of Gamaliel*.

*Titles*: "Cy aprés s'ensuit la Vengeance de la mort de Nostre Seigneur Jhesu Crist et Destruction de la cité de Jherusalem"

"... Si escript et fist la Destruction de Jherusalem et Vengence de Nostre Seigneur Jhesu Crist ... la Justice et mort de Pylate."

A10. Paris. Bibliothèque Nationale, fonds français 24438

ff. 202$^{r}$, line 1 to 238$^{v}$, line 21; late fifteenth, early sixteenth century; 1 column per folio, 23-27 lines per column; no decoration, but blank spaces left for paragraph capitals; manuscript damaged: hole lower right of verso, ff. 234-237; f. 238 severely damaged.

Text preceded by the *Gospel of Gamaliel*.

*Titles*: None visible because of damage to manuscript.

A11. Paris. Bibliothèque Nationale, fonds français 1370

ff. 78$^{r}$, line 4 to 126$^{v}$, line 11; fifteenth century; 1 column per folio, 27-28 lines per column; no decoration.

Text preceded by "Traicté de la vie Nostre Seigneur et Redempteur Jhesu Crist" and followed by "Une Epistre que Pilate envoya a Cesar, empereur de Romme, soy excusant de la mort de Jhesus de Nazareth."

*Titles*: "La Destruction de Jherusalem et la Cruelle Vangence que Nostre Seigneur prinst des juifz qui pour lors estoient en Jherusalem, de Pilate et des maistres de la loy"

"La Destruction de Jherusalem et la Vangence qu'il avoit faicte de Noustre Seigneur Jhesu Cirst ... et aussi la Mort de Pilate."

A12. Paris. Bibliothèque Nationale, fonds français 979

ff. 50$^{r}$, line 3 to 80$^{v}$, line 12; mid-fifteenth century (the date 1464 appears on f. 80$^{v}$ in a hand other than the scribe's); 1 column per folio, 29-33 lines per column; no decoration.

Text preceded by the *Gospel of Gamaliel* and followed by a tract in French entitled "C'est l'oppinion des docteurs que le Roy a demandé touchant le fait de la Pucelle envoyee de par Dieu."

*Titles*: "Cy commance la Vengeance de la mort et passion de Nostre Seigneur Jhesu Crist, et aussy De la Destruction de Jherusalem et des juifs"

"Cy finist le romain de la Destruction de Jherusalem et de la Vengeance de la mort et passion de Jhesu Crist."

A13. Lyons. Bibliothèque Municipale 864

ff. 158$^{r}$, line 2 to 180$^{v}$, line 19; 1450; 1 column per folio, 25-28 lines per column; no decoration; first line of each paragraph in larger script; résumé of paragraph content indicated in left margin.

Text preceded by "L'istoire de la Passion Nostre Seigneur Jhesu Crist, le benoit Filz de Dieu" and followed by "Lettre fausse d'Aristote a Alexandre."

*Titles*: "Cy commence la Destruction de Jherusalem"

"Ceste Destruction de Jherusalem a esté copiee par Piret d'Altena."

b. Family B:

B. Salins. Bibliothèque Municipale 12

ff. 257$^{r}$, line 4 to 281$^{r}$, line 6; fifteenth century; 1 column per folio, 30-31 lines per column; no decoration.

Text preceded by "Briefve doctrine pour enseignier toute personne ou lit de la mort, compilee par maistre Jehan Jarson" (= Jean Gerson) and followed by "Demandes d'ung empereur et responses d'ung enfant."

*Titles*: "Destruction de Jherusalem"
"Ainsi fut la Vangance de Nostre Seigneur faite."

B1. Paris. Bibliothèque de l'Arsenal 2114

ff. 141$^{r}$, line 1 to 173$^{r}$, line 16; fifteenth century; 1 column per folio, 25-28 lines per column; no decoration, but spaces left blank for paragraph initials.

Text preceded by "Cy commancent les meditations sainct Bernard" and followed by "Le Purgatoire de saint Patrice."

*Titles*: "La Vengence de Nostre Seigneur Jhesu Crist par Vaspasien"
"Icy fine la Vengence de Nostre Seigneur Jhesu Crist par Vaspasien."

B2. Lyons. Bibliothèque Municipale 1235

ff. 118$^{r}$, line 1 to 144$^{v}$, line 9; fifteenth century; 1 column per folio, 28-31 lines per column; no decoration.

Text preceded by "Passio Domini nostri" (in French) and followed by "Cy commancent les Meditacions monseigneur saint Bernard, abbé de Clervaulx...."

*Title*: "Destructio Jerusalem."

B3. Paris. Bibliothèque Nationale, fonds français 17061

ff. 239$^{r}$, line 1 to 261$^{v}$, line 28; fifteenth century; 1 column per folio, 30-33 lines per column; no decoration.

Text preceded by "L'Histoire de Daniel" in French.

*Titles*: "Cy commance la Vangeance de Nostre Seigneur Jhesu Crist"
"La Vangeance de Nostre Seigneur par l'empereur Vaspasien."

B4. Lyons. Bibliothèque Municipale 918

ff. 62$^{r}$, line 6 to 97$^{v}$, line 23; fifteenth century; 1 column per folio, 30 lines per column; no decoration.

Text preceded by "Chronique en prose de Richard II, roi d'Angleterre."

*Titles*: "Cy commance la Destruction de Jherusalem faicte par Vaspasien, empereur de Rome"
"Explicit la Destruction de Jherusalem faicte par Vaspasien, empereur de Rome."

B5. Vatican City. Biblioteca Apostolica Vaticana Reginensis 1728

ff. $35^r$, line 1 to $47^r$, line 33; fifteenth century; 1 column per folio, 48-55 lines per column; no decoration.

*Titles*: "La Vengence de Nostre Seigneur"
"Explicit la Vengence de Nostre Seigneur et la Destruction de Jherusalem."

B6. Carpentras. Bibliothèque Municipale 472

ff. $152^r$, line 1 to $176^r$, line 15; fifteenth century (the date 6 April 1483 occurs on f. $179^r$); 1 column per folio, 39-43 lines per column; no decoration; beginning f. $167^r$, blurring and bleeding of text which becomes progressively worse from that point on; beginning f. 173, various holes in paper, likewise becoming progressively larger and more frequent.

Text preceded by a life of Jesus: "Sur toutes choses et mesmement entre les aultres pensees espirituelles..." and followed by "Lettre du prestre Jean a l'empereur des Romains et au roi de France."

*Title*: "Si comence la Destruction de Jherusalem faicte par le tresvaillent seigneur Vasparien, empereur de Romme."

B7. Paris. Bibliothèque Nationale, fonds français 2273

ff. $155^v$, line 8 to $206^v$, line 23; fifteenth century; 1 column per folio, 20-23 lines per column; no decoration.

Text preceded by the "Passion de Nostre Sauveur et Redempteur Jhesu Crist" translated by Jehan Jerçon ( = Jean Gerson).

*Titles*: None.

c. Family C:[42]

Paris. Bibliothèque Nationale, fonds français 17229, ff. $218^d$-$222^b$
Oxford. Queen's College 305, ff. $6^a$-$7^d$
Paris. Bibliothèque Nationale, fonds français 23117, ff. $31^a$-$35^a$
Paris. Bibliothèque Nationale, fonds français 413, ff. $26^c$-$30^b$

[42] The manuscripts of families C through I will be examined in a future volume.

d. Family D:

London. British Library Harleian 2253, ff. 39[c]-41[a]
London. British Library Egerton 2710, ff. 132[c]-133[d]
Paris. Bibliothèque Nationale, fonds français 19525, ff. 59[b]-61[a]
Aberystwyth. National Library of Wales 5028C, ff. 131[r]-133[v]

e. Family E:

Dublin. Trinity College 951, ff. 5[r]-12[r]

f. Family F (Roger d'Argenteuil's *Bible en français*):

Paris. Bibliothèque Nationale, fonds français 1850, ff. 24[r]-37[r]
Paris. Bibliothèque Nationale, nouvelles acquisitions françaises 13521, ff. 263[a]-271[d]
Paris. Bibliothèque Nationale, fonds français 1555, ff. 192[r]-200[v]
Paris. Bibliothèque Nationale, fonds Moreau 1718, pp. 192-281
Brussels. Bibliothèque Royale 10394-414, ff. 48-70
Brussels. Bibliothèque Royale 10574-85, ff. 4-56
Salins. Bibliothèque Municipale 12, ff. 192-231
Paris. Bibliothèque Nationale, fonds français 25549, ff. 32[r]-44[r]
Paris. Bibliothèque Nationale, fonds français 25553, ff. 18[r]-27[v]
Lille. Bibliothèque Municipale 190 (130), ff. 17[r]-55[v]

g. Family G:

Paris. Bibliothèque Nationale, fonds français 187, ff. 68[c]-70[d]

h. Family H:

Paris. Bibliothèque Nationale, fonds français 181, ff. 184[a]-197[d]
London. British Library Royal 16.G.iii, ff. 193[a]-212[b]

i. Family I:

London. British Library Egerton 613, ff. 21[r]-25[r]

### 2. *Selecting the Base-Manuscript*

As is evident from the preceding lists of manuscripts containing the *Vengeance de Nostre-Seigneur* in prose, it was undoubtedly a very popular work in the French Middle Ages, extant then in hundreds of manuscripts. Of these, as we have seen, at least twenty-two survive in the version ascribed to Japheth. The manuscripts fall clearly into two families, here called A and B. As the differences between the two groups are not differences of content, but only of expression, the decision was made not to present an edited text of each version, but rather to edit just one, and record the readings of the manuscripts of the other family in the variants. Since there are fourteen manuscripts in the A family and eight in B, it seemed reasonable to select the base-manuscript from A, as that group probably was the most frequently read. Within A, eight manuscripts can be eliminated from consideration for the following reasons: A11, A12 and A13 present versions quite distinct from all the others, including frequent expansions; A4, A5 and A10 are incomplete; A6 follows the B family beginning with paragraph 12; and A7 was copied by a scribe who does not seem to have understood his exemplar.

This leaves us with six manuscripts: A, A1, A2, A3, A8 and A9, all of which contain "correct" versions of our narrative. Again, the stemma (p. 26) shows that A8 and A9 are not as typical of the surviving manuscripts as are the other four. Although not free from errors, MS A (Grenoble 468) was finally selected as base-manuscript as it is the earliest of all the manuscripts, dating from the fourteenth century, whereas all the others are from the fifteenth.

### 3. *Corrections Made in the Base-Manuscript*

The guiding principle employed in deciding if the base-manuscript were to be altered was a conservative one: changes would be made only if clarity would suffer by not making them. As indicated, our scribe did not have total control of his written language, and tends frequently to spell phonetically or to confuse homonyms. He therefore will use *se* for *ce*, *dist* for *dis* or *atacher* for *ataché*. In the first case, no changes have been made as the syntactic context clearly shows whether the reflexive pronoun or the demonstrative adjective is intended. But in the case of verb forms, where syntactic confusion might occur in the reader's mind, they have been corrected to conform to the norms of the period. Similarly, our scribe does not always distinguish between initial *b* and initial *v*. In the name *Beronique / Veronique*, this has not been changed, but *boucirent* (l. 560) has been corrected to *voucirent*, as it is the third person plural in the preterit tense of *vouloir*.

In all, ninety-eight changes were made. Of these, thirteen (those in lines 61, 143, 189, 212-213, 365, 436, 529, 638, 697, 795, 999, 1136, 1156) resulted from the scribe's failure to expunctuate; and twenty-eight changes (those in lines 16, 17, 20, 134, 144, 237, 283, 330, 396, 432, 542, 551, 560, 595, 604, 746, 779, 780, 787, 800, 883, 995, 1011, 1053, 1061, 1064, 1080, 1086) were made because the scribe chose the incorrect homonym, most frequently in the case of verb forms. Twenty-one omissions (in lines 131, 165-167, 183-184, 192-193, 234, 518, 555, 570-

571, 577, 708-709, 715, 725, 729, 791, 809, 811, 969, 1047, 1086, 1130, 1139) which made the text incomprehensible or of unsure interpretation were supplied from other manuscripts.

The largest group of changes (thirty-six) consists of those words in the base-manuscript that are partially or completely incorrect and needed to be adjusted or replaced to assure understanding of the text. Here again corrections were made, whenever possible, on the basis of the readings of the other manuscripts. These fall into several categories: 1) an extra letter, a missing letter, or a wrong letter (18, 107, 261, 310, 578, 586, 652, 675, 684, 714, 715, 1059, 1082, 1133); 2) an incorrect pronoun or possessive adjective reference (43, 72, 554, 976, 1123); 3) an incorrect verb tense, person, or both (65, 66, 357, 448, 1165, 1177); and 4) an inappropriate word (10, 118, 149, 269, 360, 458, 743, 778, 1048, 1116, 1145). All rejected readings are to be found in the critical and explanatory notes.

All abbreviations have been resolved on the basis of forms fully written-out elsewhere in the text. These are limited to cardinal and ordinal numbers, plus the names *Jhesu, Jherusalem* and *Nostre-Seigneur*. Modern capitalization, paragraphing and punctuation have been supplied.

*4. Stemmata*

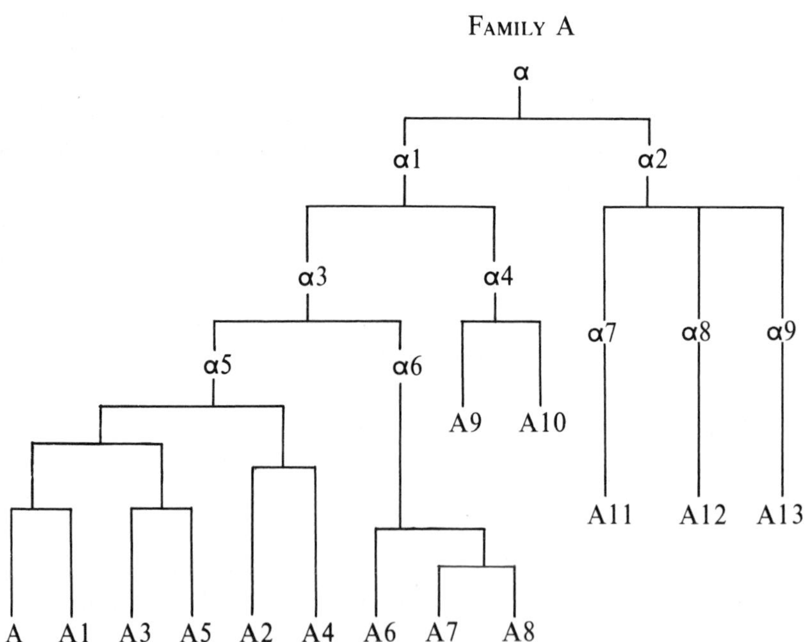

FAMILY B

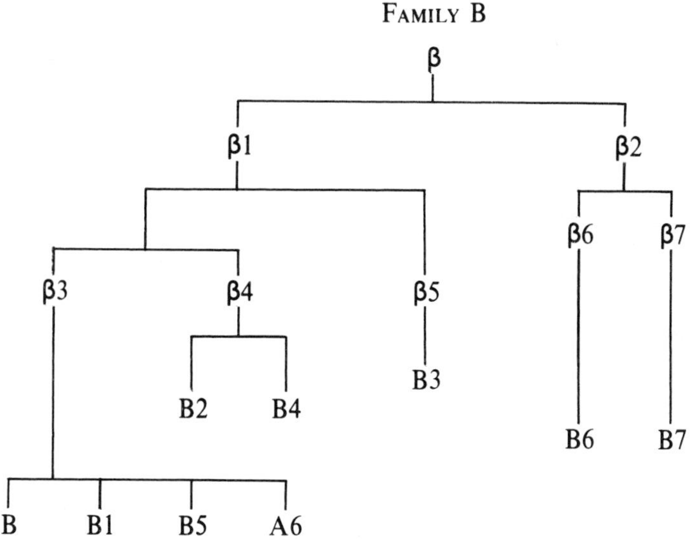


The symbols "α" and "β" represent unknown *Urschriften*. Each symbol may indicate a single manuscript or multiple manuscripts. The symbols "α1" through "α9" and "β1" through "β7" indicate an undetermined and undeterminable number of manuscripts between the *Urschriften* and the surviving manuscripts. Note that MS A6 is shown in both *stemmata* as its scribe used exemplars from both families.

## C. Résumé of the Text of the Base-Manuscript

### *1. Preamble*

(1) Forty years after Jesus' death, Vespasian is emperor of Rome and master of Jerusalem. Both he and his son Titus believe in pagan idols and the pleasures of this world. But Jesus, in order to dissuade the emperor and his people from this error, proceeds as follows. (lines 1-14)

### *2. The Curing of Vespasian*

(2) Ill with leprosy at Our Lord's will, Vespasian summons his best doctors, but to no avail. Only God can cure this illness which is becoming progressively worse. (lines 15-25)
(3) At this time, Clement, a disciple of Jesus Christ, arrives in Rome where he must preach in secret. Gaius, the head of the emperor's household, is converted by Clement's sermons and laments Vespasian's suffering. (lines 26-34)

(4) Gaius, when he hears the emperor's claim that his illness has been visited on him by the gods, tells him of Jesus Christ who in Jerusalem cured many illnesses. If the emperor could only touch some object that had touched Jesus' body, he would be cured instantly. After a brief résumé of the tenets of the Faith, including Judas' role in the Crucifixion, Gaius recommends that someone be sent to Jerusalem to find such an object. (lines 35-70)

(5) Vespasian wishes Gaius to go himself. If the object does indeed cure him, he will avenge Jesus' death. While in Jerusalem, Gaius is to seek out Pilate to see why he is no longer sending the yearly tribute money. (lines 71-79)

(6) Gaius leaves on his mission: by horse to Barleta, then by boat to Acre and Caesarea, and finally overland to Jerusalem, where he stays in the home of Jacob, the father of Maria Jacobi. (lines 80-92)

(7) Believing Jacob to be an honest man, Gaius tells him of the emperor's illness and of his own mission. (lines 93-121)

(8) After insisting on faith in Jesus as a prerequisite to being cured, Jacob tells of the cloth owned by Veronica, which was used to wipe Christ's face during the Crucifixion and onto which His face was transferred. (lines 122-147)

(9) Summoned by Jacob, Veronica agrees to return to Rome with Gaius and the Holy Face. (lines 148-161)

(10) But before returning, Gaius must speak to Pilate. To him he explains the emperor's displeasure, but promises forgiveness if the tribute money is paid immediately. (lines 162-173)

(11) Pilate convenes his council to discuss the request. Barlabam, one of his councillors, recommends that Vespasian no longer be recognized as emperor of Jerusalem, for even if the Romans besieged the city, they could not prolong the siege because of the lack of water. Pilate agrees and suggests that Gaius be killed, but Barlabam insists it would be wrong to kill a messenger. Gaius is sent away with Pilate maintaining that the emperor is no longer his lord. (lines 174-188)

(12) After recompensing Jacob for his kindness, Gaius and Veronica retrace their route to Rome, where the emperor remains gravely ill. (lines 189-199)

(13) Upon his return to Rome, Gaius finds the nobility of the empire assembled for the crowning of Titus as emperor. When he announces that he has the Holy Face with him and that it will cure the emperor if the latter believes in Jesus, Vespasian declares that he does believe and that if cured, he will avenge Jesus' death. Gaius recommends that the miracle

take place the next day when the nobility will all be present at Titus' coronation. (lines 200-225)

(14) When informed of the emperor's decision, Veronica prays for the curing of Vespasian. (lines 226-240)

(15) Arising from her prayers, Veronica notices Clement in the street and after summoning him, explains her role in the Crucifixion and the reason for her presence in Rome, and requests that Clement accompany her the next morning. (lines 241-257)

(16) The following day before the assembled nobles, Clement outlines the Christian faith. (lines 258-275)

(17) Clement and Veronica pray again for the emperor's health, and when the Holy Face is unfolded, Vespasian is immediately cured. After giving thanks to God, he crowns Titus as co-emperor. (lines 276-284)

(18) The next morning, after preaching before the emperor and his people, Clement requests that they be baptized. (lines 285-293)

(19) Vespasian does not reply but offers Veronica any reward she might like except the city of Rome. She refuses, insisting that Clement should receive any recompense, for she is in his service. The emperor agrees but Clement wants no material reward, only the baptism of Vespasian and of his nobles. (lines 294-305)

(20) Vespasian makes Clement bishop of Rome, but refuses baptism until he has avenged Jesus' death. To this end, he announces his imminent departure for Jerusalem. The Holy Face is placed over the altar of St. Simeon's church. Veronica and many others receive baptism. (lines 306-320)

(21) Gaius explains privately to Vespasian his treatment at the hands of Pilate and the reasons for not pressing the matter of the tribute money. He reveals that during the interview with Pilate, various Jews prophesied that soon mothers would eat their children and Jerusalem would be destroyed. (lines 321-339)

### *3. The Destruction of Jerusalem*

(22) Angered by Gaius' report, Vespasian immediately mobilizes his armies. They set out, arriving five weeks later at Acre. The city capitulates without delay and is spared. (lines 340-350)

(23) After resting in Acre, the Romans besiege the castle of Caffe, the home of Japheth, a first cousin of Joseph of Arimathea. All the inhabitants are killed except Japheth and eight friends who hide in a cavern under the castle. Realizing the hopelessness of their situation, the men begin to kill each other rather than starve to death. When only Japheth and one other

remain alive, they decide to ask the emperor for mercy, as Japheth is convinced that once Vespasian realizes who he is, they will be spared. (lines 351-372)

(24) Vespasian has the castle destroyed. Japheth and his cousin emerge from the cavern, explain who they are, and assure the emperor how useful they can be to him in the taking of Jerusalem. Vespasian pardons them and names them to his council of advisors. (lines 373-389)

(25) Vespasian and Titus decide to go on to Jerusalem. We are reminded of St. Luke's prophecies concerning the destruction of the city. (lines 390-396)

(26) In Jerusalem, Pilate, Archelaus (the king of Galilee), and many Jews have assembled for the holy days, unaware of the approaching danger. A great wind prevents them from leaving the city. (lines 397-403)

(27) Jerusalem is besieged, but Pilate is again advised (this time by Archelaus) that there is no need for fear as the besiegers would not have enough water to sustain them. Pilate orders all those in the city to arm themselves and to carry stones up onto the walls. Unarmed, Pilate goes up on the wall and summons Vespasian. (lines 404-426)

(28) Vespasian reminds Pilate of the latter's loyalty to the former's father, Julius, and reveals once again the reason for his presence before the city: Pilate's refusal for seven years to pay the annual tribute money. The emperor orders the gates to be opened so he can deal with Pilate. (lines 427-441)

(29) Pilate again summons his council and again hears from Archelaus and Barlabam that there is no real danger as the nearest water supply is a day's journey away. Pilate agrees with this opinion and defies the emperor, ordering him to return to Rome. (lines 442-467)

(30) The emperor refuses to return and assures Pilate no one will be spared. Pilate again defies him, refusing to recognize him as emperor. (lines 468-475)

(31) Back in his tents, Vespasian tells Titus of Pilate's obstinancy. Titus is overjoyed, seeing it as God's will, in that Pilate will have no more mercy from Vespasian than Jesus had from Pilate. (lines 476-485)

(32) The grooms come to announce that the horses lack water and that the nearest supply is fifteen miles away. Japheth recommends as a solution that their animals be slaughtered and the hides be sewn together and stretched out in the Valley of Jehoshaphat. While this is being done, two thousand horses bring water which, when poured into the hides, miraculously remains pure. (lines 486-510)

(33) When Pilate sees the valley filled with water, he regrets not having given up the city to Vespasian. Again Archelaus and Barlabam encourage

him, but Jacob advises Pilate to turn over the city as he believes Vespasian will be merciful. Pilate berates him, accusing him of being responsible for sending Veronica to Rome, and emprisons him in one of the towers of his palace. (lines 511-534)

(34) Jacob, in prison, prays to Jesus that he not die in such a place. His daughter, Maria, also prays for his liberation. (lines 535-544)

(35) As a result of her prayer, an angel appears to Jacob, frees him, and leads him to the emperor's tent without him being seen by the Roman guards. (lines 545-558)

(36) Gaius recognizes Jacob as his host in Jerusalem and presents him to the emperor. Jacob relates his story and is appointed to Vespasian's council of advisors. (lines 559-572)

(37) Vespasian consults with his council on how best to deal with Jerusalem. Jacob, when called on by the emperor to speak first, tells of the lack of food within the city, a fact that will prevent them from withstanding a long siege, and advises that a ditch be dug around the city to prevent anyone from escaping. (lines 573-595)

(38) Vespasian accepts his advice and commands that the ditch be dug, the workmen to be under the orders of Jacob and Japheth. (lines 596-605)

(39) Upon seeing the ditch being dug, Pilate recognizes the work of Jacob and Japheth and accepts the recommendation of Archelaus that Joseph of Arimathea, their cousin, be sent for. Joseph suggests that the only thing to do is to attack the Romans early in the morning when the latter will be facing the sun. Pilate accepts this and orders his men to assemble at dawn in front of the Temple of Solomon. (lines 606-621)

(40) The next morning Pilate orders his men into battle and twenty thousand soldiers come forth from the city. (lines 622-628)

(41) Alerted by a guard, Vespasian orders his men to arms. (lines 629-641)

(42) The two armies attack each other from nine in the morning to three in the afternoon. Three thousand of Pilate's men die, eight hundred of the emperor's. After resting, they again engage until sundown. Pilate loses thirty-seven hundred men, the emperor twelve hundred. (lines 642-654)

(43) Then Our Lord, who wishes His death to be avenged, works a miracle. At sundown the sun rises again in the east. (lines 655-660)

(44) The emperor sees this as an indication that he and his men are not to leave the battlefield. The battle continues until noon, Pilate losing twelve hundred and fifty men, the emperor one thousand and fifty. (lines 661-666)

(45) After resting until vespers, they again fight until sundown. Twenty-two hundred and fifty of Pilate's men die, only three hundred and fifty of

the emperor's. Pilate's forces are routed and chased back to the gates of Jerusalem.
(lines 667-674)

(46) As they return to the city, a voice is heard crying: "Vespasian, go into Jerusalem." The people think it must be a prophet. During the return, Joseph of Arimathea is wounded between the thighs. (lines 675-679)

(47) Back in the city, Pilate, Archelaus, and the people lament their losses. (lines 680-683)

(48) In their tents, the emperor and his men rest after the battle. Japheth and Jacob are ordered to proceed with the digging of the ditch. (lines 684-691)

(49) Pilate and his men are very upset when they see the ditch and are berated by the people who say that the man heard shouting at the gates was Jesus, and that Pilate has been ill-advised by those who recommended not turning over the city, for people are now dying in the streets. (lines 692-701)

(50) Joseph of Arimathea recommends the immediate digging of ditches to bury the dead and the careful preservation of the food supply, especially because of the presence in the city of thirty thousand outsiders. (lines 702-711)

(51) Joseph is ordered to have the ditches dug and to bury the thirteen thousand, seven hundred who have died. The food supply is quickly exhausted, even the rats and the leather on the city gates are eaten. And the people are dying without number. (lines 712-741)

(52) And there is in the city a woman named Marie, the widow of the king of Africa, who is living with her daughter, her companion Clarice, and the latter's son. Since arriving in Jerusalem, they have converted to Christianity. And now that there is no more food, their children have both died. Both mothers grieve, but Clarice suggests that they roast a part of her son. The queen is horrified at the suggestion and faints, but is raised up by an angel who reveals that it is God's will that this be done, for it was prophesied that in this generation there would be in Jerusalem such famine that mothers would eat their children and the city would be destroyed. The mothers, still in tears, prepare to roast one quarter of the child. (lines 742-774)

(53) Pilate and Archelaus, walking in the street, smell the roast cooking and send a servant to inquire as to its source. He is welcomed by the queen and her companion who offer him a quarter of the child for Pilate. The servant is so shocked that he runs from the house and explains to Pilate what he has seen. Pilate is equally distressed and retires to his bed for three days. (lines 775-804)

(54) Having consumed the companion's child, the two women begin to eat the queen's daughter. (lines 805-813)
(55) Pilate leaves his bed and summons his council. He now sees no hope for Jerusalem as there is no food and mothers are even eating their own children. He recommends that the city be turned over to Vespasian as it is better for him to die rather than all the people. A great cry goes up from the people when they hear the news, a cry heard in the emperor's camp. (lines 814-830)
(56) Pilate orders that what he has said be done. He comes to the ditch with five thousand men and addresses the emperor with his ten thousand, asking for mercy. Vespasian refuses, saying that the city must be handed over to do with as he sees fit. Archelaus steps forward and identifies himself as the son of Herod, the faithful subject of the emperor, but Vespasian, on hearing that this is the son of the man responsible for the slaughter of the Holy Innocents, refuses him any mercy. Archelaus commits suicide. Pilate returns to the city to relay the news to his people. (lines 831-866)
(57) Pilate summons Joseph of Arimathea, Barlabam and his people and asks for their advice. Joseph replies that he has no more recommendations to make, for in the past Pilate has been given bad advice. (lines 867-876)
(58) Pilate suggests that what they can do is to prevent the emperor having the city's treasure. This they can accomplish by grinding up the precious metals and stones and eating them. The people do this and then again come before Pilate who asks their pardon for any offence he may have committed against them. The people are very upset as they believe they must all soon die. (lines 877-897)
(59) Pilate now decides to throw himself on Vespasian's mercy as this is better than the certainty of dying by starvation. He and his people come forth from the city and send word to Vespasian through Titus whom they encounter near the city walls. Vespasian accepts the surrender of the city but refuses to be merciful. Pilate surrenders Jerusalem, recognizing Vespasian as its rightful ruler. (lines 898-927)
(60) Vespasian orders the ditches to be filled in and has ten thousand of his men go into the city, closing the gates behind them, to prevent anyone from escaping. After all seventy thousand, six hundred inhabitants are tied up, the gates are reopened to allow the entrance of Vespasian who goes directly to the Temple of Solomon to give thanks for the victory. (lines 928-941)
(61) Vespasian, in order to avenge Jesus' death, orders that the Jews of Jerusalem be sold, that just as they sold Jesus for thirty denarii, they will

be sold, thirty for one denarius. Thirty-five solders are commissioned to do the selling. (lines 942-951)

(62) One soldier, having purchased a group of thirty Jews, runs one through with his sword and is amazed to see that gold and silver flow from the wound. A second Jew reveals Pilate's deception and how they had lived twenty-one days on the city's treasure. When this becomes known, the Jews are purchased quickly and killed for the treasure. Jacob and Japheth remind Vespasian that some of these people, especially Joseph of Arimathea, the queen of Africa, her companion and their children, are friends of God and should be spared. (lines 952-978)

(63) The emperor sends Jacob and Japheth to locate them, but only Joseph is found alive. He is spared by Vespasian because of his role in the Crucifixion. (lines 979-987)

(64) Vespasian orders that the remaining six groups of thirty Jews not be killed. In all, seventy-two thousand, three hundred and fifty have died, many of whom would have been spared, had it not been for the advice given by Pilate. (lines 988-998)

(65) The entire city of Jerusalem and its walls are destroyed, with the exception of the Temple of Solomon and the Tower of Sion. (lines 999-1011)

(66) When this has been done, Vespasian and Titus ask Jacob, Japheth and Joseph to take them to Calvary, Jesus' tomb, and other sites. (lines 1012-1018)

(67) The emperor and his son decide to return to Rome, taking with them as far as Acre Pilate and the six groups of Jews. There, two groups are put in each of three ships that are put out to sea without food or captain. The ships and their contents are not lost but arrive in Narbonne, in Bordeaux and in England. This miracle occurs so that Jesus' passion and death will always be remembered. The Romans continue their journey by sea to Barleta, then on to Rome. (lines 1019-1036)

(68) When Clement hears of their arrival, he comes in procession to meet them and there is much rejoicing in Rome. After preaching for a week, Clement reminds the emperor of his promise to be baptized, if he is able to avenge Jesus' death. The emperor and many of his court accept baptism, and all who are ill are miraculously cured through being baptized. The lords of the empire request and are granted permission to return to their homes, taking with them a written statement of their new faith. In their own countries they baptize their own people. Saint Clement sends his disciples to every land. (lines 1037-1070)

### *4. The Punishing of Pilate*

(69) Vespasian summons the Roman Senate so that Pilate may be judged. After being apprised of his crimes, the senators deliberate and decide that since they were committed outside of Rome, Pilate must be sent to Vienne for punishment. There, he is to be attached to a pillar in the public square, covered in oil and honey, and progressively dismembered over a period of twenty-one days, this figure representing the twenty-one extra days the Jews lived in Jerusalem because of Pilate's deceit. This punishment is prescribed since Pilate is a traitor both to God and to the emperor. (lines 1071-1120)

(70) Ten soldiers accompany Pilate to Vienne, where, while the pillar is being prepared, he is held in a well. (lines 1121-1137)

(71) But when Pilate is removed from the well, his face is so changed that he looks like a devil. He is put in the middle story of a three-story tower on a bridge over the Rhône, with guards above and below him. (lines 1138-1149)

(72) The next morning, when the soldiers come to the tower to take Pilate to the public square, they find the tower covered with devils crying: "He is ours; let us have him !" The tower then falls into the river and the water begins to boil. All attempts to get close to where the tower fell are unsuccessful. Nothing further is known of the death of Pilate. The pillar is still in the square, and it is believed the devils did this to prevent Pilate from converting to Christianity during his punishment. (lines 1150-1179)

### *5. Conclusion*

(73) The soldiers return to Rome and relate the events of Vienne to the emperor and the people. Japheth then puts into writing the story of the destruction of Jerusalem and the death of Pilate; (lines 1180-1185)

(74) Here ends the Destruction of Jerusalem, and the Vengeance of Jesus Christ, and the Punishment and evil end of Pilate. (lines 1186-1187)

# La "Vengeance de Nostre-Seigneur"
# The Version Ascribed to Japheth

## Apparatus Sigla

*Base Manuscript*:

A Grenoble. Bibliothèque Municipale 468

*Collated Manuscripts*:

A1 Valenciennes. Bibliothèque Municipale 541
A2 Bern. Bürgerbibliothek A260
A3 Paris. Bibliothèque Nationale, fonds français 981
A4 London. British Library Additional 32090
A5 Paris. Bibliothèque Nationale, nouvelles acquisitions françaises 1357
A6 Besançon. Bibliothèque Municipale 588
A7 Paris. Bibliothèque Nationale, fonds français 12481
A8 Brussels. Bibliothèque Royale IV.509 (formerly Phillipps 3657)
A9 Chantilly. Condé 38 (olim 898)
A10 Paris. Bibliothèque Nationale, fonds français 24438
A11 Paris. Bibliothèque Nationale, fonds français 1370
A12 Paris. Bibliothèque Nationale, fonds français 979
A13 Lyons. Bibliothèque Municipale 864

B Salins. Bibliothèque Municipale 12
B1 Paris. Bibliothèque de l'Arsenal 2114
B2 Lyons. Bibliothèque Municipale 1235
B3 Paris. Bibliothèque Nationale, fonds français 17061
B4 Lyons. Bibliothèque Municipale 918
B5 Vatican City. Biblioteca Apostolica Vaticana Reginensis 1728
B6 Carpentras. Bibliothèque Municipale 472
B7 Paris. Bibliothèque Nationale, fonds français 2273

## Commentary

The notes accompanying the text are in two sections. The first section includes all the variants from the manuscript families A and B. The second section includes critical and explanatory notes. In the critical notes the symbol [ is to be read as: "has been corrected from." Full publication information for the books and articles cited is to be found in the Bibliography. The minimal citation given here includes only the author's name and the pages to be consulted. Only in the case of multiple titles by the same author is a short title given in addition.

## [1. Preamble]

[34r] [1] Aprés quarante ans que Jhesu Crist fust mis en croys en Jherusalem, Vespesian, filz d'August Sesar, estoit empereur de Rome et d'Almaigna et de toute Lombardie, et ossy detenoit Jherusalem et Judea en sa subjection.

1 *A13* a. le sainte passion que *B, B1, A9, B3, B4* que nostre seigneur i. *A12* que dieux i. *A5, B5, B2* que nostre seigneur (*B2* s. dieu) f. *A6* c. print mort et passion en c. *A8* i.f. *B6* q. et deux ans que i.c. nostre seigneur f. *A13* f. leuve en *A12* en la c. 1-2 *B7* En jherusalem regnoist v. qui pour lors es. *A10, B5* c.v. *A11* en la c. regnoit v. 2 *A11* v. qui lors es. *A12* v.s. qui es. leur empereur et estoit f. *B, B1, B2, B3* v. empereur qui fu f. des iulius (*B2* da.) s. es. (*B3* s. iadis) em. *A7* v.s. *B5* v. fut regnant em. *A13* v. estoit en ce temps e. de r. et estoit filz de iulius cesar lequel fut em. *B4* v. empereur de r. *A3* s. qui es. *A12* s. em. 2-3 *A10* f. de lempereur a.s. dal. et de t.l. et tenoit ih. 2-5 *B5* r. qui e. seigneur de tout le monde et fut homme de grant abstinence et souvent iunoit et se abstenoit de boire et de manger maiz il f. 2-9 *B6* v. qui fut fut f. de iulius cesar em. de r. et de toute barbarie et tenoit en sa s. ih. et toute guacien de iuifs et si e. sire de tout le monde et de toute la loy paigne mais cedit vasparien iunoit et faisoit pluseurs abstinences mais il aouroit les y. et estoit le plus grant ydolatre qui fut en son empire aussit il avoit des biens de cest m. a son vouloir il a. un f. lequel avoit non t. moult noble et tres saige et ce filz tenoit si g.p. et aussit ce filz estoit paroillement ydolatres et prenoit g. plaisir aux y. lesquelles e. 3 *A8* o. de toute ih. et iu. tenoit en *A11, A13* en grant s. 3-4 *B7, A13* l. et r. 3-5 *B, B1, B2, B3, B4* l. et tenoit en destroit la cite de (*B2* d. en) ih. et les iuifs de romme (*B3, B4* de rommenie) et e. seigneur de t.p. (*B1* t. espaigne) et (*B4* et ledit) lempereur (*B3* f. maintez) abstinance et f.a. les y. (*B4* f. a croire les y. qui estoient maintenues par lart du dyable) et aoroit

2 *Vespesian* Titus Flavius Vespasianus (9-79 AD) was emperor from 69-79 AD. Between 66 and 68, Nero put him in charge of the war against the Jews, a task that fell to his son Titus after Vespasian was made emperor. See note to line 7, Robert de Boron (vv. 961-2256) and Bertrand de Bar-sur-Aube (line 4886 *et passim*).

*August Sesar* Caius Julius Caesar Octavianus (63 BC-14 AD) was emperor from 29 BC on. He was therefore emperor when Vespasian was born, but that is the only link between them. He was certainly not Vespasian's father, although he was the step-father of Tiberius, who replaces Vespasian in those narratives known as *The Curing of Tiberius* (*Cura sanitatis Tiberii*). As is so often the case in "historical" documents of the Middle Ages, the names of historical personages are frequently cited merely to lend credence and respectability to the apocryphal tale being told. See also notes to lines 27, 432, and 1080.

2-3 *Almaigna, Lombardie* Although both these areas were subjugated by the Romans, the terminology, particularly in the case of Lombardy, is anachronistic, more suitable to the period of the Holy Roman Empire.

3 *Jherusalem* In addition to its importance in the history of Christianity and its destruction by Titus in 70 AD, Jerusalem was the much-disputed capital of the medieval Kingdom of Jerusalem (beginning 1099).

Et Rome estoit chief de toute paiengnie pour quoy l'empereur tenoit a Rome son siege. Et aouroit et fesoit aourer les ydoles. Et sy estoit le greigneur seigneur du monde et avoit tout le plaisir et bien de cest monde. Et sy avoit un filz sain et noble qui s'apeloit Titus, lequel avoit grant puissance et si avoit grant esperance et grant delit aux biens de cest monde. Et sy creoit moult fort es ydoles qui estoient maintenues par les [34v] deables, car il parloient par elles par lesquelles tout le monde / se perdoit.

4 *A10* de toues ses provinces et de *B7* et lors r. *A6* de tous espaigne pour *A13* t. pour *A9* pa. et pour ce t. le. a 4-5 *A11* e. lors c. de tout icelluy pars et pour ce il se t. a r. tousiours et iceluy empereur aouroit *B7* de toutez les espaignez et pour ce ilz se t. tousiours a r. et aussi ledit empereur adoroist *A10* t. son s. a r. et a. *A12* t. espaigne et pour se t. la a r. tousiours si que ledit empereur vaspesian adouroit 4-8 *A13* q. ilz se t. illec tousiours et faisoit son filz thitus lequel f. estoit saint homme n. de g. 5 *A8* s. et yceluy empereur aouroit 5-6 *A3, A4, B7* le plus grant s. *B3* le plus grant maistre du m. *A10* le plus grant de tout le m. et a. tous b. et tous les p. de 5-7 *B5* y. car il estoit paien et sy *B2* le plus grant maistre de tout le m. et a. tous b. et tous p. a son vouloir et sy 5-8 *B, B1, B4* le plus grant maistre du (*B1* g. sire de tout le *B4* g. sire et m. du) m. et avoit tous les b. et les (*B4* b. desirez a son) p. (*B1* p. et desirs) a son vouloir et sy a. un f.m. et saige qui avoit nom t. et tenoit tant g. 6 *A9* et aussi a. *A5, A7* g. du *A11* g. de tout le m. *A7* a. tous les b.p. de 6-7 *A4, A6, B3, A12* m. et sy *A11* a. de tous b. a son p. et avec ce a. un sien f. moult n. et puissant lequel avoit non t. et iceluy filz a. *B7* m. a son plaisir et a. ung f. moult bel et n. nomme t. 7 *A1* f. saige et *A6* f. saige et leur loy et sa. *A2, A4* a. a f. ung saige et n. home en leur loy qui 7-8 *A3* f. saige et n. en leur loy qui se nommoit t.l. estoit grant seigneur et a. *B3* f.n. et sage qui avoit nom t. et tenoit tant g. *A4* t. et a. *A8* t.a. *A12* n. lequel avoit nom t. et celluy filz a. *B7* l.a.e. 7-9 *B5* f. moult n. et moult g.p. et merveilleuse et estoit entour les y. 7-10 *B2* f.n. et sage qui avoit nom t. et estoit moult puissant et prenoit et avoit en icelluy temps tous les plaisirs et tenoyt lerreur des y. lesquelles e.m. par lart du d. qui parloyt dedans elles par 8 *A6, A8* p.g. *A11, A12* si que il a. *A6* a.g. desir des b. *A9* d. prenoit aux *A10* e. de g. *A11, B7* e. de d. au temporel (*B7* e. o t.) de 8-9 *A10* b. mondains et *B4* g. plaisir en icelluy temps et estoit et se genueroit entour les y. *A12* d. au temporel du m. *B, B1, B3* a. tant grants plaisirs en cellui temps et estoit entour les y. 8-10 *A13* g. temporelz mais ilz en c. point en dieu mais son pere et luy adoroyent les y. et estoit vaspasien seigneur de tout le monde et t. 9 *A10* cr.f. *B7* cr. es y. lesquelles e. tenues 9-10 *A6* e. par les d.m. car il se p. *B, B1, B3, B4, B5* par lart du d. qui p. dedens e. *B6* par lart du d. lequel p. dedens ces ydoles et par aussit t. 10 *A11* p. en e. *A5* pour lez par *A12* e. mesmes par *A8* car par ces ydoles t. *B7* par itelle t. *B7* d. qui p. dedens e. *A12* d. qui p. *B3, A11* le peuple se 10-11 *A10* d. et p. pour quoy le m. en estoit plus abuse sy *A13* p. pour ces faulses ydoles et le doulz i. *B, B2, B4, B5* le peuple se p. (*B5* p. estoit perdu) mais (*B2* m. nostre seigneur dieu) i. *A2, A4* p. pourquoy i. *B1* p. mes i. 10-15 *B6* p. mais i.c. qui avoit voulu mourir en la croix par toute u. nature vouloit tirer le. et titus avecques toulx leurs gens de celle erreur par pugnicion il envoya a

7 *Titus* Titus Flavius Sabinus Vespasianus (40-81 AD) co-ruled with his father Vespasian from 71 to 79 and then ruled alone from 79 to 81. He alone (i.e., not with his father) subdued and destroyed Jerusalem.

10 *parloient par elles* [ *parloient pour elles*

Sy que Jhesu Crist, qui avoit souffert passion pour racheter l'umain linnage, afin qu'il donast recognoissance a l'empereur et pour le geter hors de celle erreur et ces gens ossy, ovra par telle maniere comme il s'ensuit sy desoubz.

## [2. The Curing of Vespasian]

[2] Avint le temps que Nostre Seigneur donna a l'empereur Vespesian une maladie qui s'appeloit chancre, qui lui menga le nes du visaige et les

11 *A6* que nostre seigneur i. *B7* i. qui *A5, A6, A7, A8, A10, A11, B7, A12, A13* s. mort et p. 11-15 *B5* s. mort pour pour r. toute u. creature pour oster le. et toute ses gens dicelle e. et luy faire recongnoistre d. a v. 11-16 *B1, B2, B3, B4, B* s. mort et p. pour r. toute u. (*B4* r.u.) creature (*B* u. lignage) et pour recognoistre et oster (*B2* p.o. le. et toute sa gent dicelle e. car pour (*B, B4* e. et p. *B3* e.p.) ce d. dieu v. (*B2* e.d. dieu a v. empereur) une 12 *A5* pour lez g. *A6* le mectre h. 12-13 *A7* g. de celle tour et *A2, A4, A5, A7* g. ovra 12-15 *B7* l. vollust ouvrer comme vous orrez cy apres dieu envoya et d. a v. *A12* l. et pour recognoistre et g. lempereur et ses gens de celle e. voulsist ovrer ainsi dieux d. a v. le. 12-16 *A11* l. pour g.h. lempereur et ses g. de c.e. ou ilz estoient voulut ouvrer ainsi que vous orrez cy apres dieu d. a v. le. une telle m. *A13* l. pour g. le. de son malvous e. car ainsin comme vous orez apres dieu d. ung m. a v. terrible comme c. 13 *A6* et o. ces g. si ovra *A9* e. cy apres et o. *A3* e. luy et toutes ses *A10* ossy il ovra 13-15 *A3, A4, A8* sy apres a. 14-15 *A1* d. il a. que *A5* d. a celluy t.a. que dieu d. 15 *A2, A3, A6* que dieu d. *A4* que d. *A10* a v. 15-16 *A1, A2, A4, B6* e. une 16 *B, B2, B3, B4* quon appelle c. qui tout le *B6* que on appelle c. *B1* que on a.c. que tous levres du 16-17 *B2* v. les mains la bouche et les oreilles lui mangia d. *A11* qui le nez et le v. et les l. luy mengea i. *A12* c. laquelle le nas du v. et les l. en iusques aux d. le m. et les s. *B5* que on a.c. si horrible que tout le et les temples du v. les mains les oreilles et la bouche luy pelerent d. *A6* les balevres i. *B, B1, B3, B4* v. les mains et les (*B4* v. et les) oreilles et la 16-18 *A13* nez et la bouche i. a s.d. luy et *B7* m. tout le nez et le v.t. 16-26 *B6* m. tout le v. le nefs et les orailles et se luy p. toute la b. et adoncy quant le. praint si g.d. luy et toulx ces gens car il estoint toulx esbais et cedit vasparient fist mander toulx les medecins que on put t. mais rien ny valoit leur medicine et disoit que nul ny pouroit garir cest maladie et de fait abandonnerent lempereur car tant plus il luy metoient les mains et de tant plus croissoit tant quil devint tout mesel et tout poacre et de tant si malde quil ne se povoit soustenir sur ces pies aucunement en

16 *nes* [ *nef* Reading of all other manuscripts.

levres juques aus dans. Et les sourcis et la barbe lui pellerent dont l'empereur et toutes ses gens en eürent grant duel, si que il firent venir les meilleurs mires qu'il peürent onques trouver. Et tant plus y mettoient les mires les mains, et tant plus croysoit la maladie, en tant que les mires n'y

17 *A7* les oreilles et *A11* s. des yeulx et *A1* b.d. *A3, A8, B, B1, B3, B4* luy pelerent d. 17-18 *A10* d. ses *A6* p. de quoy luy et 17-19 *A11* luy pelerent d. il fut long temps en g. doulleur et martire et de ce e. tous ses barons chevaliers et escuiers et tout le peuple g.d. lors fist vaspasien lempereur v. tous les me. phisiciens et mi. que len peut au monde t. et quant ilz furent tous venuz et eurent veue et apparceue icelle griefve malladie de lempereur tous en furent esmerveillez et ny pouoient trouver nul remedde de aucune garison dont tout le peuple quanllement furent moult dolans et couroussez car t.
18 *A2, A4* et ses *A6, A10, B, B1, B2, B3, B4, B5, B7, A13* g.e. *A12* e. tres g.d. et f. *B7* e. moult g.d. et fist v. *A3, A5, A7, A9, A10* d. et pour ce (*A10* d.p. quoy) ilz *A2, A4* g. doleur et pour ce ilz *B, B1, B3, B4* g. doulour (*B1, B3* g. paour) et f. *A13* d. et f. 18-19 *B2* g. doleur et ferant v. tous les me. medecins quil *A6* d. et pour celle cause il f. advenir les m. phisiciens qui puissent o. 18-26 *B5* g. douleur puis f.v. les phisiciens tous ceulx que on povoit t. maiz rens ny valoit leur medecine et disoient que autre chose ne povoient faire se la grace de dieu ny ouvroit y adont la la m. descendit ou corps de lempereur tant quil fust tout mesel et ne se p. soustenir sur ses piez et iceluy *B, B1, B3, B4* les me. meges et fisiciens (*B1* les les merveilleux mi. et surgiens *B3* les me. medicins *B4* les me. mi. et serorgiens) que on peut t. mais rien ne valoit leurs medecines et d. qu autre (*B4* q. eulx ne a.) ny (*B1, B3* a. autre ny) pourroient faire (*B1, B4* p. riens f.) ce non la grace (*B4* la voulente) de d. adonc la m. va venir (*B1* a. va v. la m. *B3* d. avint que la m.) au corps de lempereur tant que fut tout mesel et f. tant mal appareille (*B1* m. adobe *B3* m. ordonnez *B4* t. malaide) de l mesellerie quil ne p. sur se piez ester (*B1* sur p. se tenir ne e. *B3* ne se p. tenir sur p. *B4* ne se p. tenir sur ses p.) en 19 *A9* me. medicins quils *A13* me. phiseciens que lon pehu t. et comme p. *A1, A9, A10, B2* p.t. *A4* tant y 19-20 *A2* tant y m.p. les ma. les mi. la maladie p.c. et t. *A4* me. les mieges les *A5, A7* et quant p. y me. (*A7* q. il p. me.) les ma. *A6* me. les ma. les phisiciens de t. *A9* me. iceulx medecins les ma. *A11, A13* me. la ma. 19-23 *B7* me. medecin que ilz poeult t. et tout le royaumes mais t.p. y touchoient les medecin et p.m. de lempereur et les medecin ce voyant d. a lempereur que ne pouet g.f.d. soulement et le laisserent du tout en tout p. la m. duy empreulx crust tant quil devint ladre et si p. de lepre *A12* me. mieges et fisiens que lon peut t. et quant p. les fisiisiens y me. les ma. et p. fort c.m. si que les mieges et les piziciens le vont laissier et le vont dire que riens ne len pourroit g.f. que d. puis tousiours la m. vait c. a lempereur v. tant quil f. tout lepreus 19-26 *B2* t. mais riens ne valloit leur medicine et d. que autre chose ny povoyent faire si non par la grace de dieu adonc la m. va venir du corps de lempereur si fort et tant quil fut tout mesel et f. si firut malade de la meizellerie quil ne se p. tenir en piedz en 20 *A10* mi. leurs ma. *A11* p. fort c. *A8* et p. *A10* p. luy c. *A10* m. et f. quilz ny *A3, A4, A5, A7* maladie et t. *A6* maladie t. *A4* les megez ny *A6* les phisiciens ny *A9* ladicte m. et adonc les medecins ny *A11* la m. si que 20-23 *A11* m. et phisiciens le vont habandonnez du tout et vont dire que riens ne le porroit garir f. que d.p. tousiours la m. va c. a v. lempereur tant quil 20-25 *A13* maladie avint que une fois les phizeciens le laisserent em pais et luy dirent que se dieu de sa puissance ne le garissoit quil ny savoient nulz remede et icelle m. cruyt tellement quil fut plains de mesellerie et ne se p. ne lever ne soubstenir nullement mais gisoit n.

17 *pellerent* [ *pella* Correction from MSS *A3, A5, A11, B, B1, B3, B4, B5*. MSS *A2, A4, A5, A7, A9, A10* agree with *A*. MS *A1* omits.
18 *que* [ *ques* Reading of MS *A1*.
20 *croysoit* [ *croysoient* Reading of MSS *A2, A3, A4, A5, A6, A7, A8, A9, A10*.

vousirent plus mettre les mains. Et lui distrent qu'il n'estoit chose en cest monde, ne mire ne autre, que le peüst guerrir fors Dieu. Puis aprés va croistre la maladie a Vespessian par telle maniere qu'il fust tout lepreus. Et sy fust sy plain de celle lepre qu'il ne pouoit aler ne seoir ne tenir droit, mes failhoit qu'il se tenist au lit couchiés et nuit et jour.

[3] En cel temps vint a Rome ung disciple de Jhesu Crist qui s'appeloit Clement, lequel pour la malice de l'empereur et de ces gens, il n'ausoit parler ne prediquer de Jhesu Crist se ce n'estoit secretement. Et avint un jour qu'il parloit de la pacion de Jhesu Crist et de la foy a aucunes gens

21 *A8* p. les ma.me. et *A10* me. leurs ma. 22 *A4* ne miegne ne *A9* ne medecin ne *A6* monde qui *A10* monde qui y p. mectre remedde si non d. *A1* f. tant seullement d. *A8* f. que d. *A6* f. que d. tant seulement p. *A3* d. du ciel p. *A4* d. tant seulement p. 22-23 *A8* a. la m. va c. a 23 *A1, A3* m. de v. *A5* m.v. *A10* m.v. en t. A6 tout mesiaul et 24 *A11, A12* de leptre *A2, A4* ne se (*A4* ne) p.s. ne soy t.d. ne aler *A5* a. ne t. *A6*c. maladie que il ne se p.s. ne aler ne *A3, A7* s. ne soy t. *A9* ne se s. ne soy t. 24-26 *A11* ne se p.t.d. mais convenoit quil s.t.n. et i. en son lit moult desconforte de ce quil ne povoit trouver nullement garison en *B7* ne se p.t.d. mais n. et i.c. en 25 *A3* lit out c. *A5* t.c. au lit et *A6* se mist a lit couchier n. *A7* t.c. *A9* t. tousiours tousiours c. ou lit n. *A10* il feust tousiours au *A12* lit et 25-26 *A8* il fust touriours c.i. et n. en 26 *A8, A12* v. ung d. de i.c. a r. qui *B7* v. ung prophete de 26-27 *B, B1, B2, B3, B4, B5* v. un d. de i.c. a r. qui (*B3* c. qui) avoit nom (*B5* a.a.n.) c. et celluy pour (*B2* c. disciple p. *B3* et p. *B4, B5* c. lequel p.) la paour de *A6* d. qui avoit nom c. 26-28 *A13* c. nomme c.l. pair paour de *B6* de dieu lequel avoit nom c. et icelluy disciple na. prescher la loy de i.c. pour la paour quil avoit de lempereur et de ces gens a. 27 *A7* p. doubte de *A9* m. mauvaise de *B7* ladite maladie de le. et ausi pour crainte de *A6* la malaidie de le. il *A10* le. na. 27-29 *B, B1, B2, B3, B4, B5* a preschier de i.c. ne pa. un i. (*B1* pa. au i. *B2* c. mays un i. *B4* pr. ne pa. de i.c. ung i. *B5* pr. de i.c. ne parole dire ung i.) q. que il prescha de 28 *A1, A2, A3, A4, A5, A7, A8, A9, A11, A13* ne preschier de *A6* ne a luy ne a ces gens de *A10* ne prescher de la passion de nostre seigneur se *B7* pa. de *A13* e. bien s. *A11* e. celeement si a. *A6* et il a venir ung 29 *B6* il preschoit de *A11* p. et preschoit de *A13* que clement preschoit ou temple de lempereur et parla tres affectueusement de *B7* il preschoist du baptesme de i.c. a *A6* pac. et *B5* pac. et de nostre seigneur et *A11* la sainte foy en la presence de au. 29-30 *B, B1, B2, B4* et de sa foy et au.g.av. (*B1* g. y av.) c. et (*B2* foy tellement que a.g. furent c.) g. *B6* c. secretement et aussit de la loy novelle et cedit iour c. pluseurs g. de lempereur et ad ce sermon fust g. *B3, B5* foy au.g.av.c. et (*B5* et gueriz et ung appelle) g. *A8* foy a.g. dient quil 29-31 *A13* foy et au.g. quil av. desia c. estoient au

27 *Clement* Generally regarded as the fourth pope, having been preceded by Sts. Peter, Linus, and Cletus. It is thought he reigned as bishop of Rome from 88 to 97, that is, after the events of this narrative.

qu'il avoit converti, sy que Gaius, qui estoit seneschal de l'empereur, vint au sermon. Et quant il l'eüt oÿ, il se converti a la foy de Jhesu Crist. Et quant il se parti de la, il s'en ala a l'empereur et le vist moult desfaissonné gesir en son lit. Et commensa a pleurer et a fere trop malement grant duel du grant mal que son seigneur l'empereur avoit.

[4] Lors dist l'empereur a Gaius, son seneschal: "Amis, ne ploures point

30 *A4, A5, A7, A8, A2* c. et (*A2* c. en) tant que *A6* g. convertir et tant que *A11, A12, B7* sy que ung bon chevalier qui sappelloit (*B7* se nommoist) g. *A8* s. a le. *B, B2* e. son s. *A2, A4* sem. v. 30-31 *B1, B2, B3, B4, B5, B* v. au preschement et lescouta moult voulentiers (*B4* le.v.) et (*B* et il) se *B6* de vasparien et cedit seneschal escoutoit moult vouluntiers se disciple et se *A13* le. et 30-32 *B7* s. dicelui disciple de ihesus et lescouta moult volluntiers et puis appres le s. il se c. et crust en la foy nostre seigneur ihesus et puis adora dieu et apres sen 31 *A1* et il *A7, A8, A9, A11, A12* il eut *A9* a ung s. *A10* a ce s. 31-32 *A10* et sen *B, B1, B3, B4* c. et print grant plaisir au sermon du disciple et (*B2* s. dicelluy apostre et *B3* s. de ihesu crist et) puis adoura dieu et sen *B2* c. et print grant plaisir du sermon dicelluy apostre et adora dieu et q. *A11* cr. et tantost quil se p. de son sermon il *B5* foy cristiene et print tresgrant plaisance au sermon de clement puis adoura dieu et sen ala vers le. *B6* c. et incontinent il leissa ces ydoles et adoura ihesu crist et ung peu apres sen vint a le. vasparien et le *A12* cr. et tantost quil p. du sermon il sen vait aler a son seigneur le. 32 *A6* sen vint a *B2* p. du lieu il *A13* p. dillec ilz sen ala vers le. *A8* sen vint a la maison de le. 32-33 *A6, A7* d. gesant en *A8, A13, B, B1, B2, B4* m. deffigure gesant (*B, B2, B4* d. et si estoit *B1* d. et se couchoit *A13* d. et defformez) en *A9* v.g. en *B6* m. defigure alors lempereur se prist fort a *A11* et adonc c. *A10* le. de rome ou il estoit en son lit m. defforme si c. a p. et a mener moult g. 32-35 *B3* m. diffiguray et gisoit en son lit adont c. a p. quant il luy vit avoit tant de malx l. *B5* m. deffigure et se seoit sur son lict et adoncques c. a p. quant il luy vit tant de mal a son seigneur lequel d. au s. mon amy ne *A12* d. en son lit out il se gisoit et c. moult fort a p. car le faisoit si mal voir l. le d. a g. le s. 33 *A9* son son lit m.d. et si c. icellui g. a *A1* p.t.m. et f.g.d. *A3* f. moult g. 33-35 *A6* p. du g.d. quil a. de son s. le.l. *B, B1, B2, B4* p. quant il vit tant de mal a son s. (*B2* p. pour la pitie quil a. de sons. *B1* son maistre) l.d.le. (*B1* s. didonc d.le. *B2, B4* s. adonc le.d.) a *A13* c. fort a p. du mal quil veoit avoir a son moustre adoncque le.d. a *B7* c. forment a p. pour le grand mal que lui veoist souffrir l.le. commenca a dire a son s. *B6* p. et son senechal aussit de la g. pouvrete en quoy il vouyet le. adonques le.d. a 33-39 *A11* p. moult fort et alla f. tres g.d. du mal que le. son s.a. et luy dist telles parolles l. iceluy g.s.d. a le. sire ie 34 *A4* mal qui creoit que le. son *A1* s.a. *A2, A3, A5, A7, A8, A9* que le. son s. (*A8* son maistre) a. *A10* mal quil veoit que son maistre a. 35 *A9* a a g. *A10* g.a. *B4* s. quil ne *B6* s. mon amy 35-36 *B4* po. et luy dist que n.d. ma do. *A6* pl. plus car 35-40 *B7* po. pour moy car d. de c.m. me guerirast q. il luy p. lors seigneurs ie c. pas quil soict si puissant pour v.

35 *Gaius* Although nothing is known of this particular Gaius, the name has probably been chosen for both its biblical and secular resonances. It occurs several times in the New Testament: Rom 16:23, Cor 1:14, Acts 20:4, 19:29. In addition, 3 John is addressed to a Christian with the same name. In MS B.N.fr. 17229 (f. 222[a], family c) a Gaius is named as the successor of Tiberius. This is a reference to Gaius Caesar (Caligula) who did indeed succeed Tiberius and reigned from 37 to 41 AD.

quar nostre dieu qui me ont donné ceste maladie me guerront bien quant il leur plaira. Mes prions les fort qu'il me veullent guerir, car s'il me guerrissent, je leur promés que je leur edifiray le plus bel temple que [35r] onques / fust edifié par home. — Sirre, dist Gaius, le seneschal, je ne croy point que vostre dieu aient pouoir de vous guerir. Mes j'ay ouÿ dire au temple de August Sezar, vostre pere, qu'il avoit en Jherusalem ung saint prophete qui s'apeloit Jhesu Crist, lequel fesoit moult de miracles en sa

36 *A7* car les dieu *B6* car d. le grant ma do. *A2, A4, A6* qui nous ont *B, B1, B2, B3, B5* dieu ma (*B5* d. a) do. *A2, A4, A6* m. nous g. *A4, A10, A12* q.g. 36-37 *A13* m. et q. il p. ilz le me hosteront mais noz leurs en p.f. car 36-38 *B6* m. et aussit q. il luy p. de me garir il est tout puissant mais si ne veult garir ie luy p. de luy fere faire en lonneur de luy le *B, B1, B2, B3, B4, B5* me garira q. il luy p. et il me garist ie (*B2* me veult guerir ie) luy p. que ie luy bastiray (*B5* p. de luy gaire bastir) le 37 *A9* pl. et prie leur f. car *A3* les bien f. *A7* mes pour les srurd quil 37-38 *A12* les en f. ie l.p. que se me g. que ie l. feray massonner et fere le *A8* me vueillent garir et g. 37-39 *A10* sil me g. ie leur e. ung t. que o. ne f. plus bel e.s. 38 *A13* l. feray maisonner le 39 *A1, A8* o. mais f. *A8* par nul h. *A12* o. mais f. maisonne ne fait s. *A13* f. maisonner s. *A1* h. du monde s. *B5* f. fait s.d.g. ie *B6* f. fait adoncques quant g. eut escoute ce que disoit son sire il va dire a lempereur mon sire ie *A4, A13* g. ie 39-40 *A6* ie c. que v.d. nont povoir *A10* ne cuide p. 39-41 *B, B1, B2, B3, B4* f. basti seigneur se d. (*B3* s.d.) g. ie c. (*B4* g. le s. ne c.) que v.d. ayt point de p. (*B3* de puissance) mais au temps de v.p.s. (*B1, B4* t. que v.p. iulius s. *B2* p.a.s. *B3* t. que iulius s.) ie (*B1, B4* s. vivoit ie *B3* s.v. nobe p. vivoit ie) oy d. que en i a. ung 40 *B5* d. ait point de p. *A11* d. ne voz puissances a. *A13* que nous d. *B6* d. ait point de puissance de vous bailler garison ne sancte mais 40-41 *A7* au temps de *B5* mais ou temps que o. vivoit iay ouy dire que en l.a. ung *B6* d. que ou temps que v.p. iulius s. vivoyt en i.a. ung 40-42 *B7* d. durant que v.p. rennoit estoit ung s.p. en i. que lon a. 41 *A13* s. et vostre quil *A8* en en i. 41-42 *A11* a. ung s.p. en i. qui 42 *A2, A4, B, B1, B2, B3, B4, B5, B6* qui havoit nom i. *B, B1, B3, B4, B5, A11* f. (*B5, A11* f. moult de) grans mi. *A9* de beaulx m. *A12* mo. grans mi. 42-43 *A13* i. de nazareth et f. a sa vie m. de beal m. car il garissoit les mesealx quil e. 42-45 *B6* f. moult grans m. car il garissoit les meseaulx qui e. malades come vous de vostre maladie et ceulx qui estoient aveulgles les f.v. les s.f.o. les mus 42-46 *B2* f. grans m. car il guerrissoyt les meseaulx qui e. malades de voustre m. ceulx qui ne veoyent rien il enluminoyt les a.f.o. et les malades il r.s. et f. partir les deables des corps des personnes bref il g. 42-49 *B7* l. tous maladez mais les i. eurent se grand despis des m. quil faisoit quil fut mis a m. a une c. entre deulx larrons et sy

42-47 For the diverse miracles of healing performed by Jesus, see Mt 7:22-23, 31-37; 8:1-4, 28-34; 9: 1-8, 27-34; 20:30-34; Mk 1:40-45, 7:31-37, 10:46-52; Lk 5:12-16, 17:11-19, 18:35-43, etc.

vie, car il netteyoit les lepreux qui estoient entachés de vostre maladie et fesoit veoir les avugles et fesoit oïr les sours et dressoit les boyteux; et les parletiques rendoit tous sains et les mus fesoit parler, les endemoniés guerrisoit et ressuscitoit les mors et guerrisoit tous ceulx qui venoient a lui de toutes maladies. Et les juifs pour envie qu'il avoient sur lui, pource qu'il lui veoient fere tieux miracles, le livrerent a mort et le crucifierent en croys. Et Pylate, vostre prevost, le juga a mourir en crois. Et sy ay ouÿ

43 *A12* vie et pares sa mort aussy tieulx car *A6* vie et garisoit les mesiaulx qui *A7* il guerissoit ceulx qui *A8* il garissoyt les *A5* es. estoient en. *A10* en. et 43-45 *A12* m. et f.o. les s. et f.v. les a. les b. il d. et les p. 43-46 *B1, B, B3, B4, B5* vie car (*B* vie et) il garissoit les meseaulx qui e. malades de voustre m. et ceulx qui ne voioient goutes (*B* v. rien) il les f.v. (*B5* g.f.v.) les s. il les f. parler (*B* les s. il les f.o. et les malades r. *B3* les malades r. *B4* les s. il les f.o. les malaides il les r. *B5* les s.f.o. et les maldes r.) les muets (*B* s. et f.p. les diables *B3* s. et garis et f. parler lez dyablez *B4* s. et f.p. les m. et *B5* s. et haitiez et f.p. les dyables et les ames) et r. *A11* es.g. les demoniacles et r. 44 *A2, A3, A4, A5, A6, A7, A9, A10* a. oir *A6, A10* s. et les b. 44-45 *A13* s. les b.d. les p. 45 *A1* p. estoient t. *A9* p.t.s.r. et 45-46 *A1, A7, A8* les demoniacles g. *A13* les mors f.p. sauvoit les demoniacles g. *B6* p. et *A6, A12* p. et g. les e. (*A12* les demoniacles) et r. 45-47 *A10* et t.c. qui e. malades il les g. et les *A1* e.g. et qui venoit a luy il les guarissoit de *A2, A4* e.g. de t.m.t.c. qui et 46 *A8* g.c. *A9* g. et les m.r. et 46-47 *A11* g. les gens de t.m.t. et *A12* g. de toutes maladies t. et *A13* g. de t.m.c. quil v. a luy et 46-48 *B4* t. malaides et toutes gens qui le prioient de bon cuer avoient ce quilz demandoient mais les i. eurent si grant despit des m. quil faisoit quilz le iugerent a *B, B1, B2, B3* t. et toutes qui (*B2* t.c. qui) le prioyent de bon cuer mais les i. en eurent si grant despit des m. que il faisoit que ilz le iugerent a 46-51 *B6* g. de toutes maladies t.c. qui le prioient de bon cuer mais les i. en eurent envie et desplessance et le prevost et le baillerent a pilate et pilate qui est v.p. pour paour de perdre son office si le i. a mort par faulce malice le fist cruxifier en croix mais iay o.d. que trois i. apres ce quil fust mort il r. de mort a vie et p. *B5* qui le prioient de bon cuer maiz les i. qui en eurent si grant despit pour les m. quil faisoit ilz le i. a mourir en la c. et iay o.d. et est vray que au t.i. il r. et apres m. es c. et en oultre iay ouy 47 *A7* et quant les *A12* lui car il 47-49 *A13* pour les m. quil luy v.f. le mirent a m. en 48 *A1* lui verint f. *A6* v.t.m.f. qui le *A8* f. ses m. *A9* f. tant de si beaulx m. *A1* le mirent a *A12* le iugerent et le 48-49 *B, B1, B2, B3, B4* le firent crucifier et *A10, A12* c. et sy 49 *A6, B, B1* a mort en *A7, B3* a mort et sy *B2* al mectre en *A11* i. icelui ihesus a m.

43 *vostre* [ *nostre* Reading of MSS *A1, A2, A3, A4, A5, A6, A7, A8, A9, A12, A13*.

49 *Pylate* Pontius Pilate was procurator of Judea from 26 to 36 or 37 AD, after which little is known of his life. In all probability he was dead by the year 70 AD, the date of the events of this narrative. For his role in the Crucifixion of Jesus, see Lk 3:1, Mt 27, Mk 15, Lk 23, Jo 18-19. He was the subject of numerous apocryphal works, including various letters attributed to him (see, for example, the "Epistre que Pilate envoya a Cesar, empereur de Romme, soy excusant de la mort de Jhesus de Nazareth," beg. f. 127$^{r}$ of MS *A11* [Bib. Nat. fr. 1370]), and the *Acta Pilati* incorporated into the *Gospel of Nicodemus* (see my edition [pp. 12-14]). See also note to line 1080.

dire qu'il ressussita le tiers jour, et puis s'en monta sus au ciel avec Dieu tout puissant. Et sy ay encoures ouÿ dire que qui pouroit avoir aucune chouse qui eüst touché au cors du Saint Prophete, pour tant que hom y eüst sa foy, qu'il seroit tantost gueri. Pour quoy, Sire, je croy que cy vous pouiés avoir aucune chose qui eüst touché a lui, vous seriés tantost gueri de vostre maladie. — Dis moy, dist l'empereur, ses tu point sy cest saint prophete croy a nostre dieux? — Sire, dist Guaius, coment poués vous penser que cest saint prophete creüt en vostre dieux? Car j'ay ouÿ dire

50 *A13* d. les chouses quil sensingent premierement quil *B, B1, B2, B3, B4* que au t.i. (*B1, B2, B4* i. il) r. et apres sen *A2, A4, A6, A7, A8, A9, B, B1, B2, B4, B6, A12, A13* m. au 50-51 *B7* d. que au t.i. il r. et se m. es c. ausi iay ouy *B3* m. es c. et aussi ay ouy *A2, A10* d. le t. *B, B1, B4* c. et aussi iay ouy *A11, A12* c. comme roy et seigneur t. *B2* c. et ie croy que *A13* p. qui 50-52 *B6* d. le pere mais mon sire ie croy car qui auroit au 51 *A9* e. plus ouy *A6, A7* ay ouy d.e. que 51-52 *B4* av.c. *B7* p. au.c.av. qui *B1* av. une c. 52 *A6* quil y 52-53 *B5* a ce s.pr. et eust bonne esperance en luy quil gueriroit de toute maladie que ce fut p. *A13* a son c. mais que *A9* pr. pourveu que on deust tenir sa *A12* pr. et que lon e. sa foy en luy quil *B, B1, B3, B4* pr. et lon ait bonne esperance en luy de (*B3* e. de) garir (*B1* de garison) de (*B4* luy de) toute maladie que lon auroit lon s. tout (*B1* g. et s. on t. *B3* g.f.m.) que on s. (*B1* t. sain) g. *B6* de ce s.pr. et en eust bonne esperance en luy car on auroit t. garison et sancte p. *A11* pr. et que en luy on e. sa foy on s. 52-55 *B7* t. aulx s.pr. de tout le mal que lon eust on s.g. mais que lon eust bonne esperance en luy de guerir lors le. demanda a son senechal se *B2* pr. incontinent v.s.g. ce dit le. dist ie vueil que tu me dies se 53 *A8* quil croye fermement en luy quil en s. *A13* foy que lon s. *A10* s.g. *B4* g. et tout sains p.q. mon s. *A8* p. tant s. *A2* s. ne c. *A1* c. se v. *A12* c. et suis certain que *A13* ie dys et c. *A13* v. faiciez ceci v. 53-54 *A6* v. aviez au. *B6* ie conseille que vous faissies chercher par toute vostre empire si en trouveres au. 53-56 *A10* v. voullez bien croire en ihesus v.s.g.le. dist mon senechel se ihesus croioit en n.d.s. 54 *A8* av. riens qui *A1* qui le.t.v. *B, B1, B3, B4, B5* a celluy sant prophete v. *A11, A12* t. au saint prophete (*A12* p. que) v. *B5* s.g. *B4* t. tout sains et g. 54-55 *A3* g. dis 54-56 *B6* chose adoncques lempereur eust ouy aussit parler son seneschal si luy demanda ce cest pr. 55 *A2, A4* m. or dis *A13* m. seigneurs dist *B, B1, B3, B4, B5* m. se dist le. (*B1* m. cest bien dist d.le. *B4* m.le. respondit au senschal) ie vueil que tu me dies se *A12* si le s. 55-56 *A6, B4, A11* cest pr. 56 *A8* c. en mes d. *B* pr. croyoit et adouroit n.d. respondit g. son seneschal c. que le s.p. adourast v. *A13* c. en n. loy s. *B1, B2, B3, B4, B5* pr. (*B2, B4* pr. creoit et) adouroit n.d. (*B1, B3, B4* d. respond g. son seneschal) c. *B7* pr. adoroist son d.g. respondit seigneurs c.p.v. croire quil adore v. *A9* s. ce d. *A12* g. le senneschault c. 56-57 *B6* c. en leur dieu et si la adoroyt adonc gay luy respond mon seigneur c. pances v. que *A1* v. croire que *B1* c. que le s.p. adourast v. 56-58 *A10* c. dictes vous il *A11* g. le seneschal nennil mais est *A13* c. ce pourroit ce fere car il est

57 *A2* en nos d. *A12* cr. point en *B3, B4* que le s.p. adourast v. *B6* pr. adorast v.

57-58 *B5* que le r.p. adourast v.d. quant il estoit sire de vostre d. 57-59 *B2* que le s.p. adorast v.d. respondit le seneschal car il estoyt dieu luy mesmes de paradis et de t.l.m. mais il vint sur t.pe.c.h. et souffrir passion pour racheter toute humaine creature et qu'il est seigneur des dieux et de tout le monde et si est Dieu tout puissant qui descendi en terre pour penre char humaine. Et sy ay ouÿ dire que quant il aloit par terre, il avoit soisante et douze disciples qui aloient avec lui. Et de ceulx soisante et douze, il avoit esli douze qui estoient plus ces prochains que les autres. Et de ses douze, il en y eüst un qui s'apeloit Judas Scariet, qui le vendi es juifs trente deniers d'argent, quar ensi se devoit fere segont les escriptures des juifs. Et puis ycel diciple se repanti et retourna

58 *B6* il estoit sire de vostre d. *A10* de tous vos d. *B, B1, B3, B4* de vostre d. *A11* et roy et sire de *B7* est maistre de vostre d. *A12* d. roys et sire de *A12* d. du ciel t. *A8* est d. de tout le monde t. 58-59 *A2, A3, A4, A5, A6, A7, A9* p. ie ay encor oy (*A6* ay oy) dire (*A5* oy d.e. *A7* ay oy d.e.) quil d. *A11* m. et celuy qui forma le ciel la terre la lune le souleil les estoilles la mer les poissons les oyseaulx et les bestes et d. du ciel en *B, B1, B2, B3, B4, B6* m. car il d. en t. en (*B1, B4* p. pr. *B6* p. racheter) c.h. en laquelle print (*B6* l. il souffrit) mort et passion pour rachapter (*B6* pour toute) humaine creature et 58-60 *A13* m. et q. 59 *B7* d. en t. pour [ ] de c.h. en laquelle ilz souffrit mort et passion pour racheter humaine creature aussi *A12* d. du ciel en *B5* d. du ciel en terre come dieu po.pe.c.h. en laquelle comme homme non mie comme dieu il print mort et passion pour racheter lhumain lignage en oultre iay ouy *A1* t. et prist c. *A10* pour racheter h. lignage et *A11, A12* h. en la vierge marie si *A2, A4* h. ou precieux ventre de la verge marie et que *A3, A5, A7, A9* h. que 59-60 *A6, A8* h. et q. *A11* que il av. lxxii compaignons d.q. il al. par t. 60 *A4* a. en t. *B2* a. sur t. *B1* par vie il *A12* lxxii compaignons d. *A13* av. les xij d. *A2* qui avoit avec *A10* qui en al. *A4* d. avec *A7* d. il en a. 60-62 *B6* av. lx et deulx d. desqueulx il y en a. xij pour son secret desqueulx doze 60-63 *B7* d. desquelz en print douze de son secrest dont ung des douze que lon a.i. le 61 *A8* lxxii disciples il y en a. xij esleux qui *A12* c. il *A2, A3, A4, A5, A6, A9* il en a. 61-62 *A9* qui pl.l. ces pr. *A6* doze de ses plus pr. *A5* e. ses plus pr. *A12* plus pr. *A10* e. ses plus pr. et *A11* et entre iceulx la il en y a. xij qui e.pl.pr. *B, B1, B4* desquelx il (*B1* d. en *B4* d. il en) print xii de son secret desquelz xii il en (*B1* d.) y *B2* desquelz il print douze de son secret et *B3* desquelz il en print xii de son secret desquelz en *B5* et en avoit xij especialment avecques lui desquelx 62 *A1* il y en e. *A4* d. y en e. *A13* a. desquelz lung sa. 62-63 *B6* ung nomme i.s. lequel iudas si le 63 *B, B1, B2, B3, B4, B5* qui avoit nom i. et celluy (*B2* c. disciple *B5* a. a nom i. lequel) le *A12, A11* s. et celluy (*A11* c. iudas) le *A13* v. son maistre es *A4, B4* i. pour t. *B, B1, B2, B3, B4, B6, A11, A12, A13* de.q. *B7* de. ensi *A10* a. par ensi *A8* q. se *A6* d. il f. 63-64 *B6* d. il estre fait s. 63-65 *B5* de. maiz apres iudas son d. qui avoit trahy ihesu crist sen r. et sen retourna aux i. et leur rendit leur argent en d. 64 *A11, A12* s. ce que disoient les *B2* s. quil estoit escript apres y. *A3, A10, B6* es. et *B, B1, B4* s. escript des *B1, B3, B4, A11, B7, A12* i. et apres ledit (*B3* i.a. le *A11* i. en a.l. *B7* i. en a.l. *A12* i. et le) d. *B* i. et apres y. 64-65 *B6* p. apres ceucy iudas se r. et randit largent en d. *A10* et rapporta les *B, B1, B2, B3, B4* sen (*B2, B3, B4* se) rep. et leur rendit leur argent (*B1* et r. la.) en di. *B7* et [ ] renditz largent en di. *A11, A12* ret. aux i. les xxx de. en di. 64-68 *A13* i. lequel iudas se r. et se d. car il ne v. reprendre largent dont la. de iudas est en e. puant doncques seigneurs ie vous prie que en.

61 *il avoit* [ *il is avoit*
62-67 *Judas Scariet* See Mt 26:15-16, 20-25, 47-49, 27:3-10, Acts: 1:16-20.

[35v] les trente deniers es juifs disant / que mal avoit fet. Mes les juifs ne les voussirent onques panre et il les geta au temple. Et puis se desespera et se pendi, et l'arme s'en ala en enfer. Mes laissons, dist il, ces paroles em pais et sy envoiez en Jherusalem sy hom poura riens trouver qui soit du Saint Profete ou qui ait touché a son saint corps, car sy vous en pouvés riens avoir, vous serés tantost gueris."

65 *A8* de. dargent es *A2* i. en di. *A1, A10, B1, B2, B4, B5* quil a. mal fet (*B1* a.f. mal) mes 65-68 *B6* quil a. mal fait davoir vendu le sang iuste et gecta leur argent dedens le t. et puis come despere sen ala pandre pour despit et son a. est ale en e. avecques toulx les dyables en compaigne a tousiours mais sans paigir mes l. toutes ces choses et d. gay le seneschal a son seigneur mon seigneur en. 66 *A2, A4, A8, B, B1, B4, B5, B7, A10, B3* v.p. *A11* o. et *B2* v. pas p. adonc il *A11* t. de sallemon et se 66-67 *B, B1, B2, B3, B4, B7* g. dedens le t. et par despit se p. *A12* v. point p. et le disciple les vait gitter au t. de salamon et sen allast et sen p. et son arme 66-68 *B5* g. dedens leur t. et par despit se d. et ala son arme en e. aprez toutes cez choses l. ester gay le seneschal dit a lempereur seigneur en. 67 *A2, A4, A5, A6, A7, A9* et son arme *A3* et sen ala son a. en *A10, B, B1, B3* et son arme alla *B2* arme de luy alla *A11* p. mes *A2, A4, A6, A7, A8* pais et (*A6* p. mais) envoyons en *A1, A10* l. ces *A6* e.l. huy m. ces *A9* l. ces p.d. gayus em 67-68 *B, B1, B3, B2* e. mes (*B1* e. et) toutes ces choses l. ester ce d. le seneschal a lempereur et (*B2* e. mais advises que vous) en. *A11* l. ces p.d. le senechal et *A12* e. pour ce qui se deseperast mes l. ces p. em p.d. il et *B4* p. en son arme ala en e. atout les dyables de toutes ces chouses et p.l. ester se dit le seneschal a lempereur en. *B7* et son arme fust transportee es e. mes toutez ces chosez l.d. le seneschal a lempereur en.
68 *A2, A3, A4, A5, A6, A7, A9, A10, A11, A12* i. (*A11* i. pour) scavoir (*A12* i. pour voir) sy *B, B1, B3, B4, B5, A13* i. savoir se trouverez r. (*A13* i. pour sarcher se lon p.t. nouvelle) du *A1, A6, A10* t. du 68-69 *B6* i. savoir ce vous en trouveres nulle chose qui aye t. au c. du s. prophete car p. trouver aucune chose v. 68-70 *B2* i. pour savoir se vous trouveras r. qui ait t. le c. du saint prophete car se aucune chose en peust estre trouve t.v.s.g. 68-71 *B7* i. savoir chose qui ait t. au s. prophete lo.le.d. a son senechal sil est vray ce que tu 69 *B, B1, B4, B5, A10* ou (*A10* ou aulcune) chose qui *A13* ou chouses a quoy il heusse t. et se v. en p. *A2* ait a son c.t. car *A12* t. en son *A11* p. trouver r. *B4* son c. *A11* son precieulx c. 69-70 *B3* ou chose quil ait t. le s. prophete car se en p.r. trouver t.s.g. *B4* car se r. en p. trouver v. *A6* p.a. *B5* p. trouver ne a. *A12* p.a. aucune chose v. *A9* r. trouver v. 69-71 *B1* c. si en p.r. savoir tost s.g.le. respondit si est vray ce qe tu *B* v.p.r. trouver t.s. bien g.le. respont se ce est vray ce que tu 69-80 *A10* v. en s.t.g. adonc le. lui dist ie te commande que tu y voises et que preignes or et argent tout a ton plaisir le s. lui d. ie 70-73 *B6* g. de vostre maladie adonques le. luy d. certes ce que vous dictes est vray ie vous p. que vous ne me veilles fallir a cest besoing et va veoir en iherusalem si en trouveres a.c. qui et et touche ou corps du saint prophete et si me rapporte

65 *avoit* [ *aves* Reading of all other manuscripts.
66 *geta* [ *gete* Reading of all MSS, except *A12, A13*.

[5] Lors dist l'empereur: "S'il est ainsy comme tu me dis, je te pri que tu ne l'esloignes plus, mes que incontinent tu y voyses. Et si tu treuves aucune chose, pourte la moy et saches que si le Saint Prefete me veust guarir, je vengeray sa mort et destruiray juifs tant que j'en donray trente pour ung denier, comme il vendirent le Saint Profete trente deniers. Et si voeil que tu dies a Pilate, mon prevost, puisque tu vois de par dela, qu'il sache qu'il me desplest moult fort de ce qu'il ne m'envoie le treüt qu'il

71 *A7, A12* lors le.d. (*A12* d. a gaye) sil *A6* le. ie te pri si est a.c. tu dis que *B2* le.d. si a. est c. *B3, B4, B5* le. respondit (*B4* r. au seneschal) cil est vray ce que tu *A9* tu dis 71-72 *B2* dis ne.es. 71-73 *B, B1, B3, B4, B5, B7* que tantost (*B3, B7* que) tu (*B5* tu ten) v. en iherusalem savoir si tu (*B7* se la) trouveras du saint prophete (*B1* t. riens qui ayt touche son corps et *B3* t. riens de son saint corps et) si me laporte (*B1, B3, B5* si le ma. *B7* t. chose qui ait touchie au saint prophete *B4* p.) et 71-74 *A13* pri que tu y ailles et se ie puis g. 72 *A2, A3, A8* ne es. *A4* ne tardes p. *A9* nes. ne se tardez p. *A6* ne demeures gaires mes *A1, A7, A11, A12* mes i. que tu *A4* que tu y v.i. et *A5* si tu en t.
72-73 *A6* tu v. veoir se tu trouveras a.c. du saint prophete si le me apporteras et *B2* mais va ten tantost en iherusalem et pour savoir se tu trouveras rien ne nulle enseigne du saint prophete si le me apporteras et 73 *A9* s. de certain que *A11* c. de luy aporte *A12* c. du saint prophete que tu le me aportes et *B7* s. de vray que 73-74 *A11, A12* me garist ie *B4* v. gary ie *A9* v. faire g. que ie 74 *B6* ce celuy s.p. me garist ie *A8* v. la m. de luy et *B5* v. de sa *A13* m. si cruellement que ie d. tous les i. et sy en *A1* d. tous les i. *A3* d.t. de i. que *A6* d. tous les i. et en 74-75 *B7* et feray doniez au temps de iuif pour *A12* t. iuifs p. *B, B1, B2, B4* et feray t. (*B2* f. tellement) que do. xxx iuifs pour .i. de. aussi c. ilz le v. (*B2* de. ansi c. il v. *B1* ilz lachepterent *B4* ilz acheterent pour) t. *B3, B5* et feray t. que do. xxx iuifz p. lil de. et *B6* m. et travaillere t. que ie baillere xxx iuifz pour ung de. et 75 *A2, A3* de. aussi c. *A4, A5, A9, A11* de. ainsi c. *A6, A8* de. ainsi c. il acheterent le *A1* il acheterent le *A12* de. ainsi c. il out donne du s. *A7* ung et si 75-76 *A13* de. ainsin que ont la chaer du s.p. et aussy que tu me die 75-89 *B7* de. que il lachettere de de d. cestassavoir xxx pour ung de. feray donnez au tamps que fest vendre et v. a pi. quil me. largement de iherusalem il y a sept ans que riens nen receu dont ne suis pas bien content seigneurs bien acompliray v.c. sil d.p. et tantost gay sapparella et sen alla en 76 *B1, B4* tu me diez *A13* pr. quant tu seras par
76-77 *B, B1, B2, B3, B4, B5* pr. quil *A6, A11, A12, A13* de la quil *B6* p. quil
77 *A7, A11* d.f. *A6* m. qui ne *A12* m. grandement de *A13* m. de *B, B1, B4* d. quil *B2* d. quant il *B3, B5, B6* d. de *A5, B5* me. mon tresor *B, B1, B4* le tresor quil *B6* t. de iherusalem qui 77-78 *A12* quil me devoit e. et lequel il envoyet a *A7* que autresfoys a envoye a mon p. por t. et *A2, A4* a nostre p.

72 *tu y* [ *ty y* Reading of all MSS except *B6*.

souloit envoier a mon pere. Et ossy le m'envoya il par trois ans, mes hors m'a il failhi par sept ans, mais je ne les ly pardoing pas.

[6] — Sire, dist le seneschal, je feray vostre commendement, s'il plest a Dieu." Et lors le seneschal s'apresta sy honnourablement comme il appartient a messagier d'empereur. Toutesfois, il ne mena pas trop de gens, mes que tant seulement quatre chevaliers et d'autre gent a sa voulenté. Et si prist de l'argent de l'empereur ce qu'il luy pleüst, et puis ala penre congié de l'empereur et monta a cheval et s'en ala a chival avec ses

78 *A1* p. il le me. par *A4* o. il le me. par *A6* o. quil me. par *A7* t. mes *A8* ans h. 78-79 *A3* h. il *A4* ans et pour ce ie *A6* mes il ma f.h. par *A9* ans et pour ce dist lempereur vaspasien ie *A11* mes il ma f. *A12* h. il ma f.p. troys annees mais ie ne luy quitte ne ne luy *A2, A3, A5, A6* ans et pour ce ie *A11* an dont ie *A13* p. ilz ma ia f.s. ans tous entiers ie *B5* mon predecesseur car il y a vij ans que ie nen eubs rien pour quoy ie ne luy 78-80 *B, B1, B2, B3, B4* p. car il a vii ans que rien nen eu pour quoy ne luy (*B1* que nen eu r. par q. ie ne luy *B2* que nen ay r. eu et luy dy que ie les luy) s. 78-84 *B6* p. iulius cesar et luy die car ie le veul avoir et que ien suis malcontant alors gay le s. respondit a lempereur s. ie acomplire v. volunte avecques la ayde de d. laquelle est mout grande adoncques gay sen va par soy apareiller pour aler en iherusalem si p. 79 *A8* f. et ie *A7* f. de sept ans et pour ce ie 80 *A2, A4, A6* d. gaius le *A6* f. voluntier v. *A10, A12* c. tres voullentiers (*A12* c.v.) sil 80-81 *A11* f. bien v.c. et feray tant que ie trouveray aucune chose de celuy prophete en iherusalem ou a lentour et 80-82 *A13* s. se d. le s. se d.p. ie f.v.c. il 80-86 *B, B2, B4, B5* seigneur d. le s. bien acompliray (*B2* s. ie compliray b. *B4* s. iacompliray b.) v.c. se d.p. et tantost sen ala le s. appareiller pour sen aler et ne voult pas mener t. de (*B5* t. grans *B4* ne mena pas t. de) g. print q.c. et tant de nobles comme luy pleut (*B2* p.q.c. et de escuiers tant que bon luy sembla *B4* g. avec luy mais il p.q.c. et autant de n. quil l.p.) et de chevaulx aussi et sen (*B1, B4* et p. du tresor de le. a son bon plaisir et des c.a. *B2* et du tresor de le. et de ses c. a son p. *B5* et du tresor de le. a sa voulente et aussi des c.) et sen alerent par terre i. *B1, B3* seigneur d. le s. bien acompliray v.c. et se d.p. et tantost sen ala le s. appareiller pour sen aller et ne veult pas mener t. de g. avecques lui mes il (*B3* g. il) print t. de c. (*B3* p.q.c.) et tant de nobles comme luy pleut (*B3* p. et de chavaulx aussi) et p. du tresor de le. a son bon plaisir et des chevaulx aussi et (*B3* a. et) sen allerent par terre i. 81 *A8* l. se apareillie sy *A12* l. gay le *A10* l.sa. moult h. *A9* sa. moult h. ainsi c. *A3* h. il 81-82 *A8* il peult et a. 82 *A12* a seneschault et a embassadeur de. *A10* m.t. 82-83 *A2* pas guerres de g. avec luy mes *A4* pas guaire de g. *A13* m. avec luy que q.c. quatre escuiers et des varlet a 83 *A6* c. avec luy et *A11, A12* s.c. (*A12* s.q.c.) et escuiers et sonmiers et varletz (*A12* e. et v. et s.) a *A4* da. a *A9* g. avecques lui mes *A1, A6, A12* g. fors (*A12* f. que) t. 83-84 *A10* g. si son que trois c. et si 84 *A2, A4* le. tant quil *A5, A6* a. a le. *A7* a. ce *A10* de lor et de la. de le. tant quil voult et *A11, A12* e. a sa voulente et *A5* puis ala *A6* puis sen ala 84-85 *A8* le.m. *A11, A12* puis print c. *A2, A4, A6* pl. et puis m. 84-86 *A13* e. a sa voulente et entrirent en mer a p. de b. et n. *B6* de la. du tresor de le. et des gens darmes pour le conduire et gardes et aussit print des chevaulx a son son commandement et adonques il sen partirent pour aler en iherusalem a mort belle noblesse et sen alirent au 84-89 *A11* pl. et puis monterent a c. et tant cheminerent par leurs iournees quilz vindrent en 85 *A10* c. a le. *A12* de son seigneur le. *A1, A2, A3, A4, A6, A7, A8, A10* ala avec *A9* m. a c. avec 85-86 *A12* m. a c. et ses g. aussi et alarent par terre i.

gens jusques au port de Barleta. Et la il se mirent en mer et nagerent tant que par la voulenté de Dieu il ariverent au port d'Acre. Et quant il furent en Acre, il se mirent en un lin et alerent par eau jusques en Sezaria. Et de Sezaria, il se mirent en terre chevauchant jusques en Jherusalem. Et la il se logierent bien seleement afin que on ne seüst qu'il y fussent. Et sy se logierent a la meson d'um preudomme qui s'apeloit Jacob, pere de Maria Jacobi. Et la il sejourniere[nt] par trois jours.

86 *A1* au pont de *A5* b. a cheval et *B5* de hostia qui est le port de romme qui autrement se appelle la boucque de rome et quant il furent a hostia il *A9* en nef et *A10* mer et quant ilz furent au port de barbete ilz se mirent en mer et 86-87 *A12* mer et navigarent t. que la v. de d. fust quil a. par dela la mer au *B* mer et dilecques a. par la grace de d. au *B1, B4* mer et dilecques (*B4* et dez la) vindrent par la grace de d. au *B2* mer et de la a. ou p.da. par la v. de d. et *B6* la sen allerent au *B3* i. au 86-88 *B5* mer luy et ses gens et sen alerent par eaue de la iusques au p.da. et de la sen alerent par t.i. 87 *A4* la grasce de *A9, A10* par le plaisir (*A10* le voulloir) de *A7* p. daciel et *A8* f. arrives il *A13* il venirent au *B, B2* et sen a. en 87-88 *B6* dacre et dilecques sen allerent par t.i. *A1* f. au port da. *B3, B4* f. a a. *A10* f. dacre la il se *B1* f. dacre f. et a a. 88 *A6, A12* ung lieulx et *A7* ung vaissel et *A9* ung autre vaissel appelle ung lut et *B3, B4* une nave (*B4* ung bateaul) et sen a. *A12* par mer i. as s. 88-89 *A6* sarasenemie et quant il furent en sareseneme il m. sur t. *B, B3, B4* i. au port de s. et de la (*B4* p. de azarias et dillec) sen alerent par t.i. *A13* ceparie et dillec se m. sur t. et chevacharent i. *A3* de la ilz *A12* et la ilz *B2* de la sen allerent par t.i. *A8* m. en eau i. a s. et la se m. a t. *B1* une navire et sen a.i. au port de s. par eaue de dela sen allerent par pie i. 89 *A3* m. a t. *A10* t.i. *A12* m. a t. et vont chevauchier i. 89-91 *B, B1* et la (*B1* et illecques) furent logies en lostel dun sages iuif et bon p. *B3, B2, B4, B5, B6, B7* et (*B2* et en iherusalem) fuirent logiez en ung hostel dun sage homme et boin (*B2* dun bon iuif et s. *B4* s. iuifz et *B5* s. iuif et bon *B6* h. qui estoit iuifz et *B7* et print son logis sus ung s. iuif et bon) p. *A12* se vont logier secretement en la *A13* la se l. en la 90 *A1, A7, A10* b. secretement a. *A9* s. et secretement tellement que onques on *A4* s. quelz ilz f. *A6* s. quel gens cestoient et *A8* quil f. venus et 90-91 *A11* l. seullement en la 91 *A1, A2, A3, A4, A5, A6, A8, A9, A10* l. en la *A8* dung homme *A13* dung bon p. *A4* dum qui *B, B1, B2, B3, B5, B6* qui avoit nom i. qui estoit p. *B7, A10, A12* iacob lequel estoit (*A10* i. et e. *A12* i. le sage) p. 91-92 *A5, A8* iacob et *B4* qui avoit nom i. et la 92 *A3* iacobi ou il 92-93 *B7* iacobi et q. *A9* par lespace de t.i. tous entiers et *A1, A11, A12, B, B1, B2, B4* s. et q. *A8* s. et la sy advint que q. 92-94 *A13* et illec s.t.i. que onques ne se firent congnoistre et iacob lui *A10* i. et iacob lui 92-95 *B6* iacobi et furent leans t.i. et parloit les ungz aveques les aultres adoncques i. luy va dire i. vostre persone si me s. estre dung grant lieu ie v. prie quil vous plaise moy dire donc v. *B3, B5* iacobi et la s.t.i. (*B5* iacobi et illecques s. et) se firent c. a i. et parlerent avec luy (*B5* p. ensemble) et i. leur d. (*B5* d. iacob) hoste v. me resemblez eistre n. (*B5* r.n.) gens et vous (*B5* et pour ce silz v.) plaist d. moy de

87 *Acre* The Modern Akko (also known as Accho, Ptolemais, and St. Jean d'Acre) is a Mediterranean port of N. Israel. It was an important military objective during the Crusades.

88 *Sezaria* A city of S. Palestine. It was the capital of Herod the Great.

91-92 *Jacob ... Maria Jacobi* The name Jacob, assigned here to Gaius' host in Jerusalem, is probably a back-formation derived from the name of his more important

[36r] [7] / Et quant le seneschal et ses gens eürent sejourné par trois jours sans se fere cognoistre, et Jacob, son hoste, lui dist: "Sire, il me semble que vous estes home puissant et noble. Si vous suppli que vous me dites de quel terre vous estes, ne que vous querés, quar sy vous le me dites, je vous promés come loyal home, que je vous ayderay sy c'est chose a quoy je vous puisse aidier tout a mon povoir." Lors le seneschal respont a Jacob,

93 *A11, A12, B, B1, B2, B4* s. gayus et ses compaignons (*B, B1, B4* et sa compaignie *B2* s. et a compaignie) e. *B7* s. eust s. *A8* g. seiournerent par *A5* e. demoure par *A1, B, B1, B2, B4, B5* s.t. 93-94 *A1, A3, A9* sans eulx f. *A2, A4, A5* sans soy f. *A7, A6* sans leurs (*A6* l. a) f. *A11, A12* i. qui onques ne se fist (*A12* se firent) a c. 93-95 *B, B1, B2, B4* i. ilz se firent c. a i. et parlerent avec (*B2, B4* p. a) luy et i. leur d. (*B1* et luy distrent) v. (*B4* d. iacob hostes v.) me samblez n.h. (*B2* d. ainsi honeste et n.h. me s.) se vous plaist d. moy de 93-127 *B7* i. il se fist a c. a s.h.i. en luy disant la cause pourquoy il estoict venus en iherusalem en apres que le se. eust contez de poinct en poinct la cause pourquoy ilz estoient venus en iherusalem i. demanda se le. adoroist icellui p. que non mais les y.i.d. au seneschal quil se retournast a son sire en lui disant que sil ne adoroist ledit s.p. ilz ne porroist estre gueri car il souffrist mort et pa. pour racheter toutez humaine creature et saches que ie le vis d. 94 *A4* i. lui *A12* s. dist il il 95 *A10, A13* e.n.h. et p. (*A13* e.p.) seigneur et n.h. ie v. 96 *A9* ne aussy que v.q. et ie *A13* q. en ceste terre et se *A8* sy v. me le d. 96-97 *A11* que v. estes venuz querir en ce pays ie 96-98 *B, B1, B2, B3, B4, B5* q. quar sy (*B2* q. et se ie *B5* q. et se le) v. puis a. (*B2* p. de rien a.) ie le feray moult voulentiers (*B2, B3* f.v.) et de boin cuer le (*B2* v. le *B5* p. faire plaisir ie le f. tres v. et de bon c. le) s. 96-100 *B6* que v. demandes ne pourquoy v. estes venus en ces pais alors gay come prins home va dire a i. sire il me semble car vous estes home saige et secret ie vous prie car vous me veilles avouer adoncque iacob luy dist en verite sire non feraige mais aincoys ie vous aidere le mieulx car ie pourray ce cest mon seigneur que ie puisse adoncques gay se va deceuvrir a luy et si luy dist par ceste maniere ie s. nomme gay s. 97 *A13* p. par la foy que ie doy a saint prophete que *A11, A12* p. que *A10, A11* si (*A11* si c. est de q.) ie *A3, A9* c. en q. 97-98 *A6* ie puis de t. mon *A7* ie p. *A13* a. de t. mon p. se ce c. en q. ie v.p.a. gaye le *A1* a. de t. mon p. sy cest c. a q. ie v.p.a.l. *A8* h. que ie suis que v.a. de t. mon 98 *A3* a. a *A9, A11* a. a (*A11* a. de) t. mon *A12* p.t. mon *A10* a.l. 98-99 *A1* l.r. gaius le s. a son h.i. et *A12* s. gay dist a son h.i. par *A8* r. et *A10* r. par *B, B1, B3, B4, B5* a son h.i. et *A3* s. a i. son h.r.v. *B2* a son h.v.

---

daughter who was present at the Crucifixion. In two gospels (Mt 27:56, Mk 15:40), she is defined as being the mother of the disciple James the Less (Maria Jacobi mater). And in John 19:25 she is described as the wife of Cleophas and sister of Jesus' Mother. Mary Jacobi, according to popular French tradition, was expelled with Mary Magdalene, Mary Salome and others from Palestine in approximately 40 AD. Their ship, without sails, oars, or food, but under divine protection (cf. lines 1021-1031, and see also Aurélien, p. 252), came ashore at Saintes-Maries-de-la-Mer, in the Camargue region west of Marseilles. Mary Jacobi and Mary Salome remained there while the others proselytized throughout Provence (Aix, Tarascon, Sainte-Baume). Pilgrimages to the area date from the earliest centuries and the present church was constructed during the twelfth century. Devotions to her intensified in the mid-fifteenth century (after 1448), when King René located and exposed the remains of the two Marys.

son hoste, et lui dist: "Per Dieu, hostes, vous me resemblés preudome. Et pour ce je le vous diray. Sachiés que je suis seneschal de l'empereur de Rome, qui est mon seigneur et le vostre, et sy se fie moult en moy. Et sachiez que mondit seigneur, l'empereur, par qui Rome et Jherusalem se gouvernent, est surpris d'une maladie qui s'apelle chancre, qui lui a mengié tout le visage. Et son corps est si mal apareillié de lepre, qu'il ne se puet soustenir. Mes le convient tenir au lit nuit et jour, si que il le fet trop mal veoir. De quoy, li et toutes ses gens en ont trop grant desplesir, car il ne peut trouver gens ne mires qui le puissant guerrir. Et sy va tousjours en

99 *A4* son h.h. *A2, A5, A6, A7, A9* son h.v. *B, B1, B3, B4, B5* dist h.v. 99-100 *A13* son h.s. *A11* h. par *B5* r. est pr. et pour ce ie v.d. la verite et ne vous mentiray point s. *B, B1, B2, B3, B4* pr. ie v.d. la verite s. 100 *A2, A4* pour tant ie *A7* s. de r. et de le. qui *B3, B4* s. a le. 100-101 *A12* se. de vaspazian cesar e. et 101 *B2, A6* r. mon *A2, A4* est vostre s. et le mien et *A9* m. fort en *A10* m. a moy 101-102 *A8* moy et par luy r. *B1, B2* v. et s. 101-103 *B5* v. cestassavoir vaspasien sire de r. et de i. lequel est prins *B3, B4* v. et s. que vespasien (*B4* que mon s.v.) s. de r. et de i. est prins *B2* v. qui est appelle vasparian e. de r. et de i. est s. quil est prins 101-107 *B6* r. donc il me semble que vous estes a luy subiet et aussit tout iherusalem et veilles scavoir car la cause pourquoy ie suis icy venu si ceste icy car mon seigneur et le vostre est si malade dune m. que on apelle c. tant que il hap du v. de toulx ses menbres et de tout son c. et ne se p. aidier nullement et n. et i. le fault garder pourquoy luy et t. en sont en g. mesaise car on ne p.t. surriciens ne medecins qui 102 *A11, A12* que le. vaspasien (*A12* que v. le.) par *A13* s. et mon maistre par laquelle r. *B, B1* mon s. vaspasien seigneur de r. et de i. *A10* qui i. et r. se 103 *A9* une tres orrible m. *A13* m. appelle c. *B, B1, B3, B4, B5* qui est appellee c. et luy *B2* c. laquelle maladie luy 103-104 *A6, A2* m. le 104 *A12* et le c. *A13* et a le c. si mal a. quil *B2* et le c. faait quil *B, B1, B3, B4, B5* et empli le c. de mesellerie tant (*B4* m. tellement) quil *A4, A11* l. tellement quil *A6* a. quil *A12* si si entachiez de 104-105 *A10* t. son v. et le c. et si est tout plain de l. tant quil 105 *A2, A4, B, B2* s. pourquoy il (*B, B2* s. et) le *B1, B4, B5* p. sur les (*B4* sur ses) piedz et c. garder (*B5* p. aider) n. *A11, A12* c. gesir n. *B, B2* c. garder n. *A6* i. pourquoi il 105-106 *A12* i. le fet tres mal *A8* i. de *A9* fet tres mal *B5* fet mal et piteux v. pourquoy *A10* s. sur piez ne sur mains mes c. quil soit tousiours couchie i. et n. de *B2* s. et est grant pitie de le v. et le fault guarder nuit et iour dont luy 105-107 *A13* s. lon ne treuve phisicien ou monde qui 106 *B, B1, B3, B4* v. pourquoy *A11* q.t. *A6, A7, A11, B3* ont g. *A9, A12* ont tres g. (*A12* g. deul et) d. *B, B1, B4* ont si g. 106-107 *B2* ont si g.d. pour ce que on ne p.t. medecin qui *B5* ont si g.d. que on ne le pourroit croire car on ne p.t.m. *B, B1, B3, B4* car on ne p.t. mege (*B1* t. surgienne *B3* t. medicin *B4* t. seroigien ne medecin) qui *A10* et ses g. sont moult dollens on ne 107 *A7* ne se p. *A11, A12* ne pevent t. *A4* ne mieges qui *A7* m. ne aultres quil *A9* ne medecins qui *A6* t. phisicien qui *A10* t. nulz m. *A12* ne phiziciens qui *A8, A11* g. et si (*A11* g. car il) va de iour en iour en 107-108 *A13* g. mais empire de iour en iour p. *A6* g. mais va t. em. 107-109 *B, B1, B2, B3, B4, B5, B6* g. et la maladie luy empire (*B1* g. car la m. de luy est pire que nul autre et lui e. *B4, B5* m.e.) touz les iours (*B6* g. mais tant plus il luy metent les mains et tant plus il e. de iour en iour) et ie ay oy p. (*B4* ay our dire et p. *B6* ouy d. et raconter) dun

107 *qui* [ *quil* Reading of all MSS except *A7* and *B4* which agree with *A*. MS *B7* omits.

empirant. Pour quoy, biaux hostes, je suy isci venu pource que j'avoie ouÿ dire et parler d'un saint profete que les juifs crucifierent en ceste cité pour envie qu'il fesoit grant miracles en sa vie et en sa mort et aprés sa mort. Et je avoie dist a mon seigneur que s'il pouoit trouver aucune chose qui eüst touché au corps du Saint Prophete, que incontinent qu'il l'aroit, il seroit gueri, en tant qu'il creüst en sa loy. Pour quoy je vous dis que mon seigneur m'a yssy envoyé pour veoir cy j'en pouray riens trouver. Et que sy je en trouvoie riens, que je lui aporte. Pour ce, biaus hostes, je suy issy venus. Pour celle cause sy vous suppli que sy de ce vous me poués donner

108 *A2, A4* q.b. (*A4* q. mon b.) sire ie *A11* q.h. *A8* suy v. *A10* q. ie s.i.v.b.h. pour *A11, A12* v. car iay ouy 108-109 *A13* pour un *A6* ouy p. 109 *A12* pa. a romme dun *A5, A7, A11* du s. *A8* dun p. *A12* pr. qui sappelloit ihesus de nazareth que *A13* pr. quil sappelloit ihesus de nazareth que les i. ont fait morir en *B6* pr. lequel fust cruxifie en *A6* cr.p. 109-110 *A12* cr. et mis a mort en ceste ville et tout p.e. pour ce quil *B6* cite quil f. mout g. 109-111 *B, B1, B2, B3, B4, B5* cr. a tort en ce. ci. lequel f. en sa vie de moult g.m. (*B1* vie m. *B2* f.g.m. en sa vie *B4* vie moult de m.) et sa mort aussi et ie ai (*B1* m. ie *B5* a. et icelluy estoit) conseille a 110 *A4, A11* e. car il *A9* e. pour ce quil f. de beaux et g. *A10* m. et pluseurs merveilles et *A6, A13* m. a sa vie et a sa (*A13* vie moult grant et en sa) m. *A2* vie a sa *A8, A12* vie et a. *A9* mort et aussi a. 110-111 *A11* en sa mort ie *A13* m. avec et pour ce iavoye 111 *A1* ie dis a *B6* ie conseille a *A8, A9, A12, B6* s. lempereur que avoit ou (*A9, A12* que sil *B6* e. car si) p. *A6, A12, B, B3, B5* p. avoir a *A10* p. scavoir ne t.a.c. de ihesu crist ou a. *B2* si ie puys avoir a. 111-112 *B4* qui es e.t. son c. tantost quil 111-119 *A13* s. lempereur de rome que sil p. avoir a.c. dicelluy p. quil e.t. a son c. quil s. tantost g. et pour ce suy ge icy et se v. men p. aidier g.b. en a. de mon s. et s.t. iours mes de sa c. et ne 112 *A8* a son c. que *A11* au s.p.i. *A3, B3* p. tantost quil *B1* que tantost quil *B2* p. tantost quil la verroyt et adoreroyt quil s. *B5* que tantost s. *A2* lavoit vehu quil *A4* a. veu quil *A11* a. touche il 112-113 *A12* s. tantost g. *A10* t. a lui quil pourroit bien estre g. mais quil c. 112-116 *B6* c. de se s.p. car il s. tantost g. mon houste et mon amy ie s.v. 113 *A6* g. pour t. *A3* g. mais quil *A11* g. mais quil c. en luy si que *A12* t. quil eust sa creance au saint prophete si que *B, B1, B2, B3, B4, B5* g. mon 114 *A3, A12* s. lempereur ma *A6, A8, B2* p. savoir se *B2* t. de luy et que ie lui *B5* e. savoir se *A1* t. quelque chose que *A4* trouver que 114-115 *B5* pouray t. aulcune chose qui ait touche au saint prophete et p. *B, B1, B4, B3* ma e.y. savoir cy ie trouveroye r. de ces choses et p. ce h. (*B4* c. vecy h. pourquoy) ie 115 *A6* en povoye r. trouver que *A11* en tienne que *A11* ce ie *A12* t. aucune chose que *A3* lui portasse si saches b. *A2, A4* p. quoy b. 115-116 *A8* ie vous *A10* si vous en avez r. ie v.s. quil vous plaist de moy aider ou moy d. 115-117 *B2* p. quoy h. se vous me p.d.c. de ce que ie vous demande v. en a. 116 *A11* ca. par quoy ie vous *A11* se a cecy v. *A12* vous prie que se en cessy v. *A6, A8* se v. me p. de cecy aidier ou (*A8* p. ad ce) d. 116-117 *A7* ce a.c. me p.d. car v. 116-118 *B, B1, B3, B4, B5* venus pourquoy (*B4* p.h.) se me p.d. (*B1* se tu me puiz d.) c. de ce que ie demande v.a.g.b. et g.h. (*B1* d. tu auras g.b. et g.h.) de 116-121 *B6* ca. par de sa pourquoy ie v. prie quil vous plaise car vous me conseiller et v. en a. bon gardon se vous scaves chose qui me fust bon pour pourter a mon seigneur et ie vous promet que se vous le faictes vous en poures avoir ung g.h. de mon s. et de moy car i. ie ne finere de aler et de venir tant

aucun bon conseil, que vous le me donnés, car vous en arés grant bien et
grant honneur de mon seigneur, l'empereur. Et si vous dis que vous serés
[36v] tous temps mes de sa court. Et sy vous suppli que vous ne / me celés
riens, car en verité je ne retourneray jamais par devant mon seigneur
jusques a tant que j'en ay trouvé aucune chose.

[8] — Sire, dist Jacob au seneschal, dites moy, si vous plait, se mon seigneur, l'empereur, croit au Saint Prophete et s'il le adoure." Et le seneschal lui dist qu'il adouroit les ydoles et si ne les lairoit pour nulle chose. Et Jacob lui dist: "Sire, retournés vous en donc hardiement,

117 A11, A12 a.c. A4 a.c. bon que A3 c. sur ce que A10 c. et v. A1 car ie vous promectz que v. A11 a.b. 117-118 A1 et h.g. de A10 b. de mon s. et B2 b. et h. de le. mon s. et le v. [ ] s. 118 A8 s. et si A12 v. iure que 118-119 B4, B de le. mon s. et (B de le. et) le vostre ie vous prie ne A11 dis bien que tous A7 e. et sy B3, B5 s. (B5 s. et le vostre) ne A3, A6 seres a tous 118-121 B1 s. atant 119 A10, B2 tous iours de A8 tous iours mes A12 mes grant sire en sa A3 c. pourquoy ie v. A6, A11, A12, B2 v. prie que 119-120 A10 quil vous plaise de moy aider et aussi ne men celer riens 120 A11 r. pas mon 120-121 A12, B, B2, B3, B4, B5 car ie en v. (B car mais ne B4, B5 car iamais ne) r. devers mon s. (B4 s. iusques) a A2, A4, A5 i. vers mon s. (A4 s. lempereur) i. A6 i. a A7, A9, A10 par devers mon A1 d. lui i. 120-124 A13 r. point pour neant i. luy d.c. ilz ou p. neny fist gaye ilz croit es y. 121 B5 i. ad ce que 121-122 A10 c. pour sa sante s. A11 c. de celuy prophete s. 121-123 B6 a. remede adonque i. luy d. mon seigneur B5 tr. remede i. di au s. sire d. moy se le. B, B1, B2, B3, B4 c.i. (B3 c. adont i.) d. au s. seigneur se il v.p.d. moy se le. (B2 d. ainsi respondit au s. seigneur d. si v.p.le.) c. (B1 le. adouroit) au 122 A6 moy mon 122-123 A4, A10 i.d. A12 se. gay d. A2 sire sil v.p.d. moy se mon s.le.c. A10 se le. 123 A6 c. il au B6 nullement au 123-124 A10 p. le se. respond et d. A12 sil a point a comme dieux d[ ] est tout puissant et gay luy B5 le erre le s. B2 a. il adore d. le s. les 124 B, B1, B4 s.d. seigneur il (B1 s.d. il) a. A4 d. que non et quil A3, B3 lui respondit (B3 r. seigneur) quil a. B6 lui rancout il a. tousiors ces y. et saiches car il ayme tant ces y. car il ne A6 y. et faisoit adorer et qui ne B, B1, B2, B3, B4, B5 ne l. ses dieulx (B5 l. les ydoles) p. A11 l. a adourer p. 124-125 A9 n. rien ne pour n.c. A2 p. celles c. et adonc r.i.s. 125 B6 c. adoncques i.d. a gay s. A2, A4, A5, A9, A12 lui respondi s. A8, A13 d.r. B3 d. amy r. A10, A11, A12, A13 en h. A1 r. eut h. 125-126 B, B1 i.d. amy tournes v. en car se il B5 lui respondit r.v. en car sil B4, B2 d. amy r.v. en car sil A3, A7, B3 donc p. A6 an arriere h.d.p. B6 en bien toust a rome et dictes a lempereur que sy ne lesse ces ydoules et qui ne croisse au A13 h. car se ilz

118 *de* [ *et* Reading of all MSS except B7.

puisqu'il ne croit au Saint Proffete qui prist pacion si come je le vis. Et si le vis descendre de la crois et mettre au sepulcre a ung sien amic qui s'appela Joseph d'Arimatie. Et puis le vis quant il fu ressusité prediquer a ses apostres et leur dist: 'Alés vous en prediquer l'avangile par tout le monde a toute creature. Et leur dittes que qui crera au filz de la Vierge Marie et se

126 *A10* qui receut mort et pa. si *A2, A3, A4, A5, A6, A7, A9, A12* prist mort si tres amere (*A3* pr.pa. si a. *A4* m. et pa. si t.a. *A5, A7* pr.pa. si a. *A6* m. si a. et sy dure *A9* m. et pa.a. *A12* m. et pas. si) c. 126-127 *A8* ie le vis d. *B, B1, B2, B3, B4, B5, B6* qui souffrit mort et pa. et aussy ie le (*B2* s.pa. lequel ie *B3* pa. car ie le *B5* pa. il ne peut avoir guerison et sachiez que ie le *B6* pa. en la croix pour racheter toute humaine creature et aussit veilles scavoir car ie le) vy d. 126-148 *A13* s. il s.d. et ne s. point gery car ihesus dist celluy quil ny croira sera dampne et se ilz y croit il sera gery exemple comme devant es de en ceste presente passion du quevrechiez de veronne et lui dist tout alon comme la faice de ihesus fut escriptre en celuy quevrechiefs dequel elle f.g. beal h. 127 *A2, A4* et le m. *A1* s. et ly mist ung *A6* au saint s. *A10* s. par ung *A6* ung de ces amis qui 127-128 *A12* et le vis m. au s. du noble chevalier i.da. lequel estoit son bon amy et p. *A11* au monuement a ioseph de barimathie son amy et *A3* a. nomme i. 127-130 *B, B1, B2, B3, B4, B5, B6* au saint s. a son ami (*B2* au s. de son amy *B3, B5* s.s. par son amy *B6* s.s. par son bon ames) i. et apres le vy (*B1* i. de ar. et ap. le vy *B6* i. et nichodemus et puis apres au tiers iour apres sa mort il resuscite et la tout vif) prescher a ses disciples quant fut resucite et l.d.a. par trestout le (*B3* par toutez terrez par le) monde (*B6* p. a ses a. et d. et alors l.d. aler) prescher a t.c. lev. et (*B1, B3, B4* p. lev. a t.c. et l.d. que *B5* p. a t. humaine c.lev. et l.d. que *B6* p. par t. le m. la foy et la loy a t. humaine c. car) qui 127-133 *B7* c. par ung s. bon amy nomme i.da. puis apres le vist preschez a ses a. en disant allez p.t. le m. prescher lev. et d. quiconques sera baptisiez s. sera et qui ne se f. baptiser d.s.p.q. il p. estre guerir et sil 128 *A3, A9* p. aussi ie (*A9* p. apres) le *A1* vis resusciter q. *A11, A12* r. prescha (*A12* r. de mort a vie preschier) a *A1, A2, A3, A4, A6, A7, A8, A9, A10* r. preschier a 128-129 *A1* ses disciples et a. 129 *A1, A2, A3, A4, A7, A10* en preschier la. *A9* en et preschiez lav. *A12* en par t. le m. et prediquez lev. a t. 129-130 *A6, A8, A11* d. qui alassant preschie (*A8* d.a. par t. le m. et prescher *A11* d. aller par t. le m. et prescher) lev. a t.c. et l.d. (*A8* c.) que 130 *B1* d. quilz croyent au f. de dieu et de *B4* f. de dieu et de *B5* f. de dieu f. 130-131 *B2* f. de dieu et se b.s. sera *A7* la benoite v.m. et quil baptise sera sera sa. *A3, A4, A5, A1, A6, A10* et sera baptisiez sa. sera (*A4, A5* et qui se b. sera sa. *A6, A10* b. il sera sa.) et *B, B3* et qui se b.sa. sera et *B5* et quilz se faicent baptizer car qui croira et en baptesme sera sa. sera le croira sa. 130-132 *B1, B4* m. et qui se b.sa. sera p. *B6* c. et baptise sera il sera sa.p.

128 *Joseph d'Arimathie* All four gospellers attest to his role in the burial of Jesus (Mt 27:57-61, Mk 15:42-47, Lk 23:50-56, Jo 19:38-42). Matthew and John inform us in addition that he was a secret disciple of Jesus, a fact which allowed for numerous apocryphal elaborations of these minimal biblical data. He will become, for example, the custodian of the cup Jesus used at the Last Supper and in which he will collect the Holy Blood (see Micha's edition of MS Bib. Nat. fr. 187 [family G], pp. 1291-1298). The cup will be transmitted to Europe, where Joseph and the legends concerning him will be fused with Arthurian materials. For a clear résumé of the literary transmission of these legends, see Marx (pp. 343-351). Joseph is likewise an important figure in the *Gospel of Nicodemus*, where two manuscripts (Bib. Nat. fr. 1850 and Oxford Queen's College 305) even identify him as "connestable" in Pilate's household.

129-131 *Alés ... dampnés* See Mk 16:15-16.

baptizera, [sera] sauvez. Et qui ne le fera, sera dampnés.' Pour quoy je vous dis que s'il ne croit au Saint Profette et ne le adouroit come Dieu tout puissant, il ne pouroit guerrir. Mes s'il le vouloit croire, il seroit tantost guerri come ont esté grant foison d'autres. Sy vous en donray ung exemple: Il estoit une bonne dame qui s'apelloit Beronique laquelle vist ancoures et sy est de Galilee et estoit si plaine de lepre qu'elle ne s'ouzoit tenir entre les gens. Et elle avoit sa foy que le Saint Prophete Jhesu Crist la

131 *A1, A6* qui ne crera d.s. (*A6* c. il s.d.) p. *A3, A7* le sera s. *A11, A12, B, B2* ne croira s.d. (*B* c.d.s.) p. *B3* ne croyait et baptisie ne serait d.s.p. *A10* p. ce ie 132 *B6* se monseigneur lempereur ne *B1* a. lui et toute sa gent c. 132-133 *B, B1, B2, B3, B4* d. il *B5* c. iay dit il *A11* et le adourer c.d. il *B6* ne layme sur toutes choses et se ne le tient pour son pere et son creatour ie vous dy car il 133 *A12* il ne croira ou saint esperit seroit saulvez et quil s. *A9* p. iamais g. *B, B1* g. et se *B3, B4, B5* p. estre gueris et cil *B6* p. estre gari au regart se *A8* sil y v. *B2* v. adorerr et c. en luy il s. *B1* c. et adourer lui et sa gent seront t. *B, B3, B4, B5, A1, A6* c. et adourer (*B5* c. en luy et le a. *A1* c. a luy *A6* a. comme dieu tout puissant quil est) il 133-134 *A7* c. il sen c. *A10* p. iamais il se guerira si v. *A11* g. come 133-138 *B7* v. adorer il s.g. de tout c. les a. out e. ie v. dis par e. dune bo. damme appellee b. de g. laquelle e. toute meselle tant quelle no. aller parmi les g. pour sa mesellerie mais e.a. bonne esperance au s.p. et q. 133-142 *B6* c. en dieu t. il aura garison et ie v. die car il avoit une bo. fame qui e. malaidie de celle maladie mais pour la preise des iuifz ne peut parler au s.p. mais seulement avoit ferme esperance au saint prophete car se elle povoit toucher a son vestement car elle seroit tantoust garie et apres elle vit car lon menoit le saint prophete cruxifier elle fust moult dolente et marrie alor q. 134 *A6* g. comme les a. si v. en veulz dire ung *A3* e. plusseurs a. *A12* e. da. gens f.g. sy *A8, A11, A12* en dyray ung 134-136 *B, B1, B3, B4, B5* c. plusiurs autres ont e. et v.di. par e. que (*B5* e. de) une bo. femme be. (*B1* que be. une bo.f. *B3, B5* f. qui avoit nom be. *B4* f. nommer be.) de g. qui e. tant meselle (*B3* be. qui estoit du pays de g.e.t.m. *B5* be. et estoit de g. qui e.t.m.) que 134-137 *B2* g. ainsy c. ont e. plusieurs et v. dy pour e. que une bo. femme qui avoit nom b. de g. qui e. tant mezelle quelle no. estre avec les aultres g. mays elle a. esperance en la foy du s. 135 *A8* une d. *A10* b. femme qui *A3* d. nommee be. 135-136 *A11* be. et *A6* be. et estoit tout plainne de meselerie et sy. *A1* l. en a. en vie et est en g. *A12* d. encores est elle qui sa.be. et est en g. et celle damme e. lepreuse tellement que 136 *A9* est en g. *A2* g. qui e. 136-137 *A6* g. et elle et elle ne se savoit t. *A10* e.p. de l. tellement quelle t. entor les *A11* e. si lepeuse quelle t. ne approucher e. les autres g. *A12* o. se t.e. les autres g. 136-138 *B, B1, B2, B3, B4, B5* no. estre avecques les autres g. (*B1, B4* les g.) et si a. (*B3* a. tousiours) esperance a la loy du s. (*B4* e. et foy du s. *B1, B5* e. au s.) p. et (*B5* p. et en sa foy et) q. 137 *A10* a. bonne foy *A11* a. esperance que *A9* foy et sa fiance que *A6* que i. le s.p. la *A4, A5, A7, A8, A10, A11* p. la 137-138 *A1* foy au s.p.i.c. quil la gariroit et

131 *sera* Addition from all other manuscripts.

134 *guerri* [ *guerrir* Correction from all MSS except *A11,A12,A13,B6*.

135 *Beronique* For the development and diffusion of the legend of St. Veronica, see pp. 3-18 of the Introduction.

136 *Galilee* Region of northern Palestine, the principal area of Jesus' ministry. Cana, Capernaum, Nazareth, etc. are located here.

guerist. Et quant elle seüt que les juifs l'eürent mis en crois, elle eüt grant duel et s'en vint au mont de Calvaire out il estoit mis en crois. Et vist la Vierge Marie enprés la crois avec ung sien disciple qui s'apelloit Jehan, si que Beronique ne s'auzoit aprocher d'eulx pour sa maladie, mes plouroit et crio[i]t fort et fesoit grant duel. Et quant la Vierge Marie la vist et vist qu'elle pleuroit, elle lui fist signe a la main qu'elle venist a elle. Et quant

138 *A12* i. vouloyent mectre ihesu crist en la c. *A10* mis a mort en *A9* eut moult g. 138-139 *A6* c. et vist 138-140 *B, B1, B2, B3, B4* en la c.e. (*B1, B2, B4* c.e. eut g.d. et) v. au pie de la (*B3* dicelle) c. avec la v.m. et ses disciples (*B2* c. et la v.m. mere du saint prophete *B4* c. et aux piedz de la v.m. et de son d.) dont lun avoit (*B2* p. et ung de ses d. qui a. *B4* d. lequel a.) nom i. 138-142 *B5* en la c. et la estoit la v.m. et ses disciples dont lun avoit non i. et la pouvre femme nau.a.p. sa meselerie quelle avoit mes c. de loingz et se plaingnoit forment et q. *B7* i. le menoit morir et que le. mis en la c.e.v. au pietz de la c. avec la v.m. mais pour honte de sa mesellerie elle no.a. de la croix et p. de loing forment q. 139 *A3, A7, A8* au moult de *A10* sen alla au *A12* out les juifs mettoient ihesu crist en la c. 139-140 *A8* en c.a. 140 *A8* quon a.i. leuvangeliste si *A9* m. au plus pres de la c. et ung *A3* d. nomme i. *A5* d. quon a. *A6* ung de cests d. qui avoit non i. 140-141 *A11* ung de ses d. qui sa. saint i. leuvangeliste et be. *A10* i.be. *A12* m. qui regardoit comment lon mettoit son filz en la crois et il estoit son d.i. euvangeliste avec elle et la be. 141 *A6, A9* m. quelle avoit mes 141-142 *B, B1, B3, B4* ap. de luy (*B1* a. iehan *B4* a. deulx) p. la mesellerie que elle avoit mes c. (*B3, B4* c. fort) et p. et pleignoit de (*B1, B3, B4* p. de) loing et q. *B2* sa.de.a. mes c. et p. moult f. et q. *A8, A10, A11* p.c. aussy (*A10* p. viment et *A11* p. moult fort et c. et) f. *A1* p. fort 142 *A6* c. et menoit g. *A9, A12, A2* f. moult (*A2* f. trop) g. *A9* q. la la v. 142-143 *A10* vierge la vist pleurer elle *B2, B4, B3* la vit plourer (*B3* la p.) e. *A1, A2, A4, A7, A8* la vist quelle *A11, B, B1, B5* la vit et ouyt plourer (*B, B1, B5* vit p.) elle la regarde et si luy *B6* m.v. celle fame e. *A3* vist et apparceut quelle 142-144 *B7* la vit plourer e. lappella et lui f.s. quelle v. vers e. et ainsi le fist adoncques q.e.e.f. pres de la *A12* la vit elle le vait fere s. de la m. car il la veoit ainsy plourer et la veronique vint incontinent et la 143 *A1, A7, A8, A10, A11, B, B1, B3, B4, B5, A4, A5* s. de la (*A4, A5* de sa) m. *A6, A9* s. quelle *B2* s. quelle *A4* v. parler a 143-144 *A3* quant elle y f. *A4, A8* ve. a la vierge marie (*A8* v. devers luy) la *A11* quelle voulust venir a elle et veronique vint incontinent lors la 143-145 *B6* s. de la m. alors la doulce fame vint ver elle et luy bailla le crouvreche de sa t. et lestandit devant la face de

139-140 Only St. John specifically records the presence of the Virgin Mary at the Crucifixion (Jo 19:25-27). See, however, Mt 27:55-56, Mk 15:40-41, Lk 23:49, 55.

140 *Jehan* With the exception of the fourth gospel (Jo 19:26), there is no record of the presence of any of the disciples at the Crucifixion. Since John alone relates the conversation of vv. 26-27 (in which Jesus entrusts Mary's care to an unnamed disciple), it is generally assumed that he is that disciple and that he did not name himself through modesty.

143 *quelle venist* [ *quelle ven venist*

elle fust venue, la Vierge Marie print ung crevichié que Beronique avoit
en sa teste et essua le visage de Jhesu Crist. Et incontinent la figure du
[37r] visaige de Jhesu Crist fust apparant au crevichief et le bailla a Beronique. /
Et encouirres l'a et si fust guarie.

143-149 *B, B1, B3, B4, B5* a e. et tantost e. va venir la v. (*B1, B3, B4* v.m. *B2* t.e. vint a la v.m. adoncques la v.m.) p. une touaille que b. portoit sur (*B5* que p.b. sur) sa t. et lestandit devant la face de (*B5* es. sur la f.) i. (*B4* f.i.) c. et tantost la face de limage du v. de i.c. (*B2* et t.li. et la fusson du saint prophete *B3* c. laquelle se figurait dedans icelle *B4* du v. *B5* v. de nostre seigneur) d. pourtrait en la touaille et la vierge marie la ba. a be. et tantost elle fut g. de tout son mal et veronique a b. la (*B1* de son mal v. a e. la *B3* de son mal et v. ait encorres la *B4* v. a encoire ladicte *B5* g. et e. veronique a) touaille h. ce d. le s. (*B3* t. adont gay le s.d. a iacob h.) ie croy (*B5* ie scay) b. ce que vous me dictes et v.p. (*B3* d. mais ie vous prie (*B5* b. que vous estes preudome et que vous dictes vray et le croy ainsi pour quoy ie v.p.) que vous mandiez que la (*B1* v. menvoiez *B5* la bonne) f. *B2* a e. et la veronique va venir a elle adont la v.m. mere de ihesus crist p. une touaille que b. portoyt sur sa t. et lestandit devant la face de i.c. et tantost lymage et la fusson du saint prophete demoura protrait en la touaille et la b. ainsi a b. et tantost elle fut g. celle femme a e. icelle touaylle mon h.d. le s. ie v. croy fermement pour ce v. prie que vous queres la 144 *A2* quelle a. 144-145 *A12* c. et le mist devant la face de *A1, A4* b. portoit en *A6* a. et en e. *A7* a. sur sa *A10* ve. elle tenoit ung c. en sa main et la vierge marie lui demanda pour quoy elle plouroit et elle lui dist que ihesu crist la deust guerir et la v.m. print le c. et en e. 144-153 *B7* une touaille que la b.a. sus la teste et lestendictz sur la face de son enfant et quant metre loua ihesus il demoura proutraicte lors maren dar la ba. a ladicte be. et tantost quelle la tint elle f.g. et ladicte veronique a e. la touaille apres toute ses choses le s. de lempereur d. a iacob h. ie crois bien ce que vous me dictez pour ce v.p. que vous mandez ladiste veronique et luy disant quelle voeulle venir a. moy a rome p. guerir le. et sachez que se cestui s.p. le vueul guerir il v. sa m. tantost i. manda la v. et 145 *A3* t. dont elle e. *A4, A8, A9, A1* et en (*A1* en torcha) e. *A11* t. et le mist au v. *A11* c. pour ce quil suoit et i. la fasson du 145-146 *A2* i. le v. *A8* c. y fut emprainte et 145-148 *A12* la semblance de la face de i.c.f. pourtraitte au c. de la veronique et puis la benoitte vierge marie le vait bailler a b. laquelle la e.h.d. gay le 145-150 *B6* la face de i.c. demeura painte dedens celuy c. et puis ladite fame le prist et elle f. tantoust g. et celle fame havoit veronicle et ladicte veronicle garde e. ledit cravreche adoncques le s.d. mon h. ie v.p. quil vous plaise mander ladicte f. et ausit quil vous plaise venir a. moy par devers le.

146 *A5, A7, A11* f. apparissant (*A11* f. pourtraicte) au *A1,A3* et puis le 146-148 *A2, A3, A4, A5, A6, A7, A9, A10, A11* be. et en couvri la lepre et tantost elle f. (*A3* et sen c. et tantost f. *A4* et veronique en c. sa l. et t.e.f. du tout *A5* be. et t. quelle regarda la face de dieu nostre seigneur elle f. *A7* be. et incontinant quelle la vit elle f. *A9* et en c. sa teste et elle f. *A10* be. et nostre dame la donna a veronne et t. quelle le tint elle fist sa priere a ihesu crist et veronne fut *A11* et incontinent f.) g. (*A9* g.t. *A10* g. incontinent [ ] on *A7* g. beau *A6* be. et en c. la malaidie et elle f.t.g. de tout son mal et plus necte quelle navoit ester iour de sa vie) h. 147-148 *A1* g. tantost quelle leust oste dy le s. ie croi b.c. mes

144 *print* [ *prent* Reading of all MSS except *A13*.

[9] — Hostes, dist le seneschal, cecy croi je bien. Mes je vous prie que nous envoions querir la fame et qu'elle s'en viengne avec moy a mon seigneur l'empereur, car je say bien qu'il croira au Saint Profette. Et quant il sera gueris, toute crestienté sera exaucié pour lui, car je say tant de lui et de sa voulenté qu'il vengera la mort du Sai[n]t Profette." Et lors Jacob envoia querir Veronique par un sien sergent. Et quant elle fust venue, Jacob li conta coment le seneschal de l'empereur estoit la venus pour la querir. Et si li dist coment il failloit qu'elle alast a Rome pour guerir

148 *A11* d. au s. que cecy estoit tout vray lors d. le *A11* b. car bien scay que vous ne le me deigneriez dire sil nestoit vray mes 148-149 *A1, A5, A8* que vous encoie (*A5* v. envoyez *A8* v.n. envoyes) q. *A12* que vous envoies q. celle damme et 148-163 *A13* s. envoyez querir celle dame laquelle quant elle oy compter le fait fut complete daler a romme pour gerir lempereur quant furent accorde g.d. a son hoste ilz me f. parler a pi. et i. respondit quil 149 *A6* q. cest f. *A11* q. icelle veronique et faisons tant quelle *A8* elle et quelle *A3* q. celle f. et faictes tant quelle sen va a nous a *B5* elle v.a. moy vers mon 149-150 *A7* moy devers le *A11* moy a romme devers le. car iay espoir an laide que ie y mectray quil croira en dieu et *B, B1, B2, B3, B4* que venez a. moy a (*B2, B3* moy devers *B4* a mon s.) le. 150 *A1* le. et q. *B6* ie suis certain quil 150-151 *B1* et s.g. et t. *B4* p. et t. sa c. 150-152 *B6* p. et 151 *A9* g.c. *A3, A9* say bien t. *A6* say tout de 151-152 *A5, A10* lui quil *A11* g. il exaulcera la creance par t.c. et v. *A12* c.p. luy s.e. et aussy il v. *B, B1, B2, B3, B4, B5* car il 152 *A1* v. bien la *A9* p. car ainsy la il dit et 152-153 *B, B1, B3, B4* m. de nostre seigneur (*B1* de ihesus crist *B3, B4* s. ihesu crist adonc) i. manda q. *B2* m. de ihesu crist le s.p.i. manda parmy de ses serviteurs q.v. et *B5* i. mand tantost q. *A11* l. envoierent q.v. que tantost vint a leur mandement et q. *A12* i. incontinent en par un sien s. et ung escuyer de gay q. la v. et 153 *A8* v. a un *A10* v. et *A7* ung de ces villes qui estoit s. *A1* un sergent *A6* un de ces sergens *B, B1, B3, B4, B5, B6* un de ses serviteurs en *B6, B10* q. veronicle (*A10* veronne) f. 154 *A1, B, B1, B3* li dist comment *B4* li comment *B5* luy exposa comment *B6* luy dist dams le *A11* s. estoit de le. *A6, A8* e.v. *A10* v. la 154-155 *B, B1, B3, B4, B5* le.e. (*B1, B3* le. de rome) v. a elle (*B3* v. devers e.) et quil (*B3, B4* quil la) f. aler (*B5* que la convenoit a.) a *A11* la v.p. lemmener a romme p. *B7* comment le. avoit envoye son s. en iherusalem et luy demanda se elle volloist aller a 154-160 *B2* le.e.v. a elle et c. il luy convenoyt p.g.le. qui estoyt tant meseaux aller a r. pour exaucier la foy de i.c. car il sera par la vertu de la saincte t. guery v.r. que v.y. pour croistre la v. de i.c. car se le. peult guerir t. le p.c. en dieu q. 154-165 *B6* le. de rome vous est v.q.p. le g. et pour ce si vous plaist vous pourteres avecques vous le cruverche que vous aves ou est la face du saint prophete apres ces c.v.r. quelle estoit contente de y aler a rome guarir ledit empereur et aussit pour exaucer la foy de ihesu crist car se le. peust estre gari t. le p.c. en luy adoncques q. gay leust ouy aussit parler veronique il fust moult resari et dist a veronique dame ie vous remercie de ce quel vous [ ] nous faire ce plaisir et puis que cest vostre volunte ie vous prie vous aprester vous besoingnes pour nous en partir adoncques g.d. a iacob son hoste qui vouloit parler a p. lequel estoit seigneur de iherusalem et pylate estoit a celle heure devant de temple salmon et i.d. a gay mon seigneur ie veul aler a. vous si vous plaist vous tenir compaignie adoncques gay et iacob sen partirent et sen a.d. 155 *A6* a. avec luy a *A7* e. il a. 155-156 *A8* r. a le.

149 *a* [ *avec* Reading of MSS *A1, A2, A3, A4, A5, A6, A8, A9, A10, A11, B, B4*.

l'empereur lequel estoit tout lepreux. Et lui dist ces paroles afin que la foy de Jhesu Crist fust exaucié. Et sy lui dist qu'elle portast la touaille et sy lui dist pluseurs autres chouces. Et Veroniques lui respont qu'elle yroit voulentiers, car elle creoit que la vertu de Jhesu Crist gueriroit l'empereur et ossy tout le peuple qui creroit en Jhesu Crist. Et quant le seneschal le seüt, il en ot grant joye et dist qu'il s'aprestent d'aler.

156 *A6, A10* t. meseaul et *A9* et veronique lui *A10* p. veronne mamye ie vous prie que vous allez avecques ces gens cy a romme et si portez vostre cueuvrechief a. 156-157 *A9* la loy de 156-158 *A11* e. griefvement l. par a toucher au queuvrechief quelle avoit ou estoit empraínte la face de ihesus crist et la v.r. 156-160 *B, B1, B3, B4, B5* le. qui est tant mesel (*B1* e.t.m.) que cest merveille et la ires (*B1* et i.) pour exaussier la foy de ihesu crist (*B2* que cestoit grant *B5* que cestoit merveilles) et porteres vostre t. que vous donna sa mere (*B4* p. la t. que sa m.v.d.) v.r. que v.y. pour acroistre la foy et (*B3* m. et quant v. et oy cez nouvellez elle s. que v. elle y. pour a. la foy et *B4* y. pour exaulcier et a. *B5* merveilles et lre pour exaulcer) loy de ihesu crist (*B5* en nostre seigneur et pour croistre la foy) car se le. puet garir t. le p.c. en luy *B3* en i.c. et *B5* en nostre seigneur i.c. et) q. 156-176 *B7* le. et respondit que vollentiers le feroist et en prendroit largent pour lamours de nostre sauveur a. que sa foy fust plus multiplies s. ouy ce dire a la veronique il fust moult ioyeulx et luy suppliast quelle sappareilla pour venir a romme avecques son seigneur et ainsi le fist en apres toutes ces chosez g. le s.d. a iacob que vollrist aller parler a p. de par son seigneur lempereur et i. respondit que y.a. lui et sen a. tout droict au t. de s. ou pillate estoict et gay commenca a dire que lempereur estoit m.c. que pillate ne lui envoyoit largent de sa terre de iherusalem comme il solloit faire a iullez cesar son pere car il y a sept ans que nen receu riens et se par moy lui voulles envoyez ie feray vostre pays par d. luy car il sera bien content que de luy por ce vous suies que ceste terre est a luy pourtant tenez vostre conseil sur ce et me rendant responce le plus tost que porres car ie ne puis demourer lontemps p. eust escoutez gay ainsi parler il fust tres malcontent en luy faisoict mauvaise c. en disant parollez fieres et orguelieusez en le m. de la faire morir et ung 157 *A5* de nostre seigneur f. *A3* c.e. quelle *A12* sy iacob luy *A1* p. le coeuvrechief et 157-158 *A2, A3, A5, A6, A7* t. avec pl. *A4* p. sa t. avec elle et avec p. *A9* t. de quoy elle estoit garye avecques p. *A8* t. et pl.c. luy d. et *A12* le couvrechieff out estoit portroitte la semblance de la fasse de ihesu crist et da.c. se elle navoit point et v. luy dist que 157-159 *A10* e. et v.r. ie yray tres v. car ie croy bien que 158 *A1* v. dist que *A3, A5* e. y y. 158-159 *A9* e. y y. moult v. *A11* y. moult v. et disoit quelle 159 *A9, A12* c. fermement (*A12* c. et pansoit) que *A3* crist estoit si grande quelle g. 159-162 *A10* le. et adonc le senechal fut moult aise or d.g. couvient que 159-163 *A11* e. et lors le s. eut g.i. puis d. a iacob quil convenoit quil parlast a pi. et 160 *A12* et que se ainsi se pouvoit faire t. le p. creroit 160-161 *A7* lot oyt ot *A12* la oye ainsy parler il eust tres g. 160-164 *B, B1, B2, B3, B4, B5* q. (*B5* q. gay) le s. oit dire ceste chose il eut moult (*B2* ces parolles il eut *B3* ces nouvellez a iacob il oult *B5* celle c. a iacob il e.m.) g.i. et d. (*B5* et puis d.) a veronique que (*B5* que elle) se appareillast pour tantost aler (*B1* ap.t.p. aler *B2* p. aler *B3* p.t. *B4* que t. se ap.p.t. aler *B5* p. sen aler) a romme et aussi le fist (*B5* r. avecques luy et tantost le f. de bon cuer) g.s. (*B2* r. adonc le s.) d. (*B3* f. elle tantost apres d.) a iacob quil (*B4* f. et quant le s. oyt dire ces chouses et que veronique fut dacort il eust moult g.i. et d. a iacob quil) vouloit parler a p. (*B3* p. le prevost) et i.d. que v.y.a. lui et tantost le seneschal o sa c. ala (*B1* s. et iacob et sa c. alla) parler a pi. et (*B2* v. le meneroyt devers luy et a. ensemble devers p. que ilz) t. pilate d. 161 *A1, A5, A8* il ot *A9* ot tres g. 161-162 *A7* quelle sapprestat da. oste d. *A8* ap. deulx en aler or d. *A12* que tantost sapprestoit de a. ors d. *A4* den a. a rome vers lempereur or d. *A1, A2, A3, A5, A6* aler or d. *A9* aler puis apres g. le s.d. il

[10] Et dist Gaius le seneschal: "Il faut que je parle a Pilate ansois que je m'en voise." Et Jacob lui dist qu'il yroit avec lui voulentiers. Et lors il s'en alerent a Pilate avec leur compaignie et sy le trouverent devant le temple Salmon. Et lors le seneschal le salua et lui dist: "Sire [Pylate, je suis messagiez de l'empereur de Romme lequel est mon seigneur et le vostre. Et vous] mande par moy que vous li envoyés le truage de set ans que vous li devés. Et sachiez qu'il se tient par malcontens de vous car vous ne lui

162 *A1, A3, A4, A6, A7, A10* pi. avant que 162-163 *A12* pi. et 163 *A4* d. sire ie yray v.a. vous et *A6, A7, A9* y.v.a. lui et *A5* lui moult v. *A11* v. chex pilate l. 163-164 *A13* lui et toues l.c. ilz a. et le tr. *A12* et entre eulx deux et l.c. sen a. parler a pi. et sen vont trouve d. 164 *A2* il a. *A4* a. tous deux ensamble a *A9* a. parler a *A11* a. vers lostel de p.a. leurs gens et *A7* avec leurs compaignons et *A10* pi. et 165 *A1* l. gaius le *A12, A13* salmon gay le (*A13* s. le) se. *B5* et le se. *A4* se. salua pylate et *A10* se. se agenoilla devant lui et *B, B1* se. luy *B2* et le se. sa. pilate et *B3* et gay le se. luy print a dire ie *B4* et le se.d. a pylate ie *A11* d. de telles paroles s. ie 165-166 *B, B3, B5* ie s. venu de par monseigneur le. *B1, B4* ie s. venu par le. *B2* ie s. venu et suis m. 165-167 *B6* et la estoyt pylate adoncques le se. de lempereur fit grant reverance a pylate et le sa. de par lempereur cesar et puis apres luy dist ie suis icy venu de par lempereur cesar seigneur de rome et de toute terre monseigneur et le vostre lequel vous m. par moy illoique que 166 *A12* de vaspasian cesar e. *B, B1, B2, B3, B4* r. mon 166-167 *B5* r. et vous m. de par luy e. son tresor de *A1* s. mon seigneur lempereur te m. *A13* m. mon s. lempereur et le v. ilz vous *A11, A12* r. (*A12* r. mon s.) et le v. lequel vous 167 *B2* par moy que vous li d. *A13* ans ans que 167-168 *A10* e. ce que vous lui devez depuis s. ans passez et *B, B1, B4* e. son tresor que v. luy d. de .vij. ans car il *A6* ans en ca que *B5* ans que luy d. de vij ans car il *B3* t. que luy d. de vij ans car il sen t.m. 167-179 *B6* t. que vous solies anvoier a son pere iulius cesar et se vous fais assavoir car il y a vij ans quil nen heust rien de quoy il nest pas bien contant mais monseigneur si vous plaist vous luy anvoires ledit trehu par moy et ie v.e. le mieulx que ie pouray et croyes que ie fere tant que monseigneur sera contant de vous aussit monseigneur vous scavez que c.t. est toute subiecte a rome et pour ce tenes vostre c. affin que vous poures faire sur ce et quelle responce vous me feres adonques q.p. eust oy telles parolles il ne fust pas bien contant mais r.o. par parolles fieres et menassa tres fort gay en luy disant bien ie tiendray mon c. et puis vous randre response adonc pylate tint son c. [ ] les aultres du c. il en eust ung lequel e.s. dudit pilate lequel avoit non b. lequel va dire seigneur pilate ie vous conseille car nullement vous ne facies nul h. a cest empereur car pourquoy vous estes aussit grant maistre que luy et aussit tout le pays de i. et de galilee veust car vous soyes leur s. et que 168 *B2* d. depuis sep ans et s. quil nest pas c. *A4, A11, A12* t. trop (*A11* t. bien *A12* t.) m. 168-169 *A3, A10, A12, A4, A5, A6* v. pour (*A4, A5, A12* v. de) ce que v. (*A6* que) ne *A11* an. de c. 168-171 *A13* d. dont ilz est de v.m.c. et se par moy vous voulez envoyer ie vous e. et ne sera point malcomptent de vous pour causes que 168-174 *B5* t. moult m.c. car c.t. est subjecte a r. et se ainsi vous le faictes ie v.e.d. luy et pour ce tenez vostre bon conseil et *B3* lui voulez envoier et

164-165 *Salmon* Two temples have borne this name. The first, although at least partially planned by David, was built on Mount Moriah in Jerusalem during Solomon's reign and lasted from approx. 1011 BC to 588 BC, when it was destroyed by Nebuchadnezzar. The second was begun in 534 BC, was frequently modified over the centuries, and attained its definitive form under Herod the Great (died in 4 BC). It is this second temple that Titus (here, Vespasian and Titus) destroyed in 70 AD.

165-167 Addition from all other MSS except *A1* and *B7*.

avés anvoiés chascun an comme vous devés. Toutesfoys, sy vous le lui anvoiés pour moy, il ne sera pas sy malcontans comme sy vous ne le fetes pour ce que ceste terre est trop loing de Rome. Et ossy je vous escuzeray par devers ly. Et de cecy ayés conseilh et fettes que vous le lui anvoyé par moy, sy ferés que bien conseilliez."

[11] Et quant Pylate ouÿ le seneschal, il lui fist trop malla chiere et sy lui [37v] respondi moult orguilleusement en le menas/sent et lui dist qu'il en averoit conseilh. Et lors ung mauvés homes qui estoit de son conseilh et sy

---

si par moy luy a. il en s. bien c. car c.t. est subgette a r. et se ainsi le feres ie v.e. par d. luy et pourtant tenes vostre bon c. et *B4* lui a.ch. an paiez et se luy voulez envoier par moy il en sera moult content car c.t. est subiecte a r. et ainsi le faites ie v.e. par d. luy et pourtant tenez vostre bon c. et 169 *A8* an ainsy c. *A11* d. et estes tenu t. *B* an et se 169-170 *B1* an. par ch. an et si lui voulez envoyer par 169-171 *A7* d. et par moy le luy a.p *A11* v. luy voullez envoier par moy ie 169-174 *A10* an. son tribut que vous lui d. depuis sept ans lenca pour ce ie vous prie que vous le me baillez car ie prometz de faire vostre paix envers lui et o. ie v.e. car ceste t. est bien l. de rommet se autrement vous le faites mal vous en prendra et pour ce sur ce ie vous prie que vous prenez conseil et 169-179 *A12* an. de truage ainsi cov.d.ch. annee t. *B2* d. pour ce envoyes luy par moy car c.t. est subiecte a luy et luy doyt tribut et se ainsi le faictes ie vous e.d. luy pour ce tenes vostre conseil pour moy rendre response et 170 *A6* a. par par moy *A1* comme il sera se 170-171 *A12* contans p. que la t. est sy l. *A8* ne sen tendra ia sy *B, B1* il en s. moult comptant car c.t. est subiecte a r. et se ainsi le faites ie 171 *A8* est sy l. *A3* et par ainsi ie *A2* o. ne v. *A12* o. de mon pouvoir v. 171-172 *A9* e. envers lui 171-176 *A13* r. et p. luy f.m.c. disant despiteusement a. sur ce c. 172 *A11* ly et feray tant quil ne sera point mal contant de vous pour ce que cestuy pays est l. de r. et de *B1* par devant lui *A6* a. bon c. *A12* a. vostre c. *A9* et saichez que *A7* luy duges par 172-173 *A12* co. et luy a. par moy la responce et faictes comme b. 172-174 *B, B1* et pour tant tenez vostre bon c. et *A11* co. et men donnez sur ce responce et 173 *A4* f. comme saige et b. *A9* que saige et comme b. avise et c. *A2* que saige et b. 174 *A11* ouy aussi parler le *A12* ouy gay le *B, B1, B2, B3, B4* ouy gay ainsi parler (*B2* o.a.p. le s.) il *A2, A3, A4, A5, A6, A7, A9* il f. *A12* f.m. *B, B2, B3, B4* f. tres mauvaise c. 174-175 *A10* lui dist m. *B5* oy gay le s. luy r. paroles moult chieres et fierez et luy f. tres maulvaise chiere et orguelleuse en 175 *A2* r. trop o. *A6* r.o. *B, B1., B2, B3, B4* r. paroles fieres et orguilleuses et (*B2* et moult *B4* p.o. et) le menassa et lui dist (*B1* m. en lui disant *B2* d. par despit) quil *A1* en m. *A4* en luy m. *A10* m. quil 175-176 *A11* o. en disant quil en parleroit a on c. 176 *B, B1, B3, B4, B5* et ung *B2* c. adonc pilate fist appeler ung *A8* ung malheureux h. *A10* co. et son s. et se 176-177 *A11* son c. se leva et dist que fief ne 176-178 *A13* m. iuifs qui e. du c.d. quil ne devoit a le. nullement ses h. ne r. mes quil luy mesme f. *B, B1, B2, B3, B4, B7* e. du c. pilate et son s. et (*B2* s. qui *B4* s. lequel) avoit nom b. lequel (*B2* e. de son c. et sy estoit s. et a. nom b. qui luy) donna conseil que ia t. ne h. ne (*B4* c. a pylate que ia t. ne) feroient a le. (*B2* d. en conseil quil ne envoyast point de t. a le. ne ne luy fist h. aucunement *B3* le. de romme) car t. (*B7* d. en cousstre a pillate que ia tabust ne luy pairrist et t.) le p.v. que p. 176-180 *B5* e. du c. de pilate qui e. son s. qui avoit a nom b. donna conseil a pilate que ia t. ne feist a le. car t. le p.v. que p.f.s. de r.

estoit son seneschal, lequel s'apeloit Barlabat, dist ausant tous que treü ne homaige il ne recognoistroit a l'empereur. Mes conseilloit que Pilate fust seigneur de Jherusalem et non altre car tout le peuple le vouloit, et que l'empereur fust sire de Rome et de Lombardie. Et puis dist a Pilate qu'il ne lui failhoit a doubter de riens car sy l'empereur venoit devant Jherusalem avec ses gens pour gueroyer, il ne pouroit vivre pour deffaute d'eau qu'il

177 *A1, A10* d. devant t. *A4* d. devant fief ne *A5, A7* d. au seneschal de lempereur devant (*A7* s.d.) tous *A9* d. ainsi que *A2, A3, A5, A6, A7* que fief ne 177-179 *A12* d. a pilate et luy conceilla quil ne consessasse riens tenir a h. de le. mais quil dist que il mesmes estoit s. 178 *A6* h. a le. ne r. mes *A10* h. ne devoit a *A10* c.f. 178-179 *A11* mes convenoit que luy mesmes f.s. et i. et que t. 179 *B1, B, B2, B3, B7* i. et (*B* i. *B7* et de la terre en tuor et) que *A13* i. car le p.v. pilate et non a. et *A12* i. et de iudee car aussy le p. lamoyt mais pour seigneur que lempereur ne autre homme du monde et *A8* car le p. avoyt le voulloir et *A11* v. bien et 179-180 *B4* i. de l. 180 *A10* le. se tint s. *B7* r. dalmaigne et de toute l. *A10* de toute l. *A6* p. se d. 180-181 *A10* p. ne vous doubtez de *A6* d. et que ce *B, B1, B2, B3, B4, B5, A12* ne luy chaloit (*B1* ne c. le *B2* luy f. point *B4* luy f. ia *B5* c. de lempereur) d. (*A12* c. ia d. de lempereur) car 180-184 *A13* et tantost pilate teny le consel a bon et com. 180-185 *A11* et de toute l. et lors pillate tint le conseil diceluy a bon puis c. par grant yre que g. le s. fust mis a mort mais iceluy maulvais homme qui estoit appele b.d. a pilate que 180-187 *B6* et de toute l. et apres toutes ces choses pylate randit la response a gay seneschal de lempereur en luy disant quil 181-182 *A6* i.p. 181-185 *B, B1, B2, B3, B4, B5* le. et tout sa puissance (*B2* sa gent *B5* t. ses gens) v. en i.p. faire guerre eulx ne pourroient (*B1, B3, B4, B5* g. il ne p.) v. pour la souffiet deau dont eulx navoient (*B3* d. il ny ait *B5* s. et grant faulte de. quilz ne a.) point et pilate tint le conseil pour bon (*B2* g. se ne le p. ilz avoir pilate t. le c. diceluy barrabam p.b. et vouloit occire (*B2* v. faire o. *B3* o. gay) le s. de lempereur b. seneschal de pilate d. (*B2* le. mais b.d. a pilate *B3* s. mais b. le s. de p.d. *B5* le. maiz b.s. le p. luy d.) que ne se devoit faire (*B2* p. quil ne luy d.f. nul grief *B4* d. a pylate quil ne se d. point f.) car

181-186 *B7* luy chalust de d. les menasses de le. car ce lui et toute sa puissance ne porroient avoir iherusalem car ilz ne porroist finer deaue pillate tint le c. bon et vollust faire morir le s. de lempereur ce neust este b. senechal de pillate quil d. que nen message ce ne doict on poinct faire car a messages ou faire mal pour son message faire et 182 *A8* a. toutes ses *A12* a. toutes ses g. en iherusalem p. faire guerre il *A10* g. nous sommes gens pour le combatre et aussi il ny p. *A2* ny p. *A6* v. atout son lost par *A8* ne scaroyt v. *A9* pouroit nullement v. 182-183 *A6* eau car il navoi p. *A11* eau car *A10* eau qui y est car p.de. ny avoit pretz de iherusalem et

177 *Barlabat* Barlabat or Barlabam (Heb. son of Laban, laban = white) is not mentioned in any of the biblical narratives. A Laban, the brother of Jacob and the father of Rachel and Leah, is named in Gen 24:29, 29:5 etc., but he bears no resemblance to the Barlabam of our text.

avroit [quar il n'y a point de eaue pres d'ilec. Et adont Pylate se tint a son conseil et] commanda que hom tuast Gaius, le seneschal. Mes Barlabam dist que se seroit mal fet car messagier ne doit penre mal ne vilannie pour chose qu'il die, pour tant qu'il ait de commandement. Et lors Pilate dist a Gaius, le seneschal, qu'il s'en retournast la dont il estoit venu car il ne tenoit riens de l'empereur.

[12] Et lors Gaius, le seneschal, se parti de Pilate moult couroucié et se pensa de retourner a Rome. Et prist congié de Jacob, son hoste, et lui

183 *A8* p. pres *A11* p. pres iherusalem quelle ne soit bien loing et *A4, A6* pres de la et *A6* py. se crut a 183-184 *A10* a ce conseil et dist que *A11* t. son conseil a bon et *A1* a. et lors pilate commanda 184 *A13* quon mist a mort g. *A6* t. le s.g. mes *A8* t. ledit s. *A12* s. de lempereur mes 184-185 *A13* mes abraham d. *A10* b. le destourna et d. que cestoit mal 185 *A8* que non feroyt car *A9* car nul m. *A10, A1* d. avoir ne (*A1* d.a.) mal *A11* d. nul mal avoir pour *A12* d. mal p. pour *A4* d. porter ne mal ne v. ne dommaige pour 185-186 *A13* d. avoir nulz mal car ce quil dist il *A6* ne p.t. que se quil dit est de *B, B1, B4, B5* d. mal p. pour faire (*B3* pour *B5* mal avoir p.f.) sa messagerie et (*B5* et tantost) p. *A10* pour nulle parolle quil die puis quil le fait par le c. de son maistre et 185-187 *B2* mal ne avoir p. respondit ou s. de lempereur quil 185-189 *B3* d. malx p. pour sa messaigerie et 186 *A12* die mais quil *A11* die et *A4* p. commanda a 186-187 *A6* p. luy d. quil *A13* c. adoncques d.p. a g. quil 187 *A2, A11, A12, B, B1, B4, B7* g. quil *A6* r. arriere et quil ne *A13, B, B1, B2, B4, B5* r. et (*B4* et dist) quil ne *A9* v. en lui disant et notiffiant quil 187-188 *A7* ne anvoist r. 187-189 *A10* car ie ne tiens r. de le. et ne demoure plus ycy adonc sen p.g. de devant le fellon pi. *A12* r. et quil dicist a le. quil ne t. homage ne r. de luy l. *B7* r. a lempereur en luy disant quil ne t.r. de lui et *A8* r. et *A11* r. sans plus luy parler de celle matiere et quil deist a le. quil ne t.r. de luy l. se p.g. de 187-190 *B6* r. a rome le plus diligemment que faire se pourroit et qui dist a lempereur car il gardast bien rome et quil garderoit bien iherusalem alors quant g. eust ouy ces nouvelles estres telles il sen p. de p. tout merri et c. de la responce qui luy avoit faicte pylate et puis p. gay de soy partir de iherusalem pour sen re. 188-189 *B2* le. de rome et *A1* le. et de cecy a ton seigneur atant se p.g. le s. de 188-190 *A13* le. lequel sen p.m.c. et commanda a dieu son h. 189 *A8* l. le *B2* s. de lempereur se *B1, B, B3, B4, B7* g. sen (*B, B7* g. se) p. *B5* s.p. *A7* se departi de la place m. *B, B1, B3, B4* pilate tout c. 189-190 *A3* c. et se doubte de *A10* c. et sen retourna a *A12* c. et sen p. tantost a rome 189-195 *A11* c. et sen retournerent luy et sa gent chex son h.i. et la parlerent de plusieurs choses puis firent leur apparail pour eulx en retourner a romme devers lempereur quant gayus ot fait son appareil si p. de i.c. puis se mist en chemin pour sen retourner a ronme avec luy la b. a moult grant ioye car il avoient grant esp. 189-200 *B7* c. et sen alla a lhotel de i. et luy laissa grand tresors pour le conseil quil luy avoit donnez et en apres p.c. de luy puis sen p. de la citez de i. et v. avecques luy et sen allerent a r. et 190 *A4, A9, B2* de sen r. *B, B1, B3, B4, B5, A6* de sen (*A6* soy en) aler a *A6, B, B1, B3, B4, B5, B6* c. de (*B* c. a) son h.i. (*B5* h.) et 190-191 *B2* c. de son h.i. et le paya largement et le remercia et se *B* lui bailla de tresors et tantost sen p.

183-184 Addition from MSS *A2, A3, A4, A5, A6, A7, A8, A9, A10, A12*.
189 *de Pilate* [ *de de pilate*

donna de biaux joyaux et d'or et d'argent a grant foison. Et se parti de Jherusalem avec Beronique et avec ses gens et s'en ala en Sezarie [et de Sezarie] en Acre. Et la se mistrent en une nef et eürent bon vent tant qu'il vindrent au port de Barleta a grant joie que chascun avoit de retorner. Et sur tous estoit grant la joye que le seneschal avoit car il avoit esperance que Dieu li feroit grant honneur, que son travail lui seroit sauvement. Et quant il eürent ileques sejourné par deux jours, il ordennerent leur

191 *A6, A1, A3, A4* d. moult de tresor et tantost sen p. *B5* d. du tresor puis tantost se *B6* d. moult de argent pour sa despance et aussit pour la paigne quil avoit prise pour luy adoncques gay se *A8* j. et aussi dor *A12* j. et tresort g. *A1* a. puis se *A2, A10* g. plente et 191-192 *A8* p.a. 191-198 *A13* j. et emmenna veronne avec toutes sa compaingnie et sen 192 *A10* i. et amena a. lui veronne et ses *B2* ala par terre iusques a s. *A3, A7* et ses *A6* et sa compaignie et *B, B1, B3, B4, B5* et toute sa (*B4, B5* et sa) compaignie et 192-193 *A6* ala a sazarias et puis sen ala en *B6* i. et b.a. luy et sen allerent en ung lieu que on apelle azacamias et puis dilecques sen allerent a. *A12* b. et toute sa compaignie et chevacha iusques a o. et en a. ilz se boucterent en 193 *B, B1, B3, B4, B5* en s. et puis (*B5* et de la) sen ala a (*B1* p. a *B5* a. en) a. *A6* v. et tellement quil *B, B1* a. et (*B1* et puis) se *A1* m. sur mer en *A10* en mer et *B5* une galee et *B6* m. dedans ung galliot et 193-194 *B, B1, B3, B4, B5* v. a talent et (*B1* a lour t. et *B4* v. et *B5* a leur talent et puis) v. au (*B1* a bon) p. *B6* v. tout a leur plaisir et tantost il arriverent au *B2* a. et quant ilz furent la ilz prindrent une nef et la guarnierent de vivres et de tout ce qui estoy neccessayre si e. bon temps et bon v. et tres bonne fortune sur la mer tellement quil v. arrieres du p. 194 *A8* b. car c. sy a.g.i. de sen r. 194-195 *A12* b. en t.g.i. quil avoyent c. de sen r. a son pays et sur t. gay pour ce quil avoit trouve chose par laquelle il y estoit alle et aussy car *A4* r. car 194-196 *A10* a moult g.i. car ilz avoient grant e. en d. quil leur aideroit et leur f. 194-198 *B, B1, B2, B3, B4, B5, A6* b. et la firent (*B1* et f.) grant (*B2* f. moult g. *B5* et illecques f. tres g.) feste gay qui (*A6* f. et cahin qui *B1* f. car gay qui) estoit le maistre crioit que (*B2* f. et le seneschal e. moult ioyeux car il c. fermement que *B5* gay le seneschal c. que) dieu ly f. (*B1* d.f. *B5* d. y f.) vertus pour la paine quil avoit prise et q. (*B2* f. grace a son amistre et q.) furent s.d.i. ilz (*B2* q. il e.s. la d.i. il *B4* s. a barbet d.i. ilz (*B5* q. ilz e.s.d.i. ils) m. 194-200 *B6* b. et furent illecques bien aises et faisoient tres grant chiere en puis apres q. ilz e.s. iii ou quatre i. au port de barbot il sen alerent a r. la ou es. leur maistre qui estoit tres fort mercaul et fort malaide et 195 *A8* t.a. la voye quanque le seneschal a. car *A9* e. la i.g. que *A3, A9* a. pour ce quil *A2* a. grand esp. 196 *A8* f. si g. *A3* son lui *A1* s. guerredonne et *A9* s. cause et moyen du s. de plusieurs ames et aussy de la sante de son maistre lempereur et *A10* lui feroit son s. *A8* s. a lame et au corps et 196-197 *A3* sa. puis q. 196-198 *A11* d. donneroit garison a lempereur si cheminerent tant par leurs iuornees quilz vindrent a r. 197 *A1* e.s.d. *A2, A4, A10* e.s. *A12* e.s.i.d. *A8* e.s.i. par 197-198 *A12* il m. a c. et o.l.s. et sen *A10* o. de leur estat et comment ilz rendroient responce a lempereur et m.

192-193 Addition from MSS *A2, A3, A4, A5, A7, A8, A9, A10*.

194 *Barleta* A seaport on the Adriatic coast of Italy (Apulia). During the Middle Ages, it was an important departure-point for the Crusades. See Gryting (note to line 129) and Ambroise (v. 507).

196 *li* [ *le* Correction from all MSS except *A11, A13, B5, B6, B7*.

somiers et monterent a cheval et s'en vont venir a Rome, out l'empereur estoit en tres grant langueur pour sa maladie.

[13] Et quant l'empereur seüst la venue de son seneschal, il eüst grant
joye et sy grant voulonté de parler a lui. Et au tans que Gaius, le
seneschal, fu venu, l'empereur avoit anvoyé querir les princes de son paÿs
et de son empire, out il avoit roys, dux, princes, contes, vicontes, barons,
[38r] et chi/valiers. Et sy y estoit toute la noblece de sa mer et son empire. Et sy

198 A6 c. que il troverant leur chevaliers tout pret et sen vindrent a B, B1, B2, B3, B4, B5 c. et trouverent leurs sommiers touz prestz et vindrent (B1 l. vivres et sen v. B2 et vindrent sur leurs chevaulx par terre et moult brief temps iusques B3, B4 p. et sen v.) a A1, A8 vont (A8 v. venir) tout droit a A2, A4 et vont 198-199 A10 c. et vindrent a r. a le. qui e. 198-200 B, B1, B2, B3, B4, B5, A6 r. out e.le. fort malade de mesellerie (B5 le. tres f.m. de sa me.) quil avoit (B2 r. la ou le.e. moult f. affligie de la m. dessus dicte A6 me.) et A13 r. et 198-205 A11 le. gisoit griefvement mallade que desiroit moult la venue de son senechal et luy tardoit moult quil ne venoit car le cueur luy disoit tousiours que aucune chose luy pourroit apporter du saint prophete par quoy pourroit recouvrer sante et garison de son mal en celui temps que gayus fut retourne de iherusalem estoient a ronme les p.r.d.c. et c. de tous son empire car il v. 199 A8 l. de m. A4, A10 sa griefve (A10 sa grande) m. A1 en g. 199-200 A9 l. peine et douleur quil avoit et souffroit p. sa m. qui chascun iour empiroyt et A12 m. quil avoit et 200 A10 le. vaspazien s. A6, B, B1, B2, B3, B4, B5, B7 le. oyt dire que son (B1 que le B3, B4, B5, B7 que gay son) s. estoit venus (B7 v. de iherusalem) il A10 v. du s. A13 s. leurs venues ilz en e. A12 s. gay il A2, A3, A4, A7, A8, A10 e. tres g. 200-201 A9 e. tres g.v. de B7 e. tres g.i. ia crist quil fut fort malade et vollu p. B6 le. ouyst les novelles que gay son s. estoit venu il sent moult rejouy et avoit g. desir et v. 201 A2, A3, A4, A5 et tres g. A7 et v. A12 et eust tres g. B1, B4, B5 et (B5 et tres) g. desir de B2 i. il avoit moult g. desir de A6, B, B3, A13 g. desir (A13 g. envie) de A3 lui mais au A10 et quant le A12, B2 et en celuy t. B6 luy et de scavoir aussit des novelles de pylate et en celuy t.

201-202 A8 lui et lors le. 201-203 B, B1, B3, B4, B5, A6 luy et adonc le.a. mande (B5 adonc a.q.) toute sa court ou B7 luy adoncques le. fist venir tous les seigneurs de sa terre ou 201-204 B2 que le s. arriva a romme le.a. mande toute sa court cest assavoir les d.c.p. et toute la chevallerie de son 202-203 A12 q. tous les roys p. et seigneurs de tous les royx son 202-206 B6 le.a. mande tous les elus grans de ses subie cest assavoir r.d.c.b.ch. et t. la n. du pais et ilecques e. la fame dudit empereur laquelle avoit avecques elle plusieurs dames et damoyselles et de mout grant lieu celon les gens qui pour lors estoyt et saiches car la estoit assemblee la plus grant partie de roeme car le.v. instituer et ordonner de son empire et v.c. son f.t.p. 203 A1 son regne et de son e. A10 de toute son A2 e. la ou A4 e. la y a. A13 e. comme r. A5, A7, A9 dux c. A8 r.p.d.c. A7, B7 c.b. 203-204 A1 c. et A8 b. et sy avoit t. 203-205 B, B1, B3, B4, B5, A6 r.d.c. (B1, A6 r.c.d.) p.b. et toute sa chevalerie de lempereur y e. car il (A6 c. et le. B1, B4 c. et la femme de le.e. la car ilz B3 c. et le. B5 c. et) v. A13 p.b.c. escuiers car il v. A12 c. marquis et b. et t. la n. de son e. desza la mer car il v. 204 A2, A1, A3, A4, A5, A7 de sa (A3, A4 de deca la) mer de (A1 mer en) son A7 n. de son A8 n. de son e. dessa la mer et sy 204-205 A10 n.p. ce quil v. B7 c. et moult dautres seigneurs car il v.

y estoient venus pour ce que l'empereur vouloit couronner Titus, son filz, pour ce qu'il estoit si desfasonné et si afoulé quar il ne pouvoit gouverner son empire, sy que il estoit a tant venu qu'il devoit l'endemain couronne[r] son filh. Et lors vint le seneschal devant l'empereur tout lié et sy le salua et l'empereur lui. Et incontinant l'empereur lui demande s'il avoit trouvé nulle chose par qui il peüst estre gueris. Et Gaius lui dist: "Sire, fettes vous liez et fettes bonne chiere et rendés grace a Dieu car j'ay trouvé une sainte

205 *A4* e. la v.  205-206 *A6, A11, A12, B, B1, B3, B4, B5* c. son f.t.p.  205-208 *A10* c. son f.t. car il e. de desseur et aussi pour ce quil e. si mallade quil ne p. plus g.le. de rome l.  205-209 *B7* c. son f.t. novel empreulx p. cause que cuidoit morir dung iour a aultre tuit e. gastez de mesellerie et l. debvoit est c. titus empereur gay v. legerement d. son seigneur lempereulx en le saluant et tantost le.  *B2* es.p. ce quil v. faire son f.t. empereur car il e. tant deffigure et ne p. plus g. et d. estre c. tithus empereur le landemain apres le s. gay v. legierment d. son seigneur le. et le s. humblement et tantost son seigneur le. lui d.  *A13* f. adoncques d.le. a gaye se  206 *A7, A9* et afoybly car  *A4* a. de sa maladye q.  *A11* d. si desfigure et si affaibly pour sa gensucte de sa maladie quil pouvoit  *A9* pouvoit plus g.  206-207 *A8* si deffigure et quil e.a. quil  206-208 *B, B1, B3, B4, A6* e. tant deffigurez quil ne se p.g. et d. estre c.l. son (*B1* c. son) f. titus (*B3* c.le.l. adont gay *B4* c. titus lors) le s. gay v. joyeusement (*A6* v. diligemment *B1, B4* v. legierement) d. son seigneur et sy  *B5* quil ne p.g. et d. estre c. titus l. le s. gay sen v.d. son seigneur legierement et sy  206-209 *B6* e. si desfigure car il avoit grant houste de soy moustrer ne trover entre les seigneurs ne aultres gens pour qui vallissent pis de luy pour cause de sa maladie adoncques gay s.v.d.le. son maistre et son seigneur et moult noblement le s. come il apartenoit alors le.  207 *A2, A3* es.v.a. quil  *A1* il vouloit l.  207-208 *A11* e.l.  *A12* e. et pour ce le vouloit il c. le l. lors  *A2, A3, A4* c. tytus son  *A8* c. titus son f. et faire empereur et  208 *A1* f. or v.  *A3, A5* t. joyeulx et  *A12* s. gay d.le. son seigneur et sy  *A2, A4* s.t. joyeulx d.le. et le  *A9* lie et joyeulx et  208-209 *A10* d. tytus et d.le. vaspazien moult joyeulx il fut et i.  *A11* le. luy rendit son salut puis lui d.  *A8* sa. et i.  *A1, A6, A7, B, B1, B3, B4, B5, B6, B7* salua et le. lui d.  209 *A6, B1, B3, B4, B5* d. tantost sil  *A6, B, B1, B3, B4* a. riens t.  209-210 *A3* a. riens t. par  *A10* t.c.  *A2, B2* t. aulcune c.  *A11* a. rien t. du saint prophete que le p. garir et  *A12* t.c. qui luy fust bonne pour le guerir et  209-211 *B7* a. riens t. du saint prophete par quoy il p. garir gas respondit a lempereulx monseigneur donnez v. bon cuer et r.g. a nostre seigneur ihesu crist car  *A13* t.c. de quoy ilz puisse garir lequel respondit s. menez ioye tres grant et r.  *B5* a. rien t. qui eust touch[ ] au saint prophete pour quoy il p. guerir et le seneschal luy respondit seigneur donnez v. bon cuer iay  *B6* d. hellas gay mon amy ie te prie car tu me dis se tu as rien trouve du saint prophete adonc gay luy respondit tout en plourent de grant ioie quil avot sire ayes parfaite esperance en d. car  210 *A8* c. de quoy il  *A2* quoy lempereur p.  *A10* p. guerir et g. son senechal lui  *A8* et le seneschal luy  *A9* d. ouy si dieu plaist sire  210-211 *B, B1, B2, B3, B4, A6* p. garir (*A6* p.e. garis et) le seneschal respont (*B1* g. et son s.r. *B2* g. et gayus son s. lui dist) seigneur donnez vous bon cuer et r.g. a nostre seigneur (*B2, B3, B4* a dieu ihesu crist) car (*B4* crist) iay  *A8, A11* s.f. b.  *A5* s. tenez v. joyeux et  *A4* s. soyez joyeux et saichez b.c. et a ihesu crist r.g. car  *A10* s. scert b. chose et r.  *A12* s. soyes certainz r.  *A2, A3* v. joyeux et  *A7* v. joyealx et faisons b.  *A9* v. joyeulx et l.  211 *A5, A7, A8, A9, A10, A13, A11* a ihesu (*A11* a dieu i.) crist car  *A2* et a ihesu crist r.g. car  *B6* t. moienant son aide une  211-212 *A13* ay amenne ung d.  *A12* d. le prophete ihesu crist car t. iay une d.s. laquelle a sa saincte en  *A10* une femme qui  *A2, A4* une bonne d.  *B6* s. fame laquelle ha la face du

dame qui ha la figure du Saint Prophete en une touaille, de laquelle touaille elle fust guarie incontinant qu'elle l'eüt. Et sy estoit elle toute lepreuse. Et Sire, mes que vous crées en Jhesu Crist et le adourés comme vray Dieu tout puissant qu'il est et que vous ayez en lui vostra foy,vous serés tantost gueris. Mes si vous ne crées en lui, vous ne pouvés guerir mes serés tous jours en ceste langueur." Lors dist l'empereur: "Je croy

211-213 *B4* s. femme qui a la face de ihesu crist en une belle t. dont e. 211-218 *B7* une bonne d. qui f.g. de telle malladie come vous estez malladez dune t. et l. est la face du s.p. pour quoy pries luy que vous voeullez garir et se le faicte pour vray v.s.g. et aultrement ne p. estre guerist le. respondit ie oy b. ce que 212 *B1* t. belle de *B1* la face du *A6* ha sa face en une belle t. *A8* f. de ihesu crist en *B* ha sa face en une t. belle de *B3* f. de dieu nostre seigneur en une belle t. *B5* ha la face du s.p. de nostre seigneur ihesu crist en une t. 212-213 *A11* ha sa f. en ung quvreçhief par quoy e. *A13* f. de ihesu crist en ung quevrechiefz dont e. *B2* ha sa face en une belle t. par l.e. *A1, A10, B6* en ung coeuvrechief duquel coeuvrechief (*A10, B6* d.) e. *A2* t.e. *A6, A8, B3* l.e. 213 *A9* t. et f. *A4* f.i.g. quelle *A9* quelle la vit et *A5* es.t. *A9* es.l. 213-214 *A10* g. de la malladie de lespre et vrayement mon cher s. *A12* t. celle dame a estoit toute lepreuze i. eut vehue e. en fust guerie en s. 213-215 *B2* g. de semblable maladie come la voustre pour quoy pries dieu t.p. quil vous vueille guerir et se ainsi est que vous a. *A11* quelle leut atouche laquelle e. si l. quelle ne se ousoit trouver devant les gens et pour ce sire si vous voulez croire en i.c. qui est le roy et sire de tout le monde qui a forme le ciel et la terre la mer les oyseaulx vray 213-216 *B, B1, B3, B4, B5, A6* g. de mesellerie pour quoy (*B5* g.p.q.) priez dieu (*A6* p. le *B4, B5* d. le) t.p. quil vous (*B5* p. et luy rendez graces affin quil) vueille garir et (*B4* g. et se vous me c.v. en luy entierement car) se 213-218 *B6* g. de parielle maladie come la vostre et tout par la grace de dieu pour ce sire ie vous prie c. en luy car sans luy ne p. vous estre gary adonques le. lui d. ie c.b. tout ce que 213-219 *A13* g. et si estoit tellement entach[ ] de vostre maladie que merveille et se parfectement c. en luy t.s.g. certes dist vaspasien sy luy p. de moy guerir ie 214 *A2, A3, A4, A5, A7, A9* et pour ce tres cher s. *A8* l. mes *A5* v. vueillez croire en 214-215 *A2, A4, A5, A7, A1* comme (*A1* c. ung) d. 215 *A11* p. et que *A11* lui bonne foy saichez et croiez fermement quil vous donra bonne garison de voustre maladie et bien vous dy que ce v. 215-216 *A10* lui bonne foy v.s.g. *A12* et vous seres 216 *B2* c. fermement le saint prophete estre dieu tout puyssant vous guerires de ceste douleur le. respondit ie c. tout ce que *A9* p. iamais g. 216-217 *A10* ne le povez estre mais demourerez t. 216-218 *B, B1, B3, B5* luy autrement ne (*B1* luy entierement v. ne *B5* luy entierement sachez que nullement v.) p.g. (*B1* g. pourquoy veillez y croyre *B3* p. eistre g. adonc) le. respont ie c.b. ce que *B4* g.le. respondit ie c.b. ce que *A6* ne c. en luy aultrement v. ne p.g.le. respondit ie ie c. ce que 217 *A11* la. et martire lors *A12* la. et vostre maladie croistra tousiours en empirant lors

212-213 *laquelle touaille* [ *laquelle de laquelle touaille*

bien quantque vous me dites. Et si plait a Jhesu Crist de moy fere tant de grace qu'il me voeille donner santé, je vengeray sa mort. Or me fetes venir celle dame et lui dites qu'elle aporte celle touaille sy dignement comme il appartient. — Sire, dist le seneschal, demain quant toute la baronnie sera ensemble, je feray venir la dame devant vous en presence de tous, afin

217-218 *A11* le. gayus mon amy ie scay bien que vous me aymez loiaulment si c.b. que ce que v. me d. est vray et bien saichez que ie feray tout ce quil vous plaisa car sil p. *A10* c. tout ce que v.d. 218 *A10* au doulx i. *A9* a dieu de *A2, A3, A4, A5, A7, A9* b. ce que 218-219 *A8* c. a moy f.t. donneur quil *A11* c. le tout puissant quil *B7* et te promis que se i.c. me voeult guerir ie *B, B1, B3, B4, B5, A6* se i.c. me fait tant donneur quil me d. (*B5* se le benoite prophete me f.t.do. et si grant g. quil me d.) s. de mon corps ie (*B1* t. que iay s. de mon c. ie *B4* t. que ie soye garys et que ie puisse avoir s. de mon c. *B5* c. ie luy prometz que ie le) ve. *B2* se i.c. me fait t. donneur quil me donne s. de mon corps ie luy prometz de venger sa m. de sa passion or *A12* t. donneur quil *A10* f. telle g. que ie puisse estre guery et de moy d. 218-223 *B6* et croie de fait quil est vray mais se i.c. fait tant que ie guarisse certainement ie luy promes de vanger sa mort pour ce ie veul car vous fassies v.c. fame et quelle a. son couvreche honestement adoncques gay heust grant ioye de quoy son maistre se acordoit a croire en dieu alors va dira a lempereur monseigneur d. et vostre court s. toute assemblee ie suis content de faire v. celle saincte fame de laquelle il vous viandra ung tresgrant bien et tout par la grace de dieu et saiches que quant tout le peuple de vostre court sera assemble et toute la noblesse verra faire ung si grant m. car il se convertissent a la foy et a la loy de ihesu crist et l. 219 *A11* s. et garison de ceste maladie saichez certainement que ie *B, B1, B3, B4, A6* m. ie vous prie que me faciez (*B1* que farez) venir *A11* m. tellement quil en sera memoire a tousiours mais lessons ester ses paroles et me *B7* m. si te prie que tu vooy guerrir c. bonne d. et

219-220 *A10* or f.v. la bonne d. et *A13* m. de tres bon cuer or vengne c.d. quelle a. la t. *B5* m. si vous prie quelle a. vers moy sa t. sainctement comme 220 *A11* d. que vous me d. *B2* c. femme et quelle a. sa t. ainsi comme *B, B1, B3, B4, A6* et quelle (*B1* e. me) a. la t. saintement ainsi (*A6* a. sa t. et me faictes a. *B2* a. sa t.a. *B4* t.a.) celle *A10* quelle a. le cueuvrechief ainsi *A7* e. me pourte *A13* aporter ensamble le queuvechief ainsin di. *A1* ce coeuvrechief si *A11* a. celuy linge ou quvrechief ainsi *A12* comme a elle a. 220-221 *B7* quelle a.c. digne t. en laquelle est la face de nostre seigneur ihesus s. respondit le s.d. au matin q. *A12* et car ie desire de tout mon cueur de le veoir et a toucher sire 221 *A11* a.s.d. gaius d. sil plaist a dieu q. *B2, B4* a. monseigneur d. (*B4* d. gay) le *A2, A4, A12, A13* dist gaius le *A3* sire demain *A9* la seignourye et b. *B5* t. vostre noble b. 221-222 *A6, B, B1, B3, B4, B5* sera assamblee ie *B2* t. vos gents et la b.s. venue ie *B7* sera venue et assamblee ie 221-223 *A13* t. vostre noblesses s. assamblee a. que chascun voye le m. et c. 221-224 *A10* se. vous ferez d. assembler t. vostre b. devant v. et la d. en la p. de t. vous le moustrera et aussi v. couronnerez v.f. et chascun verra le m.a. quil c.t. en ihesu crist et lors d.le. que 222 *A6, B, B2* la femme de. *B4* dame en *A11* f. la dame v.de. 222-223 *A12* de.t *A9* de vous t. *B1, B3, B5* v. par davant en la p. (*B3* v. a la p.) de tous les gens (*B5* v. present toute la compagnie) pour veoirs la grant m. affin que se convertissent touz a (*B5* c. a) la foy de i.c. et l. *A6, B, B2, B4* de toutes les gens (*B2* de t. ceulx de voustre court *B4* g. celle dame avec la touaille) pour veoir le grant m. affin quil se convertissent tout a la foy de i.c. et l. 222-225 *B7* la sainte femme veronique affin que chascun voie le beaulx m. affin quil se convertissent a la foy de ihesus et le. respondit au

qu'il voient tous le miracle et qu'il croyent tous en Jhesu Crist. Et lors vous pourés couronner vostre filz. Et l'empereur dist que ce estoit bien dist et qu'il lui plaisoit bien et que au plesir de Dieu fust fet.

[14] Puis Gaius, le seneschal, retourna a sa meson et l'empereur demoura a son palais. Et quant le seneschal fust en sa meson, il trouva Vero-
[38v] nique et lui dist: "Dame, mon seigneur, l'empereur, / vieust que vous viengnés par devant lui. Mes priez Nostre Seigneur qu'il voeille monstrer

223 *A12* que tous vous barons v. *A1, A4* v. le *A11* v. le m. quil sera an laide de dieu fait en vous affin quil c. *A9* c. en 224 *A13* c. thitus v. *A9, A12* f. titus et *A3* le. respondit que *A4* le. luy d. *A9* d. adoncques que 224-225 *A2* b. et *A12* ce seroit b. fait et que au *A8* b.d. et que au *A13* le. respondist ce b.d. a plousir de de d. ce soit g. sen r. sen sa m. et a v. va dire dame *B, B1, B3, B4, B5, B6, A6* f. (*B1, B4, B5* f. titus) et le faire empereur se vous voulez (*B1, B4* sil v. plaist) et le. respondit au (*B3* r. le) plesir *A11* f. titus a vostre plaisir et le.d. a gayus quil disoit tres b. et que au 224-226 *B2* f. tithus et le fayre fayre empereur se vous voules adonc g. 224-227 *B6* f. et le feres e. sy vous voules alors lempereur lui d. certes tu dis tres bien et puis que cest le p. de d. ie le veulx bien adoncques le s. sen partit et sen vint en son hostel et laissa le. en son 225 *A2, A9* p. moult b. *A8* de ihesu crist f. *A9* f. tout ce fet 225-226 *B1, B3, B4, B5, A6* fait g.s. (*B4* f. lors g. le s.) sen r. en son hostel et *A10* p.p. *A1* b.p. 225-227 *B* fet g. le s. sen tourna a son hostel ou il 225-229 *B7* dieu soit tout fet apres ces parollez gay se r. en son hostel et t. la bonne dame v. dame ie vous doicbs demain mener a monseigneur le. si prie que n. 226 *A1, A8, A12* s. sen r. *A9* p. apres g. *A11* g. sen r. *A2, A3, A4, A5, A7, A9, A10* s. sen r. en sa 226-227 *B2* s. se r. en son hostel et t. *A10* le. se retourna en son *A1* m. il 227 *A6, A9, B3, B4, B5* d. en son *A4* q. gay f. *A8* q. il f. *A11* f. venu en *A6, B1, B3, B4, B5* en son hostelz (*B4* son hoste) il 227-228 *B5* t. trouva v. la sainte dame et *A11* il d. a la v. qui la estoit venue pour savoir des nouvelles de lempereur dame 227-244 *B6* q. il arriva en son hostel il t. la sainte v. a genoulx et prioit dieu et estoyt en orayson adoncques gay luy va dire dame le. vous veult veoir demain et veult car le m. soit fait tout devant le p. a celle fain car tout le peuple croie en dieu et qui se face baptiser apres toutes ces choses ladicte veronique retourna en son orayson ausy quelle estoit par devant en priant dieu par ceste maniere sire dieu veilles estandre vostre grace sur le corps de cest empereur et que ce soit a lauenge de vostre sain nom et pour le exaucement de vostre louange et que le tout le peuple voye ung tel miracle affin quil vienge a vostre creance apres toutes ces choses elle se leva et regardoit aval la rue et elle vit ung des d. de ihesu crist lequel avoit nom clement et celuy clement nosoit prescher la loy de ihesu crist pour la paour quil avoit de lempereur et de ces gens aussit quil p. veronique l. la teste et le c. bien adoncque elle luy va dire sire c. et la. par son non dieu vous doint honeur et sainte et adoncques se saint disciple fut moult esbahy de quoy il oy 228 *A6, B, B1, B2, B3, B4* v. la saincte femme et *A6, B, B2, B3, B4, B5* dame demain vous veult veoir monseigneur le. (*B2* veult mon s. *B3* veoir *B4* vous veuillez veoir mon s. *B5* veul mener veoir mon s.) le. (*B3* le. nostre sire) et vieust (*B2* le. que *B5* le. car il v.) que 229 *A12* viengnes demain au matin par *A3* viengnes parler a luy *A6, A7, B, B3, B4* viengnes d. *A11* viengnes demain par d. luy mais ie vous suplie que vous veillez prier n.s. ihesu crist quil *B1* viengnes d. luy et pour n.s. ihesu crist quil *B2* viengnes devers luy et pries n.s. ihesu crist quil *B5* viengnes d. luy pourquoy p. *A12* luy et pour ce faittes priere a n. *A6, A9, B, B3, B4, B5* s. ihesu crist que *A8* p. bien n. *A9* p. a n. 229-230 *A13* viengnes d. lui prier dieu devotement que le *A12* m. de ses grans m.

ses miracles en la personne de mon seigneur. Et qu'il le voeille guerir afin que tout le peuple croie que Jhesu Crist est vraie Dieu tout puissant." Et quant Beronique l'ouÿ, elle se mist en oroison et pria moult devotement Nostre Seigneur en telle maniere: "Biaux Sire, Dieux, qui vousist exaucier ton saintisme non a saint Pierre et a saint Pol et a tous tes disciples, donne ta vertu et leur donne pouoir de guerir de toute maladie et commandement sur les deables. Plaise toy de guerir ce noble home afin qu'il croie en toy et en ta puissance et afin que tout le peuple vieigne a saint baptisme. Et plaise toy, beaux Sire, Dieux, de le guerir comme je fus guerie quant

230 *A3, A4, A5, A7, A11* m. a la *A7* quil luy plaisse de le g. *A8, A9* s. lempereur quil *A10* v. par sa grace g. *A10* de lempereur et 230-231 *A6, B, B1, B2, B3, B4, B5, B7* en telle maniere que t. *A11, A12* de lempereur et quil luy plaise le g. de sa malladie a. que le (*A12* p. quil le g. de sa m.a. que t. le) p. 231 *A4* que nostre seigneur i. *A13* que chascun c. que ce d. *A8* c. en luy qui est *A11, A12* c. quil (*A12* quil est) d.e. *A1* crist quil est 231-232 *A6, B, B1, B2, B3, B4, B5, B7* c. en luy et q. la bonne femme (*B5* la sainte dame) o. secy (*B, B3, B4, B5* o. ce dire *B2* o. ces parolles *B7* f. veronique o. dire a gay) e. *A10* c. en i.c. adonc q.v. ot aye la response que gayus lui dist e. 232 *A11* q. la bonne dame o. gays parler incontinent e. sen alla mectre en *A12* q. la bonne damme v. leust oy e. se m. a genoulx et en *A13* q. la dame lo.e. se print dieu adourer d. *A6, B, B1, B2, B3, B4, B5, B7* o. en priant d. 232-233 *A7, A12* m. fort d. (*A12* m. doulcement) n. *A8* p.n.s. ihesu crist m.d. en *A9* m. doulcement n.s. ihesu crist en *A10* et depria en disant b. 233 *A4* se. dieu ihesu crist en *A1* se. disant ces parolles b. *A9* d. plase toy que tu vueillez e. 233-234 *A3* e. a ton *A1* e.s.b. 233-238 *B, B1, B2, B3, B4, B5, B7, A6* se. ihesu crist en disant s. (*B2* d. ainsi s. *B5* d. tres doulx) d. vueilles (*B2* d. ihesu crist v.) e. de ton (*A6, B4* e; vostre *B1, B3* e le vostre *B7* e. le tien *B5* e. ton saint nom et le saint) nom et de s.p. et de s. poul et vueilles (*B2* de v.) monstrer devant (*B1, B3* d. tout) le peuple (*B7* m. au p.) ta (*B1, B4* p. vostre) v. en (*B5* pol en) telle maniere quil te (*B1* quil vous) p. de g. ce n. (*B1* ce h.) seigneur lempereur (*B3* que n.s. puisse estre gary) a. quil vueille croire en toy et aussy que (*B1, B4* et que *A6* et afin que) t. le p. puisse venir a vray (*B7* v. adoray) b. et a ta foy s.d. (*B2* et a ta saincte foy s.d. ihesu crist *B3* et a ta sainte foy s.d.) vueille le g. en telle maniere c. 234 *A7* ton saint baptesme a *A10, A11* t. les di. 234-235 *A13* di. et as p. *A1* do. v. *A8* donna v. et p. 235 *A10* et le p. *A11* v. et beneisson et *A3* g.t. *A13* m. et leur as donne c. 235-236 *A12* m. et de faire c. es d. *A9* p. sur les d. et c. de les povoir faire yssir des corps des humaines creatures et aussi leur donnas povoir de g. de t.m.p. 235-238 *A11* m.p. toy par ta beningne grace de g. lempereur vaspasien a. que le p. croye en ton saint nom et v. au s. sacrement de b. 236 *A8* toy par ta pitie de g. cest h.q.a. *A7* ce h. 236-237 *A1* h. afin 237 *A8* p. et aussy que *A12* c. en ta *A13* toy et t. 238 *A7* et te p.b. *A10* s. de *A11* g. ainsi c. 238-239 *A13* b. et aussi le g.c. ie suis de ta coulceure quil me *A10* g. ainsi c. ie fus q.v. doulce mere me

234 *tes* [ *ces* Reading of MSS *A1, A3, A4, A5, A7, A8, A9, A12, A13.*

237 *croie* [ *croient* Correction from MSS *A2, A3, A4, A5, A7, A8, A9, A10, A11, A12, A13.*

vostre mere, la benoite Vierge Marie, me donna vostre douce samblance en la touaille que j'ay."

[15] Et tout ainsi que Veronique estoit en oroison, ung disciple de Jhesu Crist passa par devant la porte et elle leva ses yeux et le vist et si le conneü et l'apella et lui dist: "Frere Climent, Jhesu Crist soit avec toy." Et quant le

239 *A12* v. doulce mere me bailla et d. *A4* v. doulce m. la doulce vierge 239-240 *A1* vostre s. au coeuvrechief que 239-241 *A12* douce et sainte s. et a. comme v. *B, B1, B3, B4, A6* mere mappella et me bailla v. face en la t. (*B1, B4* en une t. *B3* en figure en une t.) que ie avoye quant vous fustes mis en la crois a. comme (*B1* a.) v. *B2* g. en la presence de ta doulce mere qui me bailla ta sainte face en icelle t.a. comme v. *B5* v.b. mere la glorieuse vierge marie me appella et me bailla v. benoite face en une t. que iavoye quant les faulx iuifs vous mirent en la croix a. comme v. *B7* q. ta mere tapelle me bailla ta face en une t. que avoye sus ma teste quant tu fut mis en la croix a. comme v. 239-243 *A11* q. ta tres glorieuse v. mere me d. sa saincte s. ou queuvrechief apres celle o. faicte ne demoura gueres que clemens d. de noustre sire i.c. vint par devers la veronique laquelle lui d. sire c. 240-241 *A10* s. tout comme v. *A13* s. en mon quevrechief a. comme v. *A7* t. et 241-242 *A2, A4, A6* o. vint (*A6* o. passoit) ung d. de i.c. passant (*A6* c.) par *B, B1, B4, B5* o. (*B5* o. il) passoit un d. de i.c. par 241-243 *B7* en maison passoit ung d. devant elle en levant sa teste et elle le c. par son non la. en disant f. 242 *A10* et ainsi comme e. *A1* p. et quand e. le *A8* e. jette a coup ses y. et lavisa et *A3* v. tantost le *A10* y. elle laperceust et si *A12* v. passer et 242-243 *A10* co. si lui *B, B1, B5, A6* l. la teste et le c. par (*A6* par son) non et la. (*B1, B5* c. et la. par nom) et lui *B2* po. de la maison ou e. estoyt adonce le v. va congnoistre si la. *B3* et la dame l. la teste et elle le c. et la. par son nom et lui *B4* po. ou elle estoit et l. la teste et le c. et la. par son nom et 242-244 *A13* po. laquelle veronne a. disant sire c. dieu s. en toy et se merveilla moult clement comme elle le savoit n. par son nom et pour ce quelle parloit de 243 *A8* d.c. *A1, A6* c. dieu s. 243-244 *A12* s. en vous et le d. fust tout merveilleux quant il oyt quil fust nomme par son nom et p. 243-246 *A11* s. en toy f.na. 243-247 *A6* toy et clement e. moult g.m. quant elle lappella par son non et o. quelle parloit de i.c. en lostel du s. de lempereur de romme et v. luy d.f.na. point de p. car se dieu plait la c.s. par vous e. et ie croy que ne *B, B1, B3, B4, B7* c. dieu s. en vous et (*B1, B4* s. et clement) e. moult g. (*B7* s. quant clement e.g.) m. quant elle lappella par son nom et o. que elle (*B1* et ainsi comme elle *B3* s. de ce quelle *B4* et estoit o. ainsi comme elle *B7* et ainsi quelle) parloit de i.c. en lostel de s. de lempereur de romme et v. luy d.f.na. (*B3* d. sire na. *B4* d. na.) p. car se dieu plaist (*B1* d.na.) p. car sil p. a dieu c. (*B7* p.c.) s. par vous demain (*B1* s.d.) e. (*B3* v.e.) ie croy que ne le *B2* c. dieu s. et clement e. moult g.m. quant elle lappella par son nom et o. quelle parloit du nom de i.c. et quant elle vit quil estoit esmerveille elle lui d.f.na.p. car se dieu plait toute c.s. par toy e.s. 243-252 *B5* c. dieu s. et clement e. moult g.m. quant elle lappella et o. quelle parloit de i.c. puis v. lui d.f.na.p. car se a dieu plaist c.s. par vous e. ie croy que ne me c. ne vous souvient il pas que q. nostre seigneur ihesu crist fut mis en la c. ie vins de g. la ou ie demouroie au lieu ou on crucifioit nostre seigneur pour querir grace et guerison de lorrible maladie de meslerie de quoy ie estoie si horriblement infecte et la ou ie estoie pour ce que ie ne me osoie approucher des gens pour ma maladie nostre dame la benoite vierge martie p. une touaille que p. sur ma teste et la mist devant la face de i.c. et tantost y parust sa face puis la benoite mere la

disciple s'oÿ nonmer, il eüt grant merveille et ossy quant il oÿ parler de Jhesu Crist a la meson du seneschal. Lors lui dist Veronique: "Frere, n'aiez paour de riens car je te dis que sainta crestienté sera exaucié par toy. Tu ne me cognoistrois sy je ne le te disoie. Sachiez que je suy celle fame qui estoit lepreuse en Gualilee. Et quant Jhesu Crist fu mis en crois, j'alay au mont de Calvaire et sa douce mere qui estoit la prist ung crevechief que pourtoie et en essua la face de Jhesu Crist qui estoit toute seureuse de la grant engoysse qu'il souffroit. Et incontinent fust la figure de la face de

244 *A9* d. ouy ce il en e. moult g. *A1* m. en especial q. 244-246 *A10* n. il entra en la maison du senechal avecques veronne et veronne lui d.f.na. de r.p. car 245 *A1, A2, A3, A4, A7, A8, A9, A13, A6* c. en la *A12* c. en lostel propre du s. de lempereur et l.v. lui d.f. *A1* s. et veronnicque f. 245-247 *A13* s. laquelle luy d.f. par toy sera e.s.c. et s. 245-255 *B6* s. car il cuidoyt que se seneschal fust le plus conternie de la loy de ihesu crist adoncques v. lui d. amy na.p. car demain au plaisir de ihesu crist la loy s.e. avecques son ayde mais ie croie car vous ne me c. point se d. mon non adonques clement luy va dire certainement non dame alors veronique luy va dire ie s. veronique lequel estoit a la passion du prophete ihesu crist qui bailla le couvreche a la mere donc il e. son visaige car pour latouchement du couvreuche ie fus g. de la maladie donc lempereur est malaide et pour ce saches car le seneschal mest v. querir en iherusalem ou ie estoye pour celle cause et non point pour autre chause et pour ce ie v.p. quil vous plaise de venir demain a. moy devant lempereur et lui monsteres le danger ou il est et aussit luy enseigneres les manieres de la passion nostre seigneur ie ne saroie adonc clement pensa que 246 *A1* car s. *A10* que la s. foy sera *A12* que c. 246-247 *A1, A11* toy ie croy (*A11* toy bien scay) que tu 247 *A12* c. pas ie suys *A6, B, B1, B3, B4, B7* d. mon non sa. *A9* d. qui ie suis sa. *A10* d. qui ie suis sa. clement bien sire que 247-248 *B, B1, B3, B4, B7, A6* celle feme qui (*A6, B3* c. dame que) tant e. meselle en *A13* celle que e. meselle en *B2* suy la f. qui e. tant mezelle en 247-254 *A13* celle que e. meselle en laquelle fut g. de la sainte face de i.c. et p.g.le. ie suis v. en c.t. venez v. la avec moy et prescherez la 248 *A10* e. moult l. *B4* galice q. *A4* ie men a. 248-249 *A12* crois au m. de ca. ie y a. et quant ie fuys la la benoitte vierge marie m. de ihesu crist prist *A10* q. le tres doulx i.c. fu cruciffie sa 248-252 *A6* en la c. ie y fut et nostre dame saincte mere p. une tualle que ie avoye sur ma teste et la mist devant la faice de i.c. et tantost sapparu sa face en la tualle et sa mere la *B, B1, B3, B4* crois ie y fu et nostre dame sainte marie sa mere p. (*B1* marie p. *B3* marie mappellait et p.) une touaille que ie avoye en ma teste (*B1, B3* a. sur ma *B4* a. a ma) teste et la mist devant la (*B1* et tantost la) de i.c. et tantost saparut sa (*B3* t. se print sa) face en la touaille et (*B1* sa. en ma touaille et *B4* et sa f.ta.sa. en la to. et) sa mere la 248-253 *B7* q.i. fust crucifie et sachez que suis ici v.p. *B2* crois ie fus ou lieu ou il estoyt et la vierge marie sa d.m.p. une touaille que ie avoye en ma teste et la mist devant le visaige du benoit i.c. adonc en la touaille fut faicte la face du saint prophete par laquelle ie f.g. quant ie la eus touchee et adoree et maintenant ie suis 249 *A11* mere men print une linge que 250 *A1* p. en mon chief et *A8* p. en ma teste et e. *A11, A12* p. en ma teste et le mist devant la *A10* f. de son doulx filz i. qui t.e. plaine de sueur de la *A1, A3* t. plaine de sueur de la *A5* t. suante de la *A9* t. sanglante de 250-252 *A8* c. au *A12* c. et i. la face de i.c.f. pourtraitte au *A11* c. son filz et i. ou linge f. empreins la semblance de i.c. et elle la 251 *A10* que son corps portoit et i. demoura la *A2* i. que la *A1* la samblance de 251-252 *A7* fi. de i. *A10* de son doulx visaige au *A3* i. la fi. de la face de i.c. fut ou

Jhesu Crist au chevichief. Et puis la me bailla et incontinent je fus guerie. Hors sui venue en ceste terre pour guerir l'empereur. Sy vous prie que vous y venés avec moy et sermonerés la foy de Jhesu Crist." Lors le diciple conneü que c'estoit par la voulenté de Dieu et lui dist: "Dame, au plaisir de Dieu soit fet. Et vous prie que vous me dites vostre non." Et elle [39r] le luy dist. / Lors le disciple prist congié de Veronique et s'en va.

252 *A1* au et *A4* ch. apparant et *A12* p. la benoitte vierge marie la me *A1* et tantost ie *A12* in. que ie leu ie le regarday ie f. toute g. 252-253 *A10* g. pour ce gayus le senechal ma admenee en cette ville p. *B, B1, B3, B4, B5, A6* et tantost ie fu toute saine (*A6* ta. fus s.) g. (*B1, B4* fu g. *B5* fu g. de ma meselerie) et pour ce ie suis 252-254 *A11* g. si suis v.p. apporter ledit linge affin que le. que par latouchement dicelluy puisse estre gary ie v.p. que vous prie que v. y 253 *A7* c. ville et t. *A12* c. ville p. *B1* c. cite p. *A10* le. au plaisir de dieu sil vous plaist que *A12* le. en layde de ihesu crist sy 253-254 *B* le. et v. y viendres a moy demain et *B3* le. se dieu plaist si *B4* le. et vous y *B5* le. et v. y v. demain a. *B1, B7* le. et v. y (*B7* et se vous plaist) vendrez demain a. (*B7* ve.a.) moy et prescherez la *B3* que demain au matin venez *A2, A5* si servirez (*A5* s. de) la *A10* si preschera la *A11* si prescherez et illecques la 254 *A2, A4, A7, A8, A9, A10, A12* v.v. *A6* v. y vindrez a. moy demain et 254 *B4* moy demain et *A12* la sainte loy et foy *A8* de nostre seigneur i. 254-255 *A6, B, B1, B4, B7* cr. et clement vit bien (*B1* cl. oyt b. *B4* vid *B7* cr. tantost cl. aperceu) que *A2, A13* cr. adont co. le d. (*A13* co. clement) que *B3* cr. devant lempereur et clement vit bien tantost que ce. par miracle de ihesu crist et *B5* cr. et clemens luy respondit dame *B2* le. et fault que demain ie ayle devers luy si vous playt v. y v. lapostre clement respondit que ce *A11* l. iceluy d. dit a la dame que au 254-256 *A10* cr. clement lui respondit dame le p. 255 *A8* d. voyant que *A6, B1, B4* la grace de *A8* v. nostre seigneur luy *A4, A12* de ihesu crist et *B* la grace de ihesu crist et *A13* d. et respondit dame 255-258 *B2* la grace de d. et que on p. de d. lempereur gueriroyt adonc demanda le nom dicelle femme veronique qui le luy d. saint clement p.c. delle et sen alla iusques le lendemain et 255-259 *B7* lui respondit dame le p. de ihesus s.f. lors clement p.c. de la dame et sen alla iusques a lendemant et le. ne v.o.a. ycelui iour les ydoles car il *B6* la grace deinque de d. adoncques lui d. quil yroit avecques elle voluntiers et p.c. de v. et saiches aussit que oncques puis que gay sen partit davecques le. ledit empereur ne v.a. ses ydoles de bon cuer pour cause que son s. 256 *B3* v. que *A3* d. fet *A10* fet or me *A6, B, B4, B5* que tantost me 256-257 *A1* fet lors *A12* e. luy d. son nom l. 256-258 *A13* fet et sen retourna en son hostel len. matin lem. *B, B1, B3, B4, A6* et tantost (*B1, B3, B4* t. elle) luy d. que elle avoit nom veronique clement d. de dieu p. (*B3* cl.p.) de la (*A6* d. toucha la) femme et (*B1, B4* la dame et) sen ala iusques a landemain et lem. celuy iour (*A6* et len. lem.) ne 256-260 *A11* fet puis parlerent de plusieurs choses et apres le d. sen alla en sa maison len. a 257 *A3* d. veronique l. *A7* d. veronique suis appellee l. *A9* d. quelle se appelloit et faisoit appeller veronique l. *A10* d. on me appelle veronne adonc climent p.c. et 257-258 *A4, A10* sen ala (*A10* a. en son repaire) et *A12* va aller en son hostel et *A3* va mais q. 257-259 *B5* d. quelle avoit nom veronique clement d.p.c. de la sainte femme et sen ala iusques a lendemain et le. ne v.o. celuy iour a. les ydoles qui estoient ses d. car il ny prenoit plus plaisir et ny a. plus fiance ne c.

[16] Et quant il vint l'endemain, l'empereur ne voucit onques adourer ses dieux pource qu'il n'y avoit fine creance par les paroles que le seneschal lui avoit dist. Et quant il vint a heure de tierce, tous les barons furent acemblés et l'empereur se fist aporter la ou estoit toute la baronnie en un lit. Et fist venir Gaius, son seneschal, Clime[n]t et Veronique tous ensemble. Et Veronique portoit le drap a la main destre et le bailla a Climent. Et quant il furent devant l'empereur, Veronique le salua et lui

258 *A12* len. a matin et lem. *A12* v. point a. *B1* v.a. *B2* v. point a. 258-259 *B* o. son d. adourer car il *A7* ses ydoles p. 259 *B1, B3, B4* d. car il *A6* d. car il na. point de bonne c. pour ce que gay le *A10* quil a sainte c. en dieu par *A1* a. mye ferme c. *A2, A7* a. ferme c. *A3* a. plus ferme c. *A4, A5, A12* a. point ferme c. *A8, B7* a. plus de c. *A9* a. plus nulle ferme c. *B3, B4* a. point de bonne c. *B1, B* a. point de bonne (*B* a. pas b.) c.p. ce que gay son s. *A8, A12, B7* que son s. *B3, B4* que gay son s. 259-260 *B5* que son bon s. gay luy *A13* que gaye son s. lui avoit deffendut et 259-263 *B2* d. et ny eut plus p. ce que gay son s. et la bonne dame veronique et saint c. vint avecques eulx et p. la touaille en sa m. 260 *A10* v. comme a *B, B1, B3, B4, B5, A6* v. landemain a h. de ti. et (*B5* de prime que) toute la court et toute la baronnie (*A6, B5* c. et les barons) f. *B6* d. quilz navoient nulle puissance sinon que par lart dyabolique et tout ce que disoient le dyable parloit illecques dedans ces ydoules et lempereur soupiroit et pensoit en son cuer come cecy povoyt faire adoncques le landemain au matin que toute la cort f. *A9* les roys ducs contes viscontes b. et autres seigneurs f. *A10* ti. que les 260-261 *A13* ti. que toute la baronnie fut a. ilz se 260-264 *B7* v. le lendemain a h. de ti. que les seigneurs f.a. en lostel de lempereur ilz f.v. a luy son s. et la v. et c. disciple de ihesus estoict avecques elle q. 261 *A10* ap. au lieu ou 261-262 *A11* ap. au lieu ou e. la ung bel lit *A2, A3, A4, A5, A7* ap. en ung lit ou (*A5, A7* ung lieu ou *A4* a. sur ung lyt et en ung lyeu ou) e.t. la b. et *A13* ap. en ung lit devant toutes la noblesse et puis f. *A8* b. et *A9* ou t. la seignourye et b. estoit assemblee et f. adoncques g. son s.v.c. 261-263 *A6* le.f.v. son s. et v. et c. et *B* le.f.v. son s. et v. et c. vint avecques veroniques et p. la touaille en la *B1* le.f.v. son s. et v. et p. la touaille et clement vint avecques eulx et bailla la *B5* le.f.v. gay son s. et v. et c. avec v. dont v.p. la touaille en sa m. *B3* le.f.v. son s. et v. et p. la touaille avec elle en sa m. et puis le donna a 261-264 *B4* le.f.v. son s. et v. et p. la touaille et clement vint avec eulx et veronique b. la touaille a la destre de c. *B6* le.f.v. son s. et v. laquelle p. en sa m.d. le couvreche adoncques q. 262 *A10* lit puis conmanda a g. quil f.v. la v. lequel tantost la f.v. avec elle saint c. *A8* v. son *A1* g. le s. *A11* v. son s.g. et c. 262-263 *A8* v.e. 262-264 *A11* et et q. 263 *A10* et lors v. qui p. le cueuvrechief a *A3, A6* p. la touaille en la *A8, A12* d. en la (*A12* en sa) m. *A9* d. ou touaille a *A13* le donna a *A13* e. laquelle p. son queuvrechief en sa m.

263-264 *B1* d. a chascun q.f. 264 *A13* et q. la dame heu salue lempereur elle lui *A11, B6* f. venzu d. *B7* f. loens d. 264-265 *B6* salua mou humblement en luy disant s. plaise vous escouter le s. du d. 264-268 *B7* salua moult humblement et puis luy pria quil voulsit escouter le s. de clement d. du saint prophete et puis a. le s. il seroit g. au plaisir de dieu lors le.c. a tous ses g. que clement f. bien e. et tantost m.c. sus une chaiere et prescha de 265 *A3, A8* sire or e. *A7* d. sy e. *B, B1, B2, B3, B4, B5, A6* sire plaise vous escouter (*B1* s.e. *B3* e. ung poc) le *A11* e. devotement le *A12* sire veilles entendre le *A10* sire sil vous plest e. ce que ce s.h. vous dira qui

261 *se* [ *le* Reading of MSS *A1, A2, A3, A4, A5, A7, A8, A9, A10, A11, A12*.

dist: "Sire, entendés le sermon de cest saint home qui est disciple de Jhesu Crist, et aprés le sermon vous serrés gueris." Et l'empereur commenda qu'il fust escoutés par toute gent. Et lors Climent monta sur un chafaut et se mist a sermoner: premierement de l'incarnacion de Jhesu Crist, de la nativité, du baptisme du fluive Jourdain, de la quarantaine, de Judas Scariot qui le traÿt et le vendi trente deniers, de la pacion de la crois,

265 *A6, B, B1, B2, B3, B4* saint proudomme (*B1* p. sil vous plaist) qui *A9* c.h.s. qui est ung des d. du benoist doulx i. *B5* saint preudomme qui est des d. *A4* est un des d. *A13* qui sz estoit d. 265-266 *A11* h. et croiez fermement en i.c. filz de dieu dont il vous preschera et lors a. 266 *A6, B, B1, B2, B3* et puis a *B4, B6* et puis a.v. *A6, A8, A10, B, B1, B2, B3, B5* sermon se dieu plait (*A8* s. de se saint home) v. *A11* sermon ie croy fermement que v.s.g. et lors le. *A12* seres au plaisir de dieux tantost g. *A13* g. de toutes maladies et 266-267 *A8* g. lors c.le. quil *A9* g. si dieu plaist et le.c. a toutes ses gens qui f.e. et *A1* le. dist voulentiers et c. quil f. racompte par t.g.c. 266-268 *B3, B4* le. incontinent c. (*B4* le. dist que voulentier et c.) a toute sa court quil f. bien e. adonc saint c.m. en chiere haulte et preschait de *B5* g. adonc le.c. a toute sa court quil f. bien e. saint c.m. en chaiere haulte et comenca a prescher de *B6* g. avecques la aide de dieu adoncques quant le. eust ouy veronique il fust moult joyeulx et demanda a tous ceulx et celles qui estoient la ce nestoient pas bien content dacomplir sa volunte et il respondirent certainement ouy sire car cest bien raison quelle se face adoncques il c.a. tous ceulx et celles qui estoient illecques escoutassent le sermon du disciple de ihesu crist alors mon seigneur saint c.m. en ung lieu hault ou tout le peuple le povoit veoir pour faire son sermon et commanca a parler de *B, B1, A6* co. a toute sa court que il f. bien e. saint c.m. en une chaiere haulte et prescha de *B2* co. a tous ceulx de sa court quil escoutassent diligenment le sermon de saint c. qui estoyt en une chayre hault et prescha de 267 *A11, A12* m. en ung *A2, A4* f. oy et e. *A11* f. de tous diligemment e. *A3* e. de t. sa g. *A10* e. adonc c. *A12* t. sa court et sa baronnie et c. 267-268 *A13* e. de t.g. de sa court et c. commensa a prescher p. *A1* ch. et comencha a *A11, A12* ch. et sermonna p. 268 *A10* se print a prescher et p. 268-269 *B, B1, B3, B4, B7, A6* in. et du *B5* in. du b. et du *A10* in. de nostre seigneur et de la n. *A12* in. de la n. du f. 268-270 *B6* in. de dieu et puis de sa n. de la circoncision de la carentene qui ieuna de son apoustre i. qui le v. 269 *A11* n. de son b. fait au f. *B2* n. et de la circuncision et du *A3* b. ou f. *A10* b. qui fut fait au f. *A1* la desperation de *A3, A5* la quaresme de *A8* la trahison de 269-270 *A11* de la trahison de i. qui v. le mercredi de devant sa passion aulx iuifz xxx *B, B1, B3, B4, B5, A6* io. et de la n. et circoncision de (*B3* de nostre seigneur) i.c. et de la xlne et de i. qui *A9* n. de la q. que nostre seigneur si ieusna comment i.s. le v. *A13* io. de io. s. quil v. nostre seigneur ihesu crist xxx *B7* io. de la n. de i.c. et coment i. le 270 *A2* s. et *A3, A5, A7, A8* qui le *B2* v. noustre seigneur lequel avoyt receu mort et p. en la *A8, A9* d. dargent de (*A9* d. aux iuifs de) la p. *A11* d.co. *B3* de sa p. quil souffrit en la *B6* d. par envie au faulz iuifs et co.p. *B, B1, B5, A6* p. quil souffrit en la (*A6* en) c. 270-271 *A10* p. et co. *A13* p.co.pi. iuga nostre seigneur co.io. le m. *B7* v. au iuif xxx d. et co.pi. la iuga a mort et co.io. le *B4* d.co.p. le iuga a mort de la p. quil souffrit en la c.co.io. le

269 *quarantaine* [ *lx*$^{e}$ Reading of MSS *A4, A10, A12, B, B1, B2, B4, B5, B6*. The erroneous reading of the base-manuscript (which is also found in MSS *A2* and *A7*) results from the transposition of the elements of "xl$^{e}$". See the variants to this line.

coment Pilate le juga, coment Joseph d'Arimatie le mist au sepulcre, comment il fu descendu de la crois, comment il espolia enfer, de la rexurrecion, de la accencion, comment il envoya le saint esperit a ses apostre[s] et coment il doit venir le jour du jugement. Et quant il eüst assés sermoné, il acheva et dist: "Amen."

[17] Et lors lui et Beronique se mistrent en oroison et prierent Jhesu

271 *B, B1, B3, B5, A6, A12* iuga a mort (*B3* a morir *B5* m. sans cause et a grant tort) et (*A6* m. et) co.io. le *A10* io. le descendit de la croix et le 271-272 *B2* iuga a mort et co.io. le descendit de la croix et le m. au s. et co. il e. *A10* s.co. il es. *A13* s.co. ihesus es. enfer apres sa mort de *B, B1, B3, B4, B7* s.co. il e. *B5* au saint s.co. 271-273 *B6* iuga faucement a tort et sans cause et co. il fust cruxifie en la croies et co.io. et nichodemus le descendirent de la crois et le mirent dedans le s. et co. il resuscita et io. il monta au ciel le iour de la. et c. *A11* iuga a mourir en croix ou mont de calvaire entre deux larrons co.io. et nycodemus le misdrent au s. et co. au tiers iour il resuscita puis de la. et conment il monta es cieulx a la fin du monde il viendra iuger les mors et les vifs et conment a la panthecoste il 272 *A12* c. le descendit de *A7* d.co. *A5* cr. il *A6, B, B4, B5, B7* enfer et aussi de *B2* enfer et en getta dehors les anciens peres de *B3* il brisait enfer et aussi de 272-273 *A4* enfer comment il resuscita de la. *A4* de son a. 273 *B4* de son a. *A10* il monta es cieulx et de la penthecoste comment il en. *B6* es. le iour de la pantecouste a 273-274 *B1, B3, B4* es. aux a. *B2* au x sins a. *A12* en. a ses a. le s.es. et 274 *A1* v. iugier le 274-275 *B, B1, B3, B4, B5* c. dieu viendra (*B4, B5* co. il v.) au iour du iu. (*B1* au iu.) iugier les bons et les mauvaiz et co. il preschera et adont fenit son sermon et *A6* iu. les bons et les mauvais et comme il preschera et adonc finit son sermon et d. *A4* iu. pour iugement des bons et des maulvais et *A9* iu. iuger les bons et les mauvais et *B2* iu. pour tout le monde iugier et adonc il fina son sermon et *A10* as. presche il 274-276 *A11* a. et de plusieurs aultres choses qui trop longues seroient a racompter et apres le sermon fine se *B6* c. au iour du iu. il viandra iugier les bons et les maulves et adoncques il finit son sermon adoncques v. et clement se 274-277 *B7* a. et parla de plusieurs aultres chosez tant quil finist son sermon en apres il se mist en o. et b. parellement en priant i. devotement quil luy pleust moustrez son m. et telle maniere que lempereur fust bien guerist et 274-278 *A13* iu. et conclut son sermon en disant amen et p. devotement luy et veronne nostre seigneur comme devant es ia dit l.o. acomplie ilz ouvrirent devant t. le quevrechief et 275 *A12* s. et il finist son sermon et 275-276 *A7* a. et l. 276 *A8* et luy *B5* et puis luy *A6, B, B1, B2, B3, B4* et puis se mit en o. et b. aussi (*B3* et a. fit b. *B2* et b.a.) et p. *A9* p. nostre seigneur i. 276-277 *A2* o. vers i.c. quil voulsist monstrer i. *A11* p. dieu le tout puissant quil *A4* o. vers i.c. et ly p. quil voulsist a leure demonstres ses mi. *B6* o. pour prier a dieu qui luy plust demonstrer de ces m. et guerir cedit empereur adoncques q. *B2* p. dieu qui luy pleut de monstrer son m. a lempereur et de luy donne sante q. *A6, B, B1, B3, B4* c. le tout puissant quil luy plaise montrer son *A8* c. tout puissant quil *A10* m. son *A12* c. tout puissant quil luy pleust de demonstrer i. son m. et sa bonne et grande vertus et q. 276-278 *B5* p. nostre seigneur qui luy pleust de monstrer son m. et guerir lempereur q. ilz furent levez de o.

272 *il espolia enfer* Jesus' descent to the netherworld (a place of waiting, not of suffering) in order to lead the just to heaven is the subject matter of the *Descensus ad inferos*, one part of the *Gospel of Nicodemus*. See Ford, 52-57, 92-98.

Crist qu'il monstra illuecques son miracle. Et quant il eürent achevee leur oroison, il desploierent veant tous la touaille et la mirant devant l'empereur et la lui firent adourer. Et incontinent il fust guari par telle maniere que onques ne lui paru ne que si jamés n'eüst eü nulle maladie. Et quant il fu gueri, il ala partout et fust aucy legier comme nul des autres.

277 *A12*, *B6* e. faicte l. 277-278 *A2* e.l.o.a. il *B*, *B2*, *B3*, *B4*, *B7*, *A6* ilz furent levez de (*B3*, *B4*, *A6* de leur) o. 277-279 *A11* mi. devant puis la veronique print le saint queuvrechief et le bailla a saint clemens qui le desploya et puis le mist devant *B1* ilz furent levez do. ilz d. la t. ou estoit la face de ihesu crist devant 278 *A2*, *A4* des. devant t. *A1* des. devant t. et v.t. le coeuvrechief et *A6*, *B*, *B3*, *B4*, *B7* des. la t. ou (*B7* t. en laquelle) estoit la face de ihesu crist d. *A10* des. devant tous le noble cueuvrechief et *A12* t. le barons le saint couvrechief et 278-279 *B2* des. la t. la ou estoyt la face de ihesu crist moult honestement et luy *A7* touaille i. *A10* m. tout d.le. adoncques lui f.a. par si bonne intencion que tantost fust 278-282 *B5* des. la t. ou estoit la face de ihesu crist et tantost quil eust adoure il f.g. de sa maladie tout ainsi come se o. nen eust rien eust q. lempereur fut ainsy guery il sen ala aussi tost et legierement c. nul de ses gens et t. sa baronnie en e. moult g.i. et tant que lempereur et toutes gens et r. *B6* des. le saint couvrechef devant lempereur et lui f. faire honeur et la adore de bon cuer aupe v. tout le peuple et f.i.g. de sa maladie ausit co. se il neust oncques este malaide et sa chair estoit renovelle et blanche come celle dung petit enffant adoncques tous les seigneurs et toulx autres en e.g. 279 *A11* a. et atoucher et puis i. *A1* a. et tantost il *A4* i. quil leut adore il creust fermement en ihesu crist et fust *A9* i. icellui vaspasien empereur qui estoit tout lepreux fust *A12* i. quil eust eust adore il f. tout sain et bien g. en t. *B7* i. quil eust adorer ilz fust 279-281 *A10* g. et tres necheut que o. en lui ne put non plus que sil ne. eu oncques m.q. lempereur si fut g. moult gracia nostre seigneur ihesu crist et aussi fist tout le peuple qui moult grant ioye lempereur se moustroit a tout le monde et alloit par

279-282 *A11* g. si ala p.t.a. legierement c. ung a. qui iamais neust eu mal dont luy et t. sa chevalerie e. grant *B7* g. tant bien que se o. neust este malade et q. lempereur f.g. il se levast du lictz ou il gisoit malade ausy legerement que home que fust en la compagnie et l. le seigneurs qui la estoyent e. *B*, *B1*, *B3*, *A6* a. ihesu crist et tantost que il leut adouree il f. tantost g. (*B1* t. tout sain *B3* f. tous g.t. tout sains et g.) de toute sa maladie comme se o. nen (*A6* se nen) eust riens (*A6* heust point) eu q. lempereur fut (*B1* eust eu r. et fut du tout *B3* eult o. eu devant le. fut) gay il sen ala aussi legierement c. nul de ses gens (*B1* c. si oncques neust este malade) et t. sa baronnie en e. moult g. plaisir et moult grant ioye (*B1* e.m.g.i. *B3* p. et i.) et r. *B2* a. et tantost quil eut adoure il f. tout sain et entierement g. de toute sa maladie aussi nettement come o. avoyt este et aussi bien come se iamais ne eut eu mal toute sa court tous ses barons et tout le monde sen e. *B4* a. ihesu crist et tantost quil eust adore il f. tantost tout sains et g. de sa malaidie et t. sa court en e. mout g.i. et g. plaisir et 279-284 *A13* fust sains et allegiez comme o. mais avoit estez dont ilz furent tous ioyeulx et louuarent ihesu crist adoncques c. son f.m. 280 *A3* p. maladye ne *A12* p. aussy peu comme sy *A1* se oncques ne. *A2*, *A3*, *A5* eu maladie *A8* o. puis ne p. ne plus que se onques ne. *A9* o. puis ny apparut nulle tache de macule de lepre ne que *A7* ne. ne maladie 280-281 *A12* maladie et incontinent quil *A4* eu nul mal et 281 *A1* t.a. *A9* l. et delivre c. *A2*, *A4* c. ung des *A7* c. les a. 281-282 *A12* t. et se leva a.l.c. il avoit oncques este par devant la maladie dont luy et t. sa court et sa baronnie en e. grant *A10* nul homme de sa court et l. lui et ses gens demenerent grant

Et lors lui et toute sa gent eürent tres grant joye et rendirent grace a Jhesu Crist coment Climent, le disciple de Jhesu Crist, leur avoit enseignié. Et puis il couronna Titus, son fil, et le fist empereur moult honorablement.

[18] Quant vint l'endemain a matin, et Climent sermona a l'empereur et
[39v] a Titus, son filz, et a toute sa gent. Et / quant il eü achevé, il rendi grace a Dieu, et l'empereur et toute sa gent distrent: "Amen." Aprés Climent dist a

282 *A8* l. toutes ses gens e. *A1* e.g. *B2* g. merveille et furent moult ioyeux et r. *A11* a dieu i. 282-283 *A12* r. grant g. et louanges a dieu i.c. ainsi co. *B3* r. tous enssemble g. a nostre seigneur i.c. ainsi co.cl.l. *A8* a dieu co. *B1* a nostre seigneur i.c. aussi co.cl.l. *B2* a dieu moult humblement ainsi co. saint cl.l. *A10* a dieu apres cr. *B6* grace et louanges a i.c. plusieurs se firent baptiser et 282-285 *B7* i. et firent grand feste en remerciant nostre seigneur ihesu pour la garison de lempereur en apres lempereur c. son filz t. novel e.m.h. en faisant grandez solempnitez comme le plus grand du monde q.
283 *A2, A3, A5, A7, A9* co. le *A7* d.l. *A2, A3, A7* a. dit et e. *A8* de dieu l.a. dit en secret et *A1* cr. de ce que cl. son d.l. *A6, B, B4, B5* cr. ainsi co.cl.l. *A4* cr.l.a. dit et e.
283-284 *A11* cl.la. ordonne et p. apres il *A12* et apres ses graces il c. son f.t. et
284 *A1* p. lempereur c. *A7* c. son filz t. et *B, B1, B2, B3, B4, B5* p. apres il (*B1, B5* a. lempereur *B3* a. apres il) c. son filz t.e. (*B4* t. nouveaul e. *B3* t.) m. *A12* e. de romme m. *A1* e.h. 284-285 *A9* h. illec presentement q. *B, B3, B4* h. a le. *B1, B5* h.le. *B2* h. le le. *A6* p. apres il c. son filz t.e.m. notablement ainsin comme il devoit faire a le. 284-286 *B6* p. apres toutes ces choses t. qui estoit f. dudit empereur fust couronne h. et puis apres c. prescha devant le. et devant t. 284-288 *A11* h. ainsi quil appartient a filz de si noble empereur apres ces choses saint c. et la veronique dirent a le.
285 *A1* le.c. *B2* m. saint c. prescha a *A6, B, B1, B3, B4, B5* c. prescha a *A10* c. oprescha encores devant le. 285-287 *B7* c. preschast devant le. et son filz t. et ainsy devant le poeuple et fust fort escoutez et q. il eust faict son sermon il dictz amen ainsi fist le. *A13* q.c.s. le l.m. chascum respondit devotement amen sire d.c. a 286 *A6, B, B1, B2, B3, B4* a son filz t. (*B, B1, B3* f.) et *A3, A8* to. leur g. *A10* f. et q. *B, B1, B3, B4, B5, A6* g. et fut moult bien escouter (*B1* m.e.) et q. il eut fine son sermon il *B2* g. et fut moult bien escoute dung chascun et apres le sermon chascun r. *B6* et par devant t. et puis rendirent g. *A3* a. son sermon il *A9* a. de sermonner il *A10* il ot sermonne il *A12* eust finy il 286-287 *A3* g. a ihesu crist et luy avec t. *A4, A5* g. a ihesu crist et tous (*A5* g. et les gens) distrent 286-288 *A7* g. a ihesu crist a p. 287 *A9* g. et t. ses g. aussy disans amen *A2* d. et t. *B, B1, B3, B4, B5, A6* d. aussi fit le. *B2* d. moult homblement et devotement et par grant devotion ap. saint c. *B3* distrent tous amen *B4* amen et puis ap.d.c. a *A1* ap. cecy c. 287-288 *B, B3* ap. se d.c. seigneurs p. que dieu v. *B1* ap.d.c.p. *A12* c. et gay le seneschal distrent a le. sire p. *A6* ap. ce d.c. seigneur p. que dieu a il si *A10* ap. ce d.c. a le. sire p. que le doulx i.c.v. a donne si *B6* d. et d. tous amen ap. toutes ces choses veronique parla avecques lempereur et luy d. monseigneur p. que dieu v. *B5* g. en disant amen ap. se d.c. seigneur p. que d.v. 287-294 *B7* g. come clement leurs enseigna ap. le sermon c. comenca a dire a le. qui devoist estre ioyeulx p. quil estoit bien gueris et quil luy pleust soy faire b. car nostre seigneur a establi b. pour homme estre saulvez et la dieu ordonez en sa loy adoncques lempereur an manda a ses gens que chascun deulx se fist baptiser et quil en estoict autent a. que creust en la foy de i.c. fust plus fort que aultre en apres le.d. ie dois grand gardon a dieu et a la sainte femme veronique qui tant

283 *enseignié* [ *enseignier* Correction from all MSS except *A11*.

l'empereur: "Puisque Jhesu Crist vous a fette sy grant grace que vous estes sy bien gueri, je vous pri que pour l'amour de lui vous vous fetes baptizer car Jhesu Crist a ordonné le batisme, sans lequel hom ne se puet sauver et c'est la loy donnee par Jhesu Crist, le Saint Profette. Et ossy commende que toute personne se batize et voeilliez crestienté exaucer afin que toute personne se puisse baptizer sans peur et tourner en la loy de Jhesu Crist."

[19] Lors dist l'empereur: "Je suis moult tenu a ceste dame qui c'est tant travaillee pour moy." Et lors il prist Beronique par la main et lui dist: "Dame, prenés de mon empire ce que vous en voudrés car je le vous

288 *A4, A8* le. sire p. *B4* que dieu v. *A13, B6* f. telle grace 288-289 *A12* f. telle grace quil vous aye g. *A10* estes sain et g. *A11* v. soiez ainsi g. *B1* grace seigneur que v.e.g. *B5* grace et qui vous a si merveilleusement donne guerison ie *B6* estes g. et aves sainte de vostre corps ie *B2* le. monseigneur ie v.p. et requiers que p. lonneur de celluy qui vous a rendue sante et guarison v.v. vueilles b. 289 *A6, B, B1, B3, B4, B5* p. que v. *B6* p. quil vous plaise de v. faire b. *A8* lonneur de *A13* de ihesu crist v. *A1* lui et pour le sauvement de vostre ame v. 290 *B5* car nostre seigneur i. *A11* le sant b. *B2* a estably b. *A9* l. nul ne *A13* l. nulz nul se 290-291 *A1* l. nul ne p. estre sauvez car cest *A11* l. nul on ne p. estre saulve et o. *A12* ne p. estre sauve et la foy et la sainte loy d. par le s.p.i.c. et 290-292 *A10* le saint b. pour estre saulve car quil ne sera baptise il sera dampne et qui sera baptise il sera saulve et o. commanda que t. le monde se

290-294 *B, B1, B3, B4, B5, A6* a estably b. pour homme estre (*B3, B5* p.e. *B4* p.e.h.) sauve car dieu le (*B3* car il le) donne en sa loy adont lempereur commanda a (*B1* a. demande le. a) t. ses gens que ilz se fissent baptiser et sans p. et aussi a toute femme pour e. (*B1* e. la) c. par tout le monde ou il yroit (*B5* m. et pour estre saulve) adonc ce (*B4* y. et puis) d. *B2* l. nul ne p. estre saulve lempereur fist commander a tout homme et a toute femme quil se fissent baptiser pour e. la foy de ihesu crist et toute c.le. va ainsi dire apres a saint clement ie doy dit il grant guerdon a c. femme qui a tant *A7* et celle loy donna i.c. le p. 290-309 *B6* a donne b. pour tout home s. adoncques le. commanda a toulx ces gens quil se fissent baptiser et qui leur en donoit congie mais ade moy ie 291 *A8* c. et o. 291-292 *A13* p. le saint esperit et p. de i.c. sy vous prie que *A2, A3, A4, A5, A7* o. commanda que 292 *A11* se vueillent fere baptiser et v. toute la c. 292-294 *A13* p.l. 293 *A3, A8* t. a la *A1* p. et puissant t. *A11* b. et t. a la *A12* p. sans doubtance et *A4, A7* t. a la foy de *A1, A5, A9* la foy de *A12* loy et foy de *293-294* *A2* la foy de i.c. nostre seigneur adont d. *A10* se baptise et tourne en la foy et en la chrestiente adonc d. 294 *A9* le. a clement ie *B, B1, B3, B4, B5, A6* ie doy grant guerdon a dieu et a la sainte femme (*B1, B4* la f. *A6* la dame) qui a tant *A10* le.m.s.t. 294-295 *A11* le. que ainsi le feroit voulentiers mais non pas encores si p. *A13* s. fort t. a c. vaillant d. qui tant a este tr. *A10* qui tant cest tr. 295 *A12* et p. 295-296 *A13* moy et la p. pour la m. disant dame *A11* dist p. de mes biens tout ce quil v. plaise car 295-297 *B5* m. disant dame p. de ma terre ce quil vous plaira car ie le veul s.v.ch. ou ci. or ou argent ou t. *B, B1, B2, B3, B4, A6* dist p. de ma terre ce quil te (*B2* t. tant que te) plaira car ie le vueil s. (*B3, B4* v. ainsi s.) v.ch. ou ci. (*A6* v. soit ch. ou aultres ci.) or (*B2* v.s. belles ci. ou ch. or) argent ou t. 295-298 *B7* m. en lui disant p. de ma terre ce quil te plaira a ton plaisir car ie le voeul ainsi dont ci.ch. ou argent ou toutes c. quil te plairons l. 296 *A13* e. tout ce 296-297 *A10* car t.e. ie le v. donne s.

291 *commende* [ *commendes*

octroie tout entierement, soient: villes, cités, chastiaus, tresor ou autres choses, excepté Rome qui est chief de mon empire." Et Veronique lui dist: "Sire, j'en remerci Dieu et vous et sy vous prie que ce que vous me voulés donner, que vous donnés a Climent qui est disciple de Jhesu Crist et je me suy donnee a lui." Et l'empereur l'ouctroya et dist a Climent: "Prenés de mon empire pour cest dame ce que vous voudrés." Et Climent luy dist: "Je ne voeil de vous autre chose mes que vous vous baptizez et fettes baptizer vostres gens et croire en la foy de Jhesu Crist qui vous a fet tant de grace, car vous savés bien qu'il est Dieu tout puissant."

297 *A13* o.e. *A12* s.ch.v.ci.t. *A13* s.ci.v.ch.t. *A10* v.ch.ci.t. *A3* v.chastiaux *A2* chastiaux ou 297-298 *A6, B, B1, B3, B4, B5* chastiaux que vous plaise en ma terre e. *A7* s.ci.v. et choses 297-300 *A11* o. de bon cueur et v. luy respondit sire ie v.r. mais si me v. riens d. si le donner a 298 *A13* choses quelxconques e. *A10* est le principal de *A3, A4* et lors v. 298-299 *B5* chief grant mercy a d. et a v. dit veronique mais ie v.p. *B, B1, B2, B3, B4, B7, A6* de ma terre v. respont grant (*B2* v. luy r. ainsi g. *B7* r.) mercy a d. et a v. (*B4* v. car ie ne vueulz riens du vostre mais *A6* v. mais) ie v.p. *A13* e. laquelle respondist s. *A10* em. adonc respondit v. sire ie 298-300 *A12* luy respont sire ien r. a d. ihesu crist et a v. mais ie v.p. que se v. me v. riens d. 299 *A10* v. aussi et *A13* v. ce que vous me presentez mais ie v.p. que se rien me voules *A1* v. pour ce ie v. supplie que *A10* que tout ce 300 *A1* que le d. *B5* d. aulcune chose quil vous plaise le donner a c. servant de *A6, B1, B4* c. serviteur de *B, B7* c. serf de *B2* c. apostre de *B3* c.d. *A1, A6, A8, A13, B, B1, B3, B4, B5* cr. car ie *B7* i. a qui me *B2* cr. a qui ie 300-301 *A10* c. adonc le.d. *A12* cr. car ie me s. a luy d. et 300-302 *A11* cr. et le. luy d. quil en estoit contant et quil demandast tout ce quil vouldroit et que luy seroit octroye et 301-303 *A13* lui adoncques d.le. a c. quil demandast ce quilz voudroit lequel respondit ie 301 *B, B1, B2, B3, B4, B5, B7, A6* e. luy acorda (*B1* e. le luy a. *B2* e. y a. voulentiers *A6* e.a.) et *A9* et luy d.c. *A10* c. clement p. 301-303 *A12* le. lui d. dame ce que v.v. me plait et c.d. a lempereur sire ie 301-303 *B, B1, B3, B4, B5, A6* de ma terre ce quil te plaira c. respont ie *B7* c. come il avoit dictz a veronique et c. respondit grand merci a dieu et a vous car ie 301-304 *B2* c. quil print de sa terre tout ce quil en vouldroyt saint c. le remercia et ne voulut riens prendre mais luy pria quil voulsist b. et quil voulsist c. 302 *A10* ceste bonne d. tout ce 302-303 *A10* voudres adonc respondit c. sire ie *A1* et lors luy d.c. ie *A3* luy respondit sire ie *A8* et il luy d. sire ie *A9, A11* dist sire ie 303 *A1, A9* voeil a.c. de vous mes que *A10* c. si non que *A11* c. fors que 303-304 *B, B1, B3, B4, B5, A6* voeil rien du vostre fors quil v. plaise de v. faire baptiser et touz v.g. et croiez en (*B4* c. a) la *A8* que v.b.v. et vostre g. *A10* et que vous faciez b. 303-305 *A13* voeil a.c. seulement fors que v. soyez b. ensamble v. peuple affin quil croyent en i.c. quil v. a garys car il 303-306 *B7* voeil riens de v. fors quil v. plaise v. faire baptiser car ainsy laves promis a ihesus le. respondit a clement a. 304 *A10* c. fermement en *A12* la saincte foy *A8* c. a la *A11* la loy de 304-305 *A8, A10* fet si grant (*A10* si belle) g. *A12* fet si grant g. car il 304-306 *A6* t. de si grans g. que sains vous a sgarir le. respondit et lui d.a. *A11* fet si grant g. comme de vous avoir gary de si griefve maladie dont estiez enteiche l. *B2* qui lui avoyte f. telle g. come de luy avoyr rendue sante entierement le. respondit et d. a saint clement a. *B4* t. de de g. que v. estre sains et gary le. respondit et luy d.a. 305 *A3, A5, A7, A9* s. quil *A10* car b.s. de verite quil est vray d. lequel est t. *A8* est t. 305-306 *B* g. qui sain vous a gary le. respondit et lui d.a. *B3* g. que saint vous ait gary adonc le. respondit a. *B5* g. quil vous a guery si miraculeusement le. respondit et luy d.a. *B1* g. que tout sain vous a gary le. respont et lui d. ainsi ie *A9* p. au miracle quil a fait et lors

[20] Et lors lui dist l'empereur: "Amis, je vieux que tu soies apostole et chief de toute crestienté et vieux que sermonés et facés sermoner par toute ma terre la sainte foy de Jhesu Crist. Et toute personne qui se voudra convertir, il me plet bien, mes sachiés que je ne me baptiseray jusques a tant que j'aie vengee la mort du Saint Prophete. Et je te promet que incontinent que je seray retourné, s'il plet a Dieu que je retourne, je me baptizeray et feray baptizer toutes mes gens. Et sy m'en yray en brief de

306 *A1* et le. lui d. a *A7* lors d. *A10* lors respondit le. a climent a. *A12* lui respont le. *A2, A4, A11* e. (*A11* e. clemens) ie *A7* s. sermonneur a. *A4* a. de romme et 306-307 *A2* a. de romme et de t.cr. le ch. et *B, B1, B2, B3, B4, B5, B7, A6* s. pere (*B2* s.a. et p.) de toute ma (*A6* de ma) terre et de *A10* a. de t.cr. *A13* le. lui respondit a. ie vous certiffie que vous serz a. de romme et le chief 307 *A12* et que *B, B1, B2, B3, B4, B5, A6* que tu presches et f. preschier par 307-308 *B7* que tu presche et que f. prescher la foy *A3* par ma *A12* par tout mon empire la s. loy et foy de i.c. et qui *A5* s.p. 307-309 *A11* cr. et vous donne congie de prescher par t. ma rie et ou bon vous semblera le non de i.c. car il 308 *A6, A7, A9, B, B2, B3, B4, B5* la foy *B1* la loy de *A10* terre et to. les p. *A13* s. de 308-309 *B, B1, B3, B4, B5, B7, A6* et que tout homme et toute femme (*A6* h. et f. *B7* h. [ ] f.) qui v. baptiser (*B3, B5, A6* v. fere b.) il *B2* c. et que vueil et commande que tout homme et toute femme soyent baptises mays vueylles scavoyr que 309 *A6, B, B1, B3, B4* mes vuillez savoir que *B7* b. et voeuille savoir que *A11* b. que toute personne se convertisse en ihesu crist mais bien s. *B5* mais ie *A1* ba. decy a *A2* ba. et feray baptiser toutes mes gens i. *A3* ba. pas i. 309-310 *B, B3, B4* ba.t. *B1, B5* i. a ce que *A8* i. iaray v. *B6* ne me sere point baptesme i. ie *A10, B7* ne me feray baptiser i. 310 *A4* t. ne feray baptisier mes gens tant que *A6, B, B1, B2, B3, B4* m. (*B3* m. et passion) de ihesu crist et *A2* m. de ihesu crist le s. *A10* m. de ce tres s. *B6* m. de celuy qui ma baille sainte et garison et *A11, A13* p. ihesu crist mais (*A13* p.m.) ie *B7* dudit s. *B5* p. ihesu crist et 310-311 *A6* et ie luy p. se ie puis retourner se dieu p. ie me *B1, B, B2, B3, B4, B5* promet que si ie puis retourner se (*B2* que quant ie s.r. si d.) dieu p. ie (*B5* r. et il plaise a d. me) me *A13* promet que sy p. a d. que ie r. que ie me 310-312 *B7* promet que se ie puis retourner par de ca ie me f.b. aussi par clement mis 310-313 *B6* promet qui si plaise a dieu que ie puisse retourner en ceste ville ie me fere b. et moy et toulx car si plaist a dieu ie men veul aller en i. moy et mes gens p. 311 *A12* d. ie me *A8* r. vif ie me *A1, A2, A3, A4, A7, A9, A10, A11* r. ie me 311-312 *A1* me feray baptisier et aussy f. 311-313 *A10* me feray baptiser et soyez certain que en b.t. ie y. veroir la cite de i. 312 *A1* g. et vous en tant que ie men *A9* y. bien en b. *A6, B, B1, B3, B4, B5* g. et tantost ie y. en i. *B2* g. laquelle ie vueil tantoust mener en i. *A12* t. ceulx qui ne se sont fait baptisier et men 312-313 *B7* g. et de b. me partiray pour aller en i. affin que puisse v. *A11* y. vraiement en i. *A12* b. par de la en i. pour sa m.v. car 312-314 *A13* g. car ie vuis aler bien b. en i. car les iuifz lont mis a m. et

310 *aie* [ *aiee* Correction from MSS *A3, A9, A10, A11, A12, B3, B5, B6*.

temps en Jherusalem pour venger la mort de Jhesu Crist car il prist mort a [40r] tort et sans cause." / Lors l'empereur leva Climent et fust apostole, et fist fere une eglise fondee de saint Symeon et ung alter. Et sur l'alter il mist la touuaille de Veronique sur deux pilers out estoit la figure de Jhesu Crist. Et fist ordener en celle eglise fons pour baptiser tous ceulz qui se

313 *A1* t. et et mes gens en *A11* v. sa m. car *A3* c. quil souffrit a *A7* c. qui p. 313-314 *A1* c. le sainct prophete car ilz le firent morir a grand t. 313-314 *A10* m. et passion en grant peine pour nous et s. nulle cause *A12* m. et passion et *B7* c. qui morust en la croix s. 313-315 *B, B1, B3, B4, B5, A6* c. qui p.m. et passion a grant t. adonc le. fist (*B5* a.f.) c. pape (*A6, B3* p. de romme) et fist (*B5* p. de romme) fere *B6* de celuy qui morut a t. et pylate mon prevost le iuga a mort et sans quil trovast en luy c. de mort et par faulx et desloyal iugement la iuge adoncques avant que le. partit de rome le constitua et ordona pere de rome et f. construyre et edifier une moult belle e. de mon seigneur sa. *B2* c. qui a souffert m. et passion a grant t. adonc le. fist saint c. pape et apostre et adonc f.f. a romme le. de 314 *A11* c. par lenvie des faulx iuifs lesquelx ie pense destruire l. print clement et le ordonna a. puis fist *A13* c. adonc fit le.c.a. de romme en grant ioye et en grant solempnitez et puis fist *B7* le. fist c. pape de rome et fist *A1* c. qui estoit devant luy a genoulx et *A12* c. et le fist a. *A4* a. de romme et 314-315 *A10* c. et le fist a. et faire ung hostel et une grande e. de sa. 315 *A6, A9, A12, B, B1, B3, B4, B5* e. de *B7* e. et *A1* sy. et fist faire ung *A10* sy. et sur cest a. il *A8* et dedans ung *A12* ung bel a. *A7* sur ycellui il *A5* sur celuy a. *A9* la.m. il la 315-316 *A13* e. de sa. clement et ung a. sur lequel il m. le quevrechiefz de *A11* e. dans laquelle il m. le queuvrechief de *B2* sy. et y fist ediffier ung a. ouquel y a quatre p. la ou est la touaille en laquelle appert la face de i. *A1, A10* m. le cueuvrechief de *B3* al. et dessus ledit a. ait d.p. ou est la touaille de v. en laquelle est la face de i. *B, B1, B4, B5, A6* la. a (*B4* a cinquante) d. (*B5* la.d.) p. ou est la touaille de v. en (*B5* t. en) laquelle est la face de i. 315-317 *A12* il fist mettre le couvrechief de v. out e. la face de i.c. a grant honneur sur d. beaulx p. de marbre et fist *B7* la. fist mettre d.p. bien ordoneement pour mettre la sainte touaille de v. en laquelle est la face nostre seigneur i.c. et ausi f. faire une eglise p. ceulz 315-318 *B6* la. des seigneurs et en icelle e. y a d.p. de yrepiare ou est atache le couvreche ou est la face de i.c. et avecque f. faire cedit empereur ij f. dedans ladicte eglise et mon seigneur s. 316 *A11* e. emprainte la digne face de nostre seigneur i. 316-317 *A8* v. ou e. lemprainte et f. de i.c. sur d.p. et *A10* v. auquel e. la face de i. sur d.p. et fist *A13* p. et fit fere ung fons 317 *A3* et la f. adorer et aussi en c.e. fit faire fons *B2, B3, B4* f. faire en *A4* f. en c.e.o. fons *A2* o. fons en c.e.p. *A11* c. fons *A12* en le. belles fons *A6, B, B1, B5* f. faire en (*B5* en ladicte) le. ung fons (*B1* le. les f.) pour c. (*B* p.c.p.c.) qui *B4* fons p.c. 317-318 *A8, A10, A11, A12, B2* b. et

315 *Symeon* Probably St. Peter (known as Simon Peter and designated as "Simeon" in Acts 15:14) is intended, and this would be acceptable in terms of the dates. However, the exposition of the Holy Veil between pillars (lines 315-316) may have recalled to the medieval mind sights seen or heard of concerning the exposition of the Holy Veil in Rome.

voudroient baptizer. Et la saint Climent baptisa Veronique sans lui remuer son nom. Et puis il sermona au peuple par pluseurs fois enprés Noyron. Et mains se baptiserent par ses sermons.

[21] Puis quant tout ceci fust fet, Gaius, le seneschal, entra avec

318 *A6, B1, B7* v. faire b. *A6, A9, B, B3* et adonc s. *A13* baptizer adoncques s. *B4* baptizer et adonc veronique b. *A12* s. apostole c. *A1* sans point r. *A7, A11, A13* sans r. 318-319 *B7* v. et ne luy muast poinct son 318-321 *B, B1, B3, B4, B5, A6* v. et la nomma par son nom et p. il (*B4* nom sans ly muer son nom apres il) prescha (*B1* nom apres pr.) souvent devant tout le peuple (*B4* p. et plusieurs se b.) q. *B2* v. et ne luy mua point son nom apres ce il precha souvent devant tout le peuple q. 318-325 *B6* baptisa illecques v. et la nomma par son nom en apres toutx ces choses monseigneur saint clement prescha pl.f. par devant lempereur adoncques g.s. dudit empereur alit visiter son maistre car il y avoit longtemps quil ne lavoit veu et e. en la c. dudit empereur son maistre et le salua moult humblement en luy disant monseigneur et mon maistre dieu me doint faire chouse quil vous plaise et vous doint bone vie et longe en servant ihesu crist vostre seigneur et le mien et en luy faisant service et honneur ausit obediance car certes vous i estes tres bien tenus veu le grant bien qui vous a fait et le grant miracle quil a demoustre sur vous pour quoy ie vous connons y meger vostre commandement et bon point et autres choses baussitoires et ie croy car se vous le volles servir car il vous fera puissans en cestuy monde et en lautre a tousiours mais sans fain car il est dit bien souvant qui bon maistre sert bon loyel en artant apres toutes ces choses gay dit a lempereur come p. son pr. luy avoit faict bone chere en iherusalem et commanca le senescal racontes audit empereur tout la response dudit pilate monseigneur et mon maistre il est vray car quant ie fuz en iherusalem par devers pilate vostre prevost pour luy demander le trehu quil vous doit a cause de lempire de vostre feu pere et ausit de vous depuis sept ans en enta ledit prevost pilate me 319 *A1* s. par *A9* f. et plusieurs si se *A10* f. puis n. 319-320 *A2, A4* n. et pluseurs aultres (*A4* n. lempereur et p.a. gens) se *A1* f. tant que m. personne se b. ses bons s. 319-321 *A12* s. par p.f. en celluy temple et de iour en iour se b. gens et p. apres t.c.g. *A7* pl. iours se b.p. 319-322 *A11* puis prescha par p.f. a romme et convertit moult de gens a la foy de ihesu crist puis ne demoura gueres apres ces choses que g. le s. alla veoir v. et *B7* et prescha souvent devant le poeuple depuis toutez ces chosez faictez le s.e. ne la c. de son seigneur et *A13* et prescha moult de fois a temple et g.e. une fois en la c. de lempereur et 320 *A8* m. aultres se 320-321 *A10* et plusieurs autres furent baptisez par les bons s. qui devant eulx estoient fais apres g. le s.e. ung iour a. *A9* s. et predicacions p. 321 *A8* fet le 321-322 *A1* p. apres quatre iours v.e. en sa c. et g. sen va apres lui et lui *B, B1, B2, B3, B4, B5, A6* fust fet (*A6* f. tout fet) le.s. sen e. en la c. a v. (*B1* c. voire de v.) empereur (*B2* s.g. va devers le. *B5* c. de le.) et

319 *enprés Noyron* Although Nero died before Vespasian came to the throne in 69 AD, he was the one responsible for sending Vespasian to Palestine. The specific reference here may be either to that part of Rome rebuilt by Nero after the fire in 64, or to the area of the city where he is said to have slaughtered Christians. The latter designation is more likely if the *enprés* is seen as a scribal error for *en pré* or *es prés*.

Vespesian en sa chambre et lui dist: "Sire, grant joie devons avoir car vous estes si bien gueri. Et Jhesu Crist en soit loué! Mes, Sire, de Pilate vous veuil parler, qui est vostre prevost, coment il me respondi quant je lui dist de par vous qu'il vous envoyast le truage. Sachiez qu'il me fist male chiere et si me dist que il ne vous envoiroit riens ne ja de vous ne connoisteroit riens a tenir en la cité. Et si vous dis que si j'eüsse guierres parlé, qu'il

322 A12 v. lempereur en A10 s. moult g. B, B1, B2, B3, B4, B5, A6 d.s. (B2, B4 d. mon s.) vous devez a.g.i. puis que v. B7 d. mon seigneur vous debvez a.g.i. que v. A12, A13 i. deves a. A1, A3, A10 a. dece que (A10 a. quant) v. A2 i. de vous havoit car A8 a. tous car 322-324 A11 s. iay g.i. de vostre garison dont i.c.s.l. mes de p. vostre p. en iherusalem ie 323 A3, A9, A2 e. tres b.g. et dieu (A2 e.g.d.) en A6, A7, B, B1, B2, B3, B4, B5, B7 et dieu en A4, A13 g. dieu en A10 g.l. en s. nostre seigneur mes A8 l. et de A2, A3, A4, A7, A9 mes de 323-324 A1, A12 p. vostre prouvost vous v.p. (A12 v. dire et compter) c. B, B1, B3, B4, B5, A6 l. ie vous (B3 l. et beny de v.) v. compter (B3 v. maintenant c. B5 l. et gracie et oultre ie v. veul c.) de pillate v.p. quelle responce il me fit q. B2 l. quant en regard de p.v.p. de iherusalem voycy la responce quil ma faicte q. 323-325 A10 p. vostre grant p. vous v. dire la chere quil me fist et quil me respondit sire quant de par v. lui d. quil v.e. le t. quil vous doit chascun an s. sire pour vray quil me 323-327 A13 l.q. ie parlay a pilate deppart v. il me respondit furieusement quil ne c. ia r.t. deppart vous en 323-330 B7 l. ie vous v. dire la responce que me fist pillate v.p.q. ie fus en iherusalem il est certain que luy demande vostre argent il me respondictz parollez fieres et orguelleusez en disant quil ne tenoit r. de vous et que vous fussez sire de romme et de lombardie se vous vollies et quil seroist sire de iherusalem et des terres environ et quil ne tenoit r. de vous et me vault faire morir ce se neust este son senschal nomme barrabam lequel luy dictz que messager ne debvoit mal avoir pour son message faire et q. 324 A4 pr. en iherusalem c. A3 il r. 324-325 A4 lui demanday de B2 d. quil 325 A3 t. quil vous devoit s. A9 t. que chascun an il vous doit s. B, B1, B3, B4, B5, A6 e. vostre tresor adonc (B5 t.s. quil) me B2 e. vostre tresor et le tribut quil envoyoyt a vostre pere il A11 t. quil vous devoit si me A12 t. il A6, A11, B, B2, B3, B4, B5, A6 f. tres maulvaise c. B2 f. tres m. 325-326 A12 c. et fiere et 325-327 A10 c. et me respondit que a r.v. ne devoit et ne tenoit r. de vous ne dedens ne dehors et 326 A6, B, B1, B2, B3, B4 v. devoit r. A7 de ne 326-327 A12 v.r. ne c. a A3, A9 c. a t.r. en A1 r.a.t. et v. A11 d. orgueilleusement quil nen feroit de r. et que de r. ne nestoit il tenu a v. et bien saichez que ie. trop p. 326-328 B5 v.c. et me dist que se ie ne luy donnoie paix qui me feroit mourir et de la grant i. B, B1, B3, B4, A6 ne que il ne v. (B1, B3, B4 ne que v.) c. et me dist que (B4 et que) se (B3 d. se) ie ne luy donnoye paiz il (A6 p. qui B1, B3 p. quil) me feroit mourir et de la grant i. B2 ne v.c. et dist que se ie luy parloye plus quil me feroit morir et pour la g.i. 326-334 B6 ne tenoit r. de vous ne de vostre pere ne de par home de par vous et que se ie ne le laissoie en pays qui vous en moy en serions courrousses alors ie fus marriz et trouble de celle responce et puis quant vis que ie ne poures aultre chose faire il le menasse fort de parolles mais il ne saroit conte de choses que ie luy povisse dere et saichez sire car iavoyes si grant ioie davoir trouve ceste face quil me faudroit qui nee son feroit [ ] et saches que ung home de sa cort se leva et d.de. tout le conseil dudit p. que le 327 A8 t. de vous en A4 c. de iherusalem et A7 c. de vous car ie v. A12 la ville de iherusalem ne par de la et A1 e.p.g. il A7 g. demoures il 327-329 A13 ie nosoye g.p. quant il me voloit fere mettre a mort et toutesvoyes b.

m'eüst fet occire. Mes je ne lui vousis guieres contraster par la joie que je avoie de ce que j'avoie trouvé se que vous estoit nescessaire. Mes bien lui dis de par vous qu'il en ceroit couroucié et destruit. Et quant je lui disoie ces paroles, ung saint juifs se leva et dist devant Pilate que dans peu de temps seroit en Jherusalem si grant chierté que les meres mengeroient les enfens de grant fain qu'elles avroient. Et un altre juifs qui s'appeloit Jacob dist que vraiement le Profette dist de sa bouche que en brief de temps seroit la destruction de Jherusalem car il n'y remanroit pierre sur autre. Et

328 *A9* o. et tuer mes *A12* o. et quant ie vis cella ie ne ly v. riens compter de vostre maladie pour la grant i. *A7* ie luy v. complaire et c. *A8* v.c. *A2* c. de la *A4* g. ne ne lui osay oncques c.p. la grant i. *A9* g. contredire ne c.p. la tres grant i. de ce que a mon advis ia. *A7, A8* i. de ce que 328-329 *A10* v. plus riens contredire p. la tres grant i. davoir t. 328-341 *A11* o. puis ne demoura gueres quil 329 *A6* a. pour tant que *B2* a. pour ce *B3, B5* a. avoir t. *B4* a. quant ie euz t. *A8* ia.t. ce que besoing vous faisoit et v. *A7* t. de se *A7* e. mester et n. 329-330 *B, B2, B3, B4, B5, A6* v. faisoit mestier ie (*B2* f. besoing ie *B4* v.e.m. ie) ne luy parle (*A6* ne p.) plus mais ie le menace (*B3, B4, B5, A6* m. bien) de paroles et luy dis que encore en seroit il d. (*A6* d. et deser) et q. *B1* a. de trouver ce quil v.e. mestier ie ne luy en parle plus mes le menasse de parolles et lui dist que encores en seroit il d. 330 *A10* v. en *A1* quil se repontiroit et quil en seroit d. *A7* il bien seroit *A8, A12* seroit encores c. *A10* co. au temps advenir et quil en seroit une fois d. 330-331 *A10* di. de par vous ces 330-332 *A13* seroit d. et tantost ung anciens i.d. que en i. auroit en peul de t. telz famine que 331 *A6, B, B1, B3, B5, B7* ung sage i. *A1* ung preudhome i.d. *A9, A12* ung i. *A10* s. preudomme i. se l. diligemment et d. que 331-332 *B2* ung sage i.d. a p. que en i. dedans brief t. auroyt si g. famine et charitie que *A9* que dedans s. *B7* pi. en disant que si g. famine auroient en i. que *B, B1, B3, B4, B5, A6* et parla de.p. et luy d. (*B4* et d.) que si g.c. auroit dedens (*B3* c. seroit d.) brief t. en i. (*B1* a. en i.d. pou de t.) que 332 *A4* g. famyne et si g. *A12* g. famine que les femmes m. leurs e. par la g. 332-333 *A10* en la ville de i. si tres g. famyne que les m. par g.f.m. leurs e. et adonc ung *A7, A9* men. leurs e. 333 *A6, B, B2, B3, B4, B7* e. par f. *B1* e. quelle portoit par f. et *A12, B3* qui avoit nom ia. *A13* e. et ung a. quil avoit nom i.d. aussi que le saint p. *B5* e. par force de f. et sage i. qui avoit nom i.d. aussi que le saint p. *A8* qui avoit nom iafet d. 333-334 *B, B1, B4, B7, A6* al. sage i. qui avoit nom i.d. aussi que (*B1* d. que *B4* a. a pylate que *B7* d. devant pillate que) le saint p.d. (*A6* p. lavoit d.) de 333-335 *B2* i. ancien qui avoyt nom i.d. ainsi que le saint p.d. bien brief s. 334 *B3* que le saint p. *A2, A3, A7, A8, A9* le saint p. *A12* le saint p. le d. *A10* d. que en *A9* sa propre b. *A8* en peu de 334-335 *A6, A13, B, B3, B4, B5, B7* b. que br. (*A13, B5* que bien br. *B7* que briefment) viendroit la *B1* t. viendroit la 334-336 *B6* t. la d. de i. viendroit tieullement qui ne demeurroit p. sur pierre et yl seroit si 335 *A10* s.i. destruit et tellement quil ny demoureroit p. sur pierre et *A2, A4, A7, A13, B3* ny demouroit p. *A1* i. et quil *A9, B2, A3* i. et quil (*B2* i. tellement quil *A3* i. telle quil) ny demoureroit p. sur pierre et *A6, B1, B5* ny demouroit p. sur pierre et *A1, A8, A12* sur pierre et 335-336 *B, B4* ny demourroit p. sur pierre et quil seroit si *B7* ny demouroist p. sur pierre et q. 335-338 *A13* autre et pilate l.d. quil ne p. plus de cela ou aultrement il

330 *dis* [ *dist* Correction from MSS *A1, A2, A3, A4, A7, A8, A9, A10, A12, A13.*

si y avroit si grant famine que la mere mengeroit son enfant. Et quant Pilate l'eüst ouÿ, il fust moult courouciez et leur dist que sy jamés il em parloient de tieux paroles, qu'il les feroit destruire. Hors agardés, Sire, coment vostre prevost vous est loyal!"

[3. The Destruction of Jerusalem]

[22] Et quant l'empereur a ouÿ se que son seneschal lui a dist, il fust
moult couroucez et incontinent il manda par tout son empire que tout
[40v] home vensist armé. Et incontinent / il vindrent chescun en la plus belle

336 *A10* si tres g. *A12* a. dedens la ville de iherusalem si *B6* que les femmes men. *A10* mere par fain men. *B, B1, B3, B4* e. par fain q. 336-343 *B6* e. alors ledit pilate se leva de son siege et sen corrousa m. fort se d. car il le f. morir et d. pourquoy seigneur vous poves veoir la volunte de v.p. pylate adoncques vaspasien e. fust fort ire et c. et plain de grant ire et de deul le menmehu encontre pilate et i. il fit mender tous les fieloges de son empire et de toute sa terre et et tantoust son conmandement fust accompli et de toutes pars vindrent a luy en luy faisant obeissance et incontinent il furent tous assembles come roys 337 *A6, B, B3, B4, A1, A7, A12, B1, B2, B5, B7* p. oyt ces paroles (*B1, B7* p. ot oy cestes p. oyt cela *B2* ouyt dire ces p. *B5* pa. dire) il *A9* m. fort c. *A10* m. dollant et c. *B7* m. esbahi et 337-338 *A7* il employent et dysoyent celles paroles *B2* sil en p.i. quil A12 i.p. de cella quil en f. iustice h. *A10* en p. il 337-340 *B, B1, B3, B4, B5* se ilz p. plus h. povez veoir la bonte de pilate (*B3* p. en son effaire) q.le. a ouy toutes ces choses (*B1* q. vaspazien eut o.t. ses parolles *B3* q. vespasien eult oy cez c. *B4* q. vaspasien ot oye ces c.t. *B5* q. vaspasian eust o.t. cez c.) il *A6* sy il p. plus qui les f. destruire se povez veoir la bonte de pylate et q. vaspasien ot oyr ses paroles il 337-354 *B7* sil en p. plus quil leur f. morir et povez veoir la bonte de pillate apres ces parollez ouye pillate manda ses subiectz qui estoient entour et quant ilz furent venus en iherusalem il y eust grand conseil tantost apres le. se partit de romme pour venir as. iherusalem et quant ilz furent pres iherusalem devant ung c. nomme alejazef ceulx de c. se vollurent rendre mais le. ne v. 338 *A2, A3, A4, A9* p. ne disoient de t. (*A3, A9* d.t. *A4* d. ces) p. *A1* f. desconfier h. 338-339 *A12* s. dit gay c. *A13* f. iustissier h. *A10* d. prenez garde s.c. pillate v.p. vous ayme et vous est 338-340 *B2* d. consideres donc la bonte de v.p. pilate et q. 339 *A8* c. pylate vostre 339-341 *A13* p. est bon et l. iuge dont le.f. bien c. 340 *A7* ouy ces paroles que *A3* que lui d. son s. il *B2* ouy dire ces parolles il *A12* s. gay lui 341 *A1, A12* et il m. (*A12* et m.) tantost par *A10* et m. tout i. a t. 341-343 *B3, B4, B5, A6* et m. querir sez subgetz par toute sa terre quil venissent a (*B5* v. par devers luy a) romme et tantost il fist faire venir (*B4, B5* il fut fait et vindrent) roys *B, B1, B2* m. marry et m. querir ses subgiez par (*B2* q. son ost et fist apprester par) toute sa terre que ilz vansissent (*B2* que tous les nobles v.) a romme et tantoust il fut fait et (*B2* fait adoncques) v. roys 341-345 *A13* et tantost m. sa puissance laquelle fut tantost prest en tres b.o. et la furent roys prince d.ch. escuiers et p.a. gens archiers arbalestriers et f.o.c. pour aller en 342 *A1* v. a romme a. *A12* h. portant armes et faisant autres artifices necessaires a faire guerre v.a. et abillies et i. tout le monde de son empire et de toutes ses terres et de ses alliez v. en *A10* v. en beaux harnois et bien a. et si tost quil les eust mandez c. vint i. en *A5, A9, A4* i.c. y vint en (*A4* v. a) la *A7, A8* a. (*A8* a.c.) en 342-343 *A11* h. frequentant les guerres se voulsist ariver et veinsissent tous a romme a ung certain iour par luy assigne si y v.m.b.o. roiz d.b.c.ch.

ordenance qu'il peüst. Et la eüst roy, dux, contes, barons, chivaliers et pluseurs autres. Et sy furent ossis bien ourdenné come s'il vouscissent entrer en bataille et sy en y eüt par nombre trois cens mile chivaliers sans l'autre menue gent. Et l'empereur eüst que nef que lins que gualees trente mile, auquelles l'empereur et toute sa gent se mistrent sur mer. Et puis

343 *A10* que chascun p. faire si ot moult belle assemblee de roys *A1* la furent assamblez roy *A8* et brief la *A4* b. vicontes princes ch. 343-344 *A12* o. que faire se povoit chescun sellon son estat et la furent royx d. princes marquis b.ch. escuyers et p.a. gens et f.b. *A1* co.ch. et a. gens et vindrent si b. *B, B1, B3, B4, B5, A6* c. princes b. (*B3* p. assez) et p.a.ch. assez et (*B1* ch. armez *B3* ch. largement et) au (*B5* ch. au *A6* b.a. et ou) mieulx que eulx porent o. (*B3, B4, A6* p. ainsi *B5* p. estre appareilliez ainsi) c. 343-345 *B2* c. princes p.ch. dauphins marquis aprestes en armes le mieulx que ilz peurent tant quilz feurent n.t. 343-347 *B6* c. vicontes b.ch. nobles et gentil anmi eulx que faire ce peut et puis apres toutes ces choses ledit empereur fit faire grant nombre de g. et plusieurs autres petiz vesseaulx et saches car de contrefait il avoit xxx m.g. sans les autres vesseaux qui estoient sans nombre et sembloit que ce fust une breft quant on regardoit en la mer pour les max de vesseaux qui estoient plains de gens armes qui voloit aler encontre iherusalem pour le destruire adoncques le. 344 *A4* a. gens et *A3* f. ainsi b. 344-345 *A1* ilz deussent e. *A11* a. tous o. pour e. *A10* a. assez et y *B3* v. bataillier et la avoit t. 345 *A1, A8* b. et furent par *B, B4, B5* et la avoit t. *A11, A12* b. et furent en (*A12* et estoyent de) n. *A13* b. et estoient en n. iiij c. *B1* b. et estoient t. *A10* n. bien t.

345-346 *A6* et la avoit t. miles c. et moult da.g. *A11* m. que barons princes et c.s.a. maniere de g. *B, B1, B3, B4, B5* ch. et moult da. (*B5* da.m.) g. 345-347 *B2* ch. et asses da.g. et tantost le. fist appareiller nefz g. iusques au nombre de t.m. et tantost le. *A1* s. les jeunes g. et orent t.m.g. et se 346 *A7, A13* a.g. *A12* a. maniere et g. *A3* et si ot le. que l. *A10* et ot le. par droit nombre que nefs que g. *A2, A4, A5, A7, A9* e. que l. *A12* e. avoit fait faire que *A13* nef que g. *A6* e. fist tantost aparoillier nacez g. et aultres fustes iusques a t. *A2* g. bien xxx 346-347 *B1, B5, B3, B4, B* e. fist tantoust apareiller (*B3* f.a.t. *B* e. appareilla *B4* e. appareilla t.) navyres g. et autres fustz iusques a laperre de (*B5, B4* la a *B3* naves g. et a. vasseaulx assez i. a *B* f.i. a t.m. et que luy et) t. *A4* g. bien xxx esq. *A12* l. que vaissialx xx m. auxq. vaissiaux le. *A11* nef g. environ tr.m. dedans lesq. luy et ses g. 347 *A6* e. a t. *A4, A11, A13* m. en (*A13* en la) mer 347-348 *A10* esq. se mist le. sur la mer et tendirent leurs v. au vent et e. *A1* m. en mer et e. *A4* p. se f. *A6* m. de dessus la mer et f. faire v. *B1, B3, B4, B5, B* et f. faire (*B* et f. *B5* f. tendre les) v. *B2* m. dedans et f. faire v. et toutes choses neccessayres desquelles ilz devoyent user sur mer et sen partirent nostre seigneur leur envoya le t. moult agreable tellement que 347-350 *B6* m. dedans lesdis gallees pour eulx en aler devant iherusalem et saches que lempereur prist congie de sa fame et chascun de la science et titus parillement de sa mere aloir quant ung chascun eust pris congie de leur gens il sen alerent dedans lesdites gallees come dist est et saiches car il y avoit tout de monde car cestoit bone nolesse de veoir celle compaignie aussit bien emproint et ny avoit celuy qui seust le nombre de celle compaignie et saiches car il ploroist fort quant ce fust a la desprie adoncques apres toutx ces choses il misent les voilles au vant alors ihesu cripst les condusoit et avoit le vant tout a leur gre et ung m. bien m. ausit que le s. commencoit a luyre vont ariver au port da. adoncques les iuifz da. se r. bientoust a la volunte de le. et saiches quil est ouit moult esbays de veoir tant de monde devant eulx car il servoit come dist est car il eust forest dedans la mer des [ ] des gallees et aultres veseaulx adoncques le. les firent lever les voilles et eürent sy bon temps que au bout de cinc semaines il ariverent au port d'Acre, sy que ung matin au soleilh levant ceulz qui estoi[en]t en Acre rendirent la ville a l'empereur. Et il les prist a mercy.

[23] Et quant l'empereur, Titus et toute leur gent furent illec refreschés, il alerent asegier un chastel qui est entre Acre et Jherusalem et sy s'apelle

348 A3, A5, A7, A8 l. leurs v. A12 f. tromper les trompetes et corner les menestriers de coustes et firent adressier et l. les v. en telle maniere que lon cuidoit que ciel et terre se adioustassent et e. si bon vent et sy A6, A1, B3, B5 bon vent et bon t. (B1 sy bon v. tant B3, B5 t. tant) que A7, A10 de sept (A10 de six) s. A12, A13 que avant (A13 que en) c. B t. tant que 348-349 A11 v. au vent et tant nagerent par leur iournees quilz A8 que c.s. apres ilz A1 t. tant quilz a. en c.s. au A6, B, B1, B2, B3, B4, B5 .v. iours il furent (B, B3, B5 i.f. B2 ilz vindrent B1 i. ariverent) au 349 A1 que au m. B, B1, B2, B3, B4, A6 a. un iour bien m. aussi comme a s.l. tantost c.da. A10 que au s.l. et adoncques c.da. A4 l. tous c. 349-350 B5 a. et r. la cite et la v. a la voulente de le. A11 a. quant ilz furent au port dacre c. qui e. en la v. dacre luy r. la A1, A8 c. da. 350 A12, A13 e. dedans (A13 e. en) la ville da. A6, B, B1, B2, B3, B4 v. a la volente de le. A13 e. lequel les A1 p. tous a 350-351 A10 m.f.r. en acre il 350-352 A11 v. car q. ilz se f.i. assez longuement r. vaspasien et t. son filz avec t.l.g.al. B6 m. apres ce quil feurent response i. un petit il partirent de acre et sen a. a ung 351 A9 et puis apres q. le ti. et aussi to. B, B1 q. vaspazien et ti. A1 ti. son filz et to. sa g. A2 e. et sa g.to.f. A5 le. lempereur et ses g.to.f. A6 q. vaspasien e. et son filz f. la ensamble l.g. ung pou r. A13 q. il f.r. ilz 351-352 A8, A12 q. ilz f. (A12 ilz se f.) i.r. vaspasien et t. et (A12 v.le. et son filz t. avec) t.l.g.al. B2 q. ilz f. la vasparien et tantost son filz t. empereur et t.le.g. sen a. en un B4, B5 q. vaspasien et t. son filz et t.l.g. (B5 t. ses g.) f.i. reposez ilz sen a. en ung B3 q. vaspasien et t. son filz f. reposey il sen a. devant ung B, B1 i. reposes ilz sen a. en ung A6 il sen a. en ung c. 352 A11 e. la ville da. 352-353 B5 c. qui estoit moult fort et puissant qui estoit a ung noble iuif qui avoit a nom iassel de cassel et q. A9 i. et la. ou c. A10 i. lequel est nomme c. A6 i. et qui en appeller altafer et estoit moult fort et puissant et estoit dung noble iuif qui avoit non iassel du cassel q. A11, A12, A13 sa. alcaffet (A12 a. de iaffa) et B2 sa. altaset qui estoit moult fort et esoyt dung nobe iuifz qui avoit nom iassel et cassel et q. 352-354 B, B3, B4 sa. alcafet et estoit moult fort et puissant et dung noble (B3 f. et estoit celuy chaistiaulx a ung n.) iuif qui avoit nom iassel et cassel q. les (B3 c. devant les) i.v. si grant host e. le c. et lavantgarde tantost se r. se 352-364 B1 i. aleafsait avoit nom et estoit moult fort et puissant et dun noble iuif que se appelloit iassel du cassel et q. les i. oirent si grant ost e. le c. et lavangarde tantoust regarderent si B6 i. lequel avoit nom atasset et estoit celuy chateau moult fort et puissant et estoit a ung molt noble noble qui avoit nom iasel de tassel adoncques ceulx qui estoient dedans le chastel ne cuydoient point que les gens de lempereur heust sy grant puissance se ressurerent audit empereur ledit chastel et incontinant le c. fust pris dassault et firent morir t. ceulx qui estoient dedans excepte ix qui estoyent dessoubz une rouche s.t. et f.t.i. et trois nuys sans boire ne sans manger et

351-389 The account of the taking of the castle of Caffe is based loosely on Josephus Flavius' recounting of the siege (in July 67 AD) of Jotapata, a city 15 km directly east of Acre (Akko). Historically, Josephus himself played the role given here to Japheth: military leader, hiding in a grotto, refusal to participate in the group suicide, the decision to trust the mercy of Vespasian, etc. See Josephus Flavius (pp. 314-340).

Caffe. Et quant les juifs du chastel virent tant de gent logiez entour leur chastel, il se rendissent voulentiers si l'empereur les vousist penre a mercy. Et quant les hostes furent en leur tantes, Nostre Seigneur envoya si grant nege et si grant vent que a paines personne se pouvoit tenir en l'ost. Et le chastel estoit bien massonné et bien garni car le sire du chastel l'avoit fet bastir, qui estoit sains homes et bon chevaliers juifs. Et si fust né de Nazeret. Et sy estoit cosin germain du noble Joseph qui mist Jhesu Crist au sepulcre, et s'apeloit Jafet de Caffe. Et sy eüst son conseil qu'il vensist a

353 *A2, A4, A13* i.v. *A5, A7* et les *A10* les gens de caffe v. 353-354 *B2* i.v.t. grans g.e. de c. ilz *A6, B5* i.v. si grant lost e. du c. et lavangarde tantost se (*B5* t. dirent quilz se) r. se *A2* g.e. du c. *A11* t. aller de g. darmes alentour du c. *A13* g. alentour du c. *A4, A5, A7, A9* e. du c. *A12* e. eulx ilz *A10* l. tout autour du c.v. se r. mais que le. 354 *A8* v. mais que le. *A9* se feussent moult v. rendiez si 354-355 *B4* m. mais le. ne les 354-362 *B7* m.a. 354-363 *A13* m. et quant le c. fut prins ilz mirent t. a mort escepte le seigneur du chastel luy ixme quil estoit muchie en 355 *A2, A3, A4, A7, A9* f. logiez en *A5* h. se f. logiez en *A6* f. estandus devant le chastel n. *A4* t. rendues n. *B2* f. la n. *B, B1, B4, B5* f. estandu n.s. manda (*B1, B2, B5* s. envoya) si *A10* q. ce vint que tout lost fut logie en *A11, A12* q. ceulx des h. de lempereur (*A12* q.le. et leurs gens) f. *A10* e. adonc si 355-357 *B3* f. estandu devant le c. 356 *A2* n. et v. *A6, B, B4, B5* n. et froidures (*B5* et si grandes f.) que *B1* n. et froidures a grant peines se p. homme de lo. soustenir et le *A7* que appoint que pe. *A9* peines nulle pe. *A6, B, B4, B5* peines se po. homme de lo. (*B5* po.lo.) soustenir et le *A10* peines se po.t. nul fu dedans lost *B2* que nul ne po. estre en *A8* t. a lost 356-358 *A11* ost or e. celuy c. moult fort et b.g. et la.f. faire ung s. et bon c.i. natif de 357 *B, B1, B2, B3, B4, B5, A6* e. moult fort basti et aussi (*A6* b. et *B2* f. et b. garde *B5* b.) g. car *A12* b. bastis et *A3* et g. *A12* g. de toutes choses car *A6* du c. estoit moult fort et la. 357-358 *A10* e. moult b. g[ ] du ch.e. moult s. *A8* a.b. *B, B3* f. bien b. *B1* a. bien f. garnir et b. *B5* a. bien f. fortiffier qui *A3* du c. qui la.f.b.e. *B2* du c. estoit mout sage c.i. 357-359 *B4* fet bien b. et garny car il e. moult saige i. et fut c. 358 *B, B1, B3, B5, A6, A12* e. moult sage c. (*A6, B3, B5* c. et estoit *A12* e. noble c.) i. *A1* s.l. et bon c. et *A3* f. de 358-359 *A6, B1, B2, B3, B5* ne en n. *A10* ne et nourry de 359 *A1* e. comme g. *A10* c. du bon n. *B2, B3, B* du (*B* dun) n. homme i. 359-360 *A8* io. darimathie qui m.i. au *A12* io. dabarmathie qui *B1, B4* dun n. homme qui avoit non i. (*B4* h. appelle i.) darimathie qui *A9* m. au s.i.c. et 360 *B1, B2, B4, B5, A6, A12* s. cestoit (*A6* s. et) i. *B3* s. ce fut ioseph du c. *B* et estoit i. *A11* s. lequel estoit nomme i. *A9, A11* e. par (*A11* e. en) son *A9* il alast a 360-361 *B, A6* que lempereur les voulsist (*A6* les vuilliez) prendre a m. *B4* que ilz se rendroient se lempereur les vousist prandre a m.a 360-362 *B2* et lempereur ne le voulut point prandre a m. mays a. *A6, B* et il ne les v. pas prendre a m. (*B* p.) a. *A10* c. et adoncques ioseph de caffe quant il vit le sort il envoya son c. a lempereur qui lui pleust de les prendre a m. mais h.le. le v. prendre ne a. a m. et ung bien peu de t. apres advint que le c. fut prins de le.o. *B1, B3, B5* que lempereur le (*B3* e. les) veulsist prandre a m.a.

357 *massonné* [ *massonna* Correction from MSS *A1, A2, A3, A4, A5, A7, A8, A9*.
360 *vensist* [ *vousist* Correction from MSS *A2, A3, A4, A5, A7, A8, A12*.

mercy a l'empereur. Et lors l'empereur ne vousist honques avoir mercy de luy. Puis aprés peu de temps l'empereur prist le chastel et fist ossire tous les juifs fors Jaffet qui se mussa, luy noefieme, en une crote qu'il avoit soubz terre out il furent musés trois jours. Et quant il virent qu'il les failloit mourir de fain, il entreprirent que l'un entretuast l'autre du coutel, afin qu'il mourissent la. Et ainsy il le firent tuit fors Jafet et ung sien cousin qui ne s'y voussirent onques acorder. Et quant lé set juifs furent

361 A4 et le. *A11* le. mais le. *A4* h. adont a. 361-362 *A12* m. a le. mais le. ne le prist point a m.p. *A1* e. mais il ne v.o. prendre a m.p. 362 *A11* luy ne de ceulx qui leans estoient p. *A8* luy ains ung petit de t.a.le. *B3, B7* t.p. *B4* c. par force et *A6, B, B1, B3, B4, A8* f. tuer (*A8* f. mourir) t. *B2* f. trestous 362-363 *A9* o. tuer et mettre a mort t. les i. excepte ia. qui se m. et n. autres iuifz avecques lui en 362-364 *B7* f. tuer ceulx qui estoyent dedens excepte iaphat et ix aultres qui se estoyent boutez en une caverne s.t. et illec f.t.i. et trois nuistz sans boire ne menger et 362-365 *B5* f. tuer les iuifs excepte ioseph et plusieurs autrez qui estoient muciez en une fosse s.t. et q. il v. que les convenoit illec demourer et m. 363 *A11* iuifs excepte ia. luy n. qui se mirent en *A5, A7* se mist ly *A8* luy onzieme en *A10* m. mesme en *A12* m. et huit autres avec luy dedens une *A8* une caverne quil 363-364 *B1, B2, B3, B4, A6, B* iuifs excepte iosef neuf autres (*B3* i. et huit a. *A6* i. et les a.n. qui) qui (*B2* e. iaffet et ix aultres anciens iuifz qui) estoient en une cave s. (*A6* une foce s. *B4* une crote s.) t. et y.f.t.i. (*B4* i. sans boire et) sans manger (*A6, B3* i. muses *B* i. estendus) et *A1* c. qui estoit s. *A12* a. fait faire s. *A10* une caverne qui estoit dessoubz t. et q. *A13* une cave dessoubz t. et la demorarent t.i. sans boire ne sans mangier et 364 *A4* t. et la f. *A1* out ilz demoureront .ii. i. sans mengier et *A8* f. par t. *A9* m. par lespace de t. *A11* f.t.i. sans boire ne sans menger et *A2* t. la out 364-365 *B, B1, B2, B3, B4, B7, A6, A11* que illec leur (*B2, B7* que l. *B3* i. lez *A6* quil les *B4* que la les) convenoit m. *A7* quil mouroyent de 365 *A9* e. entre eulx que *A2, A3, A4, A12, A13* lung tuast la. 365-366 *A11* lun tuast la. dun glayve a. que tous m. sans a. plus languir et a. le f.t. excepte i. *A6, B, B1, B2, B3, B4, B5, B7* il tuerent (*B, B3, B7* il se t.) lun la. excepte ioseph (*B4* i. du tassel seigneur dudit chastel) et son c. *A10* lun tuast la. et a. le f. si non ung s.c. et iaphet qui *A8, A13* c. et 365-367 *B6* m. il tuerent lung la. excepte ioseph et son c. car lun ne voloit occire lautre adoncques q. les i. 366 *A12* la dedens et *A1, A3, A5, A7* f.f. *A13* fi. excepte i. *A12* t. excepte i. 366-367 *A9* i. et ung autre qui estoit son c. qui a ce ne 367 *A12* ne cestoient vouluz a. a eulx oussire et q. les vj.i. *A3, A4, A11, A13* v. (*A13* v. point adce) a. *B, B1, B2, B3, B4, B5, B7, A6* v. pas tuer (*B1* v.t. *B5* pas eulx t.) q. *A7* o. actrurder et *B2, B5, B7* f. ainsi m. 367-368 *A6, B, B3* m. ioseph d. *B1, B4* f. ainsi m. ioseph (*B4* i. du tassel) d. *B6* f. ausit m. ioseph d. a son hellas or soloy ge estre s.

365 *lun entretuast* [ *lun que lun entretuast*

mors, Jafet dist a son cousin: "J'estoie seigneur de cest chastel et sy estoie [41r] tenus pour moult saint home. / Cousin, grant folie seroit sy nou mourions yssy. Mes yssons hors car nous n'y pourions vivre et si alons ardiement a l'empereur et lui crions mercy et sy nous feisons conoistre car quant il saura qui je sui, il ne nous aussira ja.

[24] Puis l'empereur fist abastre le chastel et fist emplir les fossés. Et Jaffet et son cousin yssirent de la ou il estoient et s'en alerent a l'empereur

368-369 *A1* c. beau cousin ie.t.p. ung s.h. pour quoy ie dictz que g. *A11* c.c. *A13* ch. et t.p.s.h. dont g. *A8* t.m. *A12* t. par le monde s. *A10* par ung bon s.h. ie te diray mon c. et mon amy ce s. tres g.f. si nous se nous *B, B1, B2, B3, B4, B5, A6* t. par m. (*B4* t. a m.) sage h. ne s. (*B5* h. et pour ce ne s. *B2* h. ce s.) ce q.f. (*B4* ce pas f.) de mourir ainsi mieulx (*B5* a. come ces aultrez qui sont occis m.) vault que nous ostrions (*B2, B3, B4* n. nous o.) de cy car nous 368-373 *B7* t. a m. sage h. ce s.g.f. a nous de morir ainsi mieulx vault que nous al. a le. et que nous mettions en sa merci et ie [ ] sil aura merci de nous le. 368-384 *B6* par saige h. pour ce quil me semble car cestoit a moy g.f. et [ ] a toy de nous laisser aussit morir de fain il me semble car il vouldroit mieulx nous rendre a la volunte de lempereur et par aventure il nous prandre a mercy et se ainsy est qui nous fait mourir ie laime mieulx que de mourir ausit de faim mediamment lung lautre adonques commencerent iasel qui estoit dudit lieu du cassel avequez son cousin a saillir dehors de celle caverne et i. et son c. partirent de soubz terre et sen a. devant le. a laventure et incontinent se misent devant ledit empereur en luy demandant misericorde adoncques le. 369 *A7* c. dist il g. *A4* s. a nous se *A8* h. sy s.g.f. que n.m. ainsy mes *A1, A12* mourions ceens en ceste croute (*A12* m. syans) mes 369-371 *A11* s. a nous de plus ycy languir mieulx vault se adventurer daller a m. a le. que de mourir ycy villainement al.ar. a luy et 370 *A13* y. de fain al. *A12* p. plus v. *A4, A12* ar. vers le. 370-371 *A10* al. a le.ar. et *B, B1, B3, B4, B5, A6* v. longuement mieulx vault que (*B5* l. et est pour le meilleur que) voison a le. et que luy c. (*A6* que nous c.) m. car q. 370-373 *B2* v. longuement al. a le. et il aura de n. mercy le. 371 *A12* n. noz ferons a luy c. *A10* f. a c. a luy car *A11* c. a luy car ie croy que q. 371-372 *A10* qui nous sommes il 371-373 *A13* m. et n. lui dirons que ie suis et il ne nous fera nulz mal p. *B, B1, B3, B4, B5, A6* il s. (*A6* il sera) qui nous (*B4* s. quelz n.) sommes il (*B3* que n. ne soiez mis a sa misericorde il) aura mercy de nous (*B1* a. de n.m.) le. 372-373 *A2* n. fera point occire p. *A9* ia mais aura mercy de nous deux et croy que sa fureur lui sera passee p. *A11* sui quil ne n. fera point oscire quant le. ot prins icelluy chastel si le f.a. et emplir *A1* n. feroit iamais morir et quand le. ot faict cecy il fist *A10* a. pour riens apres quant le. eust occis tous ceulx de ce c. a et fist 373 *B4* le. tantost apres f. *A4* p. apres le. *B7* a. les murs du c. et fist *A3, A13* et e. *A11* e. les les fo. 373-374 *A6* a. les murs du c. et combles les fo. adonc ioseph et *B, B1, B2, B3, B4, B5* a. les (*B1, B4* a. tous les) murs du c. et combler les (*B1* c. tous les *B2* du c. les) fo. adonc iosef (*B1* fo.i.) et (*B4* i. du tassel et) son c. sen partirent de la crote (*B1, B3* la cave *B5* la fosse) et sen *A13* fo. adoncques i. 373-375 *B7* fo. adoncques sen vindrent a le. et sa. devant luy en lui disant empereur ie. 374 *A4* y. hors de *A1* la cave ou *A7* la et 374-375 *A6* c.a. tout droit devant le. et se mirent a genoil et ioseph d. a le.ie. *A11* c. vindrent devant le. et se a. devant luy puis luy d.i.s. *A13* son nepveu se viendrent a genoillier devant le. et dirent s. *A12* il se e. musses et sen a. vers le. et se vont agenoillier devant luy et i.d. *A10* a. tout droit a le. et se gecterent a genoulx devant luy et dit i. a *B, B1, B2, B3, B4, B5* a. tout droit davant le. et se midrent a (*B5* se vindrent a) genoux et iosef si d. (*B5* g. devant luy puis i.d.) a le. seigneur empereur (*B4* le. et dist mon s. *B1* le. sire) ie. *A7* e. sire

et sy s'agenoillerent. Et Jaffet dist a l'empereur: "Sire, j'estoie sire de cest chastel que vous avés abatu et sy ay entendu que vous estes venus pour vengier la mort de Jhesu Crist qui a tort prist pacion en Jherusalem. Et ossy au ouÿ dire que vous venés pour destruire Jherusalem car elle y consenti. Sire, sachiez, Sire que cest Saint Prophete estoit moult mon ami, tant que ung mien cousin qui s'appelle Jozeph d'Arimatie le descendi de la crois et le mist en son sepulcre. Et sachiez, Sire, que sy vous voulés penre Jherusalem, que nou vous y ferons bien mestier et nostre conseilh ossy, car il sera fort a panre. Sy prions, Sire, que vous aiés mercy de nous et, s'yl

375 *A1, A9* a. devant luy et *A8* et d.i. a *A8* ie. de 375-376 *A10* ie. de c.ch. seigneur que v.a. cy abatu 376 *B, B1, B2, B3, B4, B7, A6* avez fait abatre seigneurs (*B2* ab. *B4* ab. mon s. *B7* ab. il est vray que) ie ay *A1, A3* aves fait abatre et *A13* c. et *B5* avez fait abatre seigneur iay e. dire que *A11* ay tousiours e. *B, B1, B3, B4, B5, A6, A11, A12* v. par (*A11* v. de par) deca (*A12* v. en cest pays) p. *B7* que estes par deca p.

377 *A10* a grant t.pr. mort et pa. *A11* t.pr. mort et pa. *A2, A4, A10, A12* pr. mort et pa. 377-378 *A8* et que *A12* et estes v. *A13* c. et p. 377-379 *B, B1, B2, B3, B4, B5, A6* qui a grant t. morut (*B1* en i. et *B3* d.d.i. et pilastre et) quant il le c. (*B4* il estoit en terre) vuilles (*A6* en i. car il le consentir et tantost dit v.) savoir seigneur que (*B2* et que voules d.i. vueilles scavoir que *B3* il vit que voulentiers lescoultoit et luy dist se.v.sa. que *B5* q. lempereur leur eust consenti ce quilz disoient adonc dist iassel du cassel sire empereur v.sa. que) le s.p. ihesu crist e. (*B4* p.e.) bien mon (*B5* mon seigneur et et mon) parfait amy (*B2* mon a. *A6* a. et seigneur) t. *B7* qui morust a grant t. en larbre de la croix seigneurs plaise vous savoir que icelui e. bien nostre amy parfaict t. *A11* iher. par les faulx iuifz plains denvye et sac. 378 *A10* que p. *A3* iher. pour ce quelle 378-379 *A8* d. ledit sy sa. que *A10* iher. vous avez amenee ceste noble assemblee sac. *A13, A12* iher.sa.s. que (*A12* i. pour ce car il c. sire sa. que) le saint 379 *A4* sac. que *A1* c.sa. que *A2, A4, A5, A7* c. si sac. *A9* c. si que sac. 379-380 *A10, A11* e. bien mon amy et ung 379-381 *A13* e. monseigneur et mon maistre et suis estez nez de nazareth et ung m.c. lensevelit en son monument quil se a.i.da. et se v. 380 *A2* c. germain qui *A3, A8, A11* c. (*A11* c. germain) nomme i. *A6, B1* i. le *A7* que mon c. 381 *A6, B, B1, B2, B3, B4, B5* m. au (*B5* au saint) s. *A11* m. ou s. et bien sa. *B7* m. au s. seigneurs se v. *A1, B2* sa. que *A12* se. et veilles savoir sire *B4* sac. monseigneur se v. 381-382 *A11* p. la ville de i. *B, B3* v.v.i.p. que v. (*B3* que nous) f. *B2* v.v.i.p. que *B5* que ie v. ay b. *A1, A2, A8, B1* v. y serons (*A8, B1* v.s.) b. 382 *A6, B, B1, B4, B5* m. pour donner (*B4* p. y d. *B5* p. vous d.) c. quar *B2* b. besoin pour vous donner c. car *A1* et vostre c. *A11, A12* c. car 382-383 *B3* m. pour donner c. quil s. bien malx a *A10* v. aiderons myeulx que tout le monde car il est mout f. *A13* y serons bons et o.n.c. proffitable car il s. bien f. *A6, B, B1, B4, B5* si bien mal (*B1* b. mauvais) a *B2* il est bien f. *A1* car ie vous dictz bien certainement que ce seroit forte chose de laler prendre que il ny ait des amys hors de la ville a pres de une iournee si vous p. que a. 382-384 *B7* n.v. donnerons bon c. se vollez avoir m. de nous adoncques le. 383 *A3, A5, A7, A9, A11, A12, A13* sy vous p. *A4, A10* sy vous p. que *B, B1, B2, B3, B4, B5, A6* pa. et ie vous prie que (*B2* pa. pour ce ie vous requiers que) vueilles avoir m. de nous et n.

383-384 *A10, A1* de n. et certainement n. (*A1* de n. et n.) v. *A7* d. ne n.d. *A11* de n. en lonneur de d. le tout puissant lors

plait a Dieu, nous vous donrons bon conseilh et loyal." Lors l'empereur les prist a merci et il prierent que hon leur donast a mengier. Et puis il distrent coment il avoient estés musés dans la crote. Et puis quant eürent mengié, l'empereur les fist venir et sy leur demanda s'il croient au Saint

384 *A13* d. nostre c.v. sera bon et profittable adoncques le. *B5* v. servirons et do. *A9* do. tres bon seur et l.c. lors 384-385 *A12* l. iaffet vait prier que *A6, B, B1, B2, B3, B4, B5* c. adonc le. 385 *A11* m. puis requirent que *A2* quil l. *B* p. touz deux a m. et leur p. quil l. *B1, B3, B4* m. touz deux et lui p. quil l. *A3* il lui p. quil l. feist donner a *B5* ilz luy p. que l. feist donner a *B6* m. et leur fist donner a boire et a *A6* m. tout deux et il leurs p. qui leur donnaissient a *A8* quil l. fist donner a *A9* p. aucuns que *A12* men. car ilz avoyent grant fain et *B2* prie. quil luy pleust de l. donnera m. et luy d. 385-387 *A10* les receust a m. et tantost requirent quilz eussent a m. car ilz mourroient de fain et quant ilz eurent mange ilz comencer a compter c. ilz sestoient mussez deda une caverne en terre et l.d.le. se ilz *A13* et il demandirent a mangier quant ilz heurent mangiez ilz leur leur comptarent c. ilz estoient m. en la cave et comme ilz avoient souffert grant femine le.l. *A11* meng. pour ce que a pou quil ne mouroient si leur fist lempereur donner a menger p.l. *B, B1, B3, B4, B5, A6* meng. et luy conterent (*B5* et c.) comment ilz a.e. en la c. (*B5* la fosse) et comme ceulx avoient (*B3, B5, A6* et quil a.) grant (*B1, B4* comment a.g.) fain et quant (*A6* et adonc) lempereur (*B5* et le.) leur eut (*B1* e. eut) fait donner a mangier et les fist mectre (*B1, B3, B4* et m.) a table bien (*B5* et quilz eurent este b. *A6* t. et furent b.) aiser il les (*A6* a. apres les) f. (*B1* a. apres ce le f. *B3* a. apres lez f.) devant luy v. (*B4* a. apres les f.v.d. ly) et (*B5* f.v. devant luy puis) l. 385-393 *B7* m. et leur fist bailler a manger car il en avoient bon mestier en apres quil eurent bien m.le. leur d. sil adoroient le s.p. et il luy respondictz que ouy adoncques le. les retint de son c.a. toutes ces choses v. et son f.t. se partirent de ce chasteaulx et sen alerent d.i. et quant ils approcherent devant i. la citez commenca a croller i.c.d. se 385-400 *B6* puis apres il parlerent audit empereur et luy dissirent monseigneur ie ouy dire que vous estes venu par deca pour vangier la mort du prophete ihesu crist qui fust iuge de vostre prevost pylate a mort a tort par faulce envye le faulx iuifz le firent mourir monseigneur saiches de vray que ie estoie sire de ceste terre et de se chastel lequel vous avez fait abatre adoncques lempereur leur dist lesses moy en paix toutes ces chosses et me dictes se iherusalem est forte pate et nous enseignes que nous la pourons prandre adoncques ioseph dist quil alassent bien toust afin quil trouvassent le peuple qui estoit dedans sans nombre adoncques lempereur luy demanda quel peuple cestoit alors ioseph luy va dire mon seigneur il ont a coustume de fair en iherusalem chascun an une feste en laquelle est assanblee la plus grant partie des iuifz dudit iherusalem et de galilee adoncques lempereur eust grant ioie et d. quil vouloit avoir ioseph de son c.a. toutes ces choses lempereur et t. et toust le houst sen vindrent et heurent tout le cuer resiouy de ces nouvelles et aussit gay senscal se avoiet aultre foiz conte a lempereur comment le saint prophete avoit d. de sa bouche que en brief temps viandroit la destruction de iherusalem [ ] car ung chascun il ny demoreroit p. sur p. et leur dist le iour de pasques flores que se grant famine viendroit en iherusalem or ung chascun peust bien considerer car il feroit grant mal endurer tielle chose estre si cruelle adoncques vaspasian arma tantoust illecques devant la site de iherusalem et saiches car p. ne se doubtoit mie de lempereur ne quil vansist mectre le siege devant celle cite et saiches car archolaus le 386 *A1* e. mis d. *A8* la caverne et *A8* d. quilz 386-387 *A12* crote et q. lempereur eust fait donner a manger il les f.v. devant luy et *B2* e. en une c. et comment ilz avoyent endure grant famine lempereur les eut fait donner a mangier ilz les f.v. devant luy et 387 *A4* v. devant lui et *A9* c. bien fermement au *A11, A12* c. bien (*A12* c. point) au 387-388 *A8* c. bien en dieu et

Profete. Et il lui distrent que ouïl. Et lors leur dist l'empereur: "Je vieux que dorenavant vous soiez de mon privé conseilh."

[25] Puis aprés Vespesian et Tytus, son filh, eürent conseilh qu'il alassent devant Jherusalem avec toute leur puissance. Et lors avint ce que reconte saint Luc evangeliste que dist que quant Jhesu Crist s'apreucha de Jherusalem, il ploura sur elle et dist: "Ou cité, sy tu savoies se qui avenra de toy, tu ploureroiez car ne connois les jours de ta visitacion car tu seras

388 *A2, A3, A4, A5, A7, A9* ilz d. *A10* et ilz respondirent que *A13* et ilz respondirent que oy adonques dist *A12* que certainement lors le.l.d. ie *A11* lors lem.l.d. ie *A1* lors d. 388-391 *B2* p. ihesu crist et ilz respondirent que oy adonc le. les retint de son hostel a. ces choses lempereur v. et t. son f. et tous les roys les princes et les chevaliers de leur compaignie se acorderent de aler en i. adonc fut veriffie ce 388-393 *B1, B, B3, B4, B5, A6* et il responderent (*B* et eulx r.) oy adonc (*B5* r. quilz y creoient parfaitement et a. *A6* il luy r. que oyr a.) ie. les retint de sonc.a. ces (*B, B4, B5* a. toutes ces) chouses v. et t. son f. (*B3* et son f.t.) et tous leurs chevaliers se accorderent daler en i. et (*B5* i. pour venger la mort de nostre seigneur et) quant ilz aproucherent de (*B* q. se apricha de) la cite de iherusalem (*B5* a. de i.) ilz recorderent de i.c. qui p. dessus (*B5* r. de nostre seigneur de ce quant il p. sus) la c. et d. (*B* iherusalem se print a plourer et i.c. de) se 389 *A7, A10* mon c. *A9* mon secrett et p. 389-390 *A12* mon c.p.a. ce v. lempereur et *A13* mon c. et quant lempereur et t. son f.a. A11 c. pour mon conseiller en droit et raison par tout ou iauray a fere p. 390 *A5* p. lempereur et *A1* et lempereur et t.e. par c. *A10* a.t. et v.e. *A10* c. daller *A12* e. leur c. 391 *A1* d.a. *A10* i. a t. A13 i. lors *A12* l. gent et leur a. *A7* a. celon ce 391-392 *A10* et leur a. selon ce que s.l.r. en leuvangille qui d. *A13* que dist s.l. quil d. 391-393 *A11* i. se se mirent tantost au chemin et quant il saproucherent de iherusalem aucuns de la compaignie vaspasien se recorderent de i.c. qui en son temps ploura sur la cite de i. en disant a la c. si 391-397 *A1* p.t. 392 *A8* i.sa. *A12, B2* luc qui d. 392-393 *B2* d. que i.c. dist em plourant q. il a. de la c. de i. se *A13* c. prophetisa en i. et se partit dudit lieu ilz p. sur la c. et d. cite se *A12* a. vers i. il se mist a fremir et p. 393 *B2* s. et congnoissoyes se *A6, A10, A13, B1, B3, B4, B5, A2* qui ta. (*A2* que de toy) a. 393-394 *A12* d. se tu cognoissies ce que te vendra tu p. pour ce car *A11* se quel te a. tu *B* a. tu *B7* que deviendras tu 393-398 *B2* qui te a. tu auroyes bien cause de plourer car les iours seront que tes annemis te viendront de tous coustes environner et ny leisseront p. sur pierre p. ne s. point a. que on allast vers luy en i. et adonc t. 394 *A4, A10, A11* car tu ne *A13* p. tu *A11* de la v. *A3* toy pour ce que tu ne *A8, A10* v. tu 394-395 *A9* p. car tu s.t. environnee a. et a. 394-396 *B, B1, B4, B5, A6* p. car tu (*B4* p. et tu) ne (*B1* car ne) sces le i. que la destruction et (*A6, B1, B4, B5* que tu seras destruite et) que ne lerront p. (*B1, B4, B5* ne demoura p.) sur pierre et (*B5* sur p. en toy et) les enffans qui s. dedans (*B5* d. toy) s. *B7* car tu ses le i. que tu seras destruicte car lon ne l.p. sur piere et les enfans qui s. dedens s. 394-400 *B3* p. car tu ne sceis le i. que tu seras destruite et que ny demorait p. sur pierre et lez enffans qui s. dedans s. perilz a.p. ne s. mie que aille a luy mais t. aultres i. de sa t. venoient en i. et le f. au roy

391-396 See Lk 19:42-44 and also Mt 24:2, Mk 13:2, Lk 21:6.

tout environ assicié et assaillie, sy n'y laira hom pierre sur aultre. Et les filz [41v] qui sont avec toy seront / destruis."

[26] Toutesfois Pilate ne savoit riens ancoure des gens qui venoient encontre lui. Mes en cel temps chescun an tous les juifs de toute la terre fesoient une grant feste en Jherusalem. Et lors tous ceulx de toute la terre i estoient venus et ossy y estoit venus le filz du roy Hero[de]s qui estoit roy couronné de Galilee, lequel s'apelloit Acherlant. Et quant il furent tous en

395 *A10, A8* t. advironnee (*A8* a. doz et) a. et a. *A12* t. entour a. et a. *A2* ny haura on *A5, A11, A13* ny demorera p. *A7* ny sera p. *A9* hom une p. *A4, A8* sur pierre et 395-396 *A11* les enffans qui s. dedans et toy serez d. 395-397 *A10* ny demourra p. sur pierre t. *A13* a. et p. 396 *A12* s. en toy 396-397 *A5* s. en toy s. periz t. 396-400 *B, B1, B4, B5* d.a.p. (*B4* d. et come p.) ne s.r. que lon vansist vers (*B1* on allast vers *B4* on aille vers *B5* que lempereur aille vers) luy mais t. les autres i. (*B4* les i.) de sa t. (*B5* de la t.) venoient en i. et le *B7* d.a.p.r. ne s. que lempereur allast vers luy mais tantost que les i. de iherusalem furent rains et le *A6* a.p. ne s.r. que lempereur alast vers iherusalem mais venoient tous les aultres i. de sa t. en i. et le 397 *A1, A3, A4, A5* s.a.r. des *A12* s.a. la venue de lempereur ne de ses gens 397-398 *A10* r. de lentreprinse que avoit fait vaspasien e. *A13* s. point que lon venisse e. *A11* s.a. que lempereur et sa gent viensist contre luy *A7* qui vengent e. *A8* s.a.r. de lempereur qui venoyt e. 398 *A4* e. la cyte de iherusalem ne contre luy *A13, A12* lui (*A12* lui car) en *A1* t. estoit accoustume que c. *A11* an les i. a to. *A12* an les *A13* temps les *A9* desa t. sa t. *A11* de la 398-399 *A3* c.i. de to. la te. faisoit en i. une g.f. et *A12* terre de par dela fesoient *A7* t. la 399 *A1* fesoient leur g. *A10* une moult g. *A1* et t.c. du pays i. *A8* de la contree y 399-400 *A11* fesoient chascun an une g.f. et y furent plusieurs v. et entre les autres y vint le *B2* terre le *A13* i. et ilz e.v. le *A12* en la cite de i. et si il furent la plus grant partie et le f. a h. *A10* de la t.e. arrivez et 400 *A3* estoient v. le *A10* o.e. *A5* estoit le *A8* f. au roy 400-401 *A4, B1* qui e.c.r. de *A7* roy de *B2* h. et plusieurs grans seigneurs estoyent venus en iherusalem pour la feste de pasques et 400-402 *B5* h.c. roy de g. qui avoit a nom a. y estoit venu a la f. et toute sa gent et q.t. les i.f. en i. il *B6* h.e. dedans la cite aussit que poures enyr et ausit saiches car ledit roy archelaus avoit la plus grande partie des iuifz de g. qui estoient venus pour lacompaigner come il apartient a ung roy et aussit pour la f. et ledit iour de ceste di faiste il B7 qui estoit roy de ac. qui venoit a la f. et q. il f.t. venus il 401-402 *B, B1, B4, A6* g. qui avoit nom a. y vint (*B1* a. se v.) a la f. et (*B1* f. luy et) toute sa gent et q.t. les (*B4* q. les) iuifs f. en i. il *B3* c. qui avoit nom a. y vint a la f. et tous ses gens et q.t. lez iuifs fuirent en i. il 401-403 *A11* g. qui avoit nom a. le quel vint a icelle f. avec tout sa gent et q. icelle assemblee des iuifs f. en i. il f. si tresmerveilleux v. que nul diceulx i. ne se oserent p. pour retourner en leur t. 401-404 *A12* g. lequel avoit nom a. et fut venu a la f. avec toute sa gent es sachoiz que les i. estoient dedans la ville de i. y faisoit si que nul des i. ne sen vouloient yssir pour a. en leur t. pour la cause du grant vent qui faisoit l. lempereur v. *B2* ilz i.f. ilz firent si g.v. et cheut tant de nege que nul ne sen povoyt pa. adonc lempereur v. 401-407 *A13* g. et ainsin comme il se quidoient tous deppartir pour retourner chascun en sa t. il fist si grand v. que nulz nosoit a. horrs de la cite adoncques fist lempereur mettre le siege tout alentour de la cite tellement que personne p. partir se non pardevant eulx et q.c.

396 *seront* [ *serons* Correction from all MSS except *A1, A10, B6*.

401 *Acherlant* Archelaus was the son of King Herod (the Herod responsible for the

Jherusalem a la feste, il fist si grant vent et sy mal temps qu'il n'i eüt juifs qui s'en vousist partir pour s'en aler a sa terre.

[27] Lors Vespesian et Titus, son filh, avec toute leur gent alerent assecier Jherusalem tout environ en telle maniere que nulle chose ne povoit istre ne entrer qu'il ne fallist qu'il passast par la oust. Et quant Pilate

402 *A1* i. et la f. fut faicte il *A9* i. en la *A10* i. il *A10* sy tres mauvais t. 402-403 *A4* eut nul i. qui sen osast p. pour a. en sa *A5* quilz nen porent pa. pour eulx en 402-404 *B, B1, B3, B4, A6* v. que les i. ne (*B3* que ne) en osoient pa. (*A6* i. se ce prindrent pa.) adonc lempereur et s.f.ti. et (*B4* le. et ti.l.f. et) to. 402-405 *B5* v. quilz ne sen oserent pa. adont lempereur et to. sa g.a. son f.t. furent devant iherusalem pour la. en 402-406 *B7* v. que nul nosoit issir de iherusalem adoncques lempereur et son f.t. midrent le siege devant iherusalem et povoit nul ystre *B6* si grant pluye que nul ne sen peust a. hors de la cite et tout ce fairoit par la grace de dieu car dieu vouloit acomplir sen il avoit prophetise de sa propre bouche adoncques lempereur aima devant celle moult noble cite que toute celle moult grand puissance et incontinant fist sonner tronpestes et clarons pour faire metre toust en son rang et tout a point et pouserent illecques son siege et saiches car il faisoit bon ouyr les trompestes et clerons dudit empereur car se estoit grant melodie de les ouyr adoncques q. 403 *A10* pour retourner en sa *A2, A7, A8* a. en sa *A5* a. en leur t. 403-404 *A9* v. aler ne yssir pour sen a. en sa t. et en sa maison l. *A1* a. en sa t.v.

404 *A11* l. lempereur et *A3, A4* f.al. 404-405 *A9* g. vindrent a. *A11* avec l.g. vindrent a. *A10* g. assigerent i. en *A12* g. vont venir as. la ville de i. 404-406 *B, B1, B3, B4, A6* g. furent devant iherusalem pour la (*B3* i.la.) quil (*B1* la. affin quil *A6* d. pour les a.) ne p. rien (*A6* p.) i. 404-407 *B2* f. et t.l. compaignie vindrent devant iherusalem pour y mectre le siege et firent tellement que nul ny p.e. ne ne povoyt saillir si non par la marge et commandement de lo. de lempereur q.p. et les iuifz qui estoyent en i.

405 *A11* t. tout e. que et tant que 405-406 *B5* m. quil ne pa. pas par lo. de lempereur nulle personne que on ne sceust bien quil fut et q. *A2, A5* ne sen p. 406 *A1* p. sallir ny e. *A4* p. partir dehors ne e. dedens quil *A7* i. quil *B* e. qui ne pa. *A8* p.e. ne i. et *B1* e. pour lo. de lempereur q. *A6* ne passassent par *A10, A11, A12, B3, B4, A9* ne (*A9* ne sen) pa. *A1* par les gens de lost 406-407 *B, B3, B4* o. de lempereur q.p. et les gens qui estoient en i. *A11, B1* pi. et c. qui (*B1* et les gens qui) estoient en i. *A10* pi. et ses gens v. si gr. multitude de gens assemblez si f. 406-408 *A6* o. de lempereur et p. et ses gens qui estoyent en i.q. ils v. si gr. multitude de gens en lost il heurent grant paour et pylate fut moult courrociez adonc le 406-412 *B7* e. sinon par le conges de lempereur q.p. et les iuif qui estoient en i.v. quil ne povoit personne issir de iherusalem sy eurent grand poeur et pilate fut moult courouces adoncques le roy a. commenca a dire a pillate que neust pour quelconquez car a. assez gent pour combatre lempereur et luy dictz allons as. hors de la cites car nous les esbahirons et ausi saves quil

massacre of the Holy Innocents) and the brother of Herod Antipas (the Herod who beheaded John the Baptist). He died in 6 AD, that is, long before the events of this narrative, after having been removed from his post by Augustus and exiled to Vienne (see Josephus Flavius, pp. 233-236, and note to line 1080).

et ceulx de Jherusalem virent si grant gent, il furent moult esbahy. Et lors 407
le roy Archilans prist Pilate par la main et lui dist qu'il ne se doubtast de riens, car il avoit tant de bonne chevalerie en la cité si fort et sy bien

407 *A7* c. de son conseil et c. de *B6* c. qui estoient dedans la cite oyrent et v. sy grant houst devant eulx ilz *B5* pi. et les gens qui estoient dedens i. *A12* c. qui estoient dedens la cite v. tant de gens et le grant oust entour la ville il se vont m. esbayr l. *A2, A4* v. tant de gens *A9* gr. multitude de gens *A13* v. le siege questoit si grant entour de leur cite ilz f. tous e. *A11* ilz eurent m. grant paour et espanliment pilate fut m. *A1, A2, A4, A5* f. tous e. *A9* m. fort e. 407-408 *B, B1, B3, B5* gr. host ilz eurent grant paour et (*B3* e. si g.p. quil fuirent tous e. et) pilate fut moult courroucie (*B5* c. et e.) adonc (*B1* c. et marry a.) le *B2* gr. host et tan grant puissanz ils eurent m. grant paour et pilate fut moult couroucies adonc le roy a. vint a pi. et *B4* gr. ost ilz eurent grant paour et pylate en fut moult courrocier adonques le roy a. vint a pylate et 407-416 *B6* e. et se nestoit pas de merveilles car plusieurs se esmerveillent de maint de choses et a celle heure pylate se remembra de la response quil avoit faicte a gay senechail dudit empereur et heust tresgrant paour alors le roy archilant le reconfortoit et le p. par dessoubz les bras et luy d. quil fist bone chere et quil ne devoit avoir nulle paour de chouse quil vist et quil ne d. de r. lempereur le ne la puissance quil avoit et luy dist sire pylate la c. est aces f. et tres b.g. pour ce ne d.r. car il y a dedans iherusalem dasses bons chevaliers aussi bons que lempereur en ha point pour bien garder iherusalem et saches quil disoit ces parolles mais quil ne peust aler quant la volunte de dieu adonce il se parvent par les bras et sen alerent au palaix de pylate et tiendrent leur conseil et saiches car le roy archilant dona conseil a pilate quil fist combatre et lempereur et pilate le crust don apres sen repentit et incontinant pylate come fol et mal conseille fist armer toulx ces gens darmes et le roy archillant les conduisoit et leurs disoit alons ardament car nous les assandrons tellement car il sen iront a grant honte sans fraper et se r. de la v. et de leur folue et disont que si grant peuple ne peust demeurer longtemps devant telle cite car il nont point diaeu car il nen trouveront point plus prest que a demye iournee dicy cest assavoir au fluve dyable ou fonderent les deux cites cest assavoir soudonme et gomorre et apres toutx ces choses firent c. car incontenent et sans delle chascun fust arme et que ung chascun se rendit d. le temple salmon et tantost il fust fait et puis il sen vindrent a la pourte pour cuideur saillir h. des portes de iherusalem et il ne peurent point sortir pour cause que les 408 *B, B5* pi. et *A12* a.d. a p. quil *B2* dist en le reconfortant quil neust point paour et que en iherusalem a. moult grant nombre de *A11* roy luy 408-409 *A6, B, B1, B4, B5, B3* neust nulle paour (*B5* e. point du p.) car il avoit (*B3* il seroit) t. *A11* do. et le pr. par la m. et luy dist quil a. en la e. moult grant c. et que la c. estoit si f. 409 *A13* car en la c.a.t. de b.c. si bonne et si f. *B5* a. biaucoup de *A4* de bonnes gens et de bons chevaliers et la c. est si *B3, B4* en ceste city et elle est tant f. *A12* la ville de iherusalem et si *A6* c. et cest c. est tant f. *B, B1, A3, A9* cite et ceste cite est tant (*A3* c. de iherusalem et si estoit si *A9* et quelle estoit sy tres) f. *B5* cite de iherusalem et aussi que elle estoit moult f. *A8* cite si b. *A5* cite et est si 409-410 *A10* car iay assez puissance pour le combatre si leur dist *B2* cite et que la cite estoit moult b.g. et estoyt moult f. si que

guernie qu'il ne lui failloit ja a doubter de riens. Mes dist qu'il s'armassent tuit et qu'il les alassent assaillir par telle maniere que il se repentissent de y estre venus. Et ossy vous dy que l'oust ne peut avoir duree pour ce qu'il n'ont point d'eau. Et cest conseil pleut moult a Pilate. Et lors il fist crier par toute la cité que toute personne s'armast. Et incontinant chascun s'arma. Et quant il furent tous armés, et il vont venir davant le palais ou Pilate demouroit. Et quant il vousirent issir hors de la cité, les gens de

410 *A13* ne doivent point d. mes quil *A4*, *A5*, *A12* ne (*A12* ne leur) f. *A7* ne f.d. *A11* g. vous ne devez point d. lempereur ne sa puissance mes quil *A1*, *A3*, *A8* f. mie (*A8* f. que *A3* f.) d. *A9* r. et aussy icellui roy archilent dist et conseilla audit pylate quilz 410-411 *A10* dist que tantost sans delay ilz se 410-412 *B5* g. pour quoy ne vous devez d. ne esbahir mais nous nous armerons tous et les irons combatre et as. de la cite et les esbahirons tant fort quilz sen r. tous et aussi lo. 410-413 *B*, *B1*, *B3*, *B4*, *A6* ne vous devez (*B1* ne d.) point d. mes nous armon t. (*A6* m. vous armes t.) et les alon as. dehors la cite et nous les esbayrons tant fort quilz se (*B3* quilz sen retourneront et sen) r. tous (*B1* quilz sen retourneront et t. *A6* se repartirent t.) eulx de lost qui estoient v. et (*B4* qui sont et) ossy lo. ne p. estre longuement icy pour deffault deau *B2* f. riens d. et dirent lung a lautre il nous fault tous armer p[ ] les irons as. et par ainsi nous les ferons tant esbays que tous ceulx de lost sen retourneront car ilz ne pevent icy longuement demourer pour la souffrette de leau 411 *A2* et les assalissent par *A3*, *A5*, *A9*, *A4* les assaillissent (*A4* a. celeement) par *A11*, *A12* as. si fierement que (*A12* sy tresfort que) ceulx qui estoient en lost se *A13* as. tellement quil se 411-412 *A7* et aussi lui dist que *A1* m. que il les fassent repentir de leurs v. *A12*, *A13* de ce quilz estoyent v. la et (*A13* v. devant iherusalem et) ossy lo. 412 *A9* et encores plus lui dist *A11* v. car lo. *A2*, *A3*, *A5* o. li (*A5* o. leur) dy *A8* o. ne p.lo.a. 412-413 *B5* p. estre longuement ycy par deffaulte deau *A13* p. longuement durer par deffault de. adoncques pi.f. *A11*, *A12* d. par deffaulte deau *A7* il ne pourroyent p. avoir deaue 413 *A10* eau adoncques ce *B7* deau pres pourquoy il ne poeult longuement tenir le siege ce c.m.p. a *A9* m. bien a *B* m. bien a p. tantost pilate f. *A11* pi. si f. *B1* et f. tantoust cr. *B3* f. tantost cr. 413-414 *A6*, *A12*, *B4*, *B5* pi. et f. tantost cr. (*A12* f.cr. incontinent) par *B7* pi. et f. 413-416 *B2* co. fut m. agreable a p. lequel ordonna a capitaignes luy et le roy archillens pour confuyre icelles gens et fut delibere de saillir sur lost de lempereur les 414 *A9* la ville et cite *A12* la ville que 414 *A1* et tantost c. 414-415 *A11* et ainsi le firent et *A8* sa. et voult venir *B*, *B1*, *B3*, *B4*, *B5*, *A6* que touz fussent armez et tantost fut fait et vindrent t. a d. (*B4* armez d.) le *A10* que tout chascun sa. si fut fait q. 414-416 *B7* que le matin en fust bien arme et ainsy fust faict et quant vint quil commencerent a saillir de la citez les 414-422 *A13* que chascun fuisse arme pour partir deshous pour combatre contre lempereur et ses gens mais les gens de lempereur furent desia deshous mais refermirent leur p. et commandirent que lon gardaisse bien sur iceulx et f. en nombre ceulx quil pourtoient celles pres .lx.m. personnes p. et a. 415 *A10*, *A11* f.a. *A11* venir tous d. *A4* p. la ou 415-416 *A10* ou d.p. et *A6*, *A11*, *A12*, *B*, *B1*, *B3*, *B4*, *B5* p. de pi. et 416 *A3* d. mais q. *A10* h. les *B4* i. de *A6* il saillirent de *B1*, *B3*, *B5*, *B* q. ilz yssirent de *A12* la ville de iherusalem les

l'empereur se furent sy aprochiez des murs de la cité qu'il n'ozerent issir. Mes eürent conseil qu'il fermassent les portes et missent gardes es murs l'une partie de leur gens, et l'autre partie se desarmast pour porter pieres sur les murs. Et lors Pilate fist crier que toute personne pourtast pieres sur les murs et que la cité fust bien guarnie. Et sy furent bien par compte a
[42r] pourte[r] celle pierre / soisante mile. Et Pilate et le roy Archilans

417 *A1*, *A11* f. si pres des *A4*, *A8* sy fort a. *A9* sy fort a. et logiez pres des *A10* sestoient tirez si trespres des *A3*, *A4*, *A5*, *A8* m. quilz 417-418 *A11* la ville quil ne furent si hardiz ne osez de les assaillir mais *A1* o. mes *A3* i. et pour ce e. *A4* i. hors mes *A9* o. oncques i. hors de la cite mais *A12* i. hors de la ville et vont avoir leur c. 417-420 *B6* e. si pres des m. et des pourtes qui ne pouvoient sortir hors nullement adoncques quat il virent il sen retournerent derechef dedans la cite et taindrent leur conseil et tout leur conseil fut car il fermissient les p. de iherusalem et puis sen monterent sur les murs et *B2* e. estoyent au plus pres des murs si que il ne fust homme si ardy de venir a eulx ne de saillir tantost apres le roy archillen et pilate eurent aultre conseil et firent fermer les p. et monterent sur les m. et les guarnirent de pierres pour mieulx garder la cite de iherusalem pi. *B*, *B1*, *B3*, *B4*, *B5*, *A6* e. se f. (*A6* e.f.) au plus pres des murs tant que ceulx de dedans ne (*B1* de devant ne *B4* que nulz de c.d. ne) furent si (*A6* d. estoyent ne furant si) hardis de venir a eulx et (*B4* v. dehors et) tantost firent un (*B5* c.d. ne f. ung) autre conseil et firent fermer les p. et monterent sur (*B4* et monter sur) les m. pour po.pi. et (*B1* pi. dessus et *B5* pour getter de.pi. et) pour garder la cite de iherusalem (*B5* c.) pi. 417-424 *B7* e. estoient au plus pres de ceulx qui salloient de la citez et de peur se retournerent dedans et tantost firent ung aultre c. et firent que lon fermerist les p. et monterent sur les murs pour y po.pi. et garder la citez et y estoit p. qui avoit v. ung iacquez v. bien fait et 418 *A10* e. en leur c. *A8* c. de fermer les *A12* p. de la ville et 418-419 *A10* m. bonnes g. en chascun et au dessus des murs lune *A3* murs de lune *A9* murs cestassavoir lune *A7* murs huit p. de l. signes et 419 *A9* et que la. *A12* a. et lautre se d. et portast pi. 419-420 *A11* d. et portast pi. sur *A10* pi. en la ville sur les m. et sur les autres lieux et tours adonc f.p.c. que t. le monde po. 420 *B6* que ung chascun po. *A12* et incontinent firent c. 420-421 *A8* pi. et *A9* po. sur les m.pi. et 420-422 *B*, *B1*, *B3*, *B4*, *B5*, *A6* c. par tout iherusalem (*B4* par i. *B5*, *A6* par toute la cite de i.) que touz apportassent pierres sur les murs et tantost furent .lx.m. et (*B3* f. bien lx.m. porteur de pierres et *B5* m. apportans pierres et) pi. *B2* f. donc c. par toute la cite que chascun apportast pierres sur les murs de la cite furent .lx.m. toux portans pierres pi. *A1* pi. soixante m. a porter pierres pi. 420-423 *B6* pi. en droit luy pour eulx deffandre adoncques pilate et le roy a. et barrabam qui estoit seneschal dudit pylate avec cent mille chevaliers bien au point mo. 421 *A12* m. excepte ceulx qui gardoient les murs et que *A9* furent b. en c. et en nombre fait a 421-422 *A10* que les portes feussent b. gardees et adonc chascun se mist en euvre et f.b. pour de gens portant p. iusques a lx *A8* g. et *A11*, *A12* furent lx.m. et p.pi. sur les murs et le 422 *A3* po.xl.m. *A9* m. personnes et 422-423 *A11* a. se desarmerent puis mo. 422-424 *A10* a. avec dix c. puissans s. estre point armes *B*, *B1*, *B2*, *B3*, *B4*, *B5*, *A6* a. ix.c. (*B2* a. vingt c.) et furent tout entour de la cite et avoient v. (*B1*, *B5* et pilate a.v. *B2* et chascun a.v. *B3*, *B4* et a. pilate v.) un iaques de vermeil (*B4* de veloer v.) bien (*B2* v. mout b. *B2* de veloux b. *A6* de vannet b.) fait et (*B1* de velluau v. et) t.

monterent sur les murs avec dis chevaliers sans plus. Et sy n'avoient nules armes, mes estoient vestus chescun d'un bliau vermeilh. Et Pilate tenoit ung petit baston pelé en sa main. Et puis il manderent a l'empereur que il vouloient parler a lui a fiance et qu'il venist la a eulx.

[28] Lors Vespesian avec Jaffet et avec Gaius, le seneschal, et avec vint autres chevaliers vint au murs de la cité la ou estoient Pilate et le roy Archelans. Et Titus demoura en la oust. Lors Vespesian demanda a Gaius,

423 *A1* murs tous desarmez et dix *A2, A9* x. mile c. *A8* dix mille c. qui na. 423-424 *B6* mo. et puis alerent tout a lenviron de la cite et pilate avoit ung iaquer de velour rouge tresbien fait et *A12* et furent desarmes et bien v. *A11* et a.v.c. ung habillement ver. 423-425 *A13* p.c.v. dune roube v. et man. *A1* p. et envoierent a 424 *A3, A4, A5, A9* dun beau (*A4, A5* dung vellut *A9* dun bel drap) v. *A10* de v. *A12* dung drap blanc fin et 424-425 *A10* et si t.p. en sa m. ung b. blanc et lors man. *A11* p. avoit en sa m. ung bastonnet p. et man. *A8* t. en sa m. ung p.t.p. et *A12* t. en sa m. ung b. blanc p. et luy et le roy archillaux vont mander a 424-430 *B7* t. en b. blanc en sa m.v.g. son s. et i. et moult a. grand seigneurs v. pres la citez ou p.e. adoncques lempereur d. a son 424-431 *B6* t. en sa m. ung b. blanc p. et saiches car il parlerent avecques le. lequel estoit pres des meurs acompaigne de plusieurs chevaliers tresbien em point adoncques lempereur et t. son f. et g. qui estoit s. de lempereur et x mille c. monterent a cheval et puis sen v. la ou e.p.d.l. ce qui avoit non p. alors g. luy respondit sire cest c. qui ha ung b. blanc en sa m. et puis lempereur parla avecques pi. 425 *A1* e. disant que *A9* ung b. blanc en 425-427 *A11* quil voulsist venir parler a ceulx de f.l. *A13* que il venisse p. a eulx a f.l. 425-428 *B, B1, B3, B4, B5, A6* un b. en sa m. bien p. et (*B4* m. et *B3* b.p. en sa m. et *B5* b. bien bel en son poing et) parlerent a le. qui estoit pres (*B3* e. bien p *B4* e. au plus p.) des murs de la cite (*A6* c. de iherusalem) v. (*B5* m.v.) empereur a.i. de iaffet et g. (*B1, B4, B5* de cassel et g. *B2* de casel avec g. *B3* a. ioseph du cassel et g.) son s. et xv (*A6* et avec xv) c. qui estoient avecques (*B2* e. la a.) luy v. (*B3* a.v. *B5* a. eulx v.) la (*B1* v. a lendroit *A6* c.v. la) ou *B2* en sa m. ung b. blanc p. et parlerent a le. qui estoyt pres des murs de la cite v. empereur et i. de casel avec g. son s. et xv a.c. qui estoyent la avec luy v. la ou 426 *A10* lui par tres grande affience et v. parler a e. *A1, A7* ve. a *A3, A9* la parler a 426-427 *A12* f.l. *A8* la parler a e. et v. 427 *A1, A3, A7, A9, A11* et g. *A4* et g. son s. *A8* i. et le *A10* i.g. 427-428 *A13* i.g. son s. et v.ch. *A9* xx mille a. *A7* a. xxx ch. *A10* s. et huit a. notables hommes c.v. iusques aux *A11* vint ch. *A12* s. et a.a. xl ch. 428 *A11* v. pres des m. ou *A12* v. apres du m. 428-432 *A13* v. parler a eulx adoncques lempereur d. a p. disant ie suis venus parler a toy car tu ne voloies venir parler a moy mon 429 *B, B1, B2, A6* a. au plus pres des murs et t. son filz d. aux tentes adont v. *B4* a. au plus pres des murs et t. son filz d. aux tentes adonc v. empereur d. *A11* o. de lempereur l. *A12* t. filz de lempereur d. *A1* d. a garder lo. et v. 429-430 *A10* o. adonc se print lempereur a perler a p. et d. a son *A3, A8, A12* g. le s. *A6, B, B1, B2, B4* a son *A11* g.l. *B3* a. au plus pres dez murs et t. son filz d. es tantez adont v. dit a gay son senechalx et luy d.l. 429-431 *B5* a. au plus prez des murs et t.d. aux tentes adont v. se print a

son seneschal, lequel estoit Pilate. Et Gaius lui dist que cellui que tenoit le baston pelé en sa main. Lors Vespesian commensa a parler a Pilate et lui dist: "Pilate, mon noble pere, Julius Zesar, te bailla ceste ville en garde et en commende et vousist que tu fussies son seneschal et que tu gouvernessies ceste terre pour luy. Et quant tu seüs qu'il fust mors, tu m'envoyas le truage comme tu devois par trois ans. Puis as esté set ans

430 *A10* p. parler il voulloit il adonc g. *A8, A11, A12, A7* p. et il (*A7* p. il) luy *A9* g.d. *B, B1, B2, B4, A6* p. le seneschal luy repondit seigneur (*B4* s.r. mon s.) cest (*B2* luy dit mon s. dit il cest) c. *B3* lui respondit que cestoit c. *A4, A5, A7, A9, A10, A11, A12* d. que cestoit c. 430-431 *A3* d. que cestoit c. qui t. ung b. *B7* et il luy respondit cest c. qui est vestu dung iacque vermeil et qui t. le b. blancq l. lempereur c. *A6, A10, B4* t. ung b. blanc en *A11, A12, B, B1, B2, B3* t. ung b. 431 *A1* m. et quand ilz furent approchies des murs v. *A7* v. commanda a *A6, A10, B, B1, B2, B3, B4* v. se prit (*B2, B4* v.p. *B1* se me et) a *A11* m. quant ilz furent aprouchez il sentresaluerent puis c.v. a *A9* pa. audit pi. *A12* pa. et *B3* a pi. en disant le n. seigneur mon pere 431-432 *A1* et lors d. a p. *A11* pa. en ceste maniere p. vray est que mon pere *B7* pa. a lui en luy disant le n. sire mon pere 432 *A4, A12* d. mon *A6, B, B1, B4* d. le n. sire mon p.i. *B2* d. le n. et puyssant seigneur mon pere august cesar *B5* d. le n. sire empereur mon predecesseur te *B6* d. par ceste maniere vien ca pylate trestre deshobeissant i.c. mon p. te *A10* mon amy mon pere *A12* b. iherusalem en 432-433 *A6, A11, A13, B, B1, B2, B3, B4, B5, B7* b. iherusalem en (*B1* b. la cite de i. en) g. et v. 432-437 *B6* c. cite pour este son provost et aussy que tu la gardasse ou non de luy et apres sa mort que tume. le treheu p.t. ans ausy come tu le devois faire par droit paternel et par raison et dessa il y a sept ans de quoy ie ne suis pas contant et qui plus est q. mon s. vint par devers toy tu luy dis par paroilles rebelles et fieres et qui plus est tu le menassis et 433 *A1, A3, A11, A12* son prouvost et 433-434 *A2* v. que tu g. la t. et que tu f. son s. et q. *B5* f. provost et que tu gardasse sa terre par deca ou nom de luy et q. *B, B1, B2, B3, B4, A6* son prevost et que gardasses toute sa terre ou (*B1, B3, B4* terre par deca au) nom de luy et (*B2* terre de part desste en son n. et) q. *B7* son gouverneur et son prevost et q. 433-435 *A13* son prevost pour icellui ensamble garder et gouverner bien et lealment et apres son trespassement tu mas paiez le t.p. 434 *A11* luy et au non de luy et q. il 434-435 *A10* quil estoit trespasse tu *A1* f. trespasse tu 434-436 *B5* m. tu ne m. pas le tresor ainsi que tu d. faire et maintenant il y a vij ans que riens ne menvoias et q. 435 *A4, A7* t. pour t. ans c. tu d. puis *A2* e. par vij. *A10* annees ensuivant p. *A11* as demoure sept 435-436 *B, B1, B3, B4, B7, A6* le tresor p.t. (*B1* tr. de t.) ans c. (*B2, B3, B4, B7, A6* ans ainsi c.) tu d. et maintenant il a sept ans que ne en ay rien eu et (*B1* ay receu r. et *B4* an r. receu et *B2* que iay r. eu du tresor que tu me dois et *B7* men repceu r. et) q. *B2* tu mandas le t. de t. ans ainsi c. tu d. et maintenant il y a sept ans que iay riens eu du tresor que tu me doys et q. *A13* puis le ma cessez de paier par lespace de s. ans tous entiers s.

432 *Julius Zesar* Another historical inaccuracy, as Vespasian was of humble origin, related neither to Julius nor to Augustus (see note to line 2). Julius died in 44 BC, 53 years before Vespasian's birth.

434 *seüs* [ *seust* Correction from all MSS except *A13, B6*.

sans le moy anvoyer. Mes quant je le t'envoyay querir par Gaius, mon seneschal, tu luy dis vilannie. Et si lui dis que tu ne tenois riens de moy et lui dis que je guardasse bien Rome et Lombardie, car tu garderies bien Jherusalem et sy ne me reconnoistrerois riens. Pour ce vieux que tu me faces ov[r]ir les portes de ceste cité afin que je puisse fere de toy et de tous ceulx qui sont la dedens a ma voulenté et a mon plesir.

436 *A11* a. ne que ie nen euz riens et q. *A6* ie te envoyt mon *B, B1, B3, B4, B7, A11, B5* e. (*A11* e.g. *B5* e. na gueres) mon *A8* par mon 436-437 *A13* q. mon s.g. le venit q. deppart moy tu le vilennas et le vouloies fere tuer si ne fuisse ung tien iuifz et des que *A10* par mon s.g. tu 437 *A8* et que *B4* tu luy respondiz que *B7* luy respondit parollez fieres et orguelieusez et disant que *A6, A11, B, B1, B2, B3, B5* lui respondis villainnement et *A10* tu luy dis que tu t. nulle chose du monde si lui dis v. et le manda que 437-438 *A3, A9* v. et si lui dis que ie *A8, A11, A13, B, B1, B2, B3, B4, B5, B7, A12* moy et (*A12* et encores luy dis plus) que *B6* ne devois r. de moy ne de home de par moy et que 438 *B, B6, B7* r. et que tu garderies *A11* l. et que ie garderoye b. 439 *B, B1, B2, B3, B4, B5* i. et ie v. *A10, B6* i. et p. *A6* et si te dis que *B7* i. et plus est tu volloist faire morir mon s. se neust estes le seneschal barraban et maintenant v. *A8, A11, A12* r. point dommage ne truage (*A11* ne ne me payeroys aucun t.) p. *B6* que incontinant come seigneur de tout lempire que tu 439-440 *A10* ma ouvres les 439-454 *A13* et que tu ne me r. point pour seigneurs ne ne pour fere ma v. anchillain dist a pilate ilz luy meschiet quil se mettra a sa v. et quil ne se deffendra contre lempereur adoncques pilate respondit a lempereur quil gardaisse bien romme comme devant et chascun disoit que lon ne pourroit tenir ledit sieges pour deffault deauue car il le convenoit aler q. a f. 440 *A6* f. a avoir les *B5* f. maintenant o. *B3, B5* de la c. et que de toy *A10* de iherusalem a. *B* de la c. et que de tu et *B2* de la c. de iherusalem et a. que ie fasse de *B1* p. et que toy et t. *A6* de la c. et que ie faice de t. *B4* de iherusalem et que tu et t. *A8* cite car ie y veul entrer a. 440-441 *A11* toy et de c. 440-442 *B7* p. come sire et maistre que ie suis de toy et de toute la terre p.r. quil *B5* t. ie faice a ma v. comme ie doy faire par raison comme seigneur que ie suis de la cite ceste parole dist p. quil *A10* p. de toy mavoit le lute et mon p. et de t.c. qui sont d. adont p.r. et dit a le. quil 440-447 *B6* de ma c. de iherusalem et que toy et t.c. et celles qui s.d. soient a ma v. pour en faire ce que ien doye faire par raison adoncques p.r. quil nestoit pas advise et qui tiendroit son c. et puis rendroit la ville ou autre responce alors pilate et le roy archillant et t. ceulx qui estoient avecques luy sen retournerent et puis sen allerent dedans le palais de pylate pour tenir leur conseil adoncques quant il feurent toulx asembles le roy a. va parler le premier et va dire a pylate sire naies point paour et fasies bone chere car vous ne vous deves nullement esbayr pour m. quil vous fasse car il luy pourroist pour et aussit vous aves de cy nobles chevaliers et vaillens gens de guerre pour deffandre et pour ce ne vous meleuvollies point ie vous certiffie car pour leure que est a petit il y a dausit vaillens gens dedans la cite come on en saroit trouver en la 441 *A6* c. de la citey qui s.d. *A8* et p. 441-442 *B, B1, B3, B4* s.d. face a ma v. conme ie le doy faire (*B4* c. tu dois f.) par raison ceste parole r.p. (*B3* raison a c.pa.r.p. et d.) que *B2* s.d. a tout mon p. a ma v.p.r. adonc a le. quil *A3, A5, A7* v.l. *A2, A4, A12* v. et adont p. li r. et (*A12* v.l. luy r.p. et) lui d. *A11* s.d. icelle a ma v. conme ie doy faire par raison l. *A1* d. a mon p. et a ma v.l. *A9* d. avecques toy a mon gre p. et v.l. 441-443 *A6* v. ainsi comme ie doye faire par raison a cecy p.r. a cest parolles quil a. c. et sen ala ou temple de salomon et t.

436 *mes quant je* [ *mes quant mes quant ie*

[29] Lors respont Pilate a l'empereur et dist qu'il an averoit son conseil. Et lors il se part de la et ala tenir son conseil avec tous ces barons. Et le roy Archelan lui dist qu'il ne lui failloit ja avoir doubtanse des menasses de l'empereur, car il se pouoit bien deffendre et s'y pouroit resister contre lui, car il avoit tant de bonne chevalerie dedans Jherusalem qu'il ne creoit que
[42v] en la tierce part du monde an ait autant. "Et sachiez qu'il vous seroit / grant honte se vous ne vous deffendiez contre l'empereur. Et il luy

442 *A9* p. et lui d. *A1, A3, A5, A7* et lui dist *A10, A12* a.c. 442-443 *A11* p. que sur ce il a.c.l. parla a ces b. apart et le *B, B1, B2, B3, B4, B5* et se en ala au temple salmon et (*B1* s. ou *B2,B3,B4,B5* s.a.) tous *A10* et sen vint au c. 443 *A1* b. et lors le *A6, B, B1, B2, B3, B4, B5* b. et avec le 443-444 *B7* et sen ala au temple salomon et la trouva le roy a. et daultre baron et tantost le roy archelan commenca a dire a pillate quil ne luy chalust des 443-445 *A10* b. adonc le r.a. dit a pilalte que de chose quil feist il neust nulle d. ne de m. que le. lui fist et que encontre lui il 444 *A12* a. et le roy a comence a parler le premier et luy *A1* a. parla premier et d. *B2, B5* ne eust point de paour des *A8* ia doubter ne a. *A9* ia doubter des *A7* ia ouvrir pour d. *A2, A4, A12* a. paour (*A12* p. ne d.) des *A1* ia d.a. des *A3* f. pas a. 444-445 *B, B3, A6* neust point de paour de la m. que luy faisoit le. *B1, B4* neust point de paour de la m. que luy faisoit le. car (*B4* que le. luy f. car) vous vous povez b. 445 *A12* car voz pouves b. *A2, A4, A8, A9, A11, A12* et r. 445-446 *A6, B, B3, B1, B4* d. c. luy car il a. (*B1, B4* car iay) t. *A12* c. lempereur car vous ayes d. ceste ville t. de b.c. que ie ne *B2* car il na. moult b. *B5* b. garder de luy et d. car 445-447 *A10* d. considere la grant c. que en i. estoit et 445-451 *B7* le. et quil se deffendroict bien contre luy quant le roy archilan eust parle b. commenca a dire sachez sire que le roy archilan v. 446 *A1* de b. gens et de b. *A1* c. quil *A6, B, B1, B4* i. se dit le roy (*B1, B4* roy archillant) que *B2* c. en la cite de i. et y avoyt plus de peuple que *B3* c. avec luy et si bon fait dez armez que *B5* i. ce dist le roy archelans quil croit bien que 446-447 *A11* a.d.i.t. de b.c. quon pourroit trouver en *A8* nen avoit pas a. en la t.p. du m. et 447 *A7* en cite du *A11* m. et luy dist derechief que ce se. *A12* aye tant de bonnes gens darmes et v. *A2, A3, A4, A5, A7* et disoit quil (*A4* que celuy *A7* quil vous) s. 447-448 *A9* et disoit qui lui feroit g. 447-449 *B, B1, B2, B3, B4, A6* aut. et (*B4* t. ne de meilleurs et) que ce s.g. oultrage de soy rendre a la v. de lempereur (*B3* e. si tost) q. *B5* m. on ne en pourroit tant trouver et que ce s. grant oultrage de soy rendre a la v. de lempereur q. 447-450 *B6* m. et pour ce mest advis car se s.g. simplesse a vous de rendre la ville pour si peu de chose et puis apres toutx ces choses le 448 *A2, A3, A4, A5, A7, A9, A11* h. sil (*A3, A11* h. a luy sil) ne se deffendoit 448-449 *A1* c. luy a mal meschief viengne qui *A3* et quil meschauf a celluy qui *A7* et disoit que aneschoir lui povoit il qui a soy ce rendroit p. *A8* et dist pylate qui luy mesauciust que *A9* et mescheoir lui puisse il qui se *A10* et que m. lui puist il qui a lui se sen droit p.f. *A11* et quil mescherroit a celuy que se rendroit a luy p. *A12* luy viengne meschance qui

448 *mescherra* [ *meschoe* Unsupported correction.

mescherra qui a lui se rendra pour en fere sa voulenté." Et quant le roy Archelan eüst achevee sa rayson, le seneschal de Pilate, qui s'apeloit Barlabam, dist a Pilate: "Sire, le roy vous donne bon conseil, car sachez certainement qu'il ne vous faut ja avoir doubtance de l'empereur, car il n'a puissance de demourer en cest païs l'espace de deux moys avec son host, car il ne peuvent avoir eau, sy ne la vont querir une journee loing, c'est au fleuve du Deable, la out perirent deux cités qui s'apeloient [Sodoma] et

449 *A9* r. a lui p. *A12* r. a en *A2, A3, A4, A5* f. a sa *A8* r. et 449-450 *A1* r. dist le r.a.p. en f. sa v. et puis dist le *A6* a. ost parler barrabam le *A12* e. dist et parle et le 449-451 *B, B1, B2, B3, B4, B5* e. parle b.s.p. se leva et luy d. (*B1, B3, B4, B5* et d.) seigneur (*B4* d. mon s.) saches que le roy archellan (*B5* roy) v. 450 *A11* a. de parler le *A2* sa parole et sa r. *A3* p. nomme b. 450-451 *B6* p. leurs va dire seigneurs faictes bone chere car ie vous promet car nullement vous ne deves de rien doutez lempereur et saiches car le roy archillant v. *A6* p. se levat et dit seigneur sachiez que le roy archileans v. *A8* p.d.s. *A10* p.d. sire le r. archelaus v. 451 *A3* roy archilant v. *A11* d.c. tres bon car 451-452 *A10* co. et naiez ia d. encontre le. 451-454 *B, B1, B2, B3, B4, B5, B6, A6* co.ce. et (*B2, A6, B6* co. et *B5* co. et ce.) ne vous doubtez de riens de lempereur (*B1* d. de le. *B2* d. point de le. *B3* ce car il ne v.f. point doubter de le. *B6* d. nullement de le.) car il (*B3* car pourquoy il *B5* d. car) ne peut icy estre grandement o sa (*B2* p. pas gueres i. arrester avec ses *B3* e. longuement avec sez *B4* p.e.i. longuement avec ses) gent car (*A6* i. longuement ne ses gens aussi car) ilz (*B1* p.e.i. longuement ou sa g. pour ce quilz *B6* p. longuement tenir siege car il) nont (*B5* ne nont) point deau *B7* co. et ne doubtez rien car il ne poeult estre sy longuement pour la deffaulte de le. car il nen ont poinct sil q. 452 *A9* v. chault ia *A12* f.a. *A8* f. point doubter le. 452-453 *A10* p. darrester en 453 *A1* d. cy a. son h.le. de deux m. car *A8* d. deux m. en ce p.a. *A12* d.a. ses gens en ce p.le. de d.m. car *A7* deux ans a. *A10* h. quil a car 453-454 *A11* d.a. son ost en ce p.le. de d.m. pour ce quil nauront point deau *A10* ne aura point deau *A12* nont point de dau 454 *A10* q. par une *B, B1, B2, B3, B4, B5, A6* q. a demie (*B5* a. environ demy *B6* q. icy a d.) i. (*B4* i. dicy ou *B2* a plus de d.i.l. dicy *B3* q.) au *A12* q. bien l. au *B7* q. au *A4, A9* cestassavoir ou 454-455 *B6* q. dicy a demi i.l. cest assavoir au f. iourdain ou au flanc dudit valle ou serudirent les .v. c. assavoir s. 455 *A10* d. out *B2* d. cestassavoir la *A13* d. ou furent confondue s. *B, B1, B2, B3, B4, B7, A6, A12* c. (*A6* c. estassavoir *B4* c. de) s. *B5* p. et fondirent s. *A11* p. iadis d.c. cestassavoir s. 455-456 *A1* sa.g. et s. et 455-458 *B7* g. et vous scaves que t. leur s. loing et p. de le. et ses gens ne podilent estre longuement entour nous et n. tiendrons bien contre luy s. ans se mestier et p. 455-461 *B6* g. et les aultres et par aussit il ne pourait fornir a si grant peuple dyaue pour quoy saiches pour tout vray quil sen yront sans fraper copt et daultre part nous povons t. la ville contre lempereur dicy a s. ans p. quoy mon opinion se est que vous ne luy rediez point nullement et ne vous soiclosies car nous nous serons aide et secors toulx en vous necessites adoncques pilate dist car le conseil estoit bel et bon et fust tresbien content quil fust fait aussit adoncques il 455-469 *A13* g. questoient a quatre liuue de la et quant pilate en fait response a le. disant quil sen retournaisse le. luy dist ie ne doy p.r. iusques a ce que me r. la

455 *Sodoma* Addition from all other manuscripts.

*Sodoma et Gomorra* Two of the "cities of the plain" destroyed by God because of their wickedness. See Gen 10:19, 13, 14, 18, 19, Deut 29:23, Hosea 11:8, Amos 4:11, Mt 10:15, Mk 6: 11, Rom 9:29, 2 Peter 2:6, Jude 7. It is believed they were located in the Jordan Valley, near the Dead Sea, perhaps even beneath the present water-level.

Gomorra. Et seroit trop de paine a tant de gent. Et pour ce je croy que l'empereur n'y poura longuement durer et nous nous pouvons bien tenir sis ou set ans contre lui. Pour ce je vous conseille que vous le deffiés, car a tant eü d'ardiment qu'il soit venus de par desa ou qu'il s'en retourne." Et Pylate et le roy Archelan et tous ceulz qui estoient au conseil le ont tenu a bon, et se tindrent a son conseil. Et lors il s'en partent tuit et s'en vont au

456 *A11* et t. leur s. loing de laller querir a *A12* et leur s. *A11* ie vous dy bien que ie c. 456-457 *B2* et se leur s. moult grief et p. ce vous povez considerer que lempereur ne p. icy gueres demorrer et vous scaves que n. *A10* et moult leur s. grant p. et pourtant ie c. bien quil ne pourroit d.l. et 456-458 *B1*, *B3*, *B4*, *B5*, *A6*, *B* et t. leur s. (*B* t. loin s.) loing et (*B5* long chemin et *A6* s. soing an ailler querre) p. ce le. ne sa gent ne p. estre gueres l. (*B4* p.l.e. *B5* e.l.) entour (*B* l. estre e. *A6* p.g.es.en.) nous et nous (*B3* et aussi n.) n. tiendrons bien s. ans c. lui (*B3* ans encontre eulx) p. 457 *A7* et n. saurons b. *A11* d. ne demourer entour n.n.n. tiendrons bien sis *A12* p. point demourer l. entour n. et aussy n.n. tiendrons bien sis *A2* t.v. ou vj. ans 457-458 *A8* l. demourer entour n. et n.p.t.c. luy vj ou vij ans p. *A4* t.v. ou vj. ans *B2* sis ans a lencontre de luy 458 *A10* ce sire ie *A10* que tantost v. 458-459 *A5* que dissiez quil *A4*, *A8* d. et comment il a t. (*A8* d.c. a yl eu t.) de har. de venir *A7* d. quant il a t. vu de audiance quil *A12* car il est auze passer de *B*, *B1*, *B2*, *B3*, *B4*, *A6* d. et (*B3* d. tantost et) luy dictes que sen tourne luy (*B3* t. en son pays luy) et ses (*B2* sen retourne avec ses) gens (*A3* g. adont) p. *A1* d. pour ce quil a aut. de har. et *A11* d. et 458-463 *B7* d. pillate et archilan tindren le conseil bon et sen retournerent sus les m. et p. commenca a dire a le.r. 459 *A12* d. et luy dies quil *A3* et lors p. *A10* r. briefvement adonc p. *A12* r. le plus tost quil pourra et *B5* r. luy et ses gens p. *A5* da. destre v. *A10* da. quil vous v. devers vous ou 460 *A2* qui au c.e. lon *A8* c. ont se conseil tenu 460-461 *A2* a son seneschal et a son c. *A7* bon et l. *B5* a. alerent sur les m. *A12* et toute sa baronie o.t. le c. pour bon et partent dilecques et sen *B*, *B1*, *B2*, *B3*, *B4*, *A6* t. les autres barons (*B1* t. ses b.) si (*A6* a. se) ont t. pour (*B1* ont touz t. ce p. *B3* t. ceste parolle p.) bon c. et (*B4* t. le c.p.b. et) pylate (*B2* si tindrent p.b. le c. de barrabam seneschal de pilate adonc p.) et le roy archilan avecques leur (*B1* ar. et toute l. *A6* ar. ensamble l.) compaignie sen p. du conseil et sen alerent sur (*B2* et vindrent sur) les m. *A1* e. du c. quilz ny firent aultre parlement et sen vindrent aux

460-462 *A10* qui la e. se accorderent a son c. si son dit et tantost ilz se p.t. ensemble par ung accord et vindrent sur les m. parler a le. qui la devant les a. et 460-463 *A11* et toute la baronnie o.t. le c. a bon et l. pilate revint sur les murs et d. a 461 *A8* t. et l. *A4* au c. du seneschal de pylate et 461-465 *B6* p. du palais de pilate ou il avoient tenu leur conseil et puis apres pylate et le roy archillant sen virent parler a parler a le. et luy va dire pylate empereur va ten a rome et aussit en lombardie et les g.b. car ie pansse bien garder iherusalem contre toute ta puissance et s. car ie

458 *contre* [ *comme* Reading of all other MSS except *B6*.

murs, la out l'empereur avoit ses gens, et les atandoit au pié du mur. Et lors Pilate dist a l'empereur: "Sire, retournés vous en et gardés bien vostre terre, car je garderay bien ceste yci contre vous et contre tous mes ennemis, car sachiés bien que je ne vous renderay point la cité. Et sy vous conseille que vous ne vous voeilliez destruire, mes vous en retournés. Et sy ferés que saige et que bien conseillié."

[30] Et lors dist l'empereur: "Pilate, ne m'en mandés point retourner, mes dites moy ce vous me rendrés point la cité comme a vostre naturel

462 *A3, A5, A12, A2, A4* le. avecques ses g. (*A2, A4* le. et toute sa g.) les *A1* le. et ses g.a. la responce que lui debvoit faire pilate et pi. *A8* le. avec ses g. les a. et pi. *B* le. les esperoit ses barons au 462-463 *B1, B2, B3, B4, B5, A6* le. et p. commenca a (*B2* le. les a. daultre part avec ses barons adonc p. va commencier a) parler a le. et luy d. (*B2* d. seigneur empereur *B3* d. empereur) r. *A10* pi. lui d.s. dit pillate r. *A12* mur et pi. commencza a parler et d. *B* pi. commanca a parler a le. et luy d. tournez 463 *A10, B1* g.v. *B3* t. et vostre pays car 464 *A4* c. cyte ycy *A10* b. la cite de iherusalem ceste *A8* yci co.t. *A11* ce. cite co.v. *A12* cy de v. et de t. *B, B1* ce.co.v. *B2* g.c. de iherusalem deca a lencontre de v. et de f. les aultres mes *B5* ce. par deca co.t. *B7* ce. citez co.t. *A10* yci co. vostre puissance et *B3, B4, A11* et co. mes 464-469 *B, B1, B2, B3, B4, B5, B7, A6* car la (*B7* car ia la) c. ne v.r. et (*B1, B3* r. ge p. et) pour ce que (*B5* car ia iour de ma vie la c. ne v.r. et aussi que) ne destrues v. (*B2* r. et v.r.p. la cite c. affin que *B3* ne vous destruions et v.) et vostre (*B7* r. ne ia sire ne vous appelleray et affin que ne v. destruyes et ausi vos) gent (*B5* d.v.g.) tournez (*B1* t.d.) vous en le (*B1* en et vous et voz gens le *B4* d. point et v.r. et v.g. le) plus tost que vous pourrez car autrement ferez que fol que mal c.le.d. ne men tourner (*B1* foulx le.d. ne me commande pas me r. mes *B2* g. ne me parles p.d.le. de men r. *B3* c. adont le. luy respondit ne me n.p.r. *B4* folz de r[ ]ne me m.p. queste [ ]ons *B5* fol le. respondit ne me m. que ie men retourne *B7* p. ou vous seres mal c.le. va dire dici non meniray pour toy *A6* le. luy d. ne me commande ia que ie men retourne) mes 465 *A11* c. en nulle maniere et pour ce ie v. *A7, A12* p. ceste c. *A1, A2, A3, A4, A8, A9, A11, A12, A5, A7* s. (*A5, A7* s. certainement) que *A10* s. que pour riens ne v.r. la c. de iherusalem si 465-466 *A10* co. pour le mieulx v. 465-468 *B6* la place et pour ce r. ten adoncques quant le. heust ouy toutes ces choses il d. a p. ne 466 *A11* v. ne v. fassez point d. ne mourir de fain ne de soif mes *A12* voe. point d. 466-467 *A1* que bien advisez et *A8* f. que b. 466-468 *A10* r. car vous serez destruict vous et les vostres le. respondit ne parles p. de r. 466-469 *A11* r. gracieusement en vostre pais l.le.d. ne me dictes p. que ie men retourne en mon pais mes 468 *A8* l. respondit le. *A7* le. ne *A9* et adoncques le.d. a pi. 468-469 *A3* me le m.p. mes *A8* ne me dis point que ie me retournes mes *A9* po. en disant retournez vous en mes *B6* po. que ie men aille mes 469 *A7* ce ne me *B2, A11* moy maintenant et en present (*A11* moy prentement) se *A1* mes vous respondz que me r. la c. *A10* v.r. la cite a 469-470 *A8* vostre s.n. car ie v. *A11* vostre s.n. car se ainsi ne le faictes iay esperance an laide de dieu que bien brief ie lauray a ma plaisance et vous prometz que *A12* vostre s.n. et ie vous promes si vous ne le faitte v. *A13* vostre s. que ie suis car ie vous promet que *B6* la ville ou non aussit que tu le doys faire que a ton s. *B1, B, B3, B4, B5, B7, A6* cite ainsi co. (*B, B7* cite co.) tu doys fere a ton s. en (*B3* ton droiturier s. et si aultrement en fais ie te promet en) telle maniere que v. ne (*B4* que ia *B7* que de toy ne de) h. 469-476 *B2* r. ceste cite a faire ma voulente ainsi come tu dois fayre a ton s. et p. luy respondit que la cite ne luy rendroyt point ne ne le appelleroyt p.s. et luy dist quil sen allast de la et quil feroyt de luy ce quil cuidoit f. de luy et quil ne le prisoyt pas ung denier le.

seigneur. Et sy vous dis bien que vous ne home qui soit la dedens ne trouvera ja mercy a moy." Lors dist Pilate: "Par Dieu, vous parlé[s] bien folement, car sachiez que je ne vous reconnois point pour seigneur, ne [43r] siens n'entrerés vous, mes vous deffie dore/navant. Et sy sachiés que je feray de vous ce que vous cuidiés fere de moy. Et pour ce je ne tiens compte de vous."

[31] Lors l'empereur se partit de la sans plut mot dire et s'en vient en sa tente et compta a Titus, son filz, se que Pilate lui avoit respondu ne dist. Et

470 *A1* s. toutesfois ie v. *A11* h. ne femme qui 470-471 *A8* d. naura ia m. de moy *A11* d. ne prendray a m.l. *A12* soit naura m. de moy l. luy d. *A10* que nulz de vous naura m.l. 470-474 *B6* dy car toy ne h. aussit ne fame ie ne prandre a m. adoncques p. si luy d. ia la place ne te rendray et ne tappelle p. mon s. car il me semble que ie suis ausyt grant maistre come toy et pour ce alles vous en toulx le plus toust que vous pourres et vous feres que saige car se vous y demoures guere ie f. de toy et de tous tes gens se *A13* h. de ceste cite nauray m. de moy adoncques p.d. ie v.d. et fere de *B, B1, B3, B4, B5, B7, A6* s. la d. (*B5* s.d.) ne (*B3* d. la citey ne prendray a m.) ia (*B1* m.p. respondit a lempereur ia *B4, A6* m.p. respondit ia) la (*B3* m.p. luy respont iay la *B5* m.p. respondit la *B7* m.p. respondit point la) cite ne vous rendray ne ia sire ne (*B5* r. ie ia ne ia ne) vous appelleray en luy disant alez (*B3* d. encore al. *A6* luy dit al.) vous en dicy (*B5* ap.al. *B7* r. ore vous en al. dici) car ie (*B5* dicy ou ie) *B3* dicy ou aultrement ie) f. 471 *A2, A3, A4, A5, A7, A9* m. en moy *A1* m. en moy et p. lui d. par *A7, A11* p.v. *A8* d. sire v. 471-472 *A2, A3, A4, A5, A7, A9, A10, A11* pa. (*A11* pa. trop) f. 472 *A2* ie ie ne *A12* v. rendray ia la cite ne v.r. *A1* pour mon s. 472-473 *A11* s. que la cite ne vous renderay ie point ne ia sire ne vous clameray mes *A10* point mes *A12* s. mes *A1* ne aussi ny e. 473 *A2, A4* e.v. point mes *A7* s. ne aultrement mes *A11* de. a oultrance et se vous en aller en brief dicy s. 474 *B5* de v. ainsi que *A10, A12* moy car (*A12* car certainement) ie *A8* et ne 474-476 *B7* que pensez f. de moy le. *A4* moy l. *B, B4, B5, A6* de moy car vous ne voz gens ne prise un denier froisse le. *B6* et qui plus est ie ne v. prise rien adoncques le. 474-477 *A11* moy car vous ne voz gens ne prise ung denier froisse apres ces rudes parolles dictes par le prevost pilate sen retourna le. en sa terre et dist a 474-478 *B1, B3* de moy car (*B3* de nous car) vous ne voz gens ne prise ung denier avoire le. sen retourna dilec (*B3* p. ie pas un d. froisie a ceste parolle p.le. dilec) et sen retourna a ses t. et c. touts ces chouses a son f.t. et il en eut moult g. plaisir et (*B3* e.i. et luy) d. 474-495 *A13* moy adoncques le.d. a i. quil 475-476 *A9* v. ne de vostre puissance l. 476 *A8, A10* p. (*A10* p. de pillate) s. *A12* la et et sen allast devers sa *A7* p. nul mot *A10* d. ne sonner et *A1, A2, A5, A7, A9* v. a sa 476-477 *A12* et dist a son f.t. se 476-478 *B6* p. luy et toulx ces gens et sen allerent vers leurs t. la ou estoit t. son f. et puis apres quant il fut avise il c. a son f. toute la response que luy a. faicte pilate et quant t.e. ouy la response de pilate il e. *B, B2, B4, B5, B7, A6* p. dilecques et (*B2, A6* de la et *B4* p. et) sen retourna a ses t. et c. toutes ces choses a son f.t. et (*B2* a t. son f. empereur et) en (*B5* t. lequel titus en) eut moult g. plaisir et (*B7* t. ausy parellement au seigneurs doing il eurent g. ioye et *B4* et g. ioye et *B5* m.g. ioye et) d. (*B2* et luy d. ainsi) b. 477 *A10* et commenca a compter a son *A2* r. et *A12* a.d. et 477-478 *A8, A9, A10* a.d. et r. et (*A10* r. adonc) t. *A3* r. et dont t.e. *A11* a.d. dont t.e.

Titus en eüst grant joye et dist: "Benoyt soit Jhesu Crist, car il ne veut que le traïtre Pilate viengne a vostre mercy. Car je me doubtoye que vous ne ly priciés. Mes je croy que dorenavant il ne trouvera nulle mercy a vous ne plus que Jhesu Crist la trouva en luy. Et sachiés que Dieu veut qu'il soit eincy pour ce que Pilate soufri que Jhesu Crist prist pacion et sy en fust conscens, et sy disoit il qu'il ne trouvoit nulle raison pour quoy il deüst mourir. Et toutesfois le juga il a mort, pour quoy lui et toute la cité venroit a destruction."

478 *A10* e. moult g.i.b. *A11* s. dieu i. *B6* d. par ceste maniere a son pere mon pere et mon seigneur d.s. loue car *B, B1, B2, B3, B4, B5, A6* s. dieu i.c. quant (*B3* d.q.) il (*B2* c. qui) ne *A12* s. dieu car 478-479 *A10, A3* car ie ne veulx pas que ce (*A3* v. que le) t.

478-484 *B7* c. quant p. ne voeul venir a m. mais dici en avant ne satende que lon te prende a merci ne quil aist merci de i. car luy et ses gens en v. 478-486 *B6* v. point car p. aye misericorde mais de mort mays il na que faire de en t. en p. quil eust misericorde de i.c. quat il le iuga a mort faulcement et sans cause car luy mesmes d. ie ne t.n. cause de mort sur cest prophete lequel vous maves mene et pour ce luy et t. eulx de la c. qui sont v. adoncques apres toux ces choses ceulx de lost lesquelx g. 479 *A8* ie ne me *A10* car moult ie *A11* v. a nous a m. *A12* a nostre m. *B5* le faulx t. *A2* t. iudas ne v. a m. *A8* que que v. luy 479-480 *A1, A9, A12* ne le preissiez a (*A12* ne leussies pris a) mercy mes *A7* v. le p. *A10* ly promissiez mes 479-481 *A11* iavoie grant paour que vous le prenissiez a mercy mais dicy en avant ne se actende p. que on le preigne a mercy plus quil eut mercy de i. et s. seigneurs que soit *B, B1, B2, B3, B4, B5, A6* a m. mais dicy (*B2* m. et pour ce dycy) en (*B5, A6* m. dores en) avant (*B4* m.a.) ne se atende que le (*B3* ne satendrait plux que lon le) preigne a mercy (*B2* av. il ne devroyt trouver m.) nyent p. que leut de (*B1* quil eut mercy de *B5* quilz ont eu mercy de) i. (*B4* quil fist a i.) c. et s. seigneur (*B2* s.s. se dit tittus) que d. 480 *A12* c. bien que *A8, A12* il nara n.m. de par (*A12* m.a.) v. *A7* m. en v. 480-481 *A10* que iamais il naura m. nen p. quil ot de i.c. et s. tout pour vray que d. tout puissant le v. *A2, A3, A4* m. en v. neant p. *A5, A9* t.m. en v. neant p. *A7* v. ne que i.c. ne t. 481 *A12* sa. certainement que 481-483 *B2* d.v. que e.s. et vous scaves p. a este c. de la mort du doulx i.c. et le iuga a mort nonobstant que en luy il ne 482 *A11* e. fait car p. *A10* que le felon p. *A8* quil s. la mort de i.c. et en *A1* quil pr. 482-483 *B, B1, B3, B4, B5, A6* e. car il s. que on tuast (*B4* on ly t.) son (*B1* e. il vouloit que on trahist il vouloit que on trahist trahist son) filz i.c. et pilate en fut c. de (*B5* et c. en f.p. de) le iugier a tort et (*B1, B3, B4, B5, A6* a mort et) d. il (*B4* d. bien) quil *A12* s. et f.c. de la pa. et mort de i.c. et aussy d. *A3* pa. dont il f.c. nonobstant quil d. *A10* c. souffrit mort et pa. et mesmes d. *A11* pr. mort et pa. et le iuga a mort a tort et sans cause et luy d. 483 *A8* c. combien quil d. *A3, A4* t. en luy n. *B, B3, B4, B5, A1, B2, A6, A10* t.r. en luy (*B1* t. cause en luy *B2* t. cause ne r. *A6* t. en luy *A10* t. cause) p. *A1, A9* n. cause (*A9* c. ne r.) p. 483-484 *A11* t. en luy cause de mort mais nonobstant ce le condempna il de sa faulce bouche a mourir villainement en la croix p. *A4* q. lui 483-485 *B2* q. il le d. iugier a mort et p. ce ie comment que la c. en v. a toute d. 484 *A10* lui et ses gens et t. la *A12* a morir en la croyx p. *A11* lui et t. ceulx de la *A3* t. puis le *A1* et nonobstant ce le *B1, B, B3, B4, B5, A6* m. et luy et ses (*B* et t. ses) gens et t. (*A6* luy et t.) la (*B* g. a la) c. en v.

[32] Et quant Titus eüst dist cella, les vallés et pages qui guardoient les chivaux vont venir a l'empereur et lui distrent comment il cheviroient d'eau, car a quinze miles de la ne pouvoit on trouver eau pour abrever les chevaux ne les autres bestes, ne ne treuvent chose que leur soit necessaire. "Car quant nous partons pour aler abrever a l'aube du jour, il est plus de none ansois que nous retournons, car nous ne trouvons ou abruver, se se n'est au fleuve du Deable ou il perirent deux cités, Sodoma et Gomorra.

486 *B, B1, B2, B3, B4, B5, B7, A6* t.e. (*B2* t. lempereur e.) ainsi parle vindrent adonc ceulx (*A6* v.c. *B1* v. apres c. *B2* p. a vasparien son pere a.v.c. *B4, B7* p.a.v.c.) qui *A2* d. les *A8* e.c.d. les *A10* e.c.d. les p. *A9* les paresremers et les v. qui 486-487 *A11* e. ainsi parle les gardeux de chaulx parges et autres v.v. *A12* e. parle les grans crys des gens darmes v.p. chevaulx et autres v.v. 487 *A1, A10* lui demanderent c. 487-488 *A5* le. comme ilz feroient deau *B1, B2, B3, B4, B5, B, A6* c. et tous les autres bestes de son ost et (*B, B2* c. de son o. et t. les b. et) d. (*B5* o. puis d. *A6* et adonc d.) a lempereur seigneur (*B4* e. mon s.) que ferons nous car dicy a q. leues (*B4* a sept l.) ne (*B, B3, B5* q.m. ne *A6* n. quant de cy a q.m. ne) pourrions t. (*B3* a vingt et ung m. nous ne trouverons) eau pour a. *B6* v.v. pars devers le. et d. a le. seigneur que ferons nous diau il est vray que nous ne povons t. *A11* d. sire que ferons nous car dicy a 487-491 *B7* c. et aultrez bestez en disant seigneurs ou prendrons nous de. pour boyre nos chevaulx car dici a deuxs iournee de. ne pouvons t. et se p. au matin il seroist nuistz avant que retournissions car 488 *A9* la qui valent vij heures et demye ou environ on *A10* q. lieues de *A12* m. lieuues de *A11* m. ne povons t. *A5* la on ne p.t. pour 488-489 *A10* on point on t. ne les *B6* t. eau plus pres que a demye iournee dicy et vous scaves bien que n. 488-490 *A11* les b. et q. *B, B1, B2, B3, B4, B5, A6* les bestes car elles ne pourroient durer (*B2* pas longuement durer *B3* p. plux d.) que (*A6* p. vivre sens boyre que) elles ne morussent de seuf car (*B5* b. et ne pourrions gueres d. en ce point sans mourir car se n. (*B1* b. car si n. *B2* car q.n.) p. a (*B1, B2* p. dicy a) la. 489 *A5* b. ne pevent trouver c. *A10* b. aussi ne c. *A12* b. ne nous ne trouvons c. qui nous s. 490 *A4, A11, A12, A9* p. a la. du i. pour al.ab. (*A9* la. et point du i.p.) il *B2* il sera leure de 490-491 *A1* il passe n. *B, B1, B3, B4, B5, A6* i. avant que revenission seroit (*B1, A6* que nous feussions retournez il) my iour (*B3, A6* s. iiij i. *B4* s.i. *B5* i. nous ne saurions retourner quilz ne fussent quatre i.) passe car

490-496 *B6* p. au matin il seroit nuyt quand nous serons retournes et saiches car v.

491 *A1* nous puissions estre retournez car *A4* t. a boire se 491-492 *A7, A10* n. soyons retournes et fault aller au *A8* nous soyons retournes et fault aller au *A11* r. et nen saurions trouver plus pres que le f. *B, A6, A12, B1, B2, B3, B4, B5, B7* t. eau se (*A6* t. autre se *B5* t. si) non au (*B1* non le *B2* t. point de. iusques au *A12* e. decza le) f. 491-493 *A10* r.a. y car nullement lo. 492 *B7* ou parellement pillez d. *A2, A4, B2* c. cestassavoir s. 492-493 *A5* de.p. *A11* il nous fault aller p.

492 *le fleuve du Deable* Assuming that the traditional geographical location of Sodom and Gomorrah (see note to line 455) is correct, this river would be located 15 miles east of Jerusalem, near the northernmost shores of the Dead Sea. It may designate the Dead Sea itself. See Gryting (note to line 921).

Pour quoy, Sire, avisez y, car autrement l'ost ne pouroit durer ne vivre sy nous n'avions de eau plus pres." Et quant l'empereur l'oÿ, il en eüst grant merveilles et dist a Jafet de Cafe qu'il pouroient fere. Et Jafet luy dist: "Sire, vous avés grant foyson de bestes comme de beux, vaches, brifors et

493 *A2* a. il car *A12* a. sire que ferons car *A5, A7* a. y car (*A5* a. car) certainement lost *A8* y au. *A3* y sire car *A1* car lost ne p. a d. *A11* d. se 493-494 *B1, B2, B3, B4, B5, B7, B, A6* q.s. (*B4* q. mon s.) lost (*B7* q. lost) ne puet (*B3, B4, B5* ne se p.) longuement tenir (*B* s. ne se p. grandement t. *B2* s. il nest pas possible que lost se puisse plus gueres icy t.) si n. *A12* d. en n. *A11* d.q. 494 *A9* plus quelle nest et *A1* plus que nous navons q.le. oy ce que les paiges disoient il *A9* le. ot ouy ces paroles il *A1* a. aultrement de 494-495 *A12* le. oyt les raisons et paroles de ses gens il fust moult fort esbay et *B1, B2, B3, B4, B5, B7, A6* plus et q.le. oyt ce il e. (*B* p.le.q. eut ce o.e.) moult g.m. (*B2* il fut mo. esbahis *B3* il fut mo.me. *B4* e.g.me. *B7* le. ouist ces parollez ilz fust forment esbahy) et *A10* loy si sesmerveilla moult et demanda a *A11* il fut grandement esmerveille si demanda a i. conseil conment il p. mectre remedde en ceste chose et il luy

495 *A1, A9,* c. quel chose (*A9* c. que sur ce) il 495-496 *A12* i. comment il se cheviroyent de eaue pour abevrer les chevaulx et les autres bestes et i.d. lempereurs s. *B1* i. dit c. quel conseil il donnoit et d. ie donne en conseil v.a. prou et assez de *B5* i. quel conseil il donrroit sur le fait lequel luy respondist seigneur ie vous donnrray bon conseil il est vray que v.a. assez de b. bouffles b. et bonnes vaches et *A3, A10* et i. luy respondit (*A10* i.r.) s. *A13* f. deaue lequel respondit s. 495-497 *B2, B, B3, B4, B7, A6* c. quel conseil il donneroyt de ce et iassel luy respondit ainsi mon seigneur d. il v. (*B3* d. et il d. ie vous donray moult boin conseil v.) a. largement de (*B* co. ilz donrons et il d. que vous donne en co.v.a. prou de *B4* co.v.a. prou de *A6* d. et d. il vous donra bon conseil v.a. preu de) v.b. et de c. (*B3* a. assez b.c. beufs v. bourffres et chamoix *B7* d. et il d. ie vous donne en co. veust que a. beaucoup de v. boeuf et cameaulx *B, B4* v. bouffres et chameaux *B2* v. de baissons de cameaulx et daultres bestes) f. 496 *B4* sire (MS ends) *A9* g. multitude et f. *A1* a. beaucoup de *B6* g. quantite de *A2* de beus br. buffles v. et *A9* c. sont beux 496-497 *A13* f. de b. de buches et c. *A8* v. et toureaulx et auxy de *A10* v. et griffons et c. *A11* v. et de c. *A7* v. et pourceaulx f. *A12* v. buffons chameaulx f. 496-498 *B1* v. bouffuers et chameaulx f. apparailler les cuirs et quilz soient bien nez et puis les f.c. ensemble lung 496-504 *B4* et chamoiz bien s.m. quilz tuerent et salerent la cher et les cu. firent boulir et mectre a point et en couvrerent la valee

496-515 *B6* v.ch. et autres bestes pour ce ne vous prions quil vous plaise trouver auchun bon consoil sur cecy et touchant ce que nous parlons adoncques lempereur se esmerveilla moult et demanda ou estoyt gay son senschal et tantost gay vint par devers lempereur et lempereur luy dist quil vouloit tenir son conseil et incontinent iasel du tassel lequel estoit saige home dist son oppinion tout le premier et dist qui donoit en conseil a lempereur qui f.e. beufz et vaches et grant puissance et que les ch. fussent salees p. son o. et qui fist ioureyot les cu. et quil fussent conreees bien a point et puis que on eust iii ou iiii c. chevaulx que ne fussent aultre chose que ailleuer car dedans la valee de iosephat et adoncques lempereur creust son conseil et tantoust fust fait et luy dona a luy mesmes la chairge du fait et de fere venir leau et en ung peu de temps ladicte valee f.p. dyaue ausset chancre c. de f. par la grace de dieu alors g.p. vit que la v. estoit aussit p. il fust moult esbay et moult coroce et

496 *brifors* This noun is not recorded in Godefroy, Tobler-Lommatzsch, nor in the *Französisches Etymologisches Wörterbuch*. The other MSS of families A and B have: *brisons* (*A1*), *buffles* (*A2,B4,B5*), *buffors* (*A3,A9*), *bouffres* (*A6,B*), *griffons* (*A10*), *buffons* (*A12*),

de chevaus. Fettes en escorchier grant foison et saler les chars pour les gens de l'ost. Et faites bien conroier les cuirs, et puis les fettes coudre l'un en l'autre et les fettes estendre au val de Jozafat. Et fettes aprester grant foison de somniers qui portant tant d'eau du fleuve du Deable que tout le
[43v] val en soit plain." Et l'empereur et Ti/tus tindrent son conseil a bon. Et

497 *A2* e. assez et *A9* e. quantite g. et f. *A10*, *B2* e. une partie (*B2* e. asses et) faictes s. *A12* et que les c. soient bien s.p. *A13* f. les tuer et s. 497-498 *A6*, *B* f. adoubez les cuers et qui soient bien nest et p. *B5* en adouber et appeiller les cuirs et quilz soient bres bien netz et p. *A13* p. lost *A10* de vostre ost *B7* s. de le affin quelle se puissent bien garder bonne a menger puis f. aparellez les f. coudre lun *B3* en conrer lez cuyers et quilz soient bien netz et puis les f. coudre lun 497-499 *B2* chars et adouber les c. tant quilz soyent bien netz et apres les f. tondre les ungs avec les a. et faictes bien cuere et nectoyer le val 498 *A10* f. le cu.co. si les *A13* et co. *A11* et nectment appareillez p. *A12* f. appareiller les cu. et qui soient b.c. et puys lon le fera coudre *A13* cu. et iceulx co. *A1* p. les f. lrendre ensamble lun 499 *B*, *B1*, *B3*, *B5*, *A6* et f. curer le val *A1* f. estanc ou *A12* les ferons e. *A13* et e. *A5* i. et prenez g. *A7* i. et f.g. *A12* i. et puis ferons a. 499-500 *B7* a. en telle meniere que puissent porter e. dedens puis apres faictez curer la vallee de iosaphat apres faictez appareillez assez s. *A9* i. et aussy f. appareillier et a.g. nombe et f. *B5* i. et puis aprez fe. appareillier fo. *B*, *B1*, *B3*, *A6* i. et f. apareiller preu de (*B3* a.g. nombrez de *A6* a. moult de) s. *B2* i. et puys apres f.a. plusieurs s. *A2* g. nombre de 499-501 *A13* i. tellement quil en 500 *A7* de sermes quil *A12* de bestes s. *A6* p.de. *B1*, *B2*, *B3*, *B*, *A12* p. (*B* p. de *A12* p. tous les iours de) le. *A5* deau de celluy f. que *A1* d. tant que le *A12* d. tant que 500-501 *B7* p.le. dedans faut que ladite vallee s. 500-502 *A10* p.e.t. que le val en puis estre p. et vous arez de leaue asses et quant le. et son filz orent oy ce que iaffet avoit dit ilz t. a bon c. et f. inconinent e. des b. iusques a.s. *B*, *B1*, *B2*, *B3*, *B5*, *A6* d. pour amplir la valee (*B2* d. ou v.) de iosafap et (*B1* pour nous servir deaue et) quant le. ot oy le c. (*B2* ouy ce c.) il le tient a moult (*B1* m. saige et m.) bon et (*B2* t. pour bon et proffitable et *A6* t. pour bon et) tantost f.e. buefz (*B2* ta. il commanda que on escourchast b.) vaches bouffres et chameaux (*B2* c. iusques ou nombre de *B3* c. bien *B5* beufs et b. chevaulx iusques a) lx. 501 *A11*, *A12* et quant le. *A2*, *A5*, *A7*, *A9* t. son filz tin. *A9* val de iosaphat en s. emply et le. 501-502 *A11* t. son filz eurent ouy le bon conseil de iaffet ilz t. a bon et tantost lempereur f. *A12* t. son filz oyrent ce que iaffet avoit dit et il ont tenuz a bien dit et tantost lon fist e. beufs vaches brissons chevaulx et chameaulx bien xxx m. 501-505 *A13* p. et iceulx lieu emplir tout deauue ainsin fut fait iaphet fut commis pour f. 501-510 *B7* p.le. eust ouy le conseil de iaphet il tint pour bon et tantost commanda a iaphet quil fist faire ce quil avoit conseillez et ainsi le fit et ne tarda gueres quelle ne f.p. quant lempereur eust ouy le conseil de iaphet il le tint pour bon et se gardast le. tout o.b. que celle eust crust audit lieu et ladite e. estoict o.b. que celle eust estez de

---

*bouffuers* (*B1*), *baissons* (*B2*), *bourffres* (*B3*), *boeuf* (*B7*). The etymon *bubulos* has probably been influenced by the verb *brifauder*, which in the thirteenth and fourteenth centuries had the meaning "eat voraciously, devour".

499 *au val de Jozafat* The only biblical reference to the Valley of Jehoshaphat is to be found in Joel 3:2, 12, a chapter in which several of the themes of our narrative occur: the captivity of Judea and Jerusalem, the selling of the people, a diaspora, etc. The Valley began immediately south-east of the Old City of Jerusalem (i.e., between the Temple of Solomon and the Mount of Olives), then ran due north along the wall of the city, turning west between Jerusalem and Mount Scopus. See also Gryting (note to line 929) and Eustache (pp. 7-9).

lors il firent escorcher de leur bestes que d'une que d'autre soisante mile, et puis firent seler les char et conreer les cuirs et coudre ensemble et les firent estandre par le val de Jozafat. Et quant le val fust tout prest, l'empereur dist a Jafet qu'il pensast de fere venir l'eau et d'emplir le val, car il l'en encharghoit de tous poins. Lors Jafet fit aprester deux mile chevaux qui pourtoient chescun eau du fleuve du Deable au val, tant qu'il fust tout plain. Et Dieu voscit que le val tenoit ossy bien comme s'il fust tout de une piece. Et l'eau ce tenoit ossy bonne et ossy nette comme ce elle fust de fontaine.

502 *A2* a. bien s. 502-503 *A11* e. que beufz que vaches et que veaulx bien s. 503 *A1, B5* p.s. *B1* et furent salez les *A7* lez lard et *A12* char et bien co. *A1* cuirs et lrendre e. *A8* cuirs et firent c. *A10* coudre tous e. *A12* coudre lung apres lautre e. *A2, A9* cuirs et puis (*A9* p. apres) les 503-504 *A11* char et adouber les cu. et nectoier la vallee *B, B1, B3, B5, A6* char et les cuirs firent adouber et (*B3* f. conreer et) curer la (*B1* c. furent appareillez et fut cuvee la) vallee de iosafap et q. 503-505 *B2* char et les cu.f. adober bien nectement et firent moult diligemment curer la vales de iozaphaz et le. 504 *A1* e. au val *A9* t. couvert et p. 504-505 *B, B1, B3, B5, A6, B4, A11, A12* f. curee (*B4* fust converte *A11* f. bien c. et nectoyee *A12* f. bien apprestee et bien appareillie et) le. *A8* t. plain le. 505 *B4, B5* i. du tassel quil *B5* f. bonne diligence de f.v. *A1* f.le. *A1* et quil fist e. 505-506 *A11* eau et de les couldre et mectre audit val et que de ce luy donnoit la charge en t. 505-507 *A10* val et que la charge lui en donnoit adont i. feist tantost appareille d.m. sommiers qui *B, B1, B2, B3, B4, B5, A6* leau car il luy en donna la charge adonc i. (*B4, B5* i. du cassel) f. appareiller d. (*B2* f. aprester d.) m. chameaux (*B2* m. somieres *A6* m. chevaux) qui 506 *A12* e. qui le fist du tout et i.f. tantost a. *A13* e. et avoit chascun iours d. *A7* il luy chargoit de tout l. *A9* il ly en donnoit la charge de 506-507 *A11* m. chameaulx et c. 507 *A12* c. et chameaulx qui *A9* qui chascun iour p. de leau *B2* qui tous les iours aprestoyent leau et le mectoyent dedans la val de iosaphas quant ilz lavoyent apportee du f. *A13* c.p.e. iusques il *B, B1, B3, B4, B5, A6* p. eau tous (*B5* p.t.) les iours du *A11* c. iour leau *A10* p. leau au f. au val de iozaphat tant *A6* a la valee de iosaphault t. *B4, B5* d. iusques en (*B5* d. leaue en) la valee de iosaphat t. *B2* d. et icelle vallee t. 507-508 *A12* p. leau c. iour sanz cesser du f. du d. et la faisoit mettre en la val comme se f. ung estang en tant que la val f. *B, B1, B3, A2* val de iosafap t. quil (*A2* t. quil quil) f. *A8* quil soyt p. comment sil eust este t. *A9* oudit val de iosaphat t. que cellui val f.p. 508 *A1* et par le plaisir de d. le *B, B1, B3* et la valee t. *A6* f.p. et la vallee t. *A10* quil t.a.b. eaue c. *A12* et elle t. si b. *A13* et t.o.b. ledit vault e.c. *A1, A6, B, B1* b. eaulve c. 508-509 *A11* p. en pou de temps et t. la vallee o.b. leau par le moyen des cuirs c. *A1* f. de *A11* f. une citerne et voulut dieu que le. se 508-510 *B5* et t. la vallee o.b. eaue c. une cisterne et leau fut o.b.c.fo. *B, B3, A6* f. une (*B3* f. este une) citerne et dieu vouloit que elle fust tant b. (*B3* f.o.b. *A6* f. ainsi b.) c. de *B2* f. une cisterne car il estoyt ainsi le playsir de dieu et estoyt o.b.le.c. dune belle fo. 508-511 *B4* et la valee t.b. eaue c. en une cisterne et *B1* f. vuellue et 509 *A10* t. entier dune pie et tout dune piece et le. y fut o. *A8* et se t. leau o. *A12* et dieu vouloit que leau *A1* o.n. et o.b.c. *A9* b. clere et n. *A12* o.n. et o.n. et aussy clere et o.b.c. *A13* et dieu le voloit de sa grase quelle fut tousiours tant cler c. 509-510 *A5* une pierre et 510 *A11* f. en une fo. 510-511 *B7* fo.p. et le roy a.q. il v.

[33] Et quant Pilate et le roy Archelain virent le val tout plain d'eau, il se esbahirent fort et penserent incontinent que Jafet avoit donné le conseil, car il estoit moult saint home et plaing de grant engin. Et lors Pilate s'esbahy par telle maniere qu'il vousist estre hors de Jherusalem a ung pié. Et se repenti moult car il n'avoit rendu la cité a l'empereur. Et le roy Archilain et Barlabam, qui lui avoient donné le conseil, le conforterent et

511 A1 q. le roy a. et p.v. A2, A3, A5, A7, A8, A9 a. et ceulx de iherusalem v. A12 a. et les autres gens de la cite de iherusalem v. A11 q. le roy a.p. et ceulx de iherusalem v. A13 q. ceulx de la cite v. si grant multitude deau B, B2 p. et le roy a.q. (B2 a. et toz ceulx de iherusalem) v. A10 v. que le val tenoit aussi bien eau B4, B, B1, B5, B7, A6, A12, A11 val de iozaphat t. (A12, A11 i. B7 i. tant) p. B2 val ainsy emplye deau 511-512 A1 ilz furent tous esbahis et A11 il ne fault ia a demander sil furent esmerveillez si se p. B3 val de iosaphath t.p. il eurent moult grant merveille et p. bien que B, B4 eau eurent moult grandes merveilles et (B4 eau ilz furent grandment esmerveilliez et) p. bien que i. du cascel leur a. B7 e. furent tous esbahis et se p. bien que A6, B2, B5 il heurant moult grant merveilles et (B2 g. paour et) et p. bien que (B5 ilz prindrent g.m. et b.p. que) i. du cassel leur (B2, B5 c.) a. A12 ilz se vont moult f. esbays et p. tantost que B1 se esmerveillerent moult f. et p. bien que 511-513 A13 ilz se p. bien que ce fut par le c. de i. qui e. 512 A9, A10 e. moult f. (A10 m.) et A2, A8 p. (A8 p. fort) que A10, B1, B3 i. (B1, B3 i. de cassel) leur a. 512-513 B2 c. de fayre ainsi car 512-515 B5 c. adont p. se r. quil 513 A10 car moult e.s. A7 m. saige h. A11 e.h.m. subtil et de A12 s. iuif et A9 de tres g. entendement et e. A1 engin et p. 513-514 A11 engin et esaprllement p. sen e. moult fort et eust voulu e. A10 engin tellement quil eust bien voullu e. A12 pi. en son cuer v. 513-515 B1, B, B3, B4, B7, A6 e. ung saige (B e. bien s.) h. et de g. conseil adonc (B7 h.a.) se r. (B3, B7 r. de ce) quil B2 m. saige h. et de g. conseil adonc p. fut moult espovante et se r. quil A13 et saige adoncques p. se r. de ce quil 514 A2 m. a 514-515 A11, A12 de la cite et A1, A7, A8, A10 i. et A9 pie perdu et 515 A8 r. fort quil A10 r. quil A12 r. car A11 rep. grandement quil na. des le conmancement r. A9 m. grandement de ce quil A3 rendu a le. la c. et le A13 rendu les cles de iherusalem a B5 a. donne et r. la c. le B1 a la voulonte de le. A13 le. et voulsisse estre horrs de la cite et 515-516 B, A6, B1, B3, B4, A11, A12 e. et son seneschal (B3 et le s.) b. qui (B4, A11, A12 et b.s. de p. qui A6 qui lui B1 s. abraham qui) av. A10 le. adonc le roy a. virent que le val tenoit aussi bien et son seneschal b. 515-517 B6 rep. de la responce quil avoit faicte a lempereur et se esbaissoit moult qui avoit done ce conseil a lempereur adoncques b. qui estoyt senechal de pylate dist car cestoit iasel de tassel car il savoit bien quil estoit moult saige home et alors pilate se desconfortoit et estoit tout trouble et le r.a. le va reconforter en luy disant mon seigneur pi. 516 B2 et son seneschal b. le vindrent reconforter et B, B1, B3, B4, B5, A6 conseil volurent renconforter p. (B3 r.) et A11 conseil de non la rendre le c. au mieulx quilz povoient et A12 conf. moult fort et 516-517 A13 b. le seneschault lan c. disant ne v. A1 conf. et lors d. B7 conseil a pillate le volloient reconforter en luy disant p.

lui distrent: "Sire, Pilate, pour quoy vous esbahissés? Car si l'empereur avoit yssy [a] demourer avec tout son host set ans, sy n'aroit il de quoy il peüst avoir la cité par force. Et ossy il ne peüst pas estre yssy longuement. Pour quoy je vous dis que vous y averés honneur." Et quant Jacob ouÿ ces paroles, il lé tint a grant folie et dist a Pilate: "Sire, je me merveille

517 *A6, B, B1, B2, B3, B4, B5* d.p. *A11* pi. neant v. *A1* e. vous car 517-518 *A11* e. vous ne donnez malaise car si le. et t. son h.a.d.y. sep *A1* e. vouloit y. *A8, A12* le. avec t. (*A12* le. et t.) son h. avoit y.d. vij 517-519 *B, B1, B2, B3, B4, B5, A6* v. espovantez vous car se le. et tout son h. avoient este sept ans (*A6* e. six a.) icy si (*B1, B2* e.i.s.a. si) ne pourroient prendre (*B5* ne nous pourroit il grever ne premdicier) la *B7* lem. estoit s. ans devant celle citez il ne la porroist poinct prendre et savez que tant longuement ne 517-527 *A13* e. riens de cesy car le. ne pourroit avoir iherusalem non pas la tierche partie du monde alencontre de la chevallerie quest ceans adoncques iacob dist a pilate rendez la c. et ilz noz prengnent a m. *B6* v. espouventes vous saichez car sil avoit toute leau du monde car auroue il ne sarroist nullement prandre ceste ville en cept ans et vous pouves bien pancer car il ne pourroit demourer par si longue espace de temps pour quoy il ne me semble point que vous aies cause de vous doulloir mes aincoys vous deves faire bone chere et sy suis certain que nul home qui soit ou monde ne sarroit nullement prandre celle ville par force adoncques iacob lequel estoit punt alors que archillant dysoit ces parolles iacob qui estoit vray catholique et bon chrestien parla alors a pilate et luy dist devant toulx ces gens mon seigneur pylate ie suis bien esbay comment vous croies telles parolles car vous poves estre certain car vous ne pourries longuement tenir aulencontre du lampereur certes ie ne scay qui se consoil vous ha donne mais vous estes mal conseille de faire lempereur vostre ennemy mortel adoncques pylate le va regarder par despit et luy va dire tory iacob ty renoye n. loy et nous dieulx ien suis certain non (MS ends) 518 *A9, A2, A5, A7* a.d.y. (*A2, A5, A7* a.y.d.) avec 518-519 *A10* a.d. cy vij ans avoit son h. si ne pourroit il avoir *A1* h. ung an si ne polroit il avoir *A11* si ne pourroient ilz la c. prendre par *A8* il paour davoir *A12* ar. force pour ce quil eust ceste c. 519 *B, B1, B2, B3, B4* et il *B5* et sachiez que ne *A1* ne demoura pas l. *A7* p.y.e.l. *A12* pas y. demourer l. 519-520 *A6* et il ne pourroyent tant tenir le siege icy devant quant *A11* et il ne pourroient pas tant tenir le siege devant nous par quoy ie vous dis que en la fin y aurons nous grant h. et naiez ia paour de ce que vous voiez et *B, B1, B2, B3, B4, B5* pas tant tenir y. le (*B1* tant y.t. le *B2* t. le *B3* tant y.t. son) siege devant (*B1* d. nous *B4* t. le s.y.d. et lors *B5* t. le s. cy d.) quant *B7* e. devant nous et quant 520 *A12* q. certainement nous y aurons tous grant h. *A9* que la fin v. *A10* que andiruier v. *A8* h. car il sen hyra honteusement par deffaulte de vivres et dargent et *A11* i. qui estoit la ouy 520-521 *A12* i. pere de marie iacobi oyt cecy il *B7* ouy dire ces *B, B1, B2, B3, B4, B5, A6* ouy dire toutes (*B4* o. oyr t.) ces choses il (*B2* d. ces p. et a chascun ainsi son opinion il) d. 521 *A10* a moult g. *A10* pi. ie *B7* il d. 521-522 *A8, A11, A9* m. fort (*A9* m. grandement) c. *B, B1, B3, B4, B5* ie suis moult esbays (*B5* s. bien e.) c. (*B4* s. tout merveilliez c.) v. povez (*B1, B3* c.p.) croire ce (*B4* cr. ceulx de ce) que ilz v. (*B1* que iceulx) d. *A6, B2* ie suis moult esbays co. ceulx icy v. povez (*B2* co.v.p.) croire que ce que il vous dict (*B2* cr. ce que dient ces g.) car 521-523 *B7* ie suis moult esbahi c.v. poves croire se comme v. dictz car vous saves de vray c. que ne porons t. la citez co.

518 *a* Addition from MS *A3*. See variants to this line.

moult comment vous creés se que ces gens vous dient. Car sachiés certainement que nous ne nous pouons tenir contre l'empereur. Mes si vous me voulés croire, je vous donray bon conseil." Et Pilate voult savoir quel conseil il donroit. "Sire, mendés l'empereur que vous lui voulés rendre la cité a en fere tout a sa voulenté. Et je croy qu'il vous penra a mercy." Lors luy dist Pilate: "Tu es escumunés et sy as renié nostre loy. Sy ne te doit hom croire ne ton conseil ossy, car sy l'empereur avoit ceste [44r] cité, tu te tourner[o]ies a / sa loy paygnie. Et bien y pert, car tu luy anvoyas Veronique qui est fauce fame et sorsiere de deables que le ont

522 *A12* m. fort de v.c. vous c. *A10* crees ton que 523 *A12* que vous ne n. *B3* que ie vous donray b.c. se *B1, B4, B2, A6* p. grandement (*B2* p. gueres *A6* p. pas g.) t. *A7* t. a lencontre de le. *A10* p. leur durer c. *A11* t. longuement la cite c. *A12* p. resister c. *A11* mais ie vous donneray bon conseil se *A6, B, B1, B2, B4, B7, B5* mais ie v. (*B5* m. sil v. plaist v.) d. bon c. si 524 *B, B3, B4, B5, A6* c. et *A12* ie v. diray mon avis et *B1, B2* c. dont (*B2* c. ce sera voustre proffit adonc) p. *A11* c. et lors p. *A9* et adoncques p. *A10* d. tres bon *A1* et v.p.s. 524-525 *B7* c. et iacob dictz m. *A10* s. se c. et iacob lui dist s. 525 *B4* c. iacob d. et iacob d. mon s. *A9* il luy d. *A11* il luy vouloit donner et iacob luy dist s. *B2* il luy vouloyt donner iacob et iacob d. par ceste maniere s. *A1* il lui d.s. dist iacob m. a le. *B, B1, B3, B5, A12, A6, A8* d. iacob et iacob (*A6* do. et i.) dist (*A8, A12* do. et i. luy d. *B3* et i. leur d.) s.m. 525-526 *A6, A8, A11, A12, B, B1, B2, B3, B4, B5, B7* lui rendres la *A10* que la c. lui v.r. et en f. a 526 *A1* c. et en ferez t. *A5, A7* c.t. *A12* a f. sa *A2, A6, A11, B, B2, B3, B4, B5, B7* f. a *B1* f. sa *A10* croy pour vray quil 526-527 *B, B1, B2, B3, B4, B5, A6* quil aura m. de vous et p. (*B3* de nous et p. *B2* de nous p. *B4* et tantost p. *B5* et de nous et p.) luy d. (*B1* p.l. *B2* d. ainsi adonc) tu *B7* vous p. lui d. incontinent tu 527 *A12, A11, A13* l.p. luy d. (*A11* d. fierement *A13* p.d. a iacob) tu *A10* m. et adonc p. lui d. moult despitement tu *A9* p. a tres grant fureur et courroux tu *A6* e. quar tu as 527-528 *B2* e. car tu as n. loy r. et ne te devons point cr. *A2, A3, A4, A7, A9* loy et pour ce on ne te d. (*A7* ce d. *A9* d. point) cr. *A6* loy or ne te devons pas cr. ne toy ne *B, B1, B3, B4, B7* loy or ne (*B1* l. et ne *B7* or nous ne) te devon pas cr. *B5* r. ta loy or ne debvons poinct cr. *A13* loy pour quoy lon ne d.cr. ton c. et se 528 *A6, A10* cr. quar *A10* a. pour vray c. *A11* le. de romme a. 529 *A6* tu croyroiez a *B5, B7, B2* te convertiroies a sa (*B2* a aultre) loy *B4* t. de sa *A1* loy et *A8* loy car *B, B1, B2, B3, B4, B5, B7, A6, A11* loy p. et tu luy en (*B2, B5* tu en) as bien monstre (*B1* as assez m.) semblant quant (*B7* en monstras s. car *A11* s. car) tu *A10* tu ne trouveras pour vray a sa paitimerte et *A13* t. vers luys et 530 *A6, B, B1, B2, B4, B5* a. la malvaise (*B2* a. ceste m.) femme (*B5* f.v.) s. *A8* fame et enchanteresse par h. de dyable qui *A12* s. qui 530-531 *A13* s. et ce quelle fait ce par la vertu du d. elle a g. lempereur par *A9* qui ont g. icellui empereur par ses m.h. *A10* est une tres mauvaise femme et tres mauvaise s. qui la g. *A11* v. la mauvaise femme que avoit non v. qui le g. 530-532 *B3, B7* a. la mauvaise femme s. plaine du d. qui avoit nom v. (*B7* d. appellee v.) et puis que tu las ainsi fet *B, B2, B4, B5, A6* d. qui avoit non v. et (*B2, B5* d. et) puis que (*A6* et pour ce que) tu las ainsi fet *B1* d. que se appeloit v. et puis que tu as ainsi f. ie en doy pandre v.

529 *a sa* [ *a a sa*

gueri par ses mauvés hars et par ses mauvés enchantemens. Et quar tu l'as fet, je penray vengence de toy." Et lors il le fist penre et estachier a une grant chayne de fer et sy le fist mettre en une foce grant et parfonde qui estoit en une des plus grans tours du palais.

[34] Et quant Jacob fust en prison male et oubscure, il se reclama moult a Jhesu Crist qui par sa douceur il ne le laissast pas mourir en tel lieu. Et

531 *A12* g. par ses m.e. *A11* h. et e. et poins que tu *A1, A2, A3, A5, A7, A9* e. et pour ce que tu 531-532 *A8* h. et la fet *A10* et e. et si en p. *A13* h. et e. adoncques le 532 *A10* v.l. *A12* l. pilate le *A1* penre et puis le fist e. *A13* penre pilate et lyer a 532-533 *B, B1, B2, B3, B4, B7, A6, A11* et tantost le f.e. a une (*B3* f. loier en une *B7* f. lier a une *A11* f. lyer dune grosse) c. *A12* une c. et le 532-535 *B5* et tantost le f.m. dedans une f. dessoubz le g.p. de iherusalem q. 533 *A13* et m. *A2, A10* une tour p. (*A10* une tres p.f.) qui *A3* une g.f. bien p. *A8* ung g.f. noire et 533-534 *B, B1* m. dedans une crote dessouz le (*B1* une roche soubz le) grant pa. *B2* fist mener et m. en une crocte dessoubz le plus g.pa. *A11* en une citerne dessoubz le pa. *B4* en prison dedans une crote dessoubz le g.pa. *A6* f. dessoubz le f.pa. *A12* une g. tour soubz la grant pa. *B3* une prison obscure dessoubz le g.pa. 533-535 *B7* et avalla soubz terre en une prisons obcure q. 533-537 *A13* f. dessoubz son pa. a grant tourment q. il f. leans questoit moult o. lieu il parla a nostre seigneur que le l. leans m. et q. la f.i. 534 *A3* t. de tout le pa. *A8* une grosse t. *A10* t. qui feus[ ] en tout le pa. 534-535 *A1* e. une des p.g. du p. ou demouroit pilate et leans fu bien enserrez a portes de fer i. qui estoit en 534-536 *A8* pa. lors r.i.m. doucement i.c. estatre en ycelle o.p. que par 535 *A3* en celle p. *B* f. mis en *A9, A12* p. laquelle estoit tres m. et (*A12* e. moult) o. 535-536 *A10* q. il f. en icel p. que par *B, B1, B2, B3, B4, A6* p.o. moult fort (*B4* o.f.) clamoit dieu (*B2* o. il commenca m.f. a reclamer d.) i. (*A6* c.i.) c. *B5, B7* p.o. moult fort clamoit (*B7* m. souvent c.) dieu i.c. en le priant que (*B7* i. que) par *A9* moult fort et de tresbon cueur a nostre seigneur i. *A12* r.i.h. moult doulcement que 535-537 *A11* p. il se escria et r.m. doulcment i.c. en luy priant et requerant que par sa doulce et benigne grace ne le voulsist laisser m. illecques en celluy lieu si obcur et q.m. 536 *A3* c. en luy priant que par *A9* d. et bonte il *A12* d. luy pleust quil *A10* m. et *A12* m. illecques et 536-537 *B, B1, B2, B3, B4, B5, B7, A6* d. il ne voulsist (*B7* ne v. *A6* d. me v.) laissier (*B1* v. oublier ne l.) m. (*B4* le laissast m.) illec et (*B2* l. point la m. et *B3* m. en prinson et *A6* m. icy et) q.m.

535-558 The miraculous freeing of Jacob from prison is here imitating various biblical and apocryphal sources. See particularly Acts 12:5-9 (liberation of Peter), but also Acts 5:19-25, 16:26-28. In the *Gospel of Nicodemus* (Ford, pp. 48, 88), Joseph of Arimathea is similarly liberated.

quant sa fille Marie Jacobi ouÿ dire que son pere estoit en prison et travaillé pour Pilate, elle pria Dieu moult devotement disent: "Biaux Sire, Dieu, Jhesu Crist, regarde comment ton ami, mon pere, est en prison. Je te prie que tu le me gardes que ces ennemis ne lui puissent mal fere. Biaux Sire, Dieux, qui delivras Joseph de la prison de Pilate out les faux juifs l'avoient fet mettre pour ossire, et par ta bonté le delivras des mains de ces ennemis. Einsy, Sire, s'il te plest, deslivres mon pere de la prison ou il est et des mains du fals juge, Pilate."

537 *A5* quil e. *A11* son peusse e. *B2* d. az iacob son p.e. mis en *A11* pere avoit este mis en *B, B3, B4* pere iacob e. 537-538 *A1* et mal menez pour *A10* et si fort t. *A12* et estoit ainsi t. *A5* pr. elle *A11* pr. par le commandement de pi. 537-539 *A13* pr. de pi.e.p.d. de bon ceur b. doulz s.i. *B, B1, B2, B3, B4, B5, B7, A6* pr. par (*B5* pr. mis par) pi. moult (*B4* pr. et que pi. lavoit fait faire m.) fort p. ihesu (*A6* m. pria i. *B2* f. elle va priere i. *B3* pr. moult f. se print a prier i.) crist et disoit s. (*B1* d. troyes foiz s. *B4* d. ainsi s. *B5* pr. mis par pi.m.f.d. pria nostre seigneur en disant s. *B7* pr. de pi.m. souvent reclamoit i. en disant s.) d.r. bien forz le (*B2* d. ainsi s.d.i.c.r. en pitie le *B3* r. le *B5* r. par sainte loy le *B7* r. le) mien p. (*B4* r. trois fois mon p. *A6* r. mon p.) ton (*B3* p. en pitie ton) amy (*B1* r. mon p. ton a.) qui (*B2* ton serviteur qui *B5* ton bon home qui *A6* a.) est 538 *A9* m. doulcement et de. *A1* m. doulcement disent *A11* pr.m. fort a i.c. en d.b. *A10* dieu doucsement b. *A12* elle se mist en oroyson et pr.d.m. fort doulcement et disoit b. 538-539 *A1* s.i. 539 *A8* c. veullies regarder co. *A8* est par pilate en *A10* r. croinent devisement ton *A13* ton bon ami *A10* est puis en p. a grant tort si te *A11* est villainement en p. obscure ie 539-540 *A13* p. iacob ie te p. que ses *B, B1, B2, B3, B4, B7, A6* pr. pour toy afin que ses *B5* pr. pour toy et luy veulles faire par la sainte grace et par ton sainctisme nom que les e. 539-541 *A2* dieu qui 540 *A3* g. de ses e. quilz ne *A8* le veulles guarder que *A9, A10* g. en telle maniere (*A10* g. tellement) que *A8* nayent puissance sur luy ne *A9, A13* pu. nul mal *A11* f. et ainsi b.

540-541 *B, B1, B2, B3, B4, B5, B7, A6* pu.f. grief (*A6* f. grevaige *B2* f. mal *B3* f. morir *B5* p. nuyre ne f.g.) s. *A7* f. il can sst d. *A10* f.s. ihesus qui i.d. de 540-548 *A13* f. ainsi comme tu de. de leurs mains ainsin s. te p. delivrer iacob mon pere des m. de p. le mauvais i. de la p. ou ilz est et son o. finee ung a. de dieu v. devant son pere disant i.na. point de p. car ie te vuis de. 541 *B, B1, B2, B3, B4, B7, A6* di. ainsi (*A6* di. vuilliez delivrez mon pere a.) comme tu de. (*B7* a. que de.) i. (*B2* de. sept *B4* di.de. le a. que tu de.i.) de *A9, A12* i. darimathie de *A3, A8, A12* pr. ou *B3* la main et pr. *A1, A10* les i. 541-542 *B5* di. ainsi come tu te d. *B, B1, B2, B4, A6* pi. quant les i. luy eurent (*A6* i.e.) mis par envie et tu (*B2* les f.i.le. enferme par e. et tu le delivras *A6* et que) par 541-545 *B3* pi.q. *B7* pi. voeulle deblivrer mon p.q. 542 *A3, A10, A11, A12* a. mis pour *A7* p. contire et par ta voulente le *A9* p. le tuer et o. *B2* b. des 542-543 *A8* d. einsy *A10* o. si ie te prie roy de gloire quil te plaise a despecher et delivrer mon *A11* o. ainsi aire te plaise delivrer mon *A12* o. tu sire pour ta b. ainsy sire sy te p.d. 542-544 *B1, B4* mains de pi. 542-545 *A6* le vuilles delivrez des mains de ces e.q. 543 *A9* plest vueillez delivrer mon 543-544 *B2* pere des m. de pi. *A7* est entre des *B* pr. et des m. de pi. 543-545 *B5* s. ihesu crist te plaise delivrer mon p. des m. de pi. qui sans cause et a grant tort le tient dedens sa pr.q. 544 *A9* f. et mauvais i. 544-545 *A1* p. ainsi que e. *A11* i.q. 544-546 *A10* et le mectez hors des murs du f.i. lequel ta iugie a mort q. marie iacobi ot son o. finee ung ange du ciel descendit en la p. ou i.e.

542 *delivras* [ *delivrast* Correction from all MSS except *A10, A11, A12, A13, B3, B7*.

[35] Et quant elle eüt achevee son orroyson, ung angel vint a la prison et trouva Jacob qui estoit en ouroison. Et apella Jacob et il leva la teste et vit grant clarté et eüt grant peur. Et l'angel luy dist: "Jacob, n'ayes peur de riens car je suis angel de Dieu qui te viens deslivrer par mandement de Jhesu Crist, car tu et ta fille Marie l'avés reclamé." Et Jacob luy dist: "Jhesu Crist en ait graces de ce qu'il ne me veust oublier." Et l'angel luy dist: "Jacob, deslivre toy des chaynes et viens avec moy." Et Jacob lui dist qu'il ne pouroit et l'angel [luy dist: "Secous toy les piez et les mains." Et

545 *A6, A12, B, B1, B2, B3, B4, B5* eut finer (*B1* e. ainsi f. *B2, B3* e. faicte *B5* f. sa priere et) son *B7* eust finist son o.v. ung a. en la *A9* et tantost peu de temps apres quelle eut fynie et a. son o. nostre seigneur ihesu crist envoya ung de ses angelz en la *A11* o. tantost ung 545-546 *B2* v. ia iacob en la p. qui le t. a genoulx qui prioit ihesu crist et lange le sonna i. et il *A11* p. ou e.i. en prison qui e. eu moult grant martire et trouva iacob qui adouroit ihesu crist si la. et luy dist iacob lieve toy sus et adont l. *A12* p. ou e.i. et i.l. 546 *A9* i. en *B, B1, A6, B5* i. a genoilz qui prioit ihesu crist et lange (*B5* p. devotement nostre seigneur puis la.) luy dist i. (*B5* i. et tantost i.) l. *A2, A5, A7* o. et il *A1* o. et lors langele a. *A3, A8* o. et lors i. (*A8* o. sy la. et i.) l. *A9* e. aussy en o. et il *A10* et adonc lange dist a i. et lui l. la la 546-547 *A11* teste en hault et vint g.c. entour luy si eut moult g. *B5* v. tres g.c. 546-548 *B3, B4, B7* i. en la prison a genoulx qui prioit ihesu (*B4* qui crioit mercy a dieu i.) crist et (*B7* iacob a g. ou il p. ihesu) lainge luy dit i.na. (*B7* d.na.) p. (*B4* i.p.) car *A10* teste en le reconfortant i. ne te doubte de r. adonc iacob pour la tres grant clarte qui de lange yssoit ot grant paour et moult sespoventa et adonc lange lui dist na. de r.p. car pour certain ie 547 *A2, A3, A5, A7, A9* c. dont il ot *B2, B5* eut moult (*B5* eut tres) g. *A11* d.na. *A12* a.d. a i. 547-548 *A6, B, B2* na.p. car *B1* na. point de p. car *B5* na.p. ie 548 *A10, B2* de (*B2* de dieu) ihesu crist qui 548-549 *B7* qui par son m. te v.d. de prissons car *A6, A11, B, B1, B2, B3, B4* par son m. car *A10* par les prieres que toy et *B5* de. de ceste prison par le m. de dieu car 549 *A5, A13* f.la. *A12* et m. ta f.la. *A2, A5* iacob luy d. 549-550 *A12* d. a langel dieux en soit loue de *A13* r. de bon ceur adieu d.i. ie te remercie de ce que tu ne mas pas oblie dont la. *A11* f.la. doulcement r. et il a obtenu vostre priere et lors i. luy d.i.c. le roy des roys soit loue de *B, B1, B2, B3, B4, B5, A6* f. le clamoit fort (*B1* le suivez f. *B4* c. moult f.) et (*B2* f.la. fort clame et) de (*B5* f.la. fort reclamez de) bon cuer ia.d.i. (*B3* c. adont d.ia.i. *B5* c. adont ia.d.i.) c. en (*B1, A6* d. dieu en *B2* ia. luy respondit i.c. le vray dieu tout puissant en) soit loue de ce quil (*B2* l. car il *B5* l. quant il) ne *A10* f. lui avez faictes i. se leva et rendit g. a dieu et adonc la. 549-551 *B7* f. le reclamer souvent et de bon coeur i.d. dieu soict louez de ce quil se recorde de moy la.d. 550 *A7* ne v. *B3* ne mait mie o. *A11* et i.la. 550-551 *B, B1, B2, B4* la.d. 551 *A3, A12* i. deschainez (*A12* i. deslie) toy *A7* i. iacob d. *A9, B3, B5* dist d. *A10* toy et ystz hors de ses c. *A6, B, B1, B4, B5* c.i. (*B5* c. de fer i.) luy (*B4, B5* i.) d. *A11* c. dont tu es lye et *A12* et me suys i. *A10* luy respondit ie ne 551-552 *B3, B7* c.i. luy respondit (*B7* i.r.) quil 551-553 *B2* i. quil le delivreroyt de celle chayne et tantost les chaynes tomberent a *A13* moy ilz soucoist ses m. et ses p. et les 552 *A3* p. apres la. *B5* p. deslier ses p. ne ses m. *A3* lui respondit s. *A6, B, B3, B4* a. lui d. (*B* a.d.) deslie les 552-553 *B1, B7* a. luy dist deslie les m. et les p. et ainsi (*B7* dist delivre toy m. et pa.) le *A10* dist estans toy des p. et des m. il le *A6* m. ainsi le *A11, B, B3, B4, B5* m. et ainsi le *A12* m. et il si f.

551 *viens* [ *vient* Correction from MSS *A1, A2, A3, A5, A7, A8, A9, A13*.
552-553 Addition from all MSS except *A1*.

Jacob le fist. Et incontinent les cheynes cheÿrent a terre. Adont l'angel] prist Jacob par la main et le bouta hors vean les guardes qui le guardoient en prison. Et nulles des guardes ne se peüst bougier ne plus que s'il fussent liés comme estoit Jacob. Et puis le bouta hors de Jherusalem par la porte aurial. Et le mena a la tente de l'empereur et la l'angel le layssa sans ce que
[44v] personne le vist. /

[36] Et quant Jacob fust a la tente de l'empereur, ceulx qui y estoient cuiderent que ce fust espie et qu'il y alast par aucun mal. Et le voucirent

553 *A6, A11, B, B1, B3, B4, B5, B7* et tantost les *A12* et les cheynes tomberent lors a *B7* chainez furent a *A10* cheynes rompirent et lors la. *B1* a pie adont 553-554 *A13* an. de dieu p. 554 *A3, A5, A7, A9* p. par la m.i. et *A2* v. tous les *A9* h. de la prison v. *A10* le mist fors de la prison v. *A11* m. devant les *A13* et veirent les *A3* v. ceulx qui 554-555 *A12* m.v. les g. qui le g. en la p. et le b.h. que n. *A11* qui le g. et le b.h. de p. sans que n. *A1* guardoient et 554-556 *A10* guardoient ne sceurent que dire ne que faire apres lange le mist h. 554-559 *B5, B, B1, B2, B3, B4, B7, A6* et le traict h. (*B1, B3, B4* le tira h. *B* le trahit h. *B2* le mist h. *B7* le mena h.) de la p. et le mena a la (*B4* m. en la) garde de (*B2* m. dedans lost de) lempereur (*B* de a le.) tellement que (*B3, B4, A6* e. que *B7* p. et lemporta vers la citez aux tentez de lempereur sans que) nul (*B1* e. que oncques n.) ne sen apperceust et le mist dedens lost et (*B4* d. les tentes de lempereur et) puis le (*B3* et plus le) l. et sen retourna aux sainctz cieulx q. (*B7* a.q. *B3, B4, A6, B* l.q. *B1* le baisa q.) i. 554-561 *A13* guardoient lange le prist et le menna en lost et cuidarent que ce fuisse une espie et le voloient prendre et 555 *A2* desdictes g. *A9* b. neant plus que *A11* peust mouvoir pour le recourre aussi peu que *A12, A1, A2* ne plus que 555-556 *A12* f. mors et langel luy b.h. de la ville de i. 556 *A1* le getta h. 556-557 *A11* l. de grosses chaynes de fer p. lange le mist h. de i. et *A1, A8, A10, A12* po. (*A12* po. oriental) et 557 *A3* et ladit m. *A10* m. tout droit aux *A1* e. et la le *A8* e. et le l. la s. *A9* e. et le fist passer et le la. la s. 557-559 *A10* e. et la il le la. que nul ne laperceust et retourna au ciel et *A11* le. sans que personne sen apperceust et illecques le l. et puis lange se fuauouyt de luy et sen alla au ciel et 558-559 *A8* v. ainsy comment i. *A9* v. puis apres q. 559 *B4* q. il f. *A11* f. conme dit est ainsy aulx t. *B1* f. mis au t. *A12* f. a lentre de la 559-560 *B, B1, B2, B3, B4, B5, A6* em. ilz se (*B4* em. les gens de lempereur se) penserent (*B2* ilz p.) que *A11* qui premier lapparceurent et virent c. *A10* qui e. dedans les tentes c. *A9* es. commis a la garde de ladicte tente c. *B7* qui gardoictz les tentez aurent poeur que 560 *A1, A11* quil fust venu (*A11* f. le v.) pour au. *A12* il fust pour au. *A3, A5, A7, A8, A9* al. pour a. *A2, A10* al. pour a. a (*A10* p. tresgrant) mal 560-561 *A12* le vont commensier a p. *A10* v. saisir et p. *A11* v. oscire mais daventure g. le s. furvint illec lequel tantost quil le vit le courust enbrasser et luy fist moult grant chiere et dist a ceulx qui luy vouloient faire desplaisir que *B, B1, B2, B3, B4, B5, A6* quil fust venu pour mal si fut prins q. (*B1, B3, B4, A6* mal q. *B5* f. mis hors de la cite pour mal faire q.) g. 560-564 *B7* et tantost le vont prendre et le mener a lempereur et g. qui estoit avecques lempereur le r. et le b. et puis dictz a le.s. veici mon h. iacob de i. lequel p.

554 *le* [ *les* Correction from all MSS except *A11, A13*.

555 *ne plus que* [ *ne que* Correction from MSS *A1, A2, A9, A12*. MSS *A7* and *A8* agree with *A*.

556-557 *la porte aurial* The Golden Gate was the main gate in the east wall of Jerusalem. This is a medieval designation.

560 *voucirent* [ *boucirent*

panre. Et quant Gaius, le seneschal, le vist, il reconneü et vist que c'estoit son hoste. Et le baisa, l'acola et le presenta a l'empereur. Et lui dist: "Sire, c'est cellui qui fu mon hoste en Jherusalem et s'apelle Jacob. Et sy est bon et loyal et bien vostre ami, car pour l'amour de vous il m'enseigna Veronique qui vous guery eu l'aide de Dieu. Et je vous supplie que vous lui demandés comment il est venus yssy. Lors l'empereur lui demanda comment il estoit issus de la cité, car il avoit ouÿ dire que Pilate l'avoit mis

561 A1, A3, A8, A10 r. tantost (A3 r. A5 r. bien et dist A10 r. bien t.) que A13 g.v. que 561-562 A12 g. le v. il et prist par la main et la. et le b. et A6, B, B1, B3, B5 s. de lempereur le v. (B3, B5 s.v. B4 s. le v.) tantost le r. qui avoit estez son h. en (B, B1 e. en) iherusalem et tantost le b. en sa bouche et puis le (B et le) mena a B4 r. tantost car il avoit este son h. en iherusalem et tantost le b. en la bouche et le menait a B2 q. le s. de lempereur le v. il r. bien que ce. son h. iacob et tantost le b. en la bouche et le mena a vasparien le. 562 A8 a. moult doulcement et A3 le a. et b. puys le p. A11 h. qui lavoit herberge en iherusalem ou temps quil alla querre la veronique et puis tantost le mena a A13 b. en la bouche et puis le p. 562-563 A10 h. qui lavoit herberge quant il fut en iherusalem si le b. et a. par tres grande amitie et le alla presenter a le. en lui disant s. veez cy mon A6, A13, B, B1, B2, B3, B4, B5 s. vecy (B2 v. iacob B5 s. empereur v.) mon 562-564 A11 d. ainsi s. voiez en c. bon homme qui estoit mon h. en i. lequel a nom i. qui est bon 563 A12 en ceste ville et a. en son nom iacob A1 si vous dis certainement quil est 563-564 B, B1, B2, B3, B4, B5, A6 i. mon bon amy et le vostre (B5 i. le b.a. du saint prophete et le v. et le mien) car p. A10 i. il est bon homme et l. et se nomme i. et cest monstre v. bon amy et p. 563-565 A13 sy est sens et bon proedommes et v. loyaul amy ie 564 A11 amy croiant en ihesucrist et p. A12 p. honneur et a. A1 il me feist bonne chiere et me. A12 bon homme et 564-565 A6, B, B1, B2, B3, B4, B5 e. la saincte femme (B5 la bonne f.) v. 564-566 B7 e. la saincte femme sil vous plaictz d. luy c. 565 A11 v. laquelle par la. de d.v. a g. de vostre maladie si v.s. A10 g. tout net par la vertus de 565-566 B, B1, B2, B3, B4, B5, A6 g.d. (B5 g. par la vertu du saint prophete d.) luy (A6 d. a iacob) c. A10 s. cher sire que v. lui d. par quelle maniere il A11 s. sire que v. le retiengnez de vostre court car cercoies vous pourra il donner bon conseil pour ceste cite avoir et tous plaise luy demander c. 566 A8 y. car se dieu plaist ce sera pour vostre bien et honneur l. A9 y. et que ly a admene l. A12 v. ne yssus de la cite l. A11 le. linterroga et luy B7 v. par deca tantost le. 566-567 A6 v. de B2, B, B1, B3, B4, B5 est ainsi v. (B e.v.) par (B1 e. y v. de p.) deca le.d. (B5 e.p.d.v. puis vaspasien empere de romme d.) a (B3 d. adont d.le. a B4 d. et lors le.d.) iacob c. 566-571 A13 v. lequel i. lui c.t. le fait et le. le 567 B, B1, B2, B3, B4, A8 e. venu (A8 v. et i. hors B2 e. sailly B3 e. ainsi v. de par deca) de A2 i. hors de A10 de iherusalem car A11 cite et conment et par quelle maniere il estoit illec venu car B5 cite de iherusalem car 567-568 B7 e. eschappe de iherusalem tantost i.c. a le.c. B3 d.la. fait mettre en A6, A11, A12, B, B4 a. fait mectre em 567-570 B5 a. fait mettre en p. maiz lange de dieu lavoit delivre que nostre seigneur ihesu crist le saint prophete luy avoit envoie et lavoit mis de la prison et conduict hors de la cite et amene dedans vostre ost ou il ma maintenant laisse ainsi suis eschape de la prison de pilate en laquelle il avoit este mis a tort q. 568 A1 p. et i. lui c. A8 l.c. A5, A6, B, B1, B4 c. a le.c. A2 p. adont c.t. par o. iacob a A9 l.c.i.t. 568-569 A12 c. de t. en tout p. B2 c. tout p. B3 c. a le.c. il a. estey mis en pr. et p.q. et c.

en prison. Lors Jacob conta tout par ourdre a l'empereur: comment ne pour quoy Pilate l'avoit mis et fait mestre en prison, et comment Jhesu Crist luy avoit envoyé son angel qui le delivra et [mena illecques. Et quant l'empereur l'ot oÿ, il luy fist tres grand honneur et le retient] de sa cort et de son conseil avec Jafet. Et luy fist fere tres grant honneur assa gent.

[37] Puis aprés Vespesian fist venir Titus, son fil, et se tret a part avec Jafet et avec Jacob et avec cinquante autres barons qui estoient de son

568 *A1, A12* o.c. *A10* t.c. 569 *A1, A2, A3, A5, A7, A8, A9, A11, A12* a.f. *A6* a. estes mis em *B, B1, B4, B7* q. il a. este mis en *A10, B2* mis en *A12* co. quant il estoit en prison i. 569-570 *B2* co. dieu a. 570 *B, B1, B3, B4* e. un a. *A11* a. et conment il le d. de prison et mist hors de iherusalem et amena *B7* d. des prisons de pillate et portez innesiblement aulx tentez de lempereur q. *B, A6, B1, B2, B3, B4* et le mist (*B1, B2* et m.) hors de prison (*B2* de iherusalem *B4* p. et le mena hors de la cite en lost de lempereur) q. *A10* et la lavoit admene et *A12* et boutte hors de la prison de la cite et lavoit menne 570-571 *A1* a. pour le delivrer de prison et lors lempereur le tint de 571 *A9* oy ce que iacob lui dist et racompta adoncques il luy f. et conmanda fere t. *A11* leut escoute il eut moult grant ioye et luy *B, B1, B2, B3, B4* eut escoute (*B1* es. iacob *B4* eut oyr et escouter iacob) il *B7* le. ainsi eust ouy parle iacob il *A6* e. ost escoutez tout cest choses il f. moult g. feste et vouloit que fut de *B1* luy dist et f. feste et voullut quil fust de *B5* eust escoute iacob ainsi parler il en eust g. ioie et en loerent moult nostre seigneur puis voult quil fut de *A11* g. chiere et grand feste et *A5, A8* le receut de 571-572 *B, B2, B3, B4* f.g. feste et (*B4* g. chiere et) volut que il fust de 571-575 *B7* g. chere et r. de son conseil en a.v. mandast son f.t. et tous ceulx de son conseil et quant il fust venus lempereur luy dictz ie 571-581 *A13* h. adoncques tout le conseil ensamble demandirent a iacob de lestat de la cite lequel respondit sire s. 572 *A12* c. prive et *A6, B, B2* i. du cassel et *B3* i. du cassel et luy fist g. *A3* fere h.t.g. a *A12* fere g. feste et grant h. a toutes ses gens 572-573 *A9* i.p. *B1* i. du cassel celuy fist g.h. et ses gens aussi p. *B4* i. du tassel et luy et ses gens luy firent g.h.p. *A11* i. et fut receu a grant ioye de lempereur de toute sa baronnie p. ne demoura guieres que lempereur f.v. son f.t. puis se mirent a *B5, A6* fist g.h. et aussi toutes ses g. (*A6* et ces g.a.) p. *A8* fere g. chiere par ses g. et f.v. son f.t. et le tira a 573 *A12, B, B1, B2, B4, B5* v. lempereur f. *A1* a. lempereur v. *A10* venir son f.t. et 573-574 *A6, B, B5* et allerant a une p. (*B5* a. parler a) iafet *A12* f. iafet *B1, B3* fil av.trente b. *B4* et alerent a une p. iassel du tassel iacob et titus avec trente b. 573-575 *B2* fil et midrent ensemble iacob et iassel de casel avec trente b. et princes de son c.s. et v. lempereur va dire ainsi s. 574 *A3* iacob a. lui .l. *A6, B, B5* iacob et tytus son filz a. (*B* t. et son pere a.) xxx b. *A5, A7, A9, A10* iacob et a. (*A9* a. les) au. *A8* .l. b. *A11* iacob et xx b. *A12* iacob et .xl. b. autres qui 574-575 *A8, A10* son c. *B, B1, B4* du c.s. et lempereur (*B4* e. et lempereur) pa. *A6, B3* du c. et ie croy que lempereur (*B3* de son c.s. et le.) pa. le pr. du conseil et v.

570-571 Addition is from MS *A2*, but based on all MSS except *A1*.

secret conseil. Et Vespesian parla premier et dist: "Signeurs, je vous ay fait venir afin d'avoir conseil comment nous nous chevirons du fet de ceste cité. Et sy [voeil] que Jacob en die premiere sa opinion car Dieu lui a fette si grant grace qu'il lui a envoyé son angel qui l'a gité de prison afin qu'il nous die de Pilate et du roy Archilan et de toute leur gent comment il se contenoient en celle ville ne qu'il font ne qu'il dient de nous ne de cest fait yssy que nous fesons." Lors dist Jacob: "Je vous diray verité. Saichiés que la dedens n'a guieres vivres. Pour quoy je vous dis qu'il ne se peuvent

575 *A8* et lempereur pa. *A10* pa. et *B1, B4* pr. du conseil et *B5* et puis lempereur v. *A1* v. dist *A11* c. affin quilz peussent avoir conseil ensemble comme ilz pourroient avoir la cite puis pa. premierement lempereur et leur d. en ceste maniere s. *A12* c. ie 575-576 *B, B1, B2, B3, B4, B7, A6, A11* ay icy assembles pour donner (*B7* ay mandez p. moy d. *A11* i.f.a.p. moy d.) c. comme n. ferons (*B2* p. ce que me donnes c. que ie doy fayre) de 575-577 *B5* d. son oppinion de ce pour quoy ilz y estoient alez et sa voulente toute auquel d. 576 *A2* v.com. *A10* v. pour vous demander con. *A12* a. que vous et moy ayons con. *A7* n.n. hirrons et c. 576-577 *A12* ch. de cessy et *A3* ceste ville mais ie v. *B, B1, B2, B3, B4, B7, A6* et ie conseille que 577 *A11, B, B1, B3, B4* sa voulente a qui d. *B2* i. a qui d. a *B7* p. ce que lat consable auquel d. *A3* p. car *A6* p. cur a *A7* car luy *A9* o. pour ce que d. 577-578 *A10* f. tant de grace 578 *A1* a.a. *B2* grace de luy avoir e. son a. et de lavoir delivre et amene icy quil *A2, A7* la boute hors (*A7* la porte h.) de *A11* la deslivre de la p. obscure ou le faulx pilate lavoit fait mectre et la amene icy a. *B, B1, B3, B4, A6* la delivre de la p. et la admene icy et que 578-579 *B5* grace et demanda puis a iacob a qui dieu avoit fait si grant g. quil leur die 578-581 *B7* grace quil la delivrez de main pillatte et la faict ici admener par ung de ses anglez et quil p. et de ceulx qui sont en la citez de iherusalem i. respondict seigneurs ie 579 *A11* die des nouvelles de p. et c. *A1* et de a. *A12* de l. *A7* l.c. 579-580 *A11, A12* c. leans (*A12* c. la dedans la cite) ne *B2* de ceulx de la cite ne comment il le sont en la cite et quil 579-581 *B, B1, B3, B4, B5, A6* de l.g. et que ilz f. dedans (*B1* que sont d.) la cite et que ilz d. ce d.i. seigneurs (*B1* d.i.d.s. *B3* ilz d. adonc i. leur respondit s. *B4* ilz d.i.d. sa voulente et son conseil le premier par le commandement de lempereur messires *B5* ilz d. de nous adont respondist i. et leur d.s. *A6* qui d.s. ce d.i.) ie 580 *A9* v. et cite ne *A1* quil d. *A9* n. y porterons et que n. en fait 580-581 *A12* d. de cest f. ne quelle est leur entencion de faire l. *A3* fait que *A11* de ceste chose adoncques titus et toute la baronnie disent que cestoit bien dit l. conmencza a parler i. et dist seigneurs ie *B2* de nostre f.i.d. ainsi s. ie 581 *A1* f. seigneurs d. *A10* l.i.d. ie *A12* i. a lempereur sire ie *B5* ve. sans faillir s. 581-582 *A11, A12* ve. sans mentir nullement s. (*A12* v. du fait s. que la) d. la cite na 581-584 *B, B1, B2, B3, B4, B5, B7, A6* s. que d. iherusalem (*A6* d. la cite de i.) a pou de viandes p.q. ne se p. grandement t. (*B3, B5, B7* p. longuement t.) ainsi et (*B4* g.a.t. et) si ont grant (*B1* a. et aussi eut g.) paour pour (*B5* g. famine pour) les (*B3* paour les) gens qui sont d. (*B2* se p. longuement t. pour la grant habundance de peuple qui est d.) car ie croy que en t.c.t. nest (*B7* quil ne soit) d. 582 *A12* q. ilz 582-583 *A11* q. ilz p. grandement resister contre vous et *A2, A10* pe. longuement t. *A7* pe.t.g. et 582-590 *A13* q. il ne p. longuement t. car ilz navoit i. en ceste quil ne fuisse v. en iherusalem a ceste f. dont il fauldront a vivre t.

577 Addition from MSS *A1, A2, A3, A5, A7, A8, A9, A10, A12*.
578 *qui* [ *quil* Correction from all MSS except *A1, A13, B2, B5, B7*.

guieres tenir et si sont fort esbahi de la grant gent qui est la dedens, car en toute ceste terre n'est a paine demouré juifs qui ne soit venu la dedens a la [45r] festa, car de coustume ont de fere une grant feste chescun an. / Et vous y venites en celle saison. Et quant il virent que vous aviez mis le siege, il n'y eüt nul qui s'an ausast istre. Et il ne s'en prenoient guarde de vous. Et pour ce il ne s'estoient point guarnis de vivres. Pour quoy, Sire, je pense qu'il seront tost destruit et sy ne se pouront pas longuement tenir. Toutesfois il s'en pouroient bien istre par aucun lieu. Si vous conseille que

583 *A9* g. soustenir ne t. *A1* s. moult f. *A10, A11* e. des gens (*A11* e. du grant monde) qui *A9* gr. multitude et foison de g. *A12* est d. 583-584 *A7* gr. multitude de i. *A11* d. ne de quoy ilz pourront vivre silz sont guieres la d. car ne to. la te. la iudee nest *A10* car il est force que on garde bien que nulz biens ny entrent car il y a tant de monde quil nest gueres d. 584 *A2* p.i.d. qui *B7* i. en to.c.te. quil *A3* s. la d.v. a *A10, A11, A12* v. a 484-485 *A2* s. la d. a la f.v. car *A1* d. sy vous diray pourquoy il est accoustume que chascun an on faict une g.f. et *A6* v. en iherusalem pour une f. qui se faisoit tous les ans 584-590 *B, B1, B2, B4, B5* v. a la f. en iherusalem pour une f. qui se faisoit touz (*B1* que on y fait t.) les ans et adonc v. (*B5* et q. vous estes venuz vous) et vostres gens et eulx ne (*B1* v. vous et v.g. ne *B4* et ne *B5* g. ne) sen donnoient garde et (*B5* g. de vous et) onques puis ne sen yssit homme ne femme et eulx sen pevent bien saillir (*B1* sen puet h. ne f. yssir p. bien istre *B2* ans et vous estes venu q. ilz sen cuidoyent retourner et ie scay quil ne p. pas s. *B4* sen peust h. ne f. yssir et ilz sen p.b.s. *B5* b. yssir) par *B7* v. a la f. en ceste citez que lon y solloist faire c. an et adoncques que tous les iuif furent venus vous v. et vos gens ausi pour quoy oncques puis il ne saillist iuif et sen poeulle bien saillir par *B3* s. tous v. a la f. en iherusalem pour une f. que se faisoit tous lez ans adont venist et vos gens et si ne sen donneirent garde et onques puis ne sen issit homme ne femme et il sen pouroient bien saillir par 585 *A3* car ilz ont a c. *A7* feste tout lez an *A10* f. quon a c. de f. par c. 585-586 *A12* f. la d. car lon y avoit a c. a f.c. an grant feste et q.vi. 585-590 *A11* f. quil ont acoustumee de f.c. an en la cite par quoy ad ce que homme ne fenme nen puisse i. ie v. 586 *A9* s. que ladicte feste si se fait et *A10* vi. que le s. y estoit il *A9* mis et pose le 586-590 *A6* v. et vous gens aussi et ne sen donoyent garde et oncques puis ne en saillit homme ne femme et il sen pourroyent bien saillir par 587 *A5* eut celluy qui *A1* eut riens quil en issit et *A9* nul si hardy qui depuis sen soit ose i. *A12* i. aussy nulz de eulx ne *A2* g. et *A7* ne se pourroyent g. 587-588 *A9* et adoncques quant vous venites ilz *A12* g. quant vous vintes p. quoy il 588 *A9* point fourniz et g. *A3* g.p. 588-589 *A10* s. il s. *A12* v. ne de viandes p.q.s. ie vous diz quil 589 *A9* t. tous defers et d. 589-590 *A12* te. la cite to. *A10* pas t.l.to. sire il 590 *A5, A10* b. fouyr (*A10* b. ouyr) par *A12, A13* b. fouyr par preux de (*A13* par aultre) l. *B5* l. pour ce ie v. dy que *B7* l. par quoy ie v.c. 590-591 *A7* i.e. *A11* que tout e. la c. vous f.f. des f.g. et p.a. *B, B1, B2, B3, B4, A6* l. pour quoy ie (*B2* l. tant seulement par quoy ie) c. que tout entour la cite faison faire f.g. et profondes (*B2* que nous f.f. tout a le.g.f. et si p.) tant que

586 *saison* [ *faison* Correction from MSS *A1, A2, A3, A5, A7, A9, A10*.

vous fette fere grans foucés environ la cité affin que nul n'en puisse istre sans vostre voulenté et sans vostre congié. Et quant les vivres leur faudront, il se rendront voulentiers. Et sachiés, Sire, que la cité est sy fort et sy bien guarnie que jemés ne seroit prince pour tant qu'il eüssent vivres. Pour quoy, Sire, je conseille que les foucés soient fes."

[38] Lors l'empereur et tous ceulz de son conseil se tindrent a son conseilz. Et incontinent l'empereur fit crier par tout l'ost que tous ceulz qui

591 *B5* fere fo.g. tout autour de la *A9* fere tout e. de la c.g.f.a. *B7, A12* fo. a lentour (*A12* fo.e. la ville) a. *A13* fo. a le. de la 591-592 *A9* p. saillir ne i.s.v.c. *A7* ne penssast i.s.v.c. *A2, A3, A5, A10* i.s.v.c. *A12* p. fuyr s.v.c. *A13* p. partir s.v. licence et *B, B1, B2, B3, B4, B5, B7, A6* p. saillir s.v. commandement et (*B7* p. sortir que par v. congez et) q. *A11* i. car quant vos venistes ycy il ne se prenoient point garde de vous ne ne savoient rien de vostre venue et de paour de vous noserent yssir ne ne cestoient point garniz de vivres et pour ce sire q. 592 *A1* vostre gre et c. 593 *A11, B2* f. saichez quil *B1* f.v. ilz se r. et *A1* se tendront v. *A9* v. a vous et a vostre mercy et *A10* r. plus v. *B7* r. et *B2* v. non obstant que *A7, A10, A11, A12* sa. (*A12* sa. certainement) que *A6* est tant f. 593-594 *A13* r. tres v. la cite est tant f. que 593-595 *B1* que i. homme ne la pourroit prendre se ilz avoient viandes dedans p. 593-597 *B7* fort que ne la prendries i. que par famine le. respondictz que le conseil luy plaisoit bien et autost fit 594 *A12* g. de gens que i. par force ne *A9* pr. par force tant quilz ayent nulz v. 594-595 *B, B2, B3, B4, B5, A6* g. que (*B5* g. de gens que) i. homme ne la pourroit prandre se (*B4* la prandroit si) ilz avoyent viandes dedens (*B2* a.d. que mangie) p. *A1* v. dedens p. 594-596 *A11* i. on ne la prendroit par ainsi quilz eussent tousiours saulve lonneur des autres seigneurs et barons que sont en present que fassiez faire les fo. ainsi que ie vous ay dit l. 594-606 *A13* pr. se ce nestoit par famine p.q. ie c. saulve lonneur de tous que affin quil nen puissent fouir lon faice tout a lenviron fo. et quil soient parfond et large adoncques furent prest .v. m.o. pour fere lesdiz fossez et iacob et iaphet furent esleuz pour estre a. diceulx ovriers avoient tous iours avec eulx .x. mille a.p.gu. lesdiz fossez et lesdiz ovriers lesquelx fossez avoient .xv.c. de p. et xxx de l. et 595 *A10* ie vous c. *A1* so. tantost fes 595-596 *A12* q. ie c. sauves lonneur des autres que vous fassies faire les fo. et l. *A9* f. si se facent tout entour de la cite adoncques le. 595-597 *B2* que vous sacies fayre les f. lempereur et tout le conseil dist que cestoyt bien dit tantost il fit *B, B1, B3, B4, B5, A6* que faites faires les fo.le. (*B4* fo. tout entour la cite le.) respont que ce seroit bien fait et tout son c. aussi et (*B5* fo. come iay dit le. et tout son c. le eurent a moult aggreable le conseil de iacob et) tantost le. 596-597 *A12* t. les autres du c. le vont tenir a bien dit et *A9* au c. que iacob dist et donna et *A10* au c. et *A11* ti. a bon ce que iacob avoit dit et *A3* au c. du dit iacob et *A5* c. le t. a bon et 596-600 *A1* au c. de iacob et de present le.c. que les fossez fussent faicts et furent pour les faire cincq m.o. qui estoient tous de cellui mestier et lempeur d. 597 *A6, B, B1, B2, B3, B5* par t. ces tentes que *A5* que t. qui 597-598 *A11, A12* qui s. (*A12* qui se s.) entremectre de fere *B1* qui faroient ouvierer v. touz parler a

595 *soient* [ *soiens* Correction from MSS *A1, A2, A3, A4, A7, A10*.

savoient fere foucés venissent a lui. Et quant il furent venus, il se trouverent bien cinc mile ouvriés. Lors l'empereur leur commenda qu'il ficent tout environ de Jherusalem foucés grans et parfons. Et dist a Jafet et a Jacob qu'il en fucent aministreus. Et lors il regarderent la hou il serroit bon de les commenser et les commenserent la ou bon leur sembla. Et sy

598 *B7* s. bien fere *A6, B, B3, B5* v. parler a *A11* a lempereur et *A12* a lempereur et tantost la crie fust faicte et *B4* fo. quilz v. parler a 598-599 *B7* et furent par compte faict cincq mille hommes adoncques le. *A12* venus devant lempereur ilz se vont trouver b. *B, B1, B2, B3, B4, B5, A6* fu. touz v. (*B3* f.v.) eulx furent (*B2* t. assembles ilz f.) v. (*B7* f. bien .v. *A6* v. venirent .v.) mille (*B5* f. xv.m.) hommes adonc le. (*B2* h.le. *B5* a.) leur 599 *A7* t. .v. *A11* b. ensemble c. *A11* lors leur 599-601 *A10* leur demanda comment on pourroit fere ung fosse qui assiegast toute la cite de i. bien p. et si vueil que iacob et iaffet en soient les maistres et 599-606 *B7* que entour la citez fustez faict g.f. ilz respondirent que vollantiers le feroient mais quil ordonnast arches pour les g. du traictz et tantost leurs fust baillez xxx mille archers puis apres lempereur ordonnast a iaphet et iacob quil allassent avecques les ouvriers pour ordonner les fosses et ainsi le firent et en bien peult de temps les fosses furent faict de xlv c. de hault et xxx piez de l.q.

600 *A3* fi.fo. entour i.g. *A12* fi. entour la ville g.f. et p. *A2* i.g. 600-601 *A11* de la cite de i.g.f. et p. et de ce fere bailla la charge a iaffet et a iacob que deviserent aulx ouvriers conment ilz devoient faire la *A2* d. a iacob et a iafet quilz 600-606 *B, B1, B3, B5, A6* fi.g.fo. tout autour de (*B1* t. entour la cite de *B5* t. a lem. de) iherusalem et en donna (*B5* et de ce faire fere d.) la commission a iassel et (*B3* a ioseph et) a iacob et eulx respondirent que ils le feroient moult voulentiers (*B3, A6* f.v.) et tantost iacob et iasel o. (*A6* t. iacob et iasel o. *B5* a iacob et o.) les (*B3* iacob et ioseph avec lez) ouvriers (*B1* a iassel et a iacob o.) firent venir la (*B3, B5, A6* f. veoir la besoigne a *B4* o. furent orier la besoigne la) ou se (*B1* f. la besoigne la ou elle se) devoient faire les fosses et diseroit ainsi que il (*A6* d. que il *B1* faire et d. aussi quilz) leur convenoit avoir gens (*B1, B3* c.g. *B5* d. a lempereur quil failloit aussi des g.) p. (*A6* c.g. darmes p.) les gu. du trait de ceulx de iherusalem et tantost lempereur leur bailla xxx (*A6* l. donnoit t.) mille archiers (*B1* e. mist xxx a.) avec leur escus et bien (*A6* e. et il firent les fosses b.) garniz et ilz firent (*B3* et adont f. *B5* e. et tout ce que leur failloit puis f.) les fosses de xv.c. (*B4* de quarante c.) de p. et de l. xxx piez (*B1* xxx pas *B5,A6* et de t.p. de l.) q. *B2* fi.t.e. de i.g.f. et i. quil les fissent fayre lesquels luy respondirent que voulentiers et tantost ces deux iassel et iacob ordonnerent les ouvriers la ou il devoyent besoignier et dirent que il leur convenoyt avoir aultres gens p. les gu. du tret et de ceulx de iherusalem incontinent lempereur fist venir trente mille a. avec leurs escus pour garder ceulx qui faysoyent les fosses et firent isseux fosses de .xxv.c. de p. et de trente pieds de l.q. 600-609 *B4* fi.fo. tout entour de iherusalem et en donna la commission a iassel du tassel et a iacob et ilz respondirent quil le feroient moult voulentier et tantost iacob et iassel avec les ouvriers furent orier la besoinge la ou se devoient faire les fossez et dirent aussi quil leur convenoit gens p. les gu. du trait de ceulx de iherusalem et tantost lempereur leur bailla trente mille a. avec leurs escus et bien garniz de traitz et furent les fossez de quarante c. de p. et de trente piedz de l. adont p.d. que i.

601-602 *A1* f. maistres et commenserent *A7* en feissent a. et sy *A12* et iaffet et iacob vont regarder out il feroyent c. *A11* hon il devoient c. et la ou ilz devoient fere et les firent conmancer ou 602 *A2* de c. *A1* ou meilleur l. *A10* commenserent et m.

602-606 *A11* s. misdrent avec eulx environ xx miles a.g. darmes et de traict p.ga. ceulx que faisoient les foussez que ceulx de la cite ne leur feissent encombrier lors les ouvriers conmancerent par grant diligence a fere iceulx foussez lesquelx il devoient faire de xx c. de p. et de xxx de l. et q. ceulx de iherusalem virent quil en conmanserent ung tel ouvraige et quon les t.

menerent avec eulx vint archiez bien guarnis pour guarder les premiers. Et il firent en la maniere que Jafet et Jacob leur commenderent et sy eürent de parfont quinze coudees et de large trente coudees.

[39] Et quant Pilate vit qu'il fesoient les foucés et qu'il les tenoient de cy pres, il demanda conseil au roy Archelan. Et le roy lui dist qu'il creoit que Jafet et Jacob avoient donné le conseil a l'empereur de les fere, sy dist a Pilate qu'il feīst venir Jozeph d'Arimatie a son conseil car il estoit saint chevaliers et sy estoit cousin de Jafet et de Jacob. Et dist que par aventure

603 *A2, A9, A10, A12* xx.m. (*A10* m. hommes) a *A7, A5* xxx (*A5* xxx.m.) a. *A1* xx mil a.p. 603-604 *A10* guarder et f. tout en *A12* guarder ceulx qui faisoient les fousses et les ovriers les vont encommencier et firent les fosses en 603-605 *A1* les pionniers et les f. quilz e. 604-606 *A12* l. deviserent et c. et estoient de p. xxx c. et de xxxi c. de l. et 605 *A10* e. les fossez de *A9* et aussi eurent de l. 605-606 *A1* de long vingt c. et *A3* xv.c. et *A10* et autant de l. et 606 *A13* que lempereur les *A9* fo. si parfont et 606-608 *B1, B2, B3, B5, A6, B* quilz estoient ainsi assiegez le (*B3* as. il fut bien esbahis et le *B5* as. il eust moult grant paour et) roy archilant luy d. quil c. que (*B2* d. que ie croy que *B5* c. bien que) i. (*B3* que ioseph de cassel) et *B7* p. et ses gens virent quil estoyent ainsi asseges le roy archilans d. a pilate que iaphet 607 *A5* il le manda au *A11* p. pilate d. *A7* d. au roy a. quil devoyent fere et *A11* a. de ceste chose lequel luy *A9* le roy archilant lui 607-608 *A13* p. ilz fut plus esbays que devant et d. a archillain qui iafet *A12* cr. que iacob et iafet a. 608 *B, B1, B2* d. celluy c. *A9* de f. les diz fossez si *A10* de f. ses fossez et il dirent a 608-609 *A12* c. et louyrent ainsy deviser a le. et p.d. que que lon fissies v. *B3* d. ce c. adont p.d. que i. *B, B1, B2, B5, A6* le. adonc p.d. il seroit bon que (*B2* d. quil falloyt ouir le conseil de) i. *A11* de f. telle chose si luy conseilla quil 608-610 *A13* le. adoncques manderent querir i.da. quil e.s. homme bon conseillers c. et *B7* le. et furent forment esbahis et dirent quil seroist bon que i.da. fust ici pour donner conseil sur le fait de ceste citez car il est parent de 609 *A1* quil envoyast querir i.da. qui fust a *A11* a.e. *A3* c. pour ce quil 609-610 *A1* e. saige ch. *A10* il e.co. 609-612 *B, B1, B3, B5, A6* a. qui est (*B1* a. estoit) sage c. que il nous donnast conseil car il est parent de iacob et de iasel et que par (*B3* iacob et de ioseph du cassel et par) a. il nous donroit moult bon (*B1* d. bon) conseil (*B5* a. adoncque) p. 609-614 *B4* a. qui estoit saige c. quil nous donna conseil car il estoit parent de iacob et de cassel du tassel et par a. il nous donnera bon conseil sur 609-615 *B2* a. que estoyt sage c. lequel leur pourroyt bien donner bon conseil adonc p.lef.v. et luy demande conseil et i.d. a pilate s.n.p. pou f. a lencontre toutesfoiz ie 610 *A12* ch. lequel est bon c. et s. iuif et *A11* i. et que *A12* i. et par *A1* i. et par *A3* i. cuidant que 610-611 *A13* i. et pensoient quil s.a. 610-615 *A11* a. luy pourroit d. sur ce a. bon c.l.p. le f. appeller et v. luy d. en conceil que il luy pleust sur ce f. ycy le conseiller et conment il se pourroit gouverner envers le.l. luy d.i. de barimathie s. soubz la correction de vous barons et chevaliers ie vous co.

604 *firent* [ *furent* Correction from all MSS except *A8, A11, A12, A13, B2, B4*.

savoit il aucune chose de leur coingne et de leur sagesse et lui donroit aucun conseil qu'il seroit bon et necessaire. Lors Pilate fist venir Joseph a [45v] son / conseil et lui dist que sur tout cest fait le conseillast, c'est assavoir sur le fet qui est entre lui et l'empereur. Lors dist Joseph: "Sire, nous n'y pouvons fere autre chose fors que je conseille que nous nous armons tous demain bien matin, chevaliers, archiez et autre gent et les assaillons. Et le souleil leur frapera sur le visaige et nous les desconfirons tous par telle

611 *A5* s. il quelque peu de i.s. *A1* c. de l.s. *A2, A3, A12, A13, A10, A9* l. conuure (*A3* l. convenue *A12* l. combine *A13* l. convenanche *A10* l. secret *A9* l. secret et truvine) et de i.s. 611-612 *A10* sag. et aussi il pourra donner a. bon c. et l. *A1* sag. et d.a. bon c. et n. de donner l. 611-614 *A13* sag. et pour ce aussi quil les. donnaisse a.c. contre leurs f. et cely de lem. 612 *A2* a. bon c. *A12* a. bon c. et l.p.f. appeller et v.i. dabarimathie a *A7* p. le f.v. a *B3* v. ledit i. 612-613 *B5* v. son *B7* i. et tous ceulx de son 613 *A2* sur c. *B5* et pylate demanda a ioseph quil estoit de faire sur le *A12* f. luy donnast aucun bon conceil cest 613-614 *B1, B3, A6, B* co. et luy demanda sur (*B* c. sur) le *A10* d. ie vous prie mon amy iozef quil vous plaise de moy conseiller de ce fet cy lem. 613-615 *B7* co. pour scavoir quil feroint de la cite et ordonna que conseillast le premier et quil luy sambleroit bon de faire et tantost iosepht commenca a dire comment il voult faire car ie ne scay a vous quel conseil donner mais toutesfois ie 614 *A1* fet de lui *A1* lem. et i. lui d.s. *A10* i.n. 614-615 *B1, B, B3, B4, B5, A6* lem. et i.d. (*B5* i. leur d.) s. (*B3* i. adont luy respondit s.) poy (*B4* i. respondit monseigneur pou) y povez f. (*A6* p. icy f.) mais ie *A12* et monseigneur le. et i. dabarimathie d.s. ie ne vous puis donner a. conceil fors *A13* i. a pilate ie vous donne consel que nous 615 *A3, A9, A10* p.a.c.f. fors *A1* f. aulcune c.f. que n. 615-616 *B, B3, B4, B5, B7, A6* co. que d. (*B4* c. de d.) au m. que t. les ch. 615-617 *A10* co. que n. tous au plus m. que tout le monde sailli sur eulx et les a. car le s. *B1* co. que d. eu m. que t. armez et que nous aillons encontre eulx et le ray du s. *B2* co. que d. au m.t. les c. et tous les a. de la cite soyent armes et que nous aillons alencontre de luy et le s. *A11* t. et que d. au m. nous les a. vigoreusement car le 615-618 *A12* t.c. escuiers sergens et a. et d.m. nous nous ensemblerons et puis quant le s. sera leve yssons hors de la ville contre ceulx de loust et les s. les f. par devant les v. tellement quil nauront pouvoir sur nous et los en celle m. nous les desconffirons tous et leurs ferons tant quil 616 *A13* d. a m.c. escuiers et aultres sergent a. et toutes a. meintes g. *A1* et sachies que le 616-617 *B, B3, B4, B5, B7, A6* a. et les (*B5* et tous les) sergens soient (*B3, B7* a.so. *A6* et servant so.) armes et que nous alons encontre eulx et le (*B7* ar. aulx mieulx quil porrons et puis que n.a. contre lempereur et ses gens car le) s. 617 *A3* s. sur le v.l.f. et *A6* l. sera au v. *A1, A10* d. par 617-618 *B1, B, B3, B4, B5, B7, A6* les d. en (*A6* les destruirons en) te.m. quilz *B2* v. et perdront clarte et nous les d. tellement quil 617-620 *A11* et par celle m. nous les pourrons bientous aisement desconfire car quant archilans et p. eurent ouy ce conseil ilz le t. a bon lors f. 617-621 *A13* f. contre eulx par devant leur v. et leurs ferons bataille ilz f. ce par t. la cite que le m. a p. du i. il f.t.a. a p. du i.d.

611 *coingne* This form is not recorded in Godefroy, Tobler-Lommatzsch, nor in the *Französisches Etymologisches Wörterbuch*, and does not occur in any of the other manuscripts of families A and B. The sense seems to be "knowledgeability," perhaps derived from *cognita*, "things known."

maniere que nous les destourberons qu'il n'averont voulenté de nous aseiger." Et Pilate et le roy et tous les autres se tindrent a son conseil et si firent crier a l'eure de vespres par toute la cité qu'il fussent tous armés au point du jour et qu'il venissent davant le temple Salamon.

[40] Et quant il vint au matin, il furent tous armés et aprestés et ordonnerent leurs batailles et se trouverent vint mile chevaliers et soisante mile que sergens que archiés bien armés et bien appareilliés. Et la Pilate leur commenda qu'il entrassent bien sagement a la bataille et que nul se desrangast ne se destornast, mes que chescun se tenist a l'ourdenance de

618 *A5, A10, A1* m. quil (*A10* que iamais) na. 618-619 *A7* m.p. *A6* de n. assallir ne a. *B1* v. dapproucher de n.p. *B4* nous approchier p. 619 *A1, A9* roy archilans et *A10* p. et tout le conseil se *A3* et les *B, B1, B2, B3, B4, B5, A6, A12* roy archilan t. son c. (*A6* a. truvant le c.) pour bon et si *B7* p. tint le c. pour bon et si *A3* t. tous a 620 *A12* a v. *A1, A10* que tout homme fust (*A10* t. le monde f.) a. 620-621 *A12* que landemain au p. du i.f.t.a. et *A5* a. au t. *A11* c. a son de trompe par t. la ville que le lendemain au matin t.f.a. et en point et *B, B1, B2, B3, B4, A6* c. par la (*B3* c. a valx la *B4* par toute la) cite a le. de v. que le matin bien (*B3* le lendemain b.) matin (*B4* le b.m.) f. (*B2* le lendemain b.m. sailloit quilz f.) t.a. (*A6* f. bien a.) d. 620-622 *B7* c. par toutez les rues de la citez que le matin il f.t.a. pour aller combatre lempereur et ainsi fust faict q. 620-623 *B5* c. par toute la c. a le. de v. que le lendemain au plus matin f. bien appareilliez et bien a. et se mirent tous le c. dune part et estoient bien xx *A7, A9* a. et apprestes et o. 621-622 *A12* s. en une belle plasse que la estoit et 621-623 *A13* s. et ainsin fut fait le m. et o. 622 *B1, A10* v. le landemain au m. (*A10* l.) ilz *B3, B4, A6* au landemain au m. (*B4* la. bien m. *A6* la.) il *A12* f. venus t. 622-623 *B, B1, B2, B3, B4, A6* f. bien appareilles et bien ar. (*B1* f. bien ar.) et touz les c. se mistrent a (*B1* c. estoient a *A6* c. a) une (*B2* f.t. pretz et tres b.ar. si m.t. les o. dune) part et estoient (*A6* e. par nombre) xx *A11* t.ap. et ar. au temple et puis o. toutes les b. et furent bien xx 622-625 *B7* t. prest p.l. dictz quil 623 *A2* t. xxx m. *A12, A13* et furent bien xxx (*A13* f. en nombre xx) m. *A6, B, B2* m. et 623-624 *B, B1, B3, B4, A6* m.a. et s. (*A6* et furant) b. *A10* m. tant de s. comme de a. que autres gens b. *A13* s.m. que a. que s.b. *A12* lx que escuyers s. que a. et p. 623-625 *B2* m.a.p.c. a ses gens quil *B5* m.a. et s.b.ap. et b.ar. et tantost p.c. 624-625 *A6, B, B1, B3, B4* p.c. 624-626 *A13* ap. adoncques fut crie par son de businnes qualment que 625 *A10* l. demanda et c. *A11, A12, B3, B5, B7* e.s. *A1* e.s. et *B2* e. en la *A7* nul se designant ne 625-626 *B, B1, B2, B3, B4, B5, B7* et que c. *A6* et c. *A9* nul ne se desordonnast desr. *A10, A12* nul ne se desordonnast (*A12* se destranchast) mes 626 *A2* desr. ne desordonnast mes *A3* desr. ne ne se *A5, A11* desr. mes *A1* dest. et c. fut a *B7* t. en o. 626-627 *A2* c. de eulx se t. ainsin et par la maniere que son c. lordonneroit adont p. *A11* c. se mist en lo. des c. quilz avoient l. *B, B1, B2, B3, B4, B5, A6* t. en son rant et en gouvernement de leurs maistres (*B2* et soubz le g. de son m.) p. (*B5* p. lequel) et *A12* o. des c. quilz avoient mis et ordennes l.

son capitaingne. Lors Pilate et le roy Archelan prirent les vint mile chevaliers et s'en issirent par la porte de la cité.

[41] Et incontinent une des guardes de l'empereur qui se tenoit au bort du foucé les vist issir tous armés et monta a cheval et s'en vint a la tante l'empereur et le trouva au lit, car encore n'estoit soulail levé. Et lui dist que ceulx de la cité estoient yssus hors tous armés pour courir sus a ses gens. Lors l'empereur envoya querir Titus, son fil, et Jafet et Jacob et si

627 *A5* roy p. *B, B1, B2, B3, B4, B5, A6* a. gouvernerent les 627-628 *A12* les xxx m.c. et lx.m. que escuyers que sergens que archiers et 627-629 *B7* c. quant ilz commencerent a saillir de la cite une g. 627-642 *A11* a. avec leurs gens sen i. hors de la c. et ceulx de la cite furent moult esbahiz et se lempereur qui ses nouvelles scavoit ot fait armes tous ses gens qui furent tantost prestz pour entrer en bataille et lempereur et titus son filz ordonnerent leurs gens bien ordonneement qui estoient moult grant n. puis sen vindrent erraument vers lost 627-643 *A13* c. sans eulx desrangier et quant il yssirent de la cite de iherusalem ung g. quil faisoit le guet sur les fossez les vit venir mout a chavalx et sen vint en loz et dist a lempereur et aux aultres chevaliers dudit ost comme ceulx de iherusalem estoient parti horrs de la cite tous armez adoncques lempereur fit commander et a son de trompete sonnee que chascun fuisse armez prestement et tellement que e.t. furent en la plaice ceulx de lempereur si comme pour combatre et les gens de 627-651 *A10* c. et puis r.a. ung chascun aux 628-629 *A12* i. hors de la ville par la grant p. et i. vont des 628-630 *B, B1, B4, A6* et commancierent (*B4* et adon c.) a saillir (*B1* c.s.) hors par la p. de (*A6* h. de) la c. et tantost la g. qui estoit pour le. (*B4* e. de le.) es f. (*B1* p. les f.) quant il les v. ainsy (*B1* v.) a. *B3, B5* et commancirent saillir (*B5* et commanderent a.s.) hors de la pl. de la c. et tantost la g. qui estoit pour le. es f. lez v. ainsi a. et tantost fit savoir a lempereur et (*B5* a. ung chevalier de la garde qui estoit) m. *B2* et comencerent a saillir hors de la c. par la p. et tantost lung des g. de le. qui estoit es f. quant il les v. ainsi a.
629 *A1* et tantost une 629-630 *A12* t. es f. *B7* le. qui estoict pres de murs de la citez commenca a monter a 630 *A3* f. aussitost quil les *A9* v. venir et i. *A12* i. hors de la cite t.a. et tantost il m. *A1* v. grand alure a *A12* v. courant a la 630-631 *B, B1, B2, B3, B4, B5, A6* en ala aux t.le. (*B1* t.) et 630-642 *B7* en alla a le. pour luy compta les novellez et il les t.en. dormans car il estoit fors matin et luy d. que de la c. salloient g.da. a grant nombre que le venoient combatre tantost le. se leva moult hastivement et f.c. par tout son ost quil f. tous brevement armes car il debvoit avoir b. contre p. quant ses gens o yre lempereur ne tardirent guere quil ne fusent tot armez et eurent tres grand ioye des novellez de le. car lempereur voeult estre des le premier en baptaille et son filz titus et ses g.q. 631 *A7* lit et lui *A9* t.en. ou lit car a celle heure il ne. 631-632 *A12* lui compte comme ceulx 631-633 *B2* t.en. couchie car le s.ne. pas encores l. si luy d. que de la c. sailloit g.da.p. combatre lost adonc lem. *B, B1, B3, B4, B5, A6* t. que dormoient e. car le s.e. encoires l. et d. (*B1* e. alevez il d. *B3* le conseille e.en. a lever et d. *B4* en. a lever et d. *B5* d. et nes. pas en. le conseil leve puis d.) a lempereur que de la c. (*B3* la la c.) sailloit g. (*B4* et partoient g. *A6* s. grans g.) a.p. combatre (*B5* a. en tresgrant nombre c.) son host adonc le. manda son (*B3* m.q. son *B5* m. bien hastivement son) f. titus iafet (*B3* t. et ioseph du cassel *A6* f.) et 632 *A9* e. sailliz et y. *A1* e.h. *A2* y.t. *A12* cite venoyent et yssoyent t. *A2* c. a *A12* a. de la cite p. 632-633 *A12* sur son oust l. 632-634 *A1* co. sur lempereur et ses g. tantost le.f. 633 *A12* q. tantost son f.t. iaffet *B2* t. et iassel

leur dist qu'il fiscent crier que hom s'armast bien tost. Et incontinent il fust fet. Et quant les gens de l'empereur seürent pour quoy c'estoit, il en eürent trop grant joye et incontinent il furent tous armés davant l'empereur. Et il leur dist qu'il averoient bataille et leur compta comment Pilate avec ses gens venoit contre eulx et leur dist qu'il appareillassent leurs batailles et qu'il fussent tous pres de ferir sur leurs ennemis. Et quant [46r] l'empereur et son filz et ses gens / furent armés, il se partirent de l'ost et vindrent aus champs et furent gens sans nombre.

[42] Et quant il furent venus la out la oust de Pilate estoit, il fust environ

634 *B4* d. et leur dist quilz *A12* d. que tantost f.c. que tout h. *A1* c. que chascun sa. 634-635 *B5* d. que tantost f.c. par tout lost que tous fussent armes et bien appareilliez et tantost fut *B, B1, B2, B3, B4, A6* c. que (*A6* c. par tout que) tous leurs gens fussent (*B2* g. de lost f.) armes et bien appareillez et (*B2* b. aprestes et) tantost fut *A1* et de present fust 634-636 *A9* i. il 635 *A12* fet car de leur mesmes estoyent prest de iour en iour et q. ceulx de lost vont scavoir p. *A7* q. en e. 635-636 *B, B1, B2, B3, B4, B5, A6* les chevaliers et les servant oyrent le (*A6* c. heurent le) cry ilz e. (*B2* et les archiers oyrent les nouvelles ilz e. moult) g. 636 *A12* et tantost vont venir t. 636-637 *A1* et vindrent d.le.t.a. et *B, B1, B2, B3, B4, B5, A6* et tantost f. bien a point et (*B3* f. en p. et *B1* b. armez et) alerent (*B2* et f.t. aprestes et sen a.) t.d. (*B5* f. prestz et b. a p.d.) le. (*A6* a.d.le.t.) et *A7* il fut fait et 637 *A2, A12, B5* et lempereur l. 637-639 *B, B1, B2, B3, B4, B5, A6* b. contre p. et ses (*B2* et contre ses) gens et adonc lempereur et ses gens se (*A6, B3* p. et sez g. et se *B2* a. tous se *B5* p. et dirent tous que nostre seigneur en fut loe et luy en rendirent graces puis se) midrent en (*B1* se tindrent en) ordonnance (*A6* en belle o.) pour entrer en b. et pour f. (*B1* b. contre pilate et *B3* p. frapper bon coup *B4* f. dedans *B5* f. dedens de tresbon cuer) q. 638 *A1* et d. 638-639 *A12* p. venoit a. le roy archilaux et leurs g. et commanda quil ordennassent les b. et que chascun fust t. *A7* quil appestassent l. 639 *A1* de frapper sur *A3* e. en apres q. *A4* sur eulx et 639-640 *A12* q. ce fust fait le. 640 *A3* f. et toutes leurs g. *A12* f. tithus et les royx dux contes marquis barons et chevaliers et toutes autres manieres de gens se 640-641 *A12* de leurs logemens out ilz estoient loges et estoient des g. 640-642 *B, B1, B2, B3, B4, B5, A6* le. et touz ses (*B1* et ses) g.f. bien a point lempereur (*B2* b. armes et aprestes le.) se (*B5, A6* p. il se) mist tout premier et (*B5* p. dedens et) touz les autres gens (*B3,B4* t. sez g.) apres et (*B1* les g.a. luy et *B5* t. ses gens a. luy et) estoient tant que nen savoient le n. (*B2* p. et ses g.t. apres luy *B5* le contre) et 642 *A12* out p. et ses gens e. *B3* v. en lost *A11* p.en. 642-643 *B, B1, B3, A6* p. et ia e. (*A6* et lay e.) heure de t. et en. ne e.t. saillis (*B3* nes.s.t. ceulx) de *B2, B4* ou e. lost de p. il estoit e. heure (*B4* es.h.) de t. et en. ne e. il pas t. saillis de 642-644 *B5* ou e. lost de p. quil e. ia heure de t. et en les b.f. arrengees toutes deux ilz se. 642-648 *B7* f. pres de losth de p. il e. ia heure de t. et ne es. poinct en. sailli de la citez trestous ung peupares que les b.f. arrengeez tous deulx se m. et donnerent lung a la. tant de grand coups que a la p. baptaille de p.m. viij cent et d.

638 *Pilate avec* [ *Pilate a avec*

tierce et ceulx de Pilate n'estoient encor tous yssus de Jherusalem. Et quant il furent tous hors et les batailhes furent ourdennees, il s'entremeslerent ensemble et fraperent l'un sur l'autre par sy tres grant force des lances sur les escus et des autres arnois ossy que a la premiere assemblee mourirent des gens de Pilate le nombre de trois mile que d'uns que d'autres, et de ceulx de l'empereur le nombre de huit cens. Et si dura la bataille jusques a none. Puis quant la bataille fu achevee, il se tirerent chascum a part pour eulx respouser. Et quant il furent assés repousés, il

643 *A11* et ne. *A2* encor hors y. *A9* tous sailliz ne y. hors de 643-644 *A12* p. yssoient tousiours de la cite car il nes.en.t.y. et q. ilz f.h. 643-645 *A11* y. ceulx de la cite et q. les b.f. pres lune de lautre il coururent sus moult fierement lun contre la. et f. 643-648 *A13* encor parti horrs de la cite et incontinant apres que la b. de vaspasien fut prest en la plaice ceulx de p.m. en la p. bataille t. et c. de le.h. 644 *A8* t. yssus h. *A1* h. a belles b.o. *A2* b.f. toutes o. 644-645 *A12* o. il firent corner les menestriers et tromper les trompettes et ent.ens. tellement que lon ne veoit ne oyoit cel ne terre et 644-648 *B, B1, B2, B4, B5, A6* q. les b.f. arengeez toutes ij. si e. et (*B2* f.t.a.ent. et *B5* a.ent.et) donnerent lun a la. (*A6* les ungs contre les a.) tant grant cop par (*B1* f.t.a. les ungs contre les autres t.g.c. feroient par) leurs (*B5* c. de l.) e. et de leurs espees et da. armes quil (*B5* a. et bastons quilz) avoient que la p. (*B2* a. que a ceste p.) bataille de (*B2* b. furent mors de) lost de p.m.t.m. (*A6, B1* p.m. huit m. *B5* p. y m. qui estoient bien huit m.) entre chevaliers et servans et de lost de le. morurent (*B5* c. de le.m. bien) h. cens 644-653 *B3* q. lez b.f. assembreez si se. tellement quilz se donneirent lez ung aux a. tant grans cops par leurs e. de leur armez et espees quil avoient que la p. bataille de lost de p.m. huit m. entre chevaliers et servans et de lost de le. mille et deux cens et d. 645 *A8* en. lung parmi la. 645-646 *A2* f. par sy g.f. lung sur la. des 646 *A1* f. que a celle assamblee moult des *A7* l. par sus *A11* l. despees et *A12* e. et o. par les a. arnois que *A7* ar. que *A8* ar. tant que 646-647 *A2, A8* p. bataille m. *A12* p. bataille m. de ceulx de p.t. 646-648 *A11* ar. que en la bataille p.m. de ceulx de p. environ t. et aussi en mourut de ceulx de le. environ h. 647 *A8* p. environ iiij m. personnes que 647-648 *A1* mile que chevaliers que sergans et 648 *A7* n. de vij c. *A8* le. viij.xx. et *A12* le. vij c. 649 *A1* b. cruelle et fellonneuse i. *A9* ladicte b. depuis tierce i. *A11* b. depuis le matin i. *A13* la premier b. dois treiche i. *A3* n. ou environ p. *A8* n. et se 649-650 *B, B1, B2, B4, B5, B7, A6* i. a heure de (*A6, B5* i. de) n. apres ceste b.c. se t. a (*B2* b. se t.c. a) p. devers leur host et *A13* n. adoncques se reposarent dung costel et daultres et *A2* t. iusques c. *A9* t. a pa.c. pour *A12* fu finies ilz se vont mettre c. dune p. et se vont r. 649-651 *A11* q. ilz eurent a. icelle b. et que les trompectes eurent sonne la traicte dun couste et dautres ilz se mirent chascun a part soy et se reffroichirent a. longuement et q. il se f.r. dun couste et dautre il r. 650 *A3* r. puis q. *A8* il se f.rep. *A1* f.r. grand piece et eubrent recouvre a lame il *A7* f.r.a. il 650-651 *A12* f.r. de deux parties ilz vont retourner a. 650-652 *B, B1, B2, B4, B7, A6* f. ung peu r. tantost se misdrent en (*B1* se tindrent en *B4* t. recomencerent la b. et) se frapperent tant (*A6* se batirent t. *B1* b. comme avoient fait autresfoiz et sentresires passerent t.) durement (*B2* se ferirent t.d. les deux ostz que *B4* se batirent si d.) que de lost de p.mo.t. (*B1* mo. quatre) mile 650-653 *B5* f. ung peu r. tantost rentrerent en bataille et se frapperent tant durement que lost de p. fut esbahy et d. *A13* f. refreschie la bataille commencha plus cruelle que devant et ilz m. de ceulx de p.f.m. six c.

retournerent ariere au champs et commenserent a fraper l'un sur l'autre sy durement que a la fin il y mouru des gens de Pilate le nombre de trois mile et set cens et de la part de l'empereur douze cens. Et dura la bataille jusques au souleil couchant.

[43] Lors Nostre Seigneur, qui voult que sa mort soit vengee, fist ung grant miracle car quant les gens des deux batailles cuiderent que le souleil dust acouchier, il se commenserent a partir du champ. Et le souleil par la voulenté de Dieu se retourna en ourient et se leva sy comme il fust matin et la nuit fust passee. Et si fist belle journee jusques au souleil couchant. Et par eincy il n'[e]üst point de nuit entre deux jours.

651 *A11* a. en bataille et *A12* c. arrieres a *A1, A2, A9* r. aux *A9* a ferir et a f. *A4* a ferir lung *A12* si fort et si 651-652 *A1* a huer et a f. si durement les ungs sur les a. que 652 *A11* que de la part de p. en m. bien environ t. *A12* m. de la part de p.t. 653 *A8* c. personnes et *B4* c. entre chevaliers et servans et *B7* c. homes et de loth de le. *A1, A6, B1* c. et dura *A10* des gens de *A13* de ceulx de *B, B2* de lost de *B4* le. morut mille et deux c. *A9, A12* le. vij (*A12* le. vj.) c. 653-654 *A7* b. au 653-655 *B, B2, B3, B4, B5, A6* dura la b.i. (*B5* la meslee i.) a vespres que le s. se vouloit couchier adonc n. 654 *A12* i. a vespres et a 654-655 *B1* a vespres que *A13* c. dudit iour adoncques de la grase de n. 655 *A12* l. ihesu crist qui *B7* s. ihesus qui v. la vengance de sa m.f. *A1* s. demonstra ung *A6* v. monstrer son m. *A12, B3* sa passion (*B3* sa mort et p.) fust v. 655-656 *A2, A9* ung tres g. *B2* ung moult g. 655-658 *A13* ve. le s. sen r. 656 *A11* g. et souverain m. *A12* q. les d. *A11* q. ceulx des d. ostz c. *A7* b. tindrent que 656-657 *A11* s. fust a. 656-659 *B, B1, B3, B4, B5, B7, A6* q.cu.p. (*A6* q. voulurent p.) du c. et que le s. se c. (*B1* du c. avant que s.c.) il fut (*B5* se c. tantost fut) tourne en (*B7* du c. cuident quil fust nuyst le s. se mest en) o. par la grace de (*B1, B3, B4, B5, B7, A6* la v. de) d. et se l. si c. il f. bien m. et comme (*B3, B4, B5* l. ainsi co.) se (*B1* f. *B7* d. ainsi co. sil fust m. et co.) la 656-664 *B2* q. ilz cu. de toutes les d.b.p. du c. et sen r. arriere sur lost de p. et d. 657 *A1* et tantost le 658 *A10* o. sy l. *A12* r. devers o. et se commencza a lever comme sil f. bien m. 658-659 *A11* m. et fist beau iour et cler i. 658-661 *A13* o. et la fut d.i. sans n. et q. 659 *A1* n.p. *A3* au c. 659-660 *A11* c. et ne fist p. *A12* c. et aussy ny 659-661 *B, B1, B3, B4, B5, B7, A6* p. et si f.b. matinee (*B5* et quil fut bien matin et quil fut b.m.) et (*B1* b. levee et) entre le s. (*B7* m. et par ainsy quant s.) c. et le soleil levant moult pou (*B7* c. neurent p.) de n.q. *A2* c. et 660 *A4* ei. ne fust p. *A3* en. ses d. 660-661 *A9* en. se d.i. dessusdiz et

652 *y* [ *ny* Correction from MSS *A1, A2, A3, A4, A7, A8, A9, A10, A12.*
655-660 The biblical precedent for this passage is to be found in Joshua 10:12-14, which relates the battle of Gibeon. During this battle, however, the sun stands still for a day, rather than returning to the east immediately after setting. See also 2 Kings 20:8-11 and Jenkins (pp. 177-178), note to line 2450 of the *Chanson de Roland*: "Que lo soleil facet por lui ester." See in addition Brault (vol. 1, pp. 262-263, 448).

[44] Et quant l'empereur et Titus, son filz, eürent veü le miracle, il en eürent grant joye et penserent que Dieu ne vouloit point qu'il yssirent encore hors du champ. Et lors il retournerent et commencerent a fraper sur Pilate et sur ses gens et Pilate sur eulx. Et dura la bataille jusques a midi. Et la moru de la part de Pilate douze cens et cinquante et de la part de l'empereur mile et cinquante.

[46v] [45] Lors les batailles [furent] fort eschausees l'une sur l'autre / et se repouserent jusques a vespres. Et lors il vinrent au champ et fraperent les

661 *A7* et son *B, B1, B3, B4, B5, B7, A6* le. et toutes ses (*A6* et ses) gens virent ces g.m. (*B5* g. merveilles *B3, B4* m. et merveille) il *A11* t. et toute sa gent e. veu iceluy grant m. *A9* le bel et grant m. *A12* f. lequel estoit empereur nouvel par la resignacion que son pere luy avoit faicte e. veu le grant m. que dieux avoit fait il 662 *A2* e. tres g. *A11* e. moult g.i. et dirent que *A12* i. et toutes leurs gens aussy et *A8* quil cessassent ne y. 662-663 *A7, A11* y.h. *A1* point que le c. se departist e. et *A10* et partissent e. *B, B1, B3, B4, B5, A6* et p. que (*B5* et apparceurent bien que) d.v. et (*B1* d. lavoit fait et) que e. nestoit pas heure de (*B4* pas haste de) partir du 662-664 *B7* d. ainsy le v. et que e. nestoient heure de retourner de baptaille et sen r. derechef sur loth de p. et d. *A13* i. et bataillarent i. 663 *A2* e. du *A11* c. sans pugnicion adoncques lempereur et ses gens sen r. vers lost de pilate moult fierement eulx reconmandast en la garde de ihesu crist et co. *A12* r. arrieres au champ et co. *A9* a ferir et a f. 663-664 *A6, B, B1, B3, B5* r. derechief sur lost de p. et d. *B4* c. et adonc alerent derechief sur lost de p. et d. *A3* f. comme devant sur *A8* a ferir sur *A12* c. ferir sur loust de p. et p. *A7* r. et d. *A11* f. sur lost de p. moult merveilleusement si que grant pitie estoit de les veoir dun couste et dautre tant sentie donnoient de merveilleux et horribles coups et d. icelle b. depuis le matin i. 664 *A1* sur les gens de p. et ceulx de p. *A9* p. aussy sur *A1* d. cest assault i. *A2, A3, A4, A7, A10* i. a tant quil fut m. *A9* i. a leure de m. 664-665 *B2* i. a heure de miiour et 665 *A1, A6, B, B1, B2, B3, B4, B7* m. des gens de pi. *B5* m. des gens a p. ij m. cent et ci. *A11* pi. environ mille deux cens et ci. *A12* pi.ij.m. et v.cz. et de la part *A13* de ceulx de pi. iij.m.ij.c. et ci. *A1* ci. des gens de *A6* ci. et de le. 665-667 *B, B1, B3, B4, B7* ci. et de la gent le. (*B4, B7* de le.) m. .l. (*B3* le. cent et .l.) adonc (*B1, B4* m. et a.) de chascune (*B5* et de ceulx de le. .v.c.lx a. quant lempereur et c.) partie de lost f. (*B1, B5* p.f. *B7* a.f.) bien e. *A13* ci. et de ceulx de le.m.l.fu.f.e. les b. lune 666 *A9, A10* e. trois cens .l. *A12* e.c. et .l. 666-667 *A6, A8, B2* c. adonc chascune partie du lost fu. bien (*A8* c. et fu. les b. fort *B2* des deux ostz fu. mout) e. 666-668 *A11* e. environ m. et .l. apres ce que les b.fu. reffroichiz assez longuement ilz retournerent au *A1* c. si se retrahirent ung peu pour eulx reposer et quand vint a heure de v. ilz retournerent et commencierent a fraper les 667 *A12* les deux b. *A7* fu. moult e. 667-668 *A12* et allerent soy reposer i. a v. et a heure de vespres ilz vont retourner arrieres au 667-670 *B, B1, B2, B3, B4, B5, B7, A6* et se prindrent (*B3* et sentreprinrent) derechief et (*B2* et bataillerent arriere et *B4* d. a combatre et) d. la bataille (*B3* d. ceste b.) i. a s. couchant (*A6* s. levant c.) et la (*B5* et adonc) m. 668 *A8* et puis ilz retournerent au c. et fierent lez 668-669 *A13* a nonne adoncques se refermerent i. a s. couchant et la *A11* c. et ferirent les *A3* c. et se combatirent durement i.

uns sur les autres. Et dura jusques a tant que souleil fust couché. Et la mouru de la part de Pilate deux mile, deux cens et cinquante et de la part de l'empereur trois cens et cinquante, sy que en tretout mouru de la part de Pilate treze mile et de la part de l'empereur deux mile et cent. Et en ceste derrienne bataille l'empereur leva le champ et chasserent les gens de Pilate jusques es portes de Jherusalem.

[46] Et en la chasse fesant il ouÿrent ung home qui ne sesoit de dire: "Vespesian, va en Jherusalem." De quoy tout le peuple de Jherusalem fu

669 *A10* d. la bataille i. *A11* a. moult fierement et d. la bataille i. 669-670 *A11* s. couchant puis sonnerent les trompetes dun coste et dautre puis se trayrent chascun a part soy et m. 669-671 *A1* i. a a s. couchant et a c.d.b.m. des gens de 670 *A11* pi. environ d. *A13* m. de ceulx de pi. *B3* lost de *B4, B5* m. des gens de *B7* m. des gens pi. *A12* pi. iij.m.iij. cens *B5* mi.vij. cens *B1, B4* c. ainsi fut compte en t. de (*B4* c. de la) part *B2* et fut conte que en t. 670-672 *A13* c. par tout t. 670-673 *B5* et dont le. et ses gens firent fuir le g. 671 *A1* le. ne morut que t. *A10* c. soixante si *A11* c. ou eviron oy que en toutes les batailles m. *B3* e. iiii c. et .l. ainsi fuerent compte en t. de *A8* que m. en tres t. 671-672 *B* c. ainsi fut compte en t. que de pi. *A12* e. mille et c. et cent 671-673 *B7* e.ii.c. ainsi par compte faict en t. par devers le. et ses gens firent fuyr loth de 671-674 *A6* e. morurent iiij.c. et .l. et ainsy fut compte de la partie de p. morurent t.m. et .v. cens adonc le. et ses gens en firent fuir pi. 672 *A11* pi.xxiii.m. *B1* pi. mourut t. *B2* pi.xiiij.m. *B3* pi. que morurent en cez dictez bataillez t. *B4* pi. qui morurent quinze m. cent et cinquante et *A5* e.iii.m.iii.c. et 672-673 *A13* et du costel de le.iij.m.ij.c. cinquante et en c.b.le. gaingna les champs *A11* c. honmes en c.b. fut chasse lost de 672-674 *B, B4* e. morurent d.m. et cinq cens adont b. et sa gent (*B4* mo. trois m.a.le. et ses g.) en firent fouir lost pi. *B2, B3, B1* deux m. .v.c. adonc le. et sa gent en firent fuyr lost (*B1* fo.p. et sa gent et tout son o.) de pi. 673 *A9* c. maniere d. *A1* c.b.d. les gens de le.ch. ceulx de *A8* b. le c. demoura a le. et *A3* et luy avecques ses gens chas. *A12, A13* chas. loust de 674 *A8* po. de la cite de 674-676 *B, B1, B2, B4, B5, A6* i. adonc tout le (*B4* a. le) peuple fut courroucie (*B1, B2, B4* f. moult c. *B5* p. de iherusalem f. moult c.) car il avoit ung h. sur les murs de la cite qui crioit bien v. (*B2* qui disoit vien v. vien *B5* c. vien v. *A6* b. fort v.) en 674-677 *B3* i. car *A11* i. et 674-680 *B7* i. dont tout le poeuple fust couroucés q. 675 *A9* en f. icelle c. grant partye et plusieurs de ladicte cite de iherusalem o. ung h. ou une voix qui c. *A13* et o. *A7* ilz eurent ung *A8* il adviserent ung *A10* c. virent ung 675-676 *A1* et faict la chose ilz o. la voix dung h. qui disoit v. *A12* et quant ilz les chassoyent ilz o. une voix domme qui crioit toujours va v. en *A13* quil disoit a haultes voix pilate va 676 *A8* q. le 676-677 *A9, A10* q. le p. fut moult f. (*A10* m.) c. *A13* i. dont ceulx de *A7, A13* fut mon c. *A12* p. en estoit esbays c. *A6, B, B1, B2, B4* i. car (*B2* i. et) il

675 *sesoit* [ *fesoit* Correction from MSS *A2, A3, A5, A7, A8, A10*.

fort couroucíés, car il cuidoient qu'il fust profette. Et en celle entree fu blacé Jozeph d'Arimatie d'une lance par les cuisses, mes il n'en vouscist moins.

[47] Et quant Pilate et le roy Archelan si furent rentrés dedans la cité, il furent fort lacés et eürent grant duel de la perde de leur gent qu'il avoient fette et de la bataille ossy. Et les gens menoient si grant duel par la cité que onques ne fust si grant en ung seul lieu.

677 *A1* fust aulcune voix de p. *A9* fust prophetize par ung p. *A5, A7, A9, A1* celle heure (*A1* c. cache) fu 677-678 *A6, B, B1, B2, B3, B4, B5* que celluy homme fut p. et adonc fut navre (*B3* c. fut p. qui estoit sur lez murs qui crioit vienz v. en iherualem adont fut moult courecie tout le peuple et f.n. *B2, B4* f. blesse) i. *A12* e. de la porte fu b. *A13* p. et adoncques i. fut faulse dune *A11* fut i.da.b. dune l. moult griefvement par 678 *A1* i. dune *B5* a. en la c. dune l. mais 678-680 *A6, B, B1, B3, B4, B5* ne vailit gaire m. (*B5* g. piz) q. *A7, A10* c. et q. *A8* il neust garde et *A11* nen mourut point et q. *B2* mes il fut tantost guery q. 678-686 *A13* c. ung chascun sen retourna mennant grant duel en son hostel et si estoient bien l.q. vient landemain le. 679-680 *A3* m. puis q. 680 *A11* p.a. et ses gens f. retraitz d. *B, B3* a. et leurs gens f. retournes d. *B1* a. retournerent d. *A3, A5, A7, A9, A12, A2, B5* f. retrais d. la ville (*A2* f.d.la c.r. *B5* f. retournez d. iherusalem) ilz *A1, A8, A10, B4* f. retraicte (*B4* f.) d. 680-681 *A6* a. et leurs gens f. retournes en iherusalem il fa.l. *B7* a. et leurs gens f. en la citez il estoient tous l. tant que a peine se pevent soustenir et e. *B2* a. et leurs gens f. moult l. et plains de grant doleur de la *B, B1, B3, B4* c. de iherusalem ilz fu.l. (*B1* fu. navrez et l. *B3* fu. fort l.) et 681 *B, B2* p. que 681-682 *A5* gent et de *A11* p. quilz a. eue de l.g. qui estoient demourez en la cite et en eurent si *A12* p. quilz a.f. sur l. gens et de la b. quil avoyent perdus et les autres gens de la cite m. *B1* d. opar 681-684 *A6* g. doleurs par la citey que oncques mais tant grant ne fut oyr de la p. qui avoyent fait le. et ses g. se reconseilirent en leurs tentes et la *B4* d. par la c. plus que o. mais tant g. ne fut ouye de la p. qui la.f.le. et toutes ses gens sen retournerent en leurs tentes et la *B5* l. et traveilies et e. moult g.d. et toutes les gens par la c. eurent tel d. et si g. ne fut pour la p. quil oroient eue et soufferte le. et ses gens sen retournerent a leurs tentes et *B3* d. par toute la c.le. et sez g. se reconselleirent en leurs tentez et 681-685 *B7* gent lors le. se retourna a ses tentez pour soy reposer et rafreschir car en avoit grand besoing ainsi ses gens quant vint le lendemain au matin pillate ne vault retourner en b. et eust en conseil de garder la citez car il avoit assez affaire a la bien garder q. 682 *A1* f. et les *A8* o. et sy m. les g. si *B* f. et adonc fut si *A9* gens de ladicte cite de iherusalem m. *A10* d. en la *A11* d. que 682-684 *B* que iamais on ne leut tant g. ne fut oy adonc le. et ses g. se retournerent a leurs tentez et la. 682-685 *B2* f. et adonc se menerent si grans complainctes en iherusalem que o. telles ne f. ouyes le. et ses g. sen allerent en leurs tantes et la ilz prindrent chascun a boyre et a mangier car ilz avoient moult grant soif et grant fain et se rep. car ilz e. moult l. quant vint le lendemain pilate eut en conseil quil ne retourneroyt point en b. mais garderoyt la cite car il y avoit asses a fayre a la bien garder q. *A12* d. que o. ne lavoit ont vehu mener si g. deul et le. et ses g. allerent reposer et refreschir a leurs tentes et alongemans car ilz e. bien l. et q. 683 *A1* o. mes en une ville ne *A3* g. veu en *A8* f. oye si *A9* f. veu si 683-684 *A1* g. et *A11* g. dueil et *B1* o. mes tant g. ne fut oye de la p. quilz a.f. et le. et ses g. se reconcilierent que ilz furent a leurs temptes et la

677-679 The wounding of a heroic figure between the thighs (the loss of the hero's reproductive ability usually symbolises a more extensive sterility of the land) is a widely-known folklore motif. Cf. Chrétien de Troyes' *Perceval* (ed. Roach, vv. 435-437, p. 13).

[48] Et l'empereur s'ala lougier en des trefs avec ses gens. Et la il se refrescherent et repouserent car il estoient tous las de la bataille. Et quant l'empereur vist que Pilate n'yssoit point hors de la cité, il dist a Jafet et a Jacob qu'il pensassent de fere fere les foucés. Et affin qu'il eüssent plus toust fet, il eürent plus d'ovriers tant qu'il en eürent quinze mile, si que a peu de temps lé foucés furent fet tout environ de Jherusalem, sy que

684 *A1* ala en *A3, A7, A8* en ses tantes a. *A11* l.a. ses g. en ses tentes et se *A9* t. et tentes a. 685 *A11* rep. apres certain iours et q. *B, B1, B3, B4, B5, A6* rep. car ilz avoient grant fain et grant seuf et si estoient bien l. mais quant vint landemain au matin (*B3* au bien m.) pilate ne (*B5* m. ne) volut tourner a la (*B3* v. venir en la) b. mais eut son conseil que ilz gardassent bien la cite car ilz avoient assez a faire a la (*B1* f. de bien la) garder (*B5* c. contre lempereur et toutes ses gens) q. *A5* t. travailles et *A10* las quant pillate vit le nombre des gens quil avoit perdus il fut moult esbahy et nosa plus yssir q. *A1* b. et lendemain q. 686 *A1* v.p. que luy ne ses gens ne y. *A10* v. que ceulx de iherusalem ne *A12* ne ses gens ne *A6, A5, B, B1, B2, B3, B4, B5* ne sauloit p.h. (*A5, B1, B2, B4, B5* p.) de *B3* d. a ioseph et 686-687 *A11* ne se vouloit p. rendre ne rendre la ville et que il n y. aucunement en bataille si d. a iaffet quilz *B, B1, B4, B5* d. a iacob et a iasel penser (*B4* i. du tassel p.) de 686-689 *B7* ne retourna p. en baptaille il commandast a iacob et a iafet du chastel qui firent parfaire leurs fo. ainsi le firent et fu. faict en p. de t. en telle maniere que *A6* d. a iacob et a iaffet pensez de f. les fo. se mirerant incontinant en nombre q.m. que incontinant fu. faites les fo.t 686-696 *A13* ne sailloit p. deshorrs ainsin comme par avant et adoncques avoit alentour de la cite en sommes toutes q. ouvriers a fere les fo. lesquelz furent en brief fais et q. ceulx de la cite virent les fossez de toutes pars quil ne p. plus partir deshorrs ilz disoient tous a une voix s.

687 *A7, A11, A8, B3, A1* de f. (*A1* f. la *A11* de parfaire *A8* dacomplir) les *A5* quilz feissent achever lez *A11* a. que par ce ilz peussent p.t. prendre la cite et affin quilz e. 687-689 *B, B1, B2, B3, B4, B5* et tantost en la presence se midrent a aler q. (*B2* t. ilz se m. en leuvre et estoient douvriers q. *B3* t. se m. a ouvrey q. *B4* t.m. ouvriers a ouvrer quilz furent q.) m. par (*B3* m. ouvriers par) nombre qui touz se misdrent a oubrer et incontinent (*B1* et tous se m. tout le nombre que devant y estoit et i.) fu. (*B2* t. ouvroyent tantost fu.) faiz les fo. (*B5* t.m. a ouvrer et y estoient par n.q.m. qui se prindrent a labourer fort a faire fo. et bien briefment fu. fais) t. 688 *A10* fet et prindrent p. *A1* fet que ilz preissent p. de gens et tantost le firent et furent entour q.m. ouvriers si *A2, A11, A8* o. que devant (*A8* quilz navoyent par davant et) t. *A3* ilz furent q. *A11* ilz estoient bien q. *A8* en avoyt environ xv 688-689 *A2* m. pour quoy en pou *A3* que en bien pou 689 *A11, A12* t. ilz eurent faiz les fo.t. *A2, A4* fet entour i. 689-690 *B, B1, B2, B3, B4, B5, A6* e. de la (*B1, B3* e. la) cite tant que (*B2* c. tellement que *B5* e. de iherusalem tellement que) nul ne sen p.y. ne entrer fors (*B1* p.e. ne y.f.) par (*B2, A6* e. se non par) la v. de lempereur car

684 *lougier* [ *lougieu* Correction from MSS *A2, A3, A5, A7, A8, A9, A10, A11.*

persone ne s'en peüt yssir sans leur voulenté, car les foucés estoient moult parfont, trente piés et de large quarante piés.

[49] Et quant Pilate vist que hom ne s'en pouoit issir, lui et tous les barons de la cité se desconforterent moult fort. Et tout le peuple disoit: "Cellui qui crioit: 'Va tost en Jherusalem, Vespesian' est mors, et le peuple le vouloit dire de Jhesu Crist. Et vous disiez que c'estoit profette contre nous. Et nous savions bien que c'estoit vois de Dieu ou de son angel. Sire,
[47r] Pi/late, mauvais conseil eüstes que vous ne rendissiez la ville a

690 *A5, A7* p. saillir s. *A12* y. ne entrer s. 690-691 *A2, A9, A10* v. et e. les f.m.p. quar il lavoient de parfont t. *A5, A7* v. et e. les f.p. *A1* v. et sachies que les f. avoient de p. *A3* car ilz avoient de p. 690-692 *B7* p. saillir sinon par la v. de lempereur q. *A11* v. et sceu car les f. avoient de p.t. piez ou environ et *B, B1, B2, B4, B5, A6* f. avoient .xxx. piez (*B5* a. .l.p.) de (*B2* t. coudees de *B4* a. quinze cottees de) p. et .xl. p. de (*A6* .xl. de) l. et q. *A12* f. avoient de p. .l.p. et .x.p. de l. et 690-702 *B3* f. avoient xxx piez de p. et .xl.p. de l.q. 691-692 *A8* p. et l. et *A2, A5, A10* q. et *A9* q. et par ainsi nul ne sen povoit yssir hors de iherusalem et 691-693 *A1* de loingn q. pies p. et tous ceulx de iherusalem q. ilz v. quilz ne p.i. hors de furent m. desconfortes et 692 *A2, A12* que nul (*A12* que personne) ne 692-693 *B, B1, B2, B4, B5, A6* que de (*B4* que de la cite de) iherusalem ne (*B1* que ne) p. saillir h. ne i. (*B4* p.i.) il (*B1* i. de iherusalem il *B2* i. nul ne p. entrer ne s. dehors il *B5* iherusalem nul nen p.i. ne entrer il *A6* p.h.i. ne entrer il) se 692-702 *B7* que de iherusalem ne p. saillir donc il fust forment esbahi et tous ceulx de la citez et criant forment par desconfort lors q.p. vit et o. le c. que le p. fasoict dictz au 693 *A11* b. et chevaliers se *A12* b. se vont ensembler et se *A7* la se *A2, A5, A7, A3* d. (*A3* d.f.) et *A9* f. pour lamour de la voix quilz avoient ouye et *A8* m. et *A3* t. le plus de p. de la cite d. *A12* lautre p. crioit et d. *A1* di. sachies que c. 693-694 *A10* b. se d. et le p.c. *B, B1, B4, B5, A6* m. et (*B1* m.f. et) touz ses barons et tous ceulx de la cite crioient et d.ce. (*B5* cite d. et cr.ce.) qui cr. touz iours vien v. (*A6* vien vien v.) en (*B4* v. vien en) i. est *A9* p. aussy et disoit icellui peuple audit pylate que ladicte voix ou ce. qui cr. disoit va t.v. en i. car la le prophete y est 693-695 *B2* et les barons de la cite et crioyt et d.ce. qui tousiours cr. vien v. vien en i. nous creons quil 693-696 *A11* p. crioit et d.s. 694 *A1, A3* t.v. en i. (*A3* v.i.) est *A12* cr. tousiours va v. en i. est 694-695 *A1* et leur intention estoit de ihesu crist et *A12* et ilz vouloyent dire disiez *B, B1, B4, B5, A6* et nous disions (*B1* et tous d. *A6* n. disoyent) que 694-696 *A10* t.v. en i. tout est m. il disoit verite car nous ne vallons gueres mieulx nous povons bien veoir que v. 695 *A9* d. et si entendoit de *A9* et v. pylate disiez *A9* p. qui est et estoit c. 695-696 *A9* co.n. scavions et s. *A12* co.n.s. 695-697 *B2* co.n.s.p. vous e.m.c. quant v. 695-702 *B, B1, B4, B5, A6* p. or voies le (*B1* p. et voyons maintenant le *B5* or veons nous maintenant le *A6* p. et veons nous bien le) t. maintenant (*B4* or veons le contraire m.) que (*B5* t. que) d.c. qui estoit es p. (*A6* d. es p.) de iherusalem car tu trouveras gens mors par les carrieres q.p. vit le c. que le p. faisoit (*B5* que les gens faisoient) il dit au 696 *A8* s. que *A9* v. qui estoit et est de *A1* de prophete de d. *A9, A10* a. et pour ce (*A10* a. aha) s. 697 *A1* p. sire pilate par dieu m. *A11* c. creustes que *A10, A13, B2* la cite a *A8* r. ceste v. 697-698 *A9* r. a lempereur ladicte cite de iherusalem or 697-700 *A3* v. car 697-702 *A11* r. a le. vaspasien la cite car par adventure nous eust il prins a mercy et

697 *rendissiez la* [ *rendissiez la la*

l'empereur. Or pouvons veoir que le temps s'apreuche de ce que cel home qui se tenoit a la porte disoit quant Vespesian nous chassoit. Car il dissoit tous jours: 'Vespesien, va en Jherusalem,' car tout le peuple meur en la ville parmi les rues."

[50] Et quant Pilate ouÿ le crist du peuple, il demanda conseil au roy Archelan et a ses autres chevaliers. Et sus tous Joseph d'Arimatie parla et dist: "Sire, yssy ne se peut mettre autre conseil ne autre remede mes que on face terre les gens, et que vous facés fere deux grans foucés pour mettre

698 *A8, A10, A1* p. nous bien (*A1* p.b.) v. *A12* e. lequel estoit nostre sire naturel or p. nous bien v. *A13* que cestui h. questoit a. 698-699 *A10* h. disoit qui 698-700 *A12* que celle voix domme qui se t. a la p. de la ville laquelle d. va 698-702 *B2* or veez le t. maintenant que d.c.h. qui estoyt en p. de i. car tu trouveras les gens mors plus charrieres q. 699 *A9* qui estoit a. *A10* p.q. 699-700 *A8* d.v. va *A13* d. est vray quilz disoit v. va *A1* c. que il crioit v. 700 *A10* le monte se m. 700-702 *A12* m. maintenant en iherusalem p. les r. lors p. *A13* car le p. commence fort a morir q. 701-702 *A1* r. de fain et 702 *A1* oy le parler du *A5* oy pilate oy le *B2, B3* c. que le p. faysoyt il dist au *A11* il ot moult grant paour et fut moult desconforte si d.co. de ceste chose au *A12* il se vayt conceiller au 702-704 *A13* ilz se conseilla a a. et tous les a. nobles barons estant lors en la cite de iherusalem adoncques i.da. respondit le premier disant s. le meilleur c. est comune il me samble que 703 *A12* ses barons et es a. *A11* a tous les a. barons et c. a iaffet et a. ioseph et en la fin i. *A12* da. lequel p. 703-704 *A3* t. a i.da. lequel luy respondit s. *A10* c. et a i.da. lequel d. 703-705 *B, B1, B2, B3, B4, B5, A6* ses c. et a touz ses gens que (*B2* t. les a. que *B5* g. seigneurs que) pourron nous faire de ces mors (*B2* de ceste gent m.) s. (*A6* m. et ioseph d.s.) que (*B3* sez gens m. et ioseph dabarimathie dist s. ie lairoiez que *B4* ces gens m. et ioseph abarimathie dist messires que) fa. (*B1* m. et ioseph dist s. faites) fere d. (*B2* s. dist lung il fault fayre fere une *B5* m. et ioseph leur respondist et dist s. ie vous conseille que v.fa.d.) gr. *B7* a. que vous semble bon de faire ie ne ses quel conseil donnez ung peult apres fust plus grand crit car les gens mouroient par monceaulx aulx rues tantost pillate commandast a fere 704 *A8* d. ainsy ne *A3, A5, A7, A8, A9, A2* m.a. (*A2* m.) r. *A1* c. ne r. 704-705 *A10* m.a.r. si non que v. *A11* s. entre les a. choses qui sont de necessite ie vous conseille que 705 *A13* f. tousier ce peuple et *A1, A3* on f. faire *A7* que on f. *A2* d.fo. *A10* fere trois ou quatre fo. *A13* fere g. 705-706 *A1* faces et que on y mette ceulx qui sont m. *A2* m.c. *A9* m. ces g. cy qui sont m. *A10* m. les m. *A11* faces hors de la cite p.m. les corps de ceulx qui ont este ocsis en ceste bataille car *A12* m. tous les mors car 705-708 *A13* faces vees les murs de la cite p.m. les mors dedeans pour la p. car noz en pourrions bien avoir grant maladie et que n.t. 705-709 *B5* faces ou nous les metterons car t.s.p. de nous car iay grant paour que de la punaisie ne v. grant mortalite et que faicie refraindre les viandes car sachez pour vray que bien petit en y a et sa y a plus de .l.m. hommes sans les femmes dedens la cite qui *B, B1, B2, B3, B4, A6* faces ou nous les mectrons touz car (*B2* ou lon mectra tous les corps car) t. nous s.p. (*B1* s. trop p.) et ay grant paour que par la grant p. ne v. mortalite en la cite (*B4* en ceste c.) et que (*B4* et aussi que) faites faire restraindre les viandes car (*B2* c. et si fault fayre les vivres r.) sachies que bien (*A6* car b.) petit en y a et y (*B2* en yci et vous scaves quil y) a plus (*B3* et il serait p.) de t.m. homes qui (*B2* h.) estoient 705-727 *B7* faces parfunde pres les murs pour les puantasez car ilz avoit grand peur de pestilencez en la cite car ilz en morroist bien pour ung iour iii et lx par ce quil ne trouvoyent que menger adoncques p.f.

toute ceste gent morte, car il sont trop pres et sy est peril que par le puentise vensist en ceste ville aucune enfermeté. Et ossy que nous nous tenons sagement [et que les vivres soient bien guardez quar nous en avons assez pou. Et] sy a en ceste ville bien trente mile estrangiers qui estoient venus a la feste et on ne les peut bouter hors. Sy seroit bien necessaire que chascun guardast bien les vivres."

[51] Quant Pilate ouÿ le conseil de Joseph, il dist que c'estoit bien dist, et

706 *A3* s.p. de nous et *A7* s.p. *A11, A12* p. dicy (*A12* p. de la ville) et *A9* est grant p. *A11* sy a grant p. 706-707 *A1* que la p. des mors ve. *A9* la tres grant p. quilz rendoient et pourroient rendre quil ne ve. 706-708 *A10* car par la p. qui en faudra il enpuentira toute la cite par quoy toute monde en pourroit bien mourir et aussi il faut que 707 *A12* p. diceulx ne ve. a la cite a. *A3* p. que a cause de ce il ne ve. *A9* a. grant e. et maladie et *A3* vi. une grant e. *A7* vi. et 707-708 *A11* p. diceulx v. sur nous a. grant mortalite et o. fault que n. nous gouvernons s. en touz noz afferes et que nous gardons b. les vivres dont n.a. 707-709 *A1* vi.t. 708 *A8* q. en verite n. 708-709 *A3, A5, A9, A10, A7* a. bien (*A7* a.) peu *A8* a. bien a faire sy sont bien en *A12* et faysons bien garder les v.q. en verite sellon les gens que nous summes il ny a bien paou *A13* et faisons bien garder nos v.q. en verite en ceste cite en a deput tres peul plus de t.m. personnes e. 709 *A10, A11* a bien en c.v.t. *A12* b.x.m. 710 *A11* f. conme vous scavez lesquelz on *A12* f. nulz ne *B2* f. lesquelz nous ne *A8* f. sy *A11* p. pas bonement mectre dehors pour la doubte de lempereur et de ses gens par quoy il s. *A3* s. grant necessite que *A5* s.n. 710-711 *A1* f. sy s.n. de bien garder les *A13* f. et pour ce ilz est bon de on garder les 710-712 *A7* h.q. *B, B1, B2, B3, B4, B5, A6* p. gecter dehors par nul lieu et (*B4* n. voye et *B5* n. et) que il estoit bien mestier a chascun sa (*B1, B4, B5* m. que c.g. sa *B3* et si est b.m. que c. garde bien sa *A6* qui feroit b.m. que c.g. sa) viande et pour cause du temp advenir (*B2* l. si est b.m. que c. garde ses vivres) q. 711 *A8* c. en droyt soy g. les 711-712 *A11* b. endroit soy les v. sans en fere aucun exces car grant besoing en aurons se autre remedde nest trouve briefvement en cest fait q. *A3* v. et pour cause q. 712 *A3* il respondit que *A12* i. dabarimathie avoit donne il d. que ce.b.d. et bien advise et 712-713 *A1* b. et lui d. que 712-714 *A11* b.d. si bailla audit i. la charge de fere faire les foussez ainsi quil avoit devise et incontinent par le congie de lempereur vaspasien et de pilate h. des murs de la c. firent d.g.f. moult parfons ou *A13* q. les fossez furent faiz lon y mist par 712-716 *B, B1, B3, B4, B5, A6* c. il (*B5* c. de i. il) le tint a moult bon (*A6* t. pour b.) et conmanda a i. que il f. a (*B5* f. tout a *A6* que le f. fere a) sa voulente et i. tantost f. (*B3, B4, B5* i.f.t.) fere fo. dehors les murs de la c. ou mi. (*B1* fere d. les m. de la c. deux grandes fo. et y mi.) les corps mors (*B5* ou ilz entrerent les c. des m. *A6* les m.) qui estoient par n. cent (*B3* m. xiii m. et c.) et (*B1* e. xiij m. et) x. adonc (*B4* n. quinze m.c. et cinquante a.) fist (*B5* qui furent tuez par le gens de lempereur et apres si f.) restraindre les (*B1* r. toutes les) viandes a *B2* i. dabarimate le tint pour bon si commanda a luy et es aultres quil f.f. ce quil disoient et tout a leur guise et tantost i. fere dehors les murs de la c. pres ung g. les corps m. de famine et aultrement et estoyent par n. xiiij.m. et vij.c. et apres fist restraindre les

708-709 Addition from MS *A2*, but based on all MSS except *A1*.

dist a Joseph que lui meïsmes le feïst fere. Et lors Joseph fist fere hors de la cité deux grans foucés ou il mirent tous les mors, sy y eüt par nombre treze mile et set [cens]. Et puis quant Joseph eüt fet cella, il fist guarder et estuier les vivres a ceulx qui en avoient trop. Aprés cela avint que en Jherusalem eüt sy tres grant cherté qu'il n'y demoura erbe sauvage a menger, en tant que hom la peüst avoir. Et ossy mengoient les bestes

713 *A8* i. darimathie que *A10* quil f. fere les fosses pour mectre le peuple qui estoit mors et *A8* le f. fere si quil avoit dit et *A1* l.i. dist que volentiers si f. fere h. 713-714 *A12* le f. fere a sa volente et incontinent i.f. ordonner et f.f.d.g.fo. la dehors la ville ou 714 *A10* f. pour mectre les *A7* n. xiiij m. et viij.c. et *A10* n. quatorze m. et 714-715 *A8* par compte xiiij m. et *A1* m. et en fouirent en fosse oussi les gens de lempereur comme les leurs et furent par n. quinze m. et cent vingt personnes et q. 714-716 *A11* n. xxiii.m. apres ces choses faittes allerent par toute la cite regarder ou estoient les vivres et commanderent de la bien g. a ceulx qui en a. largement et en vesquirent assez longtemps au mieulx quilz peurent ap. 715 *A5* vij et 715-716 *A12* xiii.m. et cccc et puis il f. cuiller et g. bien ses v. *A3, A5, A7, A8, A10, A1* g. (*A1* g. par gens) les 715-724 *A13* m. et une personne et lors furent sur les trespassez par leurs amis et aultres fait plussieurs clamours et lamentations et apres lon fist ordonnances sur les vivres pour iceulx gardera mieulx que lon pourroit apres cela vient en iherusalem sy grant famine que lon ny povoit trouver e.s. quelxconques et par grant fain m. toutes les b. questoient m. de fain f. chavalx vaiches chiens chaz et aultres b. quelxconques lors fut en la cite le cry si g. car cestoit abusion et les trouvoit lon mors par les rues .x.xx.xxx. et .xl. et les pourtoit lon es fossez dont cy dessus et faictes mention et trouva lon ung i. par compte faiz des mors par 716 *A10* v. et en prindrent a *A10* t. et en donner a ceulx qui nen avoient point ap. avint *A3* ap. avint 716-717 *A8* t. sy av. que non obstant sy g.c. fut en i. quil *A12* que en la cite de i. 716-719 *B, B1, B3, B4, B5* avo.ap. (*B5* avo. puis ap.) peu de temp fu si (*B5* t. eust si) g. famine en iherusalem qui ne d. nulles e.s. ne privees que eulx peussent trouver ne (*B1* p. avoir ne) b. que ilz ne m. chiens (*B3* n. bestez quil ne maingeassent et c. *B4* t. quilz ne maingassent et ainsi maingoient c.) chas chevaux ou (*B1* chas chamoilz ou) q. 716-722 *A6* avo.ap. peu de temps fut si g. famine en iherusalem qui d. nulle e.s. ne pomees qui puissient a. ne b. qui ne m. quar il morient de f. quar toutes choses estoyent tant chieres que ne povoyent trouver ne finer pour or ne pour argent adonc f.g.c. par la citey que les *B2* avo. asses et ap. pou de temps il fut si g. famine en iherusalem quil ny d. nulles e.s. quon p.a. pour donner aux b. qui moreyent de fain chestassavoyr aux chevaulx pallissioiz ne aultres b. tellement que les bestes moroient de male famine adonc f. si g. cry par la cite que les 717 *A10* g. famine qui *A11* c. de vivres quil 717-719 *A10* e. et mengerent toutes les b. et m. comme chiens 717-721 *A11* s. ne autre a m. que lon p. menger par laquelle c. beaucoup mouroient de fain l. 718 *A9* a. ne trouver et *A3* m. mais que *A8* m. qui la *A12* m. que len p. voir et 718-719 *A1* b. brules f. *A12* b. qui estoyent m.

714 *y* [ *ny* Correction from MSS *A1, A2, A3, A5, A7, A8, A9, A10, A11, A12, A13*.
715 Addition from MSS *A2, A3, A7, A8, A9, A10*. MS *A5* agrees with *A*.
*et*[3] [ *es* Correction based on MSS *A2* and *A9*. See variants to this line.

mortes, fucent chiens ou chas ou chevaux ou quelconque beste que ce fust, car sy grant estoit la cherté et la famine qu'il y estoit que quantqu'il avoient leur estoit cort. Lors fust plus grant cry en Jherusalem que davant, car les gens mouroient a grant monciaux parmy les rues de grant fain. Et quant il estoient mors, on les pourtoit es foucés la out l'on avoit mis les
[47v] autres et tant que l'en en trouva ung jour qui estoient mors de fain par/mi les rues trois cens et soisante. De quoy Pilate [eüt] tres grant duel car il n'avoit eü encore deul qui tant lui despleüt comme cesticy. Lors Pilate eüt son conseil et fist crier que toute personne qui n'averoit que menger, qu'il

719 *A2* chiens ou chevaulx *B5* chevaux et toutes aultrez b. 719-720 *A3* m. comme chatz chiens et che. car *A10* b. car 719-721 *B, B1, B3, B4, B5* f. car (*B1* f. quilz ne mengeassent car) ilz mouroient de fain (*B3* de pute f.) car toutes choses estoient tant chieres (*B5* choses que on povoit menger e. si c.) que ne povoyent finer pour or ne pour argent (*B5* f. ne p.a.) adonc f. (*B4* f. si) g. 720 *A12* e. la fain et la c. quil avoyent que q. *A2* que tout q. *A9* que tout ce quil 720-724 *A10* e. la f. quilz m. de fain l. firent p.g. cry que d. car on lez trouvoit p. les r. a g.m. tous mors t. 721 *A1* a. mengie l. *A9* c. et leur faisoit bien besoing puis peu de temps apres fut *A3* e. bon et l. y ot p. 721-722 *B, B1, B3, B4, B5* cry par la (*B3* p. toute la) cite que les *A12* i. fait que il navoit este fait par avant car a g. tropeaulx par 722 *A6, B, B1, B5, B3* mour. tous a (*B3* a g.) mon. *A5* mour. de f. a g. mon.p. les r. et *A1* grant plente sur les *A3* mon. et *A6* de f. *A11, A12* f. quil avoient et 722-723 *B1, B, A6* et ilz les p. tous (*A6* p.) es *A8* et sy tost que m.e. on *B3* f. quil avoient et il lez p. tous es *B4* mour. tous de f. a g.mon. par les r. et ilz les p. tous es 722-727 *B2* mour. a g. tropeaulx de malle fain et les charrieres et les p. tous mectre en les f. desusdictes et estoyt tel i. quil ne trouvoyent de m. par les cherrieres t.c. et s. adonc p.e. grant duel et fut moult marry adonc pilate f.c. par toute la cite que t. gens qui *B5* f. quilz souffroient et estoit tel i. quil en mouroit bien t. ou quatre c. adonc p.f. 723 *A1* les gectoit es *A9* p. a grant monceaulx es *A1, A7, A12, A9* out estoient (*A9* e. mis) les *A8* f. avec les 723-724 *A11* ou estoient les a. qui estoient mors en bataille et 723-727 *B, B1, B3, B4, A6* f. dehors et (*B1, A6* d. la cite et *B3* f. feurs la ville et) estoit tel i. que il en mouroit t.c. et .lx. tout de (*B4* s. de) fain adonc p. (*B1* c.s. de grant f. quilz avoient a tant p.) f. 724 *A10* i.p. *A9* m.p. 724-725 *A8* et en t. bien t.c.lx. qui e.m. de f. de *A5* i.t.c.s. qui e.m. de f.p. les r. de *A11* i.p. les r. que e.m. de f. environ t. *A12* i.p. les r. de m. qui e. mors de grant f.v.c. et q. *A1* i.t.c. et s. personnes qui e.p. les r.m. de f. et quand ilz estoient la mors p. en eubt t.g. et merveilleux d. 725 *A13* c. et quarante de *A7* q. ilz faisoyent t.g.d. et p. aussy car *A3* d. plus grant quil 725-726 *A10* ot moult g.d.l. *A11* p. et les autres out g.d. plus encores que iamais navoient eu l. *A12* d. plus e. quil navoit eu p. 725-728 *A13* d. adoncques f.c. pillate par toutes la cite de iherusalem que ceulx quil na. de quoy vivre en 726 *A3* eu ne qui *A9* eu en son cueur d. comme il disoit qui *A2* des. adont p. *A8* des. et pour ce eut 726-727 *A3* des. adont p. et son c. firent c. par toute la ville que qui 727 *A10* co. de ceste grande famine que *A6* qui a. que vivre quil 727-728 *A11* crier par la cite que na. des vivres en pour tout ou *B1* t. gens que na. que m. en parte la 727-734 *B7* que lon prinst tource en tous les lieus ou on en pourroist trouver et lors les p.g. furent moult ioyeulx et commencerent a aller de maison en maison pour trouver a mengez et par ainsi furent les v.g. tant que lon ne t.

725 Addition from MSS *A1, A2, A3, A5, A8, A9, A10, A11, A12*.

en presist la ou il en trouveroit. Et de cest crist eürent grant joie les povres gens et alerent parmi les rues a grans monceaulx espiant [ou] il trouveroient que menger. Et incontinent qu'il veoient aucune fumee ou sentoient aucune oudeur de viandes, il entroient dens cel houstel et le prenoient tout. Et qui plus en pouvoit avoir plus en avoit. Et en celle maniere que tous les vivres furent gastés en peu de temps en temps qu'il ne trouvoient plus que mengier. Et a la fin il alerent es portes de

728 A1 en penssent prendre la A1, A3, A7 cest e. 728-729 A10 cest e. les p. moult g.i. et a.p. la ville et la rue a A12 cry la p.g. en e.gr.i. et A8 i. le p. peuple et B, B1, B2, B3, B4, B5, A6 il en t. et (A6 il pourroyent trouver et) adonc (B2 et avoir a.) les (B5 t. puis les) p.g.e. (B3 g. en e.) gr.i. et A11 t. pour menger et de c.cr. les p.g.e.gr.i. et 728-732 A13 t. dont les p.g. en furent comptent et tellement que en prenoient a source tout ce quil t. car la fain les contraingnoit et en c. 729 A6, B, B2, B3, B4, B5 r.e. B1 a.e.p. les r. ou A1 grans plente e. se il A12 grans tropeaulx e. A11 e. par tout ou 729-730 A8 m. pour scavoir ou il en pourroyent trouver et 730 A1, A6, B, B1, B3, B5 et tantost quilz B4 et tantost quilz v. ou B5 f. aulcune chemine ou 730-731 A11 v. yssir la aucun h. ou quil s. A10 ou veoient a. 730-733 B2 t. si que ceulx qui en povoyent avoir en a. ainsi gasterent dedans pou 731 A10 d. et 731-732 A7 h. et qui A12 v. en aucune mayson ilz e.d. et p.t. ce quil 731-733 A8 v. en aulcune maniere et maison ilz e.d. et p.t. ce quil en povoyent a. et par se point t. les biens estoient g.

731-734 B, B1, B3, B4, B5, A6 v. en quelque h. que (B1, B4 q. lieu que) ce fut ilz entroient d. et roboyent tout ce (B3 r. ce) que povoient trouver ne prandre ainsi que ceulx (B4 a. que tous c.) qui p. en povoient avoir en a. si (B1 tout ce que p.a. si) gasterent dedans (B5 e.d. et prenoient t. ce que on y povoit f.d.) peu de t. les viandes toutes t. (B1, B3 de t.to. les v.t. B4 d. brief t.to. les v.t. B5 pau t. les v. tellement) que ne 732 A9 t. ce quilz trouvoyent et A11 pr. ce quil povoient attraper et A3 po. prendre plus en avoit A10 en prenoit p. A11, A12 po. prendre plus en prenoit et en celle A9 avoir et prendre p.

733 A2 que les A2 f. tous g. A1 m.f.g. en peu de temps t. les v. en tant quilz A9 f. en bien p. de t. rifflez t. A10 f. et en t. quilz A11 m. gasterent en p. de t. tous les v. de i.t. A12 m. ilz gasterent t. les v. en p. de t. en B2 de t. tous les vivres de iherusalem t. quil 733-736 A13 m.f.t.g. les v. de iherusalem et avec ce mangirent la comre de leurs p. et pas si grant chier temps que ung 734 A7 p. riens et A12 ny demoura p. a m. dedens la ville de iherusalem et a B, B1, B2, B3, B4, B5, A6 t.p. que m. et iusques (A6 t. a m.p.i.) au (B1 m. au) derrenier que les gens a. (B4 quilz a. dedans brief temps B5 i. ad ce quilz se adviserent et a.) es A1 m. ilz B5 po. de la cite de 734-736 A11 m. et advint en iherusalem si grant c. de ble que B7 m. ilz firent tremper les cuirs en eaue et puis les firent cuire et par faulte daultre viandez les mengoient car la c. y fust si g. que B, B1, B3, B4, A6 po. la ou (B1, B3, A6 p. out B4 p. de i. ou) e. les cuirs des bouffres des portes (B1 des baussorz es p.) de iherusalem (A6 b. de i.) et prindrent iceulx (B1 p. tous i.) cuirs et les misdrent tremper et puis les (B1 c. et les) firent cuire (B4 e. les c. et les p. et les m.c.) et par f. les m. car la c. y fut si g. que ung

729 Addition from all MSS except A1, A13, B7.

Jherusalem qui estoient couvertes de cuir et la il les mengerent de la grant fain qu'il avoient. Et avint en Jherusalem si grant cherté que ung petit pain valoit soisante piesses d'or et une pomme valoit une piece d'or. Et quant tous les biens furent gastés et on ne trouvoit riens a vendre pour or ne pour argent, lors fu le grant duel car il leur failloit menger les ras et les chas quant il les pouoient trouver et rongoient le bois et la terre. Et lors mouroient les gens par la ville sans nombre.

735 *A9* e. qui e.co. *A12* cuirs de brissons boullis et *A1* co. et les m. a la fin de la g. *A12* m. et r. de 735-736 *B5* cuirs de beufz et prindrent iceux cuirs et les misrent temprer et firent cuire et par force de f. les mengerent et la c. et la famine fut si g. que *B2* cuirs de brussons lesquels peaulx ilz mengoyent par force de f. et la c. y fut si g. que ung 736 *A2* et en i.a. si *A10* avint si g.c. en i. que ung 736-737 *A2* p.p. blanc v. *A11* pain dune maille v. 737 *B4* v. deux cens cinquante escus dor et *A12* lx. besans dor *A11* po.v. son pesant dor *A12* po.v. .xx. bezans dor 737-738 *A7* et on *B5* v. xl. besans dor et ung besant valoit cincq escus dor et une poire ou ung oignon v..v. besans quant les viandes f. *B, B1, B3, A6* lx. besans dor et chascun besant valoit v. escuz et une p. un bezant (*A6* p.va. vint b.) et un oignon v. besans (*B1* ung escu ung b.) et q. les (*B3* q. toutes les) viandes f. *A7* et on *A10* or et ainsi f.t. les b.g. *B2* lx. besans et une poire ung besant et ung ongnion .v. besans et q. toutes les viande f. *B7* lx. besans et chascun besans .v. escus quant les vivres f. *B4* po.v. cinz escus dor et ung oignon valoit vint cinq escus dor et q.t. les viandes f. *A11* q. les 738 *A12* les vivres f. tous g. *A11* on neust peu trouver a v.r.p. menger ne pour or *B, B1, B3, B4, B5, A6* tr. plus que (*B4* t. que) prandre ne que v. *B2* tr. plus r. *A10* r. de biens a 738-740 *B7* tr. plus que prendre fors ras soris crapaulx et toutez aultres verminez que trouver povent et la fiente de pourceaulx et l. 739 *A2* leur convenoit m. 739-740 *A3* et les souris q. *A8* et les souriz et les chiens et les chas *A10* ras et mengier les b. *A13* a. mangoient raz soriz la ou ilz *A11* a. dont en la fin l. convint m. les bestes qui estoient mortes fussent chiens ou chatz chevaulx ou raz ou quelque beste que ce fust mortes ou vives la ou ilz *A12* a.r. 739-741 *B, B1, B3, B4, B5, A6* a. mais mangerent les ras et souris crapaux (*B5* s. lez serpens c.) et mourons couleuvres (*B1* cr.co.) et toute (*B4* s. et les tarpes toutes co. et t.) vermine et la fuste des (*B3* t. aultres v. et le boix dez portes et des maisons et (*B1* m. adonc *B5* t. autrez v. et adonc) m. 739-742 *B2* a. mais mangoient la terre lez ratz qui en povoyt avoir les bois tellement quil m. de g. par force de famine s.n. adonc fut une d. qui avoit nom m. 740 *A11* p. atrapper et r. les ungs les b. et la t. et les aucuns alloient es portes de iherusalem qui estoient couvertes de cuir boilly et les mengeoint de grant fain quil avoient et l. *A12* b. et mengeoyent la 740-742 *A13* b. et mangoient la t. dont ilz m. dont ilz m. par les rues s.n. silz a. 741 *A8* m. de iour en iour s. *A10* et commencerent a mourir s. *A1* parmi les rues s. 741-742 *A9* v. pour la tres grant famine qui y estoit en si grant n. que nulle personne ne le pourroit extimer dire ne penser et adonques a. *A12* par les rues s.n. et apres ce a. *B4* m.gr.n. de g. de fain et adonc fut une d. qui avoit nom m. *A11* par les rues s.n. or y avoit en celluy temps en iherusalem une moult noble d. qui avoit nom m. *B, B1, B3, B5, B7, A6* g. grant n. (*B7* g.s.n.) par fain (*B3* n. de pute f. *B5* g. tres gr.n. par force de f.) adont (*B1* f. quilz avoient a.) fut une (*B5* a. et y avoit une) d. qui (*A6* a. une d.f. qui) avoit nom (*B7* a. avoit une femme en iherusalem que lon a.) m.

[52] Lors avint que une dame qui s'apeloit Marie et avoit esté fame du roy d'Efrique lequel mouru ou temps que Jhesu Crist fu mis en crois cy que celle dame ne c'estoit plus voulue marier. Et avoit une fille et une noble dame qui estoit sa compaigniere, laquelle s'apelloit Clarice et sy avoit un filz. Et ses deux dames avec leur enfanz vindrent en Jherusalem et se convertirent a la foy de Jhesu Crist et se firent baptiser. Et elles estoient bien garnies de vivres si comme il s'apartenoit a royne, jusques a

742 *A3* d. nommee m. *A12* d. laquelle a. *A13* qui avoit nom m. 742-743 *A6* dung grant roy 743 *A13* roy l. *B3, B4, B5* l. roy m. *A10* t. de de i. quant il fut *A1* que fu crucifiez et mis *B5* que nostre seigneur fut 743-744 *A11* crist souffert mort et passion et pour ce icelle *A8, A13* crois et (*A13* et par devocion) ne *A6, B, B1, B4, B5* crois et depuis ne v. (*B* d. navoit v.) prandre mary et (*B5* m. laquelle) a. 743-745 *B7* crist quant il fust crucifie et depuis ne v. point prendre mary et par c. avoit une d. que lon a. *B2* crois et depuis elle ne v. prandre mari elle a. avec elle une bonne dame pour c. qui avoit nom c. laquelle dame a. *B3* crois et depuis ne v. pranre mary et a. celle dame une f. et une c. pour d. et avoit nom c. laquelle dame a. 744 *A1* ne v. depuis m. *A8* m. ladicte dame sy a. *A13* a. une belle f. 744-745 *A10* f. et avoit avec elle une n. 744-746 *A11* v. aucunement m. mais sen vint en iherusalem avec une sienne f. et avoit avec elle une n.d. qui sa.c. laquelle a. *A6* et une c. pour d. et avoit non c. laquelle dame a. *B, B5* f. et une c. pour d. et avoit (*B5* c. laquelle a. a) non c. laquelle dame a. *B1, B4* f. et une c. pour d. que avoit (*B4* d. et a.) ung f. si (*B4* f. la compaigne et) v. 745 *A10* d. sa *A9* e. en sa *A3* c. nommee c. *A9* l. avoit nom et sa. *A7* sa. sappelloit c. 746 *B7* un petit f. et la royne une petite fille et elles *A3* f. lesquelles dames *A10* dames puis ces deux e. *A6, B, B2, B3, B5* f. et v. *A12* et celles dames v. 746-747 *A11, A13* f. si (*A13* f. lequel) se 747 *A10* de de i. *A12* la sainte foy *A13* b. par aucun des disciples de ihesu crist secretement elles 747-748 *A12* b. et celles dames es. 748 *A1* de viandes et de v. *A9* g. de tout ce que leur estoit necessaire et c. *A11* g. de tous biens et de *A6, B, B1, B3, B4, B2, B5* de viandes (*B2, B5* de vivres) i. 748-749 *A13* c. a leur estat a. mes les *A11* i. au temps dicelle grant chierte et famine et que *A8* r. mais les 748-751 *B, B1, B3, B2, B4, B5, A6* i. a t. que (*B1* a ce que) on commanda (*B2* que pilate c.) que on prist les viandes la (*B2* les vivres partout la) ou lon les pourroit trouver et adonc (*B1, B5* les trouveroit a.) on leur tollit toutes leurs viandes (*B2* on l. print t.l. vivres *B3* ou on lez trouveroit *B5* toutes les v.) e. 748-753 *B7* v. mais on leurs osta tout quant le cris desusdit fust faict et ne leurs demoura sinon le e. du vergers qui e. derriere la m. et navoient aultre mengez et tousiours adorerent ihesus de bon coeur et q. les e.f. fillye la

743 *que* [ *de* Correction from all MSS except *A10*.

*Efrique* Although the Roman desire to control the coast of North Africa dated from the First Punic wars of the third century BC, their domination of the area began only with the destruction of Carthage in 146 BC. The Roman province of Africa remained a part of the Empire until the break-up of the Western Empire in the fifth century AD.

746 *ses* [ *sest* Correction from MSS *A1, A2, A5, A7, A8, A9, A10*.

tant que les gens de Pilate les leur robirent. Et elles estoient tous jours en oroison vers Jhesu Crist car elles y avoient fort leur foy et leur fiance. Et [48r] quant hom leur eüt ousté leur vivres excepté erbes / qu'elles avoient en un jardin qui estoit en leur meson, desquelles erbes elles vivoient. Et quant toutes les erbes furent mengés, la fille de la royne fust fort afeblie de fain et mouru sans autre maladie. De quoy la royne eüst moult grant duel et ploura moult fort. Et ossy le fil de la compaigniere mouru de fain. De

749 *A8* p. leur osterent et *A12* leur r. leurs vivres et *A11* r. leurs vivres et *A10* et t.i.e. en 749-750 *A11* i.v.i.c. en o. luy priant et requerant quil luy pleust les regarder en pitie par sa grant misericorde car *A12* en priere v. 749-752 *A13* et prindrent a fource et elles labouroient fort en o.v. nostre seigneur et furent tant executee de vivre quelle nen a. plus que ung petit vergier en 750 *A10* a. ferme foy et l. esperance et en l.
750-751 *A11* a. grant foy a ihesu crist or navoient elles que menger e. *A12* foy et comme il est dist les gens de pilate l. 751 *A8, A9* o. tous l. *A3, A11* ung vergiers qui
751-752 *B, B1, B2, B3, A6* erbes du vergier qui es. en l. hostel et (*B1, A6* l.m. et) celle e. mangerent (*B2* es. dedans lo. lesquelles e. elles m.) et adourerent souvent ihesu crist car bien y avoient leur (*B1* car elles y avoient leur (*B1* car elles y a.b.l.) foy (*B2* car elles a.l.f. en luy) q. *A12* ung vergier et *B5* ex. viandes et les e. du vergier qui e. en l. hostel et icelles e. mengoient et adouroient et prioient forment nostre seigneur ihesu crist car bien y avoient leur foy et q. 751-753 *B4* erbes de leur vergier et f.m. toutes et la 752 *A8* m. dont elles *A10* des e. *A9* d.v. lesdictz dames et *A11* v. en grant abstinance et 752-753 *A13* d. elles mangirent les e. et q.f. faillis la fille *A2* q. les 753 *A8* t.f. *A2* f.t.m. *A6, B, B1, B3, B5* e. du vergier f. *A8* fust moult fort *B, B3, B4* fust feible de 753-754 *B2* m. icelle r. avoyt une f. laquelle devint si foible par force de grant fain quelle m. *A9* fort debilites et a. de f. en tant quelle m. *A11* r. devint si feible quelle en m. *A12* fort affamee et de grant f.m. *A7* a. de sang et m. *A3* fain tellement quelle en m.sa. avoir a. 753-755 *A6* r. heut grant deul et commanca a plorer et le *B7* r.m. le
753-759 *A13* fut moult fort malade et m. de f. aussy fist la fille de la compaingne dont il mennoient grant doleur tous ensamble adoncques d. la noble d.l. cesy en 754 *B1* s. avoir a. *B, B3, B4, B5* ma. adonc la 754-755 *B1, B2* ma. adoncques la r. commenca (*B2* r.e.m.g.d. et c.) a plourer en faisant g.d. et (*B2* p. et) le *A8* et sesbahyt m. *B3* e.g. douleur et commancait a plorer et le *B4, B5, B* et commanca a (*B5* c. tres fort a) plourer et aussi (*B* et) le 755 *A9* et pareillement le *A6, A9, B, B1, B3, B5* c. de la royne m. *A10* la roine m. *A12* mouru de grant f. 755-756 *A1* et lendemain apres que la faille de la royne si m. le f. de la c. de q. *A11* o. pareillement m. de f. le f. de sa c. clerice de q. sa mere ot tres grant dueil et grant angoisse au cueur et quant les d. *B, B1, B4, B5, A6* fain adonc sa mere fist (*B1* a. famme f. *B5* f. puis sa m. en f.) g. 755-759 *B2* mouru apres de dont sa mere fist moult g.d. et ainsi la mort de sa compaigne furent moult dollantes et enduroyent si grant faim que a grant paynes se povoyent soustenir quant la compaigna de la royne vit quelles avoyent si grant fain elle d. *B3* fain et desconforterent moult fort et avoient cez deux dame si grant fain que a poinne se povoient soustenir quant la compaigne de la royne eult si grant fain elle d. 755-762 *B7* c. dont il menerent g.d. en rompans leurs cheveulx et avoient si grand fain que a peine ellez se povent soustenir ung peu apres clarette d.d.l. ce crist et p. ung cartiers de mon f. que m.p. que na.a.
756 *A1* e.m.c. et plouroit moult fort et *A8* m. troublee et 756-758 *A12* q. sa mere eust tresgrant d. et ploura moult fort et ainssy faisoyent les bonnes d. moult g.d. pour ce que elles avoyent grant fain et aussy de leurs enfans qui veoyent mors et 756-759 *A11* d. eurent grant piece pleure et demene g.d. clerice d.

quoy elle fust moult couroucié. Et ainsy les deux dames fesoient grant duel car la royne fesoit duel de sa fille et la compaigniere fesoit duel de son filz. Et quant la compaigne de la royne vist le grant duel qu'elle fesoient, elle dist a la royne: "Dame, laissons cest duel em pais, mes prenons mon filz et en menghons ung cartier. Et sy le mettons roustir puis qu'il est mors, car ossy se pouriroit il. Et deslivrons nous car ossy n'avons nous autre chose que menger." Et quant la royne l'ouïst, de hideur qu'elle eüst elle cheüst a terre toute pasmee. Et lors vint ung angel qui la leva et la conforta et ly dist: "Dame, Dieux vous mende par moy que vous mengés de l'enfant afin que ce que Dieux dist soit fet. Car il dist le jour de pasques

757 *A9* fesoient et menoient g. *A10* d. de la *A9, A10* f. grant d. de *A5* d. et *A8* d. chascune de son enfant et *A9* c. de ladicte royne aussy f. moult grant d. de son 757-759 *B, B1, B4, B5, A6* r. aussi et se desconforterent moult fort et avoient si (*B5* f. adont eurent si) grant fain que a paine se povoient soustenir quant la compaigne de la royne eut si grant fain elles d. (*B5* e. ala) a *A1* f.d. chascune de son enfant que elles amoient moult q. 758 *A7* c.v. *A8* r. cognut le 758-759 *A5* r. eust assez ploure elle d. *A8* fe. chascune de son enfant si d. *A12* e. menoyent elle 759 *A10* r.l. *B, B1, B2, B3, B4, B5, A6* r.l. (*B5* r. dire l.) tout ester et (*B4* t. et) pr. *A4* l. en p.c.d. mes *A8* c. grand d. *A11* l. le plourer et le gemir car nous ny povons riens proffiter mes 759-762 *A13* pr. ung c. de mon f. le rotissons sy le m.p. que a. 760 *A11, A12* en prenons (*A12* en tranchons) ung *A11* le faisons r. 760-762 *B, B1, B2, B3, B4, B5, A6* f. et le m.r. ung (*B2* et le m. en c. et en cuirons ung) c. (*B1* et les faisons r. par c. *B3, B4, B5* r. par c.) p. que na.a.c. que m. (*B3* a. chose *B5* que n. ne av.au.) q. 761 *A12* et en mangerons car 761-762 *A1* n. car n. ne a. que m. aultre chose et *A11* et mieulx nous vault le menger que mourir de fain et 762 *A1* q. le vit devant elle le h. *A9* o. et entendy ce que sa compaigne lui dist de la grant h. et effroyheur quelle *A12* h. et deul quelle 762-763 *A8* o. et c.to.p. de h. quelle e. et *A10* o. elle c. *A11* r.o. ainsi parler sa compaigne qui parloit de roustir lenfant si fut si tres esbahye et si tres courroussee quelle c.to.p. a te. et ne luy peut respondre et *B, B1, B2, B3, B4, B5, A6* o. dire a sa compaigne ces choses elle (*B3* co.e. *B5* ces paroles e.) c. a (*B2* d. ces parolles a sa c. elle tomba a) te. comme morte et tantost v. *A13* m. adoncques la r.c.to.p. a te. et 763 *B7* m. lors la r. commenca a crier plus fort que devant et par desconfort se laissa c. a te. et tantost v. *A9* c. et tomba a *A10* p. et de la grant h. que elle eust et *A12* c.p. a te. et *B, B1, B2, B4, B5* a. de dieu et (*B1, B2* d. que *B5* a. et) la 763-764 *A3* qui la c. la l. et *B7* a. de dieu quil d. 763-765 *A13* a. de dieu quil la l. lequel len feist a mangier pour acomplir la parolle de ihesu crist quil 764 *B3, B5* m. que 765 *A12* quil dist *B, B1, B2, B3, B4, B5, B7, A6* e. si sera la voulente de d. acomplie (*B2* s.a. a v. *B3, B5, B7, A6* s. sa v.a.) car *A10* se qui est d.s. acomply car *A11* quil a dit en son temps s. acomply car 765-766 *A12* fet et acomply car ihesu crist le dit quant il e. en c.v. le i. de p.f. quil estoit monte sur *B2* dist quant il e. en iherusalem sur 765-767 *B1, B3, B5, B* i. du ralme palme quant il monta sur une a. et (*B* sur la somme et) vint en i.c. nation s. (*B5* c. generacion s. *B* i. et dist c. generacion s.) en p.

764-771 The Palm Sunday prophecies concerning the destruction of Jerusalem and the overthrow of the Jewish state are found in the first three canonical gospels (Mt 23:37-24:14, Mk 13:8-23, Lk 19:43-44, 21:5-28). Nowhere, however, is it a question of mothers eating their children.

flouries, le jour qu'il entra en ceste ville sur une asnesse, que en ceste generacion seroit en Jherusalem sy grant pestilense et famine, si grant que la mere mengeroit son enfant de la grant famine qui seroit en ceste ville, laquelle seroit destruite en telle maniere que piere n'y demoureroit sur autre, et ossy grant destruction de peuple que jamés ne seroit sa per. Pour quoy, dist l'angel, il faut qu'il soit einsy fait pour vous, car Dieux le veut." Et atant l'angel s'en despartit des dames et s'en va. Et la les dames demourerent plourant et prirent l'enfant et en trancherent ung quartier avec l'espaule et puis le mistrent roustir.

766 *A1, A8* f. que *A3, A5, A10* f. a la heure quil *A7* f. en haibt quil *A6, B4, B7, A11* f. quant il montast (*A11* il e.) sur *A9* f. a leure quil e. dedans la cite et v. de iherusalem sur *A11* a. en iherusalem c. 766-767 A6 a. et vint en i. et dist cest naction sera en i.p. *A10* a. que en i.s. si g.f. et si grande p. que *A12* a. quil chevauchoit que on c. ville et g.s.p. *B4, B7* a. et vint en i. et dist de sa bouche c. (*B7* i.c.) g.s. en p. 766-801 *A13* f. comme devant et deen en comencement de cestui livre et a commandement de lange elle m.r. ung q. de lenffant lequel flairoit si bon que merveille tellement que pilate quil passoit par la r. le s. et commanda que lon lui alaisse querir dicellui roz car il en avoit grant desir de en mangier et quant les sergens furent leans pour prendre dicellui roz la dame leurs dist prenez de de chaer crue si le faictes cuirre pilate tout a son plaisir quant il virent lenfant ilz sen fuirent courrant a pilate en lui disant le fait q.

767 *A2* ge. en i.s. sy *A9* g. cest a dire en ceste ville de iherusalem s. sy *A5* si g.f. que *A11* en p. de mortalite si g. fain que *B2* ge. auroyt p. et endureroyt si g.f. que *A1* en iherusalem et si g.f. que *A6, B, B1, B3, B4, B5, B7* et auront tant g. fain (*B4* a. telle f. *B7* a.g.f.t.) que *A3* f. que *A9* et si grant f. que 767-768 A7 f. que lautre men. 768-769 *A1* e.s. *A8* e. par rage de fain et s.d. *A10* e. et aussi que c.v.s. *A12* en la cite l. cite s. 768-770 *A11* e. quelles auront portez en leurs ventre et s. la cite d. tellement quil ne d.p. sur pierre et y sera g. 768-772 *B, B1, B3, B4, B5, B7, A6* e. quelles auront portes et (*B1* p. en leurs ventres et) la cite sera d. (*B7* e. par fain et s. la c.d. *B4* et aussi s. la c.d.) tant que (*A6* d. tellement que) ne d.p. sur pierre (*A6* sur a.p.) p. ce d.la. a la dame (*B4* la.d.) quil vouloit que la voulente de (*B5* vouloit et failloit que la verite de) d. fust (*B4* que sa v.f.) acomplie (*B1* f. fete et a.) et tantost se (*B7* pierre et tantost lange se) partit des (*B4* p.la. des) d. adonc (*B3* p. lange des d. et *B5* p. lange a.) les 768-773 *B2* e. a g.f. et que la cite devoyt estre d. ne ny d.p. sur pierre p. tant d.la. a la dame qui failloit acomplir la voulente de d. et puis la si se va delles de partir et les d. si se prindrent a plourer a la fin elles pr. 769 *A9* l. ville si s. *A3* dem. lune sur 769-770 *A10* m. qui ny d.p. sur pierre et *A8* quil ny d.p. sur pierre et si g. 770 *A1* et seroit o. *A3, A12* o. y auroit si g. *A9* s. veu son per *A3, A8, A10* s. veue sa pareille (*A8* s.p. *A10* v. telle) pour *A11* pe. pour 770-771 *A12* pe.po.q. ce d.la. a la royne f. 771 *A1* d. leuvangille il f. *A2* a. quil *A11* a. a la dame il f. *A9* fait car *A11, A12* fait et d. 771-772 *A11* v. quil soit acomply par vous a. lange se *A12* v. quil soit acompli par vous et 772 *A1* a. sesvanuy et sen alla et la *A7* dames et la *A11* dames de devant la d. et les *A3* sen ala incontinant et la *A9* sen ala sans plus mot dire adoncques les 772-773 *A8* va et elles d. 773 *A8* et puis t. *A9* le filz de la compaigne de la royne dauffrique et en *B4* e. de la compaigne et en leverent ung *A11* pr. ung q. de le. *A1* d. et puis mirent rostire et plouroient et pr. *A6, B, B1, B2, B3, B5* e. et enleverent ung 773-774 *B7* pr. ung q. du filz a clairette et le *A9* q. de devant a. *A6, A7* q. et (*A7* et p.) le 774 *A8* e. de celuy enfant mort et le *B3* et m. 774-775 *A11* r. au feu apres que les dames eurent mys lenfant roustir conme dist est et quil ot este une piece au feu il en y.

[53] Et de cest rost yssi sy douce oudeur et sy grant que hom le santi de
[48v] la rue. Et Pilate et le roy Artilan alerent par la ville pansant qu'il /
pouroient faire. Et quant il furent davant la meson de la royne, Pilate senti
celle douce oudeur de cest roust et li em prist grant desir. Et lors il apella
ung sergent et sy li dist: "Va veoir out est cest rost. Et dis a cellui a qui il
est qu'il m'en envoie car onques mes je n'eüs sy grant voulenté de chose
du monde." Lors le sergent ala par la rue assentent out estoit le roust. Et

775 *B4* et saichiez que de *A12* et quant il se rostissoit il en y. si g. et si bonne o. *B5* si grant o. que on *B, B1, B3, A6* r. sailloit si g.o. que par toute la terre (*B1, A6* la cite *B3* te. de la citey) on *A1* o. que 775-776 *B2* si tres bonne o. que toute la rue la s. adonc p. *B4* r. sailloit si g.o. que lon le s. par toute la cite adonc p. *B7* r. sailloit si g. fumee et o. que on les s. tout la rue lors p. *A11* o. et si savoureuse quon la s. par toute la cite ou demouroient icelles dames or advint que a celle heure p. *A6, B, B1, B3, B5* s. adonc (*B5* s. par toute la cite a.) p. 776 *A2* par la rue et par *A3* par la p. *A9* al.p. par la v. quilz *B, B1, B2, B3, B4, B5, B7, A6* par la rue conseillant (*B1* r. sentant et c. *B3* la cite c. *B2* c. entre eulx) que *A12* pa. et advisant quil 776-777 *A11* a. passoient daventure par icelle rue devisant de plusieurs choses et 776-884 *A10* parmy les rues p. et 777 *A12* et fu. *A6, B, B1, B3, B4, B5* fa. et passoyent par d. lostel de *B2* d. lostel de 777-778 *A6, B, B1, B3, B4, B5* s. tant bonne o. *B2* s. tant bonne o. qui issoyt de *A3* s.lo. 777-782 *B7* fa. et q. pilate passast par d. il s. le r. et eust g. desir den avoir quil mandast deulx de ses serviteurs pour savoir ou on le rotissoit et tantost les deulx serviteurs vindrent tout droit eurtes a 778 *A1, A11* o. du r. *A7, A8* o. et lui *A12* c. bone o. *A9* r. luy p. *A11* et en eut moult g. *A12* et en voit avoir tes g.d. de mangier et *A3, A9* d. den mangier (*A9* den avoir) et 778-779 *B, B1, B2, B3, B4, B5, A6* en eut g. (*B1* e. si g.) talent et (*B4* t. que merveille et) a. (*B5* e. si g. envie de en manger lors a. *A6* e. si g. envie quil a.) deux servans et (*B2* t. den mangier si a.d. de ses serviteurs) leur d. alez v. de c. (*B4* v. ou est c.) r. ou se fait et d. (*B2* v. ou est c. que lon fait celluy r. dont ie sens si bonne odeur et d.) a c. a (*B5* r. pour scavoir de quoy il est et d. *A6* de quoy il est et luy dit) qui 779 *A1* va tost v. *A11* r. que ie sens fleurer si bon et d. a c. ou a celle a 779-781 *A7* dis quon men e.dic. par iay g. desir den manger l. 780 *A11* est conment quil soit quil *B3* e. ung pou car *A11, A12* car ie ne.o.m. si 780-781 *B2* car iay g. desir den mangier adonc les s. sentirent icelluy r. *B, B1, B3, B4, B5, A6* mais de c.ne. si g. talent les (*B4* m.ne. si g. de c. les *A6* g. envie les *B5* m. iour de ma vie ne e. si g. envie ne si g. desir de c. qui fut en ce monde les) s. sentirent le (*B3* t. adont lez s.s. la flaroin du *B4* se. celluy) r. *A3* v. de mangier de c. qui feust en ce m. *A9* v. de manger de c. du m. comme iay de ce rost l. 781 *A8* l. allerent lez s. par *A9* as. flerant et odorant pour scavoir la ou *A12* rue attendant et a. ou e. celluy bon r. *A5* le (MS ends) 781-782 *B, B1, B2, B3, B5* r. et vindrent (*B3* et sen v.) a *A6, B4* et venirent en lo. *A11* r. puis a.

778 *de* [ *et* Correction from all MSS except *A7, A8, B7*.
779 *dis* [ *dist* Correction from MSS *A1, A2, A3, A5, A8, A9, A12*.
780 *eüs* [ *eust* Correction from MSS *A1, A2, A3, A5, A8, A9, A11, A12*.

va venir a l'oustel de la royne et appela a la porte. Et la dame lui alast ovrir. Et quant il fu dedans, il salua les dames et leur dist: "Dame, mon seigneur, Pilate, vous mende que vous lui envoiés de vostre rost car onques mes jour de sa vie il n'eüst si grant desir de nulle chose de cest monde." Lors lui dist la conpaingne de la royne: "Par Dieu, amis, voulentiers." Et lors elle prist les trois quartiez qui estoient demourés de son enfant et prist ung coustel et luy dist: "Tenés moy de la et sy vous en tailleray et vous l'emporterés et qu'il le face apareillier a sa voulanté." Et quant le sergent vit l'enfant detranchié et qu'elle le vouloit ancore

782 *A7* v. et entrer en lo. *A12, B, B1, B2, B3, B4* r. et vont parler (*B* et frapperent *B1, B3* et hucherent *B2* et appellerent *B4* et hurterent) a *A8* p. et on leur a. *A11* p. de la bonne d. et 782-783 *A7* r. ou le rost ce faisoit et *B7* p. des deulx damez q. *B, B1, B2, B3, B4, B5, A6* p. et tantost la d. leur ovry et (*B4* l. fist ovrir et *B5* d.o. luys et) q. il (*A6* o. et) fu 783 *A12* o. la porte et *B7* fut en lhotel il s. *A11* fut leans il d. aux d. mon 783-784 *B7* dames en disant p. nostre maistre v. *B, B1, B3, B4, A6* dame p. nostre s. (*B1* n. maistre *B3* d.n.s.p. *B4* s. et le vostre) v. *B5* dame nostre s.p.v.m. par nous que 784 *B2* s.v. *A12* v. prie que *A7* que de *A11* r. convient que ce soit car 784-785 *A12* vostre bon r. car il dist que o. 784-786 *B, B1, B3, B4, A6* car iamais (*A6* c. mes) ne. (*B1, B4* c. oncque mes ne.) de c. aussi g. talent la (*B3* t. adont la *A6* g. envie la) dame c. *B2* car iamais de rien ne e. telle envie adonc la dame clarette qui acompaignoit la *A7* car il en ast tres g.d. den manger l. 784-789 *B7* car oncques ne. si g. desir de menger rost que de cestui ici les damer luy respondirent que v. et auroist ung q. de cuist affin quil 785 *A3* d. de mengier de c. qui feust en cest 785-786 *A8* ch.l. *A9* d. davoir de ch. du m. quil a du rost adoncques lui *A11, A12* de ch. du m. comme il a de menger diceluy rost (*A12* du m.) l. *B5* g. talent ne si grant d. de menger de quelque viande que ce soit come de celle dont il a eu loudeur la dame et c. 786-787 *A2, A3, A7, A9* a. vous en aurez v. *B2* r. leur dist par dieu mon a.v. nous luy envoyerons et p. *B5* r. respondit tres v. nous luy en envoierons adont la dame p. *B, B1, B4, A6* r. leur dist moult v. luy en donray et (*B4* en donnerons et l. *A6* luy envoyray et) p. 786-788 *B3* r. leur dist que moult v. luy en donrait et p. ung 786-789 *A11* r. certes a.v. vous en bailleray une partie et v. 787 *A7* p. le demourant de 787-788 *A12* q. de son enfant et 788 *A6, B1, B2, B4, B5* son filz et *A2* en bailleray et 788-789 *A7* v. en trenchere sy luy en p. 788-790 *B, B1, B2, B3, B4, B5, A6* t. bien et ie en t. un quartier que e. (*B5* que vous e.) tout cru et (*B4* crud a nostre seigneur pylate et *B5* cru a mon seigneur et) il le (*B2* b. de laultre part et ie luy t. que v. luy p. et le *A6* que v. luy p. se le) fera rostir a sa v. et (*B2, B4* a son plaisir) q. 789 *A1* t. et puis le. a pilate et quil *A12* e. a vostre maistre et 790 *A3* e. et *A12* e. que la dame le *A11* que la dame le 790-791 *A6* e. ainsy depecier p.e. *B, B1, B3, B4* e. ainsi depecie et que la dame le v. mieux (*B3* que icelle d. le v. encoirres m.) despecier p.e. es servans (*B1, B3, B4* e. a p. les s.) eust *A7* d. il *A8* q. ilz virent le. que la dame leur en v. trencher p. 790-792 *B7* e. ainsi par pieces ilz e. tant g. esmai que apres sen y. 790-794 *B2* e. ainsi despicier p.e. moult g. paour et pou sen fallut quilz ne perderent le sens si sen retournerent tous e.d.p.p. leur dist comment venez vous tout esbays et pour quoy faictes si maulvaise chiere vous ne 790-805 *B5* s. de pilate virent celle chose ilz furent tous esbays et tous espovantez tant que bien sen failly que ne perdissent tout le sens et la memoire et tantost sen retournerent devers leur maistre pilate et ne en vouldrent point prendre pour la grant abhorautіon quilz eurent et

787 *demourés* [ *demourer* Correction from all MSS except *A10, A11, A13*.

detrancher pour en envoier a Pilate, il eüst si grant ydeur que [a] paine qu'il n'yssit hors du sens. Et s'en va hors de l'ostel et vint davant Pilate tout efreés et tout espouventé. Et quant Pilate le vist venir, il lui demanda dont il venoit sy esfreés. Et lui dist: "Ne me pourte tu pas de rost que je t'avoie dist?" Et le sergent lui dist: "Sire, sachiez que une dame a detranchié son enfant et si en fet roustir ung cartier qu'elle veust mengier. Et quant je lui en demanday, elle prist l'enfant et vous en vouloit anvoier un autre cartier et que vous le ficiez apareillier a voustre voulenté. Et

791 *A1* p. lui donner quil emportast il *A6, B, B1, B3, B4* g. paour que *A11* g. paour de ce que *A9* g. paour et y 791-792 *A1* a peu il ne se y. tout h. 792 *A7* ne saillist h. *A8* v. a p. 792-793 *A12* sen retourna tout espavante d.p. et q. *B7* et tantost se retournerent a leurs sires puis riens porter q. 792-794 *B, B1, B3, B4, A6* et tantost sen tournerent d.p. touz e.p. dist (*B3* e. adont p. leur d. *B5* p. leur d. *A6* p.p. leur d.) comme venez vous ainsi eschauffes et (*B3, A6* a. esbahis et *B4* a. espaontez et esbays et) comment faites vous tant malle (*B1* a. esbays et pour quoy f. si m.) chiere et ne *A11* sen retourna hastivement t. ainsi e. come il estoit devers pilate lequel q. il le v. retourner lui 793 *A9* es. de ce quil avoit veu et q. 793-794 *A12* lui dist dont 793-795 *A8* vist sy esperdus il fut esbahy et leur d. quilz avoyent et silz apportoyent point de ce r. et 793-801 *B7* vist ainsy esbahy ilz leurs manda quil avoient et luy dirent coment les dames se gouvernerent et comment il mengent leurs enfans par fain q. 794 *A12* sy esbay ne *A3* e. et si luy demanda ne 794-795 *A7* et il respondit sire *A11* r. duquel ia. senty lodeur si bonne lors le *A12* r. et *B, B1, B2, B3, B4, A6* r. les s. luy (*B3* lez adont luy) d. seigneur (*B4* d. mon s.) une 795 *A3* luy respondit sire *A11* d. tout effroye ha sire grant pitie et horriblete est de veoir iceluy rost cest une d. que a *A12* sire une 795-796 *B, B1, B3, B4, A6* a depecye son 795-801 *B2* a fait mourir son e. et la despice en quartier et le fait roustir et nous la mostre et vous en voulyt envoyer qui estoit tout crux pour le fayre rostir q. 796-798 *B4* fet ung c. et la mys rostir et le v. encoire mieulx despecier p. vous en an. ung c. pour rostir a *B1* c. et en v. de pecer ung *B, B3* c. et v. mieulx (*B3* et le v. ancoires m.) vous en an. ung c. a rostir a *A6* c. et v. mieulx depecier p. vous an. ung c. pour le faire a. 797 *A12* d. ainsy comme vous mavies enchargie du rost elle *A11* p. le demourant de celluy e. 797-798 *A12* an. et detranchier ung c. 798 *A7* c. pour ap. *B1* c. pour vous envoyer affin que le f. roustir a *A11, A12* f. roustir ap.

791 Addition from all MSS except *A10, A13, B2, B5, B7*.
795 *et le sergent lui* [ *et le sergent le sergent lui*

quant je le vy, j'eü sy grant ydeur que a peu que je ne perdi le sens. Et sy
m'enfuÿ hors de liens au plus tost que je peüs car de la grant hideur que je
avoie je ne savoie ou j'estoie." Et quant Pilate l'ouÿ, il en heüt grant
[49r] hideur. Et lors il se doubta / moult fort et s'en ala au palais. Et la il se mist
sur ung lit du grant duel qu'il avoit. Et il se tint par trois jours moult
tristes.

[54] Et les dames estoient en leur meson qui plouroient et plaignoient

799 *A3, A9* g. doleur et (*A9* g. paour et) y. *A9* a grant peine cuiday perdre le s. et memoire et 799-800 *A8* et nous saillismes h. de la maison au *A12* s. et yssis de *A7* s. car *A6* q. nous avons cecy vehu nous avons ester tout esbay et en avons heuz g. paour tout que a p. navons p. le sens et tantost nous en sumez tournez et nen avons point pas de

799-801 *A11* g. paour et abhominacion de veoir les pieces de celuy enfant que ie cuiday hors du sens et *B1, B3, B4* q. nous veismes ce nous feusmes tous esbahyz et en eusmes (*B4* es. et espaontez et e.) g. (*B3* e. tres g.) paour tant que pou sen faillit que ne perdismes (*B4* pou nen p.) le scens (*B3* pou ne sen saillis du sens) et tantost nous en retournasmes et nen voulismes point prandre de (*B4* pr. du rost de) la g. paour (*B3* la p.) que nous eusmes q. *B* q. nous veismes ce nous fusmes touz esbays et eusmes g. paour tant que poy en failloit que ne perdismes le sens et tantost nous en tournasmes et nen voulusmes point prendre de la g. paour que avions les dames demoururent en leur hostel plorant et plaignant et commencerent a mangier leur enfant par la grant fain que ilz avoient et aussi que dieu leur avoit mande et ne douste que eulx mangassent de lenfant et que ce devoit avenir ainsi comme dieu lavoit dit de sa bouche et quant elles eurent mangie de lenfant elles mangerent de la fille de la royne adonc eult si grant doulour quant commanca a mangier de sa fille que toute personne qui loist ne se peust tenir de plourer et avoit grant douleur au cuer q. 800 *A2, A3, A9* de lostel au *A9* g. paour et h. 800-801 *A6* hi. que nous avons heuz q. 800-802 *A8* que nous peusmes et l. pylate d.

801 *A7* ne partis de lostel et 801-802 *A7, A12* p.o. ce que le sergent rappourta (*A12* o. le s.) il *A9* o. son sergent et serviteur ainsi parler il en h. tres g. paour et h. *A11* p.o. ce dire au sergent il en fut moult esmerveille et fut en grant doubte que brief il ne luy mescheust et a ceulx de la cite adonques sen *B, B1, B2, B3, B4, A6* o. les nouvelles il eut (*B3* il en fuit moult courrecie et e.) moult g. (*B2* e.g.) paour et sen *A13* il sen ala en sa chambre et se 801-815 *B7* o. les novellez sy horribles et espoventablez ilz sen ala en sa chambre puis il se l. 802 *A12* d. et 803 *A6* sur son lit de g. douleur quil *B, B1, B3, B4, A12* g. douleur (*A12* g. ydeur) quil *A11* lit faisant moult g.d. et la se *A1* a. et ainsy il *A7* et si fut par *A9* par lespace de trois 803-804 *A1* m. a malainse et m.t.

803-805 *B2* lit tout plain de douleur et la demoura trois i.m. doulant et courrocie les *A13* tint triste et doulant trois i. et *B1, B4, A6* et illecques fut (*A6* et fut) trois i.m. marry et courrouce des nouvelles (*B4* m.c. et marry *A6* m.c. et moult marrir) et *A11, A12* m. dolant et m. (*A12* et desconforte) et 803-806 *B3* et illec fut trois i. moult doulant et plaingnant et c. 803-814 *B* et illeuc fut trois i.m. courroucie et moult marri q. 804-805 *A8, A9* t. et moult dollent (*A9* t.d. et courroucye) et *A1* et quand les 805 *A11* d. desusdictes e. *A12* m. et pla. 805-806 *B1, B2, B4* d. demorerent en l. hostel plourant et plaignant (*B2* p. et de) l. *B5, A6* les deux d. demoureren t en (*A6* les d. en) l. hostel plourans et en eulx complaingnans (*A6* p. et plangnant) et c. *A11* plo. moult l.p. 805-812 *A13* d. tout plourant pour obeir a lange mangirent la fille de la roynne mais grant fut la douleur quant la roynne commenca a m. de sa fille car

800 *peüs* [ *peust* Correction from MSS *A1, A2, A3, A9, A12*.

leur enfans, et puis commenserent a menger pour la grant fain qu'elles avoient, et ossy car Dieu le leur avoit commandé. Et tandis qu'elle mengoient, elle fesoient grant duel. Mes il se devoit fere qu'elles en mangassent car [Dieu l'avoit] dit de sa bouche. Et quant elles eürent mengé l'enfant de la compaigne, elles commenserent a menger l'enfant de la royne. Mes la fust la douleur [plus grant] quant la royne commensa a menger sa fille, car toute personne qui les veoit plurer et mener douleur pleuroit de la grant pitié et douleur qu'elles fesoient.

806 *B4, B5, B3, A6* m. de leur (*B3* m.l.) enffans par  807 *A7* a. et t.  *A3, B5, A1, B1* et o. pour (*A1* et p.) ce que (*B1* o. que que) d.  *A11* o.d.  *A8* d. par son angle l.  807-808 *B1, B2, B3, B4, B5, A6* c. et demonstre quelle (*B2* c. par son ange q.) m. et (*B3, A6* m. de lanfant et) que ce  807-809 *A11* c. quil convenoit que ce fust acomply ce que dessus est dit et apres et apres quelles  *A3* c. et devant ce quelles  808 *A1* m. elles plouroient et f.  A12 e. plouroyent moult fort mes il convenoit que  *A9* f. et menoient moult g.  *A1* d. estre que  808-809 *A7* d. ainsy f. car  *B4, B5, B1* d. avenir ainsi comme (*B1* a. car) d.  *B3* d. avenir ainsi comme lavoit dit et demostre de  *A6, A8* fere car  *B2* fere ainsi come d.  809 *A2* a. ordonne et dit  *A1* dit estoit de la b. de dieu et  *A8* q. ilz deul eu.  810 *A12* en. et e.  *A8, A9* c. a la (*A9* c. de la) royne e.  *A9* comm. apres a  810-811 *A11* le filz ne demoura gueres que leur convint m. la fille de la r. marie mes  *B3, B5, A6* en. ellez maingeirent la (*B5* m. aprez de la *A6* m. apres de la) fille la r. adont eult si grant d.q.c.  *A12* m. de la fille de la r. et lors f. la d. tres grant q.  *B1, B4* el. mangerent la fille de la r. adonc eurent si grand d. (*B4* d. au cuer) q.c.  810-814 *B2* en. apres e. vont m. la fille de la r. qui en eut si grant d. qui cestoit moult grant p.q.  811 *A1* r. sa fille que elle amoit tant et de grand amour comme la mere doibt aimer son enfant si f.  *A8* f. lorrible d.  *A11* f.g.d.q.  *A1* g. que devant q.  *A9* f. la grant pitie et d.  812 *A7* m. son enffant car  *B1* f. a la royne que t.  *B5* m. tellement que t.  812-813 *A1* f. quil nest nul quil la v.p. en mengant que il ne pl.  *A2* mener dueil p.  *A8* mener telle d. lez plaingnoyent moult de  *A12* pl. et guementer ne se pourvoit tenir que ne plorast de  812-814 *A11* f. et disoit o dieu conment me seuffres tu vivre si longuement quil me fault maintenant menger le doulx fruit que iay porte en mon ventre que iay nourry et alaictie si doulcement esperant que au temps advenir ien eusse ioye et confort et aide ainsi demenoit grant dueil la royne et sa compaigne tant que tous ceulx qui les v. ne se povoient tenir de plourer et  *B3, B4* qui loioit ne se p. tenir de p. au cuer (*B4* de p. et davoir g.d. en son c.) q.  *A6* qui loyent ne se pevent tenir de p. et davoir g.d. a cuer q.  *B1* les oyst crier ne se p. tenir de p. et avoient g.d. en leurs cuer et grant p.q.  812-815 *B5* v. ne se eust sceu tenir de p. tant avoit g.d.q. les serviteurs de pilate quil avoit envoie pour avoir du rost desusdit furent retournez vers luy et luy eurent dit ce quil avoient vu il fut si marry et si courouce quil en fut trois iours au lict couche du grant douleur quil en eust qui q. il eust ainsy este marry et d.  812-816 *A13* t.p. en pourroient p. de p.q. vient a tier i.p. se leuva et ala a a. et f.  813-814 *A8* pi. quilz en avoyent et  *A1* pi. que elles f. et grand d. en especial la royne et  *A12* f. et menoit q.

809 Addition from MSS *A2, A3, A6, A7, A8, A9, A12, B1, B2, B3, B4, B5*.
811 Addition from MSS *A1, A3*, but see variants, this line. MSS *A2* and *A7* follow *A*.

[55] Et quant Pilate eüt esté par trois jours en son lit doulant et desconfortés, il se leva. Il s'en ala au roy Archelan davant le temple Salamon et la il fist venir tous ses barons et tout son conseil et leur dist: "Seigneurs, je ne voy point quel conseil nous puissons penre contre cest empereur, car nous summes en grant destresse de vivres et sy est avenu en ceste ville une grant merveille, c'est assavoir que les meres menguent leur enfans de grant fain, si que je conseille que nous rendons ceste ville a l'empereur et que s'il me veut destruire qu'il le face, car j'ay plus chier a mourir que sy tout le peuple mouroit, car l'empereur set bien que nul n'a

814 *B1* eut t.i. este en *B, B1, B4* lit marry et *A11* en sa chambre d. *A6* i. a lit bien d. 814-815 *B2* lit tant marry et courroucye il *A8* d. il sen *A11* d. il sen ala parler au *B5* d. apres ces trois iours il se 815 *B3* alait devers le roy *B7* ala tout droyt d. 815-816 *A11* a. et si assemblerent avec t. les b. et chevaliers d. le t.s. et t. 816 *A12* s. ou il le trouva et la *A12* b. chevaliers et escuyers et t. *A13* b. estant lors en la cite et *B5* v. illecques t. les b. et les chevaliers qui estoient en iherusalem et *B, B1, B2, B3, B4, A6* b. et tous ses chevaliers et l. (*A6* et *B4* c. de la cite et l.) d. 816-817 *B7* s. la ou estoit le roy archilen et les aultres b. et tantost pillate mandast le poeuple de la citez et quant ilz furent tous venus ilz commenca a dire s. 816-818 *B5* d. en telle meneire s. ilz fault que n. prenons conseil c.le. car il nous a fort destrainctz de v. et de viandes et ung grant fait et esclande est 817 *A6, A8, A13, B, B1, B4* v. que n. *A9* p. de party ne assentement aussy et pareillement se me semble il ny a nul bon c. que n. *A12* v. ne ne scays p. *B3* ie veulx que n. *B7* p. comment n. 817-818 *B2* s. il nous fault avoyr c. que nous fersons alencontre de le. car il nous a fort destruytz de v. et ung grant cas est *A8* pu.c. tenir c.le. quar *A13* pu. ceste cite tenir a lencontre de c.e. pour deffault de *B, B1, B3, B4, B7, A6* pe. conseil c.le. car il nous a fort destruis de viande et un (*B3* et aussi ung *B7* a d. tellement de vivres que navons plus que menges et ung) grand fet (*B1* ung f. *A6* ung cas) est 818 *A11* g. tristesse de la greinde que nous avons de viandes et v. *A12* sy scay de certain quil est *A13* vivres car ilz est 819 *A6, B2, B4* c. citey c. *B, B1* c. terre c. *A11* ville depuis na guieres ung grant et horrible cas c. *B3, B5* c. cite car les *B7* c. citez cest que *A8* m. car les *A12* g. ydeur et esclandre que les femmes men. 819-823 *A13* c. cite ung fait comme devant et et escript pour quoy ilz me samble que noz n. devons rendre et ie say bien que nulz ne colpable en ce fait mais que moy et pour iayme mieulx m. se le v.d. ien sui comptent et quil 820 *B3, B, B1, B2, B4, B5, B7, A6* e. par f. (*B5* par force de f.) sachiez que (*B1* s. sires que) ie (*B* s. ie) veulx et donne par conseil (*B2* par force de famine ie d. en c. *B1* d. en c. *B4* d.c. *B7* par faulte dau et viandez ie d. en c. *A6* v. donner c.) que n. *A2* f. pourquoy ie *A3* f. quelles ont si *A9* f. et famine quelles ont et souffrent si *A11* f. quelles avoient dont ie me doubte que brief ne nous adviengne ung grant mal et pour ce ie vous c. pour le meilleur que n. *A12* f. que elles ont si que ie veil et c. *A6, A11, B, B1, B2, B3, B4, B5* r. la cite a *B7* r. la v. 821 *A11, A12* v. fere (*A12* v. prandre a mercy ou) d. *B, B1, B3, B4, A6* d. il me destruira (*B3* il nous d.) car ie ayme mieulx a *A9, A12* iayme p. 821-822 *B5, B7* le. et me deust il d. (*B7* deust il deust il d.) car iayme mieulx m. *A11, B2, A2* iaume mieulx (*A2* a. trop p. a) m. 822 *B, B1, B3, B4, B5, B2* p. ce ceste cite (*B2* de la cite) m. *A11* m. pour moy car *B7* p. de ceste citez ie s. *A11* b. que na 822-823 *A6* p. perilloit pour moy car nulz ny a culpe senon moy et ie *B1, B2, B4, B5, B7, B* b. quil ny a nul qui (*B2* a personne q.) ayt coulpe (*B* c. fors *B2,B5* que n. ny a c. *B4* n. sur ce *B7* a home coupable) que *B3* b. quil ny ait personne qui y ait coulpe f. moy seulement p.

blasme en cest fet fors que moy. Et pour ce je croy qu'il avra mercy de vous." Et quant il eürent ouÿ ce que Pilate leur eüt dit, il furent moult doulans et dirent en plourant: "Aÿ, Dieux, que ferons de nostre bon seigneur et de nostre bon gouverneur?" Et lors les plours et les cris se leverent sy grans par la cité que onques mais sy grans ne furent, car hom les pouvoit bien ouïr de l'ost de l'empereur. Et si estoit le crit si grant pour la cause car il n'estoit jour qu'il ne mouricent dens la cité de fain le
[49v] nombre de quatre cens personnes. /

823 *A12* b. que moy en cest fait sy croyes quil *A3* fet sinon moy *A1* f. moy seullement et *B2* et ie *A11* et ie c. que en ce faisant il *B5* ie cuide quil *B7* p. quoy il 823-824 *A9* de moy et pitie adoncques q. les iuifz e. *A6* a. de v. aultre m.q. heut dit ces paroles il f. *B2* de tous les aultres q. pilate e. dit toutes ces choses ilz f. 823-828 *A13* des aultres adoncques criarent tous a haulte voix plus fourt que oncques mais disant helas par trois fois n. bon s. que f. nous et criarent si hault que lon les oyt en lost 824 *A3* v. aultres et *B* v. et autres q. *B5* v. tous q. *A11* q. les barons et chevaliers et autres qui a celuy conseil estoient ouyrent ce *B3*, *B4* v. aultres q. pilate e. dit cez chosez il (*B4* dit toutes ces paroles les seigneurs et tout le peuple) f. *B*, *B1* e. dit toutes ces choses ilz f. *B5* ouy ces parole ilz 824-825 *A12* v. mercy et q. le roy archillaux et ses barons et tout le autre peuple oyrent le conceil que p. donnoit ilz en f. moult tristes et do. *B7* q. pillate e. ainsi parle tout le poeuple commence a plourer en disant ay *A1*, *B4* m. esbahis et (*B4* m. marrys et) do. 825 *B2* do. et marris et *A6* di. ay *A9* p. que 825-826 *A1* f. de n. bon g. *A12* de mon bon s. pilate et l. 825-827 *A11* f. nous sil nous convient perdre n.b.s. et tantost de la cite sceurent ceste chose qui firent moult grans criz par 826 *A6*, *B*, *B1*, *B3* s. et g. *B4* s. et g. pylate adonc les *A1* l. les c. et les p. se *A12* p. et les grans c. 826-827 *B2* s. et g. qui nous veult delessier adon le c. fut se g. par 826-828 *B5* s. et g. et fut l.p. et le cry si g. par toute la cite que o. tel ne f. ouy tant que ceulx de lost *B7* s. et g. le crist estoit si g. ceulx qui estoient en lost 827 *A2*, *A8* l. parmi la *A3*, *A7*, *A9* l. par *B* c. fut si g. en la *A9* m. ne f. ouyz si g. car 827-828 *B3*, *B4*, *B1* c. fut si g. que (*B4* c. furent si que) ceulx (*B1* g. quil fut oy des gens) de lost *A11* cite et tant que on les ouoit de lost *A8* m. sy g. que o.m. sy g. ne f. et les *B* o. si g. ne fut oy il e. si g. que ceulx de lost *B2* m. sy g. duel ne fut oy tant que ceulx de lost 827-829 *A6* c. fut sy g. que ceulx de lost de le. le p.b.o. et ne. 828 *A12* les oyoit de lost *A8* em.p. 828-829 *B*, *B1*, *B3*, *B4*, *B5* ost de le. le povoient bien ouir (*B1* e. *B3* ost le bien o. *B4* e. les p.o. *B5* ost le p.o. clere) car *A1* em. tant pour les parolles de pilate que p. ce quil *A11* es. pour lors la mortalite si grande et si merveilleuse quil ne *A7* pour la pour la c. *A12* g. que pourtant ne. 828-831 *A13* em. et en la cite es. si grant f. que chascun i. du moins m.q.c.p. de f. et p. *B7* em. le povent clerement o.p. vault que *B2* em. les entendoyent plainement et de la en avant commencerent moult for a mourir de f. tous les i. ilz m. bien q.c.p. de fain adonc p. et le 829 *A8* c. que par f. il ne m. 829-830 *A8* m. bien de trois a q. 829-831 *B*, *A6*, *B1*, *B5* que de f. il ne m.q.c. en la (*B5* quil ne m. de f. quant c. ou plus de ceulx de la) cite p. (*A6* m. en la c.q. cent p. *B1* quil ne m.q.c.p. en la c.) d. *B3*, *B4* m. de f. bien q.c. en la citey adont p. leur d. ancores une foy (*B4* f. en la c.b.q.c.a.d.p.) que *A11* cite bien trois c.p. de fine f. et *A12* m. en la ville de iherusalem bien trois c.p. de la grant f. et apres ce p.d. quil feroit ce

[56] Et lors Pilate dist que ce qu'il avoit dist fust fait. Et lors lui et le roy Archelan se armerent avec cinc mile chevaliers et s'en vinrent aux foucés, la out estoit l'empereur. Et lui manderent qu'il vouloient parler a lui a fiance. Et incontinent l'empereur avec son filz Titus et Jacob et Jafet et avec dis mile chevaliers vint la ou estoit Pilate. Et quant il fu venu, et Pilate commensa a parler a lui. Et lui dist: 'Sire, empereur, aiés pitié de moy et de tout ton peuple, s'il te plaist. Et si prenés la cité et tresour et quantqu'i est et nous en laissés aler en estranges terres exillés par tout le

831 *A11* p. qui voullout que *A8* a. ordonne fust *A6, B, B1, B3, B4, B5* fait adonc pilate et *A12* a.d. au roy 831-832 *A7* l. sarma luy et le roy a. avecques *A13* a.d. se feisse adoncques se a.vi.m. 832 *A6, B, B1, B2, B4* arc. et .v. *A11* arm. bien honnestement a .v. cesn m. *B3, B5* arc. et .v.c.ch. *A12* et quant ilz se furent armes ilz sen vont ensemble aux *B2* ch. furent aux 832-833 *B7* arc. et plussieurs aultres grand seigneurs sen allerent sus les murs et quant il furent illec pillate dictz a sires de le. quil *A11* f. que lempereur avoit fait faire et *A1* f. dehors la ville et m. a le. quilz 832-834 *A13* et vont p. a lempereur a f. 833 *A12* et lors pilate et le roy archilaux luy *B2* es. les gens de le. *B, B1, B3, B4, B5* et m. dire a (*B1* m. a) lempereur (*B3* d.) que

833-834 *B2* et m. dire a lempereur quil v. a luy p. a f. *B5* a luy a seurete et *B7* p. a lempereur et 833-835 *A6* p. a lempereur a f. et t. son f. et iaffet et iacob a. .v.m. 834 *A8* a.t. son f. iacob *A7* le. vint a pilate acompaigne de t. son f. iacob *A13* e.t. 834-835 *A2, A3* a.t. son f. et iaffet et iacob (*A3* iacob et) a. *A9* e.a. dix *B2* e. et t. son f. et iassel et iacob et a. *A12* e. et t. son f. avec iaffet et iacob et xx.m.c. bien armes vont venir la ou p. et le roy archilaux les attendoient et *B7* e. sceust les novellez vint p. a luy et q. *A11* t. avecques iaffet et iacob et certain nombre de chevaliers bien armez v. *B, B1, B4* t. et iafel (*B4* i. du tassel) et iacob et a. *B3* t. et ioseph et iacob et xx.m. *B5* t. et iassel et iacob a.v.c.c. 835 *A6, B, B1, B2, B3, B4, B5* c. tous armez (*B5* c.a.) alerent la (*B* a. *B1* a. au lieu) ou *A8* ou p.e. et *A12* q. lempereur fu *B5* e. et *A6, B, B1, B3, B4, B5* q. lempereur et toutes ces gens f. 835-836 *A13* c. venirent parler a p. et pi. *A7* c. lors d. pilate s. *B2* q. lempereur fu v. et toutes ses gens p.c. a p. a lempereur son seigneur et a dire ainsi s. 836 *A8* c. a compter sa rayson et *A11* p. a vaspasien et *A12* parler et *A6, B5, B, B1, B4* pa. a lempereur et (*B* p. et) lui *A13* c. a dire s. 836-837 *B7* c. a dire a. misericorde de moy *A11* s. en ceste maniere tresnoble prince et trespuissant sur tous princes terriens gloire et victoire te soit donnee sire ie te requiers mercy comme ton servant qui suis et metz en ta main mon corps et mon ame mais sire ains que ie meure ie te requiers baptesme affin que mon ame ne soit dampnee car ie croy certainement que ihesu crist fut cruciffiez par envie et est saulvere du peuple et dieu de toute creature et ie lappelle a tesmoing que ie nay coupe en sa mort fors que pour lavoir iuge a tort par le commandement de faulx iuifz et pour ce sire ie vous requiers que vous a. mercy de moy et faictes enquerir se ce que ie vous ay dit est vray ou mensonge et vous plaise avoir p. du pouvre pe.pr. *B5* s.a. de moy misericorde et defaut ce pl. *A6, B, B1, B2, B3, B4, A3* a. misericorde (*A3* a. mercy) de moy *A9, A12* pitie et mercy de moy 837 *A6, A12, B, B1, B2, B3, B4* t. ce (*B3, B4* t. le) p. *B7* t. le p. de ceste citez sil *A9* pl. et tout quil y a et 837-838 *A13* moy et t. et tout ce quest dedeans et q. *B7* pr. tout ce que vous playra pour en faire a vostre et n. *A6, B, B1, B2, B3, B4, B5* c. et tout ce que est dedens et n. *A3* c. et tout q. *A11* pl. et tout le t. qui y *A12* tr. qui est dedens et q. est aussy et q.

838 *A8* q. il a dedens a ton plaisir et *B* et l. *A9* ex. et banniz a tousiours mais par *A12* par le 838-839 *B, B1, B2, B3, B4, B5, B7, A6* a. a nostre (*A6* a tout n.) aventure adonc (*B5* n. voulente et av. la ou il vous plaira) le. dist a pilate (*B2* d. *B7* av.le.r.) se *A11* es. contrees l.le.r. se *A13* t. pour essayer le m.le.d.l. a pilate se

monde." Lors respont l'empereur et dist: "Sy tu me vieux rendre la cité et toy et tous ceulx qui y sont a en fere ma voulenté, je les penray voulentiers. Mes autrement non, car de personne n'aray ja merci ne que tu eüx de Jhesu Crist." Et lors le roy Archelan dist a l'empereur: "Sire, je suis filz du roy Herodes, vostre ami, qui estoit roy de Galilee, et puis aprés sa mort j'ay esté roy. Sy vous suppli qu'il vous plaise de moy penre a mercy car mon pere ne moy ne fimes onques riens contre vostre pere ne contre vous ne ne consentimes point a la mort de Jhesu Crist. Et sy vous dis que

839 *A3*, *A1*, *A2* m.l.le. (*A1* m. et le.) r. et *A9* m. icelles parolles dictes et par pylate requises et proposees l.le.r. et d. *A12* e. a pilate et 839-840 *B1* c. et tous *A13* c. en maniere que ensamble le peuple ie 839-841 *A11* c. ie men rapporte a toy mais an laide de dieu iay esperance de y entrer bien brief et feray adoncque ma v. de tous ceulx qui sont dedans car 840 *B7* v. come sire que suis ie la p. 840-841 *B*, *B1*, *B2*, *B3*, *B4*, *B5*, *A6* ie le feray et a. (*B5* ien suis content ou a.) rien ne feray (*B1*, *B4* le f. *B2* le f. mais non point a. et ne la prendraye *A6* a.) car *A13* p. mais 841 *A9* v. a mercy mais a. ie nen feray riens car *B7* a. riens nen feres car nul ne aray *A1*, *A9* p. qui y. soit na. *A13* car ie te prometz que toy ne p. quil soit en la cite na. de moi m. ne plus que *A6*, *B*, *B1*, *B3*, *B4* de nulz na.m. *A11* na. nulle m. *A1* m. non plus que *A2*, *A3*, *A6*, *A7* ne plus que *A9* neant plus que 841-842 *A12* car ie te promett que de p. qui soit na.m. aussy peu comme vous eustes de *B2* de nul na.m. au plus que vous eustes de i. *B5* de vous m.na. non plus que vous eustes de nostre seigneur i.c. quant pylate ouyt ces nouvelles il eust moult grant paour et sen retourna a son palais et se mist sur son lict et illec fut trois iours et trois nuyctz moult courouce et moult marry et le *A1* neant plus que toy et eulx eurent de *B*, *B1*, *B3*, *B4*, *B7* ne plus que vous eustes de nostre seigneur (*B1* de *B7* que eurent de) i. 842 *A6* de nostre seigneur i. *A13* c. lequel par toy pilate fut faulsement iugiez a. lui d. lors sire *B3* et adonc dist le roy a.s.e. ie *A6*, *B*, *B1*, *B4* d.s.e. ie *A11* a. que ces choses ot ouyes d.s.e. ie 842-843 *B2* e. ie s. dist ilz f. 842-844 *B7* a. commenca a dire a les.e. de s. sien du roy h. lequel quant il vivoit e. bien vostre parfaict amy et ainsi seray le vostre sil vous plaist et quant il fut mort ie fus couronnez roy 843 *A11* v. filz ami *B5* e. de 843-844 *A11* e. de g. et quant il fut roy par droicte succession ie fu fait roy apres luy si *A13* et a. luy ie *A2* g. sy *B7* g.p. vous me prenez a *B*, *B2*, *B3*, *B4*, *A6* et quant il morut ie fu roy p. (*B3* roy apres luy p.) v. que me prenez (*B2*, *B3* v. de me prendre *B4* v. moy prendre) a 843-845 *B1* et quant il fut mort ie fuz roy paisible p.v. avoir m. de moy *B5* et quant il fut mort ie fu fais roy apres luy p.v. que vous me prenez a m. moy ne mon p. ne 844 *A11* s. et requiers humblement que *A12* s. sire quil *A13* que aiez de moy m. *A1* de nous p. 845 *A6*, *B1*, *B3*, *B4*, *B7* car moy ne mon p. ne *A2* o.c. *A8* o. chose qui desplust ne fust c. 845-846 *B* car moy ne mon p. ne f. iamais c. vous ne contre vostre noble p. ne oncques ne *B2* car moy ne mon p. ne mesfeismes o.r. vers vous ne nay point consenty a *A6*, *A11*, *B4* o.c. vous ne contre vostre noble p. ne oncques ne *A9*, *A12* c.v. voulente (*A12* v. ne contre vostre p.) ne c. *A13* c. le vostre honneur et ne c. a *B1* o.c. vous ne contre vostre pere aussi ne fu onques consentant de la *B3* o. ne ne c. a *B5* o.c. vous ne contre les vostres ne oncques ne me consentis a *A8* p. et ne fusmes oncquez consentans de la 845-848 *B7* o.c.v. noble p. iulles cesar et durant mon pere estoit bien amy du sainct pere le. luy r. tu es f. du roy h. 846-847 *A6*, *B*, *B1*, *B3*, *B4* du saint prophete i.c. et durant (*B1* d. la vie de *B3* d. son temps *B4* d. la vye de vostre pere) mon *A8* sy e. mon p. de *A12* et treschier sire mon *A11* cr. et e. mon p. de la c. et aussi le seray sil vous plaist toute ma vie adonc le. 846-848 *A13* et e. mon p. de la c. du v. et estoient tous ungs le.r. es *B5* du saint prophete i.c. et quant mon p. vivoit il e. bien son amy et fut toute sa vie et ie seray le vostre amy et serviteur si vous plaist quant le roy a. eust tout dit le.r. en celle maniere est tu f. au roy h.

mon pere estoit de la court du vostre." Lors l'empereur respont a Arthelain et lui dist: "Es tu donc filz de Herodez qui fist la persecucion des enfans en voulent ousire Jhesu Crist, le profette, en son enfance? Home qui n'a merci ne doit trouver mercy. Ton pere vouloit ossire Jhesu Crist, le profette, quant il fu né et si fist ossire tous les enfens qu'il pouoit trouver qui estoient de deux ans en jus afin qu'il peüst ossire Jhesu Crist sans en avoir nulle mercy. Et sy en fist ossire par nombre cent quarante et quatre mile. Et pour ce je n'averay ja mercy de toy car tu compereras les

847 *A1* c. de v. pere l. *B, B1, B3, B4, A6* e. bien amy de mon pere et (*B3* b. son boin a. et *B4* b. son a. et) fut toute sa vie et ie seray le vostre se il (*B1* b. son a. et ie o.v. amy sil *B3* v. boin amy sil) vous (*A6* b. son a. et pourtant si vous plaist que vous ayes mercy de moy et ie s.v. amis si v.) plaise adonc le. 847-848 *A12* e. bien prive de la c. de v. noble pere et lors dist le.a. es *B2* p. le roy e. moult amy de august cesar vostre pere le.r. au roy a. es tu f. du roy h. *A2, A3* r. au roy a. *A9* v. et quant le roy archilant eut ainsy dit et parle l.le. lui r. et d. *A6, A7, A11, B, B1, B3, B4* r. au roy a. es tu f. du roy (*A7, A11* f. de) h. 848 *A2, A7, A11, A12* du roy h. *A13* de celuy qui *B2* fist si grande p. 848-849 *A11* des petits e. innocens pour ce quil v. *B, B1, B3, B4, B5, B7, A6* des petits e. pour ce que v. (*B5* e. qui v.) tuer le (*B1* v. et cuidoit o. le *A6* v.o. le) saint p. (*B3* lenfant p.) i.c. en 848-851 *A13* des innocens pour cuider mettre a mort i.c.q. 849 *A8, A9* v. et cuidant (*A9* c. tuer et) o. *A2, A3, A7, A8, A9, B2* c. en *A12* e. de bethleem en *A11* o. le saint p.i.c. en *A1, A9* enfance saches que (*A9* e. et pour ce ie te dy que) h. 849-850 *A12* c. et car en sa fausse envie il neust pitie ne m. en soy aussy ne doys tu avoir ne le trouvera ton 849-851 *B2* enfance comme qui ne prant nul a m. ne doyt point t. mes ton pere f. 849-852 *B3* enfance et h. qui nait eu point de m. nen doit point avoir ton p. afin 849-854 *B1* enfance sans nulle m. et on fist occire c.lx.iiij.m. enfans soubz le age de d. ans et p. ce ne a. 850 *A7* qui m. *B7* m. ia ne t. *A8* d. avoir m. *A11* t. nulle m. *B4, B5, B* ne trouvera ia (*B* ne trouve ia) m. *A9* o. et tuer i. 850-851 *A8* le bon p. 850-854 *B, B4, B5, B7, A6, A11* p. affin que peust tuer i. (*B5* t. le saint prophete i. *A6* p.o.i.) c.f.o. par (*B5* quil fist t. le saint prophete i.c. fist o. et t. par *B7* p. avant quil p.t. le saint prophete f. morir par) compte fait c.lx. et iiij.m.e. (*B5* cxlviiij.m. et petis e.) de laage (*B4, A11* e. soubz la. *B7* c.xl.e. soubz la.) ij ans (*A6* cxlviiij m. petits e. soubz le aige de sept ans) p. ce (*A11* ce quil nen eut aucune m. non) na. 851 *A9* p. des ce quil *A9* o. et tuer t. 851-852 *A1* e. de d. en *A3* t. de 851-853 *A12* t.a. que p. trouverent o.i.c. deys d. ans en dessoubz et sy navoit point de pitie ne de m. de eulx et en n. quarante *A13* ne s.a. 851-854 *B2* t. en tout son royaulme soubz leafe de d. ans ne navoyt m. de nul si en tu a en n. de lxiij m. par quoy ie ne doy pas avoir m. 852 *A7* ans a. *A8* e. soubz d. ans a. *A9* p. tuer et o. 852-853 *A2* s.n. 852-854 *B3* p. tuer i.c. fist o. par compte fait c.q. et quatre m. petis enffans dessoubz laaige de d. ans p. 853 *A13* m. deulx et furent c. 853-854 *A9* n. pitie ne m. de lui et p. ce te dy que sans avoir nulle pitie ne m. *A3, A7, A8, A1* quarante neuf (*A1* q.) m. 854 *A12* toy et c. 854-855 *A8* toy et q. *A11* na. ie pas de toy et sur les faulx iuifs et maistres de la loy ie prendray vangence de ihesu crist et telle quil en sera memoire a tousiours mais car a grant tort et par envie fut ihesu crist crucifie qui estoit et est roy dee tout le monde et q. *B, B1, B2, B3, B4, B5, B7, A6* m. de toy mais (*A6* de vous m. *B5* m.m.) emporteras le. de ton pere (*B5* p. le roy herode) q.

848-854 The massacre of the Holy Innocents is recorded in Mt 2:16-18.

eniquités de tes ensestres." Et lors quant le roy Arthelain l'ouÿ, il fust sy couroucié qu'a peu qu'il n'anragast. Et decendi de son cheval et ousta ses [50r] armes. Et quant il fust desarmés, / il sache son espee et dist a l'empereur: "Ja le grant Dieu ne veulle que vous ne payans ne puissant venter de ma mort." Et lors il mist la pointe de l'espee sur sa poitrine et bouta si fort qu'il fist passer oultre le corps l'espee bien ung cartier. Et incontinent il cheü mors dedens les foucés. Et quant Pilate et ses gens virent le roy Arthelan ainsy mort, il en furent moult couroucés et s'en retournerent en la cité et compterent au peuple la responce de l'empereur et la mort de

855 *A2, A3* tes predecesseurs et *A12* de ton pere herode et q. *A9* e. et mauvaistiez de tes predecesseurs et *A6* q.a. le roy *A11, A12* a.o. ainsi parler vaspasien (*A12* o. lempereur) il 855-856 *A13* de ton precedant pere adoncques d. *B, B1, B2, B3, B4, B5, A6* a.o. dire a lempereur toutes ces choses il (*B2* d.t. ces c. a le. il *B4* d. ces motz a le. il) fut tant c. *A8* sy a destroyt c. *B7* a. ainsi eust ouy parler lempereur il fust tout despitez que 856 *A1* c. quil a. de yre et de courroux et *A11* c. quil fut connme tout desespere lors d. *B7* et tantost d. *B5* d. ius de *A9* ch. a terre et 856-857 *B, B1, B2, B3, B4, B5, B7, A6* et se desarma de tout son harnois et (*A6* t. ses armures et *B2* t. ses armes et) puis (*B7* d.p.) print (*B2* et quant il fit desarme il trayt) son *A7* a. et prist son *A11* o. son harnoys et q. *A13* son destrier et se destrainsist et dist 857 *A12* il tres son *A3, A11* il tira son *A9* il s. et tira son *A13* es. pour trois fois em. 857-858 *B* em.d. le g. ne 858 *B2, B3, B4, B5, B1, B7* ia d. le g. (*B1, B7* d.) ne *A9* p. quelz quilz soient ne *B, B1, B2, B3, B4, B5, B7, A6, A7* vous ne homme pagan se (*A6* h. point se *A7* ne vous parens se) pu. *A11, A12* vous ne homme p. se puisse vanger (*A12* se p. venter) de 858-859 *B5* m. puis aprez ces paroles il 858-861 *A13* que tu parle de ma m. ne que tu ten p.v. en disant ce achillain se b. son e. par le miellieu du ventre et c. 859 *A1, A8, B4* e. contre (*B4* e. devers) sa *B3, B7, B2* e. contre son (*B2* e. au droyt de son) cuer (*B7* son ventre) et b. *A12* sa panse et la b. *A11* poit. et la frappa si 859-860 *A7* f. que passa le.o. le c.b. 860 *A12* quelle passa tout o. le c.b. *A11* quelle passa tout o. et i. *A9* p. ladicte e.o. le c. ung *A1* ung pied et tantost il *A8* p. la pointe daultre part b. ung piet et 860-861 *B3, B, B1, B4, B5* quelle passait (*B* quil la p.) tout au travers de son c. en (*B1* tr. en) telle maniere quelle passait ung pied tout o. et (*B1, B, B4, B5* pie dehors et) tantost tumbait a terre tout m. (*B* te.m. *B1* ta.c. tout m. a t. *B5* m. et c.) d. *B2* quelle luy passa par tout le c. et b. ung grant piedz dehors du couste du dos et tantost tomba es f. *A6* o. a traver de son c. en telle maniere quella passa ung pie dehors et tantost c. a terre m. 860-862 *A13* f. devant pilate lors p. et sa compaignie sen 860-863 *B7* quelle passa o. bien pietz et demy et tantost tumba par terre tout m. il sen alla en la 861 *A11* m. a terre moult laidement q. *A12* m. a terre d. *A6, B1, B3, B4, B* f. sur quoy il (*B* f. ou il) estoit q. 861-862 *A11* g. du roy archilaus le v. ainsi *A6* roy f. *A8* v. ainsi ar.m. 862 *A2* a. il *A8* m. douloureux et *A11* m. espoventez et c. de la mort du roy archilaus si sen 862-863 *B4* r. dire la r. 862-867 *A13* r. en iherusalem bien corrociez et c. es aultres la m. du roy a. et de la r. de le. dont ilz ny avoit point de reconfourt q. 863 *A6, B, B3, B5* co. la 863-864 *A11* r. que leur avoit faicte le. vaspasien et conment le roy a. se estoit octis l.t. *B7* p. comment le roy a. estoit m. adoncques t. *A2, A7, A9, A12* du roy a. *B5* du roy a. lesquelles choses ainsi dictes et racontees les 863-865 *B, B1, B2, B3, B4, A6* du roy ar. a tout le peuple adonc les g. du roy et t. le p. menerent g. (*B2* ar.ad. le p. et tous ceulx de la cite m. moult g. *B1* ar. et t. le pe.m. tant g. *B3* ar. et t. le pe.m.g. *B4* m. moult g. *A6* p. en heurent si g.) dolour et depecerent l. (*B1* et despoillerent l.) r. par desespoir (*B1* d. enragerent et *B3* par despit et *A6* et dessiroient l.r. par desprit) et a.

Arthelan. Et lors les gens de Arthelan et tout le peuple firent trop grant duel et dessiroient leur robes et aracherent leur cheveux et fesoient si grant duel que onques mes ne fust si grant duel mené en nul lieu.

[57] Et quant il vint l'endemain a matin, Pilate fist venir Jozeph d'Arimatie et son seneschal et tout son peuple et leur dist: "Seigneur, vous veés bien que nous ne nous pouons plus tenir et que Dieu nous a obliés, car onques mes cité ne fust en si grant tribulacion comme est ceste cy, car vous veés que nous n'avons nuls vivres et sy mourons de fain. Sy vous

864 *A2, A7, A12, B5* du roy a. *A12* p. menerent g. *A9* f.g. *A8* t. dur d. plus g. 864-865 *A11* p. conmancza a mener g.d. par toute la cite et de. *B5* p. menerent moult g.d. et eurent moult grant douleur au cuer et despecoient les r. par desesperance et a. 864-866 *A3* a. et adonc t. le p. plus g.d. que 864-867 *B7* p. commenca a crier plus fort que devant q. 865 *A12* c. de leurs testes et f. 865-866 *B, B1, B5* a. le poil de leur testes et menoient tant g. cri que iamais (*B1, B5* que o. mes) ne *B2* a. le poil de leur teste et menerent moult g. cris et tel que oncques navoyt ouy tel ne tan g. douleur en ung l. *A11* c. et menerent tel d. *A6, B4* c. de leurs testes et menoyent si g. (*B4* m. tant g.) cry que *B3* c. et menoient tant g. cry que 866 *A1, A7* g.m. *A2* f.m. si g. en *A3* f.m. en *B5* f. ouy si g. en place puis le l. 866 -867 *B, B1, B3, B4, A6* f. oy si g. (*B4* g. ne mener si grant) doulour en (*B1* g. duel en) une place (*B3* d.) q. *A8* f. fut ne g. quilz navoyent oncquez fait et q. *A11* o. ne fut veu tel et q. *A12* o. ne fust nomme si g. en part du monde et q. 867-868 *A8* i. son *A13* i. ensamble t. le p. de la cite pour consel disant s.d. pilate v.v. 868 *B, B1, B2, B3, B4, B5, B7, A6* et son s. barrabam et t. (*B4* et b. son s. et t.) les chevaliers et t. le (*B7* b. et t. le *B3* et le) p. et voult avoir conseil (*B4* v. oyr c.) de eulx et (*B1* et l. *B2* et le *B7* p. et quant furent venus pillate) d. *A7* s. avec tout son conseil avec t. le p. *A11, A12* s. barrabam et *A12* l. demanda conseil et l.d. 869 *B7* vees que p. *A11* plus resister contre lempereur et *A13* t. ceste cite contre cestui empereur pour deffault de vivre et que *B1, B4, B2* t. la cite et que (*B2* t. ceste c. et az) d. 869-870 *A11* o. et non pugnist moult griefvement car *B2* o. car iamais gens ne *B4* o. et que en nulle c. du monde ne fut on. menez si 869-871 *A6, B5, B3* t. la citey ne fut on.m. en telle t. ne en si grant destresse comme nous sumes car n. *A2, A3, A7, A9* t. ceste cite car v. *B, B1* o. et que ceste (*B1* que en c.) c. ne f.on.m. en telle t. ne a si grant destrece comme nous sommes car n. 869-873 *B7* t. la citez car on.c. ne f. plus tormentee come est ce. ici car v. scavez quil ny a plus que menger pourquoi ne sez que ferons doresnevant i. respondict seigneurs quel conseil v. povons n. donnez car puis que le. 870 *A8* mes ie ne fus en 870-871 *A8* co. ie suis vous *A11* t. que ceste cy est et nous qui dedans sommes car n. *B2* t. ne en si grant destroyt come nous sommes car n. *B4* t. ne si grant destresse comme nous sommes car n. *A12* t. car n.na. *A13* t. car n.m. 871 *A11* nulles nulles viandes ne aucunes choses pour menger mais m. 871-872 *A12* m. tous de f.c. *A8* f. pour tant vous s. *A13* f.c.n. que ferons l. 871-873 *B, B1, B2, B3, B4, B5, A6* nulles viandes pour mangier mais m. (*B5* me.m.) touz de f. que c.v. que (*A6* f. que voulez vous que *B2* f. que dictes v. que) n. facion i.d. seigneur (*B3* fa. adont d.i.s. *B2* d. dist s.) de ce quel (*B1, A6* d.q. *B4* fa. adonc d.i.s.q.) conseil v. povons donner car (*B5* i. de arimathie respondit en celle maniere et d. sire ie ne scay q.c. nous p. car *A6* d. sur cecy car) le. *A11* f. pour ce advisons en brief quil est de f.l. parla i. et d. sire n.

suppli que vous conseilliez que nous pourons fere. Lors dist Joseph: "Nous ne vous sarions conseiller puisque l'empereur ne nous veut penre a mercy. Mauvais conseil vous donna qui vous conseilla d'estre son enemi quar vous pouiez bien savoir que vous ne pouriez resister contre lui, ne ossy nous ne nous pouvions point tenir longuement."

[58] Lors dist Pilate: "Je ne say que nous puissons ferre fors tant que en ceste vile a grant tresor d'or et d'argent et de pierres precieuses. Et l'empereur et ses gens le cuident tout avoir. Je say coment il n'aront riens

872 *A3*, *A9* que v. me (*A9* v. nous) c. *A7* v. avises que n. *A9* f. ne que remede l. 872-873 *A12* n. ferons l.i. dabarimathie d. sire n. *A9* i. darimathie n. 873 *A13* s. donner bon consel p. *A11* s. donner conseil a ceste chose p. que il est ainsi que *A6*, *B*, *B1*, *B2*, *B3*, *B4*, *B5*, *B7* e. ne vous (*B2*, *B3*, *B4*, *B7* ne nous) v. 874 *A6*, *B*, *B1*, *B2*, *B3*, *B4*, *B5*, *B7* me. et folz (*B2* et celluy v.d. fol et ma. *B7* me. pour ce) c. *A11* me. ne ceulx de la cite m. 874-875 *A13* qui v. fist es.en. de lempereur car *A8* es.en. a lempereur car *A11*, *A12* c. que vous feussiez e. de lempereur car *B*, *B1*, *B2*, *B3*, *B4*, *B5*, *A6* c. que fussies e. de lempereur (*B5* e. a le.) car b. poviez (*A6*, *B2* car vous p.b.) s. 874-877 *B7* es.en. a lempereur car c. luy ne p.r.p.d. ie 875-876 *A12* p. deffendre ne r.c. lempereur et que n. *A8* c. lempereur l. 875-877 *A11* que c. lui ne pourriez t.q.p. ouyt ce que ioseph avoit dit il fut moult esbahy lors le conmance a dire ie *B4*, *B*, *B1*, *B3*, *B5*, *A6* que c. luy ne po. bonnement ne l. (*B5* luy vous ne po. gueres l.) t. (*A6* ne pourra t.) la cite pi.d. ie ne (*B* po.l.t.pi.d. ne *B1* po.t. la c. adonc d. ie ne *B3* po.t.l. la citey pi.d. va) say *A2* pouriez c. lui r. adont d. *B2* que c. luy ne vous po.t.l.pi.d. ainsi ie ne s. aultre chose que nous facions mais en 875-878 *A13* lui et que n. ne p. contre lui ceste cite t. adoncques p.d. seigneurs nous avons g. 876-877 *A3* pou.l.t.l. *A9* l. par faulte de vivres et puis apres p.d. ie *A12* l. contre luy ne contre sa puissance q.p. eust oy iosepht dabarimathie il d. seigneurs ie scay comment nous fersons en 877 *A11* say plus que n. ferons f. une chose que ie vous diray cest que en *B4*, *B*, *B1*, *B3*, *B5*, *B7*, *A6* que nous faissions fors (*B1* fa. sces) que *A3* t. ie considere que *A9* t. seulement que *A7* ferre mais que 878 *B*, *B1*, *B2*, *B3*, *B4*, *B5* c. cite (*B4*, *B5* c. ville) a *B7* c. citez a moult dor *A9* a tant de t. *A12* v. nous avons a grant foysons de t. *A13* t. en ceste cite dor 878-879 *A11* a. dor et le.

878-880 *B*, *B3*, *B4*, *B5*, *A11* pr. prenons les et les (*A11* pr. si conseilla que n. les) faisons m. 878-881 *B1* pr. prenons les et les mectre en telle maniere que nous les puissons m. et que en p. le temps a. que nous pourrons par defaulte de viandes et q. *A6* pr. prennons les et en faisons en m. de c. en telle maniere que nous les puissions m. et que nous en passons le temps comme nous pourrons par deffault de viandes et q. 878-885 *B7* pr. ie conseille que faccions faire pouldre tant que la puissons menger et passa le temps aulx mieulx que nous porrons puis que navons aultre chose a menger car autant trouverrons de m. atous t. que s.t. se c. pleust moult a tout le poeuple et tantost sen ala c. en son ostel pour prendre leurs or 879 *A13* e. les c. *A12* ie vous idray il *A1* na. nauront r. *A9* say bien la maniere c. 879-880 *A13* a.n. *B2* a. ie conseille que le. nen ayt r. mays fayons en nostre p. cest assavoir que nous prenons lor largent et les pierres precieuses et les faysons m.

et a nous fera aucun profet. Nous le ferons tout moudre a mortiers de cuivre que hom le puisse manger et pacerons aincy nostre vie. Et quent l'empereur penra ceste cité, il n'y trouvera nul tresor car aussy grant
[50v] mercy avrons nous de lui / sans le tresor comme eu le tresor." Quant il eüt donné le conseil, il distre[nt] tuit que c'estoit bien dit. Et chascun s'en va en sa meson. Et qui eüt or ne argent ne piere precieuse fist come Pilate l'avoit dit. Et ceulx qui en avoient trop en donnoient a ceulx qui en avoient peu et de cel tresor il visquirent vint et ung jour. Et quant le tresor fust mengé,

880 *A12* fera grant p. *A3* f.n. 880-881 *A12* feront mettre t. en m. descouvers et mouldre si que *A3, A7, A9, A11* m. tellement (*A7* m. de c. *A9* m. de c.t. et par maniere et facon *A11* m. de c. et mectre en telle maniere) que 881 *A13* c. si les mangerons car a. nous fault passer n. *B, B2, B3, B4, B5* c. en (*B3* c. et nettoyer en *B4, B5* c. et les mectre en) telle maniere que (*B2* c. et les faysons bien nettoyer affin que) les puisson m. et que en passon le (*B5* en puissons passer le) temps ainsi que nous pourron par deffaulte de viande et (*B2* m. pour passer t. et affin que *B5* po. mieulx par d. daultrez v. et) q. *A8* pu. avaller et user et pa. *A11* n. temps a. come nous pourrons par deffault daultres viandes et pour ce q. 881-882 *A13* vie car 882 *A9* c. ville il *A12* c. ville luy ne ses gens ne tro.
882-883 *A11* tresor et par ainsi il ny gaigera riens car aultant trouverons de m.s. *B5* tresor et autant trouverons nous de m. en luy s. *B, B2, B3, A6* car autant trouverons de m. (*B2* a. de m.t. nous *A6* car nous t.a. de m.) s. 882-886 *B1, B4* car autant a. de m. ou le (*B4* au. trouverons nous de m. avec le) t.c.s. le t.q. icelluy c. fut donne il le tindrent pour bon et sen ala c. a son houstel et chascun prist son (*B4* et p.c. son) t. et ses (*B4* et son a. et ses) joyaulx et les moulurent comme estoit ordonne et 883 *A12* n.s. *A13* a. lempereur de n.s. *A12* c. nous aurons avecques tout le *B2* t.q. 883-884 *A3* eu le t. et tous se tindrent a son c. *A13* eu le t. et chaschun dist lors que *A7* eu le t. a ce c. tous saccourderent et ch. *A11* q. ceulx que estoient illecques ouyrent le *A12* eut dist et d. le c. ses gens le tindrent a bon et di. 883-885 *B, B2, B3, B5, A6* q. celluy c. fut donne ilz le tindrent pour (*B2* d. chascun le tint p.) bon (*B5* t. a tres bon *A6* t. a bon) et sen ala c. en son hostel et print chascun son or 884 *A3* d. que 884-885 *A11* dit et lors fut fait assavoir icelle chose par toute la cite et alla c. a son hostel et prindrent leur or 884-887 *A13* dit et ainsin fut fait et de 885 *A1* m. et firent comme pilate avoit dist car qui *A8* m. et prindrent lor *A8* pr. sy c. 885-886 *A6, B, B3, B5* a. et ses ioyaulx (*B5* a. ne pi.pr. et les aultrez i.) et les moillirent comme estoit ordonner (*B5* m. ainsi c. pylate comme pylate lavoit o.) et *B2* pr. et *A1* a. si le pestelast au mortier et *A11* pr. ceulx qui en avoient et le molurent comme il leur estoit ordonne et c. *B7* a. ceulx *A12* av. devise et ordonne et c. 886 *A6, A8, B, B1, B2, B3, B4, B5* a. assez (*A8* a. largement *B* a. prou *B4* a. prou et as.) en *A11* a. assez desptoient a *B5* d. prou a 886-887 *B7* a. et puis en firent menuez pouldre et de *A6, A8, A11, A12, B1, B5* a c. qui nen a. point et de *B4* a c. qui en av. gueires et de 887 *A6, A13, B, B1, B3, B4, B5* ce v. *A11* ce v. et lespace de xxx i. ou environ q. *B7* icelle v. lespace de vint *A2* vis. par lespace de xxvii i. *B, B1, B3, B4, B5, B7, A6* i. en la cite sans autres (*B1* s. nulle au.) viande avoir (*B3* av. en la citez *B4* s.av.au.v. et *B5* i.s.au.v. et *B7* i.s. menger au. chosez que ceste pouldre) q. *A13* i. ung peul apres veinrent le 887-888 *A11* le tr. de iherusalem furent ainsi tous desgastez t. *B7* f. gastez il voandrent a pi. *B, B1, B2, B3, B4, A6* m. ilz vindrent devant (*A6* v. a) pi. 887-890 *B5* m. ilz vindrent devant p. en luy disant ce que avez commande a este fait nous avons g. tous le t. que ferons nous dicy en

883 *avrons* [ *avront* Correction from MSS *A1, A2, A3, A7, A8, A9, A12*.

tout le peuple vint a Pilate et lui distrent: "Sire, nous avons fet ce que vous aviés dit du tresor, et or est tout gastés. Que pourons nous fere dorenavant?" Lors Pilate fust moult desconfortés et sy commensa a pleurer davant tous et leur dist: "Seigneurs, vous m'aviés fet vostre sire et vostre gouverneur en ceste ville, mes dorenavant ne vous puis plus gouverner. Si vous pri pour Dieu, pardon, que sy je vous mefis onques riens, que vous le me veullés pardonner." Et quant les juifs l'oÿrent, il se desconforterent moult fort et sy n'i eüt nul qui ne pleurast, car du grant

888 *A11, A12* v. devant p. moult esbahy (*A12* p.) et *A13* p. a 888-889 *B2* d.s. ce que avez conseillie est fait nous avons g. le t. que 888-890 *A13* d.n.t. sont g. et failly dit n. que nous ferons de *B, B3, B4, A6* d. ce que aviez commande a este fait nous avons g. tout le (*A6* g. le) t. (*B3* g. toutez pieres precieusez et les t.) que ferons decy en *B1* d. que ferons nous decy en avant ce que avez demande a este fait nous avons gaste tous les tresors adoncques p. *B7* d.s. ce que aves comandez et faict nous avons f.g. le tr. de la citez l. 889 *A12* dist et enchargiez du *A3* t. qui sont t. *A7* qui sont t. *A9* tout maintenant g. et consume que 889-890 *A11* a. conseille et conmanday a fere car tous noz t. sont mengez et degastez et p. *A10* f.l. 890 *A8* d. sy f.p.m. *B4* p.m. courrocie et d. 890-891 *A13* p. ne sceu que dire ne que fere fors que tant quil l. *B, B1, B2, B3, B5, B7, A8* c. moult fort (*B7* c.f. *A8* m. durement) a *A10, A12* m. courrouce et d. (*A12* c.) et 891 *A6, B, B1, B3, B5* d. tout le peuple et *A11, B4* p. moult fort d. tout le peuple et *B7* p. en disant s. *B2* d. tout le peuple mes amis l.d. il vous 891-892 *B1* f.s. et g. de vous autres et de c. *A13* a. esleus g. et s. de c. terre mais *A6, B, B2, B3, B4, B5* f.s. et g. de vous aultres de (*B2* et tout g. de *B5* g. de) c. cite mais decy en *A12* sire et g. de vous tous en 891-894 *B7* f.g. de vous et de c. citez mais vous prie que ne vous attendez plus a moy pourquoy pardonnez moy se vous ay faict aulcun desplaisir q. 892 *A10* g. et vostre maistre de c. *A11* c. cite mes *A10* mes puis que tout est perdu plus ne v. 893 *A1* g. en ceste ville si *A9* pri et requier p.d. mercy et pa. *A7* d. que *A8* pri que p.d. que ie *A10* v. demande de par d. se *A11* g. dont il me desplaist par quoy ie vous requier a tous ensemble que 893-894 *A13* g. se ie v. fis o. chouses quil v. desplaisisse ie v. en crie mercy et que le *B, B1, B2, B3, B4, B5, A6* g. pourquoy pardonnes moy car ie vous requier (*B5* ie r.) p. se (*B2* pr.v. plaise me pardonner se) ie ay fait a (*B3* ay mettait a) nul desplaisir que me (*B4* quil le me) pardonnes sil v. plaist (*B1* d. il v.pl. le ma pa. *B2* d. *B4* pl. car ie vous pa. a tous et *B5* f. nul meffait silz v.pl. et ie vous en prie) q. *A9* m. ne mesdiz o. en ma vie le temps passe aucune chose qui ne soit iuste et raisonnable quil vous plaise le moy p. *A10* o. que me le pardonnez sil vous plest et 894 *A11* quil vous plaise le me p. *A12* me pardonnes et *A11* i.o. ainsi parler pilate il *A9* o. ainsi humblement et piteusement parler il 894-895 *A12* i.o. que pilate se desconfortoyt ainsy ilz se prirent moult fort a plorer car il p. bien es.d. et sy ny *B, B1, B2, B3, B4, B5, A6* i.o. cela dire a (*B1* o.d.c. a) pilate (*B2* o. ainsi parler p.) ilz furent moult desconfortez et (*B3* m. desconffis et *A6* m. dolant et) ny eut petit (*B1* ny avoit nul p. *B4* eut celluy ne p.) ne grant qui *A10* d. si 894-896 *A13* i.p. sy parfondement quil 894-899 *B7* i.o. parler pillate si durement ilz furent moult desconfortez et de grand desconfort ne p. bonnement r. a pillate s.d.p.m.n.t. a ladventure de d. le g. et 895 *A8* m. et ny ot oncques nul *A9* p. moult tendrement car 895-896 *B2* ne commencast a plourer de g. douleur quil *A7* g. quil *B1* p. tant fort quilz 895-898 *A6, B, B3, B4, B5* p. tant que a pylate ne p. riens dire (*B4* r. parler ne r.d.) pour (*B5* p. si fort que a py. ne p.r.po.) quil avoient et (*B5* et puis) p.

deul qu'il avoient, il ne lui pouvoient respondre. Mes tuit se guermentoient moult fort pour tant qu'il pensoient tous estre destruis.

[59] Lors Pilate leur dist: "Signeurs, aions bon cuer et nous mettons tous a la voulenté du grant Dieu et nous rendons a l'empereur et a sa mercy, car il vau mieulx que si nous mourions eincy de fain. Car il n'est jour qu'il ne muire bien quatre cens en ceste ville. Et par aventure nous penra il a

896 *A9* a. faisoient et menoient il ny eut oncques nul dentre eulx qui lui peust ne ne sceust r. ne dire ung tout seul mot mais *A1* ne p. riens r. *A8* luy scavoyent r. ung seul mot ains se 896-897 *A10* quil menoient ilz ne lui respondirent riens mais p. quilz estoient d. *A13* p. oncques r. ung tout seul mot car il *A9* se doulouroient et desconfortoient m. 896-898 *A11* a. oncques ne luy sceurent r. car il p. quil estoient desconfiz l. *A12* p. motz dire mes se g.t.m.f.l. *B1* p. rien dire a pillate pour la grant doulleur quilz avoient et p. *B2* mes se desconfortoyent tellement quil voulsissent e. mors s.m.n.t. 897 *A8* p. bien quilz seroyent t.d. *A13* p. bien e. 897-898 *A9* il cuidoient et p.t.e. desconfiz d. et mors l. *A2* d. et mors adont p.d. *A3* p.e.t.d. par lempereur et l. 898 *A10* l.d.p.s. *A11* d. pour leur donner confort s. *A13* p.d. *A6*, *B*, *B1*, *B3*, *B5* d. tout em plorant s.m.n.t. *B4* s.m.n.t. *A13* c. a grant dieu et 899 *A6*, *B*, *B3*, *B4*, *B5* de d. le g. et *B1* de lempereur et de d. *A10* r. tous a la voullente de le 899-900 *A13* v. de le. il *B2* r. a la voulente de le. car *A8*, *A12* e. a faire de nous toute sa (*A12* n. sa) voulente car *A6* a la voluntey de l. et faire de nous sil quil ly plaira car m.v. que *A11* e. a faire de nous a sa voulente puis que autrement il ne peut estre car a laventure aura il pitie de nous si v.m.e. mourir le fere que de mourir e. tous les iours de *B3*, *B*, *B1*, *B5*, *B7* e. et face de (*B* e. a faire de) nous a (*B5* f. a) sa voulentey car m.v. (*B1* et devons faire a sa v. car m.v. faire ainsi) que *B4* e. et face le. de nous a sa voulente car m. le v. ainsi faire que se mo. 900 *A10* car n.m. tous de f. il nest *A1* que n. laissier ainsi morir de *A3* mi. ainsi le faire que ce que n. *A6*, *A9* mo. tous (*A9* t.e.) de *A12* mi. nous allons rendre que nous sy nous mo. *A13* mo. en sa mercy que se n.m. icy de *A9* i. quelque iour que ce soit quil *A12* i. par autre que 900-901 *B3* f. car tous tous les i. en m.q.c. et plux et *A10* i. quen c. cite ne m. vij.c. personnes ou plus et *B7* i. quil se m. tous les i. plus de trois c. et 900-902 *A6*, *B*, *B1* f. car tous les i. en m.q.c. ou plus et par a. (*B* p. et que a la. *B1* m.p. de q.c. et a la.) dieu ly mectra en courraige a lempereur quil aura m. de nous et mieulx vault que se que nous (*B*, *B1* v. fere ce que n.) m. tous de *B4* f. car vous vees que chascun i. en m. plus de q.c. et a la. dieu mectra en couraige a lempereur quil aura m. de n. et vault mieulx que se m. 900-903 *B2* f. vous vees que tous les i. en m. en c. cite b.q. cinq c. ou par a. que dieu fera ier le courage de lempereur et quil aura m. de n.a.p. et t. ses gens y. 900-904 *B5* f.a. toutes ces choses p. et t. ses gens alerent h. de la c. de coste les f. que a.f.f.le. et son conseil et 901 *A8* m. de trois a q. *A9* b. xxxx c personnes en *A12* m. en c.v.b. de trois a q.x. personnes et *A13* m. en c.v. plus de q.c. personnes et *A1*, *A3*, *A7* c. personnes en *A12* a. luy venra en courage quil n. *A13* p. tous a 901-902 *A1* a. il aura m. de nous ou *A8* a. luy p. courage et voulente de n. prendre tous a m. au moins une p. sans n. gaster e. ne mourir de *B3* a. dieu mettra en couraige a lempereur quilz auray m. de n. car mieulx vaulx que se m. de 901-903 *A11* c. personnes et peut estre que luy viendra en couraige de n. prendre tous a m. ou aucune p. et ne m. point ainsi de f. adont p. et t. son pe. conclurent quil yroient a mercy a lempereur or est assavoir que durant les batailles devant dictes qui furent dehors la cite cayphas levesque de la loy estaut en son chastel pour cantif qui moult estoit fort quant il vit le deluge et la grant destruction des iuifs lors luy

souvint de la profecie quilz avoient dicte aulx iuifs devant la passion de nostre sauveur ihesu crist disant il ment venu en songe quil convient que ung homme iuste meure a ce que tout le peuple ne perisse si seroit bon que nous feissons lexcusacion de cestuy que ce fait filz de dieu pour savoir mon si cest celuy dont les prophetes dient quil devoit souffrir mort pour le peuple saulver et par ce congneut que il fut cause de la mort de ihesu crist et aussi luy souvint des merveilleux signes que estoient venuz ia piessa sur iherusalem comme gens darmes et en batailles les ungs contre les autres charioz et autres plusieurs signes et oyez plusieurs voix que estoient grant demonstrance de la vangence que dieu prendroit en brief des iuifs comme dit est si descendit au chastel portatif fait par engin ou il estoit tout desespere luy xiie des maistres de la loy et sen cuida fouir luy et sa compaignie en la cite mais cent des chevaliers de vaspasien leur furent devant qui les prindrent tantost tous douze et leur lierent les piez et les mains et leur banderent les yeulx en signe de grant derision que ceulx et les iuifs firent aulx xij chevalliers de vaspasien lesquelx il avoit envoie en iherusalem pour savoir leur entencion et quilz voulsissent croire en iherucrist et recevoir le saint baptesme car a iceulx chavliers firent reze les barbes et leur monstroient les armeures et les garnisons leurs chevaulx et leurs destriers et leurs chameaulx et elephans puis prindrent douze grox bastons et despoillerent les douze chevaliers tous nudz for de brais et puis leur lierent les mains derriere a iceulx gros bastons et puis les mirent en celuy estat hors de la cite de iherusalem et leur nercirent le visaige de charbon et pendirent a chascun deulx ung frommaige au col et leur dirent allez a voustre maistre vaspasien et luy dictes que nous ne ferons riens de son conmandement et que pour ce vous envoions a luy ainsi atournez conme foulz et quil ne sen fuit en brief nous le irons destruire et luy et tout son ost quant les cent chevaliers de vaspasien eurent ainsi prins les xii maistres de la loy et liez conme dit est ilz les misdrent derechief dedans leurs chastel dont ilz estoient descenduz puis menerent celuy chastel avecques les elezphans qui le menoient et les xij maistres dedans iusques aux trefz de vaspasien et quant lempereur les vit il en fut moult ioieulx et conmanda quilz fussent bien gardez et apres la bataille finee lempereur appella tous ses conseillers et leur demanda de quelle mort il feroit mourir cayphas et ses compaignons quil tenoit en sa prison si trouva en son conseil quilz fussent escorchez tous vifz et puis oings de miel et penduz par les piez devant les portes de iherusalem et tantost lempereur les fist amener devant luy et les fist lier sur boys tous estanduz et fist mectre cayphas ou meilleu des autres et puis le conmanda fere tous vifz escorchez et quant il les eut fait escorcher il les fist oingdre de miel par tous puis fist fere ung gibet de troys toyses et sur celuy gibet tout en hault fist dresser unes fourches et la fist pendre cayphas par les piez come souverain evesque des iuifs les mains pendans contre val et luy fist pendre aulx possez et aulx doiz plommees de fer et puis luy fist atacher aulx cuisses a deux chesnes de fer deux chiens deux chatz et deux singes tous vifz que luy pendoient aval la teste et le mordoient toutes icelles bestes moult durement puis fist pendre a celuy gibet au dessoubz de cayphas les autres xi maistres de la loy qui avoient este escorchez et oings conme cayphas et leur fist pendre es cuisses a chascun deulx chiens et en cel estat demourerent cayphas et ses compaignons ainsi penduz au chault et aulx mousches de puis leure de tierce iusques a vespre et estoient penduz pres la cite au plus hault lieu que len peut trouver affin que ceulx de la cite les peussent mieulx veoir et de fait en avoient les iuifs si grant pitie et si grant dueil que ceux plusieurs se laisserent cheoir dessus les murs de la cite en bas par desesperance et quant vint a leure de vespres vaspasien les fist tous despandre et leur fist trancher les testes et puis desmembrer a force de chevaulx et mectre par quartiers apres fist allumer ung grant feu ou il fist mectre souffre et bousche seiche et puis fist bouter leurs charoinges dedans avec les chiens chatz et singes que avoient este penduz a leurs corps et fist tout ardre emsemble et quant tout fut fait ars il fist prendre la pouldre et la fist venter tout entour de la cite de iherusalem et mectre au desoubz du vent par quoy la pouldre en allast en la cite et de ainsi villaine et cruelle mort moururent cayphas et les xi. maistres de la loy pour ce que par leur malice par leur conseil et par folle envie fut mis a mort nostre seigneur ihesu crist les chiens que furent penduz et ars avec eulx signifioient

mercy ou en pitié et ne nous gasterons. Einsy ne mourons de fain. Aprés cecy Pilate yssy hors de la cité avec tou son peuple et s'en vint au foucé que l'empereur avoit fet fere. Et Titus, le nouvel empereur, s'aloit esbatant avec ses chevaliers la environ. Et Pilate l'a conneü a ses armes signees a l'aigle. Et lors il lui fist signe en son gan qu'il vouloit parler a lui. Et quant [51r] Titus le vy, il vint celle part avec / ses chevaliers. Et Pilate lui dist: "Sire, Titus, empereur, nous vous prions qu'il vous plaise de prier vostre pere

---

quil estoient plains de felonnie et de cruaulte et les singes signifioient lengin et la malice deulx et les chatz signifioient laquet et la trahison dont ilz estoient plains car il devoient loiaulment garder et enseigner le peuple et il le trahissoient car par leurs faulx engin et malice il firent consentir forment tout le peuple a la mort de ihesu crist ce quil neussent pas fait sil eussent este bien introduiz a bien fere et pour ce leur en prenist mauvaisement a que tous les tresors de la cite furent degastez conme dit est cy dessus et que pilate ot donne conseil aulx iuifs de eulx aller rendre a mercy a lempereur y.g. de la c.p.a. 901-905 *B7* a. quil aura m. de n. tantost a.p. et ses gens alerent h. la c. luy et les aultres vers les f. que a f.f.le. et puis t. et moult de ses gens estant au fossez vidrent pillate et tantost p. 902 *A9* m. en tout ou *A12* p. et ne m. *A7* p.a. se y.h.p. de 902-903 *A10* m. et a.p. et son peuple y. *A13* et ne m. pas icy de f. adoncques p. et t. *A3* a.y.p.h. 902-904 *A6, B, B1, B3, B4* a. cest choses p. et t. ses gens allerent h. de la c. iusques es fo. (*B* c. empres les fo. *B4* c. sur les fo.) qua.f.f.le. (*B1* fo. de le. *B3* c. de coste les fo.) et 903 *A2, A9* ce y.p.h. *A12* la ville de iherusalem a. *A10* cite et sen 903-904 *B2* cite et allerent devant les f. que a.f.f.le. et *A11, A13, A12* sen allerent pres des (*A13* a. sur les *A12* sen allast au) f. 904 *A12* t. filz de le. *B* fere lempereur et *B2* t. qui estoit n. *A10* t. son filz sen a. *A11* fere et a celle heure t. le filz de le.a. chevauchant a. 904-905 *A2* e.a. ses c. estoit la *A6, B1, B* t. son filz a. chevauchant luy et ses c. entours les fosses et *B4, B5* t. son filz a. a cheval chevauchant (*B5* a. chevau.) luy et de ses c. entour les foussez et p. *B3* et p. 904-906 *A13* t. filz de le.c. pilate a laigle quil pourtoit en sa devise car t. sen aloit e. avec aucuns de ses c. pilate lui 905 *A1* c.e. les fossez et *A10* c. et *B2* a. luy et ses gens dessus les fosses chevauchant et *A8* e. sy le c.p. a *A12* e. les fosses et *B2* p. le vit et le c. *A10* ar. a 905-906 *A11* c. entour les f. de la ville soy e. et lors p. lui *A7* ar. et l. 905-907 *B4, B, B1, B3, B5, B7, A6* c. bien aux (*B1* c. aux) a. (*B3* b. tiltus a sez a.) de laigle et (*A6* de baille et) a son grant cheval aussi et (*B5* ch. grisart et *B7* c. a son g.ch. et a ses ar. et) lors p. (*B, B1, B3, B4, B5, A6* et p.) luy (*B7* et lui) commanca a dire s. 906 *B2* ai. et q. *A11* quil viensist p. *A12* gant et 906-907 *A13* gant et lors t. se tira vers luy ou ilz estoit et pi. 907 *A10* vy en icelle place avec ses chevaliers il alla a luy et *B2* vy venir a. ses c. il luy *A1* v. a lui a. *A7* p. et pi. *A11* et quant p. vit quil estoit pres de luy commancza a dire s. *A13* pi. commensa a parler et d. 908 *A10, A11* t.n. *B7* t. novel e. *A3* v. supplions quil *A12* e. noel n.v. supplions tous quil *A13* e. nouvel pl.v. prier *B2* n.v. supplions et requerons nous et tout le peuple que v. vueilles dire lempereur v.pl. *A12* vostre noble pere *A6, B, B1, B3, B4* pl. dire a lempereur ton pere *B7* pl. mandez dire a ton pere 908-909 *B5* de dire a ton pere lempereur pl. aussi en avoir mercy et de cest 908-911 *A10* pl. de prendre toute la cite et nous aussy et a pitie et r.v.g.n.

qu'il ait mercy de nous. Et qu'il vous plaise de penre aucune pitié de cest peuple qui vous en prie tout em plourant. Et qu'il vous plaise de non reguarder noustres iniquités mes vostre bonté et vostre noublece." Et quant Titus ouÿ cela, il le manda a son pere par deux chevaliers. Et quant il eüt ouÿ les chevaliers, il envoya querir toute sa gent et leur menda qu'il s'armassent. Et quant tuit furent prest, il s'en vint au foucés, la ou estoit

909 *A13* quil vuille avoir m. *A12* a. mercy et p. 909-910 *A11* m. et pitie de n. *A7* n. et aussy de ce pouvre pe. *A6, B, B3* pl. en avoir mercy et de *B1* n. et de ce peuple que le prie *A8, A11* pl. de 909-911 *B2* et de tout le peuple de ceste cite qui vous en regnies tant piteusement et ne vueilles par r. *B4* quil ne vueille r. 909-912 *B7* n. et te prions parellement et ne nous voeulle r. selon nos pechez mais celon ta grand n. et conninilite q. *A13* n. et vous aussi car ainsin le v. prions et somme contens de rendre la cite et quil ne regarde point n. grant i. mais sa n. et b. adoncques t. le 910 *A1* p. car ilz v. en prient t. *A3* en requiert t. 910-911 *A6, B1, B3, B5* pl. et ne (*B5* p. que ne) vuilliez r. 910-912 *B* et ne vueilles r. mon i.m. regarde ta noble grace se il te plaist q. 911 *A9* i. et mauvaistiez mais avoir regart a v.b. *A11* mes regardez v.b. *A7* mes v. voulente et v.n. 911-912 *A1* mes v.n. et v.b. et q. *A6, B1, B2, B3, B4, B5* mes regarde ta (*B1* mes octroier leur ta) noble grace si (*B4* r. sa n.g. et la vostre si) te plait (*B2* mes v.n. et g. *B3* g. *B5* p. et tu feras bien et moult grant aulmosne) q. 911-912 *A12* n. vous preignes misericorde et pitie de nous tous et q.t. filz de lempereur oyt et vyst c. 912 *B2* ouy ses parolles tantost le m. a son p. lempereur par *A9* ouy ce que pylate lui ot dit et propose il *A11* m. par d.c. a son p. dire ceste chose et *A12* m. tantost par d.c.a. son p. la out il estoit a sa tante avec ses autres c. et ses deux chevaliers ou distrouent a lempereur et q. 912-913 *A8, A9* q. lempereur (*A9* q. vaspasian) eut 912-914 *A13* ch. lequel incontinant se arma et toutes sa baronnie et sen 912-915 *B, B1, B3, B4, B5, A6* ouy ces nouvelles il m. ij c. a (*B5* ces paroles il les m. par d.c. a *B3, A6* il lez m. par d.c. a) son p. et tantost (*B4* m.c. quilz t.) y alerent pour luy compter les nouvelles et tantost que (*B1* ces n. et incontinent que) vaspazien les oyt il (*B5* v. le sceut il *A6* v. oyr ses nouvelles il) manda ses c. a armer et aussi il sarma (*B5* et luy mesmes se a.) de ses meilleurs armes et v. ou son (*B5* v. vers son *A6* v. a sona son) filz t. latendoit ampres du (*B4* at. au plus pres des *A6* at. es f. *B3* at. aux piedz des) f. et pilate estoit de lautres part o ses (*B1, B5* a couste avecques ses) gens adont (*B4* pi. et ses gens estoient da.p.a.) titus commanca a parler a lempereur son p. et (*B5* a son p.le. et) luy d.s. (*B4, B5* d. mon s.) v. *B7* ouy ainsi parler pillate tantost il m. perre pour le faict de la citez et tantost lempereur m. son oste quil v. avecques luy quant il furent pres des fossez ou pillate estoit dung cordez et titus de lautre titus commenca a dire a son p. *A11* q. lempereur ouyt ce il fist armer certain nombre de gens des meilleurs quil eust et puis sen vint a titus son filz qui lactendoit es f. et quant il fut la venu t. son filz luy conmancza a dire s. *B2* et tantost quez vaspasien eut ouy les nouvelles il manda et fist armer tous ses gens et se a. de ses meilleurs armeures et sen alla la ou t. son f. lattendoyt et pilate estoyt de laultre part avec ses gens adonc titus commenca a parler a lempereur son p. et luy d.s. 913 *A9* les deux c. 913-914 *A1* c. il fist armer tous ses g. et sen 913-915 *A12* q. par tout loust ses g. darmes quil venissent tous armes et il se vait armer de ses meilleurs armes et des plus riches et sen vint vers tithus son filz avec toutes ses gens qui se tenoyent tout environ iherusalem et ny avoit sans nombre et lors tithus fist reverence a son p.s. dist il v. 914 *A2, A3, A7, A9* a. et aussi il sarma et q. *A8* q. ilz f.t. armes il se misdrent au 914-915 *A13* f. parler a pilate adoncques commencha t. a dire a *A2, A3, A7, A9, A10* e. tytus lequel t.

son filz. Lors Titus dist a son pere: "Sire, veés yssy Pilate qui c'est accourdé a vous rendre la cité mes que vous les preignés a mercy." Et l'empereur dist qu'il n'est pas temps car c'est par force. Lors dist Vespesian a Pilate: "Se tu me veux rendre la cité et tous ceulx qui sont avec toy a ma voulenté, je sui tout prest de le fere. Mes je te dis bien que j'aray ausy peu mercy de toy ne des autres comme tu ne eulx eüstes de Jhesu Crist quant vous le jugates a mort et le pendites en crois.Et veux que vous sachiez que

915 *A6, A8, A10* v.p. *A10* c. de iherusalem mes   916 *A8* c. en tant que le p. *A13* c. de iherusalem pourveu que vous le p. ensamble le peuple de leans a   916-917 *A11* c. par ainsi quil v. plaise de le prendre a m. et tout le peuple aussy et vaspasien d. *A12* c. en tant quil v. plaise v. les p. a m. luy et tout le pouvre peuple car il le vous supplient en plourant et lors d.le. quil ne scoit pas   916-918 *B, B1, B2, B4, B5, B7, A6* que v. le (*B1, B3, B4, B5, B7* que le) vueilles prendre a m. et vaspazien respondit (*B4* v. empereur r. *B7* m. lempereur r. en ceste maniere biaul) filz il nest pas maintenant t. (*B7* pas t.) que il le die car il ne (*B5* die quant ne) la puet plus tenir en (*B1* p. en *A6* la plus t. plus en) nulle maniere et (*B7* car pl. ne la p.t. contre moy et) se il le meust dit au premier quant (*B5* au commencement q.) fusmes venuz autre (*B7* dit des le commencement a.) chose feust mais ores nen (*B1, A6* m. maintenant nen) feray rien (*B5* o. nous nen ferons r.) car (*B7* m.r. nen f. car) le temps est passe quil le devoit faire adonc (*B2* pas t.m. de ainsi dire quant il ne p.pl.t. la cite a. *B7* quil ne d. dire l.) v. dist a (*B5* v. respondit a) p. pilate (*B1, B2, B4, B5, B7, A6* a.p. *B7* d.) se   916-928 *B3* que le veillez pranre a mercy adont vaspasien respondit a son filz filz il nest pas maintenant saison qui le die car il ne le puelt plus tenir en nulle maniere et sil le meust dit au premier quant fusmes venus autre chose fust mais ores men feray riens car le temps est passez que le debvoit faire adonc v. fit combley lez   917 *A3, A13* e. (*A13* e. vaspasien) respondit quil *A1* l. t. ains estoit f. *A11* t. par gre que par *A12* cestoit grant f. *A9* f. et quil ne se povoit plus tenir l. 917-918 *A13* t. mais ce dit lempereur a *A10* f. et non de voullente l.d.p. sire prenez la cite et tout ce que vous y trouverez et v.d. a *A11* d. a *A12* l. lempereur v.d. a 918 *A9* tu te v.r. et aussy la *A12* me peulx r. *A13* et fere du tout a *B7* et toy pour en faire a *A1* toy et en faire ma *A2* qui y sont a *A7, A10* s. dedans a *A6, B, B4, B5* c. et celles (*B* et toutes c.) qui s. dedans pour faire (*B4, B5* p. en f.) a (*B* f.) ma   918-919 *A11* toy en la cite a mercy ie *A12* s. a ma mercy ie *B2* s. dedans ie *B1* ceulx et celle que s. dedans ie me apparaillere de la prendre et ie   919 *A8* sui p. mes *A13* de la recevoir mais *B, A6* sui appeille de la prendre et ie *B4, B5* p. et appareillier de le prandre et (*B5* de vous recevoir et) ie   919-920 *B2* de la prendre mais ia na. du nul m. ne plus que vous eustes *B7* ie la prendres et aultrement riens nen feray car de toy ne de home que soict dedens na. ia m. non plus que vous eustes *A6, B1, B4* aray m. *B5* que autant auray m. *A13* diz certainement que ia creature na m. de moy ne plus que vous eustes *B* aray de toy m. ne nul qui soit dedans que vous eustes m. de   920 *A1* toy c. tu as eu de *A12* de tous ceulx qui y sont c. vous eustes de i.c. le prophete q. *B1, B4* toy et de tous ceulx que sont dedans c. vous eustes (*B4* e.m.) de *B5* toy et de tes gens c. vous eustes de sainct prophete nostre seigneur i. *A3, A10, A11* c. vous eustes *A7* tu eux de   920-921 *A6* ne de tous ceulx qui sont dedans c. vous heustez m. de i.c. et le fites mory en la c. a grant tourt et s. *B7* i. et s.   920-923 *A13* c. car sa m.s. sur vous v. et   921 *A12* i. et la myttes a *B5* i. sans cause a *A12* et s. *B, B1, B2, B4, B5* et le feistes mourir (*B2* et les aultres iuifz le firent m.) en la c. a grant tort et s. *A11* c. a tort et sans cause et s. *A9* s. tous tant que vous estes que *A10* le feistes mourir et que le feistes pendre en

sa mort sera vengee sur vous. Et car il ne trouva nule mercy en vous, vous ne l'arés ja en moy." Et quant Pilate oÿ la responce de l'empereur, lui et toute sa gent furent moult couroucíés et sy ne seürent que fere ne que dire, mes que distrent a l'empereur: "Sire, prenés la cité et quantque vous y trouverés et nous ossy, et sy en faites a vostre vouloir comme seigneur que vous estes."

[60] Lors Vespesian fit emplir les foucés qu'il avoit fet fere. Et quant il furent plains, il envoya Titus, son fil, et Jacob et Jafet et dis mile chevaliers

922 *A2, A3, A8* et tout ainsin (*A8* et pour ce) quil *A9* ve. par moy et toutes mes gens sur v. autrez tous et tout ainsi quil 922-923 *A12* vous et pour ce que v. neustes m. de luy v. ne *A7* vous et q. *A10* vous et sur toy le premier tu nen trouveras point a moy *B2* sur toy ne en moy ne trouveres ia mercy q. *B, B1, B4, B5, B7, A6* vous autres car (*B4, B7* v. car) vous nen eustes point de m. me point de me. ne trouveres (*B1* t. en moy et *B7* e.p. de m. ne m.t. en moy) q. *A2, A8* v. tout ainsin nen trouverez (*A8* v. ne t.) vous point en *A3* en v. aussi nen trouveres v. point en moy ne en mes gens et *A9* n. pitie ne m. en v.v. ne la trouverez v. ia em moy ne en mes gens et 922-924 *A11* vous tous car vous meustes m. de luy en aucune maniere et aussy ne laurez vous ia de moy et q.p. et ceulx qui avec luy estoient eurent ainsi ouy parler vaspasien ilz f. si tres c. et esbahiz quil ne 923 *A1* la trouverez en *A1* oy le reproche de 923-924 *A8* e. il fut m. *A12* e. et tout le peuple f.m. doulens et vont faire ung grant cry en plourant et ne 923-925 *A13* p. et sa noblesse oirent ces nouvelles oncques mais navoyent estez sy esbayz adoncques d. *B2* oyt ces parolles il fut m.c. et tout le peuple aussi et adonc ilz d. a 923-928 *B, B1, B4, B5, B7, A6* oy telles parolles il (*A6* oy ses choses il *B1, B7* oy ces p. il *B5* oy ces nouvelles il) fut m. (*B5* m. espovante et m.) c. (*A6* fut bien c.) et tout le peuple aussi et ilz (*B5* p. pareillement maiz il) nen povoient autre chose dire ne faire mais (*B1, B4, B5, A6* ch.f. ne d.m.) d. (*B7* p.f.a.c. et d.) s. (*B5* d. tous a une voix s.) e.p. vostre c. et ce qui est dedens et (*B7* c. et) faites de n. autres a v. (*B5* n.v. voulente et) bon plaisir c. (*B7* n. a v. vollentez c.) s. et maistre que v.e. adonc lempereur fist (*B5* s. que v.e. et m.a.v.f.) combler les 924 *A8* et auxy toute sa gent et sy 924-925 *A12* fere mais que vont dire a *A8* dire fors tant que pylate d. *A11* dire car quant il virent quil ny avoit aucun remedde en leur fait si d. 925 *A13, B2* s. empereur p. *A12* et tout q. *A8, A9, A10* et tous ce que 925-926 *A13* c. et nous aussy et en f. vostre bon plaisir c. *A11* et ce qui y est et en f.v. plaisir et voulente comme s. et maistre que 925-928 *B2* c. et tout le peuple qui est dedans et faictes de tout a v. plaisir adonc lempereur v. fist comblier les 926 *A12* n. tous o. *A10* t. et en *A9* s. et maistre que 926-928 *A8* vou. si dist ve. que on emplit *A10* voul.l. *A12* f. vostre plaisir ainsy c.s.l.v. lempereur fit tantost e. 927-928 *A11* e. adoncques lempereur fist comblez les 928 *A13* v. lempereur fit *A11* fere entour la cite et *A12* et puis il 928-929 *A13* fo.e. en la cite de iherusalem t. iacob 928-930 *B7* fere entour la citez puis e. son f.t. a grand compagnie et leurs commandast quant ilz seroient dedens quil 929 *A6, B, B2, B3, B4, B5* f. combles il *A11* f. empliz il e. dedans la cite son *A9* e. querir t. son f. iaffel et iacob et dix *A12* e. son f.t. iacob *A6, B, B2, B3, B4, B5* t. et iaffel et (*B, B4* i. de tafel et *B3* t. et ioseph et) iacob avec dix (*B2* iassel de cassel et i. et xv) m. *A10* e. son f.t. iaffet et iacob et mle c. 929-930 *B1* f. comblez c. quentrerent dedans la *A12* iafet avec xxx.m. en la c. de iherusalem et *A11* iafet avec certain nombre de gens bien appareillez et armez de tout ce quil leur failloit et entrerent dedans sans nul contredit et puis f. *A6, B, B3, B4, B5* c. qui entrassent dedans la *A9* c. et leur dist quilz entrassent premiers dedans la *A10* c. de iherusalem et *A13* c. quil prindrent pilate ensamble tout le peuple et quant il furent dedeans il *B2* ch. dans la c. et pour fermer les p.e.a.

en la cité et leur dist qu'il fermacent les portes de la vile, afin que nul juifs ne s'en puist istre ou fouïr. Et lors Titus avec ses gens s'en entra dedens la [51v] cité et prist Pilate et le bailla en guarde a dis chevaliers / et commanda qu'il fust bien guardé. Et puis fist penre et lier tous les juifs et juives qu'il trouva. Et en trouva par nombre en tretout setante mile et sis cens. Et quant tout cela fust fet, il commanda que l'en ouvrist les portes. Lors

930 *A6, B, B1, B3, B4, B5* cite et (*B4* c. de iherusalem) et fissent clore les p.a. *A9* f. et gardassent tres bien les *A11, A12* p.a. *A3* a. de garder que 930-931 *A1, A6* nul ne *A8* i. et 930-932 *A13* p. fut baillie a garder pilate a *A11* nul nen yssist puis print tout le premier pi. 930-938 *B7* p. pouis apres quil tuasserent les i. qui dedens estoyent lung a lautre puis apres ouvrrassent les portez ainsi fust faict apres lempereur entra en la citez lequel se tenoit hors affin quil ne eschappa nulz iuif de la citez et q. ilz furent dedens il a. au 931 *A1* p. aller ne f. hors de la cite t. *A10* p.f. ne i. et *A6* p. saillir dehors et que il ne sen puissient f. *B, B1* nen saillist dehors ne ne sen p. (*B1* p.i. ou) f. *A12* t. fit le commandement de son pere lempereur et sen *A6, B* t. et iaffel et iacob avec (*B* et iacob avec iafel et) les x. milles chevaliers entrerant d. *B1* f. adoncques iassel et iacob avecques entrerent d. 931-932 *B2* p. partir adonc t. lempereur et iassel et iacob garderent bien la c. 931-933 *B3, B4* ne sen saillissent et ne sen fuissent adonc (*B4* ne s. dehors et quilz ne sen p. fuire a.) t. et iacob avec ioseph du cassel et lez x.m. chevaliers furent entres dedans la cite y il firent (*B4* c. et f.) prandre t. 931-936 *B5* ne sen saillist dehors ne dedans que nul ne sen peut f. adonc vaspasien et t. iacob et iassel avecques le x.m. chevaliers entrerent dedens la cite et y avoit bien cent et x.m. et vj.c. personnes avecques ce quil en estoit bien autant mort ou plus et q. ilz les eurent bien encerchiez et mis en fermeture ils firent ouvrir les p. de iherusalem et puis vaspasien et tout lost qui 932 *A2, A10* c. avec pillate et (*A10* c. de iherusalem et) pr. *A12* c. avec les xxx.m. chevaliers esquieulx d.b. *A2* le donna en *A12* g. pilate et leur co. 932-933 *B, B1, B2, A6* et firent prendre (*A6* p. pilate) t. *A9* g. et puis *A11* ch. sur paine de la vie et puis *A13* ch. pour le bien garder et fust prins et lyez t. 933 *A1* quilz le gardassent bien et *A8,A9* penre t. 933-934 *A1* i. et hommes et femmes quil t. *A10* i. et en t. bien s. 933-935 *A12* i. vieulx et ieunes et ny avoit sans ceulx qui estoyent mors a la bataille et sans les autres qui estoyent mors de fain par la ville cent iii.m. et vij.c. et q. *A13* i. et leurs femmes qui estoient en n. .lx.m. et plus et q. il en furent seigneur il firent ovrir les 933-936 *B, B1, B2, B3, B4* i. et toutes les iuives et les firent bien l. et y en t. en la (*B2* i. et i. et l. moult destroictement et t. dans la) cite bien lxxxij et (*B4* b. quatre vins deux mille et) vj.c. avec ceulx (*B1* b.xx.m.vj.c. sans c. *B4* vj.c. sans c.) qui en estoient mors bien lxv (*B4* m. car il avoit euz de mors dedans la cite soixante et quinze) mille et (*B1* m. et *B2* vj.c. iuifz et) q. ilz les eurent bien atachiez (*B2* ilz furent tous a.) adonc firent ouvrir les p. de iherusalem adonc vaspazien et (*B1* a. lempereur et) t. lost (*B4* v. lempereur et t. son ost) qui *A6* iuives et les firent bien l. et il t. en la cite bien lxxxii.m. et vij.c. avec ceulx qui estoyent mort bien lxxi milles et q. il les heurant bien estaichier adont firent ouvrir les p. de iherusalem et adont vaspasien et t. lors qui 934 *A1* et furent par n.s. *A8* t. dont par n. furent trouves lxx. *A11* t. lesquelz estoient environ lxx. *A9* en t. en tout par n. le compte fait s. 934-935 *A3* s. seize m. et q. 935 *A1, A11, A12* il fist ouvrir les 935-936 *A2, A3, A7* p. de la cite adonc le. *A11* p. de iherusalem tantost apres que les portes furent ouvertes vaspasien et tout son hoste qui *A8* l. vaspasien et 935-937 *A13* p. adoncques vaspasien ensamble sa baronnie e.

l'empereur et tout ceulx qui gardoient les portes et les murs de la cité afin que nul juifs ne s'en fuïst s'en entrerent dens la cité et s'en alerent tout droit au temple Salamon. Et la il rendirent graces a Jhesu Crist de ce qu'i[l] leur avoit donné victore. Et s'i sojournerent et se tindrent liement. Et la pouvoit venir toute maniere de gens excepté juifs. Et sy leur pourtoient asés vivres de toutes pars.

[61] Et quant l'empereur vist qu'il detenoit prins tant de juifs, il dist a ses gens: "Seigneurs, puisque Jhesu Crist nous a fet tant de grace qu'il nous a

936 *A10* t. ses gens qui *A12* e. vaspasien et tout loust et les sommiers et les charios et toute maniere de gens qui se g. environ les m. *A2, A7, A8, A9, A10, A1* g. les (*A1* g. par dehors) les *A12* cite de iherusalem a. 936-937 *A6, B, B1, B3, B4, B5* g. que *A11* g. environ les m. que nul ne *B2* g. en tous les m. que 937 *A1* ne issist hors e. *A10* sen peust fouyr e. dedans et *A12* sen peust ystre sen vont entrer tous en la *B* sen peust saillir e. *B1* sen saillissent entrent d. *B2* sen peust issir e. en la *B3, B4* sen fuissent (*B4* f. vindrent et) e. *A2* sen peust yssir sen a. *A6, B, B1, B2, B3, B4, B5* c. de iherusalem et 937-938 *A11* sen peust yssir de la c.e. dedans la c. et quant ilz virent quil eurent la victoire sur les iuifs si sen a. tous au *A12* a. tous au *A13* a. a t. *B, B1, B2, B3, B4, B5, A6* a. devant (*B3* a. tous d.) le (*A6* a. dedens le) t. 938 *A11* s. rendre g. a nostre seigneur i. *B7* s. aussi ses gens et la *A12* la lempereur et chascun r.g. a dieu i. *A6, B, B1, B2, B3, B4, B5* a dieu (*B5* a nostre seigneur) qui *A8* a dieu de *A13* c. qui 938-939 *A11* de la v. quil avoient obtenue sur les faulx iuifs s. dedans la cite par certains iours a grant ioie et la 938-942 *B7* a dieu de la v. quil leur a.d.q. 939 *A10* v. et se t. 939-940 *A12* d. si bonne v. et la ilz firent grant feste et se t. et la venoyent t. *B2* v. sur leurs ennemis et sur la cite et la ilz s. moult longnuement et leans p. entrer t. *B5* d. tant de vertu de avoir la v. sur les ennemys de ihesu crist qui a tort et sans cause le mirent a mort et sur toute la cite de iherusalem et la s. et furent a leur aise et se repaisserent et prindrent recreation t.g. fors que les i. *B3* v. contre leur ennemis et sur la citey et la s. et fuierent ioieusement et illec p. estre t.g. fors i. *A9* t. par aucun espace de temps l. et ioyeusement et en icelle cite de iherusalem p. aler et v. *A3* l. en tant que t.m. et g. y p.v.e. 939-942 *A6* v. contre leurs ennemis et la se s. et furant alegrement et la donnerent a mangier a t.g. feur que es i. et il firent v. moult de viandes q. *B4* v. contre leurs ennemys et sur la cite et la s. certains temps et furent allegrement et firent venir en la cite pour leurs v. moult de viandes et q. *B* v. contre leurs annemis et sur la cite et la s. et furent alegrement et la p.v.t. fors i. et y firent venir moult viandes q. *B1* v. contre leurs ennemys et sur la cite et la s. et venir moult de viandes q. 939-943 *A13* a. baillie celle belle v. contre leurs ennemis et illec se reposirent et y p. aler t.g. seurement e.i. et tellement que de t.p. ilz venoient vivre a foisons adoncques dist le. a son consel p. que dieu n. 940-941 *A11* i. car il avoient a. *A12* et ilz avoient a.v. car ilz leurs venoient de *B2* et firent venir v. *A2* pour.v. 940-942 *A10* i. lors p. ou maniere de t.v. et *B3, B5* et y fierent venir moult de (*B5* et f.m. grant quantite de) viandez q. 941 *A9* v. et autres choses necessaires de 941-942 *A1* p. a grand foison et 942 *A9* quil tenoit et d. *A10* quil avoit p. *A11* quil tenoit t. *B1* que t. les i. furent p. il *B7* quil y avoit t. de i. prisonniers il *A6* d.t. *B, B2, B3, B5* d.t. de i.p. il *B4* d. tous le i. et iuyres p. il *A10* ses barons s. 942-943 *A12* e. vasparien v. que ses gens d.t. de i.p. et lies il leurs d.s. *A6* il prit dix s. barons p. *B, B1, B2, B3, B4, B5* d.s. barons p. 943 *A8* n. envoye t. 943-944 *B7* que dieu n. a d. *B, B1, B3, B4, B5, A6* que dieu n. a d. tant de (*A6* a t.d. de) v. (*B1* d.v. *B5* t. de g. et de v.) ie *A13* gr. ie que

donné victoire contre nos enemis, je veul venger sa mort et sy veuil que tous ces juifs se vendent. Et sy veuil que come il achapterent Jhesu Crist trente deniers, que hom donne trente juifs pour ung denier." Et lors il fist crier que tout home qui vouroit achapter juifs, qu'il venissent a ceulx qu'il avoit ordené pour les vendre, quar hom en averoit trente pour ung denier. Et estoient trente et cinc pour les vendres. Et pour ce qu'il les vendoient, il

944 *B2* v. ie *A11* v. sur les faulx iuifs ie veul encores mieulx venger *A10* et que 944-946 *A12* et aussy luy ay ie promis et v. 944-947 *B, B1, B3, B5, A6* ven. la m. ihesu (*B5* m. de nostre seigneur i.) crist et v. vendre t. ces i. que tenons prins (*B1* que avons p.) et en donner (*B5* en veulx d.) autant pour un d. come a. dieu de (*B1* a.i.c. de *B5* a. le saint prophete de) d. ce est assavoir que ie en vueil donner xxx pour (*B5* xxx iuifs p.) un denier et f. (*B5* d. come ilz acheterent le saint prophete de deniers puis f. *A6* de d. et f.) c. que toute personne qui 944-952 *B4* ven. la m. du saint prophete ihesu crist et v. vendre t. ces i. et iuyres que nous tenons prins et en donneray autant pour ung d. comme a. dieu de d. cest assavoir que ien vueil donner trente pour ung denier et establist lempereur trente chevaliers a en estre marchanz et leur ordonna lempereur que c. personne qui en vouldroit avoir quilz en eussent trente pour ung denier pour en faire a sa voulente et ainsi fut cryer de par lempereur q. 945 *A1* i. soient vendus et *A11* veuil vendre t. les i. que nous tenons en noz mains et v. que nous en devons aultant pour ung denier c. *A12* veuil que nous tenons prys ainssy c. *B2* veuil vendre t. les i. que nous tenons prins et ainsi c. *A12* il vendirent i. 945-946 *A9* veuil que ces *A11* a. dieu de d. cestassavoir t.d.l. 945-952 *B7* veuil vendre t. ces i. que avons prisonniers et en voeult autant donner pour ung d. que dieu fust vendu de d. cestassavoir xxx pour ung deniers et ordonnast xxx chevaliers p. repcevoir des deniers des iuif q. 945-957 *A13* i. que noz tennons prins soient vendut t.p. ung d. ainsin comme ilz a.i.c.t.d. et furent o. xx chevaliers pour vendre lesdiz iuifs a prins que dessus ung chevaliers f. de sa l. par le ventre dung i. de ceulx quilz avoit achetez et en retirant la l. ung 946 *A12* de. ie veil do. *B2* de. vueil ie donner t.i. *A9* do. a ung chascun qui en vouldra achater t.i. 947 *A11, A12* c. par tout que (*A12* t. loust et la out estoyent longiez les gens darmes que) qui *A6, B, B1, B5* v. (*B5* v. avoir) v. *A9* ve. par devers c. 947-948 *B3* v.v. avant et c. qui estoit commiez p. les v. par lempereur a lez vandrez et il leur en donnoit t. *A8* quil en seroyt donner et bailler t. *B, B1, B2, B5, A6* ceulx qui estoit commis par lempereur a (*B2* c. de par luy a) les v. et (*B1* c. de les v. par le. et) leur en donroient t. 948 *A9* o. et commis p. *A11* v. et quil en 948-949 *A1* v. et lempereur donna a ceulx trente cinq chascun une daree et *A7* v. et p. *A12* quar il vouloit que lon en donnast t.d. et lors lempereur ordonna xxv chevaliers de ses gens qui les vendissent et pour ce 948-950 *A9* v. et p. ce a ceulx mesmes qui les v. pour leur peines et travail il en *A8* d. par xxv personnes quil avoyt ad ce connus pour lez bailler et a c. dieulx xxv p. la paine quilz auroyent a lez distribuer en avoyt d. une 949 *A1* c. personnes p. *A3* e. xv ordonnez p. *A10* e. vint six p. le les *A2* et p. les v.e. xxv et pour ce *A10* v. et a ceulx qui 949-950 *A3* v. et p. leur paine de les vendre il en *A1* v. et eubrent e. 949-952 *A11* et ordonna xxv chevaliers p. a qui en vouldroit pour en fere a sa voulente et q. *B, B1, B2, B3, B5, A6* et establi xxx chevaliers (*B2* e. xxv c.) a en (*B1, B3* c. pour en *B5, A6* c. pour) estre merchans et que a c. personne qui (*B2* e. xxv c. pour les vendre et les en fit m. et leur commanda quilz) en vouldroit que en (*B3* v. avoir en) d. xxx pour un denier a faire (*B3, B5* d. pour en f.) a (*B1* v. avoir a *A6* qui en avoit en fit a) sa voulente (*B2* d.) q.

en donne a chascun une danree. Et sy leur donna l'eliction de panre de ceulx qui plus leur plaisoit.

[62] Et quant le cri fust fait, ung chevaliers vint a l'empereur et lui dist: "Sire, j'en voeil une danree." Et lors l'empereur lui en fit baillier trente. Et quant le chevaliers eüt ses trente juifs et il eüt paié son denier, il tenoit sa lance en sa main et vint davant les juifs qu'il avoit achaptés. Et si en frapa ung parmi le corps de la lance tant qu'elle passa tout oultre. Et le juifs [52r] cheü mort a terre. Et au tirer de la lance, il yssi de la place du juifs / un ray d'or et d'argent. Et lors le chevaliers se merveilla moult. Et puis il prist

950 *A10* en demoura a *A2* p. pour eux de *A7* donna cong den p. 950-951 *A9* p. et choysyr de c. qui mieulx ilz aymeroient et qui 950-952 *A12* d. cestassavoir xxx iuifs tieulx comme ilz voulsirent eslire et incontinent que le *A8* donna congie de p. pour eulx desquieulx quilz vouldroyent et q. 951-952 *A1* qui mieulx amoient et que plus leur p. et en povoient faire tout ce quil leur plairoit a leur voulente ou de les faire morir a grand detresse ou de eulx faire vivre q. *A9* plus a leur gre et voulente et q. *A7* quilz vouldroyent et q. *A12* fait v. ung c. devant le. 952 *A11* v. tantost a 952-953 *A1* ch. dist a le.s. *B1* e. ie *B7* luy en demandast pour ung denier et 953 *A3, A8, A11, B, B1, B2, B5* v. avoir une *B3* d. de sez iuifz et tantost le. *B4* e. et ses commis luy *A2* f. donner t. *A7, A8* t. pour ung denier et *B1, B5* t. iuifs et 953-954 *A12* b. et q. *B* f. donner xxx iuifs q. *A11* t. iuifs q. *A1* t. iuifs il en paia son 953-955 *B3, B4, A6* luy en f. donner (*A6* luy d.) xxx iuifs pour (*B4* i. que iuyres p.) ung d. et q. il eut son d.p. de cez xxx iuifz il (*B4* d. et il eust p. le d. il *A6* i.q. le ch. eut xxx pour ung d. il) print son espee en *B7* t. et il luy baillast ung d. et les fist mener a son hostel par ses serviteurs et puis print son espee et si 953-956 *B2* f. donner t. iuifz pour ung d. adonc icelluy chevallier en mena les iuifz quil avoit achete en son hostel et en ferit ung dune espee parmy le ventre t. 954 *B* eut xxx *A8* t. et *A8* d. il print sa 954-955 *B5* eut p. ung d. et il e.t.i. il print son espee en *B, B1* il print son espee en 954-956 *A11* d. il les envoia en son hostel puis tira son espee et en ferit ung 955-956 *A1, A8* si en fery ung *A6, B, B1, B3, B4, B5* a. et les mena en son hostel et f. le (*B1, B4, B5* et ferit le) premier par le ventre de son espee (*B1, B5* v.) tant 956 *A1* c.t. *A8* c.t. que la lance p. *B7* p. le ventre tant 956-957 *A11* le ventre et persa t.o. et tantost tomba m. *A12* passa la lance o. le corps et incontinent il c.m. et le chevalier tira sa l. et quant il eust tiree de la playe vait yssir ung 956-958 *B2* et quant le i. tomba m. a t. il trait son espee du ventre du i. et ne saillit point de sang mais en y. semblance dor *B4, B, B1, B3, B5, B7, A6* i. tunba a te. (*B* tu.te.) tout (*B1* i. cheut tout *A6* tu. tout) m. et le chevalier tira son espee dehors et (*B3* c. trait son e. et) nen y. point (*A6* nen saillit p.) de sang mais y. samblance (*B5* de sa m. sailly en lieu de sang s. *A6* m. sailloit s.) dor (*B7* tu. par te.to.m. et du coup ne sailli oncques gouttez de sang m. loir) et (*B* s.) da. 957 *A1* au retraire de *A7* t. et de la playe y. ung *A9* t. quil fist de *A2, A3* p. un 957-958 *A11* t. et le chevallier tira son espee dehors et nen y. point de sang mais en y. semblance choses dor *A11* y. une piece dor 958 *B7* a. quil avoient mengez l. *B5* a. dont le *A11* a. dont le c. fut moult esbahy lors pr. *A9* me. fort et *A8* me. fort sy pr. *A12* me. fort que ce vouloit dire et pr. *B2* c. en eut m. grant m. si pr. 958-959 *A13* or bien resplendissant sailly du ventre dudit iuifz le c. dist a ung *B, B1, B3, B4, B5, A6* c. fut moult esbahy et deslia le i. (*B1* le second i.) que (*B5* et le second i.d. quil *A6* le second qui) devoit tuer segont et (*B1, B5, A6* t. et *B4* t. apres luy et) le tira a part et luy 958-960 *B7* c. fut moult esbahi et luy et ses gens et lui voiant ce va demander a ung aultre iuif que signifioit ce et l.

un autre juifs et lui dist: "Je veuil que tu me dies si tu ses que c'est a dire pour quoy cest juifs giete sanc a guise d'or et d'argent." Et lors le juifs lui dist: "Sire, se vous me vou[lé]s aseürer de mort, je vous diray sans faulte que c'est a dire." Et lors le chevaliers l'aseüra et le juifs lui conta coment Pilate leur avoit fet manger or et argent, pieres precieuses et tout le tresor, afin que l'empereur ne ses gens ne le trouvassent et qu'il n'en fussent

959 *A1* a. chevalier et *A11* i. qui devoit tirer et le tira a part et puis luy *A12* i. quil tenoit et luy *B2* a. chevallier i. quil vouloyt apres tuer et le mist a part et luy *A2, A7* i. ie *A1* v. scavoir et que 959-960 *A13* i.p.q. ilz sailloit du corps dudit iuifz en samblance dor et le *A6* dies que veult d. cecy de c.i. *B3* dies que veust ce d. et que signiffie cecy que est de c.i. *A11* ses p. *B* dies que veult d. cecy qui est sailli de c.i. qui gi. *B1* dies que vieult d. cecy que est yssu de c.i. que g. semblance dor *B2* dies que veult ce d. de c.i. qui ne ge. du corps que chose en semblance dor *B4* dies cecy quil est de c.i. qui giete s. em samblance dor *B5* d. verite que est ce que ce veult dire cecy qui est c.i. sailly en lieu de s. en semblance dor 960 *A2* a maniere dor *A8* s. si plain dor *A6, A11, A12* s. en samblance dor *B3* s. en fere blance dor *A11* a. se rien en scez dy le moy sans point le me celler l. 960-961 *B2* a. seigneur d. le i. se *A13* luy respondist s. *B1, B2* i.d. 960-962 *B7* lui respondit ce me v. garder de mort ie vous y connoistray veritez et 961 *A1* me assceurez de *B, B1, B2, B3, B4, B5, A6, A11* v. prendre (*B5* v. pardonner et p.) a mercy que ne meure (*B5* ne me *A6* mercy) ie *A13* de ma vie ie 961-962 *A1, A12* diray que *A2, A3, A7, A9, A10* s. nulle f. et 962 *A8* cest et *A6, B, B1, B2, B3, B4, B5* d. la (*B1* d. toute la) verite et adonc (*B2* v.) le *A11* d. et vous en diray toute verite sans rien celer l. *A1* c. le sauva et *A2* et adonc le *B, B1, B2, B3, B4, B5, A6, A10* a. de mort et (*A6* d. morir et *B2* m. adonc) le *B7* c. lui accorda sa demande et *A12* conta et dist tout par ordre c. 962-963 *A13* d. et le c. respondit ien suis comptent p. dist le i. noz fist m. *A11* a. quil ne mourroit point et adoncque le i. luy dist sir le provost p. nous a. *B7* i. va dire seigneurs debves savoir que quant p. vit que navions plus que m. il nous fist mouldre en pouldre tout loir *A10* conta toute la verite et lui dist seigneurs p. vous a. *B, B1, B2, B3, B4, B5, A6* conta tout (*A6* c. adonc t.) le (*B4* le fait et le) voir et (*B1, B2, B5* t. la verite et *A6* le fait et) luy dist seigneur p. (*B4* s. il est verite que p.) nous (*B5* p. nostre gouverneur n.) a. 963 *A6, B, B1, B2, B3, B4, B5* or et a. et (*B2* or et) va celles et pi. *A12* m. leur tresor dor *A11* ar. les vaisselles et les pi.pr. que estoient en la cite sans rien y demourer et tous les tr. 963-964 *A1, A10, A12, A13* pr.a. *B4, B5* tr. questoient en la cite de iherusalem (*B5* tr. de la c.) a. 963-965 *B7* pr. de la cite et de ce nous fist menger et en 964 *A6* e. et tous ces *B* e. et toute sa g. nen f. plus r. du tresor et 964-965 *A10, A11, A6* g. nen f. plus r. *B4* et quil ne f. plus r. du tresor questoit en la cite et le nous fit moldre en mortieres du cuyvre et *B1, B2, B3* g. ne f. plus r. du tresor et o. (*B2* o. que n. *B3* et ainsi) en a. *B5* g. ne f. pas r. du tresor de la cite ainsi nous a. *A2* f. robes et 964-966 *A13* g. ne t. riens en ceste cite et en a. grans temps v. car

961 Correction based on all MSS except *A1*.

riches et ossy affin qu'il en puissent vivre, car nous en avons vesqu vint et ung jour car nous n'avions autre chouse que manger." Et tantost cela fust ceü par les gens de l'empereur. Et incontinent chascun en veut achaster. Et l'empereur en fist delivrer a chescun une danree. Et quant Jacob et

965 *A9* que entre eulx iuifz en *A7* en pensent v. *A6, B, B4* o. en *A12* vivre grant temps car *A1* n. navions riens que mengier se mangasmes le tresor et en v. lespace de vint 965-966 *A2* vesqu. xxvij i. *B, B1, B2, B4, B5, B7, A6* vivre longtemps (*B5* v. ung grant temps) sans (*B7* v. xxi.i.s.) mengier (*B2* l. car n.na.) autre *A9* vesqu. dist le iuifz lespace de xxj.i. sans a.c.m. 965-967 *A10* o. en avoir v. ung longtemps sans menger au.c. et pour ce il ny a aucune chose dedans nos corps sinon les tresors de la cite et quant le chevallier oyt ces parolles il ot grant merveilles et appella deux de ses escuiers et leur dist ie veulx que les autres qui sont demourez vous les fasiez trestous mourir et la teste coupper et incontinent fut fait et puis fist fendre la pance et fist tirer le tresor qui estoit dedans et les corps fist gecter dedans les rues apres les *A11* o.a.v. grant piece sans m.a.c. quant le chevalier ouyt ces parolles il fut moult esmerveille si appella deux de ses escuiers et leur dist que les xxviii qui estoient demourez de la denree eussent les testes tranchees et tantost fut fait si les fist fendre par le ventre et traire les tresors qui estoient dedans leur corps et tantost ce fut fait et sceu par plusieurs des g. *B3* vivre loingtz temps il ny ait aultres choses en ventre sinon lez tresors quant le chevaliers oyt cez nouvellez il eult moult grant merveillez et appellait deux de cez escuiers et leur dist que lez .xxviij. iuifs estoient demorez de la danree de laquelle en avoit ung tuey et lautre assure de mort que tous lez aultres eussent la teste coppee et tantost fut fait et puis lez fit fandrez par le vantre et traire le tresor qui estoit dedans et lez corps fit gettez par lez chairrieres et tantost fut fait et lez

966 *A1* i. car il estoit moulu au mortier t. 966-967 *B, B1, B2, B4, B5, A6* c. et pour ce il na. autre chose ou (*B1* et na. cestuy iuif ou) ventre (*B2* c. que m. et nous na. rien a. dedans le v.) ce (*B4* c. ce *B5* v. des iuifz ce) non le tresor quant (*B2* non or et argent q.) le chevalier oyt ces paroles il (*B5* ces nouvelles il) ot moult grandes merveilles et appella deux de ses escuiers et leur dist que les xxviij (*B2* ch. ouyt que ces xx et viij) iuifz qui (*B1* xxviij que *B4* i. que iuyres quilz) estoient demourez de la denree de laquelle avoit un tue et lautre asseure (*B2* ung mis a mort et ung au. quil avoit as.) de mort et que (*B1* denree que) touz les autres eussent la teste couppee et (*A6* t. tranchie et) tantost fut (*B4* t. ainsi fut) fait et puis les fist faire fendre (*B1, B2, B4, A6* fist fe.) par le ventre et traire le (*B2* et en tira le) tresor qui estoit dedans et (*A6* d. leurs ventres et) les corps fist gecter par les carrieres et tantost fut fait et les (*B1* c. dont les *B4* et puis les *B5* couppee et t. fut f. puis les *B2* g. et apres fut t. sceu par les) g. 966-968 *B7* c. et pour ce navons aultre chosez que lor et largent et le pieres precieusez quant le chevalier eust ouy ces parollez il commandast que les vingt et viij qui estoient demoures eussent les testes tranchees et puis apres les ventres fenduz pour prendre le tressoirs quil avoient menges et ainsi fust faict quant les seigneurs de la court sceurent quil avoient mengez les tressoirs de la citez chascun dictz quil en volloist q. 966-971 *A13* et quant c.f. sen ilz furent plus hatiz de mettre a mort les iuifz que par avant iacob et iaffet d. a le.s. 967 *A12* par toutes les *A1, A12, A11* et lors (*A12, A11* et) ch. *A3* et pour ce i. *A12* v. avoir et a. 967-968 *B2* e. en vouldroient c. sa d. et le. *A10* e. en voullurent avoir c. pour ung denier lors le. en f. bailler a c. pour ung denier q. *B, B1, B3, B4, B5, A6* e. en vouloient avoit (*B1* v. tous a.) c. une (*B3, A6* a. une *B4* v. aussi c.a. une *B5* v.c.) denree et le. en f. donner a chascun a faire (*B1, B5* de. pour f. *B4* c. une denrie pour en f.) leur (*B3* d. a f. a c. a l.) voulente (*B5* v. come il avoit ordonne) q.

968 *A12* le. commanda que lon en delivrasse a *B2* f. baillier a *A11* a qui en vouloit trente pour ung denier et q. 968-969 *A12, B1* q. iaffet et iacob vi. *B2* de. pour en fayre sa voulente q. iassel et iacob vi.

Jafet [virent] que tuit les juifs se vendoient et que ceulx qui les achetoient les ossisoient pour le tresor qu'il avoient mengé, il s'en vindrent a l'empereur et lui distrent: "Sire, entre ses juifs en doit avoir auscun qui estoient bien ami de Dieu. Car il y doit estre Joseph d'Arimatie qui descendi le cors de Jhesu Crist de la crois et le mist en son sepulcre avec Nycodemus. Et sy y doit estre une dame qui fu royne d'Alfrique et une sienne fille et une dame qui estoit sa compaigne a la royne et ung filz que celle compaigne avoit, lesquels creoient fort en Jhesu Crist. Si vous prions,

969 *B4* iassel du tassel v. que les 969-970 *A12* ve. es chevaliers et que lon les o. tous par *A11* ve. a grant nombre il sen *A2, A8, A9* a. les tuoyent (*A9* t. et mettoient a mort) p. *A1* qui vendirent a 969-971 *B, B1, B2, B3, B4, B5, A6, A10* ve. aux chevaliers et quilz les (*B5* que les chevaliers les) tuoient pour le (*A6* les tenoyent p. avoir le *A10* les faissoient mourir p. avoir le) tresor que ilz a.m. ilz d. a le. (*B4* il sen v. devers le. et lui d.) s. 969-973 *B7* vi. que lon tuoist ainsi les iuif pour avoir loir et largent quil a.m.d. a le.s. debves savoir que en ceste gent d.a. parfaict amy du prophete lequel le d. de la 970-971 *A12* m. ilz d. a le.s. 971 *A3* d.e. *A13* e. les aultres i. 971-972 *A8* a. qui *A13* a. des gens qui *B1* a. ung nostre i.da. qui *A10* a. ung saint prophette qui a nom i. *A12* a. ung et au. qui e. ami de ihesu crist cestassavoir ung bon chevalier entre les autres qui sappelle i. 972 *A6, B, B3, B4* a. amis (*B3* au boin a.) du saint prophete car *A2* e. bons ami de ihesu crist quar *B2, B5* a. amy du saint prophete qui a i ouy (*B5* p. car) i. *A3, A11* de ihesu crist et si (*A11* et espaulement) y *A7, A8, A9* de ihesu crist car *A2, A7, A9* e. avec eulx i. 972-973 *A13* de ihesu crist car i.da. il d.e. quil le d. de la *B1* du saint prophete car il le d. de la *B5* da. y doit estre qui 973 *A11, A12* d.i. *A6, A8, A10* qui le d. (*A10* qui d.) de *B4, B5, B3, B* le saint prophete (*B* s.) de 973-974 *B, B1, B3, B4, B5, A6* et luy achapta son suayre et puis le m. en son monument que avoit pour (*B3* a. fait fere p. *B4, B5* a. fait p.) luy et n. (*B4* et doit estre n.) a. (*B1* n. estoit a.) luy et *A10* cr. lequel luy acheta son suaire et puis le m. en son monument quil avoit fait faire pour luy et puis n. estoit avecques luy et aussy *A11, B2* s. et estoit n. a (*B2* et n.e.a.) luy et *A12* s. et n.a. luy et 973-977 *A13* et le ensevelit en son monument ensamble de n. et aussi une r. et sa c. quil moult en luy c.s. 973-978 *B7* et luy acheta son suaire et puis le m. en son monument neuf quil avoit fait faire pour luy et parellement doicbt e. une femme laquelle fust femme du roy da. lequel morust au temps que ihesu cript fust mis en la croix et une s. compagne l. adouroient le saint prophete p. vous avoir merci deulx car o. ne f.c. 974 *A8* n. qui aussy y est et *A9* a. layde de n. *B4* d. avoir une r. *A2* do.da. qui *A6, B, B1, B3* une r. *A10, A11, B2* e. la r. 974-976 *A12* d. avoir une d.r.da. qui c. moult f. *A6, B, B1, B2, B3, B4, B5* r.da. et sa f. (*B2* et sa c. et sa f.) l. 975 *A11* f. et une bonne d. nonmee clerice qui *A3* c. et *A8* c. avec ung 975-976 *A10* f.l. *A1* r. et une sien f. de la c.l. *A7* ung f.l. 976 *A9* co.l. *A11* co. avec ung sien f.l. *A7, A9* cre. moult f. *A11* cre. fermement en *B, B1, B2, B3, B4, B5* cre. ou (*B2* c. bien ou) saint prophete et (*B2* p.i.c. et pour ce *B4* p.i.c. et *B5* c. et avoient parfaicte foy au s.p.) se 976-977 *A12* v. supplions s. 976-978 *A6, A10* cre. au saint prophete et si v. plaist que avez m. (*A10* p.v. arez m.) deux q.o. ne f.c.

969 Addition from all MSS except *A13*.

974 *Nycodemus* For the role of Nicodemus in the biblical narratives and in the *Gospel of Nicodemus*, see my edition (pp. 18-20).

976 *lesquels* [ *lequel* Correction from all MSS except *A12, A13*.

Sire, qu'il vous plaise de les penre a mercy quar sachiez qu'il ne furent onques consens de la mort de Jhesu Crist."

[63] Lors l'empereur leur dist: "Regardés si vous les trouverés. Et si les trouvés, faites les venir devant moy." Lors Jafet et Jacob regarderent par tout la hou estoient les juifs, et si ne trouverent que Joseph d'Arimatie. Et puis il s'en alerent a la meson de la royne car il avoient eü souvent liens
[52v] leur consolacion avec / elles. Et la trouverent morte et sa compaigne ossy. Et lors il s'en retournerent a l'empereur avec Joseph d'Arimatie. Et

977 *A2, A3, A7, A9* p. quil *A8* s. sire quil *A11, A12* quar il *A13* les avoir a m. car il 977-978 *B, B1, B2, B3, B4, B5* p. que aiez m. (*B5* p. avoir pitie et m.) de eulx car o. ne f.c. 978 *A11* m. du saint prophete i. 978-979 *A2* f. de la m. de i.c.o.c. mais en f. dolens et corrouciez l. *B, B1, B2, B3, B4, A6* m. du saint prophete adonc (*B3* p. et sil vous plaist que aiez mercy deulx a.) le. (*B4* p.i. lors le.) d. a iassel et (*B4* i. du tassel et) a iacob voyes (*B3* le. eust mercy deulx et d. a iacob et a ioseph v.) se (*B2* iacob faictes que *B4* iacob alez veoir se *A6* d. a iacob et iassel se) v. *B5* de sa m. adoncques le.d. a iassel et a iacob alez veoir se v. les pourrez trouver et *A1* cr. ains leur desplaisoit moult l. 978-985 *B7* m. du saint prophete adoncq le. commandast quil fuste cherchez et puis allerent tout drois hurter a la porte de la royne et entrerent dedens mais tout trouvirte mors en apres allerent parmi la citez tant quil trouverte i. et lors enmenerent ioseph a lempereur le.

979 *A7* l.d.le.d. *A10* e.d. a iacob r. *A11* d. allez regarder par tout se *A12* r. et faictes regarder si 979-980 *A1, A8, A12, B2* et les f.v. *A10* les pourrez trouver et les amenez adonc iafet *A11* t. aucunement car pour lamour de vous et de ihesu crist en qui ilz croient il nauront ia nul mal et l. iacob et iaffet allerent par *A6, B, B1, B4, B5* t. et si les amenez d. 979-981 *B3* t. et si lez trouverez et si lez mamenez d. moy adont iacob et ioseph r.t. lez i. qui e. prins et ne lez virent point fors io. 979-985 *A13* t. si les f.d. moy v. ilz ne t. en vie mais que i. car la roynnez sa c. furent m. de faim le.d. a iosepht se 980 *A6* moy adonc iacob et iassel les r. *A8, A12* moy sy ne tarderent point (*A12* moy et incontinent) iaffet *A7* l. iacob et iaffet r. *A9* r. et adviserent par *A12* iacob vont sercher et regarder par 980-981 *A2* iacob partent on e. les i.r. et ne *B, B1, B2, B4, A10* r.t. les i. qui e. prins et ne les virent point fors (*B2* et ny t. se non *B5* t. et ne v.po. ceulx quilz queroient f. *A10* pr. et par t. et tr.) io. *B5* iacob y alerent et r.t. et ne virent point ceulx quilz queroient fors que 981 *A6* t. ceulx qui e. pris et *A11* t. entre les *A11* et tant sercherent quilz t. le sainct homme io. *A12* t. et ne vont trouver io. *A6* tr. point fors que 981-982 *A8* tr. entre lez iuifs et ne peurent trouver fors que i. et lors sen *A6* da. si a. a lostel de 982 *A2* p. ilz ne trouverent que ioseph darimathie et p. il *A2, A10, B, B1, B2, B3, B4, B5* a lostel de *A9* p. apres il 982-983 *A6, B, B1, B2, B3, B4, B5* car s. ilz a. eu (*B1,B4* eu leur *B3* s. y aloient en) c. *A9* r. daufrique car il a. autrefoiz et s. eu c. *A10* r. dauffrique car s. alloit avec e. et y allerent tous trois et *A11* r. dauffrique et de sa compaigne ou s.a. prins c. *A1* av.s. leur c. eu a. *A2* eu layens s.c. *A3* s.c.a. *A8* av.l.s. eue leur *A12* av.s. pris avec e. leur c. et la 983 *A11* et quant il y furent il la *A6, B, B1, B3, B5* m. de fain et *A8* m. elle et 983-984 *B2* m. adonc sen *A10* com. de fain et *A11* o. dont ilz furent moult doulans puis sen *B1* o. sa compaigne dont sen 984 *A6* r. devant le. *A12* e. et luy menerent i. 984-985 *A10* e. et luy menerent i.da. quant le. le vit il luy d. *A6, A11, B, B1, B2, B3, B4, B5* a.i. et (*B2* a. iassel et *B3, B4* i.da. et) quant le. le vit il (*B2* vit ioseph il *A11* q. vaspasien vit ioseph il) ly d. (*B1* il d. a ioseph) ce *A12* a. et quant le. le vist il luy vait demander se

l'empereur leur demanda ce c'estoit celui qui descendi le corps de Jhesu Crist de la crois. Et il distrent que ouÿl. Et lors l'empereur le prist a mercy comme il avoit fet Jafet et Jacob.

[64] Et quant l'empereur vist que les juifs estoient auques mors et vendus, il demanda a ceulx qui les avoient vendus combien de danrees il y avoit encore. Et il distrent qu'il en y avoit encoure bien sis denrees. Et lors l'empereur leur dist qu'il n'en vendissent plus car il retenoit ses sis

985 *A12* des.i. 985-986 *A13* qui avoit i. descendut de la *A6, B2, A10* le saint prophete de la *B, B1, B3, B4, B5* co. du saint prophete de la *B7* des.i.c. de la *A11* des. de la croix le c. de i.c. et il respondit que 986 *A12* il luy sire oy *B, B1, B2, B3, B4* crois et iosef dist (*B2* c. quant il fut mort et il d. *B3* i. luy respondit) que *A6* crois et ioseph respondit a le. que oyr adonc le *B7* il luy respondictz que ouy adoncq le. *A8* ouyl sy le p.le. a 986-987 *A11* m. avec iaffet *B, B1, B2, B4* m. pour lamour de iasel 986-988 *A12* p. tantost a m. et *B7* m. avecques les aultres et puis apres q. 986-989 *A10* crois et iozef lui respondit ouy sire et le. le print et d. pour co. *B5* crois et ioseph luy dist que ouy et pour amour de ce et de iacob et de iassel ie te prenderay a m. dist le. a ioseph aprez toutes cez choses le. demanda aux chevaliers quantes da. *B2* oy et adont le. demandait aux chevaliers quantes da. *A6* m. pour lamour de iacob et de iassel adonc le.d. es chevaliers quantes da. 986-991 *A13* crois dist iosepht oy lors fut pris iosepht a mercy et fut retenu du consel de lempereur aux chevaliers quil avoient charge de vendre les iuifz co. ilz en a. plus a vendre lesquelx responderent que bealcopt et l. ilz leur 987 *A9* fet lesdiz iaffet 987-988 *A3, A7, A8* fet iacob et iacob puis q. *A1* fit ioseph et *B2* iacob q. 987-989 *B, B1, B4* iacob apres le. demanda (*B4* i. vaspasien le. lors d.) aux chevaliers quantes (*B1* a. ce d.le. aux c. combien de *B4* c. qui estoient per luy commis q.) da. 988 *A2, A9, B2* que tous les *A3* e. pris ou mors 988-989 *A11* et puis parla aulx chevaliers qui avoient la commission de vendre les iuifs et leur d. quantes da. *B2, B7, A12* e. (*B7* e. tous *A12* e. quasi tous) v. 989 *A8* a.v. quantes da. *A12* d. les chevaliers qui les vendoient quantes da. *B2* d. aux chevaliers quantes da. 989-990 *A9* d.co. de d. il en y a. encores et *B7* d. aulx chevalier qui les vendoient et leurs demandast co. il y en a.e. de d. et respondirent quil *A1* co. il y a. de remanant et *B1* da. de iuifz i a.e. a vendre et 990 *A11* e. si luy respondirent quil *A6, A10, B, B2, B3, B5* a.e. de iuifz a (*B2* e. a) vendre et il respondirent (*A10* a. de i. et les merchants r.) que (*B* v.d. que *B3, B5* ilz luy dirent que) tout estoit vendus fors que (*A10* v. sinon pour *B2* quilz e.b.t.v. excepte *B5* v. excepte) vj *A8* d. six *B1, B4* d. que tous estoient venduz for six 990-991 *B1* da. adoncques d.le. nen 990-992 *B7* e. pour vi deniers et il leurs dist que p. nen v. et quil voulloist garder la vie d. pour en faire a sa volluntez et plaisir l.f.f. si *B3* da. adont f.f. tant g. mort et occision de i. en iherusalem que 991 *A6, B, B4* e. dit *A10* l. deffendist quilz *A11, B, A6* p. car il vouloit avoir et retenir (*B* v.r. pour soy les *A6* p. qui v.r. pour luy les) six *A9* car il vouloit retenir ces 991-992 *A12* car vouloit garder les vi d. pour en fere sa voulente l. *B2, B4, B5, B1* p. car il (*B1* p. et quil) vouloyt retenir celles (*B4, B1* r. pour luy ses) six d. pour luy adonc (*B1* p. faore a sa voullente a. *B5* r. pour soy pour en fai a son plaisir et voulente a.) f.f. tant g. mort de (*B5* g. occision de) i. en (*B4* g. occision de i. et de iuyres en) iherusalem que *A8* car ilz les voulloyt guarder l. *A13* car il les vouloit garder et adoncques fut telles la pestilance que *A1* r. six d. pour lui si g.m. fut f. de 991-993 *A10* car il voulloit retenir pour luy le demourant des iuifs adonc fut la g. mort des i. dedans ih. tant quon

danrees. Lors il fust faites en Jherusalem si grant mortalité de juifs que hom ne pouvoit aler hors que par sur mors tant y en avoit. Et se fust par le conseil que donna Pilate quant leur conseilla qu'il mengassent leur tresor. Car si ne l'eüssent mengé ceulx qui les achaptoient en eüssient prist grant foison a mercy et fucent eschapés, mes pour l'amour du tresor il tuerent bien le nombre de setante et deux mile, trois cens et cinquante pour leur ouster le tresor de dedens le corps.

992 *A3, A7, A9* da. pour luy l. *A2* da. pour luy adont fut *A8* f.f. sy *A12* en la cite de iherusalem *A6, B* f.f. sy g. destruction des (*B* f.f. tant g. mort de) i. en iherusalem que *A7, A9, A11* g. destruction (*A9* g. occision et m. *A11* g. octision) de 993 *A3* a. mais que *A8, A11, A12, A13* a. par la ville fors (*A11* par les rues f. *A12* a. en iherusalem f. *A13* par la cite de iherusalem) que *B7* a. par les ruez pour les m. 993-994 *A6, B, B1, B3, B5* a. par les rues maisques sur (*B, B3* r. fors sur *B1* r. sans marcher sur) le corps des m. mauvais (*B5* r. pour le grant nombre de m. qui y estoient m.) f. le c. qui (*B1* c. quant) m. *A10* a. par les rues de la cite fors que pardessus les corps mauvais fut le c. de menger l. *B2* a. par la cite se non sur les corps m. mauvaiz f. le c. que leur d.p. de manger le t. *B4* a. par les charrieres fors que sur les corps m. malvais f. le c. de celluy qui l. fist mainger les t. *A11* av. et en mourut grant nombre qui a laventure ne fussent pas mors si ne f. le c. de p. qui l. 993-995 B7 av. grande destruction et fust par ce quil avoient menger le t. de la citez car 993-997 *A13* et se ce fuisse este le mauvais c. de p. plusieurs deulx heussent heu mercy car par la convoitise de lor que les iuifz avoient mangiez les gens de lempereur en t.s. 994 *A1* c. de p. car il leur *A8* p. qui l. *A12* p. quil *A11* conseilla menger l. *A7* c. quil entregasterent l. 995-996 *A6* car peu en avoit qui ne morust p. *A11* e. beaucoup p. a *A7* eussient g.f.p. a 995-997 *A10* car on en fist bien mourir quatre vings et deux m. et quatre c. *B* car prou y en eust eu que on eust p. a m. et pour ce que mangerent le t. lon fist mourir lxxxij m. *B3* car assez en y eust eu que on eust p. a m. et pour ce quil il maingeirent le t. on en fit bien morir lxxxij.m. et iiij.c. *B4* car on en fist morir quatre vins deux m. quatre c. *B2* m. plusieurs eussent este p. a m. et pour ce quil avoyent mangie le t. ilz en morurent lxxiiij.m. et iiij.c. *B7* m. aulcun f.e. par merci mais p. la les t. furent tues xl.m. et trois c.p. 995-999 *B1* car molt y en eust eu que on eust p. a m. mes p. ce quilz avoient mange leurs t. nul ne les espargna q. la destruction f.f. des i.le. *B5* car on en fist bien mourir iiij.c.lx.m.iiij.c. et

996 *A1* p. avoir le t. quilz avoient dedans leurs corps il 996-997 *A11* t. qui estoit en leurs e. en mourut bien environ de *A6* t. et en fit morir lxxxij.m.iiij.c. 997 *A9* b. environ le *A12* b. cent quatre m. et sept c.p. *A2* m. quatre c. *A7, A8* lxx.m. 997-998 *A6, B3, B4* p. avoir le *A8* l. personnes p.o. *A9* p.o. *A10* p. les t. qui estoient d. *B* p. avoir le t. quilz avoient d. 997-999 *A1* c. iuifz q. *B2* p. avoir le t.le. 997-1000 *A13* cent adoncques le.f. trayner les mors h. de la cite et sur iceulx mors il f.

998 *A2* t. quilz avoient d. *A9* t. qui estoit d. 998-999 *B7* t. quil avoyent au ventre apres que la m.f. *A7* t. quil avoyent de d. leurs ventres et *A11* c. et q. loctision des *A9* c. adoncques q. *A12* d. le ventre et

995 *mengé* [ *menger* Correction from MSS *A1, A2, A3, A7, A8, A9, A12.*

[65] Et quant la mortalité des juifs fust faite, l'empereur fist apourter les corps hors des murs. Et puis fist abatre toute la muralle de la ville en tant qu'il n'y demourast piere sur autre, ne en toute la ville que tout ne fust abatu excepté le temple Salamon et la tour de Syon qui estoit de David, car Dieu ne le vouloit. Et lors fust acompli se que Dieux dist de sa bouche le jour de pasques fleuries quant il pleura sur la cité. Mes Titus, le filz de l'empereur, paravant que la ville fust abatue, il ala par toutes les mesons et

999 *A2* m. fut *A6, A10, B, B3, B4* la destruction des *A8* loccision des *A9* m. et occision des *B5* la destruction de cez i.f. ainsi fist 999-1000 *A11* le.f.a. 1000 *A6, A10, B, B3, B5* c. entours les murs de la citey et p. apres (*A10* p.) f. *A9* les mors h. des m. de la cite et p. apres f. *A12* c. iusques es m. de la ville et *A2* a. la *A11* de la cite t. *A12* muralle t. 1000-1001 *B1, B2, B4* c. mors entour les murs de la cite et ne (*B2* et p.f.a.t.t. quil ny *B4* et ny) d. *B7* c. iusques au murs de la citez et m. sus eulx en telle maniere quil *A6, A10, B, B5* muralle (*B5* m. tellement) qui *B3, A13* muralle de la cite (*A13* ladicte c.) qui 1000-1002 *A1* v.e. 1001 *A11* sur pierre ne *B1* sur pierre de tous les murs et hostelz de iherusalem que *A11* v. chasteau ne maison ne demoura que ne 1001-1002 *A6, A10, B, B2, B3, B4, B5, B7* sur pierre et fit (*A10* p. apres il f.) abatre t. les hostel de (*A10, B5* les maison de *B2* et t. les maysons de) iherusalem e. (*B7* p. en t. la citez fors) le *A8, A13* v. (*A13* v. aussi) e. 1002 *A1* s. et fist abatre toutes les maisons tellement quil ny demourra pierre sur aultre et avoec le temple s. demoura le tour *B7* syon car 1002-1003 *A6, A7, A1* estoit dedens quar d. ne (*A1* d.) le *A11* syon et ainsi f. 1002-1004 *A13* s. adoncques f.a. ledit de ihesu crist quil avoit dit le i. 1003 *A6, B, B1, B2, B3, B4, B5, A9, A10, A12* ne v. pas quelle fut abatue adonc (*A9* quilz se abatissent et lors *A13* v. point atant) f. *B5* a. la prophecie que dieu avoit de sa *B2* dist le *B1* que nostre seigneur dist *B4* dieu vouloit et quil avoit dist 1003-1004 *B7* d. aussi le promist adoncques f. la parolle de dieu a. quil leurs avoit dist le i. 1004 *B2* q. dieu p. *B7* q. il entra en la c. de iherusalem quant la citez fust ainsi abatue t. *A9* ladicte c. de iherusalem mes *A12* c. de iherusalem t. 1004-1005 *A8* t. son filz a. que on abatist la v. il *A11* c. de iherusalem quon abatist les maisons t. qui avoit este e. nouvel ala

1004-1006 *A13* f. et lors fust visetee toute la cite et prindrent les 1004-1007 *B, B2, B3, B4, B5, A6, A10* c. de iherusalem m. lempereur (*B3* c. mes le. *B5* m.t.e.) nouvel abatit que (*A6* n. devant qui) f. (*A10* i.t.a. que tout f.) a.f. (*B2* c. mes t.e.n. devant que lon a. les ostelz et f. *A6* a. se f.) p. tout (*B2* p. et oster t.) ce que estoit dedans mes (*A10* d. iherusalem m.) il (*B2* d. et) ny t. 1004-1008 *B1* c. de iherusalem le nouvel empereur a. que les choses dessus f.a. il f.p. ce que estoit dedans mes de tresor il ne trouva nyant pour

1005 *A12* la cite f.a. fist aller par t. les estaux et *A11* les bons hostelz et 1005-1008 *B7* e. allast par t. les ostel et f.p. toutez leur armures de quoy ladicte estoit bien garnye et tous lez drap dor et dargent mais aultre chosez riens car les i. de la citez a. tous m. mes f.m.p.e. comme dessus et dictz car

999 *lempereur fist* [ *lempereur lempereur fist*

1002 *excepté le temple de Salamon et la tour de Syon* This is historically inaccurate. Titus did indeed destroy the Temple.

fist penre les armeüres et toute l'ordille paravant qu'i[l] y estoit et pluseur
autres choses que l'empereur y gaigna. Mes il n'y trouva point de tresor
[53r] pour ce que les juifs l'avoient / mengé. Mes se fust mal pour eulx car il en
mourirent tuit excepté les sis danrees que l'empereur avoit retenu et
excepté Joseph d'Arimatie et selui qui dessela les juifs qui avoient mengé
le tresor, car ses deux furent pris a mercy.

[66] Et quant l'empereur et Titus, son filz, eürent cela fait et il se furent bien sejourné et leurs gens ossy, il distrent a Jacob et a Jafet et a Joseph

1006 *A2, A7* p. toutes les *A7* et lartillerie qui *A2, A3* artillerie qui *A1* artilleries quil trouvoit et *A9* o. et utensille qui 1006-1007 *A13* a. et riche draps dor mais 1006-1008 *A11* p. toutes les a. de quoy la ville estoit garnye et aussi print tous les draps et fourreuses dont il y avoit moult grant largesse mes de tresors ne trouva il p. car comme dit est les *A12* p. les harnoys de quoy la ville estoit bien garnie et aussy tous les draps de soye dor et dargent et toutes les choses riches que lempereur il g.m. lautre tresor il ne trouva p. car les *A8* a. ce que bon luy sembla avec laultre despoulle et o.c. car le tresor estoyt m. et se 1007 *A6, B, B3, B4, B5* trouva riens de 1007-1010 *A10* tresor car ilz la.m. dont mal leur en print car tous en m.e. ceulx qui estoient demourez et i. et aussi s. qui revela au chevalier quilz av. 1007-1015 *A13* trouvarent ne or ne argent adoncques iosepht m. lempereur ou lieu ou i.c. fust mors et enseveliz et ou sepulcre et en 1008 *A1, A12* a. tout m. *A11* a. tout m. qui f. grant mal *A8* mal p. les iuifs car 1008-1009 *B, B1, B2, B3, B4, B5, A6* a.m. (*B3, B4* a. tous m.) dont mal leur print (*A6* m. luy p.) car touz en m. (*B1* p. comme dit est dessus *B2* d. ilz l.p.m. comme vous aves ouy car par ceste cause ilz m.t. *B3* t. *B5* p.) e. 1009-1010 *A6, B, B1, B2, B3, B4, B5* d. et i. *A8, B7* em. retint et auxy (*B7* e. remist et) i. 1010 *A11* i. et *A8* qui dist que les i.av. 1010-1011 *A12* s. iuif qui dist pour quoy des i. yssoit sang en semblance dor et dargent car *A11* qui dist au chevalier que tous les t.a. este m. et ces *B2* qui les revella au chevallier quil print a 1010-1013 *B, B1, B4, B5, A6* qui revela au chevalier q. (*B4* c. comment le t.a. est m.q. *B5* qui dist au c. que estoit devenu le t. et q.) cestes choses furent faites et le. et sa gent f.s. ilz *B7* et le iuif qui a dictz veritez q. ses chosez furent faicte le. commanda a ioseph *B3* qui revelait au chevaliers quil avoient maingie leur tresor fuierent tous morts et occist q. cez chosez fuirent faictez et que le. fut reposey il dist a iacob a ioseph du cassel et a ioseph 1011 *A9* t. et par ainsy ces *A9* f. a *A11* d. ycy f. 1011-1012 *A12* m. et non autres plus de la cite et q. 1011-1013 *A1* t. et q. ilz furent assez secouruez le.d. 1011-1014 *A10* t. et q. ces choses furent acomplies le. dit dit a iaffet et iacob quilz 1012 *A8* t.eu. 1012-1013 *A11* eu.f. et acomply les choses dessusdiz et se furent reposez eulx et l. *A12* furent s. 1012-1014 *B2* q. tout fut fayt et le. fut s. et toutes ses g. il dist a iassel a iacob et a ioseph quil 1013 *A2, A12, B4* d. a iaffet (*B4* i. du tassel) a iacob et a ioseph 1013-1014 *B, B1* d. a iasel et a iacob que *A6, A11, B5* i. qui

1006 *ordille* This form is not recorded in Godefroy, Tobler-Lommatzsch, nor in the *Französisches Etymologisches Wörterbuch*. It perhaps represents a blending of *ordonner* and *artillerie*.

1011 *ses* [ *sest* Correction from MSS *A1, A2, A3, A7, A8, A9, A11, A12*.

d'Arimatie qu'i[l] les menassent la ou fust mis en crois Jhesu Crist, et au moniment et au fleuve Jourdain et la out ressucita le ladre, et en tous les lieux out Jhesu Crist avoit fet de grans miracles. Et il les y menerent et illuec chescun ploura en adourant Jhesu Crist en tres grant honneur et en tres grant reverance.

[67] Aprés tout ce l'empereur et son filz et ses gens s'en pensirent retourner en leur païs de Romanie. Et si enmenerent Pilate avec les sis danrees des juifs et vindrent en Acre. Et la Vespesian fist aprester trois

1014 *A1, A8, A9, A11* m. tous la (*A8* m. la) ou (*A11* m. au lieu ou) i.c.f.m. en (*A9* m. la ou f.m.i.c. en) c. et 1014-1015 *A12* ou i.c.f. mys en la c. et au f.i. au m. et la *B5* ou avoit este mis dieu en la c. et en 1014-1016 *B, B1, B2, B3, B4, B7, A6, A10* m. la ou avoit este mis dieu en (*A10* ou i.c.a.e.m. en *A6* ou d.f.m. en *B7* m. au lieu ou i.a.e.m. en *B1* m. luy et toute sa gent au lieu ou i.c.a.e.m. en *B2* m.ic. en) c. et (*B4* ou estoit e.m. en c.i.c. et) en t. les autres (*B2, B7* et es a.) l. 1015 *A9* i. et aussi au lieu ou *A11* i. ou saint iehan le baptisa aussi au lieu ou il r. 1015-1016 *A8, A1* l. et par les l. (*A1* p. tout) out *A12* les bons l. *A11* et es l. ou nostre seigneur l. 1015-1020 *A13* les aultres sens l. de iherusalem et firent leurs oroisons en plourant moult doulcement en chascun lieu et a. sen retournarent apres ladicte destructon de iherusalem iusques a pourt da. et en e. *B5* les aultrez l. ou a. dieu nostre seigneur i.c.f.m. et ilz y alerent et en chascun lieu adourerent devotement nostre seigneur i.c. et en t.g.r. et puis a. sen voult le. aler a romme luy et ses gens et fist prendre de vi 1016 *A6, A10* ou il a. *A12* a. este et f. les g. 1016-1017 *A8* m. et i. oyans ses miracles et les fays de sa passion c. *A12* il distrent que voluntiers et quant lempereur et tithus son filz et toutes leurs gens estoyent par ses saintz lieux c. *A11* m. et en chascun lieu adouroient nostre seigneur i. 1016-1020 *B7* ou il a.f.m. et ainsi fust faict quant lempereur fust ou i. avoit este mis en croix moult devotement ladora et son filz titus parellement et tous les seigneurs que i. estoient et pareillement furent en tous les lieux ou il avoit f.m.a. toutez chosez le. retourna a romme et fist prendre p. et les *B, B1, B2, B3, B4, A6* f.m. et ilz y alerent et (*B2* m. et ainsi le firent et) en chascun lieu adourerent nostre (*B1* al. en ad. a c.l.n.) seigneur i. (*A6* s. dieu i.) c. o g. (*B2* s. en moult g.) r. et bien devotement a. (*B1* o.t.g.r. et devocion a.) ses (*B2* a. toutes ces) choses le. sen volut r. a romme luy et (*B1* luy son filz et *B2* r. et) toutes ses gens et fist prandre p. et les 1016-1021 *A10* m. adonc ilz allerent ensemble et en c. lieu ilz adorerent nostre seigneur a g.r. et moult devotement a.t. ces choses le. voullut r. a romme et luy et toutes ses gens et fist prendre p. et tous les i. qui estoient demourez et les fist lier et amener a a. 1017 *A9* c. de eulx p. 1017-1018 *A1* cr. en t.g.r. *A8, A11* h. et r. 1019 *A9* ceci fait le. et titus son *A11* a. ces choses faictes le. *A12* et thithus son *A2* f. et toutes ses 1019-1020 *A1, A2, A3, A7, A9* sen volrent r. *A11* sen voulurent r. a romme lors appresterent toutes leurs choses puis en partirent et e.a. eulx p. bien lye avec les vj *A12* sen voulsirent r. a romme et mennerent p.a. eux et les 1019-1021 *A8* sen vindrent r. en 1020 *A2* et envoyerent p. 1020-1021 *A1* a. ses d. *A6* les sept d. 1021 *B, B1, B3, B4, B5, A6* i. et les fist bien lier et (*B1* i.b. lies et) les (*B5* i. qui estoient demourez et les f. tres b.l. puis les) admena a a. *A11* i. qui estoient demourez et tant errerent par leurs iournees quilz v. au port da. *A12* i. que lempereur avoit retenues bien lies et vont venir en *B2* i. et les fist moult fort actachier et puys sen partirent et firent tant quil v. *B7* i. et les fist mener a a. puis f. appareillez t. *A12* la lempereur f. *A6, A9, A10, A11, B, B1, B2, B3, B4, B5* f. appariller t. 1021-1024 *A13* i. moitie homme et femme et les mist sur mer en t. bapteau et puis f. lever les v. pour a.

1021-1025 The topos of a ship abandoned without food or captain, but which

nefs et en chascune nefs il mist deux danrees de juifs sans nul vivres et sans personne qui les gouvernast. Et avec autre nefs il les fist mestre bien parfont en la mer et fist tendre les voiles. Et la il les laisserent aler a l'aventure, la out seroit la voulenté de Dieu. Et car Dieu ne vouloit que toux les juifs prissent mort et pericent, mes vouloit qu'il en demourast en terre pour remembrance, Dieux voult que l'une des nef arivast a

1022 *A2* c. il *A8* n. prinst deux *A9* m. on fist mettre deux *A12* il fist mettre deux *A12* s.v. 1022-1024 *A10* c. fist mectre soixante iuifz qui valloient deux deniers et les fist mectre s. pain et s.n.v.b. avant dedans la mer pour faire ainsi que dieu vouldroit et les *B, B1, B3, B4, B5, A6* c. n. fist mectre lx i. qui valoient ij deniers s. pain et sans vin et sans homme et (*B1* vin ne h. ni femmes autre a. eulx et *B4* vin et sens autre p.a. eulx et) avec a. bateaulx et f. (*B5* vin et sans autre viande et sans aultre p. et sans gouvernaulx et les f.) mener les n.p. en (*A6* et les f. mestre b. avant en *B5* m. dedens lesdis n.b. avant en) mer (*B1* m. ou p. de la mer *B3* n. ou plux p. de la mer *B4* f. les n. entres ou p. de la mer) pour perir ou pour sauver lequel que (*B1* s. ainsi que) dieu (*B5* l. il plairoit a d.) vouldroit et leverent les v. afin que alassent a 1022-1025 *B7* en fist mestre a c. deulx da.s. patron puis les f. mener b.p. en la mer avecques aultres bateaulx et quant furent bien avant en mer ceulx qui les avoient menez copperent les cordez et les laisserent aller pour perilz ou pour saulvez si comme il plairoist a dieu mais d. ne 1022-1026 *B2* c. il fist mectre deux d. de i.s. pain sans vin ne sans nulle ayde du monde et les f. mener b.p. dedans la mer pour les perir ou pour les sauver et firent lever les v. et les envoyerent a leur a. et pour ce que d.v. quil 1023 *A12* et ses troys n. *A11* et puis les f. 1023-1024 *A2, A3, A7* b. avant en *A9* b. avant dedans la mer et puis apres f. *A12* m. en la mer b.p. et f. lever les *A11* m. en mer b.p. et les v. au vent et dist quon les l. 1025 *A6, A10, B, B1, B3, B4, B5* av. et d. (*B5* d. qui) ne *A9* v. et plaisir de *A11* out il plaisoit a d. quil ne *A12* out ihesu crist plairoit et *A13* av. ainsin quil plairoit a d. lequel ne *A7* de ihesu crist car *A1* et d. 1025-1026 *A1* que les 1025-1027 *A13* quil morissent t. affin que a tous iours mais fuisse par eulx memoire entre les crestiens de la passion a doulz ihesu crist et v. nostre seigneur par sa grace que *B7* que perissent affin que t.i. eust memoire de sa passion et a. 1026 *A8* les les i. *A2, A7, B, B3, B4, B5* i. perissent m. (*A2* p. ne prinssent m.) mais (*B5* i. fussent perdues mais) v. *A10* t. perissent mes *A11* i. mourussent par ains v. *B1* v. pas quilz mourissent mes v. *A6* i. perissent mes v. dieu que en *A12* i. perissient ne fussient m. mais quil *A1* m. mais *A9* v. et lui pleut quil 1026-1027 *A8* m. mes voult que de eulx a tousiours fust memoire en terre pour r. de sa mort et passion pour quoy d. ordonna que *A11* d.p. 1027 *A12* p. ce quil fust r. de sa passion et de sa mort et a tous iours mais souvenance a tous les bons crestiens avint que d. *B2* p. avoir memoyre de luy et de sa sainte mort et passion une nef vint arriver a *A2, A3, A7, A9* r. de sa mort affin quil en fust a tout temps mais remembrance (*A7* mort *A9* en eust t.t.r.) d. *B, B1, B3, B4, B5, A10, A11* r. de sa mort et de sa passion (*B4* r. de sa p.) et v. (*B5* v.d. *A11* p. affin quil en fust memoire en tout temps dont il v.) que *A6* r. de sa benoite passion et v. que une nef 1027-1028 *A12* a. nef a b. *A13* a. a b.la. a n. et la. en

miraculously arrives at a safe harbor, is part of the legend of St. Maria Jacobi's arrival in Provence.

Narbonne et l'autre a Bourdeaux et l'autre en Engletere. Et les juifs qui estoient dedens les nefs cuiderent que Dieux l'aut fet par miracle et par grace d'eulx. Mes Dieux le fist afin que tous jours mes fust remembrance

1028 *A11* n. la cite et *A1* b. et la. arrivast en *A8* b. et la tierce en *A12* b. et la. nef en *B4* b. en e. et lautre a ung autre port et les i. et iuyres qui 1028-1029 *B2* e. et ainsi fut fayt 1028-1031 *B7* n.la. en e. et la. a b. et les i. penserent bien que d. le f. par m.a. toutez ses choses le. fist 1028-1034 *A11* e. apres que vaspasien ot ainsi fait mectre le six denrees de iuifz dedans les nefz a laventure comme dit est il fist a. beaulx n. et grans et prindrent des v. tant que leur en failloit puis se mist dedans avec titus son filz et toute leur gent et d. 1029 *A12* les troys n. *A7* d. tindrent que *A13* d.c. *A10* la nacie se pensserent bien que 1029-1030 *B3* d. se panseirent bien que d. le f. pour m. et a. *B, B1, B4, B5, A6* n. se penserent bien que d.f. (*A6* que f.) ce pour m. (*B1* d. le f. par m.) et a. *A7* m. mes *B2* m. pour avoir a iamais memoyre de la passion du filz de dieu a. ces choses le. fist *A10* m.a. 1030 *A12* d. ne le fist mais a. quil en fust *A3* e. non mes *A8* g. quil leur eust faicte mes *A8* fist come dit est a. *B, B1, B3, B4* t. temps fust *A8* i. par eulx fust *A2* i.r. 1030-1031 *A13* e. mesme mais non fist mais pour avoir t.i. memoire de *A6, A10, B5* t. temps fust memoire de sa benoite pa.a. (*A10* sa pa. sy retournerent au partement de le. qui estoit a acre a. *B5* m. et r. de sa m. et p.a.) ces choses le. fit *A7* r. de sa mort et p. mais a.

1028 *Narbonne ... Bourdeaux ... Engletere* Why these three locations? Although we are told that the distribution of the survivors of the destruction of Jerusalem occurs so that there will be a "remembrance," it is undoubtedly significant that throughout the Middle Ages, these areas were outside the purview of the kingdom of France. Bordeaux, for example, remained in English hands until 1453. Assuming a French author for our documents, the selection of these areas may be seen as a political punishment visited on the enemies of France. Berman (p. 11), Gygès (p. 9), and Prado-Gaillard (pp. 19-20) all relate an alternate tradition current in the Jewish community of France that such a diaspora did take place, but that the cities involved were Bordeaux, Arles, and Lyons.

Another explanation for the choice of Bordeaux and Narbonne is the historical fact of the existence in these communities of a large – and depending on the moment, flourishing – Jewish population. Malvézin assures us that "Dès le neuvième siècle, l'histoire nous indique à Bordeaux l'existence d'une population juive; ... à la fin du onzième siècle, les Juifs établis à Bordeaux depuis longtemps, occupaient ... toute la partie occidentale d'un coteau ... près de l'Église Saint-Seurin" (p. 34). Two other events served to increase the number of Jews in Bordeaux: first, the edict of Charles VII in 1394, which theoretically banned all Jews from the kingdom of France, resulted in the settling in Aquitaine in general and Bordeaux in particular of many French Jews (Prado-Gaillard, p. 83); second, after the expulsion of the English from Bordeaux, the city was authorized to accept the nominally Christian, but in reality Jewish, *maranes*, who arrived from Spain and Portugal.

Narbonne enjoyed an even stronger position in the Jewish community in France, a position based initially on the legendary arrival of Jews there during the time of King David, that is, in the eleventh century BC. Later, Narbonne's primacy depended on the existence there by the mid-ninth century AD of an important Talmudic center, serving a community that may have represented a tenth of the total population. See Lunel (p. 15), Catane (p. 29), Bourdrel (p. 22), and Schwarzfuchs (p. 21).

de sa pacion et de sa mort. Puis aprés l'empereur et Titus, son filz, firent apareillier navilles et firent mettre dedens grant foison de vivres, quar ossy [53v] il se mistrent dedens et leur gent / avec eulx, et ossy avec Jacob et Jafet et Joseph d'Arimatie. Et Dieux leur donna bon vent en tent que dedens nuef jours il ariverent au port de Barleta. Et puis il s'en vindrent a Rome sains et liez.

1031 *A2* de sa m. et de sa pa.p. *B3* sa m.a. cez chosez le. fit *B, B1, B4* p.a. ces chose le. (*B1* a. ce le. *B4* p.le. vaspasien a. ces c.) fist *A12* puis le. et son f.t. firent 1031-1034 *A13* p. et quant les gens de le. furent sur mer d. 1032 *A9* a. leurs n. *A7* a. leurs n. et g. *A12* a. deux biaux mavilles et grant et les garnyrent de g. *A9* g. quantite et f. 1032-1033 *B, B1, B3, B4, A6* a. belles n. et grans et (*A6* g. vassel et) y midrent moult eau et (*B3* mo. de pain et *A6* mo. de chars et) moult vin et bestint chappons (*B1* mi.mo. chaars mo. de ung buctars c. *B3* v. bestes c.) et gelines et chers (*B5* mi.mo. de c.) salees et dautres viandes assez et se *A8, A1* v. et (*A1* et se) se *A12* v. vin eau et autres viandes et incontinent se 1032-1034 *A10* a. ses n. pour soy en aller a romme et se mist sur la mer dedans les navires et sen partirent du port et *B2* n. et gallees et y midrent largement v. chappons poulailles pain vin eaue vestuitz et toutes choses neccessayres et se partirent dicelluy port et d. *B5* a. belles n. et grandes et y fist m.g.f. pain chair et bestes chappons gelines chairs salees et aultrez viandes assez et se m. luy et toutes ses g.d. icelles nefz et puis se partirent du port dacre et d. *B7* a.m. grandez et largez et moul daultres vaisseaulx et les f. garnir de v. et apres entrast en mer et ses gens avecques luy et quant ilz furent sus mer d. *A7* v. et l.g.a.e. ioseph da. iacob et iaffet et d. 1033 *A1* d. avec tous l.g. et o. *A12* d. les nefs qui estoyent belles et grans et bien ornees et toutes l. 1033-1034 *A6, B, B1, B3, B4* d. et tout l.g. puis partirent du port et *A2* o. iaffet et iacob et i. *A8* g. et iaffet iacob et i. *A12* a. iaffet iacob io.da. et pilate et *A1* a. et eubrent bon

1034 *A11* do. si beau temps et bon *B7* l. envoyast si bon *A1* que au boult de n. 1034-1035 *B3, B, B1, B2, B4, B5, A6, A10* do. bon v. (*B* b. temps et bon v.) a talent et (*B1* do. a leur t.b.v. et *B3* v. et *B4* a leur vouloir et) vindrent (*A6* v. tellement qui v. *A10* v. a souhait et sen v. *B2* b. temps et v.) arriver au *A12* do. si bon v. et si bonne fortune que d. x i. *A13* do. si bon v. que en x.i. ilz furent a b. *A8* d. x i. *A11* que au bout de dix i. ou environ ilz v. 1034-1037 *B7* v. que en peulx temps furent a r.q. saint c.s. que lempereur et ses gens ve.v. 1035 *A8* a. a b. *A6, A10, B, B3, B4, B5* et de la sen *B2* et de la a *A1* puis allerent a *A9* puis apres ilz sen v. tous a 1035-1037 *A12* et la ilz se mirent a terre et vont venir a r.s. et en bon point et 1035-1039 *B1* et tous s. sen v. a r.q. saint c.s. que lempereur venoit a sa gent il v. audevant a.t. ceulx qui croyoient en ihesu crist en p. ordonne moult noble le.d. *A10* r. bien ioyeux q.s.c. sceut que lempereur v. et tous ses gens il alla au devant a.t. ceulx qui creoient en ihesu crist en belle p. et en belle ordonnance et vint le. et d. 1035-1040 *A13* et dillec ar.s. et en bon point et la. ensamble ceulx des eglises v. a devant en moult noble p. adoncques le. et thitus son filz a pie d. et basirent lappostoille et fut a r.g. ioye pour le retour des seigneurs et p. 1036-1037 *A2, A8, A9* et ioyeulx et *A1* et haittiez et l.c.la. quil s. *A3* l. a tresgrant ioye et *B, B3, B5, A6* et saufs q. saint c. (*A6* q.c.) s. (*B5* q. monseigneur saint c. pape de rome s.) que lempereur venoit et sa gent il (*B5* e. et ses g.v. il) l. vint *A11* et saulves q. la c.s. que lempereur et sa gent ve. 1036-1038 *B2* et saufz q. saint c.la.s. que lempereur venoyt et ses gens il l. alla au devant et mana a. luy la p. de tous ceux qui crooyent en ihesu crist et

1036-1039 *B4* et saulx q. saint c.s. que lempereur vaspasien et son filz tithus les leurs gens ve. et quilz furent pres de rome il l.v. au devant contre eulx a.t. ceulx qui creoient en ihesu crist en p. adonc le.d.

[68] Et quant Clement, l'apostole, seüt qu'il venoient, il leur vint a l'encontre avec toute sa clergie en la prosession. Et quant l'empereur les vit venir a son encontre, il descendi de son cheval et le besa et Titus ossy. Et lors fust feste grant feste a Rome pour la vengence de la mort de Jhesu Crist que l'empereur et son filz avoient fette. Et lors l'apoustole sermonnoit chascun jour de la pacion et mort de Jhesu Crist et de sa foy.

1037 *A12* a. vait scavoir que lempereur et son filz ve. 1037-1040 *A11* vint au devant de luy a. luy le c. et ceulx qui croioient en ihesu crist en belle p. et q. il furent les ungs pres des aultres lempereur et t. son filz se d. de dessus leurs c. et vindrent baiser saint clemens et sentrefirent grant ioye et g. honneur et reverance adoncques y eut g. ioye a 1038 *A7* e. deux a. *A8* e. il descendit a. *A9* e. en p.a. sa c. et *A8* sa chargie a p. *A12* c. bien ornes en tresgrant p. *B5* t. ceulx qui creoient en ihesu crist a tout p. tous honnourablement et *A7* et le. 1038-1039 *B7* e. en p. bien ordonnee le. laperceu et tantost d. ius de *B* t. ceulx qui creoyent en ihesu crist en p. bien ordonnee q. vaspazien vit *A6, B3* t. ceulx qui croyent en ihesu crist en belle p. (*B3* en p.) et le.d. *A12* e. et son filz tithus virent *B2* le. vit v. saint clement a grant procession il *B5* le. approucha du saint clement il *A7* ve. il *B* ve. clement a grant procession il 1039 *A12* e. lapostole clement ilz 1039-1040 *A12* c. a terre et vont baiser clement et lors il eust moult grant ioye et firent g. *B, B1, B2, B3, B4, B5, A6, A10* et baysa (*B1* et lempereur et tictus son fils b.) clement (*B4, A6, A10* b. saint c.) pappe et (*A10* p. de romme et) son filz t.o. (*B1* p.o.) adonc (*B3* p. et o. fit son f.t.a. *B4* b. saint c. et o. le fist ainsi t. filz de lempereur a.) eut g. (*B2* c. et t. pareillement a.f.f.g. *A10* a. les rommains eurent g.) ioye a r.p. lamour de (*A10* i. de la venue de) le. et (*B4* le. leur seigneur et de son filz tithus et) de (*B5* et ala baiser le p.c. et o.t.f. de le. et de) ses gens qui estoient venuz et (*B4* v. sains et saulx et *B5* v. sains et haitiez et) que ilz avoient (*B2* r. de la venue de le. qui e. retourne et qui a. *A10* g. et aussi pour ce quilz a.) vangie la (*B3* v. de nostre seigneur i.c. la) m. *A7* b. et o.t. son filz et 1039-1043 *B7* et va baisant saint clement en la bouche ainsi fist titus novel empereur l. eust par tout r.g. feste de ce que lempereur estoit retournez sains et en bon point et quil avoit eust victoire contre ses enemis sainct clement preschoit la foy de i. et le. et ses g.les.

1040 *A3* et leur f. *A8* fut g. *A12* r. par tout le pays pour lonneur et lamour de lempereur et p. *A11* la venue de lempereur et de ses gens et de ce quil avoient ainsi vangee la m. *A12* de la passion et m. 1040-1041 *A13* m. du doulz i.c. et le. 1040-1042 *B2* m. du filz de dieu saint clement prechoyt tous les iours la foy de ihesu *B3, B5* m. et estoient retournez en leur pays sains et haitieez et ioieulx pape (*B5* m. et passion de nostre benoit saulveur i.c. et puis p.) clement preschoit tous lez iour de (*B5* de la foy de) ihesu 1040-1043 *A11* de nostre seigneur i.c. et de ce quil estoient retournez sains et saulves et en louerent moult dieu tous les crestiens apres la venue de vaspasien et de sa gent le pappe clemens prescha par plusieurs iours la foy catholique au peuple en la presence de le. qui les. 1040-1044 *A10* de nostre seigneur et quilz estoient retournez sains et ioyeulx en leurs [ ] apres pappe clement prescha tous les i. la foy crestienne et lempereur lempereur les.v. et tous ses gens et q. 1041 *A8* e. et thitus a. 1041-1042 *A6, B, B1, B4* c. et qui estoient retournez sains et ioyeulx en (*A6* en saul en) leur pais pape (*B4* r.i. en l. pays par la grace de dieu pape) clement prescha (*B4* c. lors p.) tous les iours de la (*A6* les iuifz la) foy de ihesu *A12* ap. clement se mist a sermioner c. *A13* ap. clement s. 1042 *A1* s. tousiours de la *A1* p. de *A2* la m. et p. de 1042-1043 *A12* la foy et de i.c. et le. *B5* cr. et le. *B, B1, B2, B3* cr. et le. (*B1* le. et ses g.) les. *B4* cr. devant lempereur et le peuple et le.les. 1042-1044 *A13* i. faiz de la p. et m. de i.c. et q. *A6* cr. et le.les. tresbien et m.v. et toutes ses gens et q.

Et l'empereur et son filz et toute sa gent l'escoutoient moult voulentiers. Et quant l'empereur eüt sejourné par huit jours et l'apoustole l'ala veoir et lui dist: "Sire, Nostre Seigneur vous a fet grant honneur de ce qu'i[l] lui a pleü que vous avés desconfis vos enemis. Pour quoy, Sire, vous vouroie prier que les couvenens que vous li avés [promis] vous li tenés liement et de bon cuer. — Quelz couvenens sont ce?" se dist l'empereur. "Sire, dist

1043 *A2* le. et titus son *A9* f. titus et *A1* e. et titus et t. *A7* t. ses e. *A8* es.v. *B3* m. bien et moult v. *B, B2, B3, B4* et et toutes ses gens (*B2, B3* g. aussi *B4* g. et tout le peuple aussi) et 1043-1044 *A1* g.e.v. le sermon et q. ilz eubrent s.h. *A11* v. aussi fist titus son filz et toute sa gent q. 1044 *A7, B7* q. il eut *A9* par lespace de h. *A6, A10, B3, B5* i. pape (*B5* i. saint p.) clement le vint v. *B, B1, B4* i. le (*B4* i. a rome le) pappe clement vint v. lempereur (*B4* le. en son hostel) et *A1* a. alla v. lempereur et *A11* a. clemens lalla 1044-1045 *B2* eut sermone sept i. il a.v. lempereur et lui *A7* i. il dist a lempereur s. 1044-1047 *B7* i. sainct clement allast parler a luy en sa chambre en lui disant s. puis que dieu v. a donnez victoire contre vos e. ia vous prie que 1044-1053 *A13* i. ilz se feit baptisier ou *A12* v. en son palays et 1045-1046 *A12* h. qui vous ha donne victoyre de vos 1045-1047 *A11* fet telle grace et h. quil vous a donne victoire contre voz e. et la foy de dieu dieu congnoistre ie v. suplie et requiers que le c. 1045-1052 *B2* s. puys que dieu v.g. grace quil vous a fayt vengier tous voz e.p. ce s. ie vous prie que v. luy vueilles tenir la promesse que v. luy a. faicte et le. luy demanda que cestoyt quil avoit promis et il luy respondit seigneur v. vous devez fayre baptiser et il respondit quil le feroyt moult voulentiers saint clement adoncques fayre aprester et sanctiffier les f. et se departit 1046 *A9* a. eu victoire a desconfire ses e. *A2* q. ie vouldroye *A12* s. vous viens p. *A9* s. ihesu crist v. *A11* s. puisque dieu v. *A10* s. puis que dieu v. a donne victoire contre vos 1046-1047 *B, B1, B3, B4, B5, A6* s. puis (*B5* s. empereur p.) que dieu v. a f. telle grace (*B1* a donne ceste g.) que vous a donne victoire contre voz e. et la (*B3, A6* e. pour la) foy de (*B5* e. et les vreis e. de la foy catholique et de) dieu pour (*B1* d. congnoistre p.) ce seigneur ie v. prie que (*B4* d. cognoistre ie v.p. mon seigneur que *A6* d. erancier s. que v. plaise que) les c. que luy promistes que de 1046-1048 *A7* p. que luy tenes ce que p. luy a.q. 1046-1052 *A10* e. ie vous prie quil v. plaise de lui tenir ce que vous luy a. promis ce que de bon c. vous lui t. car sire vous luy promistes que vous feriez b. car ainsi le devez faire le. respondist ie le feray moult voullenties et dist a saint clement faictes santiffier les f. adont saint clement sen p. 1047 *A2* a. fais v. luy vueilliez tenir l. *A8* a. fectes v. *A12* li fistes v. luy vueilles tenir de *A9* p.v. les luy vueilliez tenir l. *A11* p. ia piessa de *A1, A8* t. lealment et 1047-1052 *B7* c. que v. luy promiste tenez de bon c. et lempereur demandast a clement quel estoit ce c. et lui respondit seigneurs cest que vous debviez faire baptizer a vostre retour de iherusalem lors le. lui respondit que ce feroist volluntiers et luy ordonnast quil sainctiffiat les f. adoncques clement se 1048 *A9* co. ce d. *A1* d. il s. 1048-1051 *A11* cuer vous luy tiengnez et le. respondit s. ce feray ie voulentiers car cest bien raison que ie vive et meure soubz la foy et creance du bon prophete ihesu crist qui a fait si beau miracle quil a f. en moy de me avoir gary de horrible malladie que iavoye et aussi de la victoire quil ma donne en iherusalem et pour ce sire appostolle faites appareillez et ordonnez les f. ainsi quil convient et quant il vous plaira moy et les miens serons baptizee l. le saint ap. 1048-1052 *B, B1, B3, B4, B5, A6* cuer luy (*B5* c. sans fainte v. luy) tiegnes le. (*A6* luy

1047 Addition based on MSS *A1, A3, A6, A7, A9, A10, A11, B, B1, B3, B4, B5, B6.*

1048 *quelz couvenens* [ *qui ele comment* Correction based on MSS *A1, A2, A3, A6, A7, A8, A9, A12.*

l'apostole, que vous vous baptizés." Lors dist l'empereur: "Sertes, je l'outroy de bon cuer et qu'il soit fet au plaisir de Jhesu Crist. Et que les fons soient prestés et santifiez ainsi comme il se doit fere." Lors l'apostole se parti de l'empereur moult lieux, louent Dieux et sa vertu. Et fist apareillier les fons, et au tier jour aprés il baptisa l'empereur ou non du Pere et du Filz et du Saint Esperit, et ne lui mua point son non. Et puis baptisa son filz, Titus, et puis le seneschal, Gaius, Jafet, Jacob, Jozeph

---

vuilliez tenir le.) demanda quel (*B4* d. au pape q.) est le c. clement respondit (*B3* t. adont r.) seigneur (*B4* c. lors r. mon s.) que (*A6* d. a saint cl.q.co. cestoyent saint cl.r. a le. que) v. faciez baptiser car ainsi le devez faire le. (*B5* f. ou vous ne povez estre saulvez et le. luy) respondit ie (*B4* f. et puis le.r. a clement ie) le feray moult voulentiers et dist a clement (*B5* r.m. bonnement ie le f. et v. et puis d. a saint c.) que tantost feist (*A6* a saint c. qui fit) sanctiffier les f. adonc pappe clement (*A6* a. saint c.) sen p. 1049 *A8* l. respondit le. *A12* v.v. feriez b.l. luy respont le. 1050 *A9* o. dist lempereur de *A12* o. et 1050-1051 *A1* cr. et faictes aprester les f. et les sa. *A12* cr. et faittes sanctiffier et appareiller belles f. et l. 1051 *A3* p.a. *A9* a. quil appartient et c. *A7* p.l. *A2, A3* il appertient et (*A3* et comme il) se *A2* s.s. *A8* s. fais et 1051-1052 *A8* l. se p.la. de 1052 *A1* e. bien ioieulx loant *A6, A10, B, B1, B3, B4, B5* e. et sen alast lo. *A9* m. ioyeulx et li. *A11, A12* le.lo. *B2* e. et va louer d. *B7* e. et sen alla remercye d. et puis f. *A11* d. moult fort de ce lempereur avoit ferme creance en dieu et quil vouloit estre baptisie et puis fist *B4* d. ihesu crist de sa 1052-1053 *A7* d. de sa promiz et f. aprester les f. et quatre i. il *A6* et appereilat les *B5* fist tantost a. 1053 *A12* a. belles fons *A11* fons et puis les saintiffia et ordonna et avant quatre i. *A12* au bout de troys i. il *A2, A3, A8, A9* et quatre iours a. *A10* au quart iour vint vaspazien et le b. saint clement au non *B2* et a. troys i. lapostre clement b. vaspasien le. *A6, B, B1, B3, B4, B5* au quart i. (*B5* au conv[ ] i.) pape clement b. vaspasien (*B* v.e. *B3* v.le. *B4* i. apres le p.c.b.le. *B5* v.le. de rome) ou 1053-1054 *B7* au quatriesme i. clement b. vaspasien et ne *A12* le. et son filz tithus en nom 1054 *B5* du benoit s. *A10, B1* e. amen si ne *A6, A9* luy changat (*A9* c. ne mua) p. 1054-1055 *A13* e. son *B5* p. ne osta son propre nom de vaspasien et *A10* puis apres b. son f.t. nouvel empereur iaffet *B4* non et apres clement pape b. son f.t. nouvel empereur et aussi iassel du tassel et iacob 1054-1056 *B3* puis apres tous b. chevaliers et g. 1055 *A8* b.t. *A1, A2, A7* b. son f.t. et (*A7* b.t. son f.) g. le s. iaffet *B, B1, B2, B5, B7, A6* et p. apres b. (*B1* et a. ce b. *A6* p.b.) t. (*B5* b. son f.t.) nouvel empereur (*B2* t.f. de le.) et (*B7* a.t. et apes i.) iafel *A9* b.t. son f. et aussy son s. *A11* t. nouvel empereur puis babtiza g. le s. et iaffet *A3* f. son filz g. son s. iacob iaffet ioseph 1055-1056 *A6, B, B1, B2, B4, B5* iozeph da. et puis apres tous (*B2* i. et a. il baptisa t.) les b. chevaliers (*B2* b. les contes les c.) t. la (*B* c. et *B5* c. et aultrez) g. 1055-1057 *A10* iozeph et tous les b. et tous les chevalliers et t. les g. de lem[ ]r *B7* iosepht et tous les seigneurs de 1055-1058 *A13* t. et toutes ses maisniez et aussi toutes ses gens comme r. duc conte b. chevaliers escuiers et toutes aultres gens adoncques demandirent a la. quil leur baillaisse et enseingnaisse la 1055-1060 *A11* iozeph et puis baptiza tous les autres r. les ducz les contes les b. et chevalliers et t. les g.e. et grant nombre de p. et quant il ot tout ce fait il

1053 *apareillier* [ *apareilliez* Correction from all MSS except *A6, A7, A11*.

d'Arimatie et les roys, les princes, les barons et toute la gent de l'empereur. Et quant tout le peuple fust baptisez, il s'en vindrent a l'apostole et lui distrent: "Puisque tu nous as baptizés, enseigne nous la foy de Jhesu
[54r] Crist." Et quant l'apostole eüt achevé de baptiser, tout le peuple qui / c'estoit baptisé de bon cuer, il eüt tres grant joie et rendi grace a Jhesu

1056 *A1* r. contes p. *A9* p. le contes les dux les b. les chevaliers et t. 1056-1057 *A12* a. et puys baptiza les royx les p. comtes marquis b. et tous ceulx qui se vouloyent baptizer et q.t. les gens de lempereur et des autres aussy f. 1057 *A9* e. et de titus son filz et 1057-1058 *A6, B, B2, B3, B5* q. le (*B3* q. tout le) p. (*B5* q. tout le menus p.) vit que tous (*B5* que lempereur titus son filz et t.) les grans seigneurs (*B3* les s.) estoyent (*B2* les barons et chevalliers e.) baptizer il d. baptizer nous a (*B, B3, B5* d. a) pape clement et (*B* c.b.n. et) ce n.e. (*B2* d. a lapostre c. seigneur b.n. et nous e. *B3* c. seigneurs b.n. et nous e. *B5* c. sire pape b.n. et nous e.) la *B1, B4, B7* q. le p. (*B7* q. tout le menus p.) vit que les (*B4* que tous les) grans seigneurs se firent baptizer (*B7* que leurs sire estoient b. *B4* s. estoient b.) ilz d.e.n. (*B7* e. *B4* d. a clement b.n. et nous e.) la 1057-1059 *A10* p. vit [ ] seigneurs f. tous b. ilz b. appappe clement pere saint b. nous et n.e. la foy de i.q. saint clement vit que t. 1057-1060 *A1* b. et la. vit que tous e. 1057-1061 *A12* a clement la. et rendirent graces a dieu ihesu crist et t.c. et tous ceulx qui 1058 *A2, A3, A7, A8, A9* d. sire p. *A3* e. la 1059 *A6, B, B1, B2, B3, B4* c. et q. (*B1* c. car nous nous voulons baptiser q. *B4* c. car nous nous voulons baptisier de nostre grey et q.) saint clement vit que (*B, B2, B3* c. oit que) t. *A2* b. le 1059-1060 *B7* q. le pape clement vit que t. se vollient faire baptizer il eust moult g. *A7* p. il *A8* p. eut g. *B, B1, B2, B3, B4, A6, A10* p. se vouloit baptiser de son gre (*B1, A10* son bon g.) il (*B4* v. de son g.b. il) eut moult (*A6* v. faire b. il e.t. *A10* eut tres) g. 1059-1063 *A13* c. et bien le feit tellement quil ne fut homme en toute la t. de 1059-1066 *B5* et puis le peuple aprez dist aussi a pape clement seigneur pape b. nous et aussi nous enseignez la foy de ihesu crist puis fist emplir l[ ] fons et y fist mettre plus ce cent tines deaue et puis le seig[ ] et sainctifia et leur dist que chascun entrast dedens ou nom du pere et du filz et du saint esperit et serez tous baptisez chascun le fist voulentiers et leur dist sires se aulcun de vous a auld[ ] maladie si sera g. quant il sera baptise ou nom de dessus cestass[ ] ou nom du pere et du filz et du benoit saint esperit et puis tantost alerent fondre et abatre toutes les y. qui estoient au[ ] t. et nen ny demoura nulz puis aprez quand laccord de lempereur fut fait et la seigneurie sen fut alee aprez quilz eurent c. et licence de r. 1060-1061 *A11, B1* a nostre seigneur i. 1060-1062 *B, B1, B2, B3, B4, B7, A6, A10* grace a i. (*B4* g. et mercy a dieu i.) c. et (*B2, B3, B7* a dieu et *A6* a dieu i. et) fist emplir les fons et (*B4* f. deaue et) y fist mectre plus de cent tines deau (*B2* c. toneaulx de. *B1* c. cuvees de.) et puis (*A10* a dieu adont f. mectre de leau dedans et p.) les signa et (*A6* les menat et) leur dist que (*B4* d. a tous que) chascun entrast dedans ou (*B2* dist clement lapostre e.de.c. ou *B3* d. en disant en *B7* f. plains deaue et p. leurs enseignast comment il debvoyent entre et p. tous entrarent au) nom du pere et du filz et du saint esperit et serez (*A10* e. amen si s.) touz baptisez (*B2* s.b.) et chascun le fist moult voulentiers (*B7* f.v.) et leur dist seigneurs (*B7* d. le pape clement s. *B2* c. entra dedans et luy dirent mon s.) se (*B3* et lempereur d. se *B4* d. ainsi messires se) aucun de vous a nulle maladie (*B2* a. avoyt aucune m. *B1* a m. *B3, B4, A6, A10* ait aucune m.) il sera g. (*B1, B2, A6* s. tantost g. quant sera baptise et (*B2* et ainsi fut fait et) q. (*B7* a aulcune m. si tot) quil s.b. il s.g.q.) il (*B4* q. chascun) v.

1059 *baptiser* [ *bapsiser* Correction from all other manuscripts.

Crist. Et tous ceulx qui se baptisoient et estoient malades, estoient tous guaris a l'issue de l'eau. Et quant il virent le miracle, en toute la terre de Rome creoit ou Jhesu Crist. Et sy ydifierent les temples et abatirent et diruerent tous les temples ou estoient les ydoles tant qu'il n'y demoura temple ne ydoule qu'om le puïst trouver. Et puis quant l'empereur eüt

1061 *A7* b.m. *A8* qui e.m. furent tantost g. 1061-1062 *A1* b. se il y avoit moult de m. de quelconques maladies que ce fut ilz c.g. *A3* b. qui e.m. furent g. *A2* m.e.g. *A9* m. a lillus du baptesme cestassavoir des fons ilz e. tantost g. et *A11* m. de quelconque maladie que ce fust tantost quil e. baptizes estoient en leure t. sains et hectiez et ne demoura guieres de peuple en *A12* m. quant ilz estoient baptizes ilz e.g. et tous sains et q. le peuple v. le m. que par baptisme ilz guerissoyent de toutes maladies par toute 1062-1063 *A8* la cite de r. chascun crut 1062-1064 *A6* m. ne demeurast a romme qui ne se fit baptiser ou non de dieu et tantost allerent fendres les y. et le t. tant 1062-1066 *B, B1, B2, B3, B4, A10* m. ne (*B4* m. de dieu il ne) demoura personne en r. qui (*B3* en la citey qui) ne se fist baptiser ou nom de dieu et tantost (*B2* d. a r. nulle p. que tous ne fussent b.t.) alerent (*B3* d. ihesu crist et a.) fondre les te. des y. tant (*B3* les y. tant *B4* les y. et les te. tant *A10* a. gecter les y. et les te. abatre tant) que (*B1* fo. leurs y. et tous leurs te. que *B2* y. affin que) nul ny en d. quant (*B2* ne les adoura q. *A10* nulz rien demourerent q. *B3* d. tout le peuple entierement q.) la court de le. sen fut alee et (*B3* sen volut aler et) que il leur d.c. et licence que sen peussent tourner (*B2* d.l. et c. retourner *B3* sen retournassent *B4* d. et puis apres lempereur d.c. et l. a ses seigneurs b. chevaliers escuiers et autres gens de eulx en aler chascun en son pays quant le congie fut donne de lempereur et la court de partir et quilz sen voulsirent aler avant quilz partissent pour t. *A10* c. [ ]our retourner) en *B7* le grant m. ne demoura ne petit ne grand quil ne se fist baptizez au non du pere et du filz et du sainctz esprilz quant il furent tous baptizes et allerent par ronme pour destruire tous les yd[ ]ez que estoient maintenus par les diablez en apres les gens de lempereur prindrent congez pour r. chascun en 1063 *A3* r. se convertit a i. 1063-1064 *A1* a. tous *A3, A9* a. et destruirent t. *A7* a. les *A12* r. vont croyre et creoyent tous en la saincte loy et foy de i.c. et incontinent vont abatre tous le t. des y. *A2* t. et destruyrent et a. tous *A9* t. qui y sont de nouvel et a. 1063-1066 *A11* r. qui ne creurent en i.c. et se firent baptiser comme vrays catholiques et bons cristiens apres ces choses faictes lempereur fist abatre le t. de leurs y. par tout ou il en y avoit puis d. *A8* t. pour adourer ihesu crist et ceulx la ou on adouraoyt les y.a. et ardirent t. et p. le d.c. a tous ses *A13* et d. y es mostiers ne ou t. de romme quil ne fuisse abbatue et tous les seigneurs retournirent en 1064-1066 *A12* que en toute romanie ny d. nulz et q. cella fust fait le.d. *A1* te. des y. puis le. donna c. a tous ses b. quilz puissent r. 1064-1067 *A6* de. quant la court de le. sen fut aller et qui leur euz d.c. pour aler en l. pais mais avant qui partissent il voulirent a. la c. 1065 *A2* com p. scavoir et *A3* tr. ne savoir et *A9* tr. ne scavoir p. apres q. 1065-1066 *A7* tr. ne savoir et qu[ ] a

1061 *estoient*[2] [ *estoiens* Correction from *A2, A7, A9, A11*.
1064 *estoient* [ *estoiens* Correction from *A2, A3, A7, A9*.

donné congié a ses barons pour eulx retourner en leur terres, et chascun des barons vieust avoir la foy et la creance de Jhesu Crist par escript de l'apostole: "Credo in deum, et cetera." Et quant il furent en leur terres, chescun fist baptiser ses gens. Et lors sainte crestienté creüt moult fort et l'apostole, saint Clement, envoyoit ses disciples precher par toutes terres.

1066 *A12* a tous ses princes b. et autres gens quilz sen retournassent en *A11* r. chascun en *A7* t. et pais c. 1066-1067 *B, B3, B4, B5* l. pais mais avant (*B3* p.a.) que partissent voulurent (*B4* pays ilz v.) a. (*B5* pays devant ce quilz se p. de romme ilz v. tous a.) la c. *A10* l. [ ]derent la c. a saint clement pour savoir la foy de crestienne lors pappe clement leur dit escoustez tous nostre creance est crist 1066-1068 *A11* t. et les contenta tout a leur gre et plaisir et puis prindrent congie de lempereur et de son filz titus et de leurs gens et sen allerent en leurs contrees a grant ioye et q. *A13* et heurrent pour e.c. in d. omnipotentem et c. *B1* l. pays mes avant quilz partissent ilz vouldrent a. la foy de i.c. et sa c. en e. et pape clement leur dist credo *B7* l. pays mais il vollurent a. la foy de i. par e. et sainct clement leur bailla en disant c. in d. patrem omnipotentem et ce. 1067 *A1* b. se fist donner la foy *A8* a. de lapostole en e. la foy *B2* a. la c. *A12* v. prandre et eust de lapostolle la saincte foy et loy de *A9* foy de *A1* e. de la main de 1067-1068 *A2* a. la c. et la foy de i.c. de la. et il la leur bailla credo *A6, B, B3, B4* e. et (*B4* et la demanderent a clement pape et) le pape clement leur dit credo *A8* crist estassavoir credo *B2* e. et la. clement leur dist c. in d. patrem omnipotentem et ce. 1068 *A3, A9* a. cestassavoir credo *A7* a. cestassavoir credo in dominum patrem omnipotentem creatorem celi terre etc *A1* d. et q. *A9, B* d. patrem et (*B* p. omnipotentem et) ce. *B5* credo et puis pape clement leur enseigna et bailla et leur dist la creance de nostre seigneur ihesu crist c. in d[ ] patrem omnipotentem et ce. 1068-1069 *A12* t. et en leurs pays tournes c.f. sanctiffier belles fons et firent b. leurs g. et leurs homme et 1068-1071 *B, B1, B2, B3, B4, B5, A6* q. sen (*B5* q. il leur eust ainsi enseigne et baille la creance de nostre saulveur ihesu crist et quilz sen) f. alez en (*B4* a. chascun en) l.t. (*A6* l. pais en diverses t.) ilz (*B2* a. ilz) firent b. touz leurs g. adonc (*B5* g. hommes femmes et petiz enfans a.) acreut fort la (*B4* a.m. la) foy et (*B3* la loy et) creance de (*B1, B4* et la loy de) ihesu (*B5* fort et avanca la foy e la loy et la c. de nostre seigneur i.) crist a. (*B2* g. par ainsi toute cres. croissoit m.f.a. *A6* c. nostre saulveur a.) toutes ces choses un bien m. vaspazien (*B2* c. advint que ung i.b.m. apres ce que le.v. *B3* v.e. *B5* m.le.v. *A6* c. que v.) et 1068-1072 *A10* d. cest la grande credo et la petite et de la sen allerent en l. pais et f.b. toutes leur g. adonc commenca la foy de ihesu crist a. que tous ses gens furent en repos et q. vaspazien et t. nouvel em. eurent *B7* t. il firent baptizer leurs g. comme il avoient estez adoncques eurent forment la foy de ihesus a. toute ses chosez ung bien m. que le. eust ouy m. et son f.t. il sen allerent au 1069 *A2* fist ses g.b. et *A12* s. eglise creust *A1* cres. fut exauchie et *A9* cres. augmenta et creut 1069-1070 *A11* ses femmes et enffans adonc creut m. et augmenta sainte esglise et e.s.c. ses *A12* f. et saint clement la.e. 1069-1071 *A7* g.p. 1069-1074 *A13* g. adoncques c. lempereur aux sennateurs de romme quil 1070 *A8* a.c. *A9* par tout pays et par to. 1070-1071 *A12* d. par t. le pays et t. de lempereur p. *A11* p. le nom de ihesu crist par tout le pais de rommanye et baptizer ceulx qui se vouldroient baptizer a. toutes ces choses ung i. apres que le. et son

[4. The Punishing of Pilate]

[69] Puis aprés ung jour a matin, quant l'empereur et Titus, son filz, eürent oÿ messe de l'apostole, il s'en retournerent au palais. Et la Vespesian envoya querir les sanateurs de Rome. Et quant il furent venus, il leur commanda qu'il juegassent Pilate selon ses meffais. Et lors les senateurs vousirent savoir les meffais. Et quant les leur eüst dist, il se tirarent a conseil. Et quant il eürent tenu leur conseil, il vindrent davant l'empereur et lui distrent: "Sire, nous connoissons bien selon les meffais de Pilate qu'il doit mourir. Mes Sire, vostre pere, Julius Sezar, ourdena

1071 *A7* ung ieudi a *A12* ung m. *A1* i. au le. 1071-1072 *B1, B, B3, A6, B4, B5* f. nouvel empereur quant (*B* f.e.n.q. *B3* f. alirent a leccleise et q.) ilz (*A6* e.) eurent *A1* f. allerent oyr m. *A12* de clement la 1072 *A12* sen allerent en leur p. *B, B1, B2, B3, B4, B5, A6, A10* m. que chanta pappe clement (*B2* m. laquelle avoit dicte saint c.) ilz (*B4* que p.cl.ch. ilz *A10* que saint cl. leur ch. il) sen alerent au. 1072-1073 *A11* m. que saint clemens celebra manda q. *A12* la lempereur e. *B, B1, B2, B3, B4, B5, B7, A6, A10* et puis manderent (*B2* et m.q. *B3, B5, B7, A6* et m.) les 1073 *A9* et apres ce quilz *A11* r. et tout son conseil lesquelx vindrent tantost a son mandement et q. 1073-1074 *A8, B2* r. et les (*B2* et leur) c. *A6, B, B1, B3, B4, B5, B7* v. lempereur l.c. (*B3, B7* l. dist *B5* l. dist et c.) quil 1074 *A2, A12* l. dist et c. *A11* il sen allerent tous au grant palaix et la leur dist lempereur quilz *A9* m. quilz avoit faiz commis et perpetuez et *A11* m. affin den faire iustice l. *A13* ses fais les 1074-1075 *A1* m. et q. 1074-1076 *A6* quil amenassent p. et qui le i.s. quil avoit forfait adonc les s. se tirerent a part au c. et voulirent scavoir le fait de pylate et *A10* s. son cas et selon ce quil avoit fait a ihesu crist adonc les s. tirerent apart a conseil et v.s. le fait le pillate et *B, B1, B3, B4, B5* p.s. ce (*B1* p. se ce) quil avoit forfait adonc (*B3* av. deservy ad.) les s. se (*B4* s. de rome vindrent devant lempereur et se) tirerent a part au c. et volurent savoir le fait de pilate (*B1* part avecques leur c. *B4* c. et quant ilz e. fait et t. a c.) et *B2* s. ce quil avoyt forfayt les s. se midrent en c. et sceurent le fait de pilate et apres v. 1074-1077 *B7* s. ce quil avoit deservi et leur compta la trahison et faulcete quil avoit faict et adonct se tirerent a part et iugassent ledit pillate selon se quil avoit deservi se leurs sauvtrist en apres v. tous a le. 1075 *A9* sa. quelz estoient ses m. 1075-1076 *A11* se. se misdrent apart pour eulx conseiller emsemble de ceste chose et q. il e. assez parle ensemble il v. *A12* m. de pilate et lempereur le l. fist scavoir et dire et puis quant ilz leurent sceu ilz se vont tirer a *A2, A3, A7, A8* se trahirent (*A8* se misdrent) a *A9* se tirerent a part en leur c. *A1* se trayrent en c. puis v. 1075-1078 *A13* m. et se mirent a c. hault ensamble plusseurs saiges l.c. finy il d. a lempereur selon les faiz de 1076 *A8* t.c. *B, B3, B5, B1* e. eu (*B1* e. fait) l. *B4* v. derechief d. *A12* ilz vont retourner d. 1077 *A2* e. lempereur et 1077-1078 *A10* et d.n. voions b. que p.s. son forfait d. souffrir mort mais *B, B1, B2, B3, B4, B5, B7, A6* s.n. (*B4* s. empereur n.) voyons b. que p.s. son (*B2* s. pilate selon son) forfait quil (*B1* b.p.s. son m. quil *B3, B4, B5, A6* son m. quil) d. souffrir mort (*B2* d. prendre m. *B5* s. et prendre m. *B7* p. a grandement deservi m.) mes *A11* c. que s. le grant m. de p. a commis envers le saint prophete ihesu crist quil d. prendre mort et m. de malle mort mes

1078 *A13* m. de tres horible et tres deshonneste mort mes *A11* s. bien saichez que v. feu p.i.c. iadis o. *A12, A13* v. noble p. *A6, B, B1, B3, B7, B4* v. honnorable (*B4* h. et noble) p. *A9* pere et predecesseur i. 1078-1079 *B5* v. noble predecesseur [ ] empereur establist que *B7* sezar fist une ordonance que *B2* v. noble p. august s. establit une chose cestassavoir que t. les h. de d. *A6, A10, B, B1, B3, B4* sezar establi que

que tout home qui seroit dehors de Rome qu'il ait meffet a l'empereur doit penre mort et estre justicié a Viene et par le justicier de Vienne. Et pour ce

1079 *A13* s. natis horrs *A9* s. natif d. de la cite de *A11* qui ne s. de *A13* r. et destraingne terre quil *B1, B3, B4* ait forfait a 1079-1080 *B5, B7* qui a. forfait en aulcune maniere a (*B7* qui nestoient nasquist de r. et fourfaisoient a) lempereur d.e. *A6, B, B1, B3, B4* doit e. *A13* m. a lencontre de le.d.e. 1079-1081 *A12* e. devoit et d.p.m. par la iustice de v. et e.i. et par ainsy nous le 1079-1082 *B2* ait forfayt fussent i. a v. si fut ordonne que *A10* e.q. [ ]s i. de v. [ ]les [ ]ont et adont lempereur en fut bien contant [ ] fut iugie pillate a mourir en [ ] que 1080 *A1* et doibt e. *A6, A11, B, B1, B3, B4, B5, B7* i. par *A1* par la iustice de *A7* le iuge de 1080-1081 *A13* i. par la iustices de v.p. quoy sire nous le *B, B1, B3, B4, B5, A6* de i. de (*B5* i. de la cite de) v. sur le rone et fut iugie a mourir (*B4* r. et lors fut pilate i. a m. et la sentence pronunciee et escripte *B5* et puis le [ ] pylate fut iustice et i. a v.) en 1080-1125 *B7* de v. sus le ronnez sil vous plaictz iusticers de par luy et tantost fist faire lectres de par luy pour porter aux iusticiers et quant furent faicte il les bailla aus chevaliers et aussi leurs bailla la s. pillate par escripst que avoyent pronuncee les senateurs de romme et leurs fist delivrer pillate et apres les c. se partirent et enmenerent

1080 *Viene* Already in the first century AD, the city of Vienne enjoyed considerable prominence in the Roman world, thanks in part to the birth in nearby Lyons of the Emperor Claudius (nephew of Tiberius, who himself had been sent to Vienne to put down local disturbances), and to its designation as an "Urbs senatoria," that is, a city entitled to send senators to Rome. The clearest proof of this honor is the document in the Musée de civilisation gallo-romaine in Lyons, dated 48 AD, and known as the "Table claudienne." It preserves in bronze a speech made by Claudius before the Roman Senate, in which he praises the excellence of Vienne: "Ornatissima ecce colonia valentissima que Viennensium quam longo iam tempore senatores huic curiae confertex...." See also Collombet (vol. I, p. 127, n. 1), and Longueval (vol. II, p. 270).

Under Diocletian (279 AD), Vienne became the capital of the *Provincia viennensis*, a territory that included much of south-eastern France and western Switzerland, and the episcopal see of the *Dioecesis viennensis*, which ultimately included seventeen provinces and covered all of southern France (Bazin, p. 16; Leglay, pp. 31-32). In the ninth century, it was made the capital of the kingdom of Burgundy and Provence, and was not united to the kingdom of France until 1448.

As for the curious linking of the fate of Pontius Pilate with the city of Vienne, the most thorough treatment of the stages of the legend is to be found in Cavard (pp. 32-71). In simplified form, the steps are as follows: a) Pilate dies of his own hand in Rome, rather than face the Emperor's punishment (see Tischendorf, pp. 456-458); b) his body is thrown into the Tiber but becomes the cause of violent storms; c) the Romans send his body to Vienne where it is thrown into the Rhone with the same results; d) his body is finally buried in a pit high in the mountains (Bazin, ch. 5); e) under the influence of the historical exile of Archelaus in Vienne, Pilate is also exiled there. Cf. the ninth-century *Chronicon* of St. Ado Viennensis: "Herodes tetrarcha ... Romam venit, sed accusatus ab Agrippa, etiam tetrarchiam perdidit; relegatusque exsilio, apud Viennam Galliarum urbem post mortem Caii, inde in Hispaniam cum Herodiadi, fugiens moerore periit. Pilatus, qui sententiam damnationis in Christum dixerat, et ipse perpetuo exsilio Viennae recluditur" (col. 77); f) the elaboration of the specifics of our narrative (well, bridge, tower, devils on the ramparts, etc.). Details of these developments are also given in the *Legenda aurea* (ed. Grässe, p. 234), in Kornmann (Pars IV, cap. LXXII), Du Méril (p. 367, where Vienne has been misread as Ingemia), and in part in Du Choul (p. 69), Bazin

le jugons qu'il soit menés a Viene au justicier. Et jugons qu'il meure en 1081
celle maniere: premierement que le justicier de Vienne face fere au milieu
de la place de Vienne un piler aut et gros de trois toises sur terre. Et dessus

1081 *A2* m. au i. de v. et *A11* m. et quil *A12* s. envoye aux i. de v. et quil *A7* i. quil m. en 1081-1082 *A9* i. et sentencions quil s.m. et remis au i. de ladicte cite de vienne et i. aussi le dit pylate quil m. et preigne mort en telle forme et m. comme cy apres sensuit et sera dit p. *A8* s. envoye audit v. et quil soyt hure a tel mort p. *A13* quil meure ainsin audit lieu de vianne ainsin horriblement comme cy dessoubz es escriptes et tout p.

1082 *A11, A12* i. face *A12* fere ung grant p. au *A13* i. de pilate se faice ou 1082-1083 *A6, B, B1, B3, B4, B5* m. que (*B4* m. cestassavoir que) les iusticiers de v. feissent (*B4* v. sur le rone f.) en (*B1* f. ung pilier en *B5* f. faire en) la *A10* v. feroient en la *B2* f.f. en la 1083 *A8* pl. ung *A12* pi. de la ville de v. aut *A11* pi. grant et *A13* v. que lon faice ung *B1* v. aut *A6, A10, B, B2, B3, B4, B5* et grant dessus terre trois caves et (*A10* te. de tr. aulnes de long et *B2* te. bien tr. quaynes et que *B3* tr. quarres et *B4* tr. cainnes de hault et *B5* tr. toises et) d. 1083-1085 *B1* et grant dessus terre et y auroit trois caves dessoubz et d. y avoit une v. de fer dune cave de hault et quelle fust tant f. *A11* terre que s.

---

(ch. 5), and Chorier (pp. 30-31). The insistance on Vienne as the place of exile for Pilate may have resulted from the folk-etymology: *via gehennae* or "way of suffering." An alternate version, perhaps preserving an earlier tradition, has him banished to Lyons, of which he becomes a native-son (Vincentius Belvacensis, Book VII, ch. CXXIV, based on Comestor; Massmann, p. 597). This tradition is also incorporated into the *mystère* versions of the *Vengeance* (see Douhet, col. 999).

Popular interest in the story of Pilate's presence in Vienne developed a new local topography, involving sites important to the legend. Even in the seventeenth century, a tourist such as the Sieur du Verdier could write after a visit to Vienne that: "L'Église de Nostre-Dame de la Vie, ou la Vieille bastie en forme quadrangulaire, avec 8. colomnes de long, & quatre de large, est selon quelques-uns le Pretoire de Pilate, ou autre audience publique des Romains. On y void escrit au dehors, c'est la ponme du Sceptre de Pilate. On y monstre sa maison dans la ville possedée par des particuliers, la Tour où il fut gardé, & / une pyramide hors la ville, qu'aucuns croyent avoir esté sa maison, le lac ou abysme où il se precipita, & autres choses de son nom" (pp. 281-282). The "pretoire" is now known to have been a Roman temple; the "pyramide" (also referred to as Pilate's tomb) has recently been identified as part of the Roman circus (Rey, plates XXVI and XXVII). Similarly, a dark mountain, visible from Vienne and the legendary site of the pit which became Pilate's final resting place, is to this day called "Mont Pilat." There have been many bridges spanning the Rhone at Vienne, from Roman times to the present, many of which, singly or in combination, could have suggested aspects of the bridge that plays such an important role in Pilate's final moments. The pilings of the original, second-century Roman bridge may still be seen when the water is low, and remains of a second Roman bridge (or perhaps a wharf) have recently been discovered somewhat upstream, where it would have joined Vienne with the Roman residential community of Saint-Romain-en-Gal (Durand and Durand, pp. 24-25, photos of pp. 25, 55). The downstream bridge collapsed in the thirteenth century, as did a replacement bridge in 1407. Those interested in possible *etyma* for the sites identified with the name Pilate should see Charvet (pp. 40-41), and Chorier (pp. 31-32).

1082 *celle* [ *telle* Correction from all MSS except *A10, B7*.

le piler ait une gresse verge au milieu dudit piler qui ait une toise de aut et [54v] soit forte / que hom puïst atachier Pilate. Et puis que Pilate soit mis sus le piler et bien ataché a la verge tout droit et tout [nu], et soit oings de miel et d'uille. Et que hom face escripre sur le plus aut de la verge: 'C'est Pilate qui desconneü Jhesu Crist et regna l'empereur, son seigneur.' Et qu'il tiengne le visaige vers le souleil. Et quant il ara demouré de tierce jusques au vespre, qu'il en soit descendu et que hom lui hoste une des aureilles. Et

1084 *A1, A9* v. de fer au *A8* ledit p. *A7* v. qui *A13* v. de fer quil sera bonte a debout dicellui p. qui *A8* m. qui 1084-1085 *A10* une v. de fer dune aulne de long et quelle feust sur le p. au plus hault et quelle feust tant f. *B, B2, B3, B4, B5, A6* une v. de fer dune cave de hault et quelle (*B2, B4* une quayne de h. *B3* une aulne de h. *B5* fer de h. dune t. de h. et) s. *A12* v. mise pardessus le p. et que telle verge aie une t. de hault laquelle p. soustenir pi. 1085-1086 *A10* puist soustenir p. apres sur le p. si mis [ ]a *A13* s. grosses affin quel p. mieulx soubstenir p. et soit lye ledit p. a celle verge de fere sur ledit p.t.d. *A11* puist soustenir p. et dessus ait une grosse v. de fer ou il sera lye t. nud et debout de la haulteur dune toyse et s. *B, B1, B2, B3, B4, B5, A6* quelle pu. soustenir pi. et dessus sera mis p. et (*B2* pi. car la d. il devoyt estre mis et *B3* pi. et d. seroit mis pi. et) lie (*B1* p. et lie) a la (*B4* et quil soit lie contre la) v. de fer en (*B5* pi. et dessus pyller attach a icelle v. de fer seroit mis pylate et bien lie en) telle maniere que s. en piez et que s. tout nuz et que s.o. (*B2* lye tout en p. en ceste v. et la devoyt estre t. nu et le devoyt on oindre tout le corps) de 1086 *A12* b. lie a *A8* a.t.d. a la v.t. nu *A1* nuds et quil s. *A10* v. de fer en telle maniere que soit sur les piez et quil s. [ ] et quil s. *A12* v.t. nus o. 1086-1087 *A13* o. deuille et de m. et que lon escrpve sur le piler a p. *B2* m. et devoyt lon e. sur sa teste cestuy pi. 1086-1088 *A6, A10, A11, B, B1, B3, B4, B5* m. et qui ayt escript sur la teste cest (*B1* que dessus sa t. ait e. cest *B5* et fut e.) celluy qui d. (*A10* qui iuga *B5* et fut e. sur sa t. cest c. qui iuga a mort a grant tort et sans cause nostre seigneur) i. 1087 *A2* f. sur le p. hault de la v.e. cest *A12* la grosse v. 1087-1088 *A1* u. et quil 1088 *A12* qui iugia i.c. a mourir en la croix et r. *A12* son droitturier s. *A6, A10, B, B1* e. et *B5* r. et deshobey a le. et avecque ce quil 1088-1089 *A13* quil destruit i.c. son seigneur et quil soit le *B2* qui iugea a mourir en la croix le saint prophete et qui a r. son s.le. et auroyt le *A8, A11, B4* quil ayt le v. *A10* quil [ ] quar le s. et q. il avoit este la depuis tierce 1089 *A6* vers le conseil et *A1* s. et que on mecte dessus le plus hault de la v. escrips qui dient cest pilate qui descongneult ihesu crist et renoia lempereur son seigneur et *A12* s. levant et *A13* s. et demmouroit illec depuis tierce *A6, A11, A12, B, B1, B2, B3, B4, B5* ara este doy (*A11, B5* e. depuis *A12* a.d. la deys *B, B3, B4* e. de *B1* a. depuis *B2* a. la e. tous les iours depuys leure de) tierce 1089-1090 *A9* d. depuis leure de t.i. a leure de v. 1090 *A6, B* s. desvalee et 1090-1091 *A10* quil s. devalle et mis *A11, B1, B3* quil s. (*B1, B3* quil en s.) devalle et quon le mecte en *B4* s. devalez et que on le remecte en *B2* v. que on le face mectre en une fosse et luy oster une o. et que *B5* qui fut devale et fut mis en p. et luy fut d. *A6* hom le mecte em *A13* lui cope une a. et cuire a fere chault et soit miese en lieu quil la puisse veoir et

1086 *ataché* [ *atacher* Correction from MSS *A1, A2, A3, A7, A8, A9, A13*.
[nu] Addition from all MSS except *A10, A11, B7*.

puis soit mis em prison. Et qu'om lui donne asés a menger et qu'il n'ait point male prison, afin qu'il puisse vivre vint et ung jour en tourment comme il vesqui vint et ung jour du tresor que les juifs avoient mengé pour famine. Et que l'oureille soit mise en lieu out Pilate la puisse voir quant il sera sur le piler. Puis l'endemain qu'om li donne bien a diner et puis [qu'om le] retourne sus le piler bien oing. Et qu'il y soit jusques a vespres. Et puis que hom l'en descende et lui face hom courper l'autre

1091 *B* puis que on le mecte en *A1* pr. et que la prison ne soit point mauvaise et *A12* en chartre et *A12* a boire et a m. *A13* d. bien a boire et a m. 1091-1092 *A1, A6, A11, B, B1, B3, B5* m. afin *A10* d. bien a m. afin *B4* a boire et a m. afin 1091-1097 *B2* d. gueres a m. et le. et les aultres iours devoit estre mis dessus le p. et o. par tout le corps et apres que on luy f. oster la. 1092 *A13* quil vive plus longuement iusques a xxj *B1* pu. durer xxi *A1, A9* v. lespace de v. 1092-1093 *A10* v. au t. autant quilz *A7* v. xxi.i. du *A11* i. autant c. il v. luy et les iuifs v. 1092-1094 *B5* pu. plus longuement v. en t. ainsi c. les iuifz avoient longuement vescu du t. de iherusalem cestassavoir xxj ior et puis que on luy osta une o. et fut pendue en tel l. que on la *A12* t. ainsy c. il fist vivre soy et les autres i. du tresor qui estoit en la ville de iherusalem quilz mangerent quant leurs viandes leurs furent faillies et *A1* quil fist mengier aux i.p.f. et pour mauvaisete et 1093 *A3* t. quil avoit m. 1093-1094 *A11* t. qui estoit en iherusalem et puis quon luy oste une o. et la mecte len en *A6, B, B1, B3, B4* v. de tr.xxj. (*B* tr. luy et toutes ses ges xxx) i. et (*B1* et les autres aussi et *B3* xxi. quil maingeirent et) quon face prendre lo. (*B1* f. perdre une o. *B4* v. et fist vivre ceulx de iherusalem xxi.i. du tr. affin que lempereur ne ses gens ne trouvassent les tresors et on luy f. perdre une o.) et mectre en (*B1* et en faire pendre lo. en *B3* f. copper une o. et la pandre en *B4* et pendre en) tel l. qui la 1093-1096 *A10* t. que [ ] lui couppe une oreille et quon la [ ] en v. [ ] le p. apres au matin [ ] de ses mere et quon le[ ]xcileur b. 1093-1099 *A13* c. il fit vivre ceulx de iherusalem xxj.i. quil mangirent leurs t. quant leurs vivre furent failly et le lendemain que lon lui cope lautre o. a descendre du piller et que tous iours lon pensoit bien de lui et que lon lui faice doulce prison et que chascun iours ilz soit o. comme dessus le t.i. que 1094 *A7* m. ou *A8* l. la 1094-1096 *A6, B, B1, B3, B4* v. de dessus le pillier apres que le l. (*B* a.l. *B1* v.a.l. *B4* p. et sera le premier iour de son tourment le l.) au matin que (*B4* m. second iour que) on le face b. (*B4* f. pilate b.) d. et p. le mectre sur *B5* v. clerement de dessus le piler et le le. que on le fist b.d. et p. fut mis sus le p. et fut tres b. 1095 *A11* s. remis sur 1095-1096 *A11* e. au matin luy soit d. bien a boire et a manger et p. le remecte len sur *A8* et quon le r. 1095-1099 *A7* p. le t.i. que 1096 *A2, A9, A3* p. le face on retourner (*A3* p. que on le f.r.) sur *A1* piler et soit b. 1096-1097 *B4* o. comme dessus est dit et *B5* et la fut i. a heure de v. 1097 *A11* v. sur ledit pillier et *A12* on luy couppe la. 1097-1098 *B, B1, B3, B4, B5, A6* p. que (*B4* p. apres que) on le devale et (*B4* d. pour le remectre en prison et) que on luy oste (*B5* p. aprez luy fust o.) la. *A10* et pour que on lui couppe une autre 1097-1101 *B5* la. puis luy fut couppee une main et fust mise et pendue de coste les oreilles et au iiij.e luy fut oste et c. lautre m. et au vje iour que on luy osta une courroye du coste des le col iusques a la cuisse et le s.

1096 Addition from MS *A8*.

oureille et mettre avec l'autre. Et que hom lui donne assez a menger. Le tiers jours outel, et qu'om lui courpe le membre virili; le quart jour outel et courpe une main; le quint jour outel et c'om luy courpe l'autre main; le sisiesme jour outel, du cousté une couroye juques au rains; le setiesme jour outel et c'om lui face lever une autre couroie du travers; le huitiesme

1098 *B, B1, A6* et que elle soit mise coste (*B1* m. iouxte *A6* que on la mecte de c.) la. *B4* et quelle soit mise de coste lautre en tel maniere qui la puisse veoir dez sur le pilier le *A8* autre et tous iours a. *B2* la. que on luy avoyt ostee premierement le *A6* d. prou a 1098-1099 *A10* autre et [ ] lautre i. semblablement et 1098-1101 *B3* et quelle soit mise de coste la. et que on luy face semblablement et que on luy tranche une main et le vje 1099 *A2* i. com ly faice o. *A12* i. aussy que *A6, B* i. que on luy face semblablement et *B1* i. que on face semblant de luy coupper une main et le q. *A6, B* c. une main et le q. *A12* lui oste le *B4* i. que on luy face comme dessus et que on lui c. une main le *A13* m. secret le 1099-1100 *A2, A3, A7, A8, A9, A13* q.i.o. et com (*A7* i. com) luy c. *A12* q.i. que lon luy oste une *B1* q.i. de luy coupper lautre m. et le *B4* q.i. que on luy c. lautre m. *A6* q.i. semblablement que lon ly c. lautre main et le ve i. que on luy ostoit une courroye du costel doy le col iusques a la cuisse et le *B* i. semblable que lon luy oste lautre et au ve i. semblable que lon luy oste une courroye du coste du col iusques a la cuisse le *B2* i. que on luy face ainsi come devant et que on luy oste une mayn et laurtre i. ainsi come devant et que on luy oste laultre m. *A1* o.c. 1099-1101 *A11* i. quon le remecte sur ledit pillier conme dessus est dit et puis quon lui oste une main le q.i. quon luy oste lautre main le v.e.i. quon luy c. une couroye depuis le coul iusques a la cuisse le s. *A10* c. une main et au q. quon lui oste lautre main et au v.e.i. quon lui oste une courroie du coste du col iusques a la cuisse et au vj.e 1100 *A8* q.o. *A7, A12, A13, B4* i. que *A12* luy oste la. 1100-1101 *B2* i. que on le mecte ou pillier come devant et que on luy oste une corroye de la char du dos depuys le col iusques a la cuisse le s. *B1, B4* luy oste une grant couroye du col (*B4* o. de son corps une c. du couste dez le col) iusques a la cuisse le s. 1101 *B1* vje quon face semblant de luy oster une c. au travers du corps le *A1* o. et lui faire oster une iour. du coste i. *A2* o. et com lui oste du *A3* o. et que on luy hoste dun coste une *A7* iour que on lui oste du *A8, A12* iour o. et que (*A12* i. que) on luy fasse oster une cour. du coste du (*A12* luy oste dung c. une cour. du) col i. *A9* o. et que on lui couppe hoste et escorche du *A6, A10, A11, A13, B, B2, B4, B5* iour semblablement et (*B2* i. quil soit mis et la ou pilier et) que (*A10, A11, A13* i. que) on luy ostoit une cour. du mener du (*A11* une autre c. du travers du *B, B5* cour. de travers du *B4* i. luy soit oste de son corps une autre cour. du travers du) corps et (*A13* luy cope ung cour. dors le col i. es mains *B2* cour. de la char du travers du dos) le 1101-1102 *B3* iour semblablement et quon luy oste lautre main et au vij.e.i. semblablement et que on luy oste une c. de son costelz du col iusquez a la cuisse et le *B* vij. que *A11* s. quon luy f. oster la solle de pie le 1102 *A6, A7, A10, A12, A13, B4, B5* i. que *A1* o. et l. *B1* i. que on luy arrache les ongles des doiz et le *A8* f. oster une *A13* luy hoste une c. du costel droit le *A6, A10, A12, B, B5* l. la seulle des pies et (*A12* l. les trines une c. et) le *B4* luy liefve semelle de lung des piedz le 1102-1103 *A8* t. le corps le h.o. *A10, B, B1* h. quon 1102-1104 *B2* i. quil soyt amene et lye ou pillier et que on luy oste la solle de lung de piedz lautre iour apres que on luy face ainsi et que on luy oste laultre solle du piedz le

jour outel et que om lui face lever une semelle du pié; le nueviesme outel et que om lui face lever l'autre semelle; le disiesme jour que hom lui face lever une couroie despuis le nombril jusques au fondement; le onziesme jour que hom enlieve une autre du travers du lie[u] mesmes afin qu'il porte la crois comme il la fit porter a Jhesu Crist; le doziesme c'om lui coupe ung des bras jusques au cousde; le treziesme jour l'autre; le

1103 *A6, A7, A12, B5* i. quon *A11* i. oster lautre solle du *B3* i. pareillement que on luy oste une courroie de son corps et le vvvje pareillement que on luy luy f. *A13* i. ung s. du piz droit le *B4* i. quil soit mys oudit pillier comme dessus et que on luy liefve la s. de lautre p. le *A8, A12* f. oster une *B* l. lautre solle le *A2, A3* n. iour o. 1103-1104 *A6* f. oster lautre seule des p. et le ixe iour que *A10* l. la solle de lautre pie et le n. quon *B5* l. la sole de lautre p. et le n. iour que *A11, B, B1, B3* n. que *A12* n. iour que *A13* n. iour la. *B4* n. iour que on luy oste de son corps une courroye de son corps des le col iusques aux piedz le 1103-1105 *A7* n. iour que on lui f.l. 1104 *A6, A10, A11, A12, B, B1* f.l. une courroye du corps iusques (*A10, B, B1* du col i. *A11* f. oster une cour. depuis le col i.) aux pies (*A12* f. oster la.s. du pie) et le *A8* f. oster la *A3* la s. de la. pie le *A2, A8* i. autel et com *A9* s. du pie le xe i. autel et que *A10, B, B3* d. quon 1104-1105 *A13* i. ung c. dois la lamberuz i. *B1* x. e que on f. semblant de luy lever lautre corroie et le *B5* l. une couroie du travers du corps affin quil semblast quil portast la croiz devant et derriere aussi come il la fist porter a nostre seigneur ihesu crist et le o. *A8, A12* i. que hom lui f. oster une *A1* i. que hom lui oste une autre c. de hault i. *A11* i. que hom lui f. oster une autre c. du travers du corps affin quil semble quil porte la croix devant et derriere comme il fist porter a ihesu crist le 1105 *B4* l. de son corps une autre c. *A6, A10, B, B3, B4* c. du travers du (*A10* c. autroauter du) corps affin (*B3* c. du corps au travers a.) qui sembloit qui pourtoit la croix devant et derriere aussi comme la fit pourter a nostre seigneur ihesu (*A10, B* a i.) crist et le *A9* au pie le *B2* le col i. au piedz le 1105-1106 *B1, B2* xi.e que (*B2* xi.e i. que) on luy face lever une courroye de travers du corps (*B2* cour. devant et derriere et de t.) afin 1105-1107 *B, B4* xie que on luy rompe une espaule le 1106 *A8* i. autel que *A8* une de t. *A12* on luy fasse lever une a. corroye des trines du l. *A13* on lui hoste ung a. courroye afin *A1* au. corroie du t. afin *B1, B2* afin quil luy semble quil p. la c. devant et derriere aussi co. (*B2* p. une c. ainsi co.) il 1106-1107 *A11, A10, B3* on lui rompe une (*A10* lui couppe une) espaulle le *A6* on luy rompe une espaule et le xije iour que *B5* e. une a. couroie le 1107 *A13* c. ainsin quil *A1, A12, A13, B2* d. iour que *A9* xije iour autel et quon *A12, B1* a nostre seigneur i. 1107-1108 *B1* xije iour lui rompre une espaulle et le xiije *A6, A11, B, B3, B4, B5* lui rompe lautre et (*A11, B4* a. espaulle *B5* luy fut rompu ung des bras) le xiije *B2* luy rompe une espaulle lautre i. apre que on luy rompe la. espaulle le xiiije 1108 *A9* b. le xiije *A11* c. lautre le xiije *A1, A3, A12* a. bras le *A2* t.la. *A6, A9, A13* iour que on luy rompe ung bras (*A9* i. autel et quon lui couppe la.b. *A13* lui cope la. brase) et le xiiije 1108-1109 *B, A10, A11, B1, B3, B4, B5* t. quon (*A10, B5* t.i. quon luy rompe un bras le xiiije quon (*B1* t.i.la. espaulle et le xiiije i. que *A10* xiiije i. que *B5* r. lautre bas le xiiije i. que) on luy rompe lautre et samblera gavache le (*B1* r. ung braz et le *A1* xiiije i.la. braz le *A10, B4* a. bras le *B5* luy crieve les yeux le) xve que (*B4* xve iour que) on luy escorche la (*B5* luy fut escorcee la) barbe (*B1* xve a. braz et semblera gars casse et *B3* e. et) le *B2* xiiije que on luy rompe lung des bras et lautre apres le xve i. que on luy face arrachier la barbe le s. *A13* q.i. que lon lui cope lune *A6* q.i. que on ly rompe lautre et semblera guaniache et le xve i. que on ly escourchoit la barbe et le s. *A9* q.i. autel et que on lui couppe une e. le xve i. autel et quon lui couppe lautre le s. *A12* q.i. que on luy escorche la barbe le xve i. que on luy couppe lune des e. le s.

quatorziesme jour l'une des espaules; le quinziesme jour l'autre espaule; le seziesme jour c'om lui escorch[e] la barbe; le dis et setiesme jour c'om lui [55r] hoste l'un des pié; / le dis et huitiesme jour l'autre; le dis et nueviesme jour que hom lui rompe les cuisse comme il les fist rompre es deux larons qu'il fit pendre avec Jhesu Crist; le vintiesme jour le corps avec tous les membres soit trainé et pandu, et que c'om lui courpe la langue et qu'il la tiengne hors de la bouche; et le vint et uniesme jour c'om lui face hoster la

1109 *A2, A3, A7, A8* a. le *A9* i. autel et quon lui hoste ung des piez le *A12* i. lautre et le 1109-1110 *A11, B, B3, B4* s. quon luy couppe ung pie (*B4* luy rompe lung des p.) le 1110 *A6, A10* lui rompoit ung piez et le *B1* luy fera escorcher la *B2* on luy oste lung des piedz le *A3* s. que *A1, A7* i. com lui coppe lun 1110-1111 *B5* luy couppe le pie dextre et le xvije que on luy couppe lautre le xviije que on luy rompe une cuisse le dis et n. *A9* i. autel et quon lui couppe lautre le *A6* i. que on ly rompe lautre et le *A10, A11* i. com lui rompe lautre (*A11* lui couppe la.) pie *B, B3* xviie que luy couppe lautre le *B1* i. com lui fera couper ung pie *B2* xviie que on lui h. lautre p. *B4* i. que on luy rompe lautre p. 1111 *A9* i. autel et que *A13, B1* i. que lon lui hoste la. (*B1* luy couppera la.) pie le *B, B3, A6* xviije que (*A6* xviije i. que) on luy rompe une cuisse le *A10* i. que on luy rompe [ ] le *A11* h. quon luy rompe une cuisse le *B4* i. que on luy rompe lune des iambes le *A1* a. pied le 1111-1112 *B3* xixe que on luy face romppe lautre ainsi quil f.r. lez cuissez aux *A8* lui fasse rompre les 1111-1113 *B2* i. que on luy face rompre les deux cuisses ainsi come il les fist rompre aux deux larrons qui furent pendus avecques ihesu crist le *A10* lui [ ] ainsi quil f. plour[ ] l. qui fure[ ] le *A12* luy fasse casser une des c. et le 1112 *A9* r. une des c. et le xixe iour autel et quon lui face rompre lautre c. *A11,B* r. lautre c. ainsi c. il f.r. les c. aulx *A1* il f. *A8* il f. faire aulx d. *A7* f.r. aux l. 1112-1113 *B4* r. lautre iambe et sera ainsi comme il f.r. les deux cuisses aux d.l. qui furent pendus a. nostre seigneur i. *B5* r. lautre et le *A6* r. lautre ainssi c. il f.r. les cuisses des d.l. que furent pendus de coste nostre seigneur ihesu crist et le xxe i. que on luy rompe le co. *A13* f. es d.l. que estoient pendut a. *B3* qui fuirent pendus a. nostre seigneur i. *A11* l. penduz avec nostre seigneur ihesu crist le co.

1112-1116 *B1* les c. et le xxe lautre cuisse aussi come fist rompre les cuisses aux deux larrons que furent penduz avecques nostre seigneur ihesu crist et le xxje que on luy rompe tout le corps et tous les membres et quon luy couppe la langue de la bouche et le xxije iour on luy face tailler la teste et que on face amasser tous les membres de luy et le mectre sur

1113 *B* a. nostre seigneur le xxe est que on luy rompe le co. *B3* xxe que on luy romppe le co. *A7* i. les a. *A8* les aultres m. *A9* i. autel et que le *B2* i. que on luy rompe le *B4, B5* i. que on luy rompe tout (*B5* r.) le 1113-1114 *A10* iour que on lui rompe le c. et tenir les m. si que on lui ost la la l. de *B, B3, B5, A6* m. et que on luy taille la l. (*B5* l. et que on luy osta) de 1113-1115 *A11* co.s.t. au gibet et quon luy taille la l. le *B2* m. et que on luy tirille la l. de la b. apres que on luy coppe la t. *A12* iour lautre et xxie i. le corps avec tous les autres membres et quil soit traitre que lon luy ostez la langue et que lon lui 1113-1116 *B4* m. et puis le xxie et derrier iour qui soit mys sur ledit pillier en sa maniere que dessus et que on luy coppe la t. et puis apres que lon f. amasser tous ses membre et mectre sur 1114 *A1* t. et que 1114-1115 *A1, A2* l. le

1115 *B5* b. dont il donna la sentence contre nostre seigneur et le condempna et iuga a mort a grant tort et sans cause et *B* xxje que *A1, B* f. copper (*B* f. tailler) la *A10, B5, A6* lui couppe (*A6* luy tailloit) la 1115-1116 *B3* xxje que on luy f. trancher la t. de dessus lez espaulles et que on face assembler tous lez membres et mettre dessus *A11* f. coupper la et puis quelle soit mis *A13* lui cope la t. et quelle s. *A6, B2, B5* om f. (*B2* om luy f.) amasse (*B5* om a.) tout les membres et mectez (*B2* et mectre tout *B5* et que fussent mis) sur 1115-1117 *A8* i. quil s. ars

teste et que hom la face seigner afin qu'il dure plus longuement. Et qu'il soit mis sur le piler en la place afin qu'il en soit remembrance, et qu'il soit ars et que les sendres soient gitees au Rousne. Et veés yssy coment nous le jugons a mort male et ourible pour ce qu'il fu traïtre a Dieu et a vous, et pour ce qu'il a fet mourir tout son peuple."

[70] Et quant l'empereur oÿ qu'il l'avoient eincy jugé a mort, et il dist es

1116 *A1* hom le mette sur *B* f. amasser touz les membres et mectre sur 1116-1119 *A10* f. amasser et tous ses membres dessus le pillier et puis apres quon face le corps et les membres et toutes les choses de luy ardre et quon gecte la s. au r. ainsi mourra de malle mort car il 1117 *A11* pi. dessus dit a. *A3, A9* r. puis apres quil 1117-1118 *A13* piler a. quil s. tous iours mais memoire de pilate et que le corps et les membres soient ars et mis en s. et g. *A11* r. et apres ce p. mis son corps par quartiers et puis apres toutes ces choses faictes quon face amassez tous les membres de luy et les face len ardre et mectre en se. et que on gecte ladite cendre au *A12* r. et puis apres x iours quil s. ars et mis en s. et g. *A8* et les s.g. 1117-1119 *B, B1, B3, B4, B5, A6* piler long (*B4* p. et la les faire tenir l. *B3* p. et quil y soit l.) temps pour (*A6* p.p.) r. et (*B5* pi.p.r. et quil y demourast pour l.t. et) puis apres que (*B4* a. ainsi fait) on face le corps et les membres et les costes de (*B3, A6* m. et toutes les chosez de) luy ardre (*B4* corps et tous les m. de luy a. *B1* corps et tous les m. de luy tout a. *B5* f. tout le corps et tous les m.a.) et mectre en (*A6* m. tout en) s. et que (*B4* et puis que) lon g. (*B5* s. et fut g.) la cendre ou (*B1* s. ou) r. ainsi mourra de male mort car (*B4* de malvaise mort pylate car *B5* mort comme il devoit car) il *B2* pillier pour en avoir memoyre et puys les faire ardoir en s. et apres que on foreigne la cendre et que on la gette dedans la riviere du r. et ainsi il moura de male mort p. 1118 *A3, A8, A11* v. (*A11* v. la) c. 1118-1119 *A7* i. de malle et o. mort p. *A8* a male mort et *A11* i. a mourir de cruelle mort nonobstant quil avoit bien desservye plus malle et o. car il *A12* a male mort et horriblement mourir p. 1118-1132 *A13* i. et quil luy poura fer plus de malx que lon luy faice car ilz la bien deservy adoncques le. lenvoya a v. par lx.c. ensamble la sentence et l. deppart lempereur et q. 1119 *B2* a ihesu crist et *B4* d. ihesu crist et *B5* d. premierement et *A10* a son seigneur et a *A12* d. ihesu crist et a lempereur son droitturier seigneur et a 1119-1120 *A9* v. sire empereur et aussi p. ce quil est coulpable davoir f. *A11* d. et a son seigneur souverain et par luy est mort moult de p. 1119-1121 *A1* o. et *A2* v. et *A6, B, B1, B2, B3, B4, B5* d. et a son seigneur lempereur et a f.m. moult de p. (*B2* le. *B5* le. de romme et avoit f. grant quantite de p.m.) q. 1120-1121 *A9* p. par le conseil quil donna de mangier le tresor et *A10* m. moult de p. mal fut conseille pillate quant il fist ainsi destruire le saint prophette dont la fin en sera mauvaise pour lui et les sciens q. *A12* m. si grant p. et mis a mal tant de bons lieux et pays et 1121 *A11, A12* ouy comment (*A12* o. eincy c.) les senateurs eurent i. pilate il d. *A1* a.i. *A10* a. ordonne il 1121-1122 *B5* i. pylate il en fut grandement content et en eust moult grant ioie puis commanda aux c. *B, B1, B2, B3, A6* a mourir il (*A6* a mort il) commanda a x. (*B1, B3, A6* aux) c. *A8, A12, A10* es (*A10* a ces) c. 1121-1123 *B4* que e. les senateurs de rome a.i. pylate a morir il manda de ces c. et leur commanda quilz g. bien pylate car il convenoit quilz le m. a v. sur le roone iusticier de part

1116 *dure* [ *vive* Correction based on MSS *A2, A3, A7, A9*. MS *A12* agrees with *A*.

dis chevaliers qui le gardoient qu'il l'amenassent au prevost de Vienne de part lui. Et leur bailla lettres seelees qu'il pourtassent audit prevost et la sentence donnee par les senateurs de Rome. Et qu'il l'eyscecutast. Lors les dis chevaliers menerent Pilate a Viene au prevost et luy porterent les lettres et la sentence. Et quant les bourgois de la ville seürent que les chevaliers estoient venus de par l'empereur, leur seigneur, il leur firent

1122 *A1* qui lavoient en garde que *A12* qui g. pilate quilz *B, B1, B3, B5, A6* g. car il (*B1* g. bien et quil *B3* g. bien car il) convenoit quilz le m. a v. iusticier (*B5* g. a v. pour le i. et mettre a execution) de *A11* a. de par luy au 1122-1123 *B2* g. et quil failloit quil le m. iusticier de par luy a v. et quil *A11* v. et 1122-1124 *A10* g. il bien et quil convenoit quilz m. iusticier de p. lui a v. et leur fist faire l. pour porter aux iusticiers de vienne a la s. de pillate [ ]stoit d. 1123 *A8* et lui envoya l. *A3* s. de son seel pour porter a p. de vienne avecques la *A7* s. pour pourter a. *A12* et aussy quilz p. la 1123-1124 *B, B1, B3, B5, A6* leur fist faire l.x. (*B5* l. closes et s.) pour (*B3* l.p.) porter aux iusticiers de vienne et la (*B5* v. avecques la) s. de pilate qui estoit (*B1* e. gectee et) d. *B4* et puis ung certain iour apres il ordonna esdits chevaliers quilz menassent pylate a vianne et leur fist baillier par escript la s. qui estoit estee d. *A11* s. esquelles estoient contenuz les proces et la s. de r. et l. *B2* po. la s. que les 1123-1125 *A8* po. comme lez s. de r. avoyent d. la sentence sur pylate et que ainsy fut fait et l. les c. 1124 *A1* par L les *A7* le putrifase l. *A9* quilz la feissent exequter et dissent audit prevost quil le. *A12* et sellee de son seel et l. 1124-1125 *B, B1, B3, A6, A10* que facent la execucion de pilate adonc les (*A10* quil meissent a e.p. [ ] s) c. *B2* r.a.d. a lencontre de pilate adoncques m. *B5* r. et commandoit quilz feissent lexecution de pylate come a eulx appartenoit de raison adont les c. de lempereur m. *B4* r. et leur dist quilz deissent aux iusticiers de vyanne que la sentence pilate feust acomplie et quilz feissent lexecucion selon le conntenu de la sentence et 1125 *A12* c. prirent congie de lempereur et m. *A1* luy baillerent les *A8* p. et les *B2* v. pour le iusticier et p. 1125-1126 *A10* p. [ ]ur iusticier et les lierent corps [ ] pillate qui estoit d. par les senateurs de romme et q. *A11* c. qui gardoient pilate le prindrent et puis se misdrent au chemin pour aller a v. quant les chevaliers dessusdictz furent a v. ilz amenerent p. tout droit au p. de vienne et luy baillerent les l. de par lempereur et q. *B, B1, B3, B5, A6* v. et aux (*B3* et le presenteirent aux) iusticiers et les (*B5* i. et leur baillerent de par lempereur les) l. closes ou (*B1* l. ou) estoit la s. de pilate et (*B3* i. avec sa s. et) q. 1125-1131 *B7* v. et quant il furent a vienne les seigneurs dilec l. fist g.h. pour lamour de lempereur et 1126 *B2* l. selees et la s. de pilate et firent tant quil vindrent arriver a vienne et q. 1126-1127 *B4* l. de lempereur aux iusticiers et la s. de pilat et q. ilz furent venus a vianne et les b. de vianne oyrent dire que e.v.c. de le. de rome l.s. *A6, B, B1, B3* les b. de (*B3* lez iusticiers de) vianne oyrent dire que e.v. des c. de le. (*B* de par le.) de romme l.s. *B2* de vienne s. quil e.v. des gens de *A10* de vienne oyrent dire quil e. [ ] c. de le. [ ] ilz eurent moult g. ioye si l.f. 1126-1128 *B5* de vienne ouyrent dire que le les c. de le. de romme e.v. ilz eurent moult g. ioie et l.fi. tres g. chiere et g.h. et lors lesdits c. 1127 *A11* c. de le.e.v. ilz allerent devers eulx et l.f. 1127-1129 *A12* fi.g.fe. et g.h. et tantost les c. firent bien leur messagie et vont bailler pi. au pr. comme iusticier et les 1127-1131 *B, B1, B2, B3, B4, A6* ilz eurent moult g. (*B2* e.g.) ioye et l.fi. moult g.f. et (*B1* fi. tous g.f. et g.h. aux c. et *B2* fi.g.f. et g.h. et) les (*B4* g. chiere et g.h. et les) c.b. (*A6* ioye et b.) aux (*B3* c. eurent delivrey pilate aux) iusticiers les l. et p. et (*B4* r. de vianne les l. de le. contre pilate et) sa s. que a. (*B2* l. et s. de pilate que la s.a.) d. les s. de r. en escript et distrent l. (*B4* d. les chevaliers aux iusticiers l.) m. et moult (*B2* d.l.m. et moult) dautres (*B3* l. dirent l.m. et plusieurs a.) n. et veu les (*B2* n. de romme et de

1123 *leur* [ *lui* Correction from MSS *A1, A2, A3, A6, A7, A9, A10, B, B1, B3, B5*. MSS *A8* and *A11* agree with *A*.

grant honneur et grant feste. Et les chevaliers baillerent Pilate au prevost et les lettres et la sentense que les senateurs de Rome avoient donnee a Pilate. Et acheverent leur messagerie [et leur dirent] des nouvelles de Rome. Et quant le prevost eüt veües les lettres et la sentance, il fist incontinent fere une chayre fetice. Et puis il fist mettre Pilate et la il estoit assés a son aise, mes il ne se pouvoit bougier. Et puis il fist mettre Pilate avec la chaiere dedens un puis, mes la chaire estoit bien atachee en chaines

---

iherusalem quant les iusticiers eurent ouy les nouvelles et visite les) l. (*B5* les nouvelles et l.) de lempereur (*B3* l.) et la 1128 *A10* h. adont les *A1* c. delivrerent p. 1128-1129 *B5* b. aux iusticiers les l. de lempereur et s. de pylate que a.d. les *A3* pr. de vienne avec lesdictes l. 1128-1130 *A11* h. et et g.f. et l. dirent les chevaliers des 1128-1131 *A10* b. aux iusticiers de lempereur qui leur [ ]oient et aussi baillerent pillate et sa s. laquelle a.d. les s. de r. en escript et dirent l.m. et moult merveilles quant les iusticiers eurent v. *A1* pr. et ainsy orent acheve l.m. et 1129 *A9* senateurs a. 1129-1130 *A12* senateurs a.d. contre p. et les chevaliers vont achiver *A8* d. sur p. *A9* d. contre p. *A7* d. contre p. et l. dirent des 1129-1131 *B5* r. en escript et dirent l.m. et plusieurs aultrez n. et veues les l. de lempereur et la 1130 *A9* a. de dire et faire l. 1131 *A3* p. de vienne ot *A11* et de lempereur et de ses choses advenues depuis la destruction de iherusalem dont tous verierent dieu et q. *A11* p. de vienne ot leu des l. de lempereur esquelles estoit contenue la *B7* q. il eurent les l. de lempereur et la 1131-1132 *A13* v. la s. et l. deppart lempereur luy et toutes la cite luy firent grant honneur adoncques le prevost luy fit fere une belle c.f. pour y m. *A12* s.i. il fist fere une 1131-1133 *A11* s. de pilate i. fist fere une chayne de fer et quant elle fut faicte il fist asseoir p. dessus et lyer a. *A10* s. de pillate et tantost firent faire une c. toute neufve et la firent ferir dedans en telle maniere quil e. a *B, B1, B2, B3, B4, B5, A6* s. de pilate tantost (*B3* p. randue par lez senateurs t.) firent faire une c. toute (*B1* c. de fer t. *B4* une bonne c. de fer t.) neuve et (*B5* t. sans delay f.f. grose c. desquellez et) lasidrent dedens (*B3* et a.p.d. *B4* et midrent p.d.) en telle maniere quil (*B5* t. guise quil) estoit bien a son aise mes il (*B2* et le firent seoyr dedans et *B5* a. combien quil) ne 1131-1141 *B7* s. pillate tantost sans delay firent faire grose chainnez desquellez lierent pillate et puis le desvallerent aupres de leaue en apres firent faire le p. selon lordonnance des senateurs de romme q. 1132 *A7* fere chayne fausse et *A8, A12* c. toute f. *A12* p. en celle chiere et e. 1132-1133 *A1* e. assis a *A13* p. bien assis a 1133 *A2* a.a. mes *A12* puys le prevost f. 1133-1134 *A11* p. mouvoir ne oster de la chayne et en icelluy estat le fist devaller en ung *A13* p. mouvoir car ilz estoit bien enchaynez puis le fist avaler a une c. de fer d. *A3* m. la c.a.p.d. 1133-1136 *B, B1, B2, B3, B4, B5, A6, A10* p. oster de (*A6* p. partir de) la chaire et (*B1,B4* la chaisne et) p. le (*B4, B5* p. apres le) firent devaler en (*A6* f. avalez en *B2* p. mouvoir ne le c. aussi et le fist on avaller en) un puis (*B1* en my le p.) iusques au pres (*B2* i. bien p. *A10* au plus p.) de leau (*A6* p. tant que les pies moilerent en le.) et une (*B1, B3* e. avecques une *A6* et avoit une *B4* e. avec la *A10* et fut devalle en une) chaine de fer et fut la a. (*A6* fut liez a.) que (*B4* la i. *B5* fut illecque a.i. ad ce que *A10* c. et fut la i. a ce que) le
1134 *A7* la chayne d. *A7, A11* la chainne e.b. (*A11* e.) a. *A8* p. et e.a. 1134-1135 *A1* p. tant que pilate ne *A12* p. et la e.a. la c. avec grans c. si que pilate ne *A13* p. en icelle chasse et ne *A9* c. la ou il e. assiz b.a. au pont a chaynnes de fer pendant aval sur le rosne en telle maniere quelle ne povoit touchier a *A7* at. de

1130 Addition based on MSS *A2, A3, A7, A8, A9, A11, A12*.
1133 *aise* [ *aiser* Correction from all MSS except *B7*.

de fer sy que elle ne touchoit point a l'eau. Et la il demoura jusques a tant que le piler fust fet. Et la hom lui donnoit assés a boire et a menger
[55v] chascun jour. /

[71] Puis le prevost fist fere le piler et ordener la plasse. Et se tint bien liement [avecques] les chevaliers qui avoient mené Pilate car il ne vouloit qu'i[l] s'en retournascent a tant que la justice fust faite. Et ossy les bourgois de la ville leur fesoient tous jours bonne compaignie. Et quant le piler fust fet et du tout ordonné le soir de quoy l'ondemain se devoit fere la justice,

1135 *A11* fer affin quil ne 1135-1136 *A13* i. le 1136 *A2* d. a 1136-1137 *A2* m.a. ung c. 1136-1138 *A10* fet et si lui donnerent aux gens assez et firent faire *B, B1, B2, B3, B4, B5* b. et luy donnerent a m.a. apres firent (*B2* m. tous les i. apres les iusticiers de vienne f. *B1* a. et f. *B4* d.a.m. et p.f.) faire (*B5* d.a.m. et firent) le *A1* a. a m. et a b. et le pr.t. *A8* m. et commanda a faire le p. et se 1136-1141 *A6* et luy donnerent a m.a.q. 1136-1143 *A13* fet et adoncques lon le tira du pues et la grant froidure de leauue luy fit tellement peler le visaige quil 1137-1139 *A11* i. adoncques commanda le p. de vienne de faire le p. conme dit est et le c. 1138 *A12* puis apres incontinent le pr. *A12* pi. en la pl. de vienne et se *A13* la pilate et 1138-1140 *B, B1, B2, B3, B4, B5* pi. en la pl. bien (*B1, B3, B4, B5* pl. de vienne b.) a point et les c. distrent (*B4* c. lors d. *B2* c. qui a.m.p.d.) aux iusticiers que (*B4* i. de vienne que) ne (*B2* pl. tres b. les c. quil ne) sen 1138-1141 *A10* le p. en la[ ]lac[ ]de vienne lors les c[ ] dirent aux iusticiers [ ] sen retourneren[ ] eurent veu la[ ] adont les iusticiers de vienne en furent moult ioyeulx et leur donnerent souvent [ ] faissoient moult grant honneur q. 1139 *A1* c. car *A7* c. de lempereur car *A12* car le prevost ne 1139-1140 *A11* ne sen voulurent partir de vienne a. quilz eussent veu la iustice estre faicte de luy et le prevost et les 1140 *A7, A8, A12* r. iusques a *B, B1, B2, B3* t. que eussent veu la iustice de (*B2* veu fayre la i. et lexecussion au corps de) pilate et les *A8* fust acomplie et 1140-1141 *B4* r. a rome devers lempereur a. quilz eussent veu la iustice de pylate pour le vray rappourter a lempereur et les iusticiers et b. de vianne en eurent grant grant ioye et les tindrent bien aise et l. firent grant honneur q. *B5* quilz eus[ ] veue la iustice mettre a execution et la fin de pilate et ce pleust moult aux b. et en eurent grant ioie et don[ ]a disner souvent aux chevaliers et firent grant honneur et gran[ ] reverence q. *A11* b.l. *A7* faite et q. *A12* b. et les autres gens destat les faysoient t.i.b. chiere et b.c. *B, B1, B2, B3* b. en eurent grant ioie et l. (*B2* b. de vienne l.) donnerent souvent a digner et l. (*B3* ioie et l.) f. grant (*B2* g. feste et grant) honneur q. 1141 *A8* v.f. *A9* v. de vienne l. *A8, A11* b. chere aux chevaliers (*A11* chiere) et 1142 *B, B1, B3, B4, B5, B7, A6* fet bien a point a leure (*B4* p. et vint que le. *B5* p. il estoit e.) de vespres et (*B1, B3, B4* v. estoit et) la. 1142-1143 *A11* s. devant que lon d. *A10* fet bien a point qant vint le l. environ vespres qui d. estre mis sur le pillier les iusticiers firent traire h. *B2* fayt bien a point a leure de vespres les iusticiers le l. firent tirer pilate h. *A11* i. dudit pilate le p. le f. mectre h. *A6, B, B1, B4, B5, B7* d. estre pylate mis dessus les (*B* e.m.d.p. les *B7* e.m.d.p. lors les *B1* d. le pillier et les *B4* e.m.p.d. le pillier pour le premier iour et les) iusticiers le (*B4* i. de vienne lors le) firent traire (*B4* t. hors *B5* e.m.p.d. le piller et le f. les i.t. *B7* i. de viennez le tirerte hors) du *B3* lo. plate d. estre mis dessus le pilier et les iusticiers le firent traire du

1136 *fust fet* [ *fust fust fet*
1139 Addition from MSS *A1, A2, A3, A7, A8, A9, A11*.

le prevost fist geter Pilate hors du puis. Et Pilate fust sy changé qu'il n'eüt pas visage d'ome mes de deable. Et lors il [le] fist mettre en ung lieu ou il fust aucunement a son aise. Et fust mis a une tour qui estoit sur le pont de Viengne en la riviere du Rosne laquelle tour estoit moult fort et si avoit trois souliers, et le Rosne aloit tout environ de la tour. Et au premier soulier de la tour le prevost fist mettre gardes, et au plus haut ossy. Et au milieu il fist mettre Pilate pour estre bien a son ayse.

[72] Et quant il vint l'endemain a heure de tierce, le prevost ala a la tour

1143 *A2* f.p.g.h. *A8* f. mettre p. *A12* f. boutter h.p. du *A11* puys mais il f. si fort c. *A12* et quant p.f. hors du puys il f. sy 1143-1145 *B, B1, B2, B3, B4, B5, B7, A6, A10* pr. et il fut tout (*A10* il le trouverent t.) c. par le v. tant que il (*B1, B3, B5* fut tant c. par le v. quil *A6* et quant il fut trait il fut t.c. par le v. que il) sambloit bien d. (*B1, B3, B4, B7* s. dun d. *B5* s. proprement ung d. denfer *A10* v. qui s. ung d.) et adonc (*B2* p. et pilate qui estoit tant c. par le v. que cestoyt grant hydeur donc) le (*A6* s. avoir ung d. et l. il le) firent m. en une t. qui (*B7* d. et non poinct home lors le midrent en une prison qui) e. (*B4, A6* t.) sur 1144 *A11* o. se sembloit mes *A8* l. le prevost le 1144-1145 *A11* d. et quant le prevost vit cecy si le fist m. au large en une *A12* et le prevost le fist m. a large en une grant t. *A13* d. et fut menne le soir que lon le devoit le lendemain mettre sur le piler en une t. qui e. a la valee du p. *A1* en une 1145 *A8* f. plus a *A7* et f. en une *A12* e. soubz le 1145-1146 *B2* le rosne et e. 1146 *A6, A10, A13, B, B1, B4, B5* v. pres de (*A10* v. qui estoit sur *A13* v. et estoit assises en *B* v. iouste *B1* v. iusques a *B4* v. de coste *B5* v. emprez) la *B7* v. du coste du *B3* v. de coste le r. qui e. *A1, A6, B* l.e. *A10* r. tout a lentour et y a. *A12* ro. qui e. moult preffont en celle t.a. *A13* ro. et e. icelle t. moult grande et moult fourb et en icelle a. *B1* ro. que e. *A11* v. ou couroit le r. tout *A1* f. et la il estoit mieulx a son aise que devant et la tour a. *B2* f. icelle tour a. 1146-1147 *B5* ri. et aloit la riviere t. a lentour et y avoit t.s. et au *B7* ri. et le rousne alloist t. alentour et estoit une t. moult forte et en celle tour avoit t. canbliers et au 1146-1148 *B, B1, B3, B4, A6* et aloit le r.t. entour et (*B1* e. de la tour) y avoit iij (*B4* a. en ladicte tour t.) s. et au (*B3* t. estaiges au) p.s. (*A6* t.s. *B3* p. estaige) f. 1147 *A10* t. planchers et au *A13* t. estaiges que le p. *A2, A3, A9* r. couroit t. *A12* et la riviere du r. *A8* e. et *A12* t. entour de *B2* s. ou 1147-1148 *A11* et dedans f. 1147-1150 *A10* p. plancher fist mectre gens darmes pour garder pillate quil ne sen fouist q. *B7* p. firent estre gens armez pour garder que p. ne poeult eschapper par maniere quelquonquez q. 1148 *A1* s. le p. mist bonnes g. *B2, B5* s. firent *A8* p. de vienne f. *A8* au segond il 1148-1149 *A12* s. il f.m. sergens et au second il 1148-1150 *A11* g. et sergnes pour le garder et q. *A13* g. sergent ou second estaiges f.m. gens darmes et ou tier f.m.p. et q. *B, B1, B2, B3, B4* m. gens darmes pour garder pi. et au segond f. (*B4* t. solier f.) m.p. et au tiers fist (*B4* t. solier f.) mettre gens (*B1* t.g. darmes) pour garder que (*B4* g. pilate quil) ne fouist (*B2* p. et avec luy g.da. qui le gardoyent de sen aller) q. *B5, A6* m. gens darmes pour garder quil ne sen fuist q. 1149 *A9* m. de ladicte tour il *A2* e. plus a 1149-1150 *A8* pour le mieulx garder et e. myeulx a son a. affin quil puist soustenir la iustice et cet. et q. *A9* pi. et q. *A12* pi. et au plus hault des gardes et les sergens pour garder pilate et q. 1150 *A13* e. matin le p. et tous les chevaliers sen alirent en la *A12* ala t. *B2* t. les iusticiers allerent a 1150-1151 *B, B1, B3, B4, B7, A6, A10* e. les (*B7* e. matin que les) iusticiers (*B1* les chevaliers et i.) volurent (*B4* i. de vyanne v.) aler (*B7* i.a.) querir p. et le (*B4, B7* p. pour le) mettre sur le pillier et (*B4* et vindrent vers le pont pres de la tour ou

1145 *aucunement* [ *ancontment* Correction from MSS *A2, A3, A7, A9*.

pour mener Pilate a la justice. Et sy mena avec lui les chevaliers que lui avoient amené Pilate. Et quant il furent a la tour, il distrent es gardes qu'il amenassent Pilate. Et tout le pont et la riviere estoit plaine de gens qui voul[o]ient veoir la justice. Et quant il voussirent penre Pilate, la tour dedens et dehors et par tout les crenelx fust toute plaine de deables qui distrent: "Il est nostre, il est nostre! Laissiés le nous!" Et toute la tour

---

estoit pilate et) les 1150-1155 *B5* q.l. le iusticiers vouldrent aler querir p. pour le mettre sur le pillier et quilz furent sur le pont et tout le peuple et que les gens qui le gardoient le cuiderent amener toute la tour commen[ ]a trembler et dessus et dessoubz et tout a lentour et sur les c. avoit tant de 1151 *A12* p. vers le pilier et m. *B2* p. au pillier et les *A1* lui dix c. *A3, A7, A12* les x.c. 1151-1152 *A11* p. pour mectre au pillier et estoient avec luy les c. de lempereur que av. *B2* c. estoyent devant et *A1* qui la. a et 1151-1153 *A13* a iugement et tellement que t. 1151-1155 *B, B1, B3, B4, A6, A10* c. estoient avec eulx sur (*B3, A6* c.a. eulx et es. sur *B7* c. de lempereur es. sur) le pont et (*B4* c. de lempereur a. eulx et) tout le peuple et (*B1* p. aussi et) q. les (*A10* et lors les) gens (*B4* p. aussi et commanderent les iusticiers aux g.) qui le gardoient le volurent admener toute (*A6* v. traire dehors t. *A10* a. et lors t.) la tour commanca a trambler (*B3* a croller et a t.) et dessus et entour et (*B4* e. la tour et) dessus les (*B1* d. la tour et e. les) c. avoit (*B4* c. de la tour a.) tant (*A10* c.t.) de *B7* c. de lempereur estoient sur le pont avecques tous ceulx de la citez quant ceulx qui le gardoient le vollure prendre et mettre hors de la prison toute la tour estoyent de d. 1152 *A12* am. et grant foyson dautre gens et *A12* g. et es sergens quilz 1152-1154 *B2* aux gens darmes qui gardoyent pi. quil venissent avec luy et doncques vindrent tant de gens a vienne et si grant peuple pour veoyr 1153 *A3* et lors t. *A11* pi. au lieu ou lon devoit fere iustice et a celle heure t. *A8* pont et la tour e. *A12* pont de vianne et environ la *A13* pont e. 1153-1154 *A8* g. pour veoir 1154 *A11* vo. fere la i. de pilate et *A13* q. les garde vous *A7* il vindrent vers pi. *A11* pi. toute la 1154-1155 *A12* vous opasser pour entrer en la t. et dedens la tour et dehors sur les *A1* t. fut toute plaine de diables par dedens dehors et c. qui 1154-1157 *B2* i. que cestoyt chose ius[ ]e quant on voulut amener pilate et mectre hors de la tour elle conmenca a tramblier moult fort adoncques les iusticiers et les gens darmes et tous ceux qui estoyent la dedans vindrent sur le pont et e. 1155 *A11* dehors et sur les *A13* dehors et dessus estoit p. *A11* f.p. 1155-1156 *B, B11, B5* qui crioient (*B5* c. forment et horriblement *A11* c. a haulte voix) il *A12* dea. et tout le peuple visiblement les veoit et crioyent tous les deables il est n.l. *A6* qui crient il est n.l. 1155-1157 *B1, B3, B4, B7, A10* qui croient il (*B4* que merveilles quilz c. moult fort il *B7* c. en disant il) est n.l. le ester et adoncques (*A10* c.l. le il est n.a.) les chevaliers et iusticiers et les gens (*B3* a. les i. et c. et les g. *B4* a. les i. de vianne les c. et g. *B5* n. quant il est n.a. les c. et les g. *A10* a. les i. de lempereur et les g.) que estoient dedens en tour (*B3* e. entour *B4* e. entour la tour *B5* qui y e.) e. 1156 *A8* il est tout n. il est tout n. *A7* d. il est n.l. *A13* d. a une voix il est mien il est mien l. *A2* il est n. il est n. et t. *A7* nous tellement que toute *A11, A13* nous car il est noustre et (*A13* est men et) la 1156-1157 *A6, B* le n. et (*B* le ester et) adonc les iusticiers et les chevaliers et les gens qui estoyent entour e. *B5* nous quant il nostre adont les chevaliers et les gens qui y estoient e.

1156 *distrent il est* [ *distrent il que distrent il est*

trembloit. Et quant le prevost et les gardes virent cella, il en eürent tres grant peür. Et puis yssirent hors de la tour et monterent sur le pont et virent les deables sur les creneaulx. Et la tour toute entiere avec Pilate et avec les deables s'en entra dedens l'eau du Rosne en abisme. Et quant le prevost, les chevaliers, les bourgois et l'autre gent virent cela, il se

1157 *A2, A3, A7, A9* p. et les v.c. et les guardes aussi ilz *A11* t. moult fort et de ce le p. et les chevalliers les g. et tous ceulx qui le v.e. *A8* g. et autres gens v. 1157-1158 *A12* t. tres fort veant le peuple et de cella le p. les chevaliers et les g. et tout lautre peuple avoyent g.p. et grant ydeur et tantost les sergens et les gardes y. 1158 *A11* paour que merveilles puis *A13* paour et grant ydeur et quant ilz furent sailly de *B, B1, B3, B4, B5, B7, A6* paour que (*B5* p. de ouyr lhorrible voix des dyables et tellement que) a poy nissirent du (*B5, B7* i. hors du) sens (*B1* i. hors de leurs s. *A6* ne seillirent de leurs s.) et adonc quant (*B4* de leurs sens et les gens questoient en la tour partirent dehors le plus tost quilz porent et q.) les gens de la (*B5* g. qui estoient en la) t. furent issus (*A6* f. saillir *B4* f. *B5* f. dehors et estoient *B7* i. il vidrent la tour et tous les diablez qui estoient) sur *A8, A11* t. et allerent (*A11* et sen a.) sur *A12* t. de la grant paeur quil avoyent et m. *A13* et furent sur 1158-1159 *A12* p. et quant ilz furent sur le pont et estoient yssus de la tour ilz v. *B4* p. ilz et tous ceulx qui la estoient v. 1158-1160 *A10* paour que a pou quilz ne yssirent hors du sens et puis quant les gens darmes quilz le gardoient f[ ]ent yssu hors de la tour toute la[ ] r[ ] pillate et les g[ ]s fondirent au rosne en [ ]t[ ] nous voullez oster et il est nos[ ]e vous nous pairions et 1158-1162 *B2* paour car il y avoyt si grant bruyt dedans la tour et dedans le r. et en yssoyt si grant fumee que cestoyt merveilles et tant que tous ceux qui la estoyent eurent moult grant paour se vo. scavoir si 1159 *A13* v. sur *A8* c. en guise de cornailles et en aultres formes quilz ne scavoyent cognoistre ne eslire les cris quilz faisoyent et la *A12* c. de la tour crians tousious il est nostre laisies le nous et venat et print tout le peuple toute la court entierement a. *A1* tour et la tour tout enthierement a. 1159-1160 *A13* c. de la t. tout plains de d. et sen e. ladicte tour avec lesdiz d. et ensamble de pilate dedeans *A11* tour et puis ne demourra guieres apres que la tour et les d.a. pilate fondirent en la riviere ou parfond de la. 1159-1162 *B7* c. de la tour et virent fondre la tours et habimez en criant vous ne leres point et maulgrez vous nous nous laurons adoncques les iusticiers et c. et parellement le poeuple furent esbahis et eurent moult grand poeur et vouldre savoir si 1159-1163 *B, B1, B3, B4, B5, A6* v. la tour et pilate et touz les d. qui (*B1* d. denfer que) fondirent (*B5* qui illecques estoient qui f.) en a. en (*B3* f. en la riviere du r. a vienne en *A6* f. en r. en) criant vous (*B4* c. moult v.) ne laures il (*B3* v. le n. aviez ostey mais il) est nostre et (*A6* ne laisselaire mie et) malgre vous nous lavon adonc les iusticiers et c. (*B4* i. de vianne c.) et b. (*B1* les c. et i. les b.) et (*A6* c. et barons et) touz les gens (*B4* et autres g.) qui estoient entour (*B4* es. en la place en.) eurent (*B1* en. la tour eu.) moult grans merveilles et volurent savoir se la t. se en es.en.p. (*B1* me. come es. en la t.p. *B3* me. quant la tour et p.es.en. et fondues ou p. de la riviere *B4* g. paour et g.m. e comment es. s[ ]t[ ] la tour en p. *A6* me. ou la t. estoit p. *B5* abisme et crioient horriblement et disoient il est n. nous laurions ma. vous car il est n. et ainsi fut mene le douleureux pylat par les dyab[ ] ses maistres et conduiseurs au plus parfont denfer et quant les i. les b. les c. et toutes aultrez g. du menu peuple qui estoient prins virent cecy ilz se donnerent grant marveille de veoir tant terribles choses) et

1160 *A8* deables virent entrer en leau *A2* dedens le r. en le. et en *A9* en parfont a. et adoncques q. *A12* a. apres que ce fust fait le 1160-1161 *A8* q. les c. le p. les b. 1160-1170 *A13* r. adoncques firent prendre ung bapteal et lathacirent a une c. qui avoit iiij t. de long et le mirent la ou la tourt estoit e. et encorre a. 1161 *A2* c.la. *A11* b.v.

[56r] merveillerent moult fort / et vousirent veoir sy la tour s'en estoit guieres entree parfont. Et distrent a ung marinier de la riviere qu'il alast avec ung bateau la out la tour s'en estoit antree. Et quant le marinier vist le lieu out estoit la tour et vist que l'eau ne fesoit que roer, il dist qu'il n'y entreroit ja, mes il veroit voulentiers s'il y avoit point de peril pour y entrer. Et lors il atacha un navile a courdes audessus du pont et la firent venir jusques la

1162 *A3* m.f. *A7* et vindrent veoir *A3, A9, A11* vo. savoir se 1162-1163 *A11* es.en.g.p. lors d. *A12* es. en de guere p. dedens leau et *B2* es. bien p. dedans leaue si prindrent ung *B7* es. bien p. en terre et 1163 *A12* ung nauchier de *A8* m. quil *A9* al. taster avec 1163-1164 *A7* m. quil regardast la *B, B1, B3, B4, B5* d. aux pescheurs que alassent avec une (*B1* al. veoir ou une) barque et avec perches (*B4* al. veoir a une verge et p. *B5* b. atout grandes p.) et cordes (*B3* et av.c. et p.) la t. *A2* r. qui la avoit ung b. quil a. la 1163-1165 *A6* d. es pescheurs qui ailassent pour avoir une bargue et dautre prescheurs avec eulx et qui heussent des cordes pour leucie la ou la t. estoit entre et diserent qui ny 1163-1166 *B7* d. aulx pescheurs quil allassent avecques une barge savoir ou la tour es.a. et il respondirent quil ne yroient point iusques ad ce quil sceusent sil 1163-1172 *A11* quil prinst ung b. et al. veoir se ladicte t.e. guieres avant si ne f. leau a lendroit que tourner par quoy le marinier leur dist quil ne leur despleust et quil la ny [ ]oit il p. car il veoit bien quil y avoit trop grant p. dy aller et t. 1164 *A12* la out estoit la t. et *B2* b. et vit *A8* q. il vit *A12* le nauchier v. 1164-1165 *A7, A8, A1* l. (*A1* l. la ou la t.e.) et 1164-1166 *B, B1, B3, B4, B5* es.a. et (*B4* a. et abysmee et) didrent que ne yroient (*B1* et nulz ne d. quilz y. iusques ad ce quilz) tant que sauroient (*B5* es. fondue et a. en abisme et ilz refuserent de y aler iusques ad ce quilz s. premierement) se 1165 *A3, A8* f. que tourner il *A9* r. et soy remuer par undes il 1165-1166 *A7* r. il ny ossa entrer mais dit quil ve. *A12* d. quil ne yroit i. et ilz distrent quilz ve. bien se la tour estoit de gueres entree ne se 1165-1167 *A6* en. point tant que il sentissent se il a. peul ou non et adonc prirent ung vasseaus et le mirent au. 1165-1168 *B2* f. que tournoyer car les aultres ny voulurent point entrer sans scavoir coment la riviere estoyt parfonde la endroit si ny avoit homme nul qui le voulsist entreprandre adonc ilz prindrent ung bateau et se midrent sur le pont ou lieu la endroyt ou tournoyt leaue et avoyent appareille q.c. brasscer de 1166 *A1* mais bien ve. se *A3* il sauroit vo. *A7* peril et 1166-1167 *A12* perilz dy aller et y vont atacher ung 1166-1168 *B7* a. danger ou non adoncques prindrent ung bateaulx et le midrent soubz le p. ou leaue tournoist et puis apareilate trois c. braces de *B1, B3, B4, B5, B* perir et (*B3* p. ou non et) adoncques prinstrent (*B4* a. les pescheurs p.) une barque et (*B5* peril toutes foiz ilz pr. ung vaisseau cestassavoir ung bateau et) la mirent soubz le (*B* m. sur le) p. et leaue y tournoit et y apparaillerent q. (*B4* et pareillement prindrent q.) c. braces (*B5* p. et a.q.c. toises) de 1167 *A3* at. une petite nef a *A8* at. une encre a *A3* v. ladicte nef la *A9* p. bien et puis la fist v. et descendre i. au lieu la 1167-1168 *A12* p. et le lieu out *A1* i. a la t. et vit et oirent q. *A6* p. la ou laigue tournoit et appereillerent q.c. bracies de

1165 *vist* [ *virent* Correction from MSS *A1, A2, A3, A7, A8, A9, A12.*

out la tour s'en estoit entree. Et si eürent quatre cens toisses de cordes pour alonger. Et quant le navile fust la, et l'eau le tira et s'en entra come la tour s'en estoit entree. Et puis il alongerent la corde et toux jours le navil tiroit en tant qu'il tira toute la corde et il vint au bout de la corde. Il firent ung vaissel fet d'escorce et puis le laiserent aler. Et tout s'en entra la dedens. Et eincy mouru Pilate que oncques n'en seüst ont noveles de lui, ne de la tour, ne du navile, ne de la corde, ne de riens qu'il y eüssent mis.

1168 *A7* sy cheurent q.  1168-1169 *A12* en. et la out leau rousoit si fort et q. *A1* co. qui falloit pour a.  1168-1172 *B, B1, B2, B3, B4, B5, A6* co. et latacherent au (*B2* et lierent la corde au) bateau et quant le bateau fut en leau (*B2* p. et le.) il sen entra la ou sen estoit entree la (*B2* il sen en. du lieu la ou es. fondue la) tour et (*B4* ou la t.es.en. et abismee et) ilz lascherent (*B5* t. puis l.) toutes les (*B3* et y attaicheirent atout lez) iiij c braces de c. et y atacherent (*B5* les c. et ratacherent) un (*B2* ilz actachierent les cordes et t. les g.c.b. de c. entrerent toutes dedans leaue et au bout de la corde avoyent actachie ung *B3* et ung *A6* bateau et puis a. a lautre chenon iiij c. et br. de c. ung) tonneau plain (*B2* t. tout p.) de liege et (*B4* de sablon et p. *A6* de samblonc et) le  1168-1174 *B7* co. et les attacherent au bateau lung bout et lautre bout liertere a ung toneau plain de liege p. laissoite a. le bateaulx et les cordes et tonneaulx entrerent ou la tour estoit en. et puis ne se trouvast riens ne de la

1169 *A3* q. ladicte nef y fut leaue *A9* la pres leau le t. a soy et *A12* la out leau rousoit et leau le t. et il y avoit de cordes bien la montance de xii cz toyses et leau les vait tirer tout assoy et sen entra c.  1170 *A3* p. tousiours ilz  1170-1171 *A1* en. tira *A3* i. la nef t. *A12* n. let t. tout assoy et au  1170-1172 *A13* c. dautant comme devant et encorre fut telle courte ilz lalongirent encorre de autant et au b. mirent ung v. de ruypt et de.  1171 *A9* t. aval en *A7* t. lui et quant v. *A1, A2, A3* et quand (*A3* q. ce) v.  1171-1172 *A9* c. et puis apres fut fait ung *A8* de la c. il ly misdent ung *A1* de la c. il mirent ung v.de. *A12* f. soure ung v. et le firent estcher qui estoit de ruche cest a dire de. darbre et le  1172 *A3* fait de cordes p.  1172-1173 *B4* a. ou la tour estoit entree et eincy *A1* a. et quand il fut la il en. tout ens et eincy *B, B1, B2, B3, A6* a. et il en. la ou la tour estoit entree (*B1* ou es. la t.en. *B2* ou es. la t. *A6* ou il es.en. la t.) et eincy *A12* en. par la mesmes et *B5* a. et il sen en. la ou la tour estoit fondue et entree et ei. fina le maleureux p. qui o. puis ne fut trouve ne luy  1172-1175 *A13* a. tout doulcement ilz sen e. en leaue come le bapteal ne plus ne moins ainsin fut perdut pilate ensamble la tourt et le bapteal le vaissealx de rupte et la corde aussi et encorre deprint y redoye leauue et sy nest bapteal quil sen  1173 *A7* d. luy *A11* p. de villanie que o. puis ne fut n. 1173-1174 *A8* on quil devint ne la  1173-1175 *A1* que de luy ne de la n. ne de la t. ne s. iamais n. mais  1173-1176 *B, B1, B2, B3, B4, A6* que puis (*A6* que o.p.) ne (*B2* que o. depuis on ne *B4* que depuis on ne) se trouva nient ne de (*B1* que plus ne sen retourna riens de) la t. ne du bateau ne de la c. (*B3* t. ne de cez c.) ne du tonneau et (*A6* b. ne du t. de samblon et) en. tourne leau et (*B2* ton. plain de liege et en. maintenant le.t. la endroyt et) le pi. demoura fait en (*B3* d. le pillier f. et est encoire en) la pl. et (*B1, B2, B3, B4* pl. de vienne et *A6* pl. de vianne et sachiez que) les  1174 *A3* t. ne de la nef ne de la c.  1174-1175 *A7* r. et en.  1174-1176 *B5* t. ne bateau ne tonneau ne des c. quelque chose que ce soit le pi. demoura et est e. en la pl. de vienne qui est ramembrance des choses dessusdictes les *B7* c. ne du tonneaulx de liege et en. y tourne leaue tousiours le pi. demeura seul et ce firent les  1174-1179 *A11* t. si est assavoir que les d. firent mourir ainsi p. affin quil ne s. pas la cruelle mort quon luy vouloit fere s. car il doubtoient que sil eust souffert quil ne se fust repenty de son malfait et quil ne se fust c. a la foy de ihesu crist en aultre lieu aussi trouvons que luy mesme se octit dun glayve et pour ce que les d. deurent avoir ilz e. en

Mes encores i roe l'eau et sy n'est navile qui s'en ause apricher. Et le piler est encores a la plasse, mes les deables vi[n]rent la en la tour afin que Pilate ne soufrist la justice longue qu'il devoit soufrir ne se convertist a Dieu. Car s'il se fust converti, les deables l'eüssent perdu, mes car il le devoient avoir, il l'eürent tout entier en cor et en arme.

1175 *A9* y fust mis et e. a present y rue et se remue par undes leaue tres fort et nest nulle n. *A12* en. roussoit leau la out il est et *A12, A13* ap. ne autre chose (*A13* c. aussi) et 1175-1176 *A3* y tourne leaue tellement quil ny a nef qui ce lieu auze ap. et si est e. le pi. en la *A9* que de ce lieu ose aucunement a. et aussi est e. le pi. en la pl. de ladicte cite de vienne mes *A7* ap. et est e. le pi. en la pl. et est assavoir que les *A8* ap. et est le p.e. a 1176 *A12* en. fait en la p. et dit lon que les *A13* en. tout fais en la *B, B1, B3, B4, B5, B7, A6* d. le firent (*B1* d.f. ce *B7* d. *B5* f. par ceste maniere) a. *A12* d. estoit venus en la t. la out pilate estoit pour la mettre en abisme a. *A13* d. prindrent pilate en 1176-1177 *A1* p. de vienne et sachies que les d. ne volrent pas souffrir que p.s. tant de martire comme on luy vouloit faire pour paour que il ne se *A7* pi. ne se convertist a dieu et quil ne *A13* quil ne 1176-1178 *B2* d. vouldrent ainsi fayre pour ce que par avanture sil eut este iusticie et eut souffert le mal que on avoyt ordonne il se fust c. et le. 1177 *B, B1, B3, B4, A6* ne fust iusticie et (*B4* i. comme il estoit ordonne et) que ne s. le mal ne la doulour car (*B1* d. a quoy il estoit iugie car) les diables avoient paour (*B4* a. moult p.) que ne se *A2, A3, A7* i. quil *A12* i. laquelle d. *A13* i. si terrible comme il *A9* i. qui lui estoit appeillee et d.s. et aussy en quoi il estoit condampnee et aussi a celle fin quil ne se *A7* s. car *A8* s. en ame et quil ne se c. a d. en corps car *A12* c. et ne cast mercy a d. ihesu crist car 1177-1178 *A13* s. car en souffrant ilz *B, B1, B3, B4, A6* d. et ilz (*A6* et ainsin ilz *B4* et quil ne se repentist car ilz) le. 1177-1179 *B5* ne fust iusticie ne excecute ainsi come il estoit iuge par les senateurs de romme car ilz doubtoient quil ne se repentist et eust aulcune consideration et oppinion de crier mercy a nostre seigneur quil ne fut dampne en cor 1177-1180 *B7* ne fust crucifiez et quil ne s. le mal que luy estoit ordonnez car avoyent poeur que en souffrant le mal quil ne tournast a la foy de nostre seigneur ihesus crist a. toutes ses choses les c. prandre conges des sires de vienne et sen 1178 *A1* c. a dieu ilz le. *A12* c. ilz e. *A2, A3, A7, A9* p. et pour ce quilz *A8* mes ilz 1178-1179 *A1* p. et par ainsy ilz le.en. *A12* mes ilz le vouloint a. entierement en cor *B, B1, B3, B4, A6* p. et ilz le (*B3* et aussi le) firent afin (*B4* f. ainsi a.) que leussent en 1178-1180 *A13* c. a dieu et dieu leusse print a mercy mes les dyables le. en c. et en a. car ilz lavoit bien gaingniez et ces chouses faittes et accomplie les seigneurs de romme sen *B2* p. et aussi ilz vouloyent avoir le c. et la. lesquelz sont en enffer a tous temps et perdurablement a. ces chose les 1179 *A8* a.t *A9* e. et pery en 1179-1180 *A7* arme comme a. *A8* ame il print son iugement et eust enfer pour y acomplir sa sentence que nul temps ne luy fauldra et se fait les *B, B1, B3, B4, B5, A6* en a. et que fust dampne a tousiours mes a. (*B5* en a. a t.m. et par ainsi leussent perdu a.) quant toutes (*B1* a iamais pardurablement sans fin a. que t. *B3* a.t.) ces choses furent faites (*B4*,*B5* f. ainsi) les *A11* arme car il avoit bien desservy a. toutes ces choses les c. prindrent congie du prevost de vienne et de tous les bourgeoys puisse mirent au chemin pour eulx en retourner a romme et quant il y furent il d.

1177 *soufrist* [ *soufrent* Correction based on MSS *A2, A3, A7, A8, A9, A10, A12, B, B1, B3, B4, B7*.

[5. The Conclusion]

[73] Puis aprés les chevaliers s'en retournerent et distrent a l'empereur les nouvelles et a toute la gent. Et Jafet, du consentiment de Jacob et de

1180 *A12* les .x.c. *B4* c. de lempereur sen *A7* r. dire a *A12* r. a romme et *B, B1, B3, B4, B5, A6* r. a romme et compterent tout le fait de (*B5* f. et la fin de) pilate a 1180-1181 *A1* c. commanderent a dieu le prouvost et sen r. vers romme et conterent a le. et a toute sa gent les *A8* d. les n. a le. et *A9* r. par devers le. et lui d. et racompterent toutes les *A11* e. et a titus son filz les 1180-1187 *A13* et racontirent a le. et a la baronnie le fait de pilate dont lempereur ordonna a iosepht da. iacob et iaphet quil escripvissent diligemment celluy livres lesquelx sen acquitarent diligemment et feirent veritablement comme ilz est cy devant escript priez dieu quilz leurs faice vraye mercy amen ceste d. de i. a este copie par piret daltena clerc demore a blecth et fut affin le iour de la decollacion saint ilz. baptesme en auost mil iiijc et cinquante ceulx quil le liront se prient dieu pour ledit piret quil sest donne paisne de le copies (MS ends) *B, B1, B3, B4, B5, A6* e. et a tithus son filz et iasel et (*B3* f. et a ioseph de cassel et) a iacob et a iosef et (*B4* e. et a son f.t. a iacob a iassel du tassel a i. dabarimathie et *B1* f. iacob iasel et iosef darimathie et *B3* i. dabarimathie et) a touz ceulx (*A6* a c.) de (*B5* i. darimathie et semblablement a t. le peuple de) romme dont furent moult merveilles ainsi fut la (*B1, B3, A6* fut fete la *B5* d. tous sen esmerveillerent a. fut faicte la) vangance de nostre seigneur faite par (*B1, B3* s. ihesu crist par) lempereur vaspazien et son (*B4* van.f. de n.s. par vas.e. de rome et par son) filz titus (*B1* et t. son f.) et la (*A6* s. ihesu crist en la) foy de (*B4* foy et la loy de) dieu exaussiee en (*A6* e. par lempereur vaspasien et tytus son filz et la foy de dieu exaucier en) iherusalem et a romme et en plusieurs lieux (*B4* i. et en p. autres l. *A6* p. aultres l.) on fut esclandre par (*B1* p. autres l. par *A6* fut respendue par) les miracles qui avoient este faiz par veronique et par clement et par (*B4* et tout par v. et par saint c. et tout par) la voulente de dieu explicit (*B1* ve. avecques la grace de d. laquelle nous doint celuy que vit et regne pardurablement in secula seculorum amen ex. icy fine la v. de nostre seigneur i.c. par vaspasien (MS ends) *B3* exaussiee par pape c. et par ve. et dez illec toute romme conquise a cristientey et baptesme et plusieurs pays et grant miracles fais par la volentey de nostre seigneur ihesu crist qui nous doint ioie sans fin amen (MS ends) *B4* d. laquelle nous doint faire et acomplir celluy qui vit sur tous les siecles amen explicit la d. de i. faicte par vaspasien empereur de rome (MS ends) *B5* s. ihesu crist par le. et fult moult grandement exaulcee ladicte ven. par la predication du benoit pape saint c. et par la benoite dame ver. la cristiente et la foy de nostre seigneur ihesu crist et tout par la voulente de dieu lequel en ce monde se nos doint sa grace en paradis et sa gloire amen explicit la vengence de nostre seigneur et la destruction de iheruslem (MS ends) *A6* d. laquelle nous dont faire et acomplir amen explicit la d. et i. (MS ends)) *B2* r. a romme et raconterent a le. tout le fait de pilate lesquelz en eurent moult grant merveilles et cl explicit destructio iherusalem deo gratias et marie virgini (MS ends) *B7* r. a romme et compterent a le. tout le fait de pillate et aulx aultres seigneurs dont ilz furent bien esbahis et moult esmervelez par ainsi fut faicte la vengence nostre sauveur et redempteur ihesus par vaspasien empereur et son filz titus et est la foy de dieu exaulcee en iherusalem ausy a romme et en plusieurs aultres lieux et fust cela par les miracles de lintercession de sainct clement disciple de dieu ainsy de veronique la saincte femme par la volluntez de dieu roy des roys qui vitz et regne sans fin amen (MS ends)
1181 *A9* n. qui estoient advenues a vienne et aussi a *A12* lautre g. aussy et *A1* n. de pilate comment il lui advint et iafet *A7* n. quilz avoyent vehus et iaffet *A9* g. et puis apres tout ce fait et acompli en la maniere que dessus est dit et escript du *A11* n. de pilate qui moult esmerveillez en furent et aussi fut tout le peuple quant il le sceurent lors dist lempereur a iaffet et a iacob

Joseph d'Arimatie escrips[t] la destruction de Jherusalem car il la savoient bien, et la justice et la mort de Pilate par le dit des chevaliers qui leur avoient dit, car il l'avoient veüe. Jhesu Crist tout puissant nous garde de tout peril et nous doint paradis aprés ceste presente vie. A.M.E.N.

[74] Si finit la Destruction de Jherusalem et la Vengence de Jhesu Crist et la Justice et la male fin de Pilate, et cetera.

1182 *A1, A11* a. mist en (*A11* a. quilz meissent en) escript la *A9* a. le noble et vaillant homme iaffet de caffe si e. et fist escripre *A12* a. le bon chevalier firent et mistrent en e. tout le proces de la passion et de la mort de ihesu crist et de la d. *A9* ih. et vengence de nostre seigneur ihesu crist car *A11* ih. et la vangence quil avoit faicte de noustre seigneur ihesu crist comme bien la *A12* ih. et aussy la m. et la i. de p. car 1182-1183 *A7* il s. la *A9* s. et avoit veu tout et en partie conseille la maniere du faire et puis apres fist et escript la i. *A11* s. et aussi la m. 1183 *A2* m. et le male fin de p. *A12* b. par le raport des x.c. *A1* des x.c. 1183-1187 *A11* p. que a tort et sans cause avoit iuge a mourir en croix nostre saulveur et redempteur ihesu crist lequel a tous bons christiens veille octroier a la fin de leurs iours sa gloire pardurable amen (MS ends) 1184 *A3* a. raporterent aincy comment ilz *A3* p. qui n. 1184-1186 *A7* vu explicit la d. *A12* v. en la ville de vihenne cy f. le romain de la d. 1184-1187 *A9* dit et relate comme ceulx qui y avoient este appellez et presens et pour ce a la fin de ces dictz prions pour tous bons xpristiens que dieu leur d. son paradis amen sine fine explicit (MS ends) 1185-1187 *A3* amen explicit deo gratias (MS ends) *A8* amen explicit (MS ends) 1186-1187 *A2* f. la v. de la mort nostre seigneur i.c. et la de iherusalem (MS ends) *A7* v. de nostre seigneur i.c. amen (MS ends) *A12* v. de la mort et passion de ihesu crist (MS ends) 1187 *A1* p. (MS ends)

# Glossary

As the Glossary assumes the reader's knowledge of the vocabulary of twentieth-century French, only items no longer in use or with meanings other than those of today's language are listed. Only the first five occurrences of each item are indicated. The symbol : is to be interpreted as "as in the expression." All references are to line numbers in the text.

**ainsi**: **tout ainsi que** adv 241 while
**aministreus** sm pl 601 administrators, those in charge
**ansois que** conj 162, 491 before
**aourer** inf 5 to worship; **aouroit** 5 imp ind 3
**appareillié de** adj 104 attacked by
**arme** sf 67, 1179 soul
**ars** 1117 past p **ardoir** to burn
**assecier** inf 405 to besiege
**assicié** 395 past p **assicier** to besiege
**aucun** adj, pro 29, 51, 54, 73, 111 some
**aucunement** adv 1145 somewhat, up to a certain point
**auques** adj 988 some
**aurial** adj 557 golden
**ausant** v **oïr**
**aut** 1029 (= **eut**) pret 3 **avoir** to have

**baillier** inf 953 to give; **bailla** 932 pret 3; **baillerent** 1128 pret 6
**bliau** sm 424 long tunic
**brief**: **en brief de temps** sm 312, 334 in a short time
**brifors** sm 496 water buffalo; see note to this line.

**chafaut** sm 267, platform
**chancre** sm 16, 103 leprosy
**cherté** sf 717, 720, 736 **chierté** 332 lack of goods, provisions
**cheviroient** 487 cond 6 **chevir** to satisfy a need
**chevirons (nous)** 576 fut 4 **se chevir** to be master of, overcome
**cheÿrent** 553 pret 6 **cheïr** to fall; **cheüst** 763 **cheü** 861, 957 pret 3
**coingne** sf 611 knowledgeability, skill; see note to this line.
**compereras** 854 fut 2 **comperer** to pay
**conroier** inf 498 **conreer** 503 to arrange, put in order
**conscens** adj 483 **consens** 978 consenting
**contraster** inf 328 to oppose, stand up to
**couroucié** adj 330 made to suffer; **courociez** 337, 341, 677, 756 angry, distressed
**courper** inf 1097 (= **couper**) to cut; **courpe** 1099, 1100, 1114 (= **coupe**) pres subj 3
**crevichié** sm 144 **crevichief** 146, 252 **crevechief** 249 piece of cloth used to cover the head
**crote** sf 363, 386 grotto cave
**cuidiés** 474 pres ind 5 **cuidier** to think, **cuiderent** 656, 1029 pret 6; **cuidoient** 677 imp ind 6; **cuident** 879 pres ind 6

**desconfirons** 617 fut 4 **desconfire** to rout; **desconfis** 1046 past p
**desconneü** 1088 pret 3 **desconnoistre** to fail to recognize
**desfaissonné** adj 32 **desfasonné** 206 overcome, overwhelmed
**destourberons** 618 fut 4 **destourber** to trouble, cause anxiety
**destre** adj 263 right
**dies** 76, 959 pres subj 2 **dire** to say; **die** 186 pres subj 1; **disent** (= **disant**) 538 pres p; **die** 579 pres subj 3
**diruerent** 1064 pret 6 **diruer** to destroy, topple

**doint** 1185 pres subj 3 **donner** to give
**doubtanse**: **avoir doubtanse de** sf 444, 452 to fear

**engin** sm 513 cleverness, talent
**entachés**: **estoient entachés de** adj 43 were suffering from
**esbahirent (se)** 512 pret 6 **se esbahir** to be amazed; **esbahy** 407 past p; **esbahy** 514 pret 3; **esbahissés** 517 pres ind 5
**eschausees** adj f pl 667 pursued
**espolia** 272 pret 3 **espolier** to remove the faithful from
**estuier** inf 716 to store, keep in reserve
**eu** prep 565, 883 with

**ferir** inf 639 to strike
**fetice** adj 1132 well-made
**fine** adj 259 complete
**foison**: **grant foison de** sf 134, 496, 497, 499-500, 1032 a large quantity of; **a grant foison** 191 abundantly
**fondement** sm 1105 anus

**gesir** inf 33 to lie
**greigneur** adj 6 greatest
**gresse** adj 1084 ( = **grosse**) large
**guermentoient (se)** 897 imp ind 6 **se guermenter** to lament

**honques** v **onques**
**host** v **ost**

**ilec** adv 183 **illec** 351 **ileques** 197 **illuecques** 277 **illuec** 1017 **illecques** 570 there
**incontinent** adv 72, 145, 251, 252, 279 **incontinant** 209, 213, 414 immediately; **incontinent que** conj 112, 311, 512, 730 as soon as
**issir**, **istre**, **issirent** v **yssir**

**ja** adv 858 certainly; **ja** ... **ne** 326, 471 never
**jus**: **deux ans en jus** adv 852 less than two years old

**lairoit** 124 cond 3 **laisser** to leave, abandon, renounce
**lié** adj 208, 211, 1036 **lieux** (lié + joyeux?) 1052 joyful; **liement** adv 939, 1047, 1139 joyfully
**liens** adv 800, 982 in there
**lin** sm 88, 346 boat

**louent** 1052 ( = **louant**) pres p **louer** to praise

**mes**: **tous temps mes** adv 119 **tous jours mes** 1030 henceforth, evermore; **mes que** conj 214 provided that
**mescherra**: **il luy mescherra** 448 misfortune will come to him
**mestier**: **faire mestier a** sm 382 to be of service to
**mirant** 278 ( = **mirent**) pret 6 **mettre** to put
**mire** sm 19, 20, 22, 107 doctor
**moult** adv 32, 77, 101, 284, 294 very much, a great deal; **moult de** 42 many
**mua** 1054 pret 3 **muer** to change v **remuer**
**muire** 901 pres subj 3 **mourir** to die
**mus** sm pl 45 the mute
**mussa** 363 pret 3 **musser** to hide; **musés** 364, 386 past p

**nagerent** 86 pret 6 **nager** to sail
**navil** sm/f 1170 **navile** 1167, 1169, 1174, 1175 **navilles** 1032 ship, flotilla
**nulle** adj f 210 any

**oïr** 44 **ouïr** 828 to hear; **oÿ** 31 **ouÿ** 40, 49, 913 past p; **oÿ** 244, 494, 923 **ouÿ** 174, 232, 520, 537, 912 **ouïst** 762 pret 3; **oÿrent** 894 **ouÿrent** 675 pret 6; **ausant** 177 pres p
**onques** adv 19, 39, 66, 258 **honques** 361 ever; **oncques mes** 780, 785, 866, 870 **onques mais** 827 never before
**ordille** sf 1006 weapons; see note to this line.
**ost** sm/f 356, 493, 498, 597, 640 **oust** 406, 412, 429, 642 **host** 453 army
**ot** 161 pret 3 **avoir** to have
**outel** adv 1099, 1100, 1101, 1102, 1103 likewise

**paiengnie** sf 4 land of the non-believers
**par** adv 168 exceedingly
**pelé** adj 425, 431 covered in hide or fur
**penre** inf 59, 84, 185, 381, 532 **panre** 66, 383, 561, 950 to take; **penra** 526, 882, 901 fut 3; **penray** 532, 840 fut 1; **presist** 728 imp subj 3; **penre a mercy** 354 to be merciful to, spare
**portant** 500 ( = **portent**) pres subj 6 **porter** to carry
**presist** v **penre**

**priciés** 480 pres subj 5 **pricier** to consider of value
**puissant** 107, 858 ( = **puissent**) pres subj 6 **povoir** to be able

**quantque** adv 218, 720, 838, 925 whatever
**que** ... **que** ... adv 346, 647-648 as many ... as...

**regna** 1088 ( = **regnia**) pret 3 **regnier** to deny, renounce
**remanroit** 335 cond 3 **remanoir** to remain
**remuer**inf 318 to change v **mua**
**riens** sf 68, 69, 114 something
**robirent** 749 pret 6 **robir** ( = **rober**) to rob
**roer** inf 1165 to boil, churn; **roe** 1175 pres ind 3

**sache** 857 pres ind 3 **sachier** to unsheath
**segont** prep 64 according to
**seleement** adv 90 secretly
**sergent** sm 153, 779, 781, 790, 795 servant
**seureuse** adj 250 covered in sweat
**siens** adv 473 in here
**souliers** sm pl 1147, 1148 levels, floors
**souloit** 78 imp ind 3 **souloir** to be in the habit of
**sus** adv 50 up

**tant**: **en tant que** conj 20, 1000-1001, 1171 **en tent que** 1034 **tant que** 74, 86, 193, 379-380, 507 with the result that, so much so that; **pour tant que** 52, 186, 594 **en tant que** 113 provided that; 718 such that; **pour tant que** 897 because; **a tant que** 1140 until, before
**tantost** adv 53, 54, 70, 133 immediately
**temps** 733 ( = **tant**)
**tenu** adj 294 indebted
**tieux** adj m/f pl 48, 338, such
**trefs** sm pl 684 tents
**tret (se)** 573 pres ind 3 **se traire** to move
**tretout**: **en tretout** sm 671, 934 in total
**treut** sm 77 **treü** 177 tribute, taxes
**truage** sm 167, 325, 435 tribute, taxes
**tuit** adj 366, 411, 461, 884, 896 all

**veant** 278 **vean** 554 pres p **veoir** to see; **veant tous** with everyone looking on
**vensist** 342, 360 imp subj 3 **venir** to come
**vertu** sf 159, 235, 1052 strength
**vieux**, **veust**, **vieust**, **veuil**, **voeil**, v **vousirent**
**voise** 163 pres subj 1 **aler** to go; **voyses** 72 pres subj 2
**vouscist** 678 pret 3 **valoir** to be of value
**vousirent** 21, 416, 1075, 1162 **voussirent** 66, 367, 1154 **voucirent** 560 pret 6 **vouloir** to want, be willing to; **voscit** 508 **vousist** 233, 361, 433, 514 **voucit** 258 pret 3; **vousis** 328 pret 1; **voeil** 303, 953 **vieux** 307, 388, 439 **veuil** 324, 959 **veul** 944 pres ind 1; **veust** 550 **vieust** 228, 1067 pres ind 3; **vousist** 354, 403 imp subj 3; **vouscissent** 344 imp subj 6

**yssir** inf 690 **issir** 416, 417, 630, 692 **istre** 406, 587, 590, 591, 931 to go out; **yssons** 370 imperative 4; **yssirent** 374, 662 (for imp subj 6 **yssissent**), 1158 **issirent** 628 pret 6; **yssy** 903 **yssi** 957 **yssit** 792 pret 3; **yssus** 632, 643 past p; **yssoit** 686 imp ind 3

# Bibliography


Ado Viennensis. *Chronicon in aestates sex divisum*. In *Patrologiae cursus completus ... series latina prior*. Ed. J. P. Migne, vol. 123, cols. 1-138. Parisiis: Apud Garnier Fratres, 1879.

Albe, E. "La Vie et miracles de S. Amator." *Analecta Bollandiana*, 28 (1909): 57-71.

Ambroise. *L'Estoire de la Guerre sainte: Histoire en vers de la Troisième Croisade (1190-1192)*. Ed. Gaston Paris. Documents inédits sur l'histoire de France, I:2. Paris: Imprimerie Nationale, 1897.

Anchel, Robert. *Les Juifs en France*. Paris: Janin, 1946.

Arbellot, l'Abbé. *Dissertation sur l'apostolat de Saint Martial et sur l'antiquité des églises de France*. Paris: Didron, 1855.

——. *Documents inédits sur l'apostolat de Saint Martial et sur l'antiquité des églises de France*. Paris: Jacques Lecoffre, 1860.

Assman, Bruno, ed. "Legende von der Heiligen Veronica (*Vindicta Salvatoris*)"; "Natanis Judaei legatio." In *Angelsächsische Homilien und Heiligenleben*. Bibliothek der Angelsächsischen Prosa, 3. Kassel: G. H. Wigand, 1889, pp. 181-192, 193-194.

Auracher, Theodor, ed. *Die sogenannte Poitevinische Uebersetzung des Pseudo-Turpin*. Halle a/S.: Max Niemeyer, 1877.

Aurélien, Dom, c.s.b. *Sainte Véronique, apôtre de l'Aquitaine; son tombeau et son culte à Soulac ou Notre-Dame-de-Fin-de-Terres, archidiocèse de Bordeaux*. Toulouse: Hébrail, Durand et Delpuech, 1877.

Baillet, Elisabeth. *Sainte Véronique*. Paris: Les Éditions du Foyer, n.d. (c. 1934).

Baluzius, Stephanus. *Miscellanea novo ordine digesta et non paucis ineditis monumentis opportunisque animadversionibus aucta et opera*. Ed. J. F. Mansi. Lucae: Apud Vincentium Junctinium, 1764, 4 vols.

Balberghe, E. van. "Bulletin codicologique, 424: Quinze Années d'acquisition" (Résumé of *Catalogues des expositions organisées à la Bibliothèque Albert Ier à Bruxelles, 34*. Bruxelles: Bibliothèque Royale Albert Ier, 1969). *Scriptorium*, 25 (1971): 195-199.

Baldi, D. *Enchiridion locorum sanctorum*. Gerusalemme: 1935.

Barbier, M. X. *Traité pratique de la construction, de l'ameublement et de la décoration des églises selon les règles canoniques et les traditions romaines*. 2 vols. Paris: Louis Vivès, 1878.

Barbier, Paul. "Sur l'Histoire de quatre mots français." In *Mélanges de linguistique et de littératures romanes offerts à Mario Roques*, 2: 23-24. Paris: Didier, 1953.

Baring-Gould, S. *The Lives of the Saints*. 2nd ed. 15 vols. Edinburgh: John Grant, 1914.

——. "Portraits of Christ." *The Quarterly Review*, 123 (1867): 490-509.

Baronius, Caesar. *Annales ecclesiastici*. 12 vols. Romae: Ex Typographia Congregationis Oratorii apud S. Mariam in Valicella, 1593-1607.

Baudot, J., P. Chaussin, et al., eds. *Vie des Saints et des Bienheureux selon l'ordre du calendrier avec l'historique des fêtes*. 13 vols. Paris: Letouzey et Ané, 1935-1959.

Bazin, Hippolyte. *Vienne et Lyon gallo-romains*. Villes antiques. Paris: Imprimerie Nationale, 1891.

Bede, Venerable. "The Book of the Holy Places." In *The Biographical Writings and Letters*. Trans. J. A. Giles. London: Bohn, 1845.

Bell, Mrs. Arthur. *Lives and Legends of the Evangelists, Apostles, and other early Saints*. London: George Bell and Sons, 1901.

Benedictus. *Ordo romanus*. In *Musei Italici complectens antiquos libros rituales sanctae Romanae Ecclesiae*. Luteciae Romanorum: Apud Viduam Edmundi Martin, et al., 1689.

Benedictus XIV. *De Servorum Dei beatificatione et Beatorum canonizatione*. In Typographia Bassanensi, 1766.

Benoît de Sainte-Maure. *Chroniques des Ducs de Normandie: publiée d'après le manuscrit de Tours avec les variantes du manuscrit de Londres*. Ed. Carlin Fahlin, 3 vols. Uppsala: Almqvist & Wiksells, 1951-1967.

Berman, Léon. *Histoire des Juifs en France: des origines à nos jours*. Paris: Librairie Lipschutz, n.d.

Bertrand de Bar-sur-Aube. *Girart de Vienne*. Ed. Wolfgang von Emden. Paris: Société des Anciens Textes Français, 1977.

*Bibliotheca hagiographica latina antiquae et mediae aetatis: Subsidia hagiographica, 6, 12*. 2 vols. Bruxelles: Société des Bollandistes, 1898-1899, 1911.

*Bibliotheca Sanctorum*. 13 vols. Roma: Istituto Giovanni XXIII della Pontificia Università Lateranense, 1961-1970.

Blouet, Léon. "Les Statues et le culte de Sainte Venisse dans la région de Villedieu et en Basse-Normandie." *Art de Basse-Normandie*, 8 (Hiver 1957-1958): 18-19.

Boissonnet, l'Abbé M., ed. *Dictionnaire alphabético-méthodique des cérémonies et des rites sacrés*. Vols. 15-17 of *Encyclopédie théologique ou Série de dictionnaires sur chaque branche de la science religieuse*. Ed. P. L. Migne. Paris: Chez l'éditeur, 1846-1847.

Bolo, Henry. *Les Gauloises et les Gaulois à la Passion de Jésus*. Paris: René Hatin, 1893.

Bonaventure de St-Amable. *Histoire de St. Martial, Apôtre des Gaules et principalement de l'Aquitaine et du Limousin, ou, la Défense de l'apostolat de St. Martial et autres de Nôtre France contre les critiques du temps*. 3 vols. Clermont: Nicolas Jacquard, 1676.

Bourdillon, F. W., ed. *Tote Listoire de France (Chronique saintongeaise), now first*

*Edited from the only two mss., with Introduction, Appendices, and Notes.* London: David Nutt, 1897.

Bourdrel, Philippe. *Histoire des Juifs en France*. H. Comme Histoire. Paris: Albin Michel, 1974.

Bourrières, Michel. *S. Amadour et Ste Véronique: disciples de Notre-Seigneur et apôtres des Gaules*. Paris: Tolra, 1895.

Brault, Gérard J. *Chanson de Roland: an Analytic Edition*. 2 vols. University Park, PA: The Pennsylvania State University Press, 1978.

Braun, Joseph. *Tracht und Attribute der Heiligen in der deutschen Kunst*. Stuttgart: J. B. Metzlersche Verlagsbuchhandlung, 1943.

Brentano, Robert. *Rome before Avignon: A Social History of Thirteenth-Century Rome*. New York: Basic Books, 1974.

Brunet, Jacques-Charles. "Vengeance." In *Manuel du libraire et de l'amateur de livres*, vol. v, cols. 1120-1122. 5e éd. 1860-1865; rpt. Berlin: Altmann, 1921.

Butler's *Lives of the Saints*. Ed. H. Thurston and Donald Attwater. 4 vols. New York: P. J. Kenedy & Sons, 1956.

Buzzard, Melitta S. G. *C'est li romanz de la Vanjance que Vaspasiens et Tytus ses fiz firent de la mort Jhesucrist, édition du manuscrit 5201 Bibliothèque de l'Arsenal, Paris*. Dissertation: U. of Colorado, 1970.

Cabrol, F., et H. Leclercq, ed. *Dictionnaire d'archéologie chrétienne et de liturgie*. 15 vols. Paris: Letouzey et Ané, 1924-1953.

Cahier, Charles. *Caractéristiques des Saints dans l'art populaire*. 1867; rpt. Bruxelles: Culture et Civilisation, 1966.

Catane, Mosche. *Des Croisades à nos jours*. Bibliothèque juive. Paris: Les Éditions de Minuit, 1956.

*The Catholic Encyclopedia: An International Work of Reference on the Constitution, Doctrine, Discipline, and History of the Catholic Church*. 18 vols. New York: The Universal Knowledge Foundation, 1907-1958.

*Catholicisme hier, aujourd'hui, demain*. Ed. E. Jacquernet. 7 vols. Paris: Letouzey et Ané, 1949.

Cautru, Camille. "L'Abbaye de Belle-Étoile." *Art de Basse-Normandie*, 5 (Printemps 1957): 10-12.

Cavard, Pierre. "La Légende de Ponce Pilate." In *Vienne la sainte*, pp. 32-71. Vienne: Blanchard Frères, 1939.

Charvet, Claude. *Fastes de la Ville de Vienne: manuscrit inédit*. Ed. E.-J. Savigné. Vienne: Savigné, 1869.

Chazan, Robert. *Medieval Jewry in Northern France: A Political and Social History*. The Johns Hopkins University Studies in Historical and Political Science, 91:2. Baltimore: Johns Hopkins University Press, 1973.

Chorier, Nicolas. *Recherches sur les antiquités de la Ville de Vienne, métropole des Allobroges, capitale de l'Empire romain dans les Gaules, et des deux royaumes de Bourgogne*. Nouvelle édition. Lyon: Chez Millon Jeune, 1828.

Chrétien de Troyes. *Perceval, ou le conte du Graal*. Ed. Wm. Roach. Genève: Droz, 1959.

Cirot de la Ville, l'Abbé. *Origines chrétiennes de Bordeaux, ou Histoire et description de l'Église de Saint Seurin*. Bordeaux: Typographie Ve Justin Dupuy, 1867.

Cocquelines, Carolus, ed. *Bullarum, privilegiorum ac diplomatum romanorum pontificum amplissima collectio, cui accessere pontificum omnium vitae, notae et indices opportuni*. 14 vols. Romae: Typis S. Michaelis ad Ripam, sumptibus Hieronymi Mainardi, 1739-1744.

Collombet, F.-Z. *Histoire de la Sainte Église de Vienne depuis les premiers temps du Christianisme jusqu'à la suppression du siège, en 1801*. 4 vols. Lyon: A. Mothon, 1847-1848.

Coulson, John. *The Saints: A Concise Biographical Dictionary*. New York: Hawthorn Books, 1958.

Cumont, Franz. *Astrology and Religion among the Greeks and Romans*. New York: Dover Press, 1960.

——. *Les Religions orientales dans le paganisme romain*. 2e éd. revue. Paris: Ernest Leroux, 1909.

Dante. *La Divina Commedia*. Ed. Carlo Steiner. 3 vols. Torino: Paravia, 1921.

——. *Vita nuova*. Ed. Michele Scherillo. Milano: Hoepli, 1911.

Darley, Dom Étienne, o.s.b. *Les Acta Salvatoris; un Évangile de la Passion et de la Résurrection et une Mission apostolique en Aquitaine*. Paris: Alphonse Picard et fils, 1913.

——. *Les Actes du Sauveur, la Lettre de Pilate, les Missions de Volusien, de Nathan, la Vindicte, leurs origines et leurs transformations*. Paris: Auguste Picard, 1919.

——. *Les Apôtres de Bordeaux*. Bordeaux: Féret et fils, 1917.

——. *Fragments d'anciennes chroniques d'Aquitaine d'après des manuscrits du XIIIe siècle*. Bordeaux: Féret et fils, 1906.

——. *Sainte Véronique*. Publication de la Société des Archives historiques de la Saintonge et de l'Aunis. La Rochelle: Imprimerie Nouvelle Noël Texier, 1907.

——. *Saint Fort et la crypte de Saint-Seurin*. Bordeaux: Imprimerie Y. Cadoret, 1918.

Delehaye, Hippolyte. *Les Légendes hagiographiques*. 4e éd. Subsidia hagiographica, 18A. Bruxelles: Société des Bollandistes, 1955.

"De S. Veronica, matrona hierosolymitana: commentarius historicus." *Acta Sanctorum*, 454-463 (IV Februarii).

Devienne, Dom Jean-Baptiste d'Agneaux. *Histoire de la Ville de Bordeaux*. 2 vols. Bordeaux: Lacaze, 1862.

Dexter, Flavius Lucius. *Chronicon Omnimodae Historiae*. Lugduni: Sumptibus Claudii Landry, 1627.

*Dictionnaire de Théologie catholique, contenant l'exposé des doctrines de la théologie catholique, leurs preuves et leur histoire*. 15 vols. Paris: Letouzey et Ané, 1930-1950.

Dobschütz, D. E. von. "Das Christusbild Abgars." *Monatschrift für Gottesdienst und Kirchliche Kunst*, 14 (1909): 265-272.

——. *Christusbilder: Untersuchungen zur Christlichen Legende*. Texte und Untersuchungen zur Geschichte der altchristlichen Literatur, N.F. III: 1, 2. 2 vols. Leipzig: J. C. Hinrichs'sche Buchhandlung, 1899.

——. "Das Schweisstuch der Veronica." *Monatsschrift für Gottesdienst und Kirchliche Kunst*, 14 (1909): 181-186.

Douhet, M. le Comte de. *Dictionnaire des mystères, ou Collection générale des mystères, moralités, rites figurés et cérémonies singulières, ayant un caractère public et un but religieux et moral, et joués sous le patronage des personnes ecclésiastiques ou par l'entremise des confréries religieuses*. Vol. 43 of *Nouvelle Encyclopédie théologique ou Nouvelle série de dictionnaires sur toutes les parties de la science religieuse*. Ed. l'Abbé Migne. Paris: Migne, 1854.

Duchesne, l'Abbé Louis-Marie-Olivier. *L'Aquitaine et les Lyonnaises*. Vol. 2 of *Fastes épiscopaux de l'ancienne Gaule*. 2e éd. Paris: Fontemoing et Cie., 1910.

——. "Saint Martial de Limoges." *Annales du Midi*, 4 (1892): 289-330.

Du Choul, Johannis. *Pilati montis in Gallia descriptio*. In Conrad Gesner. *De raris et admirandis herbis*, pp. 68-75. Tiguri: Apud Andream Gesnerum & Jacobum Gesnerum, fratres, c. 1555.

Du Méril, Edélestand. *Poésies populaires latines du Moyen Âge*. 1847; rpt. Bologna: Forni, 1969.

Durand, Johan, and Thierry Durand. *Scènes de vie gallo-romaine évoquées par les vestiges de Saint-Roman-en-Gal (Rhône), France*. Vienne-en-Dauphiné: Chez les éditeurs, 1979.

Éméric-David, Toussaint-Bernard. *Histoire de la peinture du Moyen âge, suivie de l'Histoire de la gravure, du Discours sur l'influence des arts du dessin, et du Musée olympique*. Paris: Librairie de Charles Gosselin, 1842.

Emmerick, Catherina. "Veronica and her Veil." In *The Life of our Lord and Saviour Jesus Christ*, 4: 254-259. Fresno: Apostolate of Christian Action, 1914.

Emminghaus, J. H. "*Veronika*." In *Lexikon für Theologie und Kirche*, vol. 10, cols. 728-729. 2nd ed. Freiburg: Verlag Herder, 1957-1967.

*Enciclopedia Cattolica*. 12 vols. Città del Vaticano: Ente per l'*Enciclopedia Cattolica* e per il libro cattolico, 1948-1954.

Eusebius, Pamphilus. *The Ecclesiastical History*. Ed. Valesius. London: A. and J. Churchill, 1708.

Eustache. *Le Roman du Fuerre de Gadres*. Vol. 4 of *The Medieval French "Roman d'Alexandre"*, pp. 7-9. Ed. E. C. Armstrong and Alfred Foulet. Elliott Monographs, 39. Princeton: Princeton University Press, 1942.

Evagrius Scholasticus. *Ecclesiasticae historiae libri sex*. In Theodoritus et Evagrius. *Historia ecclesiastica, item exerpta ex Historia ecclesiastica*

*Philostorgis et Theodori Lectoris graece et latine*, pp. 245-473. Cantabrigae: Typis Academicis, 1720.

Fabricius, Johannes Albertus. *Codex Apocryphus Novi Testamenti, collectus, castigatus testimoniisque, censuris & animadversionibus illustratus*. Hamburgi: Sumptu Viduae Benjam. Schilleri, 1719.

Feis, P. L. de. "Del Monumento di Paneas e delle immagini della Veronica e di Edessa." *Bessarione*, 4 (1898): 177-192.

Flavius Josèphe. *La Guerre des Juifs*. Trans. Pierre Samuel. Paris: Les Éditions de Minuit, 1977.

Fleury, Claude. *Histoire ecclésiastique*. 36 vols. Paris: Jean Mariette, 1691-1738.

Ford, Alvin E. *L'Évangile de Nicodème: les Versions courtes en ancien français et en prose*. Publications romanes et françaises, 125. Genève: Droz, 1973.

Frugoni, Arsenio. "La Veronica nostra." *Humanitas* (Brescia), 5 (1950): 561-566.

"P.G." "Il 'Sacro Volto' nell'arte." *Emporium: revista mensile illustrata d'arte, letteratura, scienze e varietà*, 7:40 (Aprile 1898), 257-270.

Gaume, Mgr. *Sainte Véronique*. Montréal: Librairie Saint Joseph, 1888.

Gesner, Conrad. *Descriptio montis fracti, sive Montis Pilati, iuxta Lucernam in Helvetia*. In *De raris et admirandis herbis*, pp. 43-67. Tiguri: Apud Andream Gesnerum & Jacobum Gesnerum, fratres, c. 1555.

Geyer, Paulus. *Itinera Hierosolymitana saeculi IIII-VIII*. Corpus scriptorum ecclesiasticorum latinorum, 39. Pragae: F. Tempsky, 1898.

Godefroy, Frédéric, ed. *Dictionnaire de l'ancienne langue française et de tous ses dialectes du IX^e^ au XV^e^ siècle, composé d'après le dépouillement de tous les plus importants documents, manuscrits ou imprimés qui se trouvent dans les grandes bibliothèques de la France et de l'Europe et dans les principales archives départementales, municipales, hospitalières ou privées*. 10 vols. Paris: F. Vieweg et Émile Bouillon, 1881-1902.

Goodwin, C. W., ed. and trans. *The Anglo-Saxon Legends of St. Andrew and St. Veronica*. Publications of the Cambridge Antiquarian Society, Octavo Series 1. Cambridge: Deighton, MacMillan and Co., 1851.

Grabar, André. *La Sainte Face de Laon: le Mandylion dans l'art orthodoxe*. Prague: Seminarium Kondakovianum, 1931.

Graf, Arturo. *Roma nella memoria e nelle immaginazioni del Medio Evo*. 2 vols. Torino: Giovanni Chiantore, 1923.

Grässe, Jean-Georges-Théodore. *Trésor de livres rares et précieux ou Nouveau Dictionnaire bibliographique*. 7 vols. in 4. 1859-1869; rpt. Berlin: Josef Altman, 1922.

Gregorius Turonensis. *Opera omnia*. Patrologiae curus completus: patres latini, 71. Ed. P. L. Migne. Parisiis: Apud Editorem, 1849.

Grimm, Wilhelm. "Die Sage vom Ursprung der Christusbilder." *Abhandlung der königlichen Akademie der Wissenschaften zu Berlin aus dem Jahre 1842*, 1844, pp. 121-177.

Gröber, Gustav. *Grundriss der romanischen Philologie*. Strassburg: Trübner, 1902.

Gryting, L. A. T. *The Oldest Version of the 12th-century Poem "La Venjance de Nostre Seigneur"*. The University of Michigan Contributions in Modern Philology, 19. Ann Arbor: University of Michigan Press, 1952.

Guénébault, Louis-Jean. *Dictionnaire iconographique des figures, légendes et actes des Saints, tant de l'ancienne que de la nouvelle loi, et Répertoire alphabétique des attributs qui sont donnés le plus ordinairement aux Saints par les artistes, peintres, sculpteurs, graveurs, etc. du moyen âge et des temps modernes*. Vol. 45 of *Encyclopédie théologique, ou Série de dictionnaires sur toutes les parties de la science religieuse*. Ed. l'Abbé Migne. Au Petit-Montrouge, Chez l'éditeur, 1850.

——. *Dictionnaire iconographique des monuments de l'antiquité chrétienne, et de ceux du moyen âge, depuis le bas-empire jusqu'à la fin du seizième siècle, indiquant l'état de l'art et de la civilisation à ces diverses époques*. 2 vols. Paris: Leleux, 1843, 1845.

Gygès. *Les Israélites dans la société française*. Villiers-le-Bel: Imprimerie Gouin pour "Documents et Témoignages", 1956.

Ham, E.B. "The Basic Manuscript of the Marcadé *Vengence*." *Modern Language Review*, 29 (1934): 405-420.

Hennecke, Edgar. *New Testament Apocrypha*. Ed. Wilhelm Schneemelcher. Trans. R. McL. Wilson. Philadelphia: The Westminster Press, 1963.

Holweck, F. G. *A Biographical Dictionary of the Saints*. St-Louis-London: 1924.

Houtin, A. *La Controverse de l'apostolicité des églises de France au* XIX$^{e}$ *siècle*. 2$^{e}$ éd. Paris: A. Fontemoing, 1901.

Jaillet, Charles. *Histoire consulaire de la Ville de Vienne du* XIII$^{e}$ *au* XVI$^{e}$ *siècle*. 2 vols. Vienne: Ph. Remilly, 1932, 1938.

Jean des Preis, dit d'Outremeuse. *Ly Myreur des histors, chronique*. 6 vols. Bruxelles: M. Hayez, 1864-1880.

Jenkins, T. Atkinson, ed. *La Chanson de Roland. Oxford Version*. New York: D. C. Heath, 1924.

Jubinal, Achille. *Mystères inédits du quinzième siècle, publiés pour la première fois*. 2 vols. Paris: Téchener, 1837.

Kerber, Bernhard. *Veronika*. Heilige in Bild und Legende, 23. Recklinghausen: Verlag Bongers Recklinghausen, 1966.

Kérédan, Amédée. *Soulac et sa plage*. Paris: Victor Masson, 1861.

Kölbing, E., and Mabel Day, eds. *"The Siege of Jerusalem" edited from Ms. Laud. Misc. 656 with Variants from all other extant Mss*. Early English Text Society, 188. London: Oxford University Press, 1932.

Kornmann, Heinrich. *De miraculis mortuorum, opus novum et admirandum in decem partes distributum*. N.p.: Typis Joannis Wolffi, 1610.

Kurvinen, Auvo, ed. *The "Siege of Jerusalem" in Prose*. Mémoires de la Société néophilologique de Helsinki, 34. Helsinki: Société néophilologique, 1969.

Langlois, E., ed. *Les Registres de Nicolas IV: Recueil des Bulles de ce Pape, publiées ou analysées d'après les manuscrits originaux des archives du Vatican*. Paris: Thonin, 1886.

Lebeuf, l'Abbé. *Histoire de la Ville et de tout le diocèse de Paris*. 7 vols. Paris: Librairie de Féchoz et Letouzey, 1883-1893.

Legeay, Urbain. *Histoire de Louis XI: son siècle, ses exploits comme dauphin, ses dix ans d'administration en Dauphiné, ses cinq ans de résidence en Brabant, et son règne*. Paris: Firmin Didot, 1874.

Leglay, Marcel, et Serge Tourrenc. *Saint-Romain-en-Gal: Quartier urbain de Vienne gallo-romaine*. Lyon: Chambre de Commerce de Lyon, 1970.

[Le Nain] d[e] T[illemont, Sébastien]. *Mémoires pour servir à l'Histoire ecclésiastique des six premiers siècles. Justifiez par les Citations des Auteurs originaux. Avec une Chronologie, où l'on fait un abrégé de l'Histoire Ecclésiastique & profane; & des Notes pour éclaircir les difficultez des faits de la Chronologie*. 8 vols. Bruxelles: Fricx, 1694-1719.

Leroquais, l'Abbé V. *Les Livres d'heures manuscrits de la Bibliothèque Nationale*. Paris: V. Leroquais, 1927-1943.

Longueval, Jacques. *Histoire de l'Église gallicane*. 8 vols. Paris: F. Montalant, 1730-1734.

Lunel, Armand. *Juifs du Languedoc, de la Provence et des États français du Pape*. Présences du Judaïsme. Paris: Albin Michel, 1975.

Mabillon, Johannes. *Iter italicum litterarium*. In *Museum italicum, seu Collectio veterum scriptorum ex bibliothecis italicis*. 1: 3-232. Luteciae Parisiorum: Apud Viduam Edmundi Martin, 1687.

Malvezin, Théophile. *Histoire des Juifs à Bordeaux*. Bordeaux: Charles LeFebvre, 1875.

Manni, Domenico Maria. *Dell'errore che persiste di attribuirsi le pitture al Santo Evangelista*. Firenze: Pietro Gaet. Viviani, 1766.

Marangoni, Giovanni. *Istoria dell'antichissimo oratorio, o capella di San Lorenzo nel Patriarchio Lateranense communemente appellato Sancta Sanctorum e celle celebre Immagine del SS. Salvatore detta Acheropita, che ivi conservasi; colle notizie del culto, e vari riti praticati anticamente verso la medesima: come anche dell'origine, ed uso di tal sorta d'immagini venerate nella Cattolica Chiesa, raccolte da Monumenti antichi, e specialmente dall'Archivio della Nobile Compagnia, che ne ha la Custodia*. Rome: Nella Stamperia di San Michele, 1747.

Maréchaux, Dom Bernard. *N.-D. de la Fin des Terres de Soulac*. Bordeaux: Imprimerie Nouvelle A. Bellier, 1893.

Marianus Scotus. *Chronica ad Evangelii veritatem, post Hebraicae sancrosancte scripture & Septuaginta interpretum variationem, magno iudicio discussam*

*& correctam, certa enumeratione temporum conscripta*. Basiliae: Apud Ioannem Oporinum, 1559.

Marucchi, Horace. *Basiliques et églises de Rome*. Vol. 3 of *Éléments d'archéologie chrétienne*. Paris: Desclée, 1902.

Marx, Jean. *La Légende arthurienne et le Graal*. Paris: Presses Universitaires de France, 1952.

Massmann, Hans Ferdinand, ed. *Der Keiser und der Kunige Buoch, oder die sogenannten Kaiserchronik, Gedicht des zwölften Jahrhunderts*. 3 vols. Bibliothek der gesammten deutschen National-literatur, 4. Quedlinburg und Leipzig: G. Basse, 1849-1854.

Maury, Alfred. *Croyances et légendes du Moyen Âge*. Paris: Honoré Champion, 1896.

——. *Essai sur les légendes pieuses du Moyen Âge, ou examen de ce qu'elles renferment de merveilleux d'après les connaissances que fournissent de nos jours, l'archéologie, la théologie, la philosophie et la physiologie médicale*. Paris: Librairie philosophique de Ladrange, 1843.

Mermet, Thomas. *Histoire de la ville de Vienne, de l'an 438 à l'an 1039*. Lyon: Chez l'auteur, 1833.

——. *Histoire de la ville de Vienne, de l'an 1040 à 1801*. Lyon: Chez les Principaux Libraires, 1853.

——. *Histoire de la ville de Vienne durant l'époque gauloise et la domination romaine dans l'Allobrogie*. Paris: Firmin Didot, 1828.

——. *Rapport sur les monuments remarquables de l'arrondissement de Vienne*. Vienne: J.-C. Timon, 1829.

Meyer, Paul. "Notice du manuscrit de la Bibliothèque Nationale, fonds fr. 25415, contenant divers ouvrages en provençal." *Bulletin de la Société des Anciens Textes Français*, 1 (1875): 50-82.

——. "Notice sur deux anciens manuscrits français ayant appartenu au Marquis de La Clayette." *Notices et extraits des manuscrits de la Bibliothèque nationale et autres bibliothèques*, 33:1 (1890): 1-90.

[Mezuret, l'Abbé]. *Notre-Dame de Soulac ou de la Fin-des-Terres: Le Tombeau et le culte de Sainte-Véronique à Soulac*. Lesparre: J. Rivet, 1865.

Micha, Alexandre. "Une rédaction de la *Vengeance de Notre Seigneur*." In *Mélanges offerts à Rita Lejeune*, 2: 1291-1298. Gembloux: Duculot, 1969.

Mills, Leonard R., ed. *L'Histoire de Barlaam et Josaphat. Version champenoise d'après le ms. Reg. lat. 660 de la Bibliothèque Apostolique Vaticane*. Textes littéraires français, 201. Genève: Droz, 1973.

Miserey, Marie de. *Sainte Véronique*. Votre nom – votre saint, 25. Tours: Mame, 1964.

Moe, Phyllis. "Cleveland Manuscript W q091.92-C468 and the Veronica Legend." *Bulletin of the New York Public Library*, 70 (1966): 459-470.

——. "The French Source of the Alliterative *Siege of Jerusalem*." *Medium Aevum*, 39 (1970): 147-154.

——. *The ME Prose Translation of Roger d'Argenteuil's "Bible en françois" ed.*

*from Cleveland Public Library MS W q091.92-C468*. Middle English Texts, 6. Heidelberg: Carl Winter Universitätsverlag, 1977.

——. "On Professor Micha's *Vengeance de Notre Seigneur: Version II*." *Romania*, 95 (1974): 555-560.

Molanus (Johannes Vermeulen, dit). *De Historia SS. Imaginum et picturarum pro vero earum usu contra abusus*. In *Theologiae Cursus completus*, vol. 27, cols. 17-424. Ed. J. P. Migne. Parisiis: Apud Editorem, 1843.

Moniquet, le R.P. Auguste-Isidore. *St. Fort: premier évêque de Bordeaux et martyr*. Les Saints de l'Archidiocèse de Bordeaux. Paris: Tolra, 1892.

——. *Les Saints de l'Archidiocèse de Bordeaux: Vie de St.-Delphin*. Les Saints de l'Église de France. Paris: Tolra, 1893.

*New Catholic Encyclopedia*. 15 vols. New York: McGraw-Hill, 1967.

Origène. *Contre Celse*. 5 vols. Sources chrétiennes, 132, 136, 147, 150, 227. Paris: Les Éditions du Cerf, 1967-1976.

Palme, Joseph. *Die deutschen Veronicalegenden des XII. Jahrhunderts, ihr Verhältnis unter einander und zu den Quellen*. Prag: Verlag des K.K. Deutschen Obergymnasiums der Kleinseite, 1892.

Paris, Paulin. "*La Destruction de Jérusalem*." *Histoire littéraire de la France*, 22 (1852): 412-416.

Pauphilet, A., ed. *La Queste del Saint Graal*. CFMA. Paris: Champion, 1923.

Pearson, Karl. *Die Fronica: ein Beitrag zur Geschichte des Christusbildes im Mittelalter*. Strassburg: Trübner, 1887.

Phillips, George. *The Doctrine of Addai, the Apostle, now first edited in a complete Form in the original Syriac with an English Translation and Notes*. London: Trübner, 1876.

Pinius, Joannes, et Guihelmus Cuperus, eds. "De Sancto Amatore eremita in Cadurcensi Galliae Provincia." In *Acta Sanctorum Augusti, ex latinis & graecis, aliarumque gentium monumentis, servata primigenia veterum scriptorum phrasi, collecta, digesta, commentariisque & observationibus illustrata*, 4: 16-25. Antverpiae: Apud Bernardum Albertum vander Plassche, 1739.

Prado-Gaillard, Henri. *La Condition des Juifs dans l'ancienne France*. Paris: Presses Universitaires de France, 1942.

Rabinis, J. *Notice sur Florimont sire de Lesparre, suivie d'un précis historique sur cette seigneurie, de notes et éclaircissements*. Bordeaux: H. Faye, 1843.

Rainoldus, Johannes. *De romanae ecclesiae idolatria, in cultu sanctorum, reliquiarum, imaginum, aquae, salis, olei, aliarumque rerum consecratarum & sacramenti Eucharistiae, operis inchoati libri duo*. Oxoniae: Apud Josephum Barnesium, 1596.

Raoul de Houdenc. *Le Songe d'Enfer*. In August Scheler. *Trouvères belges*

*(Nouvelle Série): Chansons d'amour, jeux-partis, pastourelles, satires, dits et fabliaux*, pp. 176-200. Louvain: Lefever, 1879.

Réau, Louis. *Iconographie de l'art chrétien*. 3 vols. Paris: Presses Universitaires de France, 1955-1959.

Reiske, Johannes. *Exercitationes historicae de Imaginibus Jesu Christi, quotquot vulgo circumferuntur revisae, interpolatae, figuris aeneis & multis accessionibus auctae*. Jenae: Sumptibus Joh. Christiani Wohlfartii, 1685.

Rey, Étienne , et E. Vietty. *Monuments romains et gothiques de Vienne en France*. Paris: Firmin Didot, 1831.

Ring, Maximilien de. *Symbolisme et légende de sainte Véronique*. N.p.: n.pub., c. 1869.

Robert de Boron. *Le Roman de l'Estoire dou Graal*. Ed. Wm. A. Nitze. CFMA, 57. Paris: Honoré Champion, 1927.

Robertus de Monte. *Chronica*. Ed. Ludovicus Couradus Bethmann. In *Monumenta Germaniae historica, inde ab anno Christi quingentesimo usque ad annum millesimum et quingentesimum*, vol. VI *Scriptorum*, pp. 475-535. Hannoverae: Impensis Bibliopoli Aulici Hahniani, 1843.

Rosenthal, Albi. "Le Ms. de La Clayette retrouvé." *Annales musicologiques*, 1 (1953): 105-130.

Schwarzfuchs, Simon. *Brève Histoire des Juifs en France*. Collection "Maillons". Paris: Commission du Plan d'Action culturelle, 1956.

Showerman, Grant. "Isis." *Encyclopedia of Religion and Ethics*. 1911 ed.

Solente, Suzanne. "Le Grand Recueil La Clayette à la Bibliothèque Nationale." *Scriptorium*, 7 (1953): 226-234.

Suchier, Walter. "Ueber das altfranzösische Gedicht von der *Zerstörung Jerusalems* (*La Venjance nostre seigneur*). *Zeitschrift für romanische Philologie*, 24 (1900): 161-198; 25 (1901): 94-109, 256.

C. Suetonius Tranquillus. "Divus Vespasianus." In *De Vita Caesarum libri VIII*, ed. Maximilianus Ihm, pp. 293-309. Lipsiae: Teubner, 1908.

Thomas, Dom Grégoire-Marie. *Soulac et N.-D. de la Fin des Terres*. Bordeaux: Imprimerie de l'Œuvre de Saint-Paul, 1882.

Thummius, Theodorus. *Tractatus historico-theologicus de festis judaeorum et christianorum ad disputandum propositus*. Tubingae: Apud Viduam Johan. Alexandri Cellii, 1624.

Thurston, Herbert, s.j. *The Holy Year of Jubilee: An Account of the History and Ceremonial of the Roman Jubilee*. 1900; rpt. Westminster, Maryland: The Newman Press, 1949.

Tischendorf, Constantinus, ed. *Evangelia Apocrypha: adhibitis plurimis codicibus graecis et latinis maximam partem nunc primum consultis atque ineditorum copia insignibus*. 2nd ed. Lipsiae: H. Mendelssohn, 1876.

Tobler, Adolf, and Erhard Lommatzsch. *Altfranzösisches Wörterbuch: Adolf Toblers nachgelassene Materialen bearbeitet und mit Unterstützung der*

*Preussischen Akademie der Wissenschaften herausgegeben von Erhard Lommatzsch*. 10 vols. Berlin: Weidmannsche Buchhandlung, 1915– .

Verdier, Sieur de. *Le Voyage de France, dressé pour la commodité des Français & Estrangers*. 3e éd. Paris: Michel Bobin, 1657.

Villamont, Seigneur de. *Les Voyages*. N.p. (Lyon?): N.pub., 1606.

Vincentius Belvacensis. *Speculum historiale, in quo universo totius orbis, omniumque populorum ab orbe condito, usque ad Auctoris tempus, cum sequentium annorum appendice, Historia continetur*. Vol. IV of *Speculum majus*. Venetiis: Apud Dominicum Nicolinum, 1591.

Voragine, Jacobus de. *Legenda aurea, vulgo Historia lombardica dicta*. Ed. Th. Graesse. Dresdae et Lipsiae: Impensis Librariae Arnoldianae, 1846.

Warren, F. M. "An Earlier Version of the Roland Miracle." *Modern Language Notes*, 29 (1914): 3-4.

Wartburg, Walther von, ed. *Französisches Etymologisches Wörterbuch: eine Darstellung des galloromanischen Sprachschatzes*. 24 vols. Bonn: F. Kloppe, 1928– .

Weale, Th. W. "De Legende der H. Veronica." *Dietsche Warande*, n.s. 3 (1890): 609-616.

Weiler, Ingomar. "Titus und die Zerstörung des Tempels von Jerusalem: Absicht oder Zufall." *Klio: Beiträge zur alten Geschichte*, 50 (1968): 139-158.

Wilson, Ian. *The Shroud of Turin: The Burial Cloth of Jesus?* Garden City, NY: Doubleday, 1978.

# Index of Proper Names

The titles of God and Jesus have not been included in the following list. For further details concerning most items, the critical notes should be consulted, under the first line number given.